GUIDEPOSTS

KNOW THE BIBLE IN 30 DAYS

GUIDEPOSTS

KNOW
THE BIBLE IN
30 DAYS

J. STEPHEN LANG

GUIDEPOSTS
New York, New York

Guideposts Know the Bible in 30 Days

ISBN-13: 978-0-8249-4733-0 (hardcover)
ISBN-13: 978-0-8249-4806-1 (paperback)

Published by Guideposts
16 East 34th Street
New York, New York 10016
www.guideposts.com

Distributed by Ideals Publications, a division of Guideposts
2630 Elm Hill Pike, Suite 100
Nashville, Tennessee 37214

Guideposts and *Ideals* are registered trademarks of Guideposts.

ACKNOWLEDGMENTS

Every attempt has been made to credit the sources of copyrighted material used in this book. If any such acknowledgment has been inadvertently omitted or misattributed, receipt of such information would be appreciated.

All scripture quotations, unless otherwise noted, are taken from *The Holy Bible, New International Version.* Copyright © 1973, 1978, 1984 International Bible Society. Used by permission of Zondervan Bible Publishers.

Scripture quotation marked (ESV) is from *The Holy Bible, English Standard Version,* copyright © 2001 by Crossway Bibles, a division of Good News Publishers. Used by permission. All rights reserved.

Scripture quotations marked (KJV) are taken from *The King James Version of the Bible.*

Library of Congress Cataloging-in-Publication Data

Lang, J. Stephen.
   Guideposts know the Bible in 30 days : discovering historical facts, biblical insights, and the inspiring power of God's Word / J. Stephen Lang.
     p. cm.
 ISBN 978-0-8249-4733-0
 1. Bible—Introductions. 2. Bible—Devotional use. I. Title. II. Title: Know the Bible in 30 days.
 BS475.3.L35 2008
 220.6'1—dc22
                                      2008000793

Cover design by Gayle Raymer
Cover photos by iStockphoto
Interior design and typesetting by Cindy LaBreacht

Printed and bound in the United States of America

10 9 8 7 6 5 4 3

CONTENTS

SECTION ONE
BEGINNINGS

We begin at the beginning, Genesis 1, with God's creation of the world, including human beings made "in his image." But human disobedience changes everything, sin becomes a fixture of human life, and God decides to start anew, destroying the world but saving one righteous man and his family. In this chapter we meet Adam and Eve, their sons Cain and Abel, and the faithful Noah, a moral man in an immoral world. *(Genesis 1–11)*

Today we look at the patriarchs of Israel, beginning with Abraham in Genesis 12, called by God to be the ancestor of a chosen nation. Here are some of the most memorable stories of the Bible: the sacrifice (almost) of Abraham's son Isaac, Isaac's wily son Jacob, and the saga of Jacob's twelve sons, focusing on the son Joseph and his amazing rise to power under God's protection. *(Genesis 12–50)*

God's chosen people suffer as slaves in Egypt until God sends a deliverer, the amazing Moses, a man of many miracles. *(Exodus)*

Encamped at Mount Sinai, Moses and the Israelites receive God's laws, notably the Ten Commandments. From the laws they learn that every aspect of their lives is governed by God's wise commandments. *(Exodus, Leviticus, Numbers, Deuteronomy)*

The enthralling Moses saga continues as the restless, grumbling Israelites journey on to the land God promised them, facing enemies from without and rebellions within. *(Leviticus, Numbers, Deuteronomy)*

The Israelites finally arrive in the land God promised them, led by the valiant Joshua. Tormented on all sides by their idol-worshiping neighbors, the Israelites cry out for help, and God sends them the courageous figures known as the judges, including the strongman Samson, the clever Gideon, and the amazing woman Deborah. The brief book of Ruth presents one of the most beautiful stories ever written. *(Joshua, Judges, Ruth)*

SECTION FOUR
VOICES OF WARNING AND CONSOLATION

SECTION FIVE
THE MESSIAH ARRIVES

SECTION SIX
THE FAITH GOES GLOBAL

Prepare for the Journey

Know the Bible in a mere thirty days? Impossible, you say?
Well, we will not make the rash promise that you will be an all-wise Bible scholar within thirty days. Some people study the Bible their entire lives and, late in life, stumble across things in it that they never noticed before. These people include not only the "pros"—professors, ministers, etc.—but also the many laypeople who immerse themselves in the Book day after day, year after year. In a sense, no person ever "knows" the Book completely. There is always more to discover, more to enrich the mind and the heart, more to apply to one's life in this world.

But, though you won't be an MB (Master of the Bible) upon finishing this book, you will be familiar with its key themes, its main characters, and its most important and valuable life lessons. You will know it well enough that when you hear it quoted, and misquoted, and misconstrued in pop culture, you will have a sense of what the Bible *really* says, not what its critics (and sometimes even its friends) *say* that it says. You will also have a sense of how to apply its teachings to your own life, day by day, hour by hour.

Most of all, you will—assuming you apply yourself to each day's chapter—have a sense of the Bible as a living thing, not some dry, dead document from centuries ago. You will know it not as dull ancient history, but as God's manual for life, for all people, in all times, in all situations. It is my hope that you will no longer find the Bible either dull or intimidating, but a supremely un-put-downable book.

I trust you will enjoy this thirty-day journey.

It's about You . . . and God

The Bible is never about someone else"—so said an old preacher I once knew. "It's always about you—and God." You might say the Bible is up close and personal regarding the relationship of human beings to God. Its many authors—a mixed bag of shepherds, kings, fishermen, teachers, scribes, warriors, and many more—had no intention of writing just to record history or just to entertain. True, the Bible is full of fascinating and highly entertaining stories. And, true, it does record very real history. (The more the historians and archaeologists dig around, the more obvious it becomes that the Bible is on solid historical ground.) But the aim of all those writers, all those centuries ago, was to put in writing what they believed God wanted written down: God's will, revealed in words to humankind. And for many centuries, copyists faithfully passed on the words, believing that every new generation needed to be told the old (but living) stories of God's dealings with the world, and of how God intended human beings to live rightly with each other. God meant the Bible to be a book not just about "them" and "then" but about "you" and "now."

We have to take this on faith, of course. No one can prove, scientifically, that the Bible we possess today is God-inspired or God-approved. But there are some pretty clear indications that the Bible is not a purely human invention. For one thing, it presents its many heroes—and its most important group of people, Israel—"warts and all." Amazing and saintly people like Moses and David and Solomon do terrible things, and the Bible makes no attempt to gloss over their sins. The nation that is described as "God's chosen people," Israel, constantly forgets God and wanders off the moral path. If the Bible was purely an invention of clever human writers, they would have made Israel look more faithful. They also would have "corrected" some of the discrepancies—for example, the differing details when Matthew, Mark, and Luke relate the same story.

Other things come to mind: since Israel is the most important locale in the Bible, why does the story of Noah and the flood conclude with the ark coming to rest on the mountains of Ararat—a great distance from Israel? Unless, of course, it happened to be true. The Gospels record many stories that show Jesus' disciples in a bad light—their quarrels over which of them were most important, their cowardly flight after his arrest, the chief disciple (Peter) denying that he even knew Jesus. If the Gospels were merely human documents, those embarrassing items would have been left out. No writer would have invented such scenes. They must have been included because they were true, and because God intended people to know just how human the disciples were. There is this breathtaking honesty in the Bible that purely human writings do not possess.

The Bible is an ancient book, yet it differs from other ancient writings in one important way: people actually still try to apply it to life today. That isn't true of ancient classics like Homer's *Odyssey* or the plays of Sophocles or the dialogues of Plato. Homer and Sophocles and Plato may have been inspired in some way, and the *Odyssey* does tell a rousing good story, but no one uses those old writings as a road map through life. Yet people have been doing just that with the Bible for centuries, and still do—the Bible changes lives. Its devoted readers believe that in some hard-to-define way, it says what God wanted it to say. They read it and try to apply it to life because they see in it a timeless quality that they don't find in the numerous experts spouting their advice in books and on TV talk shows. They see its ancient insights as perennially fresh. They study it and consult it because they believe that Jesus Christ and Paul and Moses and Isaiah and Solomon had a clear idea of what God intended for human beings. If they did not understand what the will of God is, then who does? Put it another way: If we can't find God in the Bible, where do we find him? We take it on faith that, when God is quoted in the Bible, the quotation has been "checked with the Author." That is why, more than any book ever written, the Bible is something we can hang our hearts upon. It gives us the comfort of knowing that a living, loving God reveals the way we ought to live, instead of believing we are alone on an indifferent planet, forced to devise the truth for ourselves.

Here is a bold statement: *If you understand the Bible, you understand the world.* It doesn't make you an expert in every subject—just in the ones that truly matter. Even if you do not fully understand science, the Bible lets you know why the world exists, and who made it and sustains it. Even if your grasp of history and politics is shaky, the Bible has timeless insights into the nature of *power* and the way human beings *abuse* it. Even if you know little of psychology, the Bible reveals all you need to know about the human *mind* and *heart*—and much of what it reveals is in striking contrast to the shallow pop psychology you encounter in the media. A recent U.S. president stated that "the Bible is pretty good about keeping your ego in check." He might have added, "the Bible reveals to us Someone bigger and more reliable than our own egos." After hearing all the shallow psychobabbling voices in our pop culture, we encounter in the Bible a divine voice so deep we can bathe in it.

And the Bible teaches us how to succeed in life—or, to put it another way, to be what we were meant to be. This won't necessarily mean becoming rich, attractive, and famous, of course. "Success" in human terms often involves spiritual and moral failure, and there are people who are "losers" by the world's standards who are highly successful in the eyes of God. Jesus promised his followers that he came into the world "that they might have life, and that they might have it more abundantly" (John 10:10 KJV). The whole Bible has that same purpose. It shows the way to "abundant life"—something that makes worldly successes and accomplishments seem small by comparison. That abundant life can be found no matter what our condition.

In one of the world's classic novels, *Robinson Crusoe*, the title character, marooned alone on an island, has a Bible among his few worldly possessions. In this difficult situation, he records that "I daily read the Word of God and applied all the comforts of it to my present state. One morning, being very sad, I opened the Bible upon these words, 'I will never, never leave thee, nor forsake thee.'"

The book you are now holding will be a strong reminder that you are never alone—God will always comfort and support you through His Word. For the next thirty days, set aside some time to read one chapter of this book—and also the suggested Bible passages for each day. In doing so, you will read some of the most-studied and most-loved sections of the Bible, encounter its most intriguing characters, discover its most important themes, see where its events fit into history, gain some valuable insights into the culture of biblical times, and find inspiration in the Word of God that will apply to your life. That last item is most important because, as already stated, the Bible is never about someone else—it is about you, and God, and you and God.

Features to Help You on the Journey

AT THE HEART OF IT ALL TODAY

Each chapter opens with this brief summary of what you will be reading about that day. This not only prepares you for each day's lesson but also makes it easy for you to review once you have completed your thirty-day journey. Here you will encounter each day's "big ideas," ideas that will challenge and touch you as you dig deeper into the Scriptures.

KEY PASSAGES TO READ TODAY

Obviously you are going to be reading the Bible itself, not just reading *about* it. The Key Passages box contains the most important passages for each day, although each chapter will always cover much more than that. In the course of this book you will be reading the lion's share of the Bible's most-quoted passages.

A word about Bible translations: the version quoted in this book is the New International Version, a popular contemporary translation that most people find easy to read. There are many other fine modern versions available today, and (obviously) if you don't already own a Bible, you should get one, and bookstore employees will usually be happy to help you pick one. You can also, on websites like Amazon.com, browse through sample pages of various translations to give you an idea of how readable each one is. I don't particularly recommend the much-loved and long-lived King James Version, since the language has changed dramatically since it was published way back in 1611, and some people find the KJV difficult to understand. But if you like the overall "flavor" of the King James Version, you might try the English Standard Version or New King James Version, two that do a good job of modernizing the more difficult words and phrases of the KJV.

THE VIEW FROM HISTORY

People argue about whether the Bible got all its historical details perfectly correct, but there is no doubt that the Bible as a whole is firmly rooted in real history. The View from History timeline shows the dates—sometimes approximate—for the events in each chapter. Included here are not only key events in the Bible itself, but events that happened elsewhere in the world, historical and cultural milestones that will help you put biblical events in perspective.

KEY TERM FOR TODAY

These are important words and phrases that every reader of the Bible ought to know. Although there are good reasons that each of these terms is connected to a particular chapter in this book, many of the terms are found throughout the Bible—for example, *covenant, angels, Messiah, sacrifice, idolatry, Satan,* etc. When you finish the thirty-day journey, consider your time well spent if you can define all or most of these Key Terms. Later, use these items as a handy way to refresh your memory about what you learned.

CHARACTER CLOSE-UPS

One goal in reading the Bible is to find more "friends for the soul." The Character Close-ups will give you an in-depth look at many of these people, the heroes of the Old and New Testaments. There are also some rogues and villains along the way, and, as already noted, even the heroes had their "warts" that the Bible made no attempt to conceal. You can learn valuable life lessons from both the saints and the sinners.

CULTURAL INSIGHTS

Stories written thousands of years ago present us with a "culture gap," and the Cultural Insights boxes help to bridge that gap, providing some historical and religious information to make the Bible passages clearer. These items include information on Israel's neighboring nations and their religions, as well as some revealing glimpses into the religious and social practices of Jews and Christians in biblical times. Part of the pleasure here is finding that, in spite of that centuries-long gap between biblical times and ours, history has a way of repeating itself.

STORIES WORTH REMEMBERING

These will highlight well-known and well-loved stories. Even with stories you may already be familiar with, you will learn some new (or neglected) aspects, letting you view the stories in a new light.

DID-YOU-KNOW FACTS

These are brief, factual odds and ends worth knowing—and sometimes, worth applying to daily life. We think you'll find these "trivoids" both useful and enjoyable.

PUTTING THE WORD TO WORK

This book—and the time you spend on it—would be a failure if your reading did not lead you to apply each day's truths to your own life. Each chapter will conclude with thought-provoking questions to guide you into applying the knowledge you've gained to your daily walk. After all, as we already said, the Bible is never just about "someone else"—it is about you and God.

Beginnings and Disasters

AT THE HEART OF IT ALL TODAY We begin our walk through the Bible at the beginning—literally, the beginning of the world. We look at the creation story in Genesis, with humankind as the pinnacle of creation, then the story of human pride and selfishness beginning with Adam and Eve and continuing on through their offspring. This mostly sad story—sin spreads far and wide—is brightened by the saga of Noah, a moral man who is preserved from the extermination of an immoral world. We might sum up this chapter in this way: God creates; man sins; God preserves the good. So despite mankind's fall from grace, we are sustained by this promise of hope: From the very start, God never gave up on his people—as he will never give up on each one of us.

It's hard to imagine an opening line better than "In the beginning..." In fact, it is probably the most famous opening of any book ever written. It is also the most appropriate, for what better place to begin the story of God's relation to the world than God's creation of it?

KEY PASSAGES TO READ TODAY

Genesis 1–4; 6:9—9:28; 11:1–9

Before we turn to the story, let's remind ourselves of the theme of the whole Bible: God revealing himself to man for the sake of man's salvation. Genesis 1–3 presents the story of Adam and Eve—who represent every man and woman who ever lived—and shows us why we need saving.

Genesis 1 tells us that in six days God created everything that is, then on the seventh day he rested—which does not mean he was tired, but simply that his work of original creation had ceased. An old title for the first chapter of Genesis was *Hexahemeron*, Greek for "the six days." Much ink has been spilled over the question of whether the "days" were meant to be literal twenty-four-hour days. Since the sun was not created until the fourth day, and since a twenty-four-hour day is measured by the earth's relation to the sun, we might assume that "day" probably meant something other than a twenty-four-hour day. Perhaps "phase" or "period" might be what is meant by "day." And perhaps God's view of time is different from ours, as the Bible itself observes: "With the Lord a day is like a thousand years, and a thousand years are like a day" (2 Peter 3:8).

Fussing over such matters makes people miss the main point of Genesis 1, which is that *God purposefully made the world*—first the earth itself, with the dry land separated from the waters, then plants, then the heavenly bodies, then the various animals, then, finally, "God created man in his own image" (1:27). God gives man dominion—rule—

Image of God

Man was made in "God's image"—meaning what, exactly? Since God does not have a physical body, it certainly doesn't mean that our bodies resemble God's. Clearly it means we are like God in some intangible way—our minds, our emotions, our ability to rule over lesser creatures. It sets us apart from animals, since God gives man permission to kill animals for food, but the shedding of man's blood is forbidden: "Whoever sheds the blood of man, by man shall his blood be shed; for in the image of God has God made man" (Genesis 9:6). This command is given after the disobedience of Adam and Eve, so even though human sin has entered the world, God still thinks of man as being in his image. And Genesis 1:27 makes it clear that both male and female are made in the image of God; woman is by no means inferior to man.

over the other creatures of the earth. Then "God saw all that he had made, and it was very good" (1:31). Then God rested on the seventh day, which is the basis for the ceasing of work on the Sabbath day, later to be of great importance for the Jews.

Let's pause here to consider something important about the Bible's view of creation: Although Genesis 1 tells us that God made the world out of nothing, and that he created everything in six "days," the Bible does not see creation as being "done." Throughout the Bible, God is not only creator, but sustainer, continuously active in the world. In a sense, creation is an ongoing thing, since every green leaf, every baby bird or baby human is a new creation of God. The Creator God of the Bible says, "I know every bird in the mountains, and the creatures of the field are mine" (Psalm 50:11).

Genesis 2 adds some details to the account of man's creation. Man is formed by God from the dust of the ground, and God breathes into man. He places the man in a lovely garden named Eden (the Hebrew word means "pleasure," and when the Old Testament was translated into Greek centuries later, *Eden* was translated as *Paradise*), and although it is a place of pleasure and contentment, the man is given a task: Tend the garden. He is also given a command: Feel free to eat anything in the garden, except for the fruit of the tree of knowledge of good and evil. The penalty for disobeying the command: death. (Presumably the man knew the meaning of death already from seeing animals die.)

The man is alone, and God sees this is not a good thing. The animals are there, and the man gives them names. (In the Bible, bestowing a name on something meant having rule over it. God gives humankind dominion over the animals. In fact, man is specifically told to *subdue* the other creatures on earth.) But the animals are not suitable companions for man. So God causes the man to fall into a deep sleep and takes from

The "E" Word

Any discussion of Genesis must touch on the issue of creation and evolution. Both religious people and skeptics express some amazement that in the twenty-first century, the old battle—science versus the Bible—is still being fought. Skeptics consider the matter settled scientifically: Evolution is no longer just a theory, they believe, but is proven beyond a shadow of a doubt. Human beings evolved from primate ancestors, and that is that.

But the matter is far from settled, and for an obvious reason: It is impossible to prove that evolution itself was not the work of a creator or to prove that it was. Real science is a matter of proof, and science has its limits. A scientist may believe that evolution is "fact," but cannot prove that evolution is purely a matter of chance. The father of evolutionary theory himself, Charles Darwin, was an agnostic but not an atheist. In 1870 he wrote, "I cannot look at the universe as the result of blind chance, yet I can see no evidence of beneficent design, or indeed of design of any kind, in the details." He had doubts, but some of his disciples do not. They see no evidence of design, but believe with certainty that the universe is the result of blind chance. So, school boards across the country fight their battles over whether to teach children that evolution is a certainty, or that there might possibly be a designer at work.

The sequence of creation in Genesis 1 seems to fit neatly with the findings of science: First there was the earth itself, then plants, then the lower animals, then man. For a document written centuries ago, Genesis seems remarkably accurate in the main points. The fact is, the real problem for unbelievers is not the six-day sequence in Genesis, but, rather, the opening words: "In the beginning, God created…" Believers choose to take those words at face value. Believers also accept Genesis 1:26: "Then God said, 'Let us make man in our image.'" It takes a leap of faith to believe that God created the universe—whether in six days or over millions of years. A creator is a creator, whether he does the work in six days or six billion years.

Scientists can acknowledge that the Bible is largely responsible for much of the growth of science itself. In many ancient religions, the world is inhabited by innumerable spirits, demons and deities, with a supernatural being literally under every bush. This isn't true of the Bible, where from the very beginning there is only one God, and everything that exists is his creation, with no malicious "spirits" inhabiting rocks and trees. God calls his creation "good," but the rocks, trees, stars, sun and moon are not seen as gods or spirits. The Bible "depersonalizes" nature, and if it were not depersonalized, modern science would not have arisen. In the Bible, then, nature is not to be worshipped or feared, but to be understood. Only God is divine, and only man is made in God's image.

him one of his ribs, which he fashions into woman. The story contains a profound truth: Man and woman are of the same flesh, not two separate species at war with one another.

Let's pause here to consider the man's name. Strictly speaking, he does not have one. The Hebrew word *adam* means simply "man." Obviously some double meaning was intended: The first man was simply named "man," so in some sense he represents all of us, every human being who ever lived. Every *adam*—every man—is made "in the image of God" and has God's "breath of life" breathed into him. So man has something of the divine in him—but also something less than divine, since man is made from "the dust of the ground." It is no coincidence that the Hebrew word for "soil," or "earth," is *adhama*. Throughout the Bible, man is depicted as having this dual nature. He is in some mysterious way made in God's image but is also "earthy."

TROUBLE IN PARADISE

At the end of Genesis 2, all seems blissful. Man and woman dwell in a beautiful, pleasant place, unharmed by anything. They work, but it is not burdensome, backbreaking toil. The two are "naked and unashamed," which indicates that in God's original plan, sex was not a source of tension between man and woman. This, Genesis tells us, is the original intention of God: man and woman living harmoniously in a lovely world. But of course, Genesis 2:17 has already told us that the fruit of one tree, the tree of knowledge of good and evil, cannot be eaten. Obviously that warning is mentioned for a reason.

Genesis 3 tells the story of what is known as the Fall of Man. A snake—or serpent, depending on the translation—speaks to the woman. We are not told why the serpent had the power of speech, or why the woman shows no surprise at its speaking. The snake raises a question: Did God make all the trees off-limits to you? The woman corrects it: No, not all trees, just the one, and if we eat from it, we die. In fact, the woman embellishes God's command: God had only forbidden eating from it, but she says: We can't even touch it. Already we sense something. She feels some resentment about that tree being forbidden. She is thinking what the serpent wants her to think: *God is not good, after all.* He is withholding something good from her and the man. The serpent tells her she is wrong about the threat of death. Not only will she not die when she eats the fruit, but she will be like God, "knowing good and evil" (3:5). Knowing good and evil really means deciding for ourselves what is right and wrong. It means relying on ourselves, rather than on God, for moral guidance. It may have an additional meaning: Adam and Eve already know good—their sweet life in Eden—but after they eat the fruit, they will know evil—the difficult life *outside* Eden. The serpent, liar that it was, might have been snickering to itself, thinking that, technically, it had told the truth. They *would* know good and evil after eating the fruit, but they would not be happy with the result once the deed was done.

Here is one of the fateful moments in the Bible—and in the history of the world. Man and woman have a perfect situation, but something tempts them. They want more than what they have; they want to be "like God"—wiser and more in control than they presently are. She eats some of the fruit, then gives it to her husband. Suddenly everything changes. First, they see each other differently. They had been "naked and unashamed." Now the nakedness seems wrong, so they cover themselves with fig leaves. Then they sense God is "walking" in the garden. They hide from him. God calls to them and asks why they hide, and the man's excuse is: I was naked. God asks the obvious question: Did you eat that forbidden fruit? The man makes an excuse: Yes, but the woman—the one *you* gave me—gave it to me. The woman has her own excuse: The snake tempted me. There is no "Please forgive us" or "We're sorry"; no sign of repentance or regret. This may explain why, in the story, God does not offer them a second chance—they do not ask for one. On top of their other folly, they allowed themselves to be led astray by an inferior being, a mere snake. Instead of listening to it, the woman could have exercised the dominion God gave them over the beasts and said to it, "Hold your tongue! God is good to us, and why should I listen to you, a snake?" But man and woman wanted to be godlike, so they disobeyed God and suffered the consequences. Their attempt at "liberation" brought disaster.

Incidentally, the Bible does not say that the snake was really Satan in disguise. Many generations of Bible readers have assumed that this was so, and at the very end of the Bible, the Book of Revelation refers to fighting "the great dragon…that ancient serpent called the devil, or Satan, who leads the whole world astray" (12:9). Perhaps it is appropriate that the final book of the Bible depicts the defeat of the serpent that caused such mischief at the beginning. But always remember: Adam and Eve were ultimately responsible for their disobedience, and blaming the snake did them no good at all.

One element in the story is often overlooked. The woman, after listening to the serpent's lies, saw that the forbidden fruit was "pleasing to the eye." Obviously this is a lesson for all of us. Things that appear beautiful and enticing can lead us astray morally. Eve was tempted not only because the serpent told her the fruit would make her godlike and wise, but because it was *pretty*. Instead of thinking like a mature adult—*God told us not to eat from that tree, and since he loves us, he must have a good reason*—Eve thought like a child, *Oooh, that looks so nice, I can't imagine God not wanting us to have it.* Judging purely by appearances gets us into trouble, which is why we are wise to rely on God's judgment, not our own.

Call the story history, call it legend, but definitely call it *truth*, for it shows a deep understanding of human nature. When people do wrong, the first instinct is to hide, then when confronted, the second instinct is to make excuses. The man and woman are each of us: We do what we know is wrong; we try to avoid the inevitable punishment;

and we try to excuse what we did, blaming someone else.

The punishment comes, but it is lighter than promised. God had promised they would die, and in time they do (which suggests that God's original plan was for them to live forever). For the time being, they do not die but are expelled from the lovely garden. Outside of Eden, the ground is "cursed," and the man must labor hard to get his food. It will bring forth weeds in addition to crops, and eventually the man will die and become part of the soil himself. The woman experiences her own punishment: She will bear children in great pain, and she will be dominated by her husband. Presumably before their disobedience, they were equal partners. Now man dominates woman. The shame associated with nakedness means that sex, instead of being beautiful, is going to cause some serious problems for humankind. Marriage and sexuality become contentious instead of blissful.

Paradise is lost. A "cherubim" (the first mention of any type of angel in the Bible) bars the way back to Eden, and so does a "flaming sword flashing back and forth." But in fact, the man and woman were already in exile before God expelled them from the garden. After they ate the fruit, they hid from him. Instead of welcoming his presence as their benevolent creator, they feared him. From this point on, God's "good" creation is constantly marred by human sin. Theologians often refer to Adam and Eve's disobedience as "original sin" ("original" meaning "at the origin"). In some sense, each person born into the world "inherits" the sin—not in the biological sense, of course, but in the sense that we all end up doing just what the original parents did: Seek our own way; make our own rules; be our own judges of right and wrong; be godlike instead of honoring God; blame others (including God himself) for our errors. The disobedience of Adam and Eve is repeated every day.

Considering how important the original sin was, it is not mentioned much in the Old Testament. In fact, Adam is not mentioned outside Genesis, with the exception of a genealogy in 1 Chronicles 1, and in the words of God reported in Hosea 6:7: "Like Adam, they have broken the covenant—they were unfaithful to me there." The Hebrews never forgot their original ancestor's disobedience, which is clear in the New Testament where the apostle Paul contrasts the first Adam, who failed the temptation test, with the "new Adam," Jesus, who was tempted to sin but did not (Romans 5:14; 1 Corinthians 15:22). Paul, like all his Hebrew ancestors, believed that sin and death entered the world thanks to their ancestor Adam, but that through the saving work of

Jesus Christ, the damage done by Adam could be undone—not by getting back to Eden on earth, of course, but by getting to heaven after earthly life ends.

Genesis 3 tells of God putting a curse on the serpent that tempted Adam and Eve. It is made to crawl on its belly forever (as all snakes do), and God decrees there will be permanent enmity between its "seed" (descendants) and the "seed" of the humans: "He will crush your head, and you will strike his heel" (3:15). Literally, this is describing how humans and snakes attack each other—the snake bites at a human's lower limbs, a human tries to strike the snake's head to kill it. But Christians have often read the verse as a kind of prophecy: The serpent is Satan, who bites and annoys mankind, but the human "seed" is Christ, who eventually deals Satan a mortal blow.

THE UNPLEASANT SEQUEL

Genesis 4 is the unhappy sequel to the sin of Adam and Eve. They begin having children, and the older son, Cain, murders his younger brother, Abel. The motive, apparently, is jealousy. For some undisclosed reason, God accepts Abel's offering but does not accept

---

CULTURAL INSIGHTS

Work

Is "work" a "four-letter word"? It may seem that way in our own culture, where fewer and fewer people engage in farming or manufacturing jobs. People today desire more leisure time, and office jobs are considered more desirable than manual labor.

The Hebrews had an entirely different view. From the very beginning, man had work to do: "The Lord God took the man and put him in the Garden of Eden to work it and take care of it" (Genesis 2:15). The Old Testament assumes that work—which for most people meant working with one's hands—is a normal and natural part of human life. Saul, Israel's first king, plows in the field, and the Bible gives no hint that this was beneath a king's dignity. Paul, the great apostle who could have lived off the contributions of the churches he ministered to, plied his trade as a tent-maker. Jesus was a carpenter, and the first Christians felt no shame that the man they believed was the Son of God worked with his hands for a living. The Old Testament prophets had harsh words for the idle and immoral rich. They must have realized that work not only enables people to make a living but also keeps them out of mischief for much of the day.

However, the fall of Adam and Eve into sin changed the nature of work. As part of his punishment for disobeying God, Adam's work became difficult and tedious, done by the "sweat" of his "brow" (Genesis 3:19). It was God's original intention for human beings to work, but the sweaty labor that most people have endured over the centuries is the result of Adam's disobedience.

The Unique Creation of Genesis

Creation is not an important consideration in the pagan religions. People seldom thought of the world around them as being "created" by a god, or being called "good" by that god. Most of the religions had some colorful (usually sexual and/or violent) story about how things came into being, such as a male Heaven impregnating a female Earth, or a god slaying a dragon and making the world from its carcass. But such stories were for amusement more than for belief. In some of those religions, there is no "beginning," just an earth that always existed. There is no conception of there being some divine purposes behind it all. In Genesis, on the other hand, there is purpose: God creates not by an act of violence, but merely by speaking: "God said, 'Let there be...' And it was so." "And God saw that it was good." The climax of this "good" creation is humankind, made in the "image and likeness of God." One God brings everything into existence by his word for the clear purpose of making a good environment for his highest creation, mankind.

The Bible never sees nature as divine. It is, as Genesis says, "good"—but it is not God. Genesis 1 does not even refer to the sun and moon directly—it calls them "the greater light" and "the lesser light." The writer was sending a message: Other religions believe the sun and moon are gods, but we don't. They are just part of the creation. Throughout the Bible there is constant conflict between those who worship nature itself and those who see it as God's creation.

Cain's. Cain sulks, and God tells him, "If you do what is right, will you not be accepted? But if you do not do what is right, sin is crouching at your door; it desires to have you, but you must master it" (4:7). Cain doesn't master it. It masters him, and he kills Abel out in the field. When the Lord asks Cain where Abel is, Cain gives his infamous reply: "I don't know...Am I my brother's keeper?" (4:9). Cain, caught in his sin, follows his parents' lead: Evade responsibility for your acts. The ruse doesn't work. God condemns him to be a "wanderer on the earth." Cain goes "out from the presence of the Lord"—which tells us he is now even further estranged from God than his parents were.

In the New Testament, 1 John 3:12 counsels people, "Do not be like Cain, who belonged to the evil one and murdered his brother. And why did he murder him? Because his own actions were evil and his brother's were righteous." This offers us one explanation of why God accepted Abel's sacrifice but not Cain's. We can also see in this verse how Cain's evil nature established a pattern, which we will see again and again in the Bible and throughout human history: Bad people persecute good people, often with no sense of guilt. Besides being the world's first murderer, Cain was also the first persecutor.

After Cain's being cursed to be a wanderer on the earth, there follows one of the great puzzles of the Bible: Cain takes a wife. Where did she come from? Presumably the only living people on earth were Adam, Eve and Cain? The only sensible answer is that Adam and Eve had daughters who were not named, and Cain married one of them.

Three generations later, a descendant, Lamech, takes not one wife but two. Things are degenerating: A handful of people exist on earth and already there is murder and polygamy, neither of them part of God's original plan. Lamech is not only the first polygamist but the first person to brag about his violent nature. He boasts to both wives that he killed a man for wounding him. He is ecstatic at being vengeful—no principle of "eye for an eye" for Lamech, but, rather, "life for a wound" (Genesis 4:23–24). He never gives a thought to whether his actions might displease God. He himself decides what is good and evil—exactly the privilege Adam and Eve sought when they disobeyed God.

Adam and Eve had another son, Seth, and it is from him that all human beings descend, since he is the ancestor of the famous Noah of the flood story. Genesis 5 tells of the generations between Seth and Noah, giving us the interesting detail that Adam lived to the ripe old age of 930 before he died. (This tells us something about God's mercy. Adam's death sentence was delayed nearly a millennium! God kept his promise that Adam would "surely die" if he ate the forbidden fruit, but a "suspended sentence" of 930 years shows a great deal of compassion.) A few generations later, Methuselah breaks the longevity record, living 969 years. But more interesting than Methuselah was his father, Enoch, who "walked with God, and he was not, for God took him" (5:24 KJV). Meaning what? We aren't completely sure. In the Bible, "walked with God" always means "lived a moral life," so the story suggests that God was so fond of this righteous man that he took him into heaven, without Enoch dying. From the generations between Abel and Noah, Enoch is the only person mentioned as being a righteous man. In the New Testament, the Letter to the Hebrews commends Enoch as "one who pleased God" (11:5).

The amazing life spans reported in Genesis can't help but raise a question. Did people really live hundreds of years? No one knows for sure. Perhaps the importance of the stories is that the gradual shortening of man's life span was the result of the increasing wickedness on the earth. By Genesis 6:3, God decrees that the days of the long, long lives are over, that man's normal life span will be 120 years. Later, of course, it will become even shorter.

Genesis 6 connects the shortening of the life span and the wickedness on the earth to the marrying of the

DID YOU KNOW?

Ever wonder where the expression "raising Cain" came from? When people are squeamish about using profanity, they are reluctant to say "raising hell." And because Cain, the first murderer on earth, presumably went to hell after he died, "raising Cain" has the same meaning as "raising hell."

"sons of God" and the "daughters of men." These verses (6:1–2) have puzzled people for centuries. Who were these "sons of God" and "daughters of men"? Verse 4 speaks of the offspring of the sons of God and daughters of men: the Nephilim, "the heroes of old, men of renown." In the Book of Numbers, "Nephilim" refers to Canaanite giants that intimidated the Israelites, and some interpreters think it is giants that are being referred to here. However, the word can also mean "fallen ones." While no one has satisfactorily explained who the "sons" and "daughters" were, there is an interesting moral lesson in this puzzling passage: The great heroes of the distant past—usually violent, promiscuous, immoral men—are not "heroes" in God's eyes. On the contrary, their exploits are part of the wickedness that leads God to shorten the human life span.

The author of Genesis was taking a slap at pagan mythology and its gods and its heroes who were often described as the offspring of gods and human women. These might have been "heroes" in their own cultures, but judged by God's standards of morality, they were selfish abusers of their fellow human beings—high station, but low morals. Following the description of these wicked beings, Genesis introduces us to a real hero.

THE GLOBAL DELUGE

Methuselah's grandson is one of the best-known men of the Bible: the great Noah, who "found favor in the eyes of the Lord" (6:8). His virtue stands out because the rest of mankind has become more and more wicked—"The Lord saw how great man's wickedness on the earth had become, and that every inclination of the thoughts of his heart was only evil all the time" (6:5). People have become so wicked that God decides to blot out the whole race and begin anew. The human race will begin fresh with Noah and the descendants of his three sons. God tells Noah to build an ark—a kind of colossal floating zoo with three decks and enough space to hold pairs of every animal on earth. The ark measured about 450 feet long, seventy-five feet wide and forty-five feet high, with a door in the side. (Note: The ark was not a real ship, since it had no way of being steered by the people inside it. It was basically a giant life preserver, and if it moved, it was God's doing.)

Part of God's command to Noah involves the first mention of a key word in the Bible: *covenant*. God says, "I will establish my covenant with you." A covenant is an agreement, a pact. God is agreeing to protect Noah and his family during the coming disaster, a global flood. The Lord himself shuts the door on the side of the ark, and rain falls for forty days. The flood is so severe that even the mountaintops are covered. All mankind, and even the land animals and birds, are blotted out. (Worth noting: Among those blotted out was Noah's grandfather, Methuselah, dying at the age of 969. Had the flood not occurred, how long might he have lived?)

There is an often overlooked moral lesson here: The people who died in the flood obviously did not see it coming. Though the Bible does not say so, it's likely they must

Noah

The people who wrote the Bible had a high opinion of Noah, and rightly so, since the world was mired in wickedness while "Noah was a righteous man, blameless among the people of his time, and he walked with God" (Genesis 6:9). We aren't given any specifics about just how he showed his righteousness, nor are we told much about the forms human wickedness took, except that God was appalled at the "violence" (Genesis 6:13). Centuries later, some of Israel's prophets recalled Noah and the flood story, remembering not only Noah's virtue, but the mercy of God in preserving a good man (Isaiah 54:9). The prophet Ezekiel mentioned Noah, Daniel and Job as being among the paragons of right living (14:20).

Centuries later, the Christian author of the Letter to the Hebrews wrote: "By faith Noah, when warned about things not yet seen, in holy fear built an ark to save his family. By his faith he condemned the world and became heir of the righteousness that comes by faith" (11:7). Noah's faith must have been monumental, since he was willing to take God's word about the coming flood, and building something so enormous (and enduring the mocking of his neighbors) required stamina that few of us possess.

Elsewhere the New Testament refers to Noah as a "preacher of righteousness" whom God saved from disaster (2 Peter 2:5). Through the centuries, the Noah story has been an illustration of God preserving the righteous man in times of disaster. No wonder the early Christians often used the ark as a symbol of God's care for his people.

have mocked Noah and his sons for building an enormous wooden barge in a climate region where there was no water. If Noah told them what was to occur, they obviously paid him no heed. In the New Testament, centuries later, Jesus warned people that living an immoral life put them in the same position as the people living in the time of Noah. The judgment of God might occur at any time, catching them unprepared: "For in the days before the flood, people were eating and drinking, marrying and giving in marriage, up to the day Noah entered the ark; and they knew nothing about what would happen until the flood came and took them all away.... Therefore keep watch, because you do not know on what day your Lord will come" (Matthew 24:38–39, 42).

We have to pause here to ask an obvious question: Was the entire world flooded, or is the story just told to remind us of how seriously God takes human sin? It is worth noting that most cultures around the world have a global flood story in some form. Obviously some great flood in the distant past impressed people so much that they believed the entire world was under water. But the Noah story in the Bible is distinct from all the other flood stories in a critical way: It has a moral. In the other flood stories, the flood just happens for no particular reason. Often a fickle god just sends it, and the human survivors are just lucky. But in the Genesis story, everything takes place because of human evil—and because God is compassionate enough to save the one good man on earth and his immediate family. Here is a theme that occurs again and again in the Bible: God saves a "righteous remnant" from disaster. People would always remember Noah as the classic example of the decent man whom God saved from destruction.

Genesis tells us that after 150 days, the waters began to subside, and the ark came to rest on "the mountains of Ararat," an area that is now on the border of Turkey and Armenia. (Many people still believe that the remains of the ark might be somewhere in that area.) Forty more days pass, and Noah sets loose a raven, then a dove, to see if they will stay away (meaning they found a place to roost) or return (meaning there is still no dry land available). Both birds return, but later he sends out the dove again, and it brings back a green olive leaf, a sign that the waters are subsiding. The next time the dove is sent out, it does not return. There is sufficient dry land for human civilization to begin again.

The time is ripe to leave the ark. Noah offers up a thanksgiving sacrifice to God, which itself is worth noting, for in Genesis there are no priests serving as the "middlemen" between God and man. People—Abel was the first—offer their own sacrifices to God, which tells us that in this early period of history, men could approach God on their own, a more direct and personal religion than in later periods when sacrifices had to be done by priests. After the sacrifice, God promises Noah that he will never again flood the entire earth. This is God's covenant—agreement—not only with mankind, but with all living things. As a sign of this promise, God sends his "bow in the clouds"—the rainbow.

AFTER THE FLOOD, MORE EVIL

Genesis never says that Noah's wife, his sons, or his son's wives were righteous—just Noah himself. But 9:20–29 shows that even virtuous people can go astray. Noah plants a vineyard and makes wine—and becomes drunk. He lies in his tent "uncovered"—meaning naked or nearly so. One of his sons, Ham, sees him in this condition and tells the other two brothers, Shem and Japheth. Out of respect for their father, they walk backward into the tent and drape some cloth over their father. Noah awakes from his drunken stupor and pronounces a curse on the less respectful Ham, but a blessing on the other two brothers.

This story puzzles us, raising some questions: Was Noah getting drunk such a horrible thing? And why was Ham cursed just for telling his brothers that their father was "uncovered"? Presumably the issue here is respect for one's parents. The fact that Ham told his brothers what he saw suggests he wanted them to share his amusement at seeing father Noah in such a condition. People in biblical times took parental authority seriously. Shem and Japheth did the right thing: They had no desire to see their father drunk and "uncovered," but apparently Ham did.

There is a memorable moral lesson here: The human evil that God blotted out with the flood still exists, with even the righteous Noah behaving badly, and one of his sons as well.

Genesis 10 is called the "table of nations" because it tells of the descendants of Noah's three sons. This group of genealogies makes for dull reading, but it is worth noting that the names of two of Noah's sons—Ham and Shem—have been used by anthropologists and linguists for centuries to label the tribes that, loosely speaking, are descended from those sons. Various languages and tribes of Africa are referred to as Hamitic, after the son Ham. Shem's name is perpetuated in the word *Semitic*, used to refer to the Hebrews and others, including today's Arabs. In the Bible, Shem's descendants are the main characters, since from Shem descends Jacob, also called Israel, the ancestor of the twelve tribes known as the Israelites, or simply Israel, the "chosen people." Jews trace their descent from Shem, which is why hostility toward Jews is known as anti-Semitism.

The genealogies are interesting for another reason: The descendants of Ham, cursed by Noah, are the ancestors of the various nations that troubled Israel over the centuries—the Egyptians, Canaanites, Babylonians, Assyrians and others.

The descendants "spread out over the earth after the flood" (10:32). At this time, all mankind spoke the same language. Some people settled in a plain called Shinar, an area that is today in Iraq. On that plain they decided to make a monument to human ingenuity: "Come, let us build ourselves a city, with a tower that reaches to the heavens, so that we may make a name for ourselves and not be scattered over the face of the whole earth" (11:4). The Lord sees the tower being built and perceives their motivation. They are trying to do what their ancestors Adam and Eve did: Be gods themselves. The old sins of pride and self-sufficiency are at work. But God frustrates their arrogant plans. He confuses their language, making it impossible for them to understand each other. They can no longer communicate enough to build the tower, so they scatter over the earth. The location of the unfinished tower is called Babel—which, purely by coincidence, resembles our English word *babble*. The literal meaning of the Hebrew word *babel* is "gate of God." The foolish builders must have believed they could open a gateway into heaven.

The Babel story provides an explanation for something humans have long wondered about: Why do people speak different languages? Asking whether the story is literally true is to miss the point of it: The tower was an attempt to be godlike. Human beings cannot, of course, build a tower into heaven. But the point of the story is, they made the attempt. In the Babel story, human alienation from God—and from each other—has become so great that humans can no longer communicate with each other.

We pause here to fast-forward several centuries to the Book of Acts in the New Testament. Acts 2 reports that Jesus' disciples, empowered by the Holy Spirit, were able to speak in languages they had never learned. This amazing phenomenon was interpreted by the early Christians as a kind of "undoing" of what happened at Babel. Because of human arrogance, God gave people different languages, but when people preached the message of the gospel, God made it possible for them to communicate in other languages.

On that somewhat hopeful note we end this chapter, looking forward to another daily lesson where the focus shifts to another Noah-like moral man, Abraham, whose close personal relationship with God will result in his descendants becoming the "chosen people," Israel, the focus of the rest of the Old Testament.

PUTTING THE WORD TO WORK

1. As you go through the day, think of what it means for human beings to be made "in the image of God." Consider what behaviors human beings exhibit that show the divine image. Put another way, what do we do that makes us distinct from the animals?

2. Consider your own and other people's attitudes toward creation. Do people view it as a good gift of God, or do they tend to worship nature itself? How do these attitudes affect our daily lives, laws, decisions?

3. Picture yourself as the man or woman tempted in Eden. Would you have behaved any differently than they did? Why? Have you ever faced any "garden of Eden moments" in your own life? Did you own up to what you did, or did you try evasion or shifting the blame?

4. Notice advertising—TV, magazines, the Internet—and how most of it holds out the classic Eden temptations: X product is "pleasing to the eye," will make us "wise" or even "godlike." To what extent is our culture in general—and yourself in particular—motivated to purchase by such temptations?

5. Think of the "Noahs"—moral people surrounded by immorality—that you've known, either personally or by reputation. What helped them maintain their integrity? Did their faith make a difference?

Making a Chosen People

ABRAHAM AND SONS

AT THE HEART OF IT ALL TODAY

In the second part of the Book of Genesis, God chooses a faithful man, Abraham, and makes a momentous agreement or covenant with him. If Abraham will live a blameless life, God will give him countless descendants, and through them the entire world will be blessed. Walking with God requires deep faith. Abraham and the other people in these stories struggle when things go horribly wrong, but in patience and trust they learn that God always delivers what he promises. In this chapter are some of the best-known stories and events of the Bible—still appealing, perhaps, because the people are so very human, and God loves them anyway.

D ay 1, the previous chapter, did not include The View from History, and for this reason: We simply don't have a very clear idea of when the events of Genesis 1–11 took place. With Genesis 12 and the story of Abraham, however, we can make some educated guesses about when events transpired. Hold on loosely to these dates, since Bible

KEY PASSAGES TO READ TODAY

Genesis 12:1–9; 15:1–6; 18:1–15; 18:22—19:26; 22:1–19; 25:19–34; 28:10–22; 32:22–31; 37:1–37; 39:1–23; 44:1—45:15; 50:15–21

scholars and historians don't agree among themselves when exactly Abraham, Isaac and Jacob lived. But as we progress further into the Bible, dates will become more and more precise, so that as we near the end of the Old Testament, we can state with some certainty that the brief Book of Haggai was written not only in a specific year, but a specific *month* in that year. And bear in mind that chronology, interesting as it is, is not the main message of the Bible. The life lessons are more important by far than the historical data.

Yet this is worth repeating: *The Bible is rooted in history, in real events*, and it never hurts to remind ourselves that characters like Abraham, Moses, David and others were real human beings, living at a specific time, not just in a "once upon a time" land of legend. Although we have no historical evidence for the patriarchs, we do know that some of the personal names found in Genesis were real names used around 2000 BC, names such as Abram, Jacob, Benjamin and Levi. And archaeologists digging in the Middle East often find items that validate parts of Genesis. For example, the childless Abraham's adoption of Eliezer (15:3) follows a custom that has been documented in the ancient site of Nuzi. Marriage contracts found at the same site point to the custom of a childless wife allowing her husband to father children by a slave woman, the practice seen in the story of Abraham, Sarah and the slave Hagar. The same contracts state that if the real wife later bears her husband children, those children take precedence over the slave's children, which is exactly the case in Genesis. The story of Rachel's theft of her father's household idols (31:19) makes sense in light of documents from Nuzi that state that such idols carry the title to inheritance of the father's property. These historical realities in Genesis are not things that some later writer would have invented out of thin air. Obviously these stories— either written or passed on orally—were rooted in real history.

Leave your comfortable and familiar space, go and live among total strangers in a completely new culture. Does that sound like a command you would eagerly obey? But that command, given by God to Abraham, is what dominates the second part of the Book of Genesis, beginning with chapter 12. In a sense, the whole Bible from Genesis 12 on is the story of Abraham's physical and spiritual descendants—people chosen by God, called by God, to be his special people on the earth, holy people. We might call Genesis 12–50 the story of the Bible's "First Family," Abraham and his descendants who will become the nation Israel that is the focus of the Old Testament.

On Day 1 we looked at the origins of the world and humankind, seeing how God created a vast, complex, beautiful universe, pronounced it all "good"—then watched as Adam and Eve foolishly, rashly disobeyed him and lost their place in paradise. Their first son murdered their second son, evil spread far and wide, and God chose to destroy the evil human race, saving the righteous man Noah along with his family from the flood. But even after the flood, the human tendency to do evil persisted. God had promised Noah never to flood the earth again, so now his response to human evil is to *choose*, to *call* one man whose descendants will become a holy people, and through them the entire world will be blessed.

That man, the most important man in the Book of Genesis, is Abram (he will be called Abraham later on), a dweller in the ancient city of Ur, in the area that is later called Babylon, and which today we call Iraq. "The Lord had said to Abram, 'Leave your country, your people and your father's household and go to the land I will show you' " (Genesis 12:1). We too easily pass over this verse, not realizing what it really means: Leave everything you know and love, settle among strangers. It could not have been a pleasant command to obey. He obeys God's call and leaves his homeland to settle in Canaan—a short distance by modern standards, but a long way in ancient times, not to mention the "emotional distance" in being far from one's home and familiar faces. Abram obeys the call of God, believing God's promise that he will become the father of many people, and that through these descendants "all families of the earth be blessed" (Genesis 12:3 KJV).

Let's pause here and consider the word *polytheism*, meaning, worship of many gods. By Abram's time, most human beings were polytheists. As a resident of Ur—already a very ancient city when he was born there—he would have seen temples to various gods, and his own family home would have had its own chapel, with wooden or stone images of the local fertility gods. Like all gods, these were thought of as powerful—but also promiscuous and violent and unpredictable. The gods of polytheism generally lacked the moral nature we associate with the name "God." But Abram turned his back on these gods

Jacob (also named Israel) has twelve sons, the ancestors of the twelve tribes of Israel.

c. 1700 BC
One son, Joseph, becomes chief adviser to Egypt's pharaoh and saves his family from a famine *(Genesis 27–50)*.

Hammurabi, king of Babylon, develops oldest existing law code.

Assyria becomes independent of Babylonia.

KEY TERM FOR TODAY Covenant

You can't really understand the Old or New Testament without grasping the idea of a *covenant*. A covenant was an agreement—a contract, to use a popular word of today. There were covenants between human beings, but the Bible is particularly interested in the covenants between man and God. These were not decided in a "committee meeting" between man and God. Each covenant was given on God's initiative.

Abraham, considered the father of the Hebrews (or Israelites) had an agreement with God: All males in his household and all his male descendants would be circumcised (Genesis 17). Circumcision was the sign that Abraham and his descendants were God's special people, the "people of the covenant." Failure to circumcise was so serious that the person could be expelled from the faith community. "Any uncircumcised male, who has not been circumcised in the flesh, will be cut off from his people; he has broken my covenant" (Genesis 17:14). Later on, the great prophets had to remind Abraham's descendants that the physical circumcision was important, but it meant nothing unless the person's heart and actions were right. Male *proselytes*, non-Israelites who chose to become full members of the spiritual community of Israel, were required to have themselves circumcised. *God-fearers* were non-Israelites who followed Israel's religion but did not take the final step of being circumcised. Among the Israelites, the surgery was performed on infant boys eight days after birth—a practice still followed by Jews today.

after he was called by the one and only God, and through his descendants, faith in this God will be passed on to the world. Abram will also pass on the habit of worshipping God as an invisible Spirit, not making idols to bow down and worship. At various places in Canaan, Abram erects altars to God, and he "calls upon the name of the Lord," but he does not make any images of his God. Centuries later, one of the Ten Commandments given to Moses will make it clear that the Almighty God of the universe is not to be represented by any visual image.

Abram did not go alone, of course. He took with him servants and livestock, also his nephew Lot, and, last but not least, his strikingly beautiful wife, Sarai. She and he were a loving and devoted couple—but childless, which in ancient times was considered a horrible thing. To believe God's promise that he would become the father of a multitude, Abram must indeed have had deep faith, since Sarai was well past childbearing age.

In Canaan, Abram and Lot divide up their flocks, with Lot taking his in one direction, Abram in another. Lot makes a fateful choice. He pitches his tents near the notoriously wicked city of Sodom, to which we will return shortly (Genesis 13:8–13).

Abram's faith seems to waver, as he laments that he is still childless. God tells him to look at the stars in the sky and to believe that his descendants will be just as numerous. Then follows one of the most quoted verses of the Bible: "He believed in the Lord; and he counted it to him for righteousness" (15:6 KJV). Sarai, unfortunately, has less faith than her husband. She has her own plan for getting him some children. He can father children by her Egyptian maid Hagar. Sarai quickly regrets this, as the pregnant Hagar begins to treat her with contempt. She abuses Hagar so badly that the maid flees to the wilderness, where an angel tells her that the son she will bear will be named Ishmael. Hagar returns to her employers and bears Abram the son he had so long desired. But Ishmael is not the son that God had promised Abram.

God tells Abram, "I am God Almighty; walk before me and be blameless. I will confirm my covenant between me and you" (17:1–2). This is one of the great promises of the Bible, the first covenant—contract, agreement—in which God agrees to bless the man who lives righteously. He changes Abram's name to Abraham—from "exalted father" to "father of a multitude." He orders Abraham to be circumcised, along with the other males in the household, with circumcision being the visible sign of the covenant.

Genesis 18 is one of the great and mysterious stories of Genesis. Abraham is resting in his tent in the heat of the day when the Lord appears—in the form of three men. He invites them—Him—to have food and drinks, and the visitors make a promise: They will return in a year and by that time Sarah will have a child. Sarah hears this and laughs to herself. *Impossible*, she thinks. But nothing is impossible for God.

The visitors take their leave, and they are on a grim mission: To pay a visit to the wicked cities of Sodom and Gomorrah. Abraham, realizing that he has been entertaining God himself, asks a question only a person of deep faith could pose: "Will you sweep away the righteous with the wicked?" (18:23). Abraham even adds, "Shall not the Judge of all the earth do right?"—one of the greatest religious questions ever posed by man, and one to which the answer is "Yes, definitely!" Abraham then pleads with God: "Would you destroy Sodom if there were as many as forty righteous people there?" *No.* "What about twenty?" *No.* "What about ten?" *No.* The Lord continues on to Sodom, where, apparently, there were not ten good people living. The Lord who at this point, (Genesis 19) is

CULTURAL INSIGHTS
Sodom and Sodomy

The word *sodomy* comes from the loose-living city of Sodom (Genesis 19). One of its residents, Lot, entertains two heavenly visitors who are about to bring down divine judgment on the immoral town. The men of Sodom surround Lot's house, demanding that he make his male visitors available for sex. The King James Version reads, "Bring them out unto us, that we may know them." More directly, the New International Version reads, "Bring them out to us so that we can have sex with them." This incident is the source for the meaning of the word sodomy.

Lot offers an alternative the men of Sodom don't like: his two virgin daughters. Though this strikes us as a less-than-fatherly gesture, by the standards of the time Lot was being a "good host," protective of his guests, keeping them from the hands of an unruly mob. The lecherous men become enraged and try to break down Lot's door. Lot's two heavenly visitors strike the men with blindness. In the end of this sordid tale, Lot's family flees, and God rains down fire on the wicked place.

Sodom and Gomorrah are mentioned many times in both the Old and New Testaments, always being seen as symbols of corruption and wickedness that are under God's judgment. Even today, people unfamiliar with the Bible will refer to an immoral place as "Sodom."

Where was Sodom? Archaeologists and historians debate that question, and one strong possibility is that the site of the doomed city is now under the waters of (appropriately) the Dead Sea.

traveling in the form of two human males, meets with Abraham's nephew Lot in Sodom, and Lot invites them to his home. There follows the perverse scene of the local men surrounding Lot's house, demanding he hand the two men over—for sex. The two visitors inform Lot that the city will be destroyed, and only he and his wife and daughters will escape. Apparently Lot has less faith than his uncle, for Genesis tells us that in spite of the dire warning, "he lingered." The divine visitors insist Lot "escape to the hills, lest you be swept away." The family flees, and at sunup the Lord rains down fire and brimstone on Sodom—which may mean he destroyed it with a volcanic eruption. From a distance, Abraham sees the smoke from the cities going up "like the smoke of a furnace."

The story has an unpleasant twist ending. The visitors had ordered Lot and the family to flee and not look back. Lot's wife *does* look back—and is turned into a "pillar of salt" (19:26). In the New Testament, the phrase "remember Lot's wife" is a reminder to Christians to flee their past sins and not look back. Lot's wife was wrong to disobey God's command—and to gaze back at the wicked city she should have been glad to escape from alive.

LAUGHTER AND DISTRESS

Genesis 21 returns to the story of Abraham and Sarah. As God promised, the aged woman gives birth to a son, named Isaac (the name means "laughter," a reminder of Sarah laughing at the prophecy that she would give birth). Regrettably, the child is not destined to get along with his older half-brother, Ishmael. At Sarah's urging, Abraham packs off Hagar and Ishmael, with only a little food and water. Far off in the wilderness, Hagar fears they will die of thirst, but God shows them a well.

One important thing about Isaac's birth that we people of the twenty-first century have trouble understanding is this: He was *not* Abraham's firstborn son. People in ancient times showed great favor to the firstborn son. He was the "opening of the womb" that every parent prayed for and doted on. From this fully understandable love for the firstborn grew the practice of *primogeniture*, giving the firstborn son the largest share of the family inheritance. The later children weren't left with nothing, of course, but they received much less than the oldest son. It was part of the ancient world's "folk wisdom" that the firstborn would be the most successful in life—and deserve to be. From the day he was born, the oldest son was a privileged character. But here is where the Bible shows God's ways as being wiser—and more surprising—than our own. Again and

Canaan

"Canaan" in the Old Testament referred to the general area occupied by the Israelites—roughly the same area as is occupied today by the nation Israel. The "Canaanites" referred to the land's original inhabitants, idol-worshippers who were driven out or killed when the Israelites settled in the area after their exodus from Egypt. Genesis states that the Canaanites were descendants of Noah's son Ham, while the Israelites were descendants of Noah's son Shem. Throughout the Old Testament, there is almost constant conflict between the Canaanites and Israelites. The patriarch Abraham obeyed God's call to leave his homeland in Ur (in today's Iraq) and settle in Canaan, where the people's violence and immorality is seen clearly in the story of God's destruction of the wicked cities Sodom and Gomorrah.

The name Canaan itself meant "land of the purple," referring to a rich purple dye that was made in the region. The Canaanites bequeathed something of great importance to the human race: the use of an alphabet. The Hebrew alphabet used in the original Old Testament developed from the Canaanites' alphabet.

Canaan happened to lie between several empires, all of them dedicated to expanding —meaning, conquering nearby territories. Egypt lay to the southwest, Babylon and Assyria to the northeast, Hittites and others to the northwest. Throughout its history, Canaan must have felt like a football, always "in play" between neighbor countries larger and more powerful than itself. No wonder the descendants of Abraham understood the need to rely on God's aid.

again in the Bible, many of the people God chooses to carry out his plans are *not* the firstborn in their families. Think back to Genesis 4, where Adam and Eve's firstborn, Cain, is a murderer. Abraham's second son, Isaac, is the one who will inherit Abraham's promises, not the firstborn, Ishmael. Among Jacob's twelve sons, the oldest, Reuben, is among the least important. Centuries later, Israel's greatest king, David, is the *youngest* of many brothers. And David's famous son, King Solomon, is not David's oldest. The pattern repeats itself many times. Primogeniture seems to be the common pattern in human custom, but God has his own way of doing things.

One of the most intense stories in the Bible follows the story of Isaac's birth. Genesis 22 tells of God's "testing" of the faithful Abraham. After years of hoping for a son to be born to him and the lovely Sarah, Abraham finally has his son Isaac. Then God delivers a shocking command: He tells Abraham to take Isaac, "whom you love," and sacrifice him on a mountain. Curiously, Genesis does not tell of Abraham's emotional state following this command. It does not need to. He must have been in shock, yet he obeyed. The

What's in a Name, Ab?

You can't help but notice that many biblical names—especially in the Old Testament—are peculiar. They seem less so when you realize that a name was picked because it had a meaning, not just because it "sounded nice," or because it was the name of some celebrity or relative.

Notice how many Old Testament names contain a -*iah* or an -*el* at the end (or sometimes *El-* at the beginning of a name). The -*iah* (sometimes -*jah* also) was actually the Hebrew name *Yah*, the name of God. *El* meant, simply, God. So every name with -*iah* or -*el* has some meaning relating to God. *Isaiah*, for example, means "Yah [God] saves." *Zechariah* means "Yah [God] remembers." *Daniel* means "El [God] is judge." *Elijah* combines the two names and means "Yah is God."

In Genesis we meet the first biblical character with the Hebrew word *Ab*, "father," in his name. This is Abram ("father of many"), later called Abraham ("exalted father"). There are numerous other biblical characters with *Ab* in their names, and all the names have meaning, such as Abiel ("father is God") and the similar Eliab ("God is father"), Abimelech ("father is a king"), Abijah ("Yah is father"), and many others. Although the Old Testament very seldom refers to God as "father," it is obvious in some of these names that the ancient Hebrews did think of God as being their heavenly Father.

next morning he departs with his son—who doesn't know what is to happen, of course—and two male servants. They travel to the mountain, and Abraham piles up wood for a fire, which will burn Isaac after he kills him with a knife. To add to the emotion of the story, poor Isaac asks his father an obvious question: "Where is the animal we are going to sacrifice?" Abraham replies, "God will provide." Abraham binds Isaac and lays him on top of the wood. Abraham is about to plunge his knife into the beloved child when he hears God's angel calling his name. The tension in the story breaks as the angel says, "Do not lay a hand on the boy... for now I know that you fear God" (22:12). The man of deep faith has passed the ultimate test. He trusted God, and the Judge of the earth did right. The angel reiterates the divine promise: Through Isaac, Abraham will be the father of many. There are few episodes in the Bible—or in all the books of the world—more dramatic than this. No wonder that Jews, Christians and Muslims all regard Abraham as a role model of faith.

We can well imagine that the near-sacrifice made a deep impression on the boy Isaac as well. However, in Genesis the story of the adult Isaac is quickly told, since the narrator seems in a hurry to get to the more interesting story of Isaac's sons. If you have the time, however, the story of Isaac's wooing of his beautiful cousin Rebecca, found in Genesis 24, is a pleasure to read.

At age sixty, Isaac fathers twin sons, Esau and Jacob. These two are definitely *not* identical twins—far from it. Calling them fraternal twins doesn't sound quite right, either, because there was no brotherly love at all between these two. In fact, poor Rebecca endured a difficult pregnancy, with the two unborn children seemingly "warring" within her. At the time of their birth, the Lord tells her that the two sons will be the fathers of two nations, never at peace with each other (Genesis 25:22–23).

JACOB THE CRAFTY

If you do a lot of reading, you're familiar with a character that has appeared in literature and folklore for thousands of years—the Trickster, the lovable rogue who engages in morally questionable behavior but somehow provokes our admiration. Mark Twain's Huckleberry Finn and Tom Sawyer are two classic examples, and many of Shakespeare's comedies (and today's sitcoms) have similar characters. We find them appealing

CHARACTER CLOSE-UP
Abraham in the New Testament

As the spiritual and physical ancestor of the Israelites, Abraham is mentioned often in the New Testament—seventy-seven times, more than any other Old Testament figure except Moses, who is mentioned seventy-nine times. Jesus' parable of Lazarus the beggar (Luke 16) shows that the Jews of that time thought of heaven as eternal fellowship with the great patriarchs, since the beggar is carried to "Abraham's bosom" (or "Abraham's side" in modern translations). The idea is that in heaven all people are "bosom buddies" of the great role models of the faith. Jesus several times mentions heaven being a feast where people are seated at the table of Abraham, Isaac and Jacob.

However, for Jesus and the apostles, the spiritual connection to Abraham was what mattered, not physical descent from him, and Abraham's descendants who rejected the truth were no better off than unbelievers. Abraham's true children are those who live by faith, as Abraham did. Several New Testament passages quote Genesis 15:6: "Abraham believed the Lord, and he credited it to him as righteousness." The apostle Paul also wrote that faith, not physical descent, makes people "children of Abraham": "Understand, then, that those who believe are children of Abraham" (Galatians 3:7). "If you belong to Christ, then you are Abraham's seed, and heirs according to the promise" (Galatians 3:29). Paul, proud of his Jewish background and his own descent from Abraham, was pleased to announce to the world that all people, if they had faith, were "Abraham's seed." In the New Testament, the Christian faith is the fulfillment of God's promise to Abraham: Through Abraham's descendants, all the earth would be blessed.

because they do things we all wish we could get away with—and, unlike us, they often don't suffer the consequences of their scheming.

The Bible's classic sneak is Jacob, the smooth-skinned twin brother of the hairy Esau. Since the ancient world placed a huge emphasis on the privileges of the firstborn son, Jacob was considered second-best. Even though he and Esau were technically twins, Esau was delivered first, and in the eyes of the ancient world, Jacob was the Number Two son, as if he'd been born years after Esau. The two sons' behavior as adults gave every indication that Esau was the more impressive character, engaging in manly pursuits like hunting while Jacob became more of a stay-at-home Mama's boy. Jacob was the favorite of his mother, Rebecca, while Esau was the favorite of Isaac. But it was part of God's plan to create his "chosen people" from Jacob's descendants, not Esau's.

By rights and custom, Esau would receive his *birthright*, the lion's share of the family inheritance, from his father. Jacob had other ideas, and so did his mother. They were helped by Esau's own dimwittedness—and letting hunger override his brain. Coming in tired from hunting, Esau begs Jacob for some of the stew he is cooking. Almost as a joke, Jacob makes an offer: "I give you stew, you give me the birthright." Rashly, Esau agrees to this very unfair trade. Later, however, this ridiculous bargain seems to be forgotten by everyone, so Jacob and Rebecca devise a plan. Jacob will go to the elderly, nearly blind Isaac, pretend to be Esau, and get his father's blessing—and the birthright. Since Esau is notoriously hairy, Jacob disguises his smooth arms and hands with goatskins, deceiving his old father. Apparently Isaac trusts his fingers more than his ears, for he notes that the voice sounds like Jacob, but the hands are Esau's, so he does indeed bestow the birthright blessing on Jacob. Esau is horrified to learn what happened, of course, and wants it all revoked. But people in biblical times took blessing and cursing seriously. Isaac has bestowed the blessing, and it can't be undone. He blesses Esau, but it is a lesser blessing than what Jacob received.

Jacob's Ladder

Did you ever sing the old camp song "We Are Climbing Jacob's Ladder"? The song is based on Genesis 28:10–22. Jacob, fleeing from his wrathful brother Esau, sleeps in the wilderness, using a stone for a pillow. Jacob dreams one of the most famous dreams in the history of the world: He sees a ladder (or "stairway," as some translations have it) going up to heaven, with angels going up and down on it. At the top of the stairway, out of sight, God repeats to Jacob the promise he made to Abraham: His descendants will be a great multitude. And he makes a life-changing promise to Jacob: "I will be with you and will keep you wherever you go."

Naturally this dream has a powerful effect on Jacob: "He was afraid and said, 'How awesome is this place! This is none other than the house of God; this is the gate of heaven'" (Genesis 28:17). He names the site *Bethel*, Hebrew for "house of God." The site will play an important part in the history of Israel. The name, thanks to its meaning, has been often used for churches, religious colleges, even for cities.

Jacob's dream has been a popular subject for artists, who have enjoyed depicting the angels on the stairs, with the snoozing Jacob lying with his head on a stone.

So far, Jacob has played his Trickster role to the hilt. But as often happens in the real world, the Trickster encounters a Master Trickster. In this case it is his mother's brother, Laban. Jacob, fearing the wrath of Esau (with good reason), goes to live with Laban and falls passionately in love with his beautiful cousin Rachel. He strikes a bargain with his uncle: He will serve him as a herdsman for seven years, at the end of which he will marry Rachel. It is worth pausing here to note that even a scheming Mama's boy is capable of deep love. No man would work hard for seven years if his love were not deep and abiding. But the impassioned man gets a surprise on his wedding night. The veiled woman he takes to the marriage bed is not the lovely Rachel, but her plain sister, Leah. Jacob the trickster has been soundly tricked. His uncle explains himself: It is their custom to marry off the older sister first, so Jacob had no choice. Laban makes Jacob serve him for another seven years in order to get Rachel. Happily for Jacob, he does not have to wait the seven additional years to take Rachel as his wife.

He is married to both sisters, a situation that will prove to be (using our modern term) *dysfunctional*, especially since the household will include not only his two wives and their children but also children by two concubines, his wives' maids. Poor homely Leah knows she is not loved—yet she bears Jacob sons, while the well-loved Rachel goes for years without bearing children. (Although polygamy is accepted as normal in the Old Testament, there is no hint that it makes for a harmonious family life—quite the opposite, in fact!)

Nomadic Assets

Genesis gives the distinct impression that a person's wealth was measured not in money or land, but in flocks—sheep, goats and other livestock. Abraham and his descendants in Genesis are nomads, meaning they lived in tents instead of houses. They had no permanent place of residence. They pitched their tents in places where the grazing was good, and when there was not enough vegetation for the flocks to eat, or the weather changed for the worse, they moved elsewhere. The flocks provided the basic necessities of life—milk and meat for food, skins and hair (wool) for making tents and clothing. In a land with many nomads, cities were far apart and small. In fact, where Genesis has "cities," mentally insert the word "towns" or "villages."

The idea of God's people as "just passing through" the world, with no permanent residence here, is found in the New Testament. The first Christians could see that their ultimate home—and destination—was heaven, with this world being only their temporary abode. They probably had in mind the nomadic life of Abraham, Isaac and Jacob, as well as the Israelites journeying toward Canaan in the Book of Exodus.

God moves in mysterious ways. Jacob—a contemptible schemer in his younger days and one who made his unattractive wife Leah feel unloved—is a roguish character, yet it is through his twelve sons and their descendants that God molds the nation Israel. In fact, Israel is Jacob's second name, a name bestowed on him after a bizarre encounter with God—in human form—wrestling with Jacob all night in the wilderness. Jacob does not give up easily in this fight, and he tells his mysterious visitor (God), "I will not let you go until you bless me." "Then the man said, 'Your name will no longer be Jacob, but Israel, because you have struggled with God and with men and have overcome'" (32:28). The name *Israel* means "struggles with God." You might say that Israel is the name of the better side of Jacob, which is why his descendants called themselves "children of Israel," very seldom "children of Jacob."

The stories of Jacob remind us of the truthfulness of the Bible. If the Bible were fiction, it probably would not have included stories showing how sneaky Jacob could be. The writers of Genesis made no effort to "clean up" history, or try to present the main characters as flawless saints.

SIBLING DEVILRY

Brother hating brother seems to be a common occurrence in Genesis. The first brother, Cain, kills his brother Abel. The twins Jacob and Esau are at odds, and for the legitimate reason that Jacob tricked Esau out of their father's blessing. Jacob spends much of his life avoiding the wrath of Esau, but in Genesis 33 the inevitable confrontation takes place. By this time Jacob is a prosperous nomad with two wives, two concubines, eleven sons, and flocks of livestock. The day following his famous wrestling match with God, Jacob sees Esau marching out with four hundred men. Jacob fears a bloodbath—or, at least, his own death and the capture of his wives, sons and flocks.

Nothing of the kind happens. Esau hugs and kisses his wayward brother, and they both shed tears. After living in fear for years, Jacob finally is at peace with his one brother (Genesis 33).

But sibling problems tend to run in this family—which seems inevitable, given that the numerous sons have four different mothers. The four women know Jacob does not love them equally. His real love goes out only to the comely Rachel—who dies giving birth to her second child, Benjamin. Jacob naturally lavishes more love on Rachel's two sons, the baby Benjamin and, more importantly, Joseph. From Genesis 37 on to the end of the book, the chief character is the spoiled but ultimately powerful Joseph.

Genesis 37 tells us that Jacob gave his favorite son a "coat of many colors" (or, in newer translations, "coat with long sleeves"). Whatever the coat was, it made him stand out from the rest of the brothers. This obviously irked the brothers, who were also irked that Joseph sometimes tattled on them. But even worse, Joseph reported having dreams where his brothers—and even his father!—were all bowing down to him. Not surprisingly, "his brothers were jealous of him." They seem determined that his dream will never come to pass—but, as often happens in the Bible, God has other plans.

Jacob sends Joseph—wearing his robe, of course—out to check on his brothers who are grazing their flocks far from home. The brothers see an opportunity. They can kill the spoiled brat and no one will know what happened. At first they plan to kill him and throw him in a pit, but then they decide to throw him alive into the pit. A caravan of traders passes by, and brother Judah has a brainstorm: Sell Joseph as a slave to the traders, make a profit from it, and ease their consciences of doing him physical harm. So his own brothers sell Joseph as a slave for twenty pieces of silver, and Joseph is taken into Egypt. The brothers dip Joseph's gorgeous robe in goat's blood, return home, and show it to the distraught Jacob, who believes some wild animal has killed his favorite son.

In fact, Joseph is alive and well in Egypt. "The Lord was with Joseph" (Genesis 39:2), and though Joseph is

DID YOU KNOW?

Our phrase "fat of the land" is from Genesis 45:18, where Joseph tells his eleven brothers, "I will give you the best of the land of Egypt, and you will eat the fat of the land." This same section of Genesis is also the source of the phrase "land of Goshen," Goshen being the very fertile area of Egypt where Jacob and sons settled. Considering that Goshen was a desirable area to live in—until centuries later, when the Israelites were enslaved by the Egyptians—"land of Goshen" was another way of saying "good heavens!"

Who Were the "Patriarchs"?

The word *patriarchs* actually means "ruling fathers." In the Bible, though, "the patriarchs" were the ancestors of the chosen people, the nation of Israel. The most important patriarchs were Abraham, the man whom God promised the land of Canaan, plus Isaac (Abraham's son), and Jacob (Isaac's son, who also had the name Israel). These figures are especially important because of God's promises to them.

Abraham, whose story is told in Genesis 12 through 25, is the patriarch par excellence. Even though it was Abraham's grandson Jacob who lent his name from God, Israel, to the whole nation, Abraham is considered the true spiritual father of Israel. This is natural, since in most ways he was a more admirable and more moral character than Jacob. But, more importantly, Abraham was called by God to leave his idol-worshipping homeland of Chaldea and settle in Canaan, "the promised land." Also very important is that Abraham endured a severe testing of his faith when God asked him to sacrifice his beloved son Isaac. This story, one of the most dramatic and most touching in the Bible, is found in Genesis 22.

Sometimes "the patriarchs" refers not only to Abraham, Isaac and Jacob, but also to their distant ancestors in the Book of Genesis: Adam, Methuselah, Noah, etc. Jacob's twelve sons—who were the ancestors of the "twelve tribes of Israel"—are also referred to as patriarchs. One easy way to remember who the patriarchs were: They were all the important men who preceded the life of Moses, related in the Book of Exodus.

a slave in the house of a high official named Potiphar, he is so wise and trustworthy that Potiphar eventually makes him head over the entire household. What ends this cozy situation is the lust of Potiphar's wife. Joseph is handsome and young, and the wife tries repeatedly to entice him into her bed. Joseph is a decent man, and he refuses her. She has her vengeance. Alone in the house one day with Joseph, she cries out that Joseph has tried to rape her. Her husband is enraged, naturally: The Hebrew slave he trusted so much has betrayed him. He throws Joseph into the royal prison. But, again, "the Lord was with Joseph." Joseph shows such intelligence that the *prison keeper* makes him his second in command.

Genesis 40 shows that Joseph is not only a dreamer but an interpreter of dreams. Two of the prisoners, both of them former servants of Pharaoh, tell him their dreams. Joseph explains that the cupbearer's dream is a prophecy that he will be freed from prison and restored to office. It happens as predicted. Joseph also explains the baker's dream: He will be beheaded with his body thrown out for the birds to eat. Sadly, this dream comes true also. In the meantime, the cupbearer, serving Pharaoh again, learns that his boss is having dreams he cannot interpret. The cupbearer remembers Joseph's amazing abilities, and he mentions it to Pharaoh, who is distraught because his court counselors have no luck interpreting the dreams. Joseph is brought in and explains Pharaoh's dream. Seven thin cows devouring seven fat cows are a prophecy of what will happen in Egypt. There will be seven years of good harvests, followed by seven years of famine. Joseph suggests that some wise man be put in charge of a program to store up food from the good years so that people will not starve in the years of famine.

Remarkably, the former slave and prisoner is made Pharaoh's right-hand man. Joseph wears the king's signet ring, dresses in fine clothes, and has a gold chain around his neck. He marries an Egyptian wife, has sons, and is even more respected when the famine he predicted really does take place.

The famine takes place in Canaan, Joseph's homeland, also. Jacob sends his sons down to Egypt to buy grain. Inevitably, they encounter Joseph, but, of course, they do not recognize him in his Egyptian clothing. (The Egyptian men also wore heavy eye makeup and had their heads shaved.) However, Joseph does recognize his brothers. Here is a tense moment: The brothers bow down to this "Egyptian" official—meaning Joseph's long-ago

---

DID YOU KNOW? # A Book of Firsts

As you might expect, there are numerous "firsts" in the Book of Genesis. For example:

- Genesis 15:1 has the first instance of a phrase used many times in the Bible: "the word of the Lord came to..." The word came to Abraham, which is why he is the first man in the Bible called a *prophet*, one who receives the word of the Lord. We will encounter "the word of the Lord" in later chapters, and meet with many other prophets.

- The first priest mentioned in the Bible is Melchizedek, who is both priest and king of Salem (Genesis 14:18). The Melchizedek story is also the Bible's first mention of *tithing*, offering *one tenth* of one's goods to God—or, more precisely, to his ministers. Abraham offered a tithe to Melchizedek. The story is also the first mention of the most-mentioned city in the Bible—Jerusalem, though here the locale is simply called Salem, a lovely name with a lovely meaning: *peace*. (The longer name, Jerusalem, means "foundation of peace.")

- Genesis 29:14 is the first use of the common biblical phrase "flesh and blood," which in the Old Testament refers to relatives and, later, to fellow Israelites. The fact that here in the twenty-first century we still use "flesh and blood" to refer to our relatives is a witness to the influence of the Bible on our thoughts and vocabulary.

Wrapping up this list of "firsts" in Genesis: the first mention of prayer, found in Genesis 20:17. The first person mentioned as praying is Abraham.

dream has come to pass. Understandably, Joseph would hate them for what they did to him. In fact, at first he treats them roughly and accuses them of being spies from Canaan. Joseph puts them to a test. He will hold them in custody until they have their youngest brother, Benjamin, brought down to Egypt. The brothers speak to each other in Hebrew, not knowing Joseph can understand them. They wonder if they are being punished for what they did to Joseph long ago. Joseph realizes his wayward brothers do possess a conscience. He is so touched he goes away from them and weeps. He sends the brothers home with the grain they bought—but when they stop to rest along the way, they discover the money they had paid for the grain has been put back in the sacks of grain.

Back in Canaan, the brothers report to Jacob that they have to carry brother Benjamin back to Egypt with them. Jacob is unwilling, of course, since his only other son by Rachel, Joseph, disappeared long ago. But the brothers, Benjamin included, return to Egypt. To their surprise, Joseph throws a feast for them. He is so touched at the sight of Benjamin that he has to leave them.

In chapter 45, Joseph finally reveals himself to his brothers. He tells them not to feel guilty for selling him into slavery, for God had used his adversity to raise him to high office, saving Egypt from famine and ensuring that Egypt would have enough food to keep Jacob's sons alive as well. "You intended to harm me, but God intended it for good to accomplish what is now being done, the saving of many lives" (Genesis 50:20). Joseph kisses his brothers and they all have a good cry. He has his old father brought down to Egypt, and the two have a tearful reunion. Jacob's brothers and their numerous wives and children settle in a region of Egypt known as Goshen. The Book of Genesis ends with the dying Jacob pronouncing blessings on his twelve sons and prophesying what will become of their descendants in the years to come. Jacob dies at age 110 and is embalmed and buried in Canaan. Joseph remembers that he himself is a native of Canaan, not Egypt, and he makes his brothers promise him that their descendants will someday rebury him back in Canaan.

All the descendants of Jacob—also known as Israel—are living comfortably in Egypt. The stage is set for a dramatic change of fortunes that will occur at the beginning of the Book of Exodus. But for now, the children of Israel are happy and content, having learned the lesson from Joseph: God can bring good out of evil, prosperity out of adversity. Joseph sets the pattern for the Israelite wise man. Instead of being crushed or driven to despair by adversity, he accepts it as a challenge and manages to rise above it.

In closing this chapter, let's remind ourselves that Genesis is the first book of what the Israelites called the Torah, a Hebrew word usually translated "law" but really meaning "instruction" or "guidance." Genesis does not contain actual commandments or instructions as are found in Exodus through Deuteronomy, but it does contain guidance in the form of moral role models, Joseph being the supreme example in the book.

PUTTING THE WORD TO WORK

1. Abraham's near-sacrifice of his beloved son Isaac shows his deep faith in God. Think of people you have known who seemed to possess such faith. Have you known any who would have given up the thing they loved most in the world, if God had asked them to? What would you have done if God asked you to make the sacrifice Abraham was asked to make?

2. God tells Abraham to "walk before me and be blameless." Based on the stories of Abraham and the other characters in today's reading, what would a "blameless" life be like?

3. Jacob's famous dream at Bethel, with the angels walking on a stairway to heaven, is one of the great moments in the Bible, showing a man who had a deep sense of God's presence. Note that the incident occurred when Jacob was fearing the wrath of his brother Esau. Can you think of times in your own life when you sensed God's presence more intensely as you faced a great challenge?

4. In the touching story of Joseph and his brothers, the most memorable words are when Joseph tells his brothers that though they meant to do him harm, "God meant it for good." Think of times in your own life when adversities led, eventually, to better things—when sickness, job loss, financial setbacks, loss of a loved one or betrayal by someone you trusted resulted in something better later on.

5. More than once in Genesis, feuding brothers forgive each other in tearful reunions. Think of times in your own life, or the lives of people you know, when old grudges and hostilities were put aside. Also, think of people you wish you had forgiven—and people you wish you had asked for forgiveness. Finally, think of people you ought to forgive *now*.

Slavery, Miracles and Freedom

MOSES AND THE EXODUS

AT THE HEART OF IT ALL TODAY The Exodus story, the high point of the Old Testament, is a story of miracles —and trust in God. In his own time and his own way, God frees the Israelite slaves in Egypt, despite the stubbornness of the oppressive Egyptian king and the constant doubting and grumbling of the Israelites. Today's chapter reminds us that a God who can free a horde of slaves from a mighty empire is a God who will do everything possible, and impossible, to save his people.

Movie director Cecil B. DeMille was so drawn to the epic saga of Moses that he filmed it twice: once in 1923 (silent and black-and-white) and again in 1956 (with sound and gaudy color). The

KEY PASSAGES TO READ TODAY

Exodus 1–4; 7; 12:29–40; 14

second version is one of the most-watched films ever made, and rightly so, for who can resist the story of a nation of slaves being delivered from bondage by a God who displays miraculous power in such dramatic fashion? DeMille understood that the story is the very heart of the Old Testament, the Big Event that ancient Israel never forgot, the event that they forever remembered as evidence of God's love for his people. He also understood that the story continues to inspire people who yearn to be free from oppression.

Although the main character in the story is God himself, the prominent *human* character is the amazing Moses, one of the great men of history, whose story is a reminder that truth is sometimes stranger (and more awe-inspiring) than fiction.

Today we'll look at the first part of the Book of Exodus, from the enslaving of the Israelites in Egypt to their pausing at Mount Sinai after their deliverance. Tomorrow we'll look at the giving of the divine Law at Sinai, and the Israelites' further progress toward their homeland of Canaan.

Before we begin in Exodus, let's pause a moment for a quick overview of the first five books of the Bible—Genesis, Exodus, Leviticus, Numbers, Deuteronomy. The collection goes by several names: Torah (a Hebrew word meaning "instruction" or "guidance"), Pentateuch (Greek for "five scrolls"), the Law, and the Five Books of Moses. They are first in the Old Testament because they cover the oldest part of history, and also because ancient Israel considered them the most important books. Tradition says that Moses was their author, or main author, so the books had the authority of the amazing man who had seen God face to face. They were the first books to be accepted by Israel as *sacred* and *inspired* and *holy*. Even after the other parts of the Old Testament were written and, in time, accepted as inspired, the Five Books of Moses held a special place, which is evident in the New Testament, where both Jesus and his opponents quoted often from the first five books. Ancient Israel did not just see the books as sacred history, but as the Law that was given by God to mankind for all time. In fact, the later books of the Old Testament are essentially the story of how the Israelites did—or more often did *not*—obey the Law of God, and the consequences they suffered. This is even so in the New Testament, where Jesus and his enemies debated the Big Question: *How do we obey the Law given by the mighty, loving God who delivered his people from slavery?*

With all that in mind, let's look at Exodus.

CHANGING PHARAOHS

The Book of Genesis ends with the word "Egypt." As we saw in the last chapter, Jacob and his twelve sons and their families were living in Egypt, having fled there to escape famine back in Canaan. And thanks to son Joseph's being second-in-command to the Pharaoh himself, the enormous clan was comfortable and happy. Genesis ends with the dying Joseph prophesying that his family will someday return to Canaan, and that his own coffin will be reburied there. What we often overlook in reading the story of Israel is that Jacob's descendants settle in Egypt and show no interest in returning to Canaan—despite God's promise to Abraham that the land of Canaan was to be their homeland. Their reluctance to go back there is understandable: Life in Egypt was easier than in Canaan, and though they were regarded as foreigners in Egypt, they were foreigners in Canaan as well, having lived there only three generations. It was easy for them to forget—or perhaps they no longer cared—about their destiny in Canaan. But something was about to change their pleasant life in Egypt.

Exodus (the book's title is Greek for "going out") opens with the statement that the twelve sons of Jacob—also known as Israel— "multiplied and grew exceedingly strong" in Egypt. But the happy situation ends at 1:8, where we learn that a new Pharaoh came to power, and he had no respect for the fondly remembered Joseph, or Joseph's kinsmen, the Israelites. In fact, this new Pharaoh feared that these foreigners in his kingdom might, if war came, side with their enemies, particularly since they lived on Egypt's frontier, the first

c. 1700—c. 1250 BC
The Israelites (Jacob's twelve sons' descendants) are enslaved in Egypt *(Exodus 1)*.

1317–1301 BC
Reign of Pharaoh Seti I

c. 1300–1200 BC
The earliest evidence of ironworking is found at the center of the developing Indo-Gangetic culture, near present-day New Delhi and Mathura.

1301–1234 BC
Reign of Pharaoh Rameses II

c. 1250 BC
Phrygians come from the Balkans to Asia Minor— the first Great Movement of Nations begins.

Moses, an Israelite reared in the Egyptian court, leads the Israelites out of Egypt, preceded by miraculous plagues on the Egyptians *(Exodus 2–15)*.

c. 1250—c. 1210 BC
The Israelites wander in the desert for forty years before entering the land of Canaan. In this period Moses receives the Law at Mount Sinai and passes on divinely given laws to the Israelites. *(Exodus 16— Deuteronomy 34).*

c. 1200 BC
Start of the Trojan War

region an invading army would pass through. So under this new king, the Israelites changed from being resident aliens to slaves, put to hard labor on the Pharaoh's colossal building projects. Apparently they still reproduced quickly despite their hard labor, so the Pharaoh ordered the Hebrew midwives to kill any male children who were born. They did not—proving they feared God more than they feared the Pharaoh, and also proving they were women of good character. In fact, they told Pharaoh a blatant lie, saying that the Hebrew women were so "vigorous" that their children were already born before the midwives arrived to assist! Pharaoh may have sensed the lie, but he could not punish them without exposing his plan to kill the infant Hebrews. Since the midwives had not cooperated, he ordered his own people to carry out the slaughter: Every Hebrew male infant was to be thrown into the Nile.

Chapter 2 begins the story of Moses. He is born, and his mother manages to hide him for three months from the Egyptians. Then, fearing detection, she places him in a basket (a sort of floating cradle) in the river, where the baby's older sister watches after him. In the plan of God, something amazing happens: Pharaoh's daughter goes to the river with her servants to bathe, and she sees the basket and has it brought to her. She knows it is a Hebrew child, but she takes pity on it and adopts it as her own. The baby's sister suggests a Hebrew woman—the child's real mother—as a wet nurse. We aren't told just how long the baby Moses remains with his real mother, but at some point Pharaoh's daughter adopts him, naming him Moses.

Here there is a gap in the story. What was Moses doing all those years? The usual answer is that as Pharaoh's daughter's son, he was raised as a prince of Egypt, living in luxury and

KEY TERM FOR TODAY ## Yahweh

God is called by many names in the Old Testament, but most commonly by the name Yahweh, used more than six thousand times—more times than all the other names of God put together. In the famous encounter at the burning bush, God tells Moses he is "Yahweh," the God worshipped by the patriarchs Abraham, Isaac and Jacob. You might say that Yahweh was Israel's distinctive name for God, since no other nation or tribe used the name.

Short forms of *Yahweh* were *Yah* and *Yahu*, and these appear in many names we recognize: Isaiah (or, correctly, *Isayah*), Elijah (*Eliyah*), Jeremiah (*Yeremyahu*). The many -iah and -jah names in the Old Testament all contain the name of God, and all the names had meaning—for example, Elijah means "Yah is God."

The Two Kingdoms, Egypt

Aside from Israel itself, the most mentioned nation in the Bible is Egypt, which throughout Israel's history was a power to be reckoned with. Egypt's dry, rainless climate means that centuries-old items are well preserved, which is why we know so much about the fascinating land. As early as 3000 BC, the Egyptians had constructed the enormous Great Pyramid and Sphinx at Giza, sights that still awe tourists. The Book of Exodus, however, reminds us that the great monuments of ancient times were mostly built with slave labor. The Pharaoh—the name means "great house"—was known as "the lord of the two lands" or "two kingdoms." These were Upper and Lower Egypt, Lower being the northern section, where the Nile flows into the Mediterranean. Around 3000 BC the two parts were united, and the Pharaohs wore a crown with emblems of a vulture and a cobra, symbols of the two kingdoms. Goshen, the area where the Israelite slaves in Exodus lived, was in Lower Egypt.

Throughout Israel's history, its people often fled to Egypt to escape a famine or trouble back home. In Genesis, Abraham lives awhile in Egypt, and later in Genesis, Joseph becomes right-hand man of the Pharaoh, saving his family from famine when they travel there. In Exodus, of course, Egypt is the oppressive slave-keeping nation. Centuries later, Egypt often invades and loots Israel, though occasionally Israelites seek refuge in Egypt. In the New Testament, the newborn Jesus is taken by his parents to Egypt to escape the wrath of King Herod.

---

probably trained as a scholar and warrior. Inevitably, he would see the suffering of his own people as slaves. Seeing an Egyptian overseer beating a Hebrew slave, Moses killed the man and hid his body in the sand. Word of it got back to the Pharaoh, and he sought to kill Moses—probably not for killing the overseer, but the threat it represented: Pharaoh may have feared that Moses, a prince of Egypt who was aware of his Hebrew roots, might have been plotting to lead the slaves in rebellion.

So Moses fled to faraway Midian, where, at a well, he encountered seven daughters of a Midianite priest named Jethro (also called Reuel). Moses was taken into the family and married one of the daughters, Zipporah. Born a son of Hebrew slaves, raised as an Egyptian prince, Moses seemed destined to live out his life as a shepherd in Midian. God, however, had other plans for Moses.

LIGHTING A FIRE IN MOSES

While Moses was making a new life as a shepherd in Midian, the oppressive Pharaoh died. (This was probably Seti I, who died in 1301 BC.) As with any tyrant, the slaves he oppressed must have hoped and prayed for a change. Their prayers and groans were heard

The Midianites were in fact related to the Israelites, both tribes being descended from Abraham. The Midianites were the descendants of Abraham and his second wife, Keturah. At the time of Exodus, the Midianites lived in the area called the Sinai Peninsula, which today is part of Egypt. Since they were nomads, they had no fixed residence, and in the Book of Judges, they became notorious as "camel jockeys" who often descended upon the Israelites, robbed them, and vanished into the wilderness. In the time of Moses, however, the two peoples were on good terms.

by God, but it would not be the new Pharaoh who lightened their burdens.

Exodus 3 tells of one of the great divine-human encounters in the Bible. Tending his flocks, Moses is near Sinai (also called Horeb), the "mountain of God." He sees an amazing sight: A bush is burning but is not consumed by the flames. God calls to him from the bush. Moses answers, and God tells him to remove his sandals, for he is on holy ground. God tells Moses he is the God of Abraham, Isaac and Jacob—the patriarchs of Israel. In other words, he is the same God who called Abraham to live in Canaan and become the ancestor of a great nation.

God reveals to Moses that he is sending his people back to Canaan—after they are delivered from their slavery in Egypt. Moses, God says, will lead the people out. As often happens in the Bible, the person God calls is at first reluctant. "Who am I, that I should go to Pharaoh?" Moses asks. God speaks words that would give anyone courage: "I will be with you."

Here Moses asks an important question of God: What is your name? God first gives an answer that is no answer: The Hebrew is *ehyeh asher ehyeh*—"I am who I am" or "I am what I am" or possibly "I will be what I will be." In other words, God is not just some ordinary being with an ordinary name. He orders Moses to tell the Hebrews that "I Am" has sent Moses to lead them out. But then he does speak his name: "The LORD, the God of our Fathers." More precisely, his name is "Yahweh, the God of our Fathers." When you see the name "the LORD" in English Bibles—note that LORD is in small capitals—it is a translation of the Hebrew name Yahweh. This practice goes back to the Hebrews themselves, who had such reverence for the divine name Yahweh that when they read the Hebrew Bible aloud, they would substitute the word Adonai—meaning "Lord"—in place of Yahweh. (One modern English translation, the Jerusalem Bible, actually uses Yahweh instead of "the LORD," but many readers find this jarring, especially in such familiar passages as Psalm 23, which in the Jerusalem Bible begins "Yahweh is my shepherd.")

God tells Moses that there will be amazing miracles taking place, for the Egyptians will not easily let go of their slave labor. As proof of his power, God shows some amazing signs to Moses. When Moses casts his staff on the ground, it turns into a snake, and then changes back again. Moses is still reluctant to take on the daunting task, pleading that he is not good with words, but "the LORD said to him, 'Who gave man his mouth? Who makes him deaf or mute? Who gives him sight or makes him blind? Is it not I, the LORD?' " (Exodus 4:11). God also assures him that his older brother Aaron will aid him in speaking.

We might well ask: If Moses were raised in Pharaoh's court, wouldn't he have spoken Egyptian well—and probably been trained in public speaking also? Probably so. But it's possible Moses had some genetic speech impediment, or, more likely, that his years in Midian had made his Egyptian rusty. At any rate, he doubted his speaking ability, but God did not. Perhaps what God desired was not eloquence or cleverness, but simplicity and directness—not the oily, false-compliment-dripping speech of a courtier, but the bluntness of a working man who hated oppression.

Moses packs up his wife and children and returns to Egypt. He meets his brother Aaron for the first time and tells him what has happened. The two then report to the Hebrew elders, and of course the people are ecstatic that God has sent them a deliverer. Thanks to the deliverer having been raised in the Egyptian court, he can be admitted to the Pharaoh's presence—something that would have been difficult or impossible for most of the Hebrews. (It is impossible not to see God's design in all of this.)

CULTURAL INSIGHTS

Hebrews / Israelites

In Exodus, the terms "Hebrew" and "Israelite" have the same meaning: a descendant of Abraham, Isaac and Jacob. Remember that in Genesis, Jacob was renamed Israel, so the descendants of his twelve sons were called Israelites, although the actual Hebrew text would translate as "children of Israel." The term "Hebrew" occurs for the first time in Genesis, where Abraham is referred to as a Hebrew. In Genesis, and also in Exodus to some extent, the term is usually used by a non-Hebrew, not by the Hebrews/Israelites themselves. (Note that in Exodus, Moses refers to his people as "Hebrews" when speaking to Pharaoh.) Among themselves, they were "children of Israel." At this time the name Israel did not apply to any spot on the map. That would not occur until later, in the Book of Joshua, when the freed slaves finally move into their homeland, Canaan. The Bible does not, incidentally, use the modern term "Israeli."

One mystery about the name Hebrew is just what the word meant. Some ancient writings use the term *Habiru*, which did not seem to refer to a specific ethnic group but to nomads who were used as slaves, low-wage workers or military mercenaries. The Israelites rarely referred to themselves as Hebrews. Although we refer to their language as Hebrew, they referred to it as *sefat Kanaan*, "lip of Canaan."

The term "Jew" was not used until several centuries after the time of the Exodus. In a later chapter we'll look at how the word came into use.

Pharaoh, as God foretold, has "hardened his heart." When Moses and Aaron confront him and tell him God wants his people freed, Pharaoh not only does not free them, he increases their labor by ordering that they make their quota of bricks without the required straw. Naturally the slaves are furious with Moses. Instead of being freed, their burdens are made heavier!

Moses and Aaron go to Pharaoh again, with the same demand. This time, Moses throws down his staff and it turns into a snake. Pharaoh is not impressed: His own court magicians perform the same trick—but Moses' snake devours theirs! Still, Pharaoh does not free the slaves.

GOD OF WONDERS VERSUS HEART OF STONE

At this point, the real miracles begin. In the morning, Moses and Aaron encounter Pharaoh on the bank of the Nile. Moses' staff touches the waters of the river, and they turn to blood. The river and every stream, pond and reservoir become foul and

---

CULTURAL INSIGHTS

Egyptians and Their Gods

The ancient Egyptians were what we might call enthusiastic polytheists—they worshipped many gods and were glad to embrace new ones. They had no real concept of only one god, or even of a chief god who ruled over the others. Depending on the locality, this or that god might be the favorite "local god." The Pharaoh, as head of the whole nation, had to pay his respects to all of them. And the Pharaoh himself was, so the Egyptians believed, divine.

Egyptian gods are usually depicted as *theriomorphic*—"animal shaped." More accurately, they were often shown as human bodies with animal heads. For example, the goddess Bast was shown as a shapely woman with a cat's head. The Egyptians were creative in adopting the heads of animals they saw every day—crocodiles, sheep, jackals, falcons, etc.—to human bodies. The Israelites, with their hatred of any kind of idol, were repelled by these grotesque images.

One very important element in Egyptian religion was their powerful belief in an afterlife. This explains their great skill in turning dead bodies into mummies, a practice first done only on the Pharaohs, but, in time, to all the rich, then to the population at large.

Aside from their many gods and their obsession with the afterlife, the Egyptians were notorious for their practice of magic, or sorcery. We see this clearly enough in the story of Moses when, amazingly, some of Pharaoh's court magicians manage to duplicate some of Moses' miracles. Their power—whether based on real magic or illusion—was certainly not potent enough to end the plagues inflicted upon Egypt.

---

undrinkable, and the fish in it die, causing serious groaning among the Egyptians.

Let's pause here to recall how important the long, wide Nile River was to Egypt. One ancient historian wrote that "all Egypt is the gift of the Nile." He was correct. Egypt is basically just a desert with one wide river flowing through it. But because the Nile flooded every year at a predictable time, the lands by the river received water and fertile silt, so in the midst of a desert there was lush farmland, supporting a very sophisticated civilization. Bible scholars tell us that the annual flooding of the Nile—the occurrence that made Egypt a fertile land—was honored with a religious ceremony of great importance. At the expected time, the Pharaoh and his court would "greet" the rising waters of the sacred river. It's probable that the meeting of Moses and Aaron with Pharaoh was at this annual ceremony. The Egyptians had a multitude of gods, and they saw the Nile itself as a god. By making the god "sick," Moses had proven that his God was more powerful than the mighty Nile that the Egyptians worshipped. Perhaps the people who witnessed the bloodying of the waters might have feared the worst: What if the river were ruined forever? The transformation was also a blow to Pharaoh, who was considered divine himself, and who tried to give people the impression that he "summoned" the Nile River every year. But Pharaoh's heart was still hardened.

> **DID YOU KNOW?**
>
> Ever wonder about the name *Jehovah*? Believe it or not, it is the same as *Yahweh*, which makes sense if you realize that in times past, a J was often pronounced with a Y sound, and a V with a W sound. It makes even more sense when you realize that Hebrew actually had no vowels, so *Yahweh* is actually only a guess at how the Hebrew name *YHWH* was pronounced. Some older versions of the Bible used *Jehovah*, including the King James Version in a few verses, and many old hymns and Christian poems used the name. It has fallen out of use, though it endures in the name of the Jehovah's Witnesses.

The second plague is an invasion of frogs from the Nile and other bodies of water. They become such a nuisance that Pharaoh agrees to let the slaves take a brief "vacation" to go to the wilderness to sacrifice to God. But when the frogs die and are no longer a problem, Pharaoh changes his mind.

The third plague is of things smaller but even more annoying: gnats. Pharaoh's court magicians had been able to reproduce Moses' earlier miracles, but not this one. They believe Moses really does have divine power backing him, but Pharaoh will not budge.

The fourth plague is an invasion of swarms of flies—which plague the Egyptians but are absent from Goshen, the region where the slaves live. Again, Pharaoh agrees to let the slaves go to the wilderness to sacrifice to God but changes his mind when the plague passes.

The fifth plague is the death of the Egyptians' livestock—while the livestock in Goshen remains unharmed. It may have been related to the previous plague: The flies

The Passover

Passover is one of the most important holidays for Jews. This is natural, since it is connected with the most important event in their history, the deliverance from Egypt. Exodus 12 tells of the first Passover. The Hebrews have been instructed to mark their doorposts with lamb's blood so that the destroying angel sent by God to the Egyptians will pass over the Hebrews' homes. The Hebrews are instructed to roast and eat the lamb, along with bitter herbs and unleavened bread. The fact that the bread is unleavened is important: The people are to be ready to exit quickly from Egypt once the Pharaoh releases them, so making regular bread—and allowing time for it to rise with the yeast in it—would not be appropriate. Thus they are to eat in haste, with their shoes on and otherwise ready to depart. They are told that this event will be remembered by their descendants forever, celebrated on the same date each year, when the curious children will be told that it commemorates the Lord "passing over" their homes while he struck down the firstborn among the Egyptians. One interesting aspect of Passover is that it was (and is) basically a holy day spent at home, with no priest or altar needed, and the sacrifice (the lamb) eaten entirely by the family.

Since the first Christians saw Jesus as the "lamb of God," who was sacrificed on the cross, they sometimes spoke of him as the "Passover lamb," since his death occurred during the Passover season (1 Corinthians 5:7).

could have caused a pestilence that infected the animals. Again, Pharaoh's hard heart is unmoved.

The sixth plague is the plague of boils on both man and beast—in Egypt, but not in Goshen.

The seventh plague is a destructive fall of hail, along with "fire that ran along the ground," which may mean lightning. The fact that hail would fall at all must have amazed the Egyptians, for they rarely saw any form of precipitation from their cloudless sky. It must have seemed to them that their powerful sun god, Ra, had abandoned them. With the great destruction of crops, Pharaoh is moved to relent—temporarily. Again, he changes his mind after the plague ends.

The threat of the eighth plague, locusts, must have frightened the Egyptians, for mankind has always feared an invasion of these voracious plant-devouring grasshoppers. Pharaoh's servants beg him to let the slaves go, but he will not, so the locusts come, devouring what little vegetation is left after the plague of hail. The swarm is so dense that "the sky was darkened." Pharaoh claims to be repentant, but after the Lord sends a wind to drive the locusts out, Pharaoh changes his mind once more.

The darkening of the sky caused by the locusts is only a preview of the ninth plague: three days of pitch-black darkness. This is another divine repudiation of the power of the sun god, Ra.

We may well wonder, after nine such dramatic and destructive miracles, how Pharaoh could continue to "harden his heart." Hasn't he learned that Moses' God is powerful—even more powerful than the mighty gods of Egypt? So why doesn't he free the slaves? The obvious answer: Evil never gives in easily. Neither does pride. The ruler of a mighty empire is simply not willing to let the god of a band of slaves push him around. Moses is seen as an awesome, even feared figure among the Egyptians (Exodus 11:3), but to Pharaoh, he is just a slave. It is worth noting here that even though all the Egyptians were guilty of maintaining the oppressive system of slavery, the evil is concentrated in the stubborn Pharaoh, who refuses the slaves freedom even after his own people beg him to let them go.

We sense that Pharaoh succumbed to the temptation Adam and Eve felt in Eden: to be like gods. Perhaps Pharaoh really believed the royal propaganda, that he truly was

STORIES WORTH REMEMBERING ## A Genuinely Lovable Father-in-Law

One neglected part of the Moses story is his good fortune in having something every man would like to have: a wise, affectionate father-in-law. This was Jethro, the priest of Midian. He is also called Reuel in some passages, but since Reuel means "shepherd of God," it's possible that this was his title as a priest. Whatever his names were, he was kind enough to take Moses in and accept him into the family after his flight from Egypt.

Moses encountered his father-in-law again as the Israelites approached Sinai, the holy mountain on which Moses was tending Jethro's flocks when he saw God in the burning bush. Exodus 18 tells us that Jethro brought along Zipporah, Moses' wife, and their two sons. Naturally Jethro—who must have wondered what happened after Moses left him to return to Egypt—rejoiced that the Israelites had been freed from slavery, and he praised Israel's God, who was the same as his own.

Unsolicited advice from a father-in-law is nothing most men welcome. Jethro, however, was wise. He saw that Moses was not only leader of this horde of people, but also their judge, and while they were encamped in an area, he spent much of the day arbitrating disputes among the people. This was wearing Moses out, so Jethro told him to *delegate*. Find some honest, decent, incorruptible men among the Israelites and let them serve as judges of minor cases, while only the more important cases would be brought before Moses. After this, Jethro "went away to his own country." Moses must have been sorry to see him go.

The Pharaoh of Exodus: Breathtaking Vanity

The Book of Exodus does not name the oppressive king, but historians are fairly certain he was Rameses II, who reigned 1301 BC to 1234 BC—a very long reign, during which he completed some grand building projects, aided (as we know from the Bible) by a large force of slave labor. His projects included the great cities of Pithom and Rameses, mentioned in Exodus 1:11. Rameses did more than just build things—he added to his grandeur by literally chiseling out the names of earlier Pharaohs on some monuments and having his own inscribed. His vanity was breathtaking.

Rameses' name—*Ra meses*—meant "Ra's son," Ra being the sun god. Being taught, as all Pharaohs were, that they were divine, Rameses had a high opinion of himself, which explains his constant refusal to free the Hebrew slaves. Exodus tells us again and again that his heart was "hardened." In fact, the meaning of the Hebrew text here isn't that the Pharaoh was hardhearted (though he undoubtedly was). When the text says his "heart was hardened," the real meaning is something like "his resolve was stiffened." In other words, the plagues, which made the other Egyptians faint-hearted, did not have that effect on him. He was determined enough—stubborn enough—to remain strong-hearted in the face of God's clear opposition. Without knowing it, Rameses, by stubbornly delaying the departure of the Hebrews, only brought on more miracles, leaving a deep impression on the Hebrews themselves but also on the Egyptian populace. Like many men who hold great power, he was deaf to any voice but his own.

divine, and as a god he could not let the god of a band of slaves defeat him—not without a fight, anyway. He was the captive of his own gargantuan narcissism—something to which all human beings are prone, unfortunately. The tragedy here is that the Pharaoh, the "father of his country," was willing to let his people suffer the consequences of his own stubbornness. The Egyptian farmers watched their livestock die and their crops beaten by hail and devoured by locusts. Why didn't their mighty Pharaoh, their divine "protector," care enough for them to do what was necessary to bring them relief?

Moses and all the Hebrews must have been in agony, amazed by God's miracles but frustrated that they were still held in bondage. But God told Moses that the final plague would break Pharaoh: The firstborn in every Egyptian house would die. Here, let's recall the importance the ancient world placed on the firstborn child, the "opening of the womb" that every parent prayed for. To lose any child was a horrible thing, but losing the firstborn was a true tragedy.

Exodus 12 tells how the plague occurred. God told Moses to order all the Hebrews to mark their doorposts (what we would call the front-door frame) with lamb's blood. The destroying angel being sent to the Egyptian homes would pass over the homes marked with the lamb's blood. At midnight, the firstborn among the Egyptians are struck down, and there is not one Egyptian house where someone does not die—including Pharaoh's own house. While it is still dark, Pharaoh summons Moses and Aaron, telling them to take their possessions and go. The Egyptians are just as eager to be rid of the slaves, so much so that they even give them money and jewelry as they depart. "So they plundered the Egyptians" (12:36).

At this point, Exodus records that the Hebrews had endured 430 years of slavery in Egypt. The freed slaves numbered six hundred thousand, plus the women and children, and also herds of livestock. The sight of this vast throng—all of them on foot—leaving Egypt must have been impressive, and perhaps the scene in *The Ten Commandments* showing the departure does it justice. The film makes a point of showing that among the items the Israelites took with them was the coffin of Joseph. His request to be reburied in his homeland of Canaan was being brought to pass.

A HEAD-SNAPPING TURNAROUND

As stubborn as Pharaoh appears in Exodus, he is also amazingly fickle, caving in and telling Moses to leave, and then changing his mind. Almost inevitably, this occurred once the slaves had made their exit. Then the willful king—and the other Egyptians as well—realized they could not let their cheap labor depart so easily. Pharaoh did a head-snapping turnaround and quickly mustered an army of charioteers, and they set out to overtake the Israelites, which was easily done, since the huge group was on foot.

The former slaves had encamped by "the sea." There has been much discussion over just what this body of water was. Was it the Red Sea, as most translations have it, or something else? The actual Hebrew text calls it the *Yam Suph*, "sea of reeds," which is not clearly descriptive of the Red Sea that lies between Egypt and Arabia. There are several guesses about the location, but all of them miss the point: The slaves were caught between the water and an approaching army of angry Egyptians, set on either capturing or killing them. The people panic, of course. Why did Moses, and God, lead them out here, only to be slaughtered in the wilderness? Weren't they better off living as slaves in Egypt? God tells Moses not to lose heart: He did not bring the people this far to let them perish. Moses stretches out his hand over the water, and "the Lord drove the sea back by a strong east wind and turned it into land" (14:21). This

> **DID YOU KNOW?**
>
> Moses is mentioned seventy-nine times in the New Testament, more than any other Old Testament figure. Abraham is second, with seventy-seven mentions. The Jews of the New Testament period honored Abraham as their physical ancestor, Moses as the liberator from slavery and the giver of the Law that governed every facet of their lives. Moses is also mentioned in many of the Psalms that recall the miraculous events of the Exodus. Psalm 90 is attributed to "Moses, the man of God."

tells us the parting of the waters did not occur so quickly as it does in movies, but it was a miracle nonetheless. The people pass through, with a wall of water on each side—and we can assume that they hurried. The Egyptians pursued them, but then the waters closed back in again, with horses and soldiers dead on the shore. And so the Israelites believed in the Lord and in "Moses his servant." Exodus 15 is the song of victory Moses utters, praising God for his deliverance. Miriam, Moses' sister, takes tambourine in hand and leads the women in a joyous victory dance. One of the great episodes in the Bible, and in human history, closes on a note of ecstasy and gratitude.

AND NOW WHAT, GOD?

Remember that the slaves departed Egypt with livestock—and with the jewelry the Egyptians gave them. Nonetheless, they faced an obvious problem: Far from the Nile, where would we find water? And where could we get enough food to sustain us on this long journey?

God provides. For a while the people encamp at a pleasant, palm-shaded oasis named Elim (15:27). But once on the road again, the people grumble against Moses: *Why didn't you let us stay in Egypt, where we had enough food? Now we will die in the desert.* God's answer is a miracle—not a one-time occurrence, but one that continues through the forty years of moving toward Canaan. He "rains down bread from heaven," the food called *manna.* What exactly it was, we aren't sure. The area they traveled even today has a cottony white sweet substance that is edible. Perhaps this was *manna,* or perhaps *manna* was some miraculous food that no longer exists. There was enough to sustain the people day to day. Moses had his brother Aaron put aside a jar of the *manna* to show to future generations. And God also sent quail to provide a source of meat. The lack of water was a recurring problem, and the people continually grumbled against Moses, but always God provided water. He was not going to deliver his people out of slavery and let them die in the wilderness. Note: The reports of the Israelites' constant grumbling are another indication of the truthfulness of the Bible. Only a truly honest author would have dared to relate that God's chosen people were constantly on the verge of rebelling against him.

Lack of provisions was one problem. Enemies were another. The closest route for getting from Egypt to Canaan would have been the Mediterranean coast—but this was the region of the warlike Philistines, and Exodus says God diverted them from this route specifically so they would not lose heart when confronted by the Philistines. But enemies were everywhere. Exodus 17 records the first battle of the Israelites, in which they faced the brutal Amalekites. While Joshua—an important character from this point on—led the men into battle, Moses positioned himself on a hill, his arms outstretched. The sight of them gave courage to the Israelites, and when Moses' arms grew tired, two men stood by to prop them up. The Israelites—slaves with no experience in fighting— defeated the Amalekites.

One element of Moses' own history is important to remember here: Moses was leading a huge band of people who had never set foot out of Egypt. Because of his years tending sheep in Midian, he alone was familiar with the sort of semidesert terrain that the Israelites were passing through. God had given the Israelites a leader who knew the sort of land the people would spend the next forty years in.

We end today's section at Exodus 19, which tells us that, three months after leaving Egypt, the Israelites encamp at Mount Sinai, the very spot where Moses received his call from God. Here occurs one of the great revelations in the history of the world.

PUTTING THE WORD TO WORK

1. Moses, like many saintly leaders in the Bible, was at first reluctant to do the work God called him to. Think of times in your own life when you felt God was calling you to a task. What were your responses? Did you doubt your own ability, or the power of God, or both?

2. Moses described himself as "slow of speech," yet we see in his confrontations with Pharaoh that he was bold enough. Think of times in your own life when you underestimated your ability to speak out when needed. Think of other times when you wish you had spoken out but did not. What kept you back? Will remembering God's words to Moses, "I will be with you," help you next time?

3. "Hardening the heart" is a recurring theme in today's lesson. Proud Pharaoh could clearly see the power of Moses' God, yet he continually resisted. What were some occasions when you, or someone close to you, seemed to resist the clear leading of God?

4. The Moses story is fairly familiar to people, probably due to the popularity of films like *The Ten Commandments* and *The Prince of Egypt*. What did you learn in today's chapter that you never learned from the film versions of Moses' life?

5. One unpleasant theme in today's chapter is the continual doubting and grumbling of the Israelites. They are privileged to witness incredible miracles, yet they still doubt God and Moses. Think hard, and make a list of things in your own life, gifts from God (or other people) that you forget to be thankful for. Make yourself a resolution: If you find the griping of the Israelites to be unappealing (and most readers do), resolve to eliminate it from your own life.

"Obey Me Fully"

THE LAW AT SINAI

AT THE HEART OF IT ALL TODAY At Mount Sinai, God makes a binding covenant with Israel: If they will be guided by his laws, they will be his treasured possession on the earth. After their years of slavery in Egypt, they learn that true freedom is to be found in putting themselves under the protective authority of the Lord. These laws seem strict by our modern standards, but God used them to shape a band of former slaves into people fit to govern themselves and live decently with each other. Even though Christians no longer observe most of the ritual laws, the moral laws still show us the wisdom and compassion of God, who taught his people how to temper justice with mercy.

Rules. *Laws. Restrictions.* These are not words we like. Many of us prefer words like "freedom" and "choice" and "self-determination." In other words, we are more like Adam and Eve than we like to admit, for we hate to think that anyone—God, parents, police, government officials, supervisors—binds us with rules. But in our saner moments, we know rules

> **KEY PASSAGES TO READ TODAY**
>
> Exodus 19:1—20:21; 23:1–9
> Leviticus 19:1–4; 9–18;
> 32–37; 24:17–22; 25:35–46
> Deuteronomy 19:15–21; 30:11–18

are important. What parent lets a child do whatever he or she wants? A world with no rules would be a mighty dangerous place, and a rude one as well. And a God who turned his people loose in the world with no rules or guidance wouldn't be a responsible Father.

Today we will look at the Father's laws, found in the last chapters of Exodus, and in Leviticus, Numbers and Deuteronomy. Many of the laws no longer apply—for example, the laws of sacrifices, which even Jews no longer observe. The laws relating to the priesthood, to the holy days, to the cure of several skin diseases loosely called "leprosy" are purely of historical interest. The kosher laws regarding "clean" and "unclean" foods are no longer observed by the majority of people today. But although many of the laws have become obsolete over time, many of the laws given by God to Moses—most famously the Ten Commandments—are timeless. There is some moral weight in those laws, and we need to recall Jesus' statement that he came not to abolish the Law, but to fulfill it. It is true that Christians believe we are saved by our faith in Christ, not by observing rules. But it is also true—in both the Old and New Testaments—that people of faith always try to please God, and that is what the commandments are all about: pleasing him, and living in a right relationship with each other.

FIRE ON THE MOUNTAIN

At the end of the last chapter, the Israelites had reached Mount Sinai three months after their happy departure from Egypt. Remember that the mountain was the site where Moses had first been called by God to lead the Israelites. Something even more dramatic and world-changing was about to happen there.

On the mountain, Moses hears God's voice. God tells him to tell the Israelites, "If you obey me fully and keep my covenant, then out of all nations you will be my treasured possession. Although the whole earth is mine, you will be for me a kingdom of priests and a holy nation" (Exodus 19:5–6). Moses informs the elders of Israel, and they agree to do what the Lord asks. Note that they agree to do so even before they know just what obligations God would impose on them. This was natural. They were not meeting God as equals. He was definitely their superior—as proven by the amazing things he performed to lead them out of Egypt. So the covenant—the divine contract—was not between two equal partners, but between a king and his subjects. How could they not accept, since they were told that though all the earth was God's, he had chosen them alone to be his "treasured possession"?

Note that God tells Moses that the Israelites will be a "kingdom of priests." The word "kingdom" here doesn't mean a place on the map, a geographical area. It means something like "those who are ruled by the king," wherever they might be. (The same idea occurs in the New Testament, with the frequently used phrase "kingdom of God," which doesn't refer to a location, but to the condition of being under God's rule.) What about the "priests"? A priest was a person who had the right of access to a god. Although Israel would soon have its own designated priests, God was promising that all Israelites would be "priests" in the sense that all of them would have access to him. (This concept is repeated in the New Testament, where Christians are referred to as a "royal priesthood.")

Three days after the Israelites agreed to be God's "treasured possession," an amazing display of power was seen and heard on the mountain. There was thunder, lightning and a thick cloud, then a sound like a mighty trumpet blast, then smoke. The people trembled, and rightly so. The King of the Universe was present, definitely, and obviously something of great importance was about to happen.

c. 1250 BC
Moses, an Israelite reared in the Egyptian court, leads the Israelites out of Egypt, preceded by miraculous plagues on the Egyptians (Exodus 2–15).

c. 1250—c. 1210 BC
Moses receives the divine Law at Mount Sinai. The Israelites spend forty years journeying to Canaan (Exodus 16 — Deuteronomy 34).

c. 1250—c. 1190 BC
The Greeks and the Trojans fight in the Trojan War.

c. 1225 BC
The Assyrians under king Tukulti-Ninurta I capture Babylon.

Mount Sinai / Horeb

There is some confusion about the name of this famous spot. Some parts of the Moses story call it Sinai, others Horeb, but these almost certainly refer to the same locale, and it was not unusual for a mountain to be called by more than one name. The first mention of it, when Moses is tending his flocks and sees the burning bush, calls it "Horeb, the mountain of God." Most famously, it was the site where God gave Moses the Ten Commandments.

The name Sinai would forever be connected with the giving of the divine laws to Israel. In a sense, what happens at Sinai is the follow-up to the deliverance from Egypt. God liberates the slaves from bondage, then gives them a law code to live by. Sinai was not just a geographical site, but a kind of spiritual landmark as well, a new beginning for God's chosen nation. Tradition holds that the mountain in Egypt called *Jebal Musa*, Arabic for the "mount of Moses," is Sinai.

"THE TEN WORDS"

The Ten Commandments are sometimes called the Decalogue, from the Greek for "ten words" or "ten sayings." They are surely some of the best-known "sayings" ever spoken, and in spite of the fact that the Israelites considered all their laws to be of divine origin, these ten were special, as evidenced by their being the first commandments God speaks. Since these are the very center of the Old Testament's moral law, and since Christians still feel bound by them, the Ten are worth looking at in detail.

It is worth noting that the Ten divide into two groups: authority commandments and neighbor commandments. Commandments one through five govern our relation to God—and to parents. Commandments six through ten govern our relation to our fellow man. The pattern of the Bible is established here: Love God, love your neighbor.

"I am the Lord your God, who brought you out of Egypt, out of the land of slavery. You shall have no other gods before me" (Exodus 20:2–3).

The First Commandment begins with a reminder of what had happened three months earlier. For us, the deliverance from Egypt is in the distant past, so the commandment reminds us that God is a loving, saving God who does wonders for his people—in the past, and in the present as well. Out of gratitude toward this God, it is not right for us to worship anyone or anything else.

At the time this Commandment was given, the Israelites may have believed that other gods existed. In other words, they were not strict *monotheists*, believers in only one God. However, they did believe this God was the only one they should serve. Today most people claim to believe in only one God—but there are other "gods"—success, money, fame, security—that people can worship besides God.

"You shall not make for yourself an idol in the form of anything in heaven above or on the earth beneath or in the waters below. You shall not bow down to them or worship them; for I, the Lord your God, am a jealous God, punishing the children for the sin of the fathers to the third and fourth generation of those who hate me, but showing love to a thousand generations of those who love me and keep my commandments" (Exodus 20:4–6).

The Second Commandment is obviously related to the First. The people are not to make or worship any picture or statue of any god—nor are they to try to make any image of the true God. This prohibition set Israel apart from almost every nation and culture and religion that ever existed, for all people everywhere create some kind of picture or statue of the things they worship or adore. But Israel was to be different. Their God, Yahweh, the Lord, was too great, too mysterious, too incomprehensible to be symbolized by any kind of image, human or animal or anything else.

Over the centuries, the Jews endured a lot of scorn for this command, but they held to it faithfully. Although art museums and churches through history have been decorated with images of Jesus, even of God himself—as in Michelangelo's painting in the Vatican depicting God stretching out his hand to Adam—most Christians do not object since they do not literally worship or bow down to them. We think of these images as aids to devotions, reminders that the Son of God was a flesh-and-blood human being. Still, the basic idea behind the Commandment is worth holding to: No visual image can really capture the essence of the Divine, and there is always the risk that we might praise the image—or the artist—more than God himself.

It is worth noting that although the Commandment prohibited representing God with any visual image, the Bible is full of references to God's eyes, hands, ears, fingers, mouth, etc. They could speak this way, as if God were human-shaped, yet could not represent him as a human. Is there an inconsistency here? Not really. The fact is, Israel thought of God as a *person*, and a person had to have some way of communicating (a mouth), perceiving (eyes, ears), moving (feet), doing deeds (hands), etc. (Remember that Genesis says man was made "in the image of God.") The alternative to thinking of God as, in some way, a person like ourselves is to think of him as some abstract kind of "Force," an idea most people don't find appealing. No one wants to enter into a close personal relationship with a "Force." Israel did not think God *literally* possessed a mouth, hands, eyes, ears, feet, which is why they did not show him in human (or animal) form.

Note that this Commandment has God referring to himself as a "jealous" God. We think of jealousy as being a negative, possibly even dangerous, quality in human beings.

Jealous spouses and lovers sometimes quarrel, fight, even murder each other. But God is the one Being who has a right to be jealous. He is our only true Protector, not the false gods or the false images that these Commandments wisely tell us to avoid.

> *"You shall not misuse the name of the Lord your God, for the Lord will not hold anyone guiltless who misuses his name"* (Exodus 20:7).

Older versions of the Bible use the familiar phrase "You shall not take the name of the Lord your God in vain." People often think this refers to swearing, using "God" as an element in profanity. This is correct, but the Commandment covers more than that. In ancient times, people often used the names of their gods as part of a magic formula, the idea being that a divine name had some power. The Old Testament is dead set against magic and sorcery of any kind, so any attempt to use the Lord's name in some kind of "spell" is prohibited. People were also inclined to call on the name of their god to back up something they said—as in, "If what I just told you isn't true, may God strike me dead." God is not at our beck and call in this way, and it is not right to misuse his name like this. Even the casual use of the exclamation "Oh my God" should be thought about more carefully.

Probably the most profound misuse of God's name, "taking it in vain," is to use it to indicate that God has put his stamp of approval on what we are doing or planning. Anyone who announces that "God told me to..." should be taken warily, since people have been known to use God's name as a way of lending authority to their own impulses.

We noted in the last chapter that the Hebrew name of God was Yahweh. The Jews, over time, took the Third Commandment so seriously that eventually they ceased to say it at all. When they read aloud from the Bible, they would substitute the Hebrew word *Adonai*, "Lord," where *Yahweh* occurred. Some Jews today make a habit of not ever writing "God," and instead writing "G-d." But essentially the lesson we can all derive from the Commandment is that we should take the name of God seriously and use it with care, just as we would refrain from flippantly using or abusing the name of any person we loved and honored.

> *"Remember the Sabbath day by keeping it holy. Six days you shall labor and do all your work, but the seventh day is a Sabbath to the Lord your God. On it you shall not do any work, neither you, nor your son or daughter, nor your manservant or maidservant, nor your animals, nor the alien within your gates. For in six days the Lord made the heavens and the earth, the sea, and all that is in them, but he rested on the seventh day. Therefore the Lord blessed the Sabbath day and made it holy"* (Exodus 20:8–11).

This harks back to Genesis 1, where God created the universe in six days, then "rested" on the seventh day. All business was prohibited on the Sabbath, and not even a person's animals could work. This rule wasn't considered restrictive. In fact, since the pagan world saw every day as a work day (a real burden for manual laborers), taking one day out of seven as a "day off" was pretty progressive. The world today owes the concept of a "weekend" to the Ten Commandments.

Remember that when this Commandment was given, the Israelites had just been freed from slavery, *with no days off*. Probably this Commandment was received with pleasure: God wanted them to work only six days out of seven! The Sabbath Commandment was also a reminder to them: Don't let yourselves become enslaved to your own work.

Throughout the Old Testament, the Israelites were constantly disobeying this Commandment. The greedy ones simply would not cease transacting business one day out of seven. This is tragic, when you consider that the Sabbath Commandment was not originally given as a burden to the people, but as a gift. The prophets spoke out against this profaning of the Sabbath, and when the people went into exile in Babylon in 586 BC, they believed one of the reasons for their punishment was their neglect of the Sabbath. This is why, in the time of Jesus, the more devout Jews took the Sabbath with great seriousness—not a bad thing in itself, except that some of them criticized Jesus for healing a man on the Sabbath, saying that the healing was "work" that the Commandment prohibited. Jesus made the observation that "the Sabbath was made for man, not man for the Sabbath" (Mark 2:27).

The Christian Sunday—"the Lord's Day"—is not the same as the Sabbath. Jesus did observe the Sabbath, though he claimed that one could do good deeds even on the Sabbath (Luke 13:15–16), and he clearly rejected all the burdensome rules that had developed concerning Sabbath observance. The first Christians, being Jews, observed the Sabbath, but in time it began to lose its importance, particularly among Christians who had not been Jews. For Christians the first day of the week—the day Jesus rose from the dead—took on a greater importance than the seventh day.

CULTURAL INSIGHTS ## Pagan "Off Days"

Though Israel was the only nation to observe the Sabbath in ancient times, other nations did not keep their noses to the grindstone 365 days per year. Every locale and every culture had its holidays, either secular or religious, festival days in which work was suspended and a party atmosphere prevailed. Most of us would agree that taking one day out of every seven was certainly more humane than the occasional festival day the pagans enjoyed. However, pagans constantly mocked Israel for its Sabbath, claiming it was a genuine waste to be idle from work one day out of seven.

In times past we left our work places on Friday and could give ourselves a respite from the world of work—a respite that God, in his wisdom and compassion, ordered for us. Today, with our contemporary technology—cell phones, e-mail, faxes, instant messaging—the idea of a weekend disappears for many people. Christians ought to take the Sabbath Commandment seriously, in the sense that we ought to try, as far as possible, to set aside some time each week—preferably on Sunday—that is our sacred "religion and rest" time, which the world of work is not allowed to intrude upon.

"Honor your father and your mother, so that you may live long in the land the Lord your God is giving you" (Exodus 20:12).

Every parent thinks this is a fine and sensible rule for his or her own child to follow. But parents have their own parents, and each generation is called upon to honor both father and mother. Young people tend to regard parents the same way Adam and Eve regarded God: the authority figures who keep them from having fun, from getting what they feel they deserve. They sometimes need to be reminded that parents are like God in a good way: They want to protect, instruct, preserve their children from danger. Adults with aging parents face different challenges in their relationships. But the family, with all its inherent dynamics, is something God ordained for humankind. It is a school where we learn to treat people with honor and respect.

Keep in mind that we are not commanded to admire our parents, or think of them as good role models, or obey them in every case (such as telling us to do something illegal or immoral). We are told to honor them, respect them—the same as we do any human authority we encounter. In fact, theologians have generally extended this Commandment to apply to all authority. We ought to respect—as far as possible—our teachers, supervisors, judges, government officials. None of them are perfect, but then, neither are we.

"You shall not murder" (Exodus 20:13).

The King James Version reads "Thou shalt not kill"—a less accurate translation than more recent scholarship indicates, because the Hebrew word here clearly refers to murder. This is a meaningful distinction to make, if people are deciding their positions on issues such as capital punishment and the morality of war based on what the Bible says. Laws in the Book of Exodus prescribe the death penalty for several crimes, and the book also describes the Israelites' going to war against their enemies. In the New Testament, Jesus gave a deeper meaning to the Sixth Commandment, saying that not only should we avoid actual murder, but also the contemplation of murder in our hearts. We shouldn't purposefully take another human being's life, nor should we let our imaginations dwell on such deeds. People of faith need to consider all aspects of this Commandment, and its applications for the world we live in today, in order to decide what they believe is right.

"You shall not commit adultery" (Exodus 20:14).

The Fifth Commandment indicates that family life, including the authority of parents, is somehow sacred. The Seventh Commandment indicates that marriage is also sacred. In fact, elsewhere in the Law, the death penalty (stoning) is prescribed for adultery. We know this from the familiar story of the woman caught in adultery, who is brought before Jesus by a group of people who are about to stone her. (According to the Law, a married man caught in adultery was also to be stoned.)

Decreeing the death penalty for adulterers certainly elevates the state of marriage to a sacred pact—with dire consequences if broken. But it is the protection of the commitment between two people that is the focus of this Commandment. Even if our present culture views adultery as a minor sin and divorce as a common occurrence, people are still drawn to the ideas of monogamy and fidelity, and hold out the hope that marriage is a partnership "till death do us part." In his infinite wisdom, God supports that commitment. And centuries after Moses, Jesus warned against committing adultery even "in our hearts," which is truly challenging in our sex-saturated world. But no one ever said that living a moral life was easy.

"You shall not steal" (Exodus 20:15).

This is the one Commandment that most people give a hearty "Amen!" to, even people with no religious inclinations. No one wants to be stolen from—but people do seem inclined to steal, not necessarily in the form of shoplifting or stealing a neighbor's newspaper from the driveway, but less visible ways, such as keeping two sets of books, cheating on one's tax returns, or lying about one's work hours or expense accounts. Stealing is not only an offense against the party stolen from, but against God as well. One common form of stealing that people don't often consider is the employee failing to do his job adequately. He is robbing his employer and, in the case of those dealing with the public, robbing the customers who are paying for his services. The employee taking an hour-long break in the storeroom or playing solitaire on his office computer is a thief.

"You shall not give false testimony against your neighbor" (Exodus 20:16).

> **DID YOU KNOW?**
>
> As any writer knows, good proofreaders are a critical part of publishing. Perhaps the printers who produced the English Bible in AD 1631 needed a better proofreader. A thousand copies of the Bible were printed with a key word missing from one of the Ten Commandments: *not.* This misprinted Bible had the verse "Thou shalt commit adultery." The printers were fined three thousand British pounds.

Strictly speaking, this prohibits lying in court in order to harm another person. Obviously this can have fatal consequences at times: A false testimony could lead someone to get the death penalty, or prison time, or a large fine. For most of us, the opportunities to do this seldom occur, since we aren't often questioned by the police or asked to appear in court. However, the opportunities to get someone in trouble with lies and slander do present themselves. We need to be wary of sharing anything someone has told us in strict confidence, since it can be so easily twisted and used against a person. Seemingly decent and respectable people sometimes pry into the faults of others, sometimes claiming to be interested in their "spiritual welfare," when often the main goal is finding fodder for gossip. The Bible speaks out constantly against the destructive power of the tongue.

Some people have raised an obvious question: Why wasn't the Commandment simply stated as "You shall not lie"? Isn't lying wrong? Yes. *Always?* Perhaps not. In Exodus 1, the two Hebrew midwives, ordered by Pharaoh to kill infant boys, lie to Pharaoh in order to avoid doing what he commanded. Were they wrong to do so? Exodus sides with the midwives, even praises them. Perhaps there are times when it is permissible, such as telling a lie to protect a human life. The key idea in the Ninth Commandment is the wickedness of lying to do someone else harm.

"You shall not covet your neighbor's house. You shall not covet your neighbor's wife, or his manservant or maidservant, his ox or donkey, or anything that belongs to your neighbor" (Exodus 20:17).

The Tenth Commandment is interesting because it prohibits something inside us. Coveting is a sin we can easily hide from the world—but not from God. The Commandment is a reminder that God is not only an observer of our acts, but of our thoughts as well.

Note that the Commandment does not say it is wrong to want things. It is wrong to want what belongs to someone else. Coveting involves a sense of unfairness: *John owns an X and doesn't deserve it, but I do.* The covetous person doesn't want the same kind of X that John owns—he wants John to be without it.

In a sense, coveting is a sin that bears its own punishment: unhappiness. We can be happy with what we have, or we can want what we don't have and resent bitterly the people who have it. It is frightening to think of the mental energy we waste on this particular sin. In our advertising-saturated culture, with its images of overpaid celebrities living in luxury, steering clear of covetousness requires us to constantly focus on the Father who gives us all that we require.

The giving of the Ten Commandments is followed by a kind of divine "exclamation point": Mount Sinai literally shakes, and the people are filled with dread. "When the people saw the thunder and lightning and heard the trumpet and saw the mountain in smoke, they trembled with fear. They stayed at a distance and said to Moses, 'Speak to us yourself and we will listen. But do not have God speak to us or we will die.' Moses said to the people, 'Do not be afraid. God has come to test you, so that the fear of God will be with you to keep you from sinning.'" Moses returns to the "thick darkness" on the mountain and receives from God the other laws for Israel.

CULTURAL INSIGHTS

Dabbling with the Demonic

The Bible is dead set against any form of magic or sorcery, including mediums who claim to be able to communicate with the dead. The Bible has no concept of "white magic." All magic is forbidden, and the Law punished practitioners with death. For Israel, God was in control of the world, and it was wrong to try to control or manipulate him—or any other spirits in the universe.

"A man or woman who is a medium or spiritist among you must be put to death. You are to stone them; their blood will be on their own heads" (Leviticus 20:27).

"The nations you will dispossess listen to those who practice sorcery or divination. But as for you, the Lord your God has not permitted you to do so" (Deuteronomy 18:14).

During their time in Egypt, the Israelites had seen plenty of dabbling with the occult, for no nation was more famous for its magicians than Egypt. God wanted to keep his people from these sinister practices.

Prescribing the death penalty for witchcraft led to the execution over the centuries of both women and men for the crime, their judges citing these Old Testament passages. This places our current acceptance of "white magic" and interest in the many "channelers" who speak for the dead (some of them well-paid authors and TV personalities) in stark contrast.

RULES, SOME OF THEM "KEEPERS"

The Ten Commandments were special, as evidenced by the fact that God with his own finger engraved them in stone and gave them to Moses (Exodus 31:18). The many laws that follow in Exodus through Deuteronomy were regarded by Israel as equally binding,

---

CULTURAL INSIGHTS

Kosher

Do you ever have a craving for bat or lizard? Probably not, but they are on the long list of "unclean" animals found in the kosher rules in Leviticus 11 and Deuteronomy 14. The rules distinguish between "clean" animals, which may be eaten, and "unclean," which may not. Most people are aware that pork and shellfish are "unclean," and so is rabbit, but most of the animals on the list are things few people would eat anyway: vultures, ravens, owls, storks, gulls, bats, rats, weasels, lizards, most insects, etc. Some of these creatures literally are unclean, being scavengers that live on dead matter—vultures, lobsters and catfish (which are prohibited because, unlike the "clean" fish, they lack scales). The bat, incidentally, is included in the list of unclean birds. The restrictions apply only to animals, since any kind of plant may be eaten.

The laws in Exodus, Leviticus and Deuteronomy also prescribe certain ways meat may be properly slaughtered and prepared, and Jews consider these to be part of their kosher laws. There is a prohibition of mixing meat and dairy products (which is why Jews cannot eat cheeseburgers, and also why some kosher Jewish households have two separate sets of dishes).

Why do Christians not observe these ancient rules? Although Jesus and his disciples, as faithful Jews, would have followed the rules, Jesus himself stated that what made a person unclean was not what went into him, but what came out of him—that is, his words and acts. In saying this, Jesus made it clear that all foods were "clean" (Mark 7:19). In Acts 10, the apostle Peter has a vision of unclean animals in a kind of tarp, with a voice from heaven telling him to "kill and eat." Peter refuses, saying he has never touched unclean food, but the voice from heaven tells him "not to call common what God has cleansed." This is a sign to Peter not only that the kosher rules no longer apply (something he should have learned from Jesus), but that he is to take the gospel message to the Gentiles. Needless to say, as the Christian message spread to non-Jews, dropping the kosher rules was an advantage, since most non-Jews thought the rules were an encumbrance. Today some Christian groups, such as the Seventh-day Adventists, choose to abide by most of the kosher laws, on the grounds that it makes for more healthy living.

The Hebrew word *kosher*, by the way, means "proper" and is not actually used in the passages dealing with the dietary laws. It occurs in the Bible only in Esther 8:5, in a context having nothing to do with foods.

---

but the Ten were in a category by themselves and, thanks to their number, fairly easy to memorize by counting off on one's fingers. For readers today, the other laws are a mixed bag: the kosher food laws that most Christians (and even many Jews) no longer follow, the laws about sacrifices (which can't be followed, since there is no longer a temple or priesthood), laws about quarantining people with various bodily discharges, etc. Some of these are interesting to read from a historical standpoint, some are puzzling. But intermingled with these are numerous laws regarding human relations that still seem valid. Many of these are expansions of the Ten Commandments, telling how to apply them in real-life situations. For example: "Do not follow the crowd in doing wrong. When you give testimony in a lawsuit, do not pervert justice by siding with the crowd, and do not show favoritism to a poor man in his lawsuit" (Exodus 23:2–3). This is a kind of expansion of the commandment against bearing false witness.

Leviticus, with all its tedious rules about sacrifices and other rituals, has some gems dealing with social justice:

"Do not steal. Do not lie. Do not deceive one another" (19:11).

"Do not defraud your neighbor or rob him. Do not hold back the wages of a hired man overnight" (19:13).

"Do not pervert justice; do not show partiality to the poor or favoritism to the great, but judge your neighbor fairly" (19:15).

"Do not go about spreading slander among your people. Do not do anything that endangers your neighbor's life" (19:16).

"Do not hate your brother in your heart. Rebuke your neighbor frankly so you will not share in his guilt" (19:17).

"Do not seek revenge or bear a grudge against one of your people, but love your neighbor as yourself" (19:18). If this verse sounds familiar, it is because Jesus stated that "love your neighbor as yourself" was one of the two greatest commandments—the other being the command to love God with all our heart, soul, mind and strength, a commandment found in Deuteronomy 6:5 (Matthew 22:37). The original law in Leviticus 19 meant "neighbor" as "fellow Israelite," but in some of his parables, Jesus extended "neighbor" further, meaning any person we encounter in life. Jesus told his followers that he came not to abolish the law but to "fulfill" it, and we see this clearly in his zeroing in on this teaching about love of neighbor.

"Rise in the presence of the aged, show respect for the elderly and revere your God" (19:32).

"If you come across your enemy's ox or donkey wandering off, be sure to take it back to him" (Exodus 23:4).

The famous "eye for an eye" laws also occur in Leviticus: "If anyone takes the life of a human being, he must be put to death. Anyone who takes the life of someone's animal must make restitution—life for life. If anyone injures his neighbor, whatever he has done must be done to him: fracture for fracture, eye for eye, tooth for tooth. As he has injured the other, so he is to be injured. Whoever kills an animal must make restitution, but whoever kills a man must be put to death" (24:17–21). This "eye for an eye" principle was designed to *limit* vengeance. The human tendency is get *more* than even, to knock out two teeth for one. God's sense of justice is greater than ours. And certainly the idea of fair restitution is a good one, one that most courts would agree on: "When a man or woman wrongs another in any way and so is unfaithful to the Lord, that person is guilty and must confess the sin he has committed. He must make full restitution for his wrong, add one fifth to it and give it all to the person he has wronged" (Numbers 5:6–7).

Consider this reasonable law against false testimony: "If a malicious witness takes the stand to accuse a man of a crime, the two men involved in the dispute must stand in the presence of the Lord before the priests and the judges who are in office at the time. The judges must make a thorough investigation, and if the witness proves to be a liar, giving false testimony against his brother, then do to him as he intended to do to his brother. You must purge the evil from among you" (Deuteronomy 19:16–19).

Consider Deuteronomy's "honeymoon laws" designed to ensure the happiness of newlyweds and engaged couples: "Has anyone become pledged to a woman and not married her? Let him go home, or he may die in battle and someone else marry her" (20:7). "If a man has recently married, he must not be sent to war or have any other duty laid on him. For one year he is to be free to stay at home and bring happiness to the wife he has married" (24:5). Do these sound like burdens—or like the laws of a God who wanted his creatures to be happy?

There were numerous laws regarding the poor, for example: "There will always be poor people in the land. Therefore I command you to be openhanded toward your brothers and toward the poor and needy in your land" (Deuteronomy 15:11). "When you reap the harvest of your land, do not reap to the very edges of your field or gather the gleanings of your harvest. Do not go over your vineyard a second time or pick up the grapes that have fallen. Leave them for the poor and the alien" (Leviticus 19:9–10). "If one of your countrymen becomes poor and is unable to support himself among you, help him as you would an alien or a temporary resident, so he can continue to live among you. Do not take interest of any kind from him, but fear your God, so that your countryman may continue to live among you. You must not lend him money at interest or sell him food at a profit" (Leviticus 25:35–37).

One wise law that was constantly broken was concerned with the future kings of Israel: "[The king] must not accumulate large amounts of silver and gold....and not consider himself better than his brothers and turn from the law to the right or to the left" (Deuteronomy 17:17, 20). We will see in later chapters that some of the kings of Israel were greedy and exploitive—and considered themselves above the laws that applied to the people they ruled.

The humanity of the laws is remarkable, compared with the other law codes of the ancient world. The crimes meriting the death penalty were relatively few, torture and mutilation were not used as punishments, and all people, regardless of their economic status, were equal before the law (because they were equal in the eyes of God). We have to keep these positive things in mind before we condemn the Law for its acceptance of slavery and polygamy.

As you browse through the various laws in these books, one thing that strikes you is the phrase "I am the Lord" occurring at the end of a commandment. The Israelites were being reminded that these laws were not some arbitrary human invention but came from God himself.

One other striking thing about the laws is that they seem to cover every aspect of human activity: work, commerce, crime and punishment, worship, sexual relations, health, even food. For the Israelites, all of life was under the watchful eye of God. There was no division between "religious" life and "secular" life. Every aspect of life was governed by the awareness of the Lord.

SIN? THEN SACRIFICE

Consider these words of Moses to the Israelites: "Now what I am commanding you today is not too difficult for you or beyond your reach. It is not up in heaven, so that you have to ask, 'Who will ascend into heaven to get it and proclaim it to us so we may obey it?' Nor is it beyond the sea, so that you have to ask, 'Who will cross the sea to get it and proclaim it to us so we may obey it?' No, the word is very near you; it is in your mouth and in your heart so you may obey it" (Deuteronomy 30:11–14). It's as if Moses were speaking as a father to a group of children who have just been told the house rules. Like most children, they were groaning, probably complaining how they would *never* be able to keep all those rules. Moses was assuring them they *could*, if they would only try. But humans are, well, only human. When we do fail, what then?

The Sinai covenant never assumed that people could be totally sinless, that they could keep every law without fail. So the Law provided a system of sacrifices: gifts of animals or grain given to the Hebrew priests. Israel's religion, like many world religions, provided that sinners could make up for their failings (and prove they were sorry) by giving something valuable to God—a sheep or cow, for example. The sacrifice did not "undo" the sin, of course. It did prove the person was aware of the sin and willing to give up something as a sign of repentance. The Old Testament's Book of Leviticus, which is mostly concerned with the various types of sacrifices, makes it clear that there is nothing "magical" about sacrifices. That is, it isn't the slaughtered animal that heals the sin, but the more important fact that the person is aware of his sin and honestly confesses it (Leviticus 26:40–41). In comparison, Israel's system of sacrifices was certainly more humane than that of its neighboring nations, which sacrificed their own infants to idols.

It is impossible to fully understand either the Old or New Testament unless we understand the basic idea of sacrifice. In a sense, the rules for sacrifice given by God to Moses are moot, since there is no longer an Israelite priesthood or temple, and neither Jews nor Christians practice sacrifice. However, Christians frequently speak of Jesus Christ as being the supreme sacrifice for human sin, and it is necessary to know the background of that idea.

CULTURAL INSIGHTS

Tithing

Tithe simply means "tenth," and tithing refers to the practice of giving ten percent of one's produce—crops, herds, whatever could be used as food—to the Lord. Of course, it is not possible to actually give anything to the Lord. Rather, the items were given to the Levites, the tribe in Israel that was responsible for administering the sacrifices. Unlike the other eleven tribes of Israel, the Levites had no land allotted to them, so they depended on the tithes to survive.

Tithing was not unique to Israel. Many countries, such as Babylon and Persia and even China, practiced it, and it was usually in the form of a tax paid to the king. Israel was unique in earmarking the tithe "for the Lord."

The tithing laws are found in Leviticus 27, Numbers 18 and Deuteronomy 14. Devout Jews took them very strictly, so much so that in the time of Jesus, some people even tithed the herbs they grew in their garden. The New Testament does not mention tithing as being required of Christians, although many do so voluntarily, giving a tenth of their income to their church. The New Testament does urge Christians to give generously, especially to aid the poor. Wealthy Christians were especially urged to aid their poorer brothers.

Canaanite Cuisine

The Old Testament contains this odd command: "Do not cook a young goat in its mother's milk" (Exodus 23:19). Archaeologists have dug around the ancient Canaanite city of Ugarit. There they found written materials describing the depraved religion of the Canaanites. Sure enough, one of the Canaanite religious rituals involved boiling a kid goat in its mother's milk. So the old law in Exodus was not only a food law but a warning to avoid the religion of the Canaanites. This prohibition against cooking a kid in its mother's milk is the basis for the Jewish rules against mixing meat with dairy products.

Most religions have some sort of sacrificial system. One explanation for this is that in order to eat meat, animals have to be killed, and in ancient times the killing wasn't done out of sight in some slaughterhouse, but in public view, and it was taken for granted by most people. Sacrificing animals was an everyday occurrence and it had a number of purposes: killing an animal for food; being connected with something spiritual; and bringing a person into a right relationship to his God. Some primitive religions imagined that their gods literally "ate" the food—or, at least, that they inhaled its aroma. This is not the idea in the Bible, where Almighty God does not need to be "fed" by his people. The sacrifice was, however, thought of as a kind of *gift* to God. Since God gives us everything we have, including food, a sacrifice is a kind of giving back to him. Offering food was, in a way, a kind of offering of oneself. God did not need the gift, but accepted it as a token of the person's gratitude.

While some cultures thought that sacrifice was the way of appeasing a cruel and demanding God, this was not so in Israel's case. The key idea was that the sacrifice was man's gift to God, the God who had given everything in the first place. The command to offer up the first fruits of each year's harvest to God assumed a sort of courtesy—giving something back to God before partaking of it oneself. Once God had received his portion, the rest was left for the people to use in a sacrificial meal. In a sense, both God and the worshippers had partaken of a meal together. Burning the sacrifice didn't mean cooking it for God but, rather, ensured that the person did not take it back for his own use. The smoke from the burning was, obviously, a symbol of the gift being "sent up" to God.

Every sacrifice also carried the idea of "expiation," meaning the person had sinned and needed to be made right with God. Everyone sins, so everyone had to make some kind of sacrifice to let God know they were aware of their sins. The sacrifice itself wasn't enough, since what God really wanted was the person's repentance—and resolution not to repeat the sin. But the sacrifice was a visible sign that the person needed to be made right with God. This idea of expiation lies behind the first Christians' belief that Christ was the supreme sacrifice, making the old system of animal sacrifices (which still existed when the New Testament was written) unnecessary. Jesus was the once-and-for-all sacrifice that made man right with God.

Any religious ritual can be done "mechanically," without feeling, and the more sensitive people in Israel constantly condemned this. "Does the Lord delight in burnt offerings and sacrifices as much as in obeying the voice of the Lord? To obey is better than sacrifice, and to heed is better than the fat of rams" (1 Samuel 15:22). If one's heart and behavior were not right, going through the motions of sacrifice had no effect. God would not be fooled by hypocritical sacrifice. Later on we will see how often the great prophets had to speak out against people merely going through the motions of sacrifice, when their hearts didn't truly follow.

PUTTING THE WORD TO WORK

1. Read through the Ten Commandments in Exodus 20. If you first heard these when you were a child, how has your perspective on these "rules" changed? Have they taken on a deeper meaning as you've faced the challenges they represent at different stages of your life?

2. What specific considerations from your own experience can you give to the Commandments? For example, are you now a caretaker of an elderly parent, and has that defined for you what "honor your father and your mother" is all about? Did discussing your thoughts about a co-worker seem harmless until a mistaken impression meant you were bearing false testimony against someone?

3. Consider the breadth of the laws in the first five books of the Bible, and how they cover every aspect of human life. Are there areas of your own life that you feel you don't put under God's command? What are they?

4. The command against worshipping idols was one of the most important in the Bible—and also one of the most frequently disobeyed. What are some "idols" in your own life that distract you from God? These aren't necessarily material objects, but could also be ambition, success, personal appearance or any other motivation that drives you.

5. Consider the commandment against coveting. Who are some people in your own life that possess things you wish you had? Do you wish you had those same things, or begrudge the other person having them? Ask yourself: *Can I be content with what God has given me?*

The Wilderness Road Home
FROM SINAI TO CANAAN

AT THE HEART OF IT ALL TODAY The Israelites in the wilderness continue to doubt and rebel against Moses and God, but God consistently forgives. Moses himself has a phenomenal experience of God's glory. Before his death, Moses predicts the coming of a great prophet like himself—a prophecy the first Christians believed was fulfilled in the life of Christ, a Prophet even greater than Moses.

Today we complete the story of Moses—even though Moses and the Law he received from God cast their long shadow over the rest of the Bible, the New Testament as well as the Old. The deliverance from Egypt and the journey to the Promised Land, Canaan, were miracle-saturated

KEY PASSAGES TO READ TODAY

Exodus 32; 33:14–23; 34:29–35
Numbers 16; 20:1–12
Deuteronomy 34

events the Israelites never forgot, and Moses was their great hero—even though their history reveals how they constantly abandoned the Law that Moses delivered to them.

Before going further, let's pause to reconsider the books we have been studying. On Day 3 we looked at Exodus 1–19, telling of the Israelites' slavery, the call of Moses, the plagues, the Red Sea crossing, and the Israelites' journey to the foot of Mount Sinai. On Day 4

KEY TERM FOR TODAY ## Chosen People

In the Bible, this name applies to the nation (or tribe) of Israel. These people are referred to as Israelites, Hebrews or Jews. The key idea in the Old Testament is that the one true God chose Israel (the descendants of Abraham) to be the recipients of his moral and spiritual guidance. The idea is expressed many times in the Bible, notably in Deuteronomy 7:6: "You are a people holy to the Lord your God. The Lord your God has chosen you out of all the peoples on the face of the earth to be his people, his treasured possession." The Bible makes it clear that the chosen people are never to be arrogant because God has chosen them. In fact, because God revealed himself and his moral law to Israel, the people of Israel will be severely punished when they break the moral law. So, being "chosen" is a privilege but also an obligation. In the words of God himself, "Be holy, for I am holy."

c. 1250–c. 1210 BC
The Israelites wander in the desert for forty years before entering the land of Canaan. Moses receives the divine Law at Mount Sinai and passes on the laws to the Israelites. *(Exodus 16—Deuteronomy 34).*

1226 BC
Mount Etna, located on the island of Sicily, erupts.

1210 BC
Merneptah, thirteenth son of the mighty Pharaoh Ramses II, assumes the throne of Egypt.

c. 1210 BC
Moses dies; Joshua leads the first wave of the invasion of Canaan *(The Book of Joshua).*

we looked at the laws given by God to Moses, found in Exodus 20–40, all of Leviticus, parts of Numbers, and parts of Deuteronomy. Today we return to the narrative of Israel's journey to Canaan, found in Numbers and Deuteronomy.

We'll begin, however, with two episodes from Exodus that are important to remember.

Moses received the Ten Commandments directly from God, carved in stone by the Lord's own finger. But while Moses was drawing close to God, the Israelites were at the foot of the mountain, losing faith in both God and Moses. Why was he so long on the mountain? Had he died? The fickle people had seen the power of the Lord manifested in smoke, thunder and lightning, but their awe soon diminished. They began to pressure Moses' brother, Aaron: Fashion us a god—an idol—to go before us. Aaron, who must have had some knowledge of metalworking, had the people gather up their gold jewelry, which he formed into an idol in the shape of a young bull. Most Bible versions say "calf," and for centuries people remembered the story of Moses and the "golden calf." But the Hebrew word here really means "young bull," a vigorous-looking animal. Bulls were symbols of fertility and strength in the ancient world and were often used as images of the pagan gods. Aaron had no doubt seen bull idols in Egypt. The people built an altar in front of the idol and the next day staged a festival day "for the Lord."

This is one of the great ironies in the Bible: At the very time God was giving Moses the commandment to "make no idols," the Israelites were making one! God saw what was happening, how the people were bowing down to their new "god." He was filled with anger, but Moses—not for the last time—begged God to show mercy, reminding him of his promises to the patriarch Abraham. The Lord relented, and when Moses went down to the people, he was met by his faithful aide, Joshua, who apparently was the only Israelite not participating in what seemed to be a sort of religious orgy. Now it was Moses' turn to be angry. He broke the stone tablets with the Ten Commandments on them. He melted down the golden bull idol and mingled it with the water, making the Israelites drink it. Aaron begged Moses to relent, excusing himself by saying the people had pressured him into making the idol—which was true. Although God did not destroy the people, he did strike them with a plague. Then he gave the order: Leave Sinai and continue on to Canaan. God showed his anger, then showed his mercy—a pattern seen again and again in the Bible. The people with whom God had just made a sacred covenant would continually test his patience.

THE WEIGHT OF GLORY

The Bible often uses the Hebrew word *kabod*, which literally means "weight," but is usually translated "glory." Sometime before departing from Sinai, Moses had an awesome experience of the Lord's *kabod*.

The Lord had assured Moses that his "presence" (the Hebrew word here literally means "face") would be with the Israelites. Moses asked a great favor from the Lord: "Show me your glory." The Lord told him, "I will cause all my goodness to pass in front of you, and I will proclaim my name, the Lord, in your presence.… But you cannot see my face, for no one may see me and live." The Lord placed Moses in a cleft in the rocky mountainside. The Lord "passed by," and Moses saw the "back" of God (Exodus 33:12–23).

CULTURAL INSIGHTS

Old Testament vs. New Testament: Two Different Gods?

Around the year AD 140 a wealthy businessman named Marcion posed a challenge to Christianity. He claimed the God of the Old Testament was not the same as the one in the New Testament. The Old Testament God, Marcion said, was a cold-hearted God of justice and violence and wrath. He was Israel's tribal God. The New Testament God was the loving, caring Father God that Jesus spoke of. So, Marcion said, let's do the obvious thing: Toss the Old Testament aside. We don't need it.

Was Marcion right? In one sense, yes. The New Testament does show a more loving, caring side of God than the Old Testament does. And the Old Testament depicts God commanding Israel to settle in Canaan and drive out the heathen inhabitants.

But the fact is, the whole Bible has the same God. Jesus, Paul and the other chief figures of the New Testament do speak of God's love and kindness and his willingness to forgive. But they also speak of his anger against sin, his justice, his final judgment of people at the end of the world. And the Old Testament does show the loving side of God. He is the Almighty, but he is also the One who desires that people turn from their foolish ways and return to him. This should be crystal clear in today's lesson and in the previous two days as well, since we see God growing angry with the unfaithful, ungrateful Israelites, yet always willing to extend mercy to them.

We need the Old Testament, and not just for historical reasons. We need its picture of God's power and (on occasion) his anger just as we need the New Testament's emphasis on God the forgiving Father. He is the Almighty—and he is loving and forgiving. There is no either/or, only a both/and. From beginning to end in the Bible, there is a wrathful God of mercy, a God who hates sin but loves sinners.

What actually happened when God passed by Moses? We don't know. God has no "face" or "back." Perhaps Moses did not see anything with his eyes. What he did see—or experience—must have been beyond words to describe. He had "seen" the glory, the "weight" of Almighty God in a way none of us can conceive.

DID YOU KNOW?

Our word *scapegoat*, which we use to refer to some innocent person taking the blame for something he did not do, is based on a ritual for the Day of Atonement. Israel's high priest would lay his hands on a goat, symbolically laying on it the sins of all the people of Israel for the past year. The goat would be driven off into the wilderness, bearing away the sins. The ritual is described in Leviticus 16.

When he came down from the mountain again, Moses was a changed man. He literally glowed. His face was radiant, and the Israelites were afraid to be near him. Moses told them not to fear—but he put a veil over his face, so powerful was the radiance. Moses departed Sinai shining—deeply aware of the presence of God and painfully aware of the ungrateful people he had to lead all the way to Canaan.

THE PORTABLE WORSHIP CENTER

Among the many instructions Moses received from God on Sinai were the specifications for making the Tabernacle, the large tent that would serve as the center of Israel's worship until, centuries later, a temple was built in Jerusalem. The Tabernacle is described in Exodus 26. Various altars and other furnishings were made for the Tabernacle, the most important being the ark of the covenant, described in Exodus 25:10–22. The ark was a wooden chest, covered in gold, and with a lid—the "mercy seat"—made of pure gold. Over the mercy seat were two figures called the "cherubim," which had human bodies but instead of arms, there were wings, and the two cherubim's wings touched each other, making a kind of arc over the mercy seat. (Some archaeologists think the cherubim were winged sphinxes— lion bodies, human heads, plus wings.) For the Israelites, the ark symbolized the presence of God. Even though God was everywhere, the ark was a visible reminder of his presence among them. They thought of the ark as a kind of "throne" for the Lord. In fact, many of the Psalms written centuries later speak of the Lord "enthroned between the cherubim."

Why was the gold lid of the ark called the mercy seat? Every year, on the Day of Atonement, Israel's high priest was to sprinkle blood on the mercy seat, symbolizing the forgiveness of the people's sins for the year.

The ark was hollow, but not empty. In it were placed the stone tablets with the Ten Commandments—not the original ones inscribed by God, for Moses had broken these when he came down from Sinai and saw the people worshipping the golden bull idol. The ark contained the second set, which God instructed Moses himself to carve in stone. It also contained a pot of manna, the miraculous food God provided for the Israelites in the wilderness, which was placed in the ark as a reminder of God's provision for his people.

The ark was the most important object in Israel's possession, and later we will see it playing an important role in Israel's history.

The entire Tabernacle was thought of as a kind of "portable Sinai," the place where Moses would meet with God as they continued on their journey through the wilderness. The Tabernacle (and, later, the Temple) was thought of as God's "house." The altar was its hearth, and just as people in ancient times always kept their homes' hearths lit, so the Law mandated that the altar fire be kept burning at all times (Leviticus 6:8–13). It was a symbol of the divine presence, as noted in Genesis, where the patriarchs would set up an altar at places where they encountered God. As in the episode of the burning bush, fire is a vivid symbol of God's presence. Fire is "alive," in motion, and though it is physical, it cannot be touched or held. There are many times in the Bible when fire indicates God's presence.

Incidentally, since the Tabernacle was the place where the Israelites encountered God, the name *Tabernacle* was borrowed centuries later by evangelists who traveled from town to town holding their meetings in large tents, called "tabernacles." The name was appropriate, for in many of those evangelism services, people found God.

SERVANTS OF GOD

Despite Aaron, Moses' own brother, caving in to the people's request to create the golden bull idol, the Lord had chosen Aaron to be the first priest of Israel, and the priesthood would be passed on to his descendants. Exodus 28 describes in great detail the distinctive garments of the high priest. He wore a turban, which had a gold plate attached to it inscribed with "Holy to the Lord." He wore a blue robe with a sash and, most distinctively, the "breastpiece," a linen rectangle set with twelve gems, each of them symbolizing the twelve tribes of Israel and engraved with the tribe's name. Yarn kept it strapped over the priest's chest so that as he went about his duties, he literally had the names of the tribes over his heart.

Prior to this, Israel had no priesthood. In Genesis, making sacrifices could be done by anyone, usually by the head of a family, as in the case of Noah and Abraham. As religions become more complex, they usually develop a clergy, a group of people who have distinctive religious duties to perform. For Israel, those duties would be performed by the tribe of Levi, the tribe from which Moses and Aaron came. The priests and their assistants in worship were all Levites. After the Israelites settled in Canaan, the Levites did not receive an allotment of land like the other tribes. Instead, they lived off the tithes that the Israelites presented to the Lord.

Since it was God who set up the priesthood for Israel, we know it was his will. However, throughout Israel's history many of the priests were unworthy and even immoral men. Jumping ahead several centuries, the priests were among the chief enemies of Jesus, seeing him as a threat to their position, and the corrupt high priest Caiaphas condemned Jesus as a blasphemer deserving of death. But even the first generation of priests was not spotless. Aaron's two sons, Nadab and Abihu, were both killed by the Lord for offering "strange fire" (or "unauthorized fire" in some modern translations)—a puzzling expression no one fully understands. What did Nadab and Abihu do that so offended God? We don't know, but God had his reasons. Their positions were filled by two other sons of Aaron, Eleazar and Ithamar, who were worthier men. For centuries, the priests of Israel were known as the "sons of Aaron."

The priests and Levites performed the sacrifices and other rituals first in the Tabernacle, then in the temple that Solomon built centuries later. When the Romans destroyed the temple in AD 70, Israel's priesthood ended forever, and when Jews created the nation of Israel in 1948, there was no attempt to build a new temple or reinstitute the priesthood. So the pages and pages of laws in Exodus and Leviticus relating to sacrifices and other priestly duties changed in relevance to the people's everyday practice of their faith.

On Mount Sinai, God had told Moses that the entire nation of Israel was to be a "kingdom of priests." He didn't mean that all were to perform sacrifices or wear the priestly garb, but that Israel—and the faith it would carry into the world—served the

---

CULTURAL INSIGHTS

Anointing

The Greek word *Christ* and the Hebrew word *Messiah* both have the same meaning: anointed. The Book of Exodus contains the first instance in the Bible of a person being anointed. The person was Aaron, Moses' older brother, who was anointed to the post of Israel's high priest. Exodus 29 describes how Aaron was dressed in the distinctive garb of Israel's priest, and Moses poured the anointing oil on his head. The recipe for the oil is in Exodus 30. It must have been very fragrant: to the base of olive oil was added cinnamon, myrrh, cassia and "fragrant cane." The mixture was only to be used for the priestly anointing or on the other sacred furnishings in the Tabernacle, and the Israelites were strictly prohibited from using the same formula for any other purpose.

The scented oil was used for the priests—the mediators between God and man—throughout Israel's history. Although the Old Testament often refers to Israel's king as "the Lord's anointed," it's worth recalling that priests were anointed long before Israel had a king. It's also worth remembering that when the first Christians called Jesus the Christ, the Anointed One, they thought of him as not only their king but also as their priest, their mediator between them and God. Jesus was never anointed as a leader with scented oil. The Gospels tell us that at his baptism the Holy Spirit came upon him. This was the better anointing.

---

kind of function that a priest did, a mediator between God and man. Israel—or, more accurately, its faith—was to bring God and humankind back together.

One passage of the Bible closely connected with Aaron the priest is found in Numbers 6:24–26. It is known as the Aaronic Benediction, and has been recited countless times by Christians over the centuries, who may not even know it is actually from the Bible. It is the blessing God gave Aaron to pronounce over the Israelites:

> The LORD bless you and keep you;
> the LORD make his face to shine upon you
>   and be gracious to you;
> the LORD lift up his countenance upon you
>   and give you peace.
>
>   (ESV)

ON THE ROAD WITH THE REBELS

One of the great curiosities of the Bible is that it took the Israelites forty years to journey from Egypt to Canaan. Take a look at any map and you may well ask: How could it possibly take that long? Did they move a few inches per day? In our time the trip could be made easily by car in a day. On foot, perhaps a few weeks. So why did the Israelites, who had God going with them, require forty years?

One obvious answer: That was the time required to make a band of former slaves ready to settle down and govern themselves in a new land. Something else happened along the way: The people died off gradually, so that when they finally arrived in Canaan, most of the ones who actually left Egypt were no longer alive. The children who were born along the way were free children, not slaves. They would be the ones to move into Canaan, conquer it, and build the nation of Israel.

Another reason for the length of the journey was that there were numerous obstacles—notably, the Israelites themselves, ever griping, ever forgetful of the favors God had showered on them.

They seemed to be always on the verge of rebellion, even threatening to go back to Egypt. Instead of being grateful to the patient Moses, the man who had talked with God face-to-face, they resented his authority. Numbers 16 tells of the great rebellion led by Korah, Dathan and Abiram. Along with 250 other Israelites—not just chronic whiners, but respected leaders among the people—these three confronted Moses, asking him, "Why do you set yourselves above the Lord's assembly?" Korah was a Levite, and perhaps the ordination of the Levites to serve in worship had given him a taste of power, and he liked it. Moses told him he should be satisfied with the office he was given and not strive for more. Dathan and Abiram were not Levites, and their complaint was the old familiar one: Moses had led them out of Egypt only to let them die in the wilderness—and he was lording it over them!

A showdown occurred. Moses told the people that if the rebels died a natural death, it was a sign that the Lord was not on Moses' side. But the Lord was very much on Moses' side. The ground split apart, and the three leading rebels were pulled down into the earth, which closed over them—they were literally buried alive. The rest of the rebels were destroyed by fire from heaven.

The other Israelites were terrified—but they got over it quickly enough, and instead of being afraid of questioning Moses' authority, the next day they accused him: "You have killed the Lord's people!" This angered the Lord so much that he sent a plague among the people, killing thousands of them. The episode reflects what was at stake: the ungrateful Israelites were on the verge of ousting the man who had clearly been chosen by God to lead them.

Another dangerous rebellion occurred after Moses sent a reconnaissance group into Canaan to spy out the land. There were twelve spies, one from each tribe. After forty days' exploration, they reported back to the people. There was good news and bad. The land was fertile, as proven by a huge cluster of grapes, so large it had to be carried on a pole by two men. In fact, Canaan really was the "land of milk and honey" that God had promised them. The bad news: The cities were fortified with stone walls, and the men were large—giants, in fact! "The land we explored devours those living in it!…We seemed like grasshoppers in our own eyes, and we looked the same to them." Two of the spies, Joshua and Caleb, were more optimistic. They could take possession of the land, as the Lord willed.

The pessimistic people grumbled all night, then the next day voiced the old lament: We ought to go back to Egypt! They were on the verge of stoning Moses and Aaron—and Joshua and Caleb as well. The Lord told Moses he would strike the people with a plague. As he did many times, Moses pleaded for his people. God relented, but swore that not one of the Israelites over the age of twenty would enter Canaan, except for the faithful Joshua and Caleb. For their lack of faith, the ten spies who gave an unfavorable report died. This is the answer to the question raised at the beginning of this section:

Why did the Israelites require forty years to get to Canaan? Some of those years were punishment for their lack of faith.

POOR MOSES!

Numbers 20 relates what could only have been a disappointing episode in the life of Moses. The Israelites were in a region without water, and as always they raised a cry against Moses for bringing them into the wilderness to die. God spoke to Moses and told him to speak to a large rock, and it would pour out its water for the people. When the people gathered in front of the rock, Moses, exasperated by these people that he rightly called "rebels," struck the rock twice with his staff. Water gushed out, and the people ceased their complaining for the moment. But at this point the people were not the main problem.

"The Lord said to Moses and Aaron, 'Because you did not trust in me enough to honor me as holy in the sight of the Israelites, you will not bring this community into the land I give them.' "

Most people read this passage and scratch their heads, wondering: *After showing such faith and obedience, Moses was denied the pleasure of entering Canaan—because of this one small act? Is this punishment in proportion to the sin?* The Lord had told Moses to speak to the rock. Instead, he struck it. Moses had always been so faithful in doing exactly what God told him; now, when he disobeyed in a small way, was he setting such a bad example?

The simple truth is, this passage is hard for us to understand. But then the ways of God aren't always clear to us. Moses was not given the pleasure of entering Canaan. But he had the greatest pleasure of all: He had served God and completed his divine mission. And we have no doubts that upon his death he entered a place much better than Canaan.

BALAAM'S TALKING DONKEY

One of the most bizarre and amusing stories in the Bible concerns a false prophet named Balaam, whose story is told in Numbers 22–24. Balaam lived in Moab, through which the Israelites were passing on their way to Canaan. Balak, the king of Moab, had heard how, with God's help, the Israelites had defeated the Amorites. Balak sent a message—and money—to Balaam and told him to ride out and put a curse on the Israelites. In ancient

---

DID YOU KNOW?

The Book of Numbers takes its name from the census that is recorded in chapter 1. The Hebrew title of the book is *bemidbar*, meaning, appropriately, "in the wilderness."

The Book of Deuteronomy takes its name from the Greek for "second law." (*Deutero*, "second," *nomos*, "law"). It repeats some of the laws found in earlier books, including the Ten Commandments. But much of the book is a sermon Moses preached to the Israelites, giving them spiritual counsel they would need as they settled in Canaan, warning them against the dangers of abandoning God's Law.

times people took blessing and cursing seriously, and Balak observes that Balaam's blessings and curses are powerful and effective. However, the prophet heard a word from the Lord: *You can't curse these people; they are blessed.* So Balaam refused Balak's request. Balak tried offering more money, and Balaam refused again—but then changed his mind and rode off on his donkey to lay his curse on Israel. God was angry at the prophet's disobedience, and he sent an angel armed with a sword to stand in the road. The angel was invisible to Balaam, but not to the donkey, who swerved off the road into a field. Balaam hit the beast, got back on the road, but the donkey swerved once more, causing Balaam to scrape his foot on a wall. Balaam beat her again. In a narrow place in the road, it could not veer off, so it did what donkeys do: sat down and would not budge. Balaam beat it again.

"Then the Lord opened the donkey's mouth, and she said to Balaam, 'What have I done to you to make you beat me these three times?' " We can assume Balaam was not accustomed to his donkey speaking, but instead of acting surprised, Balaam scolds the beast for its stubbornness and threatens to kill it. At this point Balaam himself sees the angel with the drawn sword. He falls down in terror, realizing he was disobeying God.

Balaam did ride out to where the Israelites passed through, but instead of cursing them, he blessed them, in a very eloquent passage (Numbers 23–24). In the blessing he prophesied that Israel would be a great nation, blessed by God. He speaks of Israel as "a people who live apart and do not consider themselves one of the nations" (23:9)—something that has been true for three thousand years. Balaam's blessing even includes this profound description of the Lord: "God is not a man, that he should lie, nor a son of man, that he should change his mind. Does he speak and then not act? Does he promise and not fulfill?" (23:19).

Balaam eventually came to a bad end. For trying to lead the Israelites into idolatry later on, they killed him. And the story of Balaam pronouncing a blessing on Israel is followed by the story of how the Moabites, Balaam's people, led the Israelites into idol worship—a preview of something that would happen again and again once the Israelites were settled in Canaan. This episode contains the Bible's first mention of a name that will occur many, many times: Baal, the name of the Canaanite's fertility god. This would not be the last time the Israelites found themselves involved in the worship of this rival god.

THE END AND THE BEGINNING

The great man Moses, the first man in the Bible to be called "the man of God," had suffered many things, notably the ingratitude and rebelliousness of the Israelites. And after his error of striking the rock, God denied him the joy of entering Canaan. But Deuteronomy 3 relates that Moses did see Canaan—from a distance, at least. He went to a mountain called Pisgah, which gave him an eagle's-eye view of the land. Then he commissioned his worthy successor, Joshua, who would lead the people into Canaan.

Moses' brother Aaron, Israel's first priest, had already died along the way. So had Moses' sister, Miriam. Moses died at the age of 120, "yet his eyes were not weak nor his strength gone." The Lord himself buried Moses, and no one knew exactly where. The ungrateful Israelites must have realized the loss, for they mourned Moses for thirty days.

"Since then, no prophet has risen in Israel like Moses, whom the Lord knew face to face.... no one has ever shown the mighty power or performed the awesome deeds that Moses did in the sight of all Israel" (Deuteronomy 34:10–12).

Moses was so honored in Israel—more honored in death than in life, we might add—that a whole vast literature was written about Moses' death and burial. We catch a glimpse of this in the New Testament, where the brief Letter of Jude refers to Satan and

CHARACTER CLOSE-UP ## "Meek as Moses"

"Moses was a very humble man, more humble than anyone else on the face of the earth" (Numbers 12:3). In the long-popular King James Version, the word is "meek," not "humble," and in a time when people were more familiar with the Bible, "meek as Moses" was a commonly used phrase.

Why was Moses meek? We regard him as one of the great men of history, one of history's saints, the man singled out to receive laws from the very hand of God. How could a man ascend to such spiritual heights and remain meek? Wouldn't most people become boastful and proud?

In fact, Moses' closeness to the Lord had exactly the opposite effect. The more he saw of God's power and greatness, the less he thought of human greatness. Moses had seen the Almighty—after that, what human being (even himself) could seem impressive?

In another humbling episode in the life of Moses, his own brother and sister, Aaron and Miriam, rebel against him. They feel slighted by God: *What makes Moses so special?* The Book of Numbers reveals they also don't approve of Moses' marrying a Cushite woman. Their own pettiness is in striking contrast to Moses, who was learning a hard lesson that many great men learn: It is possible to be misunderstood by one's own family.

The sibling quarrel is not settled by Moses tooting his own horn, something he would never do, but by the voice of God: "With [Moses] I speak face to face, clearly and not in riddles; he sees the form of the Lord. Why then were you not afraid to speak against my servant Moses?" After that, Miriam appears to be covered in leprosy. The frightened Aaron begs Moses to intercede for her, and her loving, forgiving brother Moses asks God to heal her. Miriam endures the leprosy for seven days before it passes.

What an amazing man Moses was. No wonder the Israelites honored him in their memory—even as they tended to disregard the divine laws he passed on to them.

The Bronze Serpent

While they were in the wilderness, the ever-complaining Israelites again spoke out against God and Moses, lamenting the "miserable food" they had to eat. On this occasion the punishment was an invasion of "fiery serpents" that caused many of the people to die. The people pleaded for mercy, so Moses set up a bronze snake on a pole, and "when anyone was bitten by a snake, and looked at the bronze snake, he lived" (Numbers 21:9).

What were the "fiery serpents"? Some translations have "venomous snakes," which is probably correct. Scientists think another possibility is that the people were afflicted by a parasite called a guinea worm, which causes intense burning and itching. Its eggs are present in water, and it grows inside the body like a small snake, visible on the surface of the skin. It can be removed—gradually and very carefully—by slowly winding it around a stick. This might explain the snake on the pole as a kind of visual aid showing the people how to remove the worm.

The Israelites apparently thought highly of the bronze snake, because they kept it—and eventually worshipped it as an idol, until it was destroyed by one of the reforming kings (2 Kings 18:4). How ironic to make an idol of something connected with Moses, the man who commanded them never to make idols!

The bronze snake is mentioned by Jesus, who compared it to himself: As the Israelites in the wilderness were healed by looking at the bronze snake lifted up on a pole, so people would be saved by looking at Christ lifted up on the cross (John 3:14–15).

the archangel Michael disputing over who would have the body of Moses. (Michael won.) There were many legends that amounted to the religious fiction of their day. The more religious Israelites stuck to the narratives of the Bible. The real life of Moses was quite fascinating in itself without adding the fanciful details of the other writings.

The Exodus and the years in the wilderness can be understood as a kind of pattern for every person's spiritual journey. There is a break with the old life, then a period of testing, then the fulfillment—leaving Egypt, enduring the wilderness, entering Canaan, conversion, life in this world, life in the next world. Note that again and again the Israelites lost faith in Moses and God and raised the cry "Back to Egypt!" True, they were slaves in Egypt—but they had food enough, and they had that comfort that many people crave: Life was predictable, no unexpected terrors, few surprises. Even today, some people prefer spiritual slavery and a life they can understand and predict to spiritual freedom and a whole array of new decisions. Some choose to turn back, and in their way "return to Egypt." Some continue on in the "wilderness," reaching for their Canaan in the hope of finding the contentment and fulfillment of resting in God.

"A PROPHET LIKE ME"

One of the greatest prophecies of the Old Testament is found in Deuteronomy 18, spoken by Moses: "The Lord your God will raise up for you a prophet like me from among your own brothers. You must listen to him." Over the centuries, the Lord raised up many great prophets, notably the fiery Elijah (who, like Moses, had a dramatic encounter with the Lord on Mount Sinai). But the Israelites always prayed for and expected a man who would be *the* prophet, a special one, the one that was predicted in the prophecy. Some of the people even expected that the longed-for Messiah and the "prophet like Moses" would be one and the same. You see this very clearly in the New Testament, where some people speculate that Jesus might be "the Prophet," which is how the Jews of that time spoke of the "prophet like me" that Moses had promised. Christians believe that Jesus *was* that Prophet, and much more. We will look more closely at Jesus as a prophet in later chapters. For now, consider just a few of the similarities between Moses and Jesus:

Moses, raised in a royal court, left the life of luxury to be among his own people, who were slaves.
Jesus, the Son of God, came to live among human beings as one of them.

Moses is almost exterminated in his infancy by the evil Pharaoh.
Jesus is almost exterminated in his infancy by the wicked King Herod.

Moses receives the commands of God on a mountain.
Jesus delivers his greatest sermon on a mountain.

Moses is tested in the wilderness for forty years.
Jesus is tested by Satan in the wilderness for forty days.

Moses is constantly misunderstood and persecuted by his people.
Jesus is constantly misunderstood and persecuted by his people.

Moses, on two occasions, is almost stoned by the people.
Jesus, on two occasions, is almost stoned by the people.

Moses is "a very humble man."
Jesus is "meek and lowly of heart."

Moses intercedes with God for the rebellious people.
Jesus intercedes with God for the rebellious people.

Moses with his arms outstretched gives hope to his people.
Jesus stretched on the cross gives hope to his people.

Moses saves people by lifting up the bronze snake on a pole.
Jesus saves people by being lifted up on the cross.

Moses leads people out of slavery.
Jesus leads people out of death.

There are many, many other parallels between the two. The early Christians, especially those raised as Jews, did see Jesus as a "second Moses," the prophet like Moses spoken of by Moses himself. In Acts, both Peter and Stephen identify Jesus as the prophet Moses predicted. But the Letter of the Hebrews says that, great as Moses was, Jesus Christ is greater—just as the builder of the house is greater than the house itself.

PUTTING THE WORD TO WORK

1. We see in today's readings that God was often angry, but just as often was eager to show mercy to the faithless Israelites. Have there been times in your own life when you felt your lack of faith angered God? Were you able to ask for and receive God's forgiveness?

2. One theme in today's study is the questioning of the leader God sets over us. It can be extremely difficult to disagree with a religious leader. If that has happened to you, did you feel that resisting the person's authority was justified? Or did it reveal more of your own doubts about God's will?

3. The ark of the covenant contained a pot of manna and the tablets with the Ten Commandments inscribed on them. These were physical reminders of God's concern for Israel. What are some physical items in your own life that you treasure as reminders of God's care for you?

4. Family members can be our staunchest supporters—and sometimes our harshest critics. What role do you most often play with your loved ones? Moses faced a problem many leaders face: being misunderstood by his own family members. Moses did the right thing and left the matter in God's hands. If you were tempted in the past to take offense easily at family members who doubted you, make a resolution to bear criticism quietly, to let God deal with the matter in his own way.

5. Every Christian's life can be compared to the Exodus story—leaving the old life behind, experiencing wandering and testing, finally coming home. Where are you in your journey? Are you ever tempted to "return to Egypt"? Have you found that enduring the tests of the "wilderness" of life on earth has heightened your yearning for God, making you more eager to get on to "Canaan"?

Settling among Evil Neighbors

AT THE HEART OF IT ALL TODAY With God's help, his people, the Israelites, conquer and settle Canaan, the promised land. In the midst of barbarity and primitive religions, they wander from their faith, but God does not abandon them. He sends military leaders, the "judges," so that his people and their faith will endure.

After the death of the great Moses, the mantle of leadership fell on Joshua, the Spirit-filled man who faced the daunting task of settling the Israelites in their new homeland, Canaan. Recall that Joshua was one of the twelve spies Moses had sent into Canaan ahead of time, and of the twelve only Joshua and Caleb were optimistic about conquering the people who already lived there. Put another way, Joshua had faith not just in the people's abilities, but in God.

KEY PASSAGES TO READ TODAY

Joshua 1:1–9; 2:1–21; 6:1–25; 10:12–14; 21:43–45; 24:14–15 Judges 2:11–19; 4:1–22; 7:19–23; 8:22–23; 11:29–40; 14:1—16:31

Let's begin this section by considering what Israel was at this time in history: a confederation of twelve tribes. Hearing the word *tribe* calls to mind the indigenous people found in the pages of *National Geographic*. But *tribe* does not have this meaning in the Bible. The patriarch Jacob, also named Israel, had twelve sons—Reuben, Simeon, Levi, Judah, Issachar, Zebulun, Gad, Asher, Dan, Naphtali, Joseph and Benjamin. The twelve "tribes" were clans claiming descent from one of these twelve sons. In the Book of Joshua, the land of Canaan was divided among the twelve tribes.

Yet, if you look at maps of Old Testament times, you won't find Joseph or Levi on the map. You'll find areas named for the other ten tribes. Why? Well, the tribe of

KEY TERM FOR TODAY ## Baal

Aside from God himself, the most-mentioned deity in the Bible is the Canaanite fertility god Baal, whose name means "owner" or "master." It is appropriate that he is mentioned so often, because for most of Israel's history he was the chief rival to God. Like most pagan gods, Baal had no moral character. He and his female consort, Ashtoreth, were personified forces of nature. Looking at the larger picture, what was at stake was not one god versus another, but the amoral religion of nature versus the religion of a moral and personal God who rules *over* nature.

1400–1200 BC
Hittite Empire
in Anatolia.

c. 1210 BC
Joshua leads the
conquest of Canaan
(Joshua).

The first recorded
sea battle occurs:
Suppuliumas II,
king of the Hittites,
defeats a fleet from
Cyprus, and burns
their ships at sea.

c. 1200–1025 BC
Military leadership
in Israel exercised by
the "judges"
(Gideon, Jephthah,
Samson and others)
(Judges, Ruth).

1190–1150 BC
The strategic location
of Cyprus and its
natural resources
attracts the attention
of many invaders
and rulers. Assyrians,
Egyptians and
Persians raid the
island.

c. 1190 BC
Greeks destroy Troy.

Levi had no land of its own. It did have certain cities allotted to it. The people of Levi—the Levites—had the duty of serving as priests in the nation. (The great leader Moses was a Levite. So was his brother, Aaron, Israel's first high priest.) The tribe of Joseph actually was divided into two "half-tribes" named for Joseph's two sons, Manasseh and Ephraim. So the maps show areas named for Manasseh and Ephraim, not for their father, Joseph. By eliminating Levi and dividing Joseph in two, we end up with twelve. Manasseh and Ephraim are sometimes called "half-tribes," but in fact they were both large, with more land and more people than several of the other tribes.

Pause a moment for a brief flash-forward into the future: Many people believe that when Jesus chose twelve men to be his disciples he was choosing to start a "new Israel"—one based not on family ties, but on being followers of Christ. He was establishing a "spiritual Israel" of people who chose to commit themselves to God. Even non-Jews could be part of this new Israel.

In the period we're studying in this chapter, Israel had no centralized government, no capital, no center of worship. Various locales scattered through the land were religious centers, usually because they had some connection with the patriarchs Abraham and Jacob. Bethel, for example, was held in high regard because it was the site where Jacob had his famous dream of a stairway into heaven. The city of Jerusalem, the most important city in the history of Israel, was named Jebus in this period, and it was not in Israel's territory. It would not become part of Israel until David conquered it centuries later and made it Israel's capital.

If the tribes were in any way united during this period, it was through their awareness of kinship with the other tribes—they all were descended from Jacob—and their worship of the same God. It was their religion more than their ancestry that made them distinct, for the nations and tribes on their borders worshipped many gods and made statues of those gods, while Israel had only one God, and they were prohibited from making images of him. The people around them were puzzled: Why would anyone serve a god they cannot see? And why were the Israelites foolish enough to think there was only one god, when everyone knew there were many, both male and female? And why engage in the dull worship of this invisible god, when the worship of the Canaanite gods involved promiscuous sex? During this period, the Israelites would ponder those same questions—and answer by abandoning their God and following the immoral fertility religion of the locals.

Now, back to Joshua 1.

A WORTHY SUCCESSOR

At the beginning of the book, the Lord strengthens Joshua: "Be strong and courageous, because you will lead these people to inherit the land I swore to their forefathers to give them.... Do not let this Book of the Law depart from your mouth; meditate on it day and

night, so that you may be careful to do everything written in it. Then you will be prosperous and successful" (1:6–8). The people assure Joshua they will fully obey him. Joshua's first act as leader is to send spies to the walled city of Jericho. The spies hide out in the home of a local prostitute, named Rahab. The king of Jericho seeks them out, but Rahab lies and says the spies have departed. In fact, she has hidden them on her roof under piles of flax. Rahab has heard that the Lord is on Israel's side, and that the Israelites will capture Jericho. She makes the spies promise that when they capture the city, they will spare her and her family. They tell her to tie a scarlet cord on the window of her house so they can recall where she lived. Then by night she lets them escape Jericho by guiding them down a rope from her window.

Soon afterward, Joshua leads the huge band of Israelites in crossing the Jordan River. As proof that God is still with them, and that the time of miracles is not past, God parts

---

CULTURAL INSIGHTS ## The First Historian

The Greek historian Herodotus, who lived around 450 BC, is often called the "Father of History" for having written a history of the wars between Greece and Persia. But the title "Father of History" rightly belongs to an earlier writer, the anonymous author of Joshua, Judges, 1 and 2 Samuel, and 1 and 2 Kings. We don't know who he was, but we do know he was a talented (and God-inspired) writer and also a careful historian who drew on earlier sources, such as the court histories of the kings of Israel. Some Bible scholars have suggested that the prophet Jeremiah might be the author, while others suggest that Samuel wrote Judges and Samuel. Whoever he was, he wrote a compelling story of Israel over a long period, from the conquest of Canaan under Joshua to the deportation to Babylon more than six hundred years later. The writing of the history was probably completed by 550 BC, a hundred years earlier than Herodotus.

the waters of the Jordan River as four priests, carrying the ark of the covenant, cross over, with the people following. The ark is the sign that God's presence is there at the head of the procession. Joshua orders them to set up twelve large stones, one for each tribe, as a reminder of the twelve tribes crossing over the river. Afterward, a sign of obedience is in order. The male children born in the forty years of the wilderness journey were never circumcised. A mass circumcision is ordered, and the site where it took place is called Gibeath Haaraloth—"hill of foreskins." Remember that circumcision was important for Israel, for God had ordered Abraham to make circumcision a sign of his covenant.

Near Jericho, Joshua encounters a man with a drawn sword, who identifies himself as "commander of the army of the Lord"—that is, an angel. He tells Joshua to have the armed men of Israel march around Jericho for six days, with the ark as part of the parade. On the seventh day, when the priests blow their trumpets and the people shout in unison, the imposing walls of Jericho will fall.

"At the sound of the trumpet, when the people gave a loud shout, the wall collapsed, so that every man charged straight in, and they took the city" (Joshua 6:20). They kept their promise to Rahab, evacuating her and her family from the city, then burning it. The story of the walls that came tumbling down spread, and the Canaanites knew the Israelites were an enemy to be feared.

The Israelites had not followed God's orders to the letter. They were told to destroy everything in the city, but one man, Achan, kept some of the loot for himself. Here we have to look at the divine mandate God gave Joshua: When a Canaanite city was taken, everything in it was to be destroyed. This is what distinguishes the conquest of Canaan from the usual pillaging that has gone on throughout human history. The usual rule in war was kill the people, confiscate their belongings. But the Israelites were told by God to capture the towns of Canaan in order to settle there and build a new life. Had God allowed them to keep the goods of the Canaanites, they would have started out their life in Canaan as looters.

Back to Achan: God told Joshua what had occurred, and assured him they would win no more battles against the Canaanites until Achan's crime was punished. Achan admitted his crime: He saw a beautiful Babylonian robe, along with some gold and silver, and he had hidden them in his tent. The sight of luxury

Cities of Refuge

As the land of Canaan was being divided up among the twelve tribes, the Lord ordered Joshua to designate certain towns as "cities of refuge." If a person killed someone accidentally and unintentionally, he could flee to one of the cities of refuge and plead his case before the city's elders. Otherwise they could be overtaken by the victim's family, who might assume the death was intentional and kill the person without giving him a chance to prove the death was an accident. The provision for this form of justice shows the compassion and humanity of the Old Testament laws (Joshua 20:1–9).

goods had made him disobey God. The people stoned Achan—partly to punish him, partly to deter anyone else from doing as he did. After God gave them victory in capturing the city of Ai, they built an altar to the Lord, and Joshua read them all the Law that God had given to Moses.

The Canaanites heard of the Israelite victory at Ai and were distressed. Some of the local chieftains planned an elaborate ruse to convince Joshua and the Israelites that their cities were not worth capturing: They sent a delegation to Joshua, all the men dressed in tattered clothing, with dry moldy bread in their provisions. Joshua made a peace treaty with the bedraggled men, who presented themselves as harmless paupers living far away. Later he learned the truth. They were from nearby cities and were neither poor nor harmless. But he had sworn to leave them in peace and could not go back on his word. He did, however, make them serve as woodcutters and water-carriers for Israel (Joshua 9).

Joshua 10 tells of a truly amazing battle. The Israelites faced a coalition army from five cities, including Jerusalem. The battle was fierce, and God rained down hail on the enemy, killing more with the hail than the Israelites did with their swords. As the battle continued, Joshua prayed for the sun to stand still. "The sun stopped in the middle of the sky and delayed going down about a full day. . . Surely the Lord was fighting for Israel!" (10:13–14). Indeed he was! The Israelites conquered many cities, so that chapter 12 of the book is a long list of the dethroned kings.

With most of Canaan conquered, Joshua divided up the land among the twelve tribes of Israel. A special allotment was given to Caleb, one of the twelve spies Moses had sent into Canaan years earlier. Only Joshua and Caleb had given Moses a favorable prediction about conquering Canaan. Caleb's faith in God was rewarded by giving him the old city of Hebron, a former home of the patriarch Abraham.

The tribe of Levi, which provided Israel's priests, was not given an allotment of land. However, they were given some towns scattered through Israel. These were called the Levitical cities.

Violent Times

The Old Testament books of Joshua and Judges show the tribes of Israel settling in the land of Canaan—and butchering the original dwellers. Is this Christian behavior? Hardly—but then, this slaughter predates Jesus and his teachings on love and nonviolence. But would God really command his people, the Israelites, to conquer—and slaughter—other people?

Consider what the Israelites faced: tribes that worshipped gods of nature and fertility. Worship of these gods—Baal, Ashtaroth, Molech—often consisted of sex with temple prostitutes and even sacrifice of children. The religion of Israel had no place for such horrors. The Israelites were constantly tempted to fall into heathen worship. The only way they saw to keep their religion pure was to exterminate the heathens. They believed that as long as idol-worshippers were at hand, there was the danger of the true religion being corrupted—and it often was.

The "holy wars" of the Book of Joshua need to be judged by the standards of their time. Compared to the terrorism that the Assyrians boasted of in their annals—mass beheadings and impaling, for example—the Israelites were admirably mild.

Chapter 23 and 24 are Joshua's farewell addresses to the Israelites. "Be very strong; be careful to obey all that is written in the Book of the Law of Moses, without turning aside to the right or to the left. Do not associate with these nations that remain among you; do not invoke the names of their gods or swear by them. You must not serve them or bow down to them. But you are to hold fast to the Lord your God, as you have until now" (23:6–8). He reminded them that in any battle, numbers are not the whole story: "One of you routs a thousand, because the Lord your God fights for you, just as he promised" 23:10). He presents them the challenge that faces every human being whoever lived on earth: to serve God or not. "Choose for yourselves this day whom you will serve...as for me and my household, we will serve the Lord" (24:15). The Israelites swore they would not forsake the Lord—a promise their descendants would break many, many times.

However, as long as Joshua lived, they remained faithful to the Lord. Joshua died, age 110. Eleazar, the priest who was the son of Aaron, also died. The coffin of Joseph, brought out of Egypt, was reburied on land that had belonged to his father Jacob centuries earlier. A chapter in history had closed. The Israelites were back in the homeland God had promised their ancestors Abraham and Jacob. The Book of Joshua ends on a happy note. But the times of trouble had by no means ended.

STOUT-HEARTED MEN

The most inappropriately named book in the Bible is Judges. The Hebrew title of the book is *Shophetim*, meaning something like "leaders" or "princes." The *shophetim* were freedom fighters, military leaders, heroes, liberators, something like the knights in the King Arthur tales, riding out to help the helpless. They were "judges" only in the sense that they brought justice by righting wrongs. When the book was translated into Greek ages ago, it was given the title *Kritai*, meaning "judges." We are stuck with the title Judges, but keep in mind that these men were not sitting in a courtroom wearing black robes and deliberating quietly. They were sweating on the field of battle, helping Israelite farmers fighting very hostile foes.

Judges 2 relates that a generation of Israelites had grown up, "who knew neither the Lord nor what he had done for Israel." They forsook the worship of God and began worshipping the local fertility gods, Baal and his female consort, Ashtoreth. Because they forsook God, he allowed them to be raided by the Canaanites who still lived in the region. They cried to God for help, and he sent them a *shophet*, a military deliverer, who would fight off their enemies and bring peace. They would be grateful to God, then soon enough forget him and fall back into idolatry, and the pattern would repeat itself.

There was a certain weird logic to the Israelites worshipping Baal. Their own God, Yahweh, had delivered them from slavery, led them through the wilderness, and aided them in conquering Canaan. He was a "mobile" God, which was a good thing (something they would find useful centuries later as they were banished from their homeland by Assyrians, Babylonians and others). But Canaan had its own native god, whose very name Baal ("owner") tied him to the soil of Canaan. And the Israelites, novices at farming, came to believe that to make crops grow, one had to pay one's proper respects to the local fertility god. Probably the vast majority of the Baal worshippers saw no conflict between worshipping both Baal and Yahweh. Plus the erotic worship of Baal and his female counterparts must have provided an obvious attraction. God's prophets continually railed against this depraved religion, and Israel's better kings tried to stamp it out, but it proved to be a deep-rooted weed.

Baal's female consort was Ashtoreth, also called Ishtar, Astarte and Asherah. The name actually means something like "she of the womb." She was usually depicted naked, and although she was seen as beneficial, bringing fertility to the crops, the livestock and people, she had a wild side, dangerous and unpredictable—in other words, as a nature goddess, she was much like nature itself. The Canaanites imagined her at times jumping naked onto a horse and riding off with a sword to slaughter people. The women attendants at her shrines were called *Kedeshoth*, meaning "consecrated women" or "holy women"—the term hiding the fact that they were prostitutes, with whom sex was seen as a way of guaranteeing the land's fertility. You have to understand this connection between nature religion and promiscuous sex to fully understand why the Bible so roundly condemns the Canaanites. But it would be wrong to think that Israel's prophets condemned Baal worship just because of its sexual element. The deeper truth is, gods of fertility and nature are generally lacking in moral character. Israel's God was known to be good, ethical, holy—and he expected the same of his people. The fertility gods were not moral themselves and did not expect their worshippers to be. Baal and Ashtoreth were not "good" in any moral sense. Their worshippers thought of them as "good" in the sense of delivering benefits—crops, livestock, children, wealth. This is the key difference—the Great Divide—between worship of God and worship of the gods of nature. A religion of nature basically has no moral center.

Geography played a role in which Israelites were more likely to worship Baal and Ashtoreth. In the northern part of Israel, the fertile land seemed blessed by the fertility gods, so the Israelites there easily slipped into worshipping them. In the southern part of Israel, rockier and less fertile, with more shepherds than farmers, more people stayed true to God. If the people of the south were more faithful to the Lord, we can't overlook the fact that there was less pressure to worship the false gods than the people in the north experienced.

There was a divine purpose in having the Israelites live near the idol-worshipping Canaanites: The Israelites' faith would be put to the test. In fact, Judges 2:23 plainly states that this is why God did not let the Israelites completely drive out the natives. Most often they failed the test, and the fact that their sons and daughters intermarried with the Canaanites' sons and daughters did not help matters at all.

Probably most Israelites who worshipped Baal wanted to have it both ways—pray to God and pray to Baal as well. But God had described himself as a "jealous" God for a reason. He understood that no one can serve two masters—or two gods. Inevitably one will edge out the other. Giving part of one's heart to the morality-free religion of Baal would inevitably lead to giving the whole heart. This is why you see the command "Choose!" again and again in the Old Testament.

In Judges it is obvious that the enemies of Israel are not only the original inhabitants of Canaan, but also the neighboring peoples: Moabites, Ammonites, Midianites and the newest migrants, the Philistines.

COLORFUL CHARACTERS

Some of the "judges" in the book are little more than names. For example, 3:31 mentions the judge Shamgar, "who struck down six hundred Philistines with an oxgoad," an implement used by farmers to prod cattle. That is all we know about him.

Some are described in more detail. One of the most interesting is the female judge Deborah, who was also called a "prophetess." Apparently Deborah really did serve as a judicial judge, for she held court under a palm tree, and people brought their disputes for her to settle. Deborah gave her encouragement to a fighter named Barak, who went off to fight the oppressive Canaanite general, Sisera. Barak's army routed Sisera's, but the general himself escaped, fleeing on foot to the tent of a woman named Jael. Not knowing she was on the side of the Israelites, Sisera was pleased to have her give him some milk to drink. The battle-weary king fell asleep in the tent. Jael took a tent peg and drove it into his temple with a mallet. She went out and told Barak that the enemy he was seeking was dead inside her tent. Chapter 5 is the song Deborah and Barak sang, celebrating their victory and praising Jael. Barak's name, by the way, means "lightning" —a rather good name for a warrior.

Deborah's victory song contains one disturbing element: In 5:15–17, she scolds some of the tribes of Israel for not joining their brothers in the battle. During the period of the judges, the tribes were not really united, and if you read Judges carefully, you will note that the heroes' activity was mostly confined to their own tribes, not Israel as a whole. The lack of unity made invasion by foreigners easier, and was the reason that, later on, Israel would unite itself under a king.

STORIES WORTH REMEMBERING

Left-handed Liberator

Ehud, a left-handed Israelite, was chosen by God to help deliver Israel from the oppression of the king of Moab, Eglon. For eighteen years Israel had to send a huge sum to Eglon—or risk being slaughtered by his men. Ehud set off to deliver this tribute money to Eglon. He took along a double-edged sword, which he strapped to his right thigh, concealing it under his clothing. Ehud paid the tribute, then said he had a secret message for the king. The king sent his servants away, and he was left alone with Ehud. "I have a message from God for you," he told the king. The "message" was not what Eglon expected. With his left hand, Ehud drew his concealed sword from his right thigh and plunged it into the fat king's belly. The handle sank in after the blade, and the king's fat completely closed in on the sword.

Since Ehud's sword was about a foot and a half long, Eglon must have been grossly obese. He was caught offguard, never expecting Ehud to have a sword strapped to his right side, since most men (being right-handed) strapped the sword to their left side.

Ehud locked the door of the chamber and escaped by another entrance. The servants wondered why they were hearing nothing from the room. When they finally entered, the fat king was lying dead on the floor. With the king dead, Moab was demoralized, and Ehud's army defeated Moab in battle. Ehud's bold and crafty scheme had bought the Israelites eighty years of peace.

GIDEON VS. MIDIAN

You might recall that Moses married a Midianite woman and had a warm relationship with his Midianite father-in-law, Jethro. That was the only episode in the Bible in which Midian and Israel were on good terms. Elsewhere the Midianites were notorious "camel jockeys," land pirates who appeared swiftly out of the deserts on their camels, plundering the Israelites and riding away into the wilderness. Apparently their looting expeditions were profitable, for their beloved camels wore gold chains around their necks. A band of Midianites descending on a place was as destructive as a swarm of locusts.

The man God chose to deliver the people from the Midianites was a farmer name Gideon. An angel appeared while Gideon was threshing wheat. The angel called him "mighty warrior" and told him he would lead the Israelites into battle. As happens so often in the Bible, the man chosen by God was at first reluctant. He also doubted if his mysterious visitor was truly sent from God. As a test, he set some meat and bread out on a rock. The angel touched the food with his staff and it burst into flame. Gideon was convinced. Gideon built an altar to the Lord—and tore down his father's altar to Baal. The locals almost lynched Gideon for this, but he defended himself by telling them that if Baal was really powerful, he could defend his own altar. For this act, Gideon received the nickname Jerub-Baal, meaning "let Baal contend."

> **DID YOU KNOW?**
>
> In the story of Jephthah, we learn that the word *shibboloeth* was pronounced differently on the two sides of the Jordan River. Jephthah used the pronunciation to determine if a man was friend or foe. *Shibboleth* was the pronunciation by friend, *sibboleth* by foe—leading to execution. In fact, forty-two thousand men were executed for saying *sibboleth*. The word *shibboleth* passed into our language to refer to a custom that is used to distinguish one group of people from another.

Gideon needed the best fighters to go against the Midianites. He made his choice in an interesting way: Watching the men drink from a stream, he saw that some lapped up the water with their tongues (as dogs drink), while others cupped their hands (Judges 7:4–6). The "lappers" were chosen. Why? Because the alert, battle-ready warrior would not be willing to cup his hands and, even briefly, have his hands away from his weapons. Gideon took his three hundred men and descended on the Midianite camp. At a signal, they all blew trumpets and broke jars, raising such a ruckus that the Midianites panicked, and Gideon was victorious.

He had such success against the Midianites that the Israelites invited him to be their king, with the crown passing on to his descendants. Gideon's reply is memorable: "I will not rule over you, nor will my son rule over you. The Lord will rule over you" (8:23). After Gideon died, however, one of his sons—Gideon had seventy in all—grew ambitious to be Israel's king. This son, Abimelech, hired some ruthless thugs to murder his

The Philistines

The seafaring people known as the Philistines probably arrived in Canaan just shortly after the Israelites did, making it inevitable that one band of newcomers would battle the other. In the books of Judges and Samuel, they were one of the most feared enemies of Israel, not only feared, but held in contempt, because they were uncircumcised, a trait which set them apart not only from Israel but from the other peoples of that region. At times the Old Testament simply refers to them as "the uncircumcised."

As people with seafaring roots, the Philistines lived near the sea, with their five cities on the Mediterranean coast. Appropriately, one of their gods, Dagon, was a kind of merman, human from the waist up, fish from the waist down. (It was in the temple of Dagon that Samson performed his last dazzling act of strength, literally bringing the house down on thousands of Philistines—and himself.) Had the Philistines confined themselves to the coast, they would have been no problem, but as they pressed inland, they locked horns with the other newcomers to Canaan, the Israelites. In fact, it was largely the aggressiveness of the Philistines that pressed the Israelites to beg for a king who would unite them against the enemy.

Based on what archaeologists have found, the Philistines were notorious party animals—or, at least, heavy drinkers, as evidenced by the numerous beer mugs, wine carafes and hip flasks found. Appropriately, their great enemy from Israel was Samson, who, as a Nazirite, had taken a vow to abstain from all alcohol.

In the 1800s, the English author Matthew Arnold began using "Philistine" to refer to any crude, uncultured person. The word passed into common use with that meaning.

The name Palestine, still used sometimes to refer to the region of Israel, is derived from Philistine.

brothers—although one son, Jotham, escaped. Abimelech did reign over Israel for three years, riding on the fame of his father Gideon. But the murderous man came to the worst end a warrior could imagine: He was killed by a woman. While he was besieging a city, a woman in a tower dropped a millstone onto his head. Before he died, he made one of his men run him through with a sword, so that his enemies would not boast that a woman had killed Abimelech.

The next judge of interest is Jephthah, the son of a prostitute. He had numerous half-brothers, but they allowed him no part in his father's estate. He lived in the wilderness, drawing a band of fighters around him. The Israelites begged him to help them fight against the Ammonites, who were descended from Lot, the nephew of Abraham that God rescued from Sodom. Despite the kinship, the Ammonites and Israelites were almost never at peace with each other. Jephthah made a vow that would come back on him: He promised that if the Lord gave him victory over the Ammonites, he would sacrifice whatever came out of his house first when he returned in victory. When he made the vow, he was thinking of a cow or sheep being the first thing to come out of the home—but instead, it was his only child, his daughter, dancing with a tambourine to welcome her victorious father home. Jephthah was horrified—he had made an oath to God and could not break it. The most touching part of the story is the response of the girl: "My father, you have given your word to the Lord. Do to me just as you promised, now that the Lord has avenged you of your enemies, the Ammonites" (11:36). She made one request: that he would allow her two months to enjoy life with her friends. He granted her request, but also kept his rash vow to God. It is the only case in the Bible of an otherwise admirable man sacrificing his own child.

MANED MUSCLE MAN

The most interesting, though perhaps not the most inspiring, man in Judges is the mighty Samson, whose story is told in chapters 13–16. Samson's parents were of the tribe of Dan, and his mother had been childless for years. An angel told her she would conceive, and that the child born to her would be dedicated as a Nazirite, set apart to God from birth, and destined to deliver the Israelites from their newest and worst enemy, the Philistines. The angel was apparently human in form, but when the parents-to-be offered a sacrifice to God, the angel ascended upward with the flames of the sacrifice.

As proof that God moves in mysterious ways, Samson as a young man told his parents he wished to marry a Philistine woman. They were scandalized, of course—marrying a woman from the nation that oppressed Israel! But in the plan of God, Samson's closeness to the Philistines would be used for their own destruction.

On the way to visit his Philistine love, Samson was attacked by a young lion. Empowered by God's Spirit, Samson killed the lion with his bare hands. Some time later, visiting the woman again, Samson saw the dead lion's carcass, in which some bees had built a honeycomb. Forgetting his Nazirite vow not to touch anything dead, Samson—who apparently had a sweet tooth—took some of the honey, eating it as he traveled.

Among the Philistines gathered for his wedding feast, Samson posed a riddle: "Out of the eater, something to eat; out of the strong, something sweet." If they could decipher the riddle within the week of the feast, he would give new sets of fine clothing to the thirty Philistine men who formed the wedding party. Puzzling over the words, the Philistines went to Samson's wife with an unpleasant offer: Coax the riddle out of her new husband, or they would burn down her father's house. Using tears and tantrums, the bride (who is never named) wheedled the answer out of Samson. Just before the week of feasting ended, the Philistines presented their answer to the riddle: "What is sweeter than honey? What is stronger than a lion?" Samson was furious. He knew his wife had told them the answer. He kept his promise to them, but in a violent way: He went to the Philistine city of Ashkelon and struck down thirty men, carrying their clothing back to pay off the wedding bet. In short, he paid the Philistines their thirty sets of clothes with thirty sets of *Philistine* clothes. More importantly, he rejected his new bride, so her father gave her to Samson's best man (a Philistine, and not necessarily an actual friend of Samson). Later, when Samson changed his mind and visited his wife, he found she belonged to the other man. His father-in-law offered her younger and more attractive sister as a consolation prize.

Samson was furious again. He caught three hundred foxes, tied their tails to torches, and turned them loose in the Philistines' grain fields and vineyards, burning the crops. In revenge, the Philistines killed Samson's wife and her father. In revenge, he killed several of the Philistines.

Under the threat of more reprisals from the Philistines, Samson's fellow Israelites bound him—with his permission—and handed him over to the enemy. But as they approached the Philistines, Samson was empowered by the Spirit. He snapped the ropes that bound him and killed a thousand Philistines with a donkey's jawbone.

In the Philistine city of Gaza, Samson spent the night with a local prostitute. The Philistines planned to kill him at dawn. But in the middle of the night, Samson made his escape. Since the city was walled (meaning, locked up at night), he tore the doors off the city gates and carried them off.

The final episode in Samson's life is the most famous. He fell in love with the woman Delilah. The Philistine rulers bribed her with silver. If she could wheedle the secret to Samson's strength out of him, they would reward her handsomely. Samson toyed with her, telling her the right way to bind him and make him helpless, but whenever she roused him with, "Samson, the Philistines are upon you!" he snapped the fetters easily. Each time she nagged and pouted and doubted his love for making a fool of her. Finally, he told her the secret lay in his long hair. If he were sheared, he would lose his strength. He fell asleep in her lap, and when he awoke, he found both his hair and his strength gone.

The joyous Philistines gouged out his eyes and made him grind on a millstone in the prison in Gaza. They planned a great festival in the temple of their god Dagon, in which they would mock the helpless hero. They overlooked the fact that Samson's hair had grown back. He happened to be positioned between the two main pillars that supported the temple—in which three thousand Philistines had gathered. Samson prayed for strength in what he knew what would be his last act. He pushed apart the pillars, and "killed many more when he died than while he lived" (16:30). Samson's twenty years of war against the oppressive Philistines ended with a mighty crash.

ALAS, SUCH TIMES

Judges ends with one of the most violent and disturbing stories in the Bible. Chapters 19–21 tell of a Levite and his concubine passing through the territory of the Benjamin tribe. They stop in the town of Gibeah for the night, and the men of Gibeah rape and brutalize the concubine, and the next morning she is found dead. The outraged Levite cuts her corpse into twelve pieces, sending a piece off, one to each tribe of Israel, asking what they intend to do about this horrible crime. The tribes hold a council and demand that the Benjaminites hand over the men who committed the atrocity. Benjamin refuses, and a civil war follows, in which thousands of the Benjaminites are slaughtered, their towns burned. In the final chapter, the Israelites realize they have almost exterminated one of their twelve tribes, so they take steps to find wives for the surviving men of Benjamin so the tribe can repopulate itself. This episode illustrates how barbaric things were in this period: gang rape and brutality, followed by a man dismembering the body of someone he supposedly loved, then sending the body parts out to inflame public opinion, followed by eleven tribes ganging up on one… One barbaric act leads to another, unspeakable acts are committed in response to unspeakable acts.

CULTURAL INSIGHTS

Nazirites

The name looks similar to *Nazarene*, but there is no connection. Nazirites were Israelites who took a vow—sometimes for life, sometimes for a limited period—not to cut their hair, never to touch wine and never to touch anything dead. The essential motive was to express a deep devotion to God. The rules for the Nazirite vows are found in Numbers 6.

A parent could dedicate a child as a Nazirite from birth. This happened sometimes when a woman who had long been childless finally gave birth. Dedicating her child as a Nazirite was a way of expressing her gratitude to God. This is what happened in the cases of the Bible's three most famous Nazirites: Samson, Samuel and John the Baptist.

In the case of Samson, his uncut hair was not only a sign of his Nazirite vow but also the source of his strength. When it was cut—following his betrayal by the treacherous Delilah—his strength was gone, but it returned as his hair grew back. Samson was not always careful in keeping his Nazirite vows, as evidenced by his scooping up honey from the carcass of the lion he had killed—Nazirites were not supposed to go near a dead body.

The New Testament indicates that the apostle Paul was a Nazirite for a brief period (Acts 18:18).

The story concludes a book in which the Israelites have been constantly plagued by foreign enemies—Philistines, Midianites and others. But in this story, the Israelites are their own worst enemies. The Benjamin tribe should have handed over the men of Gibeah for punishment, but the other tribes took too extreme a vengeance for the rape and death of one woman. The Law given to Moses specified a limit on vengeance, with its "eye for eye, tooth for tooth, life for life" rule. The story shows why the rule was so wise and humane. Once the civil war between Benjamin and the other tribes began, bloodshed led to more bloodshed, until finally the Israelites realized they had almost wiped out one of their tribes. God's chosen people, Israel, came dangerously close to national suicide. Such things happen when people forget the commandments of the Lord.

Joshua and Judges are two of the most violent books of the Bible, not only dealing with war and terrorism but with such matters as child sacrifice. But a profound truth is repeated again and again in Judges: If the people had remained loyal to God, the oppression by their enemies could have been avoided. The people constantly fell into worship of the immoral fertility gods of Canaan, forfeiting the protection of the true God—who showed them more mercy than they seemed to deserve.

The true hero of Judges is God. The various leaders he raises up—Gideon, Jephthah, Samson and the others—are admirable fighting men, but hardly ideal role models of faith. Samson is a lustful, violence-prone man, venting his anger in terrorism on his enemies—and yet, in the plan of God, his deeds helped preserve Israel from extermination. Thanks to the judges, with all their faults, the faith of Israel lives on, while the worship of Baal and the other false gods of Israel's enemies has long since passed away.

"In those days Israel had no king; everyone did as he saw fit"—thus ends Judges, reminding us of the lawlessness of the times. Such times are a burden to live through, but turbulent times do remind people that their ultimate security is in the Lord.

THE FAITHFUL RUTH

The time of the judges was a violent period. In striking contrast to the stories in Judges is a book set in the same period, Ruth. In it, an Israelite from the town of Bethlehem goes with his family to live in Moab during a famine. His two sons marry Moabite women, then both the man and the sons die, leaving behind three widows—the man's wife, Naomi, and the two daughters-in-law, Ruth and Orpah. Naomi heard that the famine in her homeland had passed, so she resolved to return home. She said

> **DID YOU KNOW?**
>
> The affirmation of devotion found in Ruth 1:16–17 is so touching as a vow of commitment that it is often recited at weddings, even though in its original context it had nothing to do with marriage.

good-bye to Ruth and Orpah, telling them she hoped they would find new husbands in Moab. Ruth and Orpah wept and insisted they wanted to go with her back to Bethlehem. Naomi pleaded with them, reminding them that her life as a poor childless woman would not be a happy one. Orpah decided she would stay in Moab. But Ruth insisted on staying with her mother-in-law: "Don't urge me to leave you or to turn back from you. Where you go I will go, and where you stay I will stay. Your people will be my people and your God my God. Where you die I will die, and there I will be buried. May the Lord deal with me, be it ever so severely, if anything but death separates you and me" (1:17–18).

Naomi and Ruth journeyed to Bethlehem, where the two were reduced to gleaning in the fields in order to have enough food to survive. (Remember that the Law of Israel required farmers to leave some stubble in the fields so that the poor could find something to eat.) In the meantime, a man named Boaz, related to Naomi's late husband, was impressed with Ruth and her loyalty to Naomi, and also by the fact that Ruth had abandoned the religion of her homeland and began worshipping the God of Israel. Boaz ordered his field hands to see that Ruth had plenty to eat and drink.

By the time the book ends, Ruth and Boaz are married, and they have a son named Obed, who will be the father of Jesse, father of the great king David of Israel. Naomi is no longer the bitter, poor widow. She has a grandson and a home, and all ends happily.

Ruth is a brief gem of a story, a tribute to family loyalty, also a tribute to the emotional bond that can exist between women. It is a "woman's story" in the best sense, and certainly a welcome relief from the masculine—and violent—stories in Judges. The Book of Ruth reminds us that even in violent, turbulent times, life goes on, people still marry, have children and form bonds of love. There is no power on earth that can neutralize the influence of a high, simple and useful life. The book is also a lesson in how God provides for the poor and the widow. Ruth is a kind of Cinderella story, with the poor foreigner marrying the rich Israelite—an unlikely pairing that brought them both happiness. One difference between Ruth and Cinderella, however, is that it is not Ruth's beauty that charms the man, but the love and loyalty he sees in her. He sees the inner beauty in this woman and knows that her loyalty to her mother-in-law proves she can be loyal to him as well.

PUTTING THE WORD TO WORK

1. One key theme of the book is the importance of moral leadership. So long as Joshua or one of the "judges" was active, the people remained relatively faithful to the Lord. Does your faith life benefit from a moral leader you know personally, or someone you admire? Is there anyone depending on you to be an active role model for their faith life?

2. "Going along with the crowd" is an important theme in Judges, with the Israelites falling into the false religions of their neighbors. How do you cope with neighbors and acquaintances whose morals and beliefs are different from your own? Has peer pressure ever led you to be one of the crowd, to behave in ways that were not true to your faith?

3. Of the various leaders discussed in today's chapter, which do you find most admirable? Why? What are some of that person's qualities you can cultivate in your own life?

4. The story of Samson is a reminder that God works through less-than-perfect people. Is it possible for people to accomplish good even when their moral character is questionable?

5. Ruth is one of the most admirable women of the Bible. Have you known any Ruths in your own life, women who have impressed you with their love and loyalty? Think of ways these women showed their devotion to people inside and outside their family circles.

King-Making

**AT THE
HEART
OF IT ALL
TODAY** Taking a close look at the leaders Samuel, Saul and David, we consider the qualities needed in leaders—or in anyone. We also consider the nature of authority in general—if God is our true King, what do we owe to earthly powers?

A ny organization—a church, a club, a company, a nation—needs good leadership. The Book of Judges presented us with some fine military leaders, as well as colorful characters like the mighty Samson. But generally the judges were not an admirable

> **KEY PASSAGES TO READ TODAY**
>
> 1 Samuel 8:10–20; 16:1–13;
> 17:1—18:9; 24:1–22

group. One of them, Gideon, knew his limitations, and when the Israelites asked him to be their king, he declined, saying, "The Lord will rule over you." But of course, the Book of Judges is all about Israel's disobedience of God's laws, which brought on all Israel's troubles in the first place. A country's moral and spiritual crisis generally leads to a political crisis.

Today we look at an important transitional period in Israel's history. The loose confederation of the twelve tribes was about to change into a united monarchy under one king. When 1 Samuel opens, we are still in the time of the judges, but Samuel himself is the last judge, and he gives in, grudgingly, to Israel's request for a king. Having a king will prove to be a mixed blessing at best.

If this all sounds political—and *boring*—be assured it isn't. The books of Samuel and Kings contain some of the most fascinating people in the Bible, as well as some of its best-known events. (Remember David and Goliath?) We can learn a lot of lessons in character—and lessons about the workings of God—from these historical books with their "warts and all" portrayals of leaders and the people who surround them.

THE BARREN WOMAN BLESSED

Childlessness in the ancient world was considered a terrible curse, since every woman wanted children, and the more the better. The history of Israel began with the miracle of the elderly Sarah, wife of Abraham, conceiving a child. The Bible abounds in other stories of long-barren women finally conceiving, such as Samson's mother in our last chapter. At the beginning of 1 Samuel, we see the plight of Hannah, one of two wives of a man named Elkanah. The other wife had borne children, and even though Elkanah loved Hannah more, Hannah suffered the indignity of being taunted by the other wife.

The polygamous family had traveled to the town of Shiloh, which at that time was the religious center of Israel, since Joshua had stationed the Tabernacle, with the ark of the covenant, there. While Elkanah was offering sacrifices to the Lord in Shiloh, Hannah was in distress, having been taunted again by the rival wife. Hannah was praying to God—and, oddly, praying silently, which in those days was unheard of. When the priest of Shiloh, Eli, saw her mouth moving but heard nothing, he assumed she might be drunk. He scolded her for being drunk at the Lord's sanctuary, but Hannah assured him she was not drunk, only distressed. Taking pity on her, Eli told her to go in peace, "and may the God of Israel grant you what you have asked of him" (1:17).

Soon after, Hannah conceived a child, giving him the fitting name Samuel—meaning "heard by God." As always happens to barren women who finally give birth, Hannah was overwhelmed with gratitude, and she dedicated the child to God. In fact, she bound him to the Nazirite vows, as Samson's mother had done (see page 90 for more about the Nazirites). The next time she went with her husband to worship at Shiloh, she gave the child into the keeping of the priest Eli. Lest we pity Hannah for having the longed-for child living far away from her, we later learn that she bore three more sons.

The boy Samuel was destined to be the surrogate son of Eli, for Eli's own sons, Hophni and Phinehas, were notorious gluttons. For them, serving as priests meant getting the best cuts of meat to eat! Devout Israelites who came to Shiloh to sacrifice were scandalized by these worthless men, and Eli himself was embarrassed at their behavior. It is neither the first nor last case in the Bible of a good and decent man having rogues as sons. Confronting the two reprobates, Eli told them, "If a man sins against another man, God may mediate for him, but if a man sins against the Lord, who will intercede for him?" (1 Samuel 2:25). His words fell on deaf ears. Later a prophet—unnamed, but referred to as a "man of God"—gave a word of warning to Eli: The two roguish sons would die—on the same day. And God would send a faithful priest to serve him.

Chapter 3 contains the well-loved story of the Lord's calling of Samuel. The chapter begins with the observation that "in those days the word of the Lord was rare; there were not many visions." By night, the boy Samuel, sleeping in the precincts of the Tabernacle, heard someone calling his name. The boy went to Eli, but Eli told him it

c. 1750–1040 BC
China's Shang Dynasty is characterized by its system of writing on oracle bones, advanced bronze-working, ancestor worship, highly organized armies, and political or religious human sacrifices.

c. 1150–950 BC
A second wave of Achaeans settles in Cyprus. Earthquakes cause the destruction and abandonment of many cities.

c. 1040 BC
Beginning of the ministry of Samuel

c. 1030 BC
Acupuncture first develops during the Chou dynasty in China.

The Israelites demand to have a king.

c. 1030—c. 1010 BC
Reign of Saul, Israel's first king

c. 1010—c. 970 BC
Reign of David

Heart

With all his faults, David is remembered as the "man after God's own heart." This is based on 1 Samuel 13:14, where Samuel says "the Lord has sought out a man after his own heart," meaning David. The Hebrew word here is *leb*, usually translated "heart." In this context it doesn't refer to the bodily organ, of course, but to the *center* of the person—his mind, will, soul. Samuel is saying that David is a man who is in accord with God's *leb*, God's mind and will.

was not he who called. Samuel went back to bed, but the voice called again. He went to Eli, but again it was not he who called. The third time, Eli realized it was God calling to Samuel. When Samuel returned to bed and the Lord called again, Samuel answered, "Speak, Lord, for your servant is listening." God told Samuel just what the prophet had told to Eli: Eli's sons would be punished for their sins. The next morning he reluctantly told Eli what the Lord had said.

"The Lord was with Samuel as he grew up, and he let none of his words fall to the ground. And all Israel from Dan to Beersheba recognized that Samuel was a prophet of the Lord." After many years, Israel again had a leader who was in close communication with God.

In chapter 4, Israel faced its old familiar enemies, the Philistines. Going out to fight them, the Israelites carried the ark with them, knowing it symbolized the Lord's presence. Eli's worthless sons went with the army—and both were killed. The Philistines had captured the ark also. A messenger brought the news to Eli. Aged and overweight, Eli literally fell off his chair, broke his neck and died, after being Israel's priest for forty years. At the same time, his daughter-in-law, wife of the worthless Phinehas, gave birth. In despair over hearing that the ark of the covenant had been captured, and the death of her husband, she named the newborn son Ichabod—meaning "no glory," because the glory of the ark was gone. Then she died.

The Philistines would be sorry they captured the ark. As a trophy of war, they put it in the temple of their god Dagon. The next morning, the statue of Dagon was lying facedown on the floor. They set it

DID YOU KNOW?

1 and 2 Samuel were originally one book, simply known as Samuel. Because of the length of the book—more accurately, the scroll, since books had not yet been invented—Samuel was divided into two parts for easier handling. The same is true of 1 and 2 Kings and 1 and 2 Chronicles. Samuel was supposedly written by Samuel himself, but the later chapters, after Samuel's death, were (obviously) written by another author, possibly a disciple of Samuel.

back in place, but the next morning it was not only facedown again, but its head and hands were also broken off. Worse, some kind of pestilence broke out among the Philistines. They moved the ark to another location, but the disease followed them there. Wisely, the Philistines returned the ark to Israel. But they did not cease to attack Israel. However, with Samuel's encouragement, the Israelites finally routed the Philistines at a site called Mizpah, and to commemorate the victory, Samuel set up a stone, calling it Ebenezer, meaning "stone of help." There was a period of peace in Israel, and the country benefited from having the wise Samuel serve as a circuit judge for all the tribes.

"LIKE ALL THE OTHER NATIONS"

Poor Samuel! His mentor Eli had two worthless sons, and so did Samuel himself! This is not surprising. Raised apart from his own parents, the only parenting model Samuel had seen was Eli—who had reared two rogues. Samuel's sons were notorious for taking bribes and perverting justice. The Israelites honored Samuel but not his sons. Since they were not willing for Samuel to pass on his authority to the two scoundrels, the

---

CULTURAL INSIGHTS

Polygamy and Concubinage

Genesis presents God's original order for marriage as "one man with one woman." Within a couple of generations of Adam and Eve, men are taking more than one wife, and throughout the Old Testament it is more or less accepted that many men—especially men with money and power—will have more than one wife. Having multiple spouses is known as *polygamy*, as opposed to God's original plan, *monogamy*. While the Old Testament does not condemn the practice, it shows that it was frequently problematic. Jacob, with his two wives and two concubines and their twelve sons, is hardly a model husband and father, and his home life was not something most wives (or husbands) would envy. In today's chapter, there are difficulties in the family of Elkanah, whose childless wife Hannah is taunted by the other wife, Penninah, who had children. Later, we will see that the household of David, with numerous wives and concubines, was in almost constant turmoil. By the time we get to the New Testament, polygamy had almost died out in Israel.

What were *concubines*? Basically they were serving women who provided their master/owner with sex. It wasn't quite the same as a mistress, or "the other woman." The concubine lived under the man's roof, had duties around the home, and had children who were legitimate, but of lower status than the children born to the man's wife. A wealthy man—such as Solomon—who had numerous concubines was in possession of what later times would call a *harem*, though that word isn't used in the Bible.

CULTURAL
INSIGHTS

Belial

"Now the sons of Eli were children of Belial" (1 Samuel 2:12 KJV). The phrases "children of Belial" and "sons of Belial" and "men of Belial" occur several times in 1 and 2 Samuel, and other places in the Old Testament—in the King James Version, anyway. Who, or what, was Belial? The Hebrew word meant something like "worthlessness," so a "son of Belial" was a "worthless fellow," a "rogue," as some modern translations have it.

In the New Testament, the apostle Paul asked, "What harmony is there between Christ and Belial?" (2 Corinthians 6:15). By the time Paul wrote, Belial had become one of many alternate names for Satan, the ultimate rogue or "worthless fellow."

In his great epic poem *Paradise Lost*, John Milton used Belial as one of the names of the demons who were in league with Satan. Building on the original meaning of the Hebrew word, Milton describes Belial as the most "lewd" of the demons, one known to "love vice for itself."

Israelite elders gathered together and presented Samuel their demand: "Appoint a king to lead us, such as all the other nations have." It sounded like a sensible request—after all, Samuel had proven the wisdom of having a wise, God-inspired man as national leader. Surely a king would help unite them and fight off their enemies.

But they overlooked one important fact: They were *not* like all other nations. God didn't intend them to be. He had told Moses that Israel was his "treasured possession." It was to be different from other nations—holy, as he was. God didn't choose Israel because it was better—but it was supposed to be better because he chose it. Israel always failed at this, but God forgave, and God sent leaders to aid the nation. But now Israel wanted to be "like all the other nations."

Chapter 8 includes Samuel's long—and honest—warning about just what having a king would lead to. We'll look at just part of it: "This is what the king who will reign over you will do: He will take your sons and make them serve with his chariots and horses, and they will run in front of his chariots.… He will take the best of your fields and vineyards and olive groves and give them to his attendants. He will take a tenth of your grain and of your vintage and give it to his officials and attendants. Your menservants and maidservants and the best of your cattle and donkeys he will take for his own use. He will take a tenth of your flocks, and you yourselves will become his slaves. When that day comes, you will cry out for relief from the king you have chosen, and the Lord will not answer you in that day" (8:10–18). In other words, there is no government without its price. Governments do not run on air—they run on money, and the man at the head of it all will want to live well—at the expense of his subjects. It has been true since the beginning of time.

The people did not heed Samuel's warning. They still wanted a king. Samuel was distressed, but the Lord told him to give them what they wanted.

SAUL AND THE BRIGHT BEGINNING

The people and the Lord had put Samuel in the position of king-maker. He would encounter the king-to-be in a curious way. Thirty-year-old Saul, a tall, handsome man from the tribe of Benjamin, was out looking for his father's lost donkeys. Samuel caught sight of him and was told by the Lord that this was the man who would govern the people. Saul was in fact seeking Samuel—because he heard Samuel was a "seer" who could help him find his lost livestock. He got more than he expected. Samuel seated him down to a fine meal with the best cut of meat. The next morning, Samuel anointed Saul with a flask of oil. He kissed him and said, "Has not the Lord anointed you leader over his inheritance?" As proof that he was indeed the seer Saul had heard of, he told Saul exactly what would happen to him in the course of the day—and, incidentally, the lost donkeys were found.

It is worth noting that when Samuel anointed Saul, he did not refer to him as "king" (the Hebrew word is *melekh*) but as "commander" (the word is *nagid*). Samuel still seemed reluctant to think of Israel having a king, and perhaps he preferred to think of Saul as just the military leader but not a king who would tax his subjects and spend their money. In fact, Samuel got what he hoped for, for Saul was really more of a *nagid* than a *melekh*.

CULTURAL INSIGHTS

Anointing of Kings

You might recall that the Law of Moses provided for the anointing of the high priest on his commissioning. Pouring a small amount of fragrant oil on the person's head marked him as being set aside by God for a special purpose. Saul is the first case of a king being anointed in the Bible. The practice would continue throughout Israel's history, and the king would often be referred to as "the Lord's anointed." The idea of a worthy anointed king serving God led to the belief in a Messiah, a Christ, the "anointed one."

In a sense, every coronation throughout history was a repeating of Samuel anointing Saul, as the kings were designated "the Lord's anointed." However, as history would prove, it is the Spirit of the Lord, not a daubing with oil, that makes for a godly leader.

At Mizpah, Samuel installed Saul as king in a public ceremony. The Bible notes that most of the people were impressed with the strikingly tall young man—but some worthless men (or "sons of Belial" in the King James Version) "despised him and brought him no gifts" (10:27). No ruler, either good or bad, has ever been universally loved.

If the people expected their king to be leading them into battle instead of idling away in a palace, they got what they wished. Saul was called to lead the army against the Ammonites—and, as a sign that he was not putting on airs, he was plowing in the fields when he got the message. Saul was enraged at hearing of the brutality of the Ammonites. He mustered a large army and set out to fight the foe.

One interesting item in this story is worth noting: The Bible tells us of the number of soldiers who came from Israel—and from Judah. Judah, in the south, was one of the largest tribes. The Bible is already giving the hint that Judah was in some sense distinct from the other tribes. Within a couple of generations, it would be a separate kingdom from Israel.

Saul was successful in his first battle. If the people had any doubts about him, their minds were put at ease. At Gilgal the people gathered and "confirmed Saul as king in the presence of the Lord" (11:15).

At the ceremony, the aged Samuel made a speech, in which he asked the Israelites if he had been dishonest or greedy in any of his dealings with Israel. He offered to right any wrongs he had committed, but the people could remember nothing he had done that offended them. Samuel reminded the people of the Lord's compassion in leading them out of Egypt and sending leaders of Jephthah to fight off their enemies. He commanded the people—*and their king*—to obey the Lord always. If they persisted in doing evil, the nation and the king would be swept away.

Samuel and Saul would soon come to a parting of ways. Saul had mustered his army and was awaiting Samuel to arrive and make sacrifices before they went into battle. When Samuel did not arrive, Saul himself made the sacrifices. When Samuel showed up

---

CULTURAL INSIGHTS ## The Technological Edge

Technology has always been a factor in war. Israel's enemies the Philistines had served as mercenaries among the Hittites, from whom they learned the craft of ironworking. This gave them a decided advantage over Israel. Consider the dire situation of the Israelites fighting under Saul: According to 1 Samuel 13:19–22, Israel had no blacksmiths (ironworkers) of its own to make swords and spears. In fact, the Israelites were in the humiliating position of having to go to the Philistines just to have their farm implements sharpened.

Companies of Prophets

After Samuel anointed Saul as king, Saul encountered a "company of prophets," a group of ecstatic men playing their flutes, tambourines and harps (1 Samuel 10:5). This is the Bible's first mention of the prophetic bands that existed throughout Israel, often connected with religious shrines. They were not really prophets in the sense Samuel was—receiving direct revelations from the Lord. We might call them "religious fraternities," laymen gathered together to sing and play music, giving the emotional side of religion full rein. When Samuel told Saul he would be "turned into another man" among these people, he meant that Saul—who was an intensely emotional man himself—would be caught up in their religious ecstasy. The "prophesyings" they engaged in probably took the form of singing and shouting out praises to the Lord. Whatever they may have been like, they must have helped deepen the faith of those who participated. The band mentioned in 1 Samuel 19 seems to have been under Samuel's leadership. Apparently the bands were not highly regarded—they were probably drawn from the poor of the land—because people asked the sarcastic question, "Is Saul among the prophets?"—implying that the king of Israel wouldn't be hobnobbing with *those* people. These bands of prophets go unmentioned until centuries later, when they seemed to be groups of disciples around the great prophets Elijah and Elisha.

immediately afterward, he was aghast. The impatient Saul had acted foolishly. For his rashness, the kingship would be given to another man. Even though it seems as if Samuel is punishing Saul for a small matter of impatience, we see later that rashness would be Saul's undoing. With his prophetic insight, Samuel could see this before others could.

"All the days of Saul there was bitter war with the Philistines" (14:52). Much of 1 Samuel is devoted to the battles of Saul. The military details can be tedious, but some of the incidents reveal a great deal about Saul's character. Chapter 14 relates how Saul swore an oath that he and his men would eat nothing before he met the Philistines in battle. The men found some honey in the woods and wanted it badly—but feared Saul's command. Saul's son Jonathan took a taste "and his eyes brightened." One of the men reminded Jonathan of the oath, but Jonathan said the oath was foolish, for the men were growing faint. The men won the battle that day, but when Saul found Jonathan had eaten the honey, he resolved to keep the oath: Jonathan had disobeyed and must die. The men would not allow it—Jonathan had fought valiantly. Though the Bible does not say so, we can only assume Saul's rashness was not forgotten by his men.

King

When you come across the word *king* in the Bible, it may refer to the ruler of a vast empire—such as the Pharaoh of Egypt—or to the ruler of a small city-state—such as the "king" of Jericho in the Book of Joshua. Whatever the size of their land, kings in ancient times were expected to be fighters, and a king unwilling to lead an army would not be respected. It was assumed that kings would not only defend their own countries' borders, but try to encroach on neighboring lands as well. You had to hope that your own king would be formidable enough to keep your neighbor nations at bay.

Israel was slow to acquire a king. In the Book of Judges, you might recall that the judge Gideon turned down the offer of being made king. Israel supposedly relied on God as its protector, but the people constantly abandoned their faith and worshipped other gods, and they often fell prey to their enemies.

The Bible generally does not have a high opinion of kings, as seen in Samuel's reluctance to give Israel one. Throughout history, many of the world's rulers have been bullies backed by armies. A number of these egotists convinced their subjects that their kings were divine—either gods themselves or the sons of gods. Immeasurable harm has been done by "divine" kings. Although the king of Israel was considered "the Lord's anointed," the prophets never allowed the people to believe that the king himself was divine. The Bible is filled with warnings to people to trust in God, not in human rulers.

Later, Saul offended Samuel again. Saul went into battle against the Amalekites, and beforehand Samuel ordered him to put everything captured to death—even the livestock. Remember that in its "holy wars," Israel was ordered to exterminate the enemy, not go to battle for loot. Saul and his army beat the Amalekites, but did not follow Samuel's order. They kept the Amalekites' livestock, and even kept their king alive. Samuel arrived, and the lowing of cattle and bleating of sheep told him Saul had not followed his instructions. Saul defended himself, saying that he intended to sacrifice the animals to God—so how could God not be pleased? Samuel answers with some of the most-quoted words of the Old Testament: "Does the Lord delight in burnt offerings and sacrifices as much as in obeying the voice of the Lord? To obey is better than sacrifice, and to heed is better than the fat of rams" (15:22). (This is one of the great themes of the Bible, one we will encounter again in the books of the prophets. A heart set on obeying God is more important than religious rituals.) God, Samuel said, had rejected Saul as king. Saul, to his credit, begged for forgiveness. Samuel would not forgive, and as he turned to go, Saul caught the hem of his robe. It tore, and Samuel said it was a sign that the kingdom would be torn from Saul. Before Samuel left, he himself killed the Amalekite king Agag—a brutal act, but before killing him, Samuel reminded him that his own violence "has made women childless." Evil, violent men often find violence turned back on them.

GIANT-KILLER

Samuel and Saul never saw each other again. The Lord told Samuel not to wallow in regret over Saul, but to anoint another—and better—man. He sent Samuel to Bethlehem, to a man named Jesse who had eight sons. One of them would be the next king. Samuel thought the oldest looked like king material. But God spoke to Samuel words that ought to be in every believer's heart constantly: "The Lord does not look at the things man looks at. Man looks at the outward appearance, but the Lord looks at the heart" (16:7). In other words, God judges the inner person, not the outer. Samuel looked over Jesse's sons—except the youngest, "but he is tending the sheep." Samuel had him brought in and was told by God, "he is the one." This handsome, ruddy lad was to be the most famous king in Israel's history: David.

In the meantime, Saul, feeling abandoned by Samuel and by God, suffered from what the Bible calls an "evil spirit." Later ages would call it melancholy; we would call it depression. Saul's attendants thought music would cheer up the gloomy king, and one of them knew a fine musician, an intelligent boy named David. The king-to-be entered Saul's service as a musician and armor-bearer. Saul had no clue that the harpist whose playing pleased him would one day replace him.

Chapter 17 is one of the most famous episodes in the Bible: the shepherd boy David versus the hulking Philistine warrior, nine-foot-tall Goliath. Clad in bronze and iron, Goliath must have been a fright. He issued his famous challenge: Israel could send out one of their men to battle him, and the nation whose man won the combat would be subject to the other. A fine proposition—but no Israelite wanted to fight him. That included David's three oldest brothers, who were in Saul's army.

Youth has optimism on its side. David, no more than a boy, asked Saul to let him go fight Goliath. Saul was skeptical, of course—but David assured him that in his days as a shepherd he had killed both a lion and a bear. Sensing his spirit, Saul sent him out—but in armor. But David wouldn't wear the clunky armor. He went out to meet Goliath with no more than his sling and "five smooth stones from the stream."

An unequal match? Hardly. David not only had the Lord on his side but also possessed, as any military expert knows, the advantage of speed and mobility. He could not match Goliath pound for pound, but he didn't need to. All he had to do was swiftly strike the giant on his one vulnerable spot, his head.

Goliath was amazed: a mere boy with no armor? He told David he would give his flesh to the birds to eat. David said, no, on the contrary, in the name of God, David would give Goliath to be eaten by the birds. David took a stone from his shepherd bag and with his sling sent it to Goliath's forehead. The hulk fell down dead. David took Goliath's own sword and cut off his head. The Philistines panicked and were defeated in battle by the Israelites.

Everyone who saw was impressed—especially Jonathan, Saul's son. "Jonathan became one in spirit with David, and he loved him as himself" (1 Samuel 18:1). One of the great friendships in history was formed. Saul himself loved the valiant youth, and he saw David go on to more successes in battle. But Saul's love would be mingled with envy: women coming out to celebrate victory over the Philistines sang, "Saul has slain his thousands, and David his tens of thousands." Saul had the last thing any person in authority wants: a rival. Saul looked at David with both admiration and jealousy.

Saul's daughter Michal was in love with David. Saul decided to use her as a means of getting rid of his rival. He told David he could marry Michal—but the price for winning her was steep: a hundred foreskins from the Philistines. In other words, David had to kill a hundred Philistines and bring back evidence. (Recall that the Philistines were unique in the region for not being circumcised.) Saul's hope was that in trying to get his "bride price," David would be killed in battle. David did not bring back the hundred foreskins—he brought back *two* hundred. Surely this was the oddest way a man ever won his woman.

Jonathan was in an awkward position: He loved his father and loved David. Being told Saul wanted to kill David, he talked his father out of it, reminding him of David's loyal service. But envy crept in again, and Saul impulsively threw a spear at David while David played his harp. David fled, aided in his escape by Michal. He hid out for a while with Samuel—who, no doubt, had his suspicions about Saul confirmed when he heard of the attempt on David's life. Jonathan sided with David, and his angry father reminded Jonathan that the throne that would logically go to Jonathan would go to David unless the rival was eliminated. Saul did not know that, later, Jonathan would go to David and assure him he would willingly serve David as his king (23:16–18).

For a while David hid out in Nob, where the priest Ahimelech lent him a weapon David knew well: the sword of Goliath. Hearing that David had been at Nob, the paranoid Saul called Ahimelech on the carpet: How dare he aid David! Ahimelech reminded him that David had been a loyal soldier for Saul. The king was furious. He ordered his men to strike down all the priests. His men would not do it. The soldier Doeg, a non-Israelite in his service, then singlehandedly killed all the people at Nob. But Ahimelech's son Abiathar escaped and fled to David—who, as evidence of his having a tender conscience, felt responsible for the massacre, since his presence there had led to Saul's reprisal.

At this point in the saga the reader is more in sympathy with David than with Saul. And yet, throughout history, readers have found themselves sympathizing with Saul. One reason we feel compassion for him is that Samuel's demands on him seem so unreasonable. Saul waited for Samuel to show up and offer sacrifices—and when Samuel delayed, Saul made the sacrifice himself, and the late-arriving Samuel was indignant. But Samuel, remember, was told by God that God does not see things as man sees. Samuel tried to see God with God's eyes—and to God, the little episodes of impatience and rashness revealed Saul's instability. Despite his undeniable bravery, Saul's devotion to the Lord was shaky. Saul's massacre of the priests—and their wives and children—at Nob was not only uncalled for, but also a dangerous precedent: Kings murdering the Lord's priests was not something that Israel should have tolerated.

One important thing to remember regarding Saul versus Samuel: Samuel was known to be a prophet, a man through whom God spoke. Throughout Israel's history, God sent

Idol-izing a Husband

How far will a woman go to protect her husband? One wife who had to face that question was Michal, daughter of Saul and wife of David—who was in a difficult situation, since her father wished to kill her husband. After David ducked the spear that Saul had hurled at him, David ran home—not a wise choice, since Saul sent men there. Michal, who apparently understood her father's paranoia, assured David that he had to flee the house. She lowered him through a window so Saul's men would not see. David fled, and Michal took an idol, laid it on the bed and covered it with some clothing, with some goat's hair at the head. (What was a daughter of the king of Israel doing with an idol, since Israel's law prohibited them? This opens up the question of hidden idolatry in Israel.) When Saul's men came to the door, Michal told them David was sick in bed. The men sent word back to Saul, who showed no mercy: "Bring him up to me in his bed so that I may kill him." But when the men returned to David's house, they discovered that the "sick man" was merely an idol with goat's hair. Saul was furious with his daughter for letting his enemy escape.

Poor Michal! Such a position to be in, and yet she showed amazing grit and ingenuity in helping keep her husband alive. Later on in their marriage this wifely devotion would not continue. But then, not many wives would feel content married to a famous man with a house full of rival wives and concubines.

Saul

Archaeologists have excavated Saul's palace at Gibeah—and found that it was anything but "palatial." Israel saw him, and he saw himself, more as the tribes' commander-in-chief, not giving orders from an office or idling away in luxury, but leading the armies in the field—a *nagid*, not a *melekh*. Samuel's famous speech to the Israelites about the burdens that a king will impose on them applies to many later kings of Israel—but not to Saul himself. Saul never imposed any tax or instituted a draft. He relied on gifts and volunteers. In some ways, Saul was more like one of the judges than a king. In fact, more than once "the Spirit of the Lord came mightily upon Saul," just as had happened with Samson and others.

Saul's faults are exposed fully in 1 Samuel. We see that he had not obeyed God completely, and that his mentor Samuel anointed a better man, David, as king. And yet it is impossible to read Saul's story and not feel sympathy. In fact, no one over the age of forty can help but feel a little resentful toward David—handsome, charismatic and with youth on his side. He was a better man than Saul, remaining loyal to the king long after others would have rebelled against him—and killed him. After all, Saul tried to kill him several times. And yet every person who has ever felt envy and jealousy—and who hasn't?—sees something of himself in Saul.

prophets to speak the word of truth to kings. Saul's disobedience of Samuel—who, after all, had anointed him king—cannot be excused. A king disobeying someone that he knew to be God's messenger was a king assuming too much power for himself. Other nations had absolute monarchs who would brook no interference from prophets or priests. But Israel was not to be that type of nation. Even the king, "the Lord's anointed," had to heed a prophet. David himself would learn that, to his great shame.

MERCIFUL FUGITIVE

The Bible tells us that while David was in hiding, he drew to him other discontents. In time he had his own private army—not an unusual situation in world history, where a rival to the ruler creates his own fighting force and overthrows the government in power. In fact, during this period David was a sort of Robin Hood figure, a folk hero but also an outlaw. David, however, did not wish to overthrow Saul, and his loyalty to the king is commendable. David was fortunate in one way: Saul couldn't pursue him constantly for he had to fight off the Philistines too. In a lull from the fighting, Saul learned David was hiding out in the wilderness of En Gedi. David and his men were hiding deep in a cave. When Saul ventured into the cave, David was stealthy enough to draw near

Saul and cut off a piece of his cloak. Saul left the cave, and David called after him—and showed him the piece of cloth, evidence that he had been near enough to kill the king, but did not. David said that if Saul's evil deeds were avenged, it would not be David who did so (1 Samuel 24: 3–12).

Saul, bless him, was a deeply emotional man—which is not always a good thing, but on this occasion it was. Saul wept, deeply touched by David's show of mercy. He called down a blessing on David—but also made him swear that David would never try to exterminate Saul's family. David swore. Saul ceased to hunt David—for the time being.

Saul soon changed his mind and pursued David again. While he and his soldiers lay in a deep sleep, David crept into the camp and took Saul's spear and water jug. David awakened the sleepers and showed them the spear and jug—evidence he was near enough to kill the king, but did not. Again, Saul was repentant. At this point, of course, David had no faith in Saul's fleeting promises to leave David alone. In fact, he was so convinced that Saul would search every inch of Israel to find him that he took his entire family—he had acquired two new wives—and his band of followers and hid out in the last place Saul would find him: among the Philistines. The king of Gath, the Philistine city in which David lived, believed he had David in a compromising position: a man who cohabited with the detested Philistines would never be allowed by the Israelites to be their king! (The future would prove him wrong about this.) As far as he knew, the valiant David—the man Saul hated—would be the perfect ally in fighting Saul. When the Philistines went to battle against Saul again, however, they did not trust David to fight on their side—with good reason. David stuck to his principles: Whatever Saul might do to him, he would do Saul no harm. David was crafty. The land of the Philistines was the perfect hiding place, but that didn't mean he had changed his attitude toward this longtime enemy of Israel.

THE END OF SAUL

You might recall that any type of witchcraft, magic or occult activity is strictly prohibited in the Law that God gave to Moses. God wanted his people to rely on himself, not on demonic (and often fake) dabbling with "spirits." It was a law that Saul enforced as king, for the Bible tells us he had expelled all the witches—or, in modern translations, "mediums" or "spiritualists"—from the land. In one of the Bible's most ironic turns of events, Saul, facing what would be the last battle of his life, decided he needed the help of…a medium. To be more specific, he wanted some word of wisdom from the long-dead Samuel, the man who anointed him king. He could no longer bear God's silence.

Saul went in disguise to a place called Endor, where there was a medium. He asked the woman to communicate with the spirit of a dead man. The woman, fearing entrapment, stated that all the mediums had been expelled from Israel by the king. Saul gave his solemn word that she would not be punished (1 Samuel 28:8–11). When she asked whom he wanted "brought up," he told her, "Samuel." The woman did call up Samuel's spirit—and the fact that "she cried out at the top of her voice" may reveal that she did not expect it to really happen. This may have been a case of a fake medium witnessing the rare event of a "spirit" being allowed to speak from beyond the grave—not through her own "powers," but in this case God allowed it for his own reasons. When the woman saw Samuel's spirit, she realized the man who had come to her was Saul. The spirit said to Saul, "Why have you disturbed me by bringing me up?" Saul voiced his lament: He felt abandoned by God, and no dream or prophet had given him any guidance. Samuel was his last hope. Samuel reminded Saul of his acts of disobedience, then predicted that tomorrow "you and your sons will be with me"—that is, dead. Saul was devastated. The medium—no doubt as shaken by the experience as the king was—begged the king to eat some food, for he had gone all day without eating. She killed a calf and made some bread for the king, serving him what would be his last meal.

The story has intrigued people, especially artists, who have shown great creativity in depicting the depressed king, the utterly shocked medium, and the ghostly form of Samuel. We wonder what truly happened. Did God allow Samuel's actual spirit to be called from the next world to give his final word to Saul? We don't know. The disturbing tale only makes us painfully aware of the sad spiritual state of the doomed king.

The following day, David lost both his best friend—Jonathan—and his enemy and father-in-law—Saul. In a tense battle with the Philistines, Saul was mortally wounded by their archers. He ordered his armor-bearer to kill him with his sword, so as not to give the Philistines the pleasure they had so looked forward to. The armor-bearer would not kill the king, so Saul ran himself through with his sword. Suicide was rare in Israel, but Saul was depriving his enemies of the chance to torture him. Finding him dead, the Philistines cut off Saul's head and hung his body on a city wall.

A lesser man than David would have been jubilant. But when he heard the news of the deaths of Saul and Jonathan, he uttered a heartfelt lament, found in 2 Samuel 1:19–27. Its ending is well known: "How the mighty have fallen! The weapons of war have perished!" He mourned for the loss of his best friend: "I grieve for you, Jonathan my brother; you were very dear to me."

The man who brought David the bad news expected to be rewarded: he had taken Saul's crown and royal armband and brought them to David. He even lied and said he had, at Saul's request, run him through with his spear. David rewarded the man, all right: He had him killed. The man had dared to say he killed "the Lord's anointed."

Thus ended the twenty-year reign of Israel's first king—the magnificent, brave, rash, foolish, paranoid, forgiving, fickle Saul. Another "Lord's anointed" would now assume power. David the former fugitive left the Philistine territory and returned to his own people.

PUTTING THE WORD TO WORK

1. Israel's desire to be "like all the other nations" deeply disturbed Samuel. Compromise with the world is always a temptation. Consider some ways that you must fight against compromising with the world, conforming not to it but to the Word of God.

2. Who do you find the most inspiring leader in today's study—Samuel, Saul or David? Why? Reflect on the best—and worst—traits of the one you admire most.

3. Divided loyalties is one theme of today's lesson. Jonathan and Michal both faced the difficulty of loving both their father and David. What were situations in your own life in which you faced this sort of difficulty? How did you deal with it?

4. Saul and David were both extremely emotional men. Have you or someone you love ever allowed emotions to get out of control and cause harm? Were there times when displays of emotion were a good thing?

5. David's constant forgiving of Saul is amazing. Have you had situations in your own life in which a "Saul" repeatedly did you harm, asked for forgiveness and continued the pattern? How did you continue to forgive, knowing that the person's change of heart never lasted long?

David and Sons

AT THE HEART OF IT ALL TODAY   The focus here is King David and his brood of sons, some of them genuine rogues. While David is a model of mercy and wisdom in most things, his lust leads him astray, a flaw that is repeated by his son Solomon, a wise and sophisticated king who backslides spiritually. There are lessons here about self-control, forgiveness and wise leadership.

Today's lesson opens with civil war. Saul and several of his sons are dead after fighting the Philistines. David has lamented over the fallen, but he knows he is by right the new king, since God told Samuel to anoint him. In 2 Samuel 2, David is pro-

KEY PASSAGES TO READ TODAY

2 Samuel 6:1–23; 11–13

1 Kings 3:5–15; 11:1–14

claimed king—but not king of all Israel, only his home territory, Judah. Abner, Saul's military second-in-command, sets up Saul's son, Ish-Bosheth, as king of Israel. The war between the two factions lasted two years. A turning point was when Abner slept with Saul's concubine. Ish-Bosheth was indignant, since sleeping with the dead king's woman was (in the eyes of the ancient world) practically the same as taking over his inheritance. Ish-Bosheth's rage led to Abner changing sides and giving his allegiance to David. Abner went to David's capital at Hebron, where David spread a feast for him. Abner wasn't long in David's service, however. Joab, David's military chieftain, despised Abner for killing his brother Asahel. Joab stabbed Abner in the belly, killing him. David was appalled at this—Abner would have been a valuable man to have, not only as a fighter, but as a sign that Saul's authority had passed to David. David called down a curse on the treacherous Joab, then went into public mourning for Abner.

Ish-Bosheth had lost his best ally, and his days were numbered. Two rogues stabbed Ish-Bosheth to death, then cut off his head and took it to David, expecting a reward. David was furious: They had killed an innocent man lying in his own bed! He had the two men killed.

With his rival gone, David was accepted as king of all Israel. At age thirty, he had a brilliant career—and much sorrow—behind him. There were forty more years ahead, with much joy and much heartache.

One of his most important acts in his early reign—important not just to Israel, but to the history of the world—was capturing the city of Jerusalem, held by the natives, called the Jebusites. It would serve as Israel's political and religious capital for many years, and even when it was in the hands of foreigners, the people of Israel looked to it as home. Thanks to David's moving of his court there, people of three different faiths—Jews, Christians and Muslims—regard it as a holy city. In fact, when David captured it, the city had no religious associations of any kind, except that in Genesis the patriarch Abraham met Melchizedek, the priest-king of Salem, there—assuming Salem and Jerusalem were the same city. But thanks to David, a temple to the Lord would be built in Jerusalem (not under David, but under his son), and from that time on people would think of Jerusalem as the site of "God's house." They would also remember Jerusalem as "the City of David."

Though David did not build a temple, he did something almost as important: He brought the ark of the covenant to Jerusalem. This was a festive occasion, since the ark had long symbolized the presence of the Lord. In a long parade of soldiers and musicians, the ark was brought in on a cart. The king was not a mere spectator when the ark entered Jerusalem. David "danced before the Lord with all his might" (2 Samuel 6:14). Dancing, shouting and loud music—this was not some boring, solemn service, but an occasion of joy.

One person who did not feel the joy was David's wife—or, to be precise, *first* wife—Michal, the daughter of Saul. You might recall that Michal had fallen in love with the young and gallant David, and on one occasion saved him from the wrath of her father. But in the years when David was a fugitive from Saul, Saul gave her to another man named Palti. After David became king, he took Michal back—leaving poor Palti in

c. 1030—c. 1010 BC
Reign
of Saul

c. 1010—c. 970 BC
Reign
of David

c. 970–931 BC
Reign
of Solomon

c. 960 BC
Solomon
dedicates
the temple.

KEY TERM FOR TODAY ## Davidic Covenant

Despite his many faults, David was God's man, and he so pleased the Lord that God promised him, "I will raise up your offspring to succeed you, who will come from your own body, and I will establish his kingdom.... He is the one who will build a house for my Name, and I will establish the throne of his kingdom forever" (2 Samuel 7:12–13). The "house" referred to here was the temple, built by David's son and successor, Solomon. But the promise extended way beyond the reign of Solomon: David's dynasty would endure forever. This is known as the Davidic covenant, and it had a powerful hold on the minds of the Israelites, even when the conquest by the Babylonians in 586 BC seemed to bring the dynasty to an end. In time, the people came to believe that God would send a righteous king, the Messiah, the Anointed One, who would be a descendant of David.

CULTURAL INSIGHTS

The Former Prophets

The Hebrew Bible—what Christians call the Old Testament—has three divisions: Law, Prophets and Writings. In earlier chapters we learned that the Law—also called the Torah or Books of Moses—consisted of the first five books, Genesis through Deuteronomy. The Prophets has two divisions, called the Former Prophets and the Latter Prophets. The Former Prophets consisted of Joshua, Judges, 1 and 2 Samuel, and 1 and 2 Kings. We think of those books as *history*, and they are, but ancient Israel thought of them as being the works of prophets, such as Samuel, plus the books are written from what we would call the prophetic point of view—judging the kings' reigns from the standpoint of God, judging whether their reigns were good or bad on the most important level, the spiritual level. The Latter Prophets are the books of Isaiah, Jeremiah, Ezekiel, and the twelve Minor Prophets, Hosea through Malachi. In a later chapter we will look at the mixed collection of books called the Writings.

tears. By this time, David had several other wives and concubines—and several children by them. Whatever motivated him to take Michal back, it was probably not love, and she probably would have remained happier with Palti. At the time David "danced with all his might," Michal, watching from a window, was repulsed. A king, making a fool of himself in the streets with all the local women watching!

David came to his palace, obviously on a "high" after the parade and the feast that followed. Michal had sharpened her tongue, and greeted him on his arrival: "How the king of Israel has distinguished himself today, disrobing in the sight of the slave girls of his servants as any vulgar fellow would!"

Michal knew exactly the effect she would have on David, who did not feel shame, only rage at the one who "killed the moment." David had a sharp tongue too. He reminded her that God had chosen him, not her father or anyone else from her family, to rule. And he assured her that he would continue to be a joyous celebrant, even if she thought him "undignified." "And Michal daughter of Saul had no children to the day of her death" (6:23). We can assume David never touched her again.

David had a fine new palace in Jerusalem, and with the ark there now, an obvious idea occurred: Build a temple to house the ark. But Nathan, a prophet of the Lord, had a dream in which God reminded him that he had never needed a "house," and that building a temple was David's idea, not his. But God was not disapproving of David— far from it! He promised him that his dynasty would endure forever, that he would always love David—even if that meant punishing him when he needed it! And it would be a son of David who would someday build a temple. Touched by Nathan's revelation, David poured out his heart in thanksgiving to God.

The Lord truly blessed David in terms of military victory. David defeated the long-time enemy, the Philistines, and seized some of their territory. He subdued the Moabites and made them pay tribute to Israel. He subdued other old enemies: the Ammonites, Edomites and Amalekites. As sovereign over so many people, David no longer ruled a kingdom but an empire. Historians estimate that there were probably more non-Israelites under his rule than Israelites. When he conquered some of the nearby nations, he took gold and silver from them, adding them to Israel's treasury. He dedicated these things to the Lord. More importantly, "David reigned over all Israel, doing what was just and right for all his people" (8:15).

THE VICE OF LUST

David's political success story in 2 Samuel 1–10 is, alas, followed by a great failing in his personal life. Arising from bed one night, David walked on his palace roof and saw a beautiful woman bathing in a nearby house. A messenger told him she was Bathsheba, the wife of Uriah the Hittite—one of David's own captains, who was away at war. David sent for the woman and they slept together. Soon after, she found she was pregnant. Learning this, and knowing the child was his, David tried to cover up his crime. He brought Uriah in from the field and gave him a furlough, assuming he would go home to his wife and, in all likelihood, have sex with her. Instead, Uriah slept on the palace porch. He told David it was not right for him to sleep in comfort while his fellow soldiers slept out in the open fields. David tried another tactic the next night: He feasted with Uriah and got him drunk, assuming he would go home to Bathsheba. He did not.

CULTURAL INSIGHTS

Tribute

In politics (and war), tribute refers to money paid by one nation to keep another nation from attacking it. It is a sort of tax imposed from the outside. Tribute is always a financial burden on any nation that pays it, but the point in paying it is that it might be cheaper—and less devastating—than being conquered and pillaged by the other nation. In the time of David and Solomon, Israel *received* tribute from some of the neighbor nations, such as Moab. But for most of its history, Israel *paid* tribute to the larger and more powerful empires around it, such as Assyria and Babylonia. Israel learned, as other nations did, that failing to pay the required tribute could lead to dire consequences. We will study those consequences in a later chapter.

David and Mephibosheth

The enmity between David and Saul had been Saul's doing, for David consistently showed kindness and forgiveness to everyone in Saul's family. This kindness continued after Saul's death, with David executing the rogues who had dared to assassinate Saul's son, Ish-Bosheth.

In 2 Samuel 9, we learn that David wished to show kindness to any survivors of Saul's family. One of these was poor Mephibosheth, the son of David's beloved friend Jonathan. Mephibosheth had been accidentally dropped by his nurse in his childhood, and he was crippled. David had Mephibosheth brought to Jerusalem, and he "ate at David's table like one of the king's sons" (9:11). "Eating at the king's table" wasn't necessarily literal—it meant that Mephibosheth was being granted a government pension. David gave his lands into the keeping of Ziba, Saul's faithful servant.

David's compassion toward Saul's family is commendable, not only on a personal level, but on a political level too. Remember that during the first years of David's reign there was rivalry between him and the descendants of Saul. In most of human history, a man in David's position would have exterminated everyone in the rival family, even the children. David did not follow that pattern, but instead showed mercy. A king with a magnanimous spirit sets an example for his entire nation.

David was frantic and furious. What kind of amazing self-control did this Uriah have? David sent a message to Joab, his general: Send Uriah into the thick of the fighting so he will be killed. David received a message back: "Your servant Uriah the Hittite is dead." Joab's message hints that he may have suspected what the king had been up to —and if Joab knew, others knew as well. In a court, with numerous servants and people coming and going constantly, keeping secrets was not easy.

Bathsheba went into mourning, as was proper. But soon after (the Bible doesn't say how soon), David married her, and she bore him a son—somewhat prematurely, judging by the date of their wedding. But for all anyone knew, the child could have been Uriah's. "But the thing David had done displeased the Lord" (11:27).

There follows one of the great confrontations in the Bible. Nathan the prophet spun a story for the king: A poor man owned one lamb, which he kept as a beloved pet, while a nearby rich man had huge flocks. When the rich man received a guest, instead of slaughtering one of his own beasts for food, he took the poor man's pet lamb and served it to his guest.

David, always wearing his emotions on his sleeve, was furious. "The man who did this deserves to die!" Nathan uttered one of the most stinging accusations in the Bible: "You are the man!" Nathan had more to say: God had blessed David, giving him a kingdom, blessing him in every way, and yet this man with a house full of wives and concubines to give him pleasure took the only wife of one of his own men—and made sure the man was killed in battle! "Now, therefore, the sword will never depart from your house" (12:10). David was grief-stricken. Nathan assured him he would not die for this sin— but the son Bathsheba bore would. The child became ill that very night. David was so devastated he lay on the ground and would not move. In a week the son died.

One item in Nathan's dressing down of the king deserves particular mention: "By doing this you have made the enemies of the Lord show utter contempt." Israel was supposed to be a holy nation, different from all the others, and as its king, David was expected to do what was right. In fact, he did—usually. But obviously his treachery in the matter of Uriah was not going to stay a secret forever. The Israelites and others would eventually know what a rogue the king of Israel was. David and Bathsheba went on to have another son, Solomon, who would rule an even greater empire than his father, and who would build the Lord's temple. But Solomon, as we will see in the next chapter, had his own problems with controlling his lust.

That was in the distant future, however. God's punishment of David would happen much sooner.

UTTERLY DYSFUNCTIONAL FAMILY

"Blended families" sometimes get along, but often do not. David's most assuredly did not. Numerous wives and their children under the same roof constituted a disaster in the making. Almost inevitably, one of David's sons fell in love—or lust, actually—with one of his half-sisters. Amnon, the son, was so lustful for the beautiful Tamar that he became ill. A rascally friend suggested Amnon try the oldest ploy in the world: Use the illness to get the girl. Amnon took to his bed, pretended to be sicker than he was, and asked his father to have Tamar fix him something to eat. Tamar obeyed her father and made Amnon some bread. Amnon sent away all the servants, and alone with Tamar, invited her to bed. Tamar was horrified. She would not give in willingly, so he raped her.

Something even worse followed: After satisfying his lust, he hated her. He sent her away gruffly and had a servant bar the door. By the standards of her time, Tamar was "damaged goods"—no longer the highly desirable princess, but a discarded woman. A few minutes of sexual pleasure for Amnon resulted in a lifetime of shame for her.

But Tamar had a comforter—and avenger—her full brother Absalom. He let his hatred for Amnon stew for a full two years (which tells us he was less impulsive than Amnon, but just as evil in his own way). At a sheep-shearing festival, Absalom got Amnon extremely drunk—and killed him. Absalom went into exile as his father went into mourning over Amnon.

David ran rich with emotion at all times, so even though Absalom's behavior grieved him, he longed to see his son. After three years, Absalom was sent for. He was allowed to return to Jerusalem, but not to see the king—yet. After two years, king and son were reconciled. But more violence was in the making.

We are told that Absalom was strikingly handsome. He had such a fine mane of hair that on the rare occasions when it was cut, the clippings weighed about five pounds. He was attractive in more than a physical way. Apparently he inherited much of his father's charm and people skills. He created a large entourage that went with him everywhere, and he set up a kind of complaints office at the gate of Jerusalem, listening to the grievances of people throughout the kingdom. He made an impression, giving people the idea he would be a caring and compassionate king—better than his father. In time, Absalom and his attendants rode off to Hebron—which had been the capital under Saul—and had himself proclaimed king.

David, of course, was devastated—his beloved son was a traitor. He was frightened as well, so he packed up his court and fled Jerusalem. The whole court—taking the ark along—was "on the road," with no destination in mind. David had left his ten concubines to manage the palace. That turned out to be a mistake when Absalom entered Jerusalem. Ahitophel, a former advisor of David who had joined Absalom's conspiracy, gave the prince some advice: Sleep with the king's concubines. Absalom did—in public. Taking his father's women was a sign that the old king's rule was over.

What was the best way to get rid of the old king? Absalom did not lack for men offering advice. Ahitophel had been a respected advisor to David. Absalom trusted him as well. Ahitophel advised Absalom on how to capture and kill David. However, Absalom's other advisor, Hushai, gave different advice—which Absalom followed. Ahitophel was so humiliated that his advice was not followed that he hanged himself—one of the few suicides recorded in the Bible.

The numbers seemed to be on Absalom's side, but David still had the Lord on his. He had thousands of loyal fighting men. As they set out to meet the forces of Absalom, David ordered them, "Be gentle with the young man Absalom for my sake." Twenty thousand men died in a battle fought in a dense forest. The forest would be Absalom's undoing: Riding on a mule, Absalom's head got caught in some branches. (Was his thick mane of hair partly to blame?) The would-be king was left dangling in the air as his mule plodded on. Joab, the faithful general of David, saw his chance: He plunged three javelins into Absalom's heart. The men took Absalom down and threw his dead body into a pit, covering it with stones. So ended the conspiracy, and so ended the life of Israel's pretty boy prince.

But not the grief. David's lament is found in 2 Samuel 18:33: "O my son Absalom! My son, my son Absalom! If only I had died instead of you—O Absalom, my son, my son!" The day of victory for the army brought no joy for David. Knowing David's grief, the soldiers had to slink quietly into Jerusalem. Joab was furious with his master, telling him that thanks to his soldiers, the king and his family were all safe, and that the men deserved thanks, not mourning. He warned the king that if he did not show some gratitude, the men would all desert him. David went out to the city gate to play the role of the king greeting his victorious troops. David had often given his emotions free reign in public—such as dancing before the ark—but this was one occasion when he buried his grief. For a while he would be the king of Israel, not the distraught father.

David's troubles were by no means over. A new conspiracy arose under a troublemaker named Sheba, from the tribe of Benjamin. Sheba proclaimed that Israel wanted no part of David. Many men from the northern tribes of Israel flocked to Sheba, while Judah, David's own tribe, stood by him. David was getting a preview of what would happen many years later under his grandson, Rehoboam, when the country would split into two nations, Israel and Judah. David actually feared this conspiracy more than the conspiracy of Absalom. He needn't have feared. The rebellion was put down soon enough, ending in Sheba's being beheaded. But, clearly, David could never again feel totally secure on his throne. Being "the Lord's anointed" did not seem to impress everyone— not even his own children!

Sheba's followers used an interesting phrase: "Each man to his tent, O Israel!" The phrase harked back to Israel's past, to the time of the patriarchs and the time of the

CHARACTER CLOSE-UP Faithful Rizpah

During David's reign there was a three-year famine. The Lord told David it was because Saul had almost exterminated the Gibeonites years earlier. David decided to set things right—and end the famine—by asking the surviving Gibeonites what he could do for them. Since Saul himself was dead, the Gibeonites asked David to hand over seven of Saul's descendants to them. The Gibeonites took the seven men and killed them, exposing their bodies on a hill.

A gruesome story? Yes, but violence and cruelty can evoke positive emotions too. Rizpah, a concubine of Saul, was mother of two of the men who were killed by the Gibeonites. She turned herself into a kind of human scarecrow, staying on the hill and keeping the birds and beasts away from the dead bodies of her sons and the others.

David was so touched when he heard of this that he ordered the remains of the seven descendants of Saul to be buried, along with the bones of Saul and Jonathan, in the family tomb in the territory of Benjamin. While the gesture was a kind one, we can't forget that it was David, after all, who had handed over the seven men for execution.

The famine ended, and the family of Israel's first king got a decent burial at long last (2 Samuel 21:1–14).

Shimei and David

When David and his attendants were on the run from Absalom, they encountered many well-wishers—and also some critics. One man, Shimei, of the clan of Saul, pelted David and his officials with stones and dirt as they passed by, calling David a "man of blood." Shimei yelled that the rebellious son Absalom was David's punishment for replacing Saul as king. Abishai, one of David's officials, asked David permission to behead this "dead dog" who dared to curse the king. David was indignant: "If he is cursing because the Lord said to him 'Curse David,' who can ask, 'Why do you do this?'…Leave him alone; let him curse, for the Lord has told him to.' "

Later, after Absalom's conspiracy failed, Shimei feared for his life. Perhaps now that David was in full control of the kingdom, he would not be so merciful. Shimei threw himself before David and begged forgiveness for his surly behavior. Abishai, David's official, suggested killing him. David swore that Shimei would not die (2 Samuel 19:19–23). However, he would not keep that oath: Just before the king died, he had a change of heart (the wrong kind, alas) and told his son Solomon not to let Shimei die of natural causes.

There is a deep theological and moral point in the story of Shimei: God can use our enemies to tell the truth and to chastise us. No man, no matter how exalted he might be, is above criticism.

Israelites' journey out of Egypt, the people living in tents, not houses. People in tents can move when they don't like the way things are. The days of living in tents was past, but the cry was a kind of declaration of independence. This would not be the last time the phrase was used. Israel had been united for a short time—it could be divided again.

Chapter 23 of 2 Samuel contains a compressed history of David's "mighty men," his most valiant soldiers. Chapter 24 contains a curious story: David orders a census of Israel's military men. For reasons that are not clear, this census displeased God. A prophet named Gad went to David and told him he could choose from three punishments from the Lord: three years of famine, three years of fleeing from enemies, or three days of plague. David chose the plague, and seventy thousand Israelites died from it. David was horrified, since it was his sin (the census) that was the cause of so many of his people dying. David offered sacrifices to the Lord and prayed. The plague stopped.

In his old age, David could not keep warm. A young virgin named Abishag was brought into the household to wait on the king—and to warm his bed at night, though he did not have relations with her.

With the king old and in frail health, the obvious question arose: Who would be the next king? There was no shortage of sons, of course. But the obvious choice of David, Absalom, was long dead. The son born after Absalom, Adonijah, wanted the throne badly. As the oldest surviving son, he was probably right to expect it. He formed a party around himself which included David's faithful soldier Joab and the priest Abiathar—two men who had helped his father become king. Adonijah hosted a grand feast and invited all the king's officials.

Supposedly David had promised the throne to Solomon, the son of Bathsheba. She and the prophet Nathan went to David and reminded him of the promise. They told him Adonijah was already acting as if he were the designated heir, and they feared he would treat them badly if he became king. David confirmed that Solomon was indeed his choice. He had Zadok the priest anoint Solomon as king. The sound of the celebration honoring Solomon's anointing was heard at Adonijah's feast. Suddenly Adonijah's supporters melted away. Adonijah himself was frightened, so much so that he went and clung to the Lord's altar, believing he could not be harmed there. Solomon sent a message: If Adonijah would behave, no harm would come to him.

Before dying, David called in Solomon and commanded him to walk in the right path, observing the laws of God. Then David, so merciful in his lifetime, ordered Solomon to take vengeance on two people: the general Joab, for committing treacherous murders, and Shimei, the one who had cursed him. David was splitting hairs: He had promised Shimei he would never harm him, and he kept his promise—*but* he ordered his son to kill him. We often assume that people mellow as they age, but not always. It would have been more to David's credit had he forgiven—or overlooked—Joab and Shimei.

David breathed his last after a reign of forty years. Solomon was supposedly settled securely on the throne—but not completely. Adonijah came and asked for a small favor: Could he have Abishag, the young virgin who had slept with David, for a wife? It did not seem like a small favor to Solomon. As you may have observed in the story of Absalom, taking possession of a woman who had belonged to the king was not a small thing—it was like taking possession of the entire kingdom. He ordered Adonijah's execution.

Soon after, following his father's last request, he had Joab killed, and, in time, Shimei as well. By our standards, Solomon's reign started on a bloody note—killing his own brother and two men whose crimes were committed years earlier. But better things were to come from Solomon.

ASK FOR WISDOM, GET THE WHOLE PACKAGE

In a dream, the Lord asked the new king what he desired. Solomon's answer was commendable: "Give your servant a discerning heart to govern your people and to distinguish between right and wrong" (1 Kings 3:9). This humble answer pleased God. Solomon had asked for the most important thing in a king. God promised Solomon he would give what he asked for—and much more. He would be given riches and honor, and he would have no equal among kings—so long as he obeyed God.

The wisdom Solomon prayed for was granted. It was evident in his most famous judgment. Two prostitutes came to him. Both had shared a house, and both bore a child at the same time. One child died, and both were claiming the surviving child. This was not simply an error—one of the women knew she was lying, and that it was her child who had died. The women continued their argument right in the king's presence, but he ended it dramatically: He ordered a servant to bring in a sword and cut the child in half, dividing it between the two women. The expected happened. The real mother of the child shouted, "Please, my lord, give her the living baby! Don't kill him!" But the other mother—the one whose child had died—said, "Cut him in two!" Solomon gave the child to the woman who said, "Don't kill him!" Israel was in awe of its new king's wisdom (1 Kings 3:16–28).

So was the rest of the world. We are told that Solomon's fame spread far and wide. He spoke three thousand proverbs, wrote more than a thousand songs, and was a bit of a scientist as well, with a vast knowledge of plant and animal life. Men from everywhere came to soak up his knowledge (1 Kings 4:29–34).

Since Solomon had asked God for wisdom and was also granted riches and honor, 1 Kings is not sparing in describing the riches. The daily provisions for Solomon's household are given in 1 Kings 4, which also tells of the extent of his kingdom, and the stalls for his thousands of horses.

Israel has never been a seafaring nation, but under Solomon it did have a navy—or, more accurately, a merchant marine fleet. Because Israel dominated Edom, it had a port, Ezion-Geber, that gave it access to the Red Sea and the Indian Ocean, meaning that Solomon's ships could export goods to faraway India. Solomon could trade the copper from his mines for the exotic goods of Arabia, east Africa and India. In the other direction, Solomon's ships sailed as far as Tarshish, probably the region that was later called Spain. Within a generation, Israel's commercial life was transformed—from a small "general store" under David to an enormous "mall" under Solomon. It sounds like a good thing, and in many ways it probably was. But by helping to create a merchant class, Solomon was laying the groundwork for economic exploitation that the great prophets would condemn loud and long.

Solomon's great achievement—other than keeping the land peaceful and secure, that is—was his building of the temple. In this he was aided by Hiram, king of Tyre, who supplied him with enormous timbers from the famous cedars of Lebanon. A detailed description of the temple's construction is given in 1 Kings 6 and 7. It is probably no coincidence that it was precisely twice as large as the Tabernacle, the large tent that had been Israel's center of worship since the days of Moses. The temple must have glowed, for according to the Bible there was gold everywhere. The magnificent place was seven years in the making. When it was completed, Solomon had the ark brought in. The priests solemnly carried the ark into the Most Holy Place (or "Holy of Holies" in some translations). When the ark was placed there, a cloud—the glory of the Lord—filled the space.

Solomon prayed a solemn and eloquent prayer of dedication. Perhaps the most memorable part is this: "But will God really dwell on earth? The heavens, even the highest heaven, cannot contain you. How much less this temple I have built!" (8:27). Clearly, God cannot "fit" into any building, no matter how splendid. And yet, in some mysterious way, God was "there" in the temple, and Israel would regard it as his "house"

CULTURAL INSIGHTS ## Holy of Holies

Depending on the Bible translation you use, the temple that Solomon built might be called the Most Holy Place or the Holiest Place. It was a section of the Tabernacle about fifteen square feet, empty except for one thing, the ark of the covenant, the gold-covered chest that symbolized the presence of the Lord. It was curtained off from the rest of the Tabernacle, and no one could enter the space except Israel's high priest, and only on rare occasions, such as the annual Day of Atonement, on which he would sprinkle blood on the mercy seat, the gold lid of the ark.

The temple Solomon built also had a Holy of Holies, and the ark was carried there, its permanent home. The Holy of Holies in the temple was decorated with imposing carvings of two cherubim, the same figures as were on the lid of the ark. The cherubim had human bodies and faces, but wings instead of arms.

The Queen of Sheba

If you have ever been to an art museum, you have probably seen a painting with a title like *The Queen of Sheba Visits Solomon*. For centuries artists have been drawn to this subject—the exotic queen visiting the splendid court of Israel's wisest and richest king. According to 1 Kings 10, her primary motive in visiting was to experience the king's legendary wisdom, so she tested him with "hard questions," and of course, "nothing was too hard for the king." His wisdom impressed her, as did the magnificence of his palace.

She praised the king lavishly, speaking of the good fortune of his subjects and all his officials. She even praised his God, since any God who could place such a wise and wealthy king in power must be great indeed. She gave the king gifts of gold, jewels and spices.

Many legends were told of the queen and Solomon, and in many of them, she conceived a child by him. The people of Ethiopia believed for centuries (and some still do) that their kings were descended from the child of Solomon and the queen. In many of the legends the queen has a name: Belkis, Malkis, Makeda and several others. In Arab versions of the legend, the queen was not human but was daughter of the *jinn*, the beautiful spirits.

Where was Sheba? Historians think it was somewhere in the Arabian peninsula, perhaps in what is the nation of Yemen today. For the writer of 1 Kings, the importance of Sheba was that it was far away, a testimony to how famous Solomon was.

until the Babylonians destroyed it in 586 BC. When they had the chance, they built another to replace it.

In the prayer, Solomon asked God not only to bless Israel, but to heed the prayer of any foreigner who came to the temple. God was Israel's God, and yet the God of the whole world as well.

The feast of dedicating the temple lasted a full fourteen days.

Solomon had built God a fine house. He also built a fine one for himself, a grand palace that took thirteen years to build. Since the temple took only seven, we might conclude Solomon regarded his palace as more important. Not so. The Lord's house was more urgent, and so was completed sooner.

NOW THE BAD NEWS...

The Bible certainly gives us a "warts and all" portrait of the previous kings, Saul and David. Solomon had his "warts" also, but 1 Kings saves them until the end of the story, after giving all the eye-pleasing details about Solomon's magnificence. As evidence of his wealth—and the standing of Israel in the eyes of the world—Solomon had married foreign princesses, including the daughter of the Pharaoh of Egypt. (Consider the irony:

The descendants of the slaves of the Egyptians had a king who married into the Egyptian royal family.) Solomon married many other foreign wives—in fact, he had "seven hundred wives of royal birth and three hundred concubines, and his wives led him astray" (11:3). The faithful young man who built a temple to God—the only true God—also built temples for his wives' gods—such as Chemosh and Molech, to whom children were sacrificed.

God did not overlook this breach of faith. He told Solomon he would tear the kingdom in two. But for the sake of David, he would not do it in Solomon's lifetime, but afterward.

Solomon's sliding into idolatry was not the only problem: You have to read 1 Kings closely to understand that Solomon's grand building projects were done with forced labor. Men—both Israelites and resident aliens—were "drafted" into working as timber cutters, stone cutters and other workers. They were not slave labor, but they had little choice. The words of Samuel warning the Israelites of how a king would oppress and tax them had come true. The fact that the men of Judah, Solomon's own tribe, were exempted was not overlooked by the other tribes. Solomon had divided the country—Judah excepted—into twelve administrative districts, disregarding the tribal boundaries at a time when people took their tribal heritage seriously. In other words, many people outside Judah thought Judah was ruling over the other tribes.

One of Solomon's labor foremen was a man named Jeroboam. One day in Jerusalem he encountered a prophet named Ahijah, wearing a new robe. Ahijah tore the robe into

---

CULTURAL INSIGHTS "His Own Vine and Fig Tree"

"During Solomon's lifetime Judah and Israel, from Dan to Beersheba, lived in safety, each man under his own vine and fig tree" (1 Kings 4:25). This phrase occurs several times in the Bible. Obviously the Israelites thought of the good life as the security of living at peace under one's own vine and fig tree. This wasn't necessarily a matter of greed, but more a matter of freedom from poverty and the problems it brings, along with the usual interrupters of human happiness—war, invasion, famine, oppressive rulers and landlords, sickness. While sickness and famine often have no human cause, the other ills of mankind have a human basis, rooted in greed and malice.

History shows that the times of "each man under his own vine and fig tree" are comparatively rare. As a small nation wedged uncomfortably between larger and more powerful ones, Israel seldom enjoyed security. In a sense, little Israel represents humankind at large, a pawn in the power games of forces it cannot control or negotiate with. In Solomon's time it found the peace it desired.

DID YOU KNOW?

Readers are often skeptical of 1 Kings, feeling that it exaggerates Solomon's wealth. But in fact the thousands of horse stalls mentioned in 4:26 have been found by archaeologists at the site called Megiddo. The Bible was not exaggerating.

twelve pieces and handed ten to Jeroboam. The ten symbolized ten of Israel's tribes. For Solomon's sins, Israel was going to be divided, with ten tribes in one kingdom and two in another. Apparently Solomon heard of the prophecy, for he tried to kill Jeroboam, who fled to Egypt for safety. We will meet him again—in the role of king—in the next chapter.

Solomon died after a reign of forty years. His son, and the whole nation of Israel, were about to pay the price for the moral backsliding of the wise, wealthy king, the golden boy who had showed such promise in his youth. The gold that was so prominent a feature of his reign was a veneer over a rotten moral and spiritual building.

In closing this chapter, we can't help but reflect that David, a fine man in so many ways, was not a particularly good father, given the behavior of his children. Certainly his problems with his sons and wives are themselves a strong argument against polygamy.

Solomon, praised for his wisdom and wealth, is never mentioned in the role of father, nor are any of his numerous wives mentioned by name. The world at large knew of the amazing Solomon, but he must have been an absentee father and husband, as the character of his successor Rehoboam will show in the next chapter. Could a man with seven hundred wives know much about deep marital love? For all his fabled wisdom, he must have had some serious—and important—gaps in his knowledge of things that matter.

People often name their children after people in the Bible. David has been a favorite name, for people seem willing to overlook his sins and focus on the better qualities. Solomon has been much less common as a name, perhaps because people remember not Solomon the magnificent or Solomon the wise, but Solomon the backslider. Perhaps another reason the name is less popular is that we don't feel we *know* Solomon in the same way we know David. For all the detail that 1 Kings gives about Solomon's reign, the man himself eludes us, while David is someone we feel we know inside and out. The Bible gives us a three-dimensional David and a two- (or one-) dimensional Solomon. This is to be expected. Saul and David, humble farm boys, had to struggle with life, had to prove to the people they were capable leaders, had to prove to God that he had been right in choosing them. Solomon was born in a palace, never knowing fear or deprivation. Solomon may have uttered thousands of proverbs, but they were probably more God-inspired than the result of his own life experience. The two previous kings knew vastly more about life that Solomon did. They had lived it, tasting the bitter and the sweet.

One other item to think of: For all the emphasis that 1 Kings places upon the glory of the temple, we know that God can be worshipped without a temple. Faith can survive the loss of a building, even one said to be the "house" of God. Solomon himself had already asked the right question: Can any building contain God? Even Solomon knew the answer: No—but a human heart can contain him.

PUTTING THE WORD TO WORK

1. David's ecstatic dancing when the ark was brought into Jerusalem expresses intense emotion. David clearly "felt" God at many times in his life. Have there been times in your own life when you felt especially "enlivened" by your sense of God's presence?

2. The confrontation between David and his wife Michal is a classic case of two spouses saying exactly the *wrong* words to each other, words they knew would do the most harm. Think back to times when you gave in to malice and let your words flow too freely. If possible, contact the person you harmed and make amends.

3. David's adultery with Bathsheba is one of the most famous episodes in his life. What is often overlooked is the fact that David, though he never forgot the incident, managed to grow beyond it, not letting it bring an end to his relationship with the Lord. Is this something you can take to heart in your own relationship with God?

4. Solomon's wisdom in the case of the two women claiming the same child is deservedly famous. Who were some people you have known who amazed you with their wisdom and insights into people and situations? Have you been a voice of wisdom for others?

5. In Solomon's life, fame and sophistication and material wealth had a negative effect on his spiritual state. In gaining the respect of foreigners, and trying to please his pagan wives, his devotion to the Lord suffered. Look at your own life and ask: In what ways have I compromised myself in trying to please or impress people instead of God?

Divided and Conquered

**AT THE
HEART
OF IT ALL
TODAY**
God's chosen nation, Israel, splits into two kingdoms, with mostly immoral kings ruling both. Despite violence and poor leadership and a falling away from the faith, God blesses the people with his prophets, who work miracles of power and compassion. Even in dark times, the faith lives on.

Solomon the magnificent was dead—Solomon the builder of the splendid temple, ruler of a nation big enough to be called an empire, with a merchant fleet bringing in goods from everywhere, and peace and security all around. The same Solomon, renowned for his wisdom, was foolish enough to let

KEY PASSAGES TO READ TODAY

1 Kings 12:1–33; 18–19
2 Kings 2:1–14; 9:30–37;
17:14–17

his heathen wives lead him into idolatry and draft his people into forced labor. Spiritually and socially, things were ripe for a rebellion. Jeroboam, one of his former officials, had been given a torn robe by the prophet Ahijah and told he would tear the kingdom away from Solomon's family. On hearing of Solomon's death, Jeroboam left his exile in Egypt and returned home.

Solomon's two predecessors as king, Saul and David, had been farm boys, elevated by God to the kingship, and forced to struggle with enemies within and without. Solomon had led a more sheltered life, and we can assume his son Rehoboam led an even easier one, since his entire life had been spent in a gilded palace. In other words, Israel's new king was a spoiled son of privilege, out of touch with his people. He proved it immediately. At a large gathering, the people told Rehoboam that they would serve him—if he would lighten the load of labor and taxes that Solomon had imposed on them. Rehoboam told them to come back in three days and he would give them a response. He consulted with the older counselors, who told him to give the people what they wanted and they would serve him well. He didn't like that suggestion but did like the one given by the young men he had grown up with. (The Hebrew word used here actually means "boys," not "young men." Rehoboam's companions were hardly adult men in terms of maturity.)

Rehoboam told the gathered Israelites what his young friends had suggested: "My father made your yoke heavy; I will make it even heavier. My father scourged you with whips; I will scourge you with scorpions" (1 Kings 12:14). Scholars debate whether "scorpions" was some nasty type of whip or whether it was meant poetically. It does not matter, because Rehoboam's words cost him a large part of his kingdom. The men of

Israel were furious at his arrogance: "To your tents, O Israel! Look after your own house, O David!" Adding insult to injury, Rehoboam sent another man to speak to the people: Adoniram, the chief of the forced labor gangs, and the worst possible man to pacify the people at that time. The men stoned him, and Rehoboam fled in his chariot. The united kingdom of Israel that Saul, David and Solomon ruled had been ended by the arrogance of a spoiled prince. Rehoboam ruled only over the tribes of Judah and Benjamin. The other tribes rallied around the returned Jeroboam and made him king. Rehoboam thought of going to war to force the other tribes to accept him, but a prophet named Shemaiah told him no, the breakup of the kingdom was the will of God. It was likely that Rehoboam would have lost that war anyway.

As already noted in earlier chapters, the breakup of Judah and Israel had been a long time in the making. However, the worship had been centered in Judah, in the Jerusalem temple, for many years now, and Jeroboam feared—wisely—that even though Israel was ready to abandon Rehoboam, they were not ready to give up worship in the temple. If the people traveled regularly to Jerusalem to worship, they might some day wish to reunite with Judah. So Jeroboam did something that the author of Kings never ceased to condemn: he set up worship centers at two locations in Israel, Dan and Bethel. He chose those two sites for sound political reasons. Bethel had long been a religious site, remembered as the place where the patriarch Jacob had his dream of angels on a stairway to heaven (Genesis 28), and Bethel's name meant "house of God." Dan was chosen because it was in the far north of Israel and would be a convenient place of worship for the northern tribes of Israel. When Jeroboam opened the shrines at Dan and Bethel, he celebrated the Feast of Booths—precisely the same annual holy day at which Solomon had dedicated the temple. Jeroboam wanted his people to form the habit of celebrating Israel's holy days at the new shrines, not in Jerusalem.

In both places Jeroboam set up a golden bull idol—in other words, an idol like the one the Israelites made at Mount Sinai, which so angered Moses. (As in the Moses story, calling this a golden "calf" is not correct. It was a young bull, a symbol of strength and fertility.) In the history in Kings, every king of Israel was condemned for continuing to encourage worship at Dan and Bethel with these golden idols.

931 BC
Division of the kingdom under Rehoboam
(1 Kings 12:1–24)

874–853 BC
Ahab reigns over Israel
(1 Kings 16:29–22:40).

c. 874–852 BC
Ministry of Elijah
(1 Kings 17–19, 21; 2 Kings 1–2)

c. 852–798 BC
Ministry of Elisha
(2 Kings 2, 4–9)

c. 850 BC
Medes migrate into Iran.

c. 800 BC
Invasion of Palestine by Egypt

The Greek poet Homer composes the Iliad and Odyssey.

776 BC
First Olympics held in Greece.

753 BC
Founding of Rome

Traditional date for the beginning of Greek colonization of southern Italy

722 BC
Fall of northern kingdom (Israel) to Assyria
(2 Kings 17:5–41)

Righteous Remnant

In the dramatic theophany on Mount Horeb, God reminded the prophet Elijah that there were still seven thousand others in Israel who had not bowed down to the false god Baal. Here we see a key theme of the Bible: God preserves a righteous "remnant" of people who hold fast to him. In a sense the original "remnant" was Noah, the one righteous man God chose to preserve from the universal flood. Israel, the descendants of the patriarch Jacob, was called to be a holy nation but consistently failed to be, yet always there were those who remained faithful to God, even when surrounded by neighbors eagerly indulging in idolatry and immorality.

Did Jeroboam really intend these golden bulls to be idols? Probably not. He probably did not see them as representing some false god, and probably he worshipped Yahweh, the true God of Israel. But the idols were prohibited in the Ten Commandments, and he still set them up. He couldn't have been ignorant of the fact that the pagan god Baal was often symbolized by a bull idol. Besides that, he installed priests who were not Levites, the tribe to which the Lord had given the priesthood. Israel and Judah were not only two different nations now, but on their way to having two different religions.

Why couldn't the people worship God at Dan and Bethel—or anywhere? The fact is, in the ancient world, having multiple shrines usually meant having multiple gods. Whatever Jeroboam's intentions were, he had paved the way for Israel to worship idols—and to worship more than one god. Ahijah, the very prophet who foretold that Jeroboam would become king, scolded him for his religious innovations, as did other prophets.

Nevertheless, Jeroboam reigned twenty-two years—longer than Rehoboam reigned in Judah. We are told that Rehoboam's mother was an Ammonite. Apparently among Solomon's hundreds of wives there was not one Israelite. Having this pagan mother (and a father who was less than committed to the Lord), Rehoboam let idolatry run riot in Judah, and worship of false gods became even more common than in Israel. As punishment for his infidelity, Rehoboam watched as Shishak, Egypt's Pharaoh, attacked Jerusalem and carried off many of the treasures his father had made for the temple. (Note the irony: One of Solomon's wives was a daughter of an earlier pharaoh. Relations between Judah and Egypt had soured.) Not surprisingly, there was also war between Rehoboam and Jeroboam throughout their reigns. In fact, Shishak's invasion had been the work of a smart politician: He was taking advantage of the war between Judah and Israel. Rehoboam's loss was his gain.

The account of Rehoboam's reign in 2 Chronicles adds an interesting detail that 1 Kings did not include: "Indeed, there was some good in Judah" (12:12). There was, but not much of it was in Judah's kings.

KINGS OF JUDAH	PROPHETS	KINGS OF ISRAEL
Rehoboam 931-913 BC (1 Kings 12:1-24, 14:21-31)		Jeroboam 931-910 BC (1 Kings 12:25-14:20)
Abijah 913-911 BC (1 Kings 15:1-8)		Nadab 910-909 BC (1 Kings 15:25-32)
Asa 911-870 BC (1 Kings 15:9-24)		Baasha 909-886 BC (1 Kings 15:33-16)
		Elah 886-885 BC (1 Kings 16:8-14)
		Zimri, for 7 days in 885 BC (1 Kings 16:15-20)
		Omri 885-874 BC (1 Kings 16:21-28)
Jehoshaphat 870-848 BC (1 Kings 22:41-50)	Elijah [reign of Ahab]	Ahab 874-853 BC (1 Kings 16:29-22:40)
		Ahaziah 853-852 BC (1 Kings 22:51-2 Kings 1:18)
		Joram 852-841 BC (2 Kings 9:14-26)
Jehoram 848-841 BC (2 Kings 8:16-24)	Elisha [reigns of Jehoram and Jehu]	Jehu 841-814 BC (2 Kings 9-10)
Ahaziah 841 BC (2 Kings 8:25-29)		Jehoahaz 814-798 BC (2 Kings 13:1-9)
Queen Athaliah 841-835 BC (2 Kings 11)		Jehoash 798-783 BC (2 Kings 13:10-13)
Joash 835-796 BC (2 Kings 12)		
Amaziah 796-781 BC (2 Kings 14:1-22)	Amos [reign of Jeroboam II]	Jeroboam II 783-743 BC (2 Kings 14:23-29)
	Hosea [reign of Jeroboam II]	
Uzziah 781-740 BC (2 Kings 15:1-7)		Zechariah, for 6 months in 743 BC (2 Kings 15:8-13)
		Shallum, for 1 month in 743 BC (2 Kings 15:13-16)
Jotham 740-736 BC (2 Kings 15:32-38)	Micah [reign of Jotham]	Menahem 743-738 BC (2 Kings 15:17-22)
		Pekahiah 738-737 BC (2 Kings 15:23-26)
Ahaz 736-716 BC (2 Kings 16)		Pekah 737-732 BC (2 Kings 15:27-31)
		Hoshea 732-723 BC (2 Kings 17:1-4)
Hezekiah 716-687 BC (2 Kings 18-20)		

Court Histories

In ancient times, history was written with a purpose, the most common purpose being to keep a record of a king's reign. Since the writers were court employees, they were not what we would call objective. They wrote to make the king look good, so if the king was a greedy, cruel tyrant, they probably would not say so. Typically a court history told how the king came to power, who he went to war with, territory he conquered, good things he did for the country (often exaggerated), and who succeeded him when he died.

We know that the kings of Israel and Judah kept court histories, for they are referred to often in the Bible—for example, "The other events of Jeroboam's reign, his wars and how he ruled, are written in the book of the annals of the kings of Israel" (1 Kings 14:19). The writer of Kings was telling us he had access to the court records—in other words, he was citing his source, as any historian would do today. However, the portraits drawn of the kings tell us that this author was aiming to tell the unvarnished truth, not make the kings look good. If the court annals painted too rosy a picture of a king's reign, the anonymous author of Kings supplied the rest of the story, something that makes the Bible such a pleasure to read.

PARALLEL DECLINES

From this point on, we see a familiar formula in the way the kings' stories are told: "In the nth year of the reign of X king of Israel, Y became king of Judah, and he did evil in the eyes of the Lord…" This can seem tedious to read, especially since it seems almost *all* the kings "did evil in the eyes of the Lord." What makes the narrative interesting, however, is that a few good kings do stand out, and the activities of a few zealous and compassionate prophets hold our interest.

After the breakup into two kingdoms, the first good king was Asa, king of Judah (1 Kings 15:9–24). Asa made an effort to end the idolatry in the land, even though it had been encouraged by his own grandmother. Asa cut down an Asherah pole that she had set up. Normally the queen mother was a respected figure, and lending her support to the Asherah cult was an abuse of her clout, and Asa was right to defy her. A prophet named Hanani spoke some wise words to Asa that are worth quoting: "The eyes of the Lord range throughout the earth to strengthen those whose hearts are fully committed to him" (2 Chronicles 16:9). While Asa was successful on the spiritual level, he was less so on the political one, for he had to take gold and silver to pay tribute to Ben-Haded, king of Aram. The days when nations paid tribute to Israel were long past. For the rest of the Old Testament, both Israel and Judah were almost always paying out tribute money to the aggressive nations on their borders.

Judah had one great advantage over Israel: Throughout its history it was ruled by the same dynasty, the descendants of David. This was something the Lord had promised David. Israel had no such stability. Although Jeroboam was succeeded peacefully by his son Nadab, Nadab reigned only two years before being killed by Baasha. Jeroboam's entire family was wiped out by Baasha, and Baasha reigned twenty-two years. But a man who makes himself king by killing a king is never too secure on the throne, nor is his son. Baasha died peacefully, but his son, Elah, reigned only two years before being killed by one of his officials, Zimri. Following the pattern, Zimri quickly killed off Elah's whole family (as Elah's father, Baasha, had killed off Jeroboam's). Zimri must have acted with lightning speed, because his reign lasted a grand total of seven days. To avenge the slaughter of Elah's family, the people plotted against Zimri and besieged the capital. With the city in the hands of his enemies, Zimri committed suicide by burning down the palace—with himself inside.

Zimri's successor would, however, have a long reign and establish a dynasty—an evil one, unfortunately. Zimri had been ousted by Omri, who, on a secular level, was a great success. In fact, he made such an impression on his contemporaries that in his lifetime and for many years afterward, Israel was called "the house of Omri." He also gave Israel a new capital city, naming it Samaria. However, he tolerated the worship of idols, and though he reigned twelve years, 1 Kings dismisses his reign in only eight verses. He was important by worldly standards, but by the standards of the Bible he was just another evil king of Israel.

However, it was his son who would become the "gold standard" for wickedness.

KING VERSUS PROPHET

Success and sophistication do not seem to go well with morality. The classic case of this was Solomon, the wealthy king who married many foreign wives—meaning that his kingdom was impressive enough that he could marry the daughters of other kings, not just ordinary commoners from Israel. But, as the Bible makes painfully clear, foreign wives with their pagan gods led Solomon astray, making him unfaithful to the only true God. We see the same pattern in the life of Omri's son Ahab, who "did more evil in the eyes of the Lord than any of those before him" (1 Kings 16:30). Because Omri had made Israel into a "player" on the world stage, he had married his son off to the daughter of the king of Sidon. Ethbaal, the king, was also a priest of the god Baal (as you might guess from his name, which means "Baal is with him"). So his daughter, Jezebel, was raised as a kind of religious zealot, not just a casual worshipper of Baal, but a sort of evangelist for his religion. Sidon was a worldly, sophisticated commercial city on the Mediterranean, and it was clear to Jezebel that Sidon's god, Baal, was certainly superior to the pitiful Yahweh, god of the backward Israelites.

Jezebel had not counted on the God of Israel having a man like Elijah speak out for him.

The prophet Elijah is introduced suddenly in 1 Kings 17 simply as "Elijah the Tishbite" —no mention being made of his father, which is an odd omission in the Old Testament, where a man was always referred to as "X, the son of Y." Elijah speaks to Ahab and predicts a long drought, "neither rain nor dew." The Lord sent Elijah into the wilderness, where he lived by the brook Kerith and was brought food by ravens. When the brook dried up due to the drought, God sent him to a widow in Zarephath. He asked the poor woman for water and food, but she had no food. She and her son were on the verge of starvation, with only a jar of flour and cruet of oil. Elijah promised her that a miracle would occur: The flour and oil would not run out until the drought ended. So she, the son, and the prophet continued to exist on the food supplied by this miracle. But the son died and the woman was stricken with grief. Elijah stretched the child on the bed, lay on top of him, and prayed for life to return. The boy came to life again.

While Elijah was away from court, Queen Jezebel was busy persecuting God's prophets. She had killed many of them, but a prophet named Obadiah had kept a hundred of them hidden away in caves. In the third year of the drought, walking in the brown fields, Obadiah encountered Elijah, who told him to tell Ahab, "Elijah is here." Obadiah was horrified—hadn't Elijah heard what Jezebel was doing to the prophets of God? Obadiah feared going to Ahab—but Elijah did not. When Ahab saw him, he greeted him with, "Is that you, you troubler of Israel?" Elijah assured him that it was he, Ahab, not Elijah, who was Israel's real trouble. Elijah wanted a showdown. He would go to Mount Carmel and meet hundreds of Baal and Asherah prophets who were on Jezebel's payroll. One prophet of God versus 450 Baal prophets and four hundred Asherah prophets—a fair contest? From the divine perspective, it was no contest at all.

With a large crowd assembled, Elijah challenged the people: "How long will you waver between two opinions? If the Lord is God, follow him; but if Baal is God, follow him" (1 Kings 18:21). This is one of the great moments in the Bible, and one of the greatest decisions Israel ever had to make. As Elijah saw it, there was no "both/and" when it came to worshipping God and Baal. In this, he and Jezebel agreed. Who would win—the merciful God who had taken his people out of Egypt and led them into Canaan, or the promiscuous, violent, temperamental fertility god Baal, more like a demon than a god?

Elijah had bulls brought in and an altar set up. Here was the challenge: The god who could set the sacrifice on fire was the winner.

An elaborate "dance" took place as the hundreds of Baal prophets called on their god for hours. Elijah told them to shout louder—perhaps Baal was asleep, or busy, or traveling.

They did shout louder, and when this did not get Baal's attention, they slashed themselves with swords and spears. (In pagan worship, the sight of human blood is supposed to attract a god's attention. Cutting oneself was only a step removed from the human sacrifice that was a part of many religions. The Law of Moses prohibited such behavior.)

Elijah had no need to go through such antics to get God's attention. He set up twelve stones to remind people that the Lord had blessed the twelve tribes of Israel. Then he set up the altar with the bull—and had it doused with water. When everything was saturated, he called on the God of Abraham and Israel: "Answer me, Lord, answer me, so these people will know that you, O Lord, are God, and that you are turning their hearts back again." Then the fire of the Lord—lightning, perhaps—fell from heaven and burned up the sacrifice. The people fell facedown and cried, "The Lord—he is God!" Then they seized the Baal prophets and killed them all.

A few minutes later, Elijah's servant spotted "a cloud as small as a man's hand rising from the sea." God had proved himself—and was about to end the drought. Feeling the power of the Lord, Elijah was able to outrun Ahab's chariot.

It's worth noting here that Elijah's name means "Yah [the Lord] is God." No name ever summed up a man's career more perfectly.

Jezebel herself was not present when Elijah called down fire from the Lord. Ahab told her what transpired, and she reacted vengefully to the slaughter of her Baal prophets. She sent word to Elijah: *You are a dead man.* This wasn't a case of her revealing her plan to the man she wished to kill—she wasn't that stupid—but more a matter of telling him to leave the country if he knew what was good for him.

CULTURAL INSIGHTS

Asherah

Since the Canaanites left few written records about their religion, we glean most of what we know about them from the Bible. The picture is confusing, because they worshipped a kind of mother-goddess called Ashtaroth, Ashtoreth or Ishtar, but also another, similar goddess named Asherah. The Canaanites would set up a kind of pole or pillar that represented Asherah and was sometimes itself referred to as an Asherah. Ashtaroth, on the other hand, was usually represented as a naked, rather wild-looking woman. Both goddesses were connected with the fertility god Baal, and all three were worshipped with religious rituals involving promiscuous sex. Jezebel, wife of Ahab, had a huge bevy of prophets of Baal and prophets of Asherah, and Ahab (probably to please his wife) set up an Asherah pole. The better kings of Israel and Judah would cut down the Asherah poles from time to time, but Asherah's followers would inevitably erect new ones.

Samaria

Samaria was the last and most important capital of Israel, with the site chosen by the powerful king Omri. For the rest of 1 and 2 Kings, it existed as a rival capital to Jerusalem in Judah, and the great prophets condemned the sins of both cities. Israel was a more prosperous kingdom than Judah, and Samaria a more glorious city, though it never had the spiritual clout of Jerusalem, for it had no worship center as Jerusalem had. It is a sign of Israel's falling away from God that the capital of their country never had a temple dedicated to the Lord, whereas it did have a Baal temple. Ahab built himself a palace of ivory in the city, and he and several kings of Israel were buried there.

Apparently Omri and his son Ahab were great builders, for the fortifications they built around the city would later hold off the mighty Assyrian armies for more than a year. What a shame their morals were not as solid as their fortresses.

We will learn more about Samaria later, when it lent its name to an ethnic and religious group that was at odds with the Jews.

Elijah fled to Horeb (the other name for Sinai, where Moses had met God). His moment of triumph had ended, and in fear and dejection he prayed to God that he might die. An angel appeared and gave him food. He spent the night in a cave on Horeb. God spoke to him: "Go out and stand on the mountain in the presence of the Lord, for the Lord is about to pass by" (1 Kings 19:11). A powerful wind passed through—"but the Lord was not in the wind." Then there was an earthquake—"but the Lord was not in the earthquake." Then came a fire—"but the Lord was not in the fire." After the fire came "a gentle whisper"—or, in the classic words of the King James Version, "a still, small voice." On the very site where Moses had encountered the glory of the Lord, Elijah had done the same—in the form of a "still, small voice" (1 Kings 19:1–12). God had proven to Elijah that he could work in dramatic ways—as he did on Mount Carmel. But sometimes he could work without fanfare, in a quiet, intimate way. God was not a force of nature, as Baal and the other pagan gods were. He was invisible and spiritual—in control of nature, yes, but not nature itself.

The Lord assured Elijah he was not alone—indeed, there were seven thousand others in Israel who had not bowed down to Baal. Even a tough-minded man like Elijah could take heart from knowing he had companions in the faith. Elijah was told to return to Israel and anoint Elisha as his successor prophet—and anoint a new man to be king over Israel. Elijah found Elisha plowing the fields with oxen. He threw his cloak over Elisha, indicating he had a protégé. Thus one of the great partnerships of the Bible was formed. Moses had his Joshua, and Elijah had Elisha.

KINGS WITHOUT SCRUPLES

The Old Testament seems so obsessed with worshipping the right God that we forget the moral dimension of worship. Worshipping God—and not worshipping the false gods—was more than a matter of knowing which name to pray to. *What people worship determines how they behave.* If you worship a holy, moral God, you will become holy and moral. If you worship a fertility god and ascribe to it capricious, violent, temperamental, promiscuous forces of nature, you will become like him. You might say that we are what we idolize. This is made tragically clear in the story in 1 Kings 21. Ahab, living in his palace in Samaria, wanted to buy a piece of choice land nearby, a vineyard belonging to a man named Naboth. He offered Naboth a fair price, but Naboth would not sell his ancestral land. So far, Ahab had acted ethically.

Jezebel changed that. Finding Ahab sulking and refusing to eat, Jezebel was appalled. Wasn't he the king? He was, but in Israel, kings could not do as they pleased, for kings had to obey the rules just like the common people. Not where Jezebel came from! She came up with a scheme to get Ahab what he desired. She held a feast, invited Naboth—and hired two scoundrels to lie and say that Naboth had cursed both God and the king. With two accusers making it clear he was guilty, poor Naboth was taken out and stoned. Ahab took Naboth's land. That, as Jezebel saw it, was how you acted when you were king: If you wanted something, you took it. She would teach these Israelites to fear their rulers.

Elijah confronted Ahab in the most obvious place—Naboth's vineyard. For his crime, Ahab's entire dynasty would be killed and Jezebel would be devoured by dogs. Amazingly, Ahab must have had a tiny shred of conscience—or fear of God—for he tore his clothes and put on sackcloth—the signs of repentance. Because he humbled himself, the Lord swore to delay exterminating the dynasty. But Ahab was not destined to die of natural causes.

At some point, Ahab joined his military forces with those of Jehoshaphat, one of the more decent kings of Judah. The two contemplated going to war with the king of Aram, and Ahab's boot-licking court prophets said, "Go, the Lord wills it." Jehoshaphat was skeptical. Wasn't there a *real* prophet who could give his opinion? There was, and his name was Micaiah, but, Ahab grumbled, Micaiah never predicted anything good. Jehoshaphat had Micaiah brought in. Micaiah told the truth: Ahab would not return alive from the battle with Aram. Furious, Ahab had Micaiah put in prison, with bread and water rations. But he must have suspected Micaiah was telling the truth, for when he and Jehoshaphat went to battle, Ahab did not wear his royal robes. A random arrow—but is there anything "random" in this world?—struck Ahab. He bled all over his chariot, and when the chariot was brought to Samaria, dogs licked up his blood. The wicked (and henpecked) king was dead. "There was never a man like Ahab, who sold himself to do evil in the eyes of the Lord, urged on by Jezebel his wife" (1 Kings 21:25).

Dogs in Ancient Israel

Dogs are so widely loved in our culture that we can't imagine people feeling any differently toward them. They certainly did in ancient Israel. Dogs were not pets, but annoying street creatures, roaming in packs, scavenging, always a nuisance and sometimes dangerous. The Egyptians kept hounds for hunting, but the Israelites despised dogs. When 1 Kings relates that Ahab's blood was licked up by dogs, this is a sign of divine displeasure. Even today, many people in the Middle East hold to their ancestors' dislike of dogs.

Interestingly, when Jehoshaphat returned home to Judah, a prophet confronted him with an unsettling question: "Should you help the wicked and make alliances with those who hate the Lord?" (2 Chronicles 19:2). He was scolding the faithful king for forming an alliance with the wicked Ahab.

With Ahab gone, Elijah's prophecy of the extermination of Ahab's family was about to come to pass.

CHARIOT OF FIRE

After Ahab's death, his idol-worshipping son Ahaziah reigned. Ahaziah sent a company of fifty soldiers to capture Elijah. The prophet called down fire from heaven, and it destroyed the company. It happened a second time. The third company was, needless to say, fearful. The captain begged Elijah for mercy, so Elijah went with him peacefully. He told the ailing Ahaziah that he was soon to die, and it came to pass.

Elijah himself was not destined to die. He and the faithful Elisha came to the Jordan River. Elijah struck the water with his cloak and it parted. Knowing he was about to be taken from this earth, Elijah asked Elisha what he desired. Elisha asked for a "double portion of your spirit." As the two men walked along, a chariot of fire drawn by horses of fire separated the two, and "Elijah went up to heaven in a whirlwind." Elisha called out, "My father! My father! The chariots and horsemen of Israel!" The words are revealing—it meant that the great prophet's spiritual strength was Israel's true defense, not the king's horses and war chariots. Elijah's mantle fell upon him—and so did Elijah's power. When he came to the Jordan, Elisha parted the waters with the cloak. Elisha became the head of a band of prophets in the wilderness. In his long career he duplicated many of the miracles of his master, and did many more.

Miracle Men

Miracles occur throughout the Bible, but miracles also seem to "cluster" around certain people, notably Moses and, in today's chapter, the prophets Elijah and Elisha. Perhaps the most inspiring thing about the miracle stories connected with these two is that they tell of miracles of compassion as well as of dramatic (and very public) displays of power. The same Elijah who could call down the fire of God on Mount Carmel, or destroy a company of fifty soldiers with fire from heaven, is the same man who made a poor widow's meager supply of food continue for many months and who restored her son to life. The fiery preacher who told the Israelites they should only worship the God of Israel was the same man who could show, in miracles of compassion, that this same God loved people. There were even more such "domestic miracles" connected with his successor, Elisha.

In a certain town the people complained to Elisha that their water was bad, and the prophet "healed" it by putting salt into the spring, rendering it drinkable from that time on (2 Kings 2:21–22). A woman who provided a room for Elisha to stay in was childless and her husband was old. Elisha promised her she would conceive; she doubted, feeling the prophet was mocking her, but she did indeed bear a child. Years later when the child died, the grieving woman went to tell the prophet, who brought the boy back to life. During a famine, some of the prophets gathered some wild plants, not knowing if they were edible, and put them into the stew. When the stew proved to be poisonous, Elisha rendered the stew edible. When his followers decided to build a larger home to dwell in, one of the axheads flew off and landed in the Jordan River, but Elisha made it float to the water's surface. An admirer brought Elisha twenty loaves of bread, and Elisha told him to feed the people with it. Miraculously, the loaves multiplied enough to feed a hundred people.

Elisha exuded such divine power that he even worked a miracle after he died. When some Israelites were burying a man, some Moabite raiders passed through and the Israelites panicked and dumped the body into Elisha's grave. When the body came into contact with Elisha's bones, the man came to life again.

In the midst of the violent stories of wicked, idol-worshipping kings, the miracles of the two great prophets stand out. While we remember the dramatic episodes such as Elijah being taken into heaven, we should not forget these miracles of compassion, evidence that God was still at work among his people, lightening the loads of common folk. To many people who came in contact with the two prophets, God seemed to be working as a "still, small voice" more than in a mighty wind or an earthquake. The life of Elisha is a kind of preview of the miracles of compassion that Jesus would perform centuries later.

Naaman the Leper

One miracle story concerning Elisha has a "sting" at the end. In 2 Kings 5 we learn that Naaman, commander of the armies of Aram, had leprosy. Naaman's Israelite slave girl told her owners that a prophet in Israel could cure leprosy. Naaman left for Israel, carrying gold, silver and ten sets of clothing. He made his way to the home of Elisha, who sent him a message: Wash yourself seven times in the Jordan River and you will be healed. Naaman was not happy. He had expected the prophet to do something dramatic—call upon God and make the leprosy vanish instantly. And weren't the rivers of Aram better than that pathetic little Jordan? He was furious, but his servants softened him: Wouldn't it be wise to *try* what the prophet said?

So Naaman dipped himself seven times in the Jordan. "And his flesh was restored and became clean like that of a young boy." Naaman went back to Elisha and praised Israel's God. He asked the prophet to accept a gift. Elisha would not—miracles were not for profit.

But Elisha's servant Gehazi was greedy. He followed after Naaman and told him that Elisha had two guests, so could Naaman please give them some silver and two sets of clothing? Naaman gladly obliged. Gehazi returned home, pleased that his lie had worked—or so he thought.

Elisha at times had the power to see things at a distance. When Gehazi returned, Elisha told him he had seen him at Naaman's chariot. He knew Gehazi had not only lied but also took money for a miracle. Gehazi received an appropriate punishment: He was struck with leprosy.

JEHU, FAST AND FURIOUS

Ahab's wicked descendants were still ruling Israel. Elisha sent one of his servants with a flask of oil to meet a military commander named Jehu and anoint him king. The servant did so, telling Jehu he was to exterminate Ahab's family completely. The anointing was done in secret, and after it was done, Jehu's fellow soldiers wondered what the "madman" Elisha had wanted with Jehu. When Jehu told them he had been anointed king, his fellow soldiers reacted speedily: "Jehu is king!"

Israel must have been dissatisfied with the rule of Joram, Ahab's son, for Jehu had no trouble gathering followers. As it happened, Jehu and Joram met at the very piece of land Ahab had taken from Naboth. The king of Judah, Ahaziah, was present also. Jehu killed them both, for Ahaziah was related to Ahab's family. (Note to the reader: This Ahaziah is not the son of Ahab mentioned earlier in the chapter. This Ahaziah was king of Judah, but since he was the son of Ahab's daughter Athaliah, and thus the grandson of Ahab, he was considered part of Ahab's family. The names in 2 Kings can sometimes be confusing. See chart on page 129.)

See chart on page 129.)

The prize in this purge of idol-worshippers was the queen, Jezebel. Knowing what fate awaited her, she "painted her eyes, arranged her hair"—not to seduce him, but to die looking like a queen. Seeing Jehu enter the palace gates, she tossed him a cutting remark: "Did Zimri have peace, who slew his master?" She was reminding him of Zimri, who killed the king of Israel but died himself only seven days later. A man who murdered kings could never feel secure as king himself.

Jehu shouted to her servants: "Who is on my side?" They pushed her from a window, and the horses trampled her underfoot. Later, when Jehu sent his men to bury her—"for she was a king's daughter"—they found nothing but her skull and hands and feet. Dogs had eaten her—as Elijah predicted. Her name passed into our language as the name for any wicked woman, particularly a power-hungry one. She is definitely the most evil female in the Bible.

Afterward, the rest of Ahab's family was exterminated. But Jehu set himself a bigger task: ending Baal worship. He did so with a clever lie. He announced that he was an enthusiastic follower of Baal and was holding a great feast in his honor. The temple of Baal was filled with all the devotees of the fertility god. Jehu made sure there were no followers of the Lord present. He ordered eighty soldiers to slaughter all the Baal worshippers inside the temple. Then they tore down the temple, "and people have used it for a latrine to this day" (2 Kings 10:27). For stamping out Baal worship in Israel, God promised Jehu his dynasty would endure for another four generations.

Jehu's story, told in 2 Kings 9 and 10, is a violent but fascinating tale, well told. It deserves to be better known. If you have the time, read both chapters through. Bear in mind that in the ancient world, voting a bad official out of office was not an option. Once in power, an evil ruler could only be removed by force, and it was prudent to eliminate his family as a possible line of succession. If you find the violence distasteful, be thankful our own political processes are more civilized.

PURGES AND PUNISHMENTS

Jehu had not quite exterminated Ahab's wicked family. Ahab's daughter, Athaliah, had married the king of Judah. Jehu had killed her son, Ahaziah, and she set herself as ruler in Judah. To eliminate rivals, she proceeded to destroy the entire royal family. But her daughter managed to send Ahaziah's infant son Joash into hiding in the temple.

For six years, Queen Athaliah ruled Judah. In the seventh year, her enemies—and she had many—decided Joash was old enough to take his rightful place as king. Jehoiada the priest brought out Joash and anointed and crowned him. A crowd of supporters clapped and blew trumpets. Athaliah rushed to the scene, shouting "Treason!" Soldiers dragged her from the temple and killed her. Jehoiada had the king and people swear to obey the Lord and tear down their Baal idols.

Even though she was a woman, Athaliah—who as unscrupulous and power-hungry as her wicked parents—was infecting Judah with the same idolatry and evil as Ahab and Jezebel had done in Israel. She had to be eliminated. Everything connected with Ahab's family seemed tainted.

Joash, who was only seven, reigned as a decent king and took pains to repair the Lord's temple in Jerusalem. Sadly, at the age of forty-seven he was assassinated by some of his officials. His son, Amaziah, executed the men who killed his father—but in accordance with the Law of Moses, he did not kill any other members of their families, since the Law taught that children should not suffer for their parents' sins (Deuteronomy 24:16). Apparently his relative compassion was regarded by his enemies as weakness, for, like his father, he was assassinated. His son, Azariah, was not assassinated, but he did contract leprosy and had to abdicate in favor of his son. Also, as a leper, he could not enter the Lord's temple.

Back in Israel, the Lord kept his promise to Jehu: His dynasty reigned for four generations. Under Jehu's great-grandson, Jeroboam, Israel expanded back to the wide boundaries it had under David, and Jeroboam's reign was good for the land—Israel's last spell of peace and security. The last descendant of Jehu, Zechariah, reverted to the old pattern, and he was assassinated after only six months. His assassin reigned one month. The next assassin, Menahem, reigned ten years, but faced an imposing enemy: Assyria, to which he had to pay a huge tribute. Worse things were to come from Assyria.

Judah, after a few decent kings (some of whom were assassinated), got a thoroughly reprehensible one, Ahaz. He is the first case of a king of Judah sacrificing some of his own children (2 Kings 16:3). Defeated in battle by the armies of Aram, he offered sacrifices to Aram's gods, using the perverse logic that if they had aided Aram, they would aid him also—which did not happen (2 Chronicles 28:23). Like the kings of Israel, he found himself looting the national treasury to pay tribute money to Assyria.

Hoshea, king of Israel, ceased to pay tribute to Assyria. Instead, he flirted with the king of Egypt, hoping an alliance with him would rid him of the Assyrian burden. He

Aggressive Assyria

Assyria was one of several empires to occupy the area known as Mesopotamia, which means "between the rivers" and refers to the area between the two great rivers, the Tigris and Euphrates, roughly corresponding to the nation of Iraq today. Assyria's great capital was Nineveh, on the Tigris. Assyria lay to the northeast of Israel, and as it expanded, it was inevitable that the aggressive empire—known for its brutal warriors—would give Israel grief. Sometime during Jehu's reign (841–814 BC), Israel began paying tribute to Assyria. (In fact, a commemorative black stone in Assyria shows Jehu—or his ambassador—kneeling down before King Shalmaneser III.) The tribute continued for a while, then Assyria went through a weak period (to the relief of Israel), but then King Tiglath-Pileser III (called "Pul" in the Bible) restrengthened the empire and began demanding tribute from Israel again, and from Judah also. Later, it was Sargon II who conquered Israel and deported its people, replacing them with Assyrians.

Sennacherib, who reigned 704–681 BC, invaded Judah and frightened the king, Hezekiah, but Sennacherib's army there was destroyed by the Lord. Later kings of Assyria demanded tribute from Judah, and wicked King Manasseh of Judah probably owed his long reign to his being totally subservient to Assyria. But the mighty empire was itself conquered by the Babylonians in 604 BC. This might have been a relief to Judah, except that from then on the Babylonians menaced Judah and eventually conquered it.

The Assyrians were notoriously cruel even by the standards of ancient times, striking terror into enemies by large-scale beheadings and impalings, all made very public.

paid dearly. The king of Assyria captured him and laid siege to Samaria. Finally he took the capital and deported the people. The Assyrians followed their usual policy: Conquer a country, deport its people and resettle it with their own. The few Israelites remaining in the land found themselves outnumbered by pagans from various countries. In time they would intermarry with them, forming the ethnic group called the Samaritans. We will be hearing more about them later.

Thus ended the northern kingdom in 722 BC. They had brought it on themselves, as 2 Kings 17:15 says: "They followed worthless idols and themselves became worthless. They imitated the nations around them although the Lord had ordered them 'Do not do as they do,' and they did the things the Lord had forbidden them to do." The name *Israel* would not be used to refer to a nation again until 1948.

PUTTING THE WORD TO WORK

1. Rehoboam is a classic case of an arrogant, spoiled man deliberately antagonizing people whom he should have treated with tact and kindness. In this he was encouraged by his like-minded friends. Have there been times in your own life when you said or did the wrong thing, urged on by friends or relatives? Were you able to make amends later?

2. Elijah's "up" moment on Carmel was followed by his "down" time when he fled from Jezebel, yet he recovered his faith and courage. What were some times in your own life when your faith "crashed" temporarily? What helped you recover? Did you experience any "still, small voice" moments at those times?

3. Elijah and Elisha were both powerful and courageous prophets, yet both performed miracles of compassion for people they encountered. Think of faith-filled people you have known who consistently performed small acts of kindness in their lives. How can their actions inspire you in your own life?

4. Are there any rulers in today's lesson that you find admirable? Can you take heart in your own life knowing that throughout Israel's sordid history, God kept communicating through the prophets and never gave up on his people?

5. Spouses sometimes can lead their partners to embrace their beliefs, but as we see in the case of Jezebel, this is not always a good thing. Do you know a couple where one spouse seemed to lead the other down a different path? Was it a case (as it seems to have been with Ahab and Jezebel) of the stronger personality leading the weaker? Could anyone ever use their influence to change what *you* believe?

To Babylon and Back

**AT THE
HEART
OF IT ALL
TODAY**
Faith can thrive anywhere because God is everywhere. That is the key lesson in this chapter about exile and persecution, with people of faith learning to "bloom where they're planted" while others try to rebuild a faith community in the promised land.

Yesterday's chapter ended on a sad note: The northern kingdom, Israel, had been conquered by the brutal Assyrian empire, its people deported and idol-worshipping foreigners settled in the land. The southern kingdom, Judah, was to suffer a similar fate, but with a happier ending.

At the time Assyria conquered Israel (722 BC),

> **KEY PASSAGES TO READ TODAY**
>
> **2 Kings 22:1—23:30;
> 24:20—25:12**
> **Daniel 3**
> **Ezra 8**

the king of Judah was the young Hezekiah, son of the idol-worshipping Ahaz, whose reign had been one unceasing, flagrant scandal. Happily, Hezekiah was radically different from his father. He destroyed idols throughout the land, believing that Israel had been punished for its idolatrous ways, and tried to be faithful to God. (As a sign of how idolatrous the people had become, they were worshipping the bronze snake Moses had

KEY TERM FOR TODAY ## Persecution

Persecution of people for their customs or religious beliefs is as old as history, but it really flourished in the period of today's chapter, mainly because so many Jews lived in exile in Babylonia and Persia. Persecution was not only the result of their being different, but of their being successful. We see this especially in the Book of Daniel, where Daniel and his three friends rise high in the Babylonian bureaucracy, provoking envy, then persecution, among the Babylonians. Since their enemies could hardly criticize their diligence, they fell back on denigrating their "odd" religious customs, then suggested such "odd" people might be disloyal traitors. Unofficial persecution—gossip and mockery and petty harassment—in time resulted in official persecution, done with government backing. As Jesus would point out to his followers, good people have always been mocked and harassed by others, all the way back to the time of Noah. The "righteous remnant," an idea we have met with many times in the Bible, could always count on being the persecuted remnant—but always God sustains his faithful ones.

made centuries earlier. Hezekiah destroyed it.) After going for centuries and not observing Passover, Hezekiah celebrated the great holy day, even sending messengers north to Israel to invite the people there (those who had not been deported by the Assyrians) to join in the Passover, and some did (2 Chronicles 29). Spiritually, Judah was back on the right path.

Politically, things were not going so well. Assyria proved to be a thorn in Hezekiah's side, and the mighty king Sennacherib captured some of Judah's cities after Hezekiah stopped paying tribute. In 2 Kings 18 we read of Sennacherib's military commander going to Jerusalem and demanding that Hezekiah surrender. (This is the first mention in the Bible of the language called Aramaic, by the way. It was a language the Assyrians and the people of Judah both understood.) Naturally the commander reminded Hezekiah of what had happened to Israel. Hezekiah, to his credit, depended on God to defend him from the Assyrians, and God repaid his faith in a dramatic way. He was encouraged by the great prophet Isaiah, who had a revelation from the Lord: something would happen to force Sennacherib to return to his own country. "The zeal of the Lord Almighty will accomplish this" (2 Kings 19:31). The angel of the Lord by night destroyed 185,000 men in the Assyrian camp. Sennacherib, as Isaiah foretold, departed. Back in Assyria, worshipping in the temple of his god Nisroch, he was killed by two of his own sons.

Sometime later Hezekiah became deathly sick, and Isaiah told him he would not recover. Hezekiah prayed and wept bitterly. As proof that prayers are not in vain, the Lord told Isaiah that the king would recover—and reign another fifteen years.

As wise and faithful as Hezekiah was, he made one grievous mistake: He received ambassadors from the king of Babylon—and showed them all the treasures in his palace complex. When they departed, the prophet Isaiah delivered an unpleasant message to the king: In the future, Hezekiah's descendants would be taken off to Babylon, and the treasures Hezekiah had shown the Babylonians would all be taken away. Hezekiah consoled himself that this would not happen in his lifetime. But Isaiah's prophecy did indeed come to pass.

Hezekiah's faithfulness to God was not repeated by his wayward son, Manasseh. In his long reign (fifty-five years), Manasseh engaged in every form of idol worship and even sacrificed his own son in the fire. He dabbled in sorcery and the occult and also placed an Asherah pole in the Lord's temple. "Manasseh also shed so much innocent blood that he filled Jerusalem from end to end" (2 Kings 21:16). However, 2 Chronicles 33 reports an episode that 2 Kings omits: As punishment for his wickedness, Manasseh was captured by the Assyrians ("with a hook through his nose") and carried off in chains. In his distress he repented, and after the Assyrians freed him, he came back to Judah a changed man.

Manasseh's son Amon was notoriously wicked, so much so that his officials assassinated him after he had reigned only two years. He was succeeded by his eight-year-old son, Judah's last good king, and one of the great men of the Bible, Josiah. "He did what was right in the eyes of the Lord and walked in all the ways of his father David, not turning aside to the right or to the left" (2 Kings 22:2).

REFORM, THEN DISASTER

In the eighteenth year of Josiah's reign, a nation-changing event occurred: The high priest Hilkiah found the Book of the Law in the temple. Bible scholars agree that the Book of the Law was probably the Book of Deuteronomy, the last of the five books of Moses. Unfortunately, 2 Kings does not explain how the Book came to be in the temple, or why it had been neglected for many years. But it is clear that the finding of it led to a major spiritual revival under Josiah. The Book was read aloud to the king. He was deeply moved—the Book was a painful reminder of how badly the nation's faith and morals had declined. God had blessed Moses and given Canaan to the people, and what ingrates they had been! God had given them his Law to live by and they had totally forgotten it!

Josiah assembled Judah's elders and read to them from the Book. The elders pledged themselves to abide by God's laws. Josiah instituted a sweeping religious reform. He destroyed all the pagan temples and idols, including the horrible place called Topheth, where people (including some of Judah's kings) had sacrificed their own children to the god Molech. He even tore down a temple to Ashtoreth that had been built by none other than Solomon himself. And at long last he destroyed the Bethel shrine that king Jeroboam had built centuries earlier as a rival to the temple in Jerusalem. Like Hezekiah before him, he ordered the people to celebrate the Passover in remembrance of what God had done for them.

The Persian king Darius I digs a canal to connect the Nile with the Red Sea, continuing work begun nearly a century ago by the pharaoh Neco.

515 BC
Completion of the temple
(Ezra 6:13–18)

499–479 BC
Persian wars against Greek states.

473 BC
Esther made queen of Persian king Xerxes
(Esther).

460–445 BC
First Peloponnesian War

445–443 BC
Restoration of Jerusalem's walls
(Nehemiah 2–6)

399 BC
Death of Greek philosopher Socrates

"Neither before nor after Josiah was there a king like him who turned to the Lord as he did—with all his heart and with all his soul and with all his strength, in accordance with the Law of Moses" (2 Kings 23:25). Josiah died at the age of thirty-nine, his life cut short when he was killed in battle with the Pharaoh of Egypt. Josiah's son reigned only three months before being captured by the same Pharaoh, named Neco, who put another son of Josiah, Jehoiakim, on the throne and imposed a huge tribute on Judah.

However, a new foreign enemy was about to do even more horrible things. The Babylonian empire had conquered the Assyrians. The Babylonian king, Nebuchadnezzar, invaded Judah, imposing tribute. When Judah ceased to pay the tribute, Nebuchadnezzar had an excuse to invade the land. The Babylonians marched against Jerusalem and took the new king, Jehoiachin, prisoner—not only him, but many of the important people of Jerusalem, including the soldiers and artisans, leaving mostly the common folk. The Babylonians also stripped the temple and the palace of all its treasures—fulfilling the prophecy of Isaiah, who had scolded king Hezekiah for showing all the treasures to Babylonian ambassadors.

KINGS OF JUDAH	PROPHETS
Hezekiah 716–687 BC *(2 Kings 18–20)*	Isaiah [reign of Hezekiah]
Manasseh 687–642 BC *(2 Kings 21:1–18)*	
Amon 642–640 BC *(2 Kings 21:19–25)*	
Josiah 640–609 BC *(2 Kings 22, 23:1–30)*	Zephaniah [reign of Josiah]
	Nahum [reign of Josiah]
	Habakkuk [reign of Josiah]
Joahaz 3 months in 609 BC *(2 Kings 23: 31–34)*	Jeremiah [reigns of Josiah, Jehoiachin, Zedekiah]
Jehoakim 609–598 BC *(2 Kings 23:35—24:7)*	
Jehoiachin 598 BC *(2 Kings 24:8–17)*	
Zedekiah 598–587 BC *(2 Kings 24:18—25:7)*	
	c. 586 BC Ezekiel
	c. 586 BC Obadiah
	c. 539 BC Daniel
	c. 520 BC Haggai
	c. 520 BC Zechariah
	c. 460 BC Malachi
	c. 400 BC Joel

The Babylonians replaced Jehoiachin with Judah's last king, Zedekiah. Zedekiah stopped paying tribute to Babylon, after he joined a coalition of other nearby nations in rebelling against Babylon. In 588 BC Nebuchadnezzar laid siege to Jerusalem. The city was taken in July 586 BC. The Lord's temple was burned after all its furnishings were looted. For rebelling against them, the Babylonians killed Zedekiah's sons in front of him, then gouged out his eyes and carried him in chains to Babylon. Along with him went most of the population of Judah, except the poorest. "So Judah went into captivity, away from her land" (2 Kings 25:21). We learn from the books of the prophets that the neighboring nations nearby, Edom, Ammon and Moab, took advantage of the devastation to do some plundering—they were the "jackals" moving after the "lions" (Nebuchadnezzar and the Babylonians) who had done the killing.

The Babylonians appointed a governor, Gedaliah, over the people who remained behind, but when he was assassinated, most of the remaining people (including the great prophet Jeremiah) fled to Egypt for fear of the Babylonians. God's chosen people were scattered everywhere—Assyria, Babylonia, and Egypt. Only a handful went on living in the land he had promised them—promised on the condition that they be true to their covenant with him.

This was the beginning of the period known as the Exile, or the Babylonian Captivity. Though it seemed like a tragedy at the time, good would come of it. God had not abandoned his people.

CULTURAL INSIGHTS

Kings vs. Chronicles

Anyone who has ever read through the entire Bible will probably tell you how incredibly bored he was with 1 and 2 Chronicles. One reason he probably found it boring is that it repeats so much of the previous books, 1 and 2 Kings. Also, Chronicles has tedious genealogies and lists of people that are hardly inspiring to read. If you want to know the history of Israel, Kings is definitely more of a pleasure to read than Chronicles. Still, Chronicles does contain some interesting stories that were not included in Kings. In fact, when the book was translated from Hebrew into Greek, it was given the title *Paraleipomenon*, meaning "leftovers" or "appendices." We have included a handful of those "leftover" stories, those that were not included in Kings.

Chronicles was written later than Kings and for a different purpose. When it was written, the northern kingdom of Israel had ceased to exist, so Chronicles shows no interest in the kings of Israel, only the kings of Judah. Thus it also omits the stories of the prophets Elijah and Elisha, since their ministry was in Israel. Chronicles tends to "clean up" history—or, to be precise, leave out some of the unpleasant parts. In Chronicles, there is no rebellion against David, and hardly anything negative said about his reign. Likewise, Solomon's backsliding is not mentioned, but lavish details of the temple he built are included. So, essentially, Chronicles takes the history from Samuel and Kings, omits the material about the northern kingdom (Israel), eliminates unflattering stories about David and Solomon, and adds a few stories about the kings of Judah—and *lots* of information about the temple and the people who served in it. Incidentally, the author of Chronicles also wrote Ezra and Nehemiah, so he continued the national history beyond what is covered in Kings.

By the way, if you are using the King James Version, you may run across verses like this: "Now the rest of the acts of Rehoboam, and all that he did, are they not written in the book of the chronicles of the kings of Judah?" (1 Kings 14:29). Some people think the "chronicles" referred to here are the Chronicles in the Bible. They are not—these are the court histories that were used as sources when writing 1 and 2 Kings. More recent translations of the Bible have tried to clarify this, using "annals" instead of "chronicles" in verses like these.

Nebuchadnezzar

Other than the Pharaoh of Exodus, no king was more of a villain in the history of Israel than Nebuchadnezzar, king of Babylon, who destroyed the temple and carried the Jews into exile. The mighty king reigned 605–562 BC. We know a lot about him not only from the Bible, but from the Babylonian Chronicle, which brags that when he found a king of Judah who would not pay him tribute, he would replace him with a king who would. He banished many of the people of Judah in 597 BC to give them a taste of what would happen if they rebelled, and ten years later he deported many more after burning the temple—and taking its sacred furnishings for use in the temples of his gods Bel and Marduk. In the course of time, when the Babylonians were conquered by the Persians, those temple vessels he carted off to Babylon were returned to Jerusalem and placed in a new temple.

Like all tyrants, he was a great builder, and one of his projects was considered one of the Seven Wonders of the World, the famous Hanging Gardens of Babylon, built for his favorite wife. He made the whole city of Babylon on the Euphrates River a thing of wonder, and visitors often gasped at the awesome buildings, especially the famous gateway of Ishtar. But in time, as some of the prophets predicted, his capital became a ruin.

Bible readers often wonder: Is the episode of Nebuchadnezzar's madness, told in Daniel 4, true? The Babylonian Chronicle does not mention it—but then, it is the sort of occurrence that official court records would not include.

DANIEL, YOUNG AND WISE

Among the people carried off to Babylon was a young, attractive and wise-for-his-age man named Daniel. The Babylonians had an astute policy of making good use of their conquered peoples: They took the young ones who showed some aptitude and trained them to be court officials. This not only made them useful, but also ensured they would not rebel or make trouble—or try to go back to their homelands. They underwent a three-year internship, during which they were given Babylonian names. Thus Daniel and his three friends—Hananiah, Mishael and Azariah—were renamed Belteshazzar, Shadrach, Meshach and Abed-nego. The new names all contained the names of Babylonian gods, whereas the men's original names all contained El (God) or Yah (the Lord). Their names had been changed, but their spiritual allegiance had not, as the Babylonians would soon learn.

Daniel found himself in a situation like that of Joseph in the Book of Genesis: captive in a foreign country, able to interpret dreams—and confronted with a king who had a dream no one could decipher. King Nebuchadnezzar summoned his court astrologers and magicians to have them interpret the dream—and none could. (The fact that he threatened to cut them into pieces and reduce their houses to rubble might have affected their concentration.) Daniel was sent for and was horrified to learn the king had ordered all the court wise men executed. Daniel had himself taken to Nebuchadnezzar, assuring him that the power of interpreting the dream lay not in man's wisdom but in the power of God.

With that, Daniel interpreted the dream. The king had dreamed of a statue of a man. The head was gold, the chest and arms were silver, the belly and thighs were bronze, the legs were iron—and the feet were a mix of iron and clay. A rock struck the statue's feet and toppled it. (The term "feet of clay" comes from this story, although in fact the feet were a mix of clay with iron.)

What did it all mean? The king himself—or, more precisely, the empire of Babylon—was the golden head. It would be followed by another, inferior, kingdom, represented by the silver. Then a third, inferior still, would follow, represented by the bronze. Then a powerful empire, represented by the iron, would arise. Then that kingdom would be divided, represented by the mix of iron and clay in the feet. The rock that smashed the statue represented a kingdom that would never end. Readers have been debating for centuries just which kingdoms or empires, ancient or modern, the metals represented. Other than knowing that the gold represented Babylon, there is no certainty here. However, the promise of a kingdom that will smash all the others and never end—the

---

CULTURAL INSIGHTS

Aramaic

Most of the Old Testament is written in Hebrew, but some of the later parts—in Daniel, Ezra and Jeremiah—are in a related language called Aramaic. Aramaic and Hebrew were, roughly speaking, similar in the way that, say, Spanish and Italian are. Aramaic was widely used as an international language in the period we are studying today, and the Bible's first mention of it is in 2 Kings 18, where Hezekiah's court converses with the Assyrian messengers in Aramaic. This passage indicates that at that time, most of the Jews still spoke Hebrew. That would change during the Babylonian captivity, since Jews had to learn Aramaic to communicate with the Babylonians and Persians among whom they lived. In the Book of Nehemiah we see that by the time the Jews returned from their exile, the Hebrew writings had to be translated for them. Aramaic had become their main language during the exile and would remain so. In the New Testament period, Jesus and his followers spoke Aramaic.

Hebrew had ceased to be the language spoken in the street by the common people, but the Scriptures were in Hebrew, and the Jewish scholars continued to learn Hebrew in order to read and comment on the sacred writings. This had an effect which is obvious in the New Testament: The intellectuals looked down on the common folk, who did not know the Scriptures in Hebrew. Paraphrases of the Scriptures into Aramaic were known as the Targums and were widely used, but were considered inferior to the Hebrew originals.

Jew

In the Bible passages we are studying today, we encounter the word Jew for the first time. It refers to a person of *Judah*, the kingdom that still existed after the northern kingdom, Israel, had been conquered and scattered by the Assyrians. The people of Judah were still aware that they were the descendants of Jacob—Israel—and they still referred to themselves as "children of Israel." In fact, they rarely referred to themselves as Jews, except in interacting with non-Jews, to whom the term *Israelite* had no meaning, since the nation of Israel had ceased to exist. The word *Jew* occurs only in the latest books of the Old Testament—Jeremiah, Daniel, Esther, Ezra and Nehemiah.

The actual Hebrew word was *yehudi*, which in Aramaic was *yehudai*, in Greek *ioudaios*, and in Latin *judaeus*.

"rock" kingdom—is something that gives us hope. Many readers believe that the rock is Christ, king of an eternal kingdom.

For interpreting the dream, Daniel was rewarded as Joseph had been. The king lavished gifts on him and made him and his three companions administrators in the empire. All seemed well. Four Jewish captives in Babylon were secure and prosperous.

But a monarch's pathological vanity intervened. Nebuchadnezzar set up an enormous gold statue—of himself. As a sign of his many subjects' loyalty, they had to fall down and worship the statue—or be thrown alive into a fiery furnace. Most people, of course, complied with the order. But some of the king's officials pointed out that Daniel's three friends—referred to as "some Jews"—had not. Furious, the king summoned the three. They assured him that their God would rescue them from the fiery furnace—but even if he did not, they still would not worship the golden idol of the king. The king had the furnace heated even hotter—and had the three bound and thrown into it. When the Babylonians looked into the furnace, they saw the three, alive and healthy—and also a fourth man who "looks like a son of the gods" (Daniel 3:25). The king was so impressed that he issued a decree: No one was to say a word against the God of Shadrach, Meshach, and Abed-nego, "for no other god can save in this way." God had rescued his persecuted people, and not for the first or last time in history.

DREAM ON, MAD KING

The king had another puzzling dream, and again Daniel interpreted it. An enormous, fruitful tree that provided shade and shelter represented Nebuchadnezzar himself. The "messenger, a holy one" who came down and gave the order to chop down the tree was a messenger from God. Nebuchadnezzar would be driven out of his court, away from all human contact, living like a beast in the wilds. Exactly a year later, the dream came to pass. "He was driven away from people and ate grass like cattle. His body was drenched with the dew of heaven until his hair grew like the feathers of an eagle and his nails like the claws of a bird" (4:33). In other words, the mighty king had gone insane, apparently having the powerful delusion that he was an animal. One minute resplendent on the gilded throne of power, the next minute crawling about on all fours. The tyrannical persecutor had become like a beast. In time, humbled by his experience, he praised God and his sanity returned, and he reclaimed his throne. This is the last the Bible tells us of Nebuchadnezzar.

Chapter 5 of Daniel tells of the great king's grandson, Belshazzar. He held a feast in Babylon and had the temple vessels from Jerusalem brought in, so that his wives and concubines were drinking their wine from vessels that had been dedicated to God. The merriment was interrupted by a disembodied human hand writing on the plaster wall. Belshazzar was so terrified he turned white and his knees knocked. He called in the magicians to interpret the mysterious words the hand had written. None knew what they meant. The queen sent for Daniel, who was said to have the "spirit of the gods" in him. Daniel was promised a grand reward if he could explain the words. Daniel reminded Belshazzar that the great Nebuchadnezzar had once been proud—until God humbled him. Belshazzar, so proud as to drink from the vessels of the Lord's temple, was about to be punished. This was the meaning of the Aramaic words on the wall: MENE, MENE, TEKEL, PERES. *Mene* meant "numbered"—Belshazzar's days were numbered. *Tekel* meant "weighed"—he had been weighed and found inadequate. *Peres* meant "divided"—his kingdom was to be divided among others. That very night Belshazzar was killed when the Persians conquered Babylon. This was in 539 BC. Daniel and all other Jews would have reason to rejoice, for the Persians would prove to be much better masters than the Babylonians.

Daniel's story has a universal appeal, with its exotic setting and its hero who combines the attractiveness of youth with faithful devotion to God. The fact that one of

> **DID YOU KNOW?**
>
> Catholic Bibles contain some additional chapters related to the story of Daniel. One of these is a psalm spoken by his three friends in the fiery furnace, and is often titled the *Song of the Three Young Men*. There are two stories added at the end of Daniel, one called Susanna, the other called Bel and the Dragon. These additions are considered part of the Apocrypha.

> **DID YOU KNOW?**
>
> An old legend said that when the Babylonians plundered Jerusalem, the prophet Jeremiah took the ark of the covenant and hid it in a cave for safekeeping. The legend probably had its origin in the fact that Jeremiah is the only prophet to mention the ark in his book (3:16). No one knows what actually happened to the ark, although since Jeremiah went into exile in Egypt, he might have taken it there—a notion that was at the center of the popular movie *Raiders of the Lost Ark*.

Safe in the Lions' Den

The young Daniel served as a respected official in the Babylonian empire, and when it was conquered by Persia, he held equally high office among the Persians. When the Persian king spoke of further promotions, some of the Persian officials were filled with jealousy. They hoped to find something negative about Daniel, but he had a flawless record. However, he had one vulnerable spot: his faith.

His enemies went to the king and suggested he issue a royal decree: Anyone who prays to any god—other than the king himself—in the coming thirty days would be thrown into a den of hungry lions. "Put it in writing so that it cannot be altered—in accordance with the laws of the Medes and the Persians, which cannot be repealed" (Daniel 6:8). Daniel, however, did not break his usual habit: praying three times a day, facing in the direction of Jerusalem. The jealous officials told the king—who was distressed, not angry. He had no desire to lose one of his best employees, but the "laws of the Medes and the Persians" could not be revoked. So, hesitatingly, the king had Daniel thrown into the den of lions.

The king spent a sleepless night. The next morning he went to the lions' den and called out to Daniel. To his great relief, Daniel answered: "My God sent his angel, and he shut the mouths of the lions."

You might remember this beloved story from your childhood. But did you remember how the king was so concerned about Daniel's safety? This detail makes the story even more appealing.

its main characters is one of the most famous kings in history only adds to the allure. But the main character in the story is God himself, giving evidence that though his people were conquered and exiled and persecuted, he was still with them. The God of Israel was in charge everywhere on earth. A man of faith could "bloom where he was planted."

RETURN TO THE LAND OF PROMISE

Living under a new master—Persia—the Jews would find their situation changed immediately. The Persians were more tolerant than the Babylonians, and their policy was to permit their subject people to practice their religions as they liked—as long as they did not rebel, of course. The Persians understood that persecution did *not* create loyal subjects. So in the first year of his reign, 539 BC, the Persian king Cyrus issued a decree: All Jews were free to return to their homeland and rebuild the temple of their God. They could take with them the temple vessels—the ones the Babylonians had plundered years earlier. Things were looking up for God's people.

We have to pause here and admit that the history of the Jews in this period is hard to piece together. The books of Ezra and Nehemiah tell much about this period, but the chronology is almost impossible to follow. Ezra and Nehemiah were originally one book, not two, written by the same author as 1 and 2 Chronicles, but incorporating the personal memoirs of Ezra and Nehemiah. The writer—often known as the Chronicler—was not a careful editor, nor did he seem to know the exact sequence of events. So we'll try to focus on some key events here, keeping in mind that they may not be in the right order.

One important fact to remember: Most Jews did *not* return to their homeland, nor wish to. The Babylonian Captivity had lasted almost fifty years, so nearly every adult taken into captivity had died, and of course, the children born in Babylon had no memory of life in Judah. Babylon, now under Persian control, was the only home they knew, and though they had probably heard their parents or grandparents talk about Judah and its temple—and its self-government—most had no burning desire to pack up and settle there. So most Jews remained behind in Babylon. Also, there was a large Jewish colony in Egypt, Jews who had fled there after the Babylonians conquered Judah. So at the time of resettlement, there were far more Jews in Egypt and Babylon than in the Jewish homeland. They were leaving the security of the only home they had ever known to live in a place where they would be regarded as strangers.

The first important name in the resettlement was Zerubbabel, who was a descendant of King Jehoiachin, meaning the dynasty of David lived on and was still entrusted with positions of leadership. Zerubbabel returned with the first wave of exiles and built an altar on which to offer sacrifices to God. They also celebrated the Feast of Tabernacles, so even though there was no temple yet, the people were seeing their religious rituals restored. When the foundation of the temple was laid, the people shouted for joy—but the shouts were mixed with the weeping of the old ones who remembered the glory of the temple Solomon had built (Ezra 3). Or were they weeping for joy, seeing the new temple begun? Perhaps both.

Work on the temple was slowed by the "enemies of Judah," which is what Ezra 4 calls the people who were living in the land when the exiles returned. These "enemies" were in fact the Samaritans, the descendants of the people of Israel, which had been conquered by Assyria. The Jews who had returned from exile did not want their help—and, understandably, the Samaritans resented this snubbing, so they harassed the builders and did what they could to delay the temple. Worse, they sent letters to the Persian king, reminding him that Jerusalem had always rebelled against foreign government, and that he was foolish to approve the Jews rebuilding their rebellious homeland. So the work was ordered stopped. A later king ordered the work to continue, and Ezra 6 tells of the dedication of the new temple, which was completed in 515 BC. The people celebrated the Passover, and it seemed the old faith had a new life. The new temple was smaller and less magnificent than the one Solomon built, but this "Second Temple" as it is known to historians, in fact lasted longer than the first. One thing notably missing was the ark of the covenant, which apparently was taken away from the first temple at some point by some of the foreign invaders (although it is odd that the Bible gives us no clue what happened to this important object). In place of the ark in the Holy of Holies there was a plain stone slab.

Worth noting: Ezra and Nehemiah use the term "house of God" many times to refer to the temple—more so than in all the rest of the Old Testament.

THE PURE BLOOD MOVEMENT

Several years after the Second Temple was completed, a priest and teacher named Ezra came to Jerusalem, with instructions from the king of Persia to administer justice in Judah and teach people the Law of Moses. Ezra learned to his horror that the Jews who had resettled the land had intermarried with non-Jews. Ezra was so appalled he tore the hair out of his beard. He convinced the Jews that they had done great wrong in intermarrying with unbelievers. God had been gracious enough to allow them to return to the promised land and build a new temple. They could not dare anger him now by mingling their own genes with those of pagans. In a great assembly, they swore to put away their pagan wives.

The next figure of importance is Nehemiah, a Jew who had the position of cupbearer to Artaxerxes, the king of Persia. A cupbearer was no mere servant: The position was of great importance, and it was considered an honor to hold it. (The cupbearer usually had the duty of tasting the king's food and drink to see if they were poisoned. More importantly, he was the king's confidant.) The king noticed that Nehemiah seemed depressed, and Nehemiah told him how it pained him to hear that the city of Jerusalem still was not rebuilt. The king granted his request to travel to Jerusalem and oversee the rebuilding of the city's walls. In fact, Nehemiah was the governor of the whole province of Judah. Work began, but again they were opposed by the Samaritans, who saw themselves being excluded from the faith community. The workers feared being attacked, so Nehemiah had them work in shifts—half doing the work while the other half stood guard with weapons. The workers themselves wore swords at their sides as they labored. Clearly these were dedicated men of deep faith. In fact, despite the opposition, the walls were restored in just fifty-two days. Jerusalem, the City of David, was a habitable place once more.

At a great assembly of the people, Ezra read from the Law for hours at a time, while aides translated it from Hebrew into Aramaic so the people could understand it. The Law affected the people so deeply that they wept. Nehemiah told them not to weep, for in fact this was a day of joy. The reading continued day after day until finally the people had heard every word of the Law read—and translated—for them. Once this was done, the people dedicated themselves to the Lord and confessed their own sins and the sins of their ancestors in disobeying the Lord. They swore on oath to follow the Law closely—to offer the required sacrifices, to tithe, to observe the Sabbath, to celebrate the holy days—and never to intermarry with foreigners. Nehemiah reminded the people that the great king Solomon had been led into sin by the foreign women he married.

"They excluded from Israel all who were of foreign descent" (Nehemiah 13:3). Faithful Jews had seen what happened when people of different faiths marry—Solomon being the classic example. The view of Ezra and Nehemiah wasn't a matter of hating foreigners, but of wanting to keep the faith pure so as to keep it alive. They didn't want to displease God and be taken into exile again. Their ancestors had a deficit of morality and responsibility. They intended to be different.

Ezra was and is regarded by Jews as a "second Moses," and with good reason. After the exile, the covenant community was re-established in its homeland, and Ezra drove home Moses' three most important conceptions: the chosen people, the temple and the Law. And note what the new community did *not* have: a king. Obviously they could live without one. But then and later most Jews hoped and prayed for a good, wise, strong king, one who was like David in the old days. That desire for a king was very much alive when Jesus Christ lived.

CULTURAL INSIGHTS

City Walls

In ancient time, a city without walls was inconceivable. Every city was thought of as a kind of fortress, and in case of foreign attacks (which happened often), people from the surrounding area fled into the city for protection. A common tactic in war was a siege, in which the invading army surrounded the city and waited, hoping to starve the city into surrendering. Walls had to have gates, of course, and these were a weak spot where an enemy might batter his way in. The walls, preferably made of the heaviest stone available, were wide enough to walk on and were used as lookout posts for sentries. As seen in the story of Rahab in the Book of Joshua, walls were even used as parts of homes, since Rahab's "house" and its windows were part of the walls of Jericho.

The Book of Nehemiah isn't comprehensible until you realize the importance of rebuilding the walls of Jerusalem, which was Nehemiah's main concern. In the eyes of people then, Jerusalem had no claim to be a real city unless it had walls with no gaps in them. Nehemiah's enemies saw the rebuilding of the walls as evidence that the Jews—who had snubbed them—were creating a fortress in their midst, which is why they did everything possible to delay the rebuilding. With the walls completed, the Jews seemed to be back on the road to self-government, even though technically they were still subject to the Persian empire.

Persia

In its heyday, Persia, the land that we today call Iran, ruled an empire spread as far as Greece in Europe and India in Asia. In fact, its territory included the three former empires that had oppressed Israel for centuries: Egypt, Assyria and Babylonia. It was the last of the great empires in the Old Testament and also the most humane, since the Persians were fairly tolerant of other religions and cultures, and they preferred to let conquered peoples stay in their homelands instead of deporting them. The Persian emperor Cyrus, who allowed the Jews to return home to rebuild Jerusalem, is spoken of highly in the Bible, the only foreign ruler ever referred to as the Lord's "anointed" (Isaiah 45:1).

In the period between the Old and New Testaments, Persia was conquered by the Greek leader Alexander the Great. Later Persia experienced a rebirth and was known as the Parthian Empire. At the time of Jesus' birth, the "wise men" or "magi" who came to see him were probably from Parthia.

Historians think that the Persians may have been the first people to practice crucifixion. They utilized it on a wide scale, particularly in putting down rebellions, when they would crucify hundreds of rebels along well-traveled roads. This was a practice the Romans later employed.

On a more positive note, the Jews borrowed a beautiful word from the Persians, a word we still use today: *pairidaeza*, meaning "walled garden," which we know better as *paradise*.

GENOCIDE IN PERSIA

What we've seen so far of the Persians is impressive. They were, for their times, relatively tolerant of different religions and cultures. But one interesting book of the Old Testament shows that even in a tolerant climate, intolerance can flourish. This is Esther, which has the distinction of being one of only two Old Testament books (the Song of Solomon is the other) that does not mention God. It does not mention prayer either, and it amazes some readers that a book about preserving the Jews from genocide fails to mention the Jews' God. Nonetheless, it is impossible to read the story and not see the working of God in it, watching over his persecuted people.

The story is set in Susa, one of the royal cities of Persia. The Persian king here is named Ahasuerus, which is probably the king known to history as Xerxes, who ruled 486–465 BC. The king hosts a lavish banquet for his officials, and Esther 1 supplies many details about the splendor of the setting. The king sends an order to his wife, Vashti, who is hosting a banquet for the women: Vashti is to come in and "display her beauty" for all the men. She refuses to come. The king is furious at being so openly defied in front of his officials. His advisers suggest getting rid of this disobedient wench and finding another queen—

otherwise all the women in Persia may start disobeying their husbands!

So the king mandates an empire-wide "beauty contest," in which beautiful young virgins will be brought in, sent through a sort of "charm school," then judged by the king, the winner becoming queen. Among these virgins is a Jewish girl named Esther, an orphan who is the ward of her cousin, Mordecai. Keeping her Jewishness a secret, Esther made a great impression on everyone, including the king himself, who married her. Good fortune fell on Mordecai also: He learned of an assassination plot, warned the king, and was rewarded with a post in the government.

The king had a right-hand man named Haman, who liked people to bow to him. Mordecai would not bow, and since he was known to be a Jew, Haman projected his hate for Mordecai onto all Jews. Haman convinced the king that the Jews were odd and disobedient—so why not exterminate them all? A decree was issued for the genocide, with the day set.

Mordecai and other Jews were mortified. But then, the queen was a Jew—surely she could intervene to save her own people. "Who knows but that you have come to royal position for such a time as this?" (Esther 4:14).

Esther hosted a private dinner for the king and Haman. At the dinner the queen revealed she and all her people were being threatened—by Haman. The king stormed out in anger, and Haman, terrified, pleaded with Esther for mercy. When the king walked in and saw Haman on Esther's couch, he thought he was seducing her. He had Haman hanged on a high gallows—the gallows Haman had built for the man he hated, Mordecai. Haman's estate was given to Esther and Mordecai. Mordecai took Haman's place as second-in-command to the king.

Because of court rules, a royal decree could not be revoked. The order still stood: Persian soldiers were to attack and kill all Jews. But Esther talked the king into issuing a second order: The Jews could defend themselves. Thus they killed the Persians—not all, but only those who attacked them. Among the slain were Haman's ten sons.

The jubilant Jews vowed to celebrate their triumph every year on the same day, to be known as the feast of Purim.

Esther is an interesting but also disturbing story. We can sympathize with the Jews and their fear of annihilation, but find it difficult to understand the joy of slaughtering the people who were about to slaughter them. We need to remind ourselves that the story is *pre*-Christian. The New Testament would teach a better way of dealing with enemies.

Keep in mind that there is no suggestion at all in the story that Esther or any of the other Jews in Persia wished to return to their homeland in Judea. They regarded Persia as their home and were happy there as long as they were not persecuted. Jews had learned they could serve God in any location, not just in Israel. Like Daniel in Babylon, the Jews in Persia had learned that living there could be God's will. After all, God is everywhere. In a sense, the Babylonian exile never ended, for most of the Jews deported there did not return, and from the time Nebuchadnezzar destroyed the temple in 586 BC, there would be more Jews *not* in their homeland than in it. This would have a powerful effect, centuries later, on the growth of a new religion called Christianity, which spread wherever there were Jews—to Persia, to Egypt, to faraway Rome and beyond. The scattering of the Jews—called the *Diaspora*—spread their faith far and wide, and prepared the world for another faith.

PUTTING THE WORD TO WORK

1. King Josiah's religious reform was a simple matter of "getting back to the Bible," a pattern repeated often in the history of religion. What were times in your own life, or the lives of friends, when reading the Bible deeply made some serious changes in your life?

2. The stories of Daniel and Esther both look at innocent people being persecuted for being "different." What can you learn from the examples of these two people about handling harassment and persecution?

3. The Bible presents both Ezra and Nehemiah in a favorable light. Which aspects of their reforms do you admire? Which do you find less attractive? Why?

4. Based on your reading of this chapter, do you think you would have remained in Babylon or returned with the Jews to help rebuild Judah?

5. The conflict between the Jews who returned from exile and the Samaritans who offered to help rebuild Jerusalem is a sad story of people of faith not seeing eye to eye. Think of situations in your own experience where you may have snubbed or ignored other believers who were different from you. Were your differences really more important than your similarities?

Soul Singing
THE PSALMS, PART I

AT THE HEART OF IT ALL TODAY	Every conceivable spiritual theme is found in Psalms, but today we focus on praise, thanksgiving and joy. We also look at the "royal Psalms" and see how Christians apply them not only to God but to Christ as well.

Psalms is the most-read, most-quoted, most-sung, most-chanted, most-commented-upon and probably the most-loved book of the Bible. It was loved by the Jews (and still is) and loved by the first Christians as well, which is evident in the New Testament, where is it quoted more often than any other book of the Old Testament. Although Israel regarded the Torah—the first five books of the Bible—as the most important writings, the Psalms had a special place in their affections. People who would never dream of sitting down to leaf through Leviticus or Numbers can open the Psalms anywhere and find inspiration. Part of the Psalms' appeal is how "user-friendly" they are—that is, most people can read and enjoy them without footnotes or commentaries. However, we'll devote two chapters to the Psalms in the hope that you can enrich your understanding of—and pleasure in—the Bible's "sacred songbook."

> **KEY PASSAGES TO READ TODAY**
>
> Psalms 1; 19; 42; 84; 103; 104; 110; 119:1–16

The Hebrew name for the book is *Tehillim*, meaning "hymns" or "praises." Our word Psalms is from the Greek *psalterion*, a stringed musical instrument. A *psalm* was a song written to be accompanied by an instrument. All the Psalms have been set to music countless times, and they are also chanted or spoken around the world. In fact, if you thumb through Psalms you will notice some of them have directions to be sung to a par-

KEY TERM FOR TODAY ## Hallelujah

This familiar term in Hebrew is *Hallelu Yah*, "praise Yah," *Yah* being a form of *Yahweh*, God's name (and remember, in times past *J* was often pronounced with a *Y* sound). Most English Bibles use *the* LORD instead of *Yah*, so in most Bibles you find "praise the Lord" instead of "Hallelujah." The phrase occurs forty-two times in Psalms, and some people have referred to Psalms as the "Book of Hallelujahs." The 1537 Matthew's Bible published in England translated Hallelujah as "praise the Everlasting."

The Psalms are unique in being written over a period of six hundred years or more. Probably the earliest are from the time of David (c. 1000 BC), although one Psalm is said to be by Moses, who lived much earlier. Many of the Psalms were written for use in the first temple (Solomon's), which was completed in 960 BC and destroyed in 586 BC, and many others were written for the second temple, which was completed in 515 BC.

640–560 BC
Solon, Greek lawgiver

c. 628–c. 551 BC
Zoroaster, Persian religious founder

606 BC
Assyrian Empire is conquered by Babylonia.

Lao-tzu, Chinese philosopher, born

ticular melody—for example, Psalm 59 is marked "To 'Do Not Destroy' " and Psalms 45 and 80 are both marked "To 'Lilies.' "

The Psalms cover every type of emotion experienced in the life of faith: praise (God is great), gratitude (thank you, God), supplication (help me, God), laments (I am so sad, God), doubt (why do the wicked prosper, God?), even curses (hurt my enemies, God). These are broad categories, and they overlap in many Psalms, some of them mixing praise and gratitude, some Psalms starting out as laments and ending as praise, some mingling supplication and gratitude, and so on.

These writings are very emotional. In fact, *the Bible as a whole is an extremely emotional book*. The people of ancient Israel were like most people in ancient times: They felt things deeply and did not try to suppress their feelings. Later chapters will look at books like Proverbs that praise self-control. Is this a contradiction, some parts of the Bible preaching self-control, and other parts running red with emotion? No contradiction at all. The self-control preached in Proverbs and elsewhere is a matter of reining in our most destructive urges—controlling our tongue so that our anger doesn't get us into trouble, controlling our physical urges so that sex, alcohol and the love of pleasure don't lead us astray. But there is nothing in the Bible urging us to hold back our emotions from God—or our emotions *about* God.

And at this point, let's state something that you have probably noticed already: In the Bible, God is very emotional. He is at times "jealous" and "angry," but also "merciful" and "forgiving," and he "delights" in people who do his will. The God of the Bible is not some cold, detached Being far off in space or on some mountaintop. Suppressing our emotions does not make us more like God—far from it! Greek philosophers like Plato and Aristotle thought of God as the "unmoved Mover" of the world, a Being too lofty to possess emotions like human beings do. The God the Psalmists prayed to, the God that Jesus called "Father," is not the god of the philosophers. He is a God of deep feelings, which is why the best parts of the Bible run rich with emotion.

I JUST HAVE TO SAY, YOU'RE GREAT

Human beings have the need to praise something or someone. We notice it in children, who rarely just *like* something, but usually *love* it, and will praise it to the skies—"I just *love* ice cream," "I just *love* this TV show," "I *love* Disney World." They can't resist telling others how much they *love* something—and neither can adults. When a person is in love with someone, they have to tell that person, and tell others. Praise is as human as breathing. Part of our pleasure in something is praising it. It is a kind of reflex, the way cats purr when they are content. When we adore something, we will express it—in words, but also in body language, in music, in any form possible. An old Christian catechism says man's chief goal is to glorify God and enjoy him forever—and in the view of the praise Psalms, glorifying and enjoying him are the same thing.

In the Psalms we don't encounter praise of small things; what is being praised is The Greatest Thing of All, God. "I will praise you, O Lord, with all my heart; I will tell of

---

Parallelism

The Psalms are poems, and poems and prose are different. We think of poetry as having rhyme and rhythm. Hebrew had no rhymes, but did have rhythm. But it also had what we might call "poetic effects," ways of phrasing that made the poem easier to memorize. One of these poetic effects is parallelism. This takes several forms. One is stating the same idea twice, in different words:

> The One enthroned in heaven laughs;
> the Lord scoffs at them (Psalm 2:4).
> You set aside all your wrath
> and turned from your fierce anger (Psalm 85:3).

It can also consist of stating something and then its opposite:

> The ox knows his master,
> the donkey his owner's manger,
> but Israel does not know,
> my people do not understand (Isaiah 1:3).

It can also take the form of simile, a comparison using "as" or "like":

> As a father has compassion on his children,
> so the Lord has compassion on those who fear him (Psalm 103:13).

One of the beauties of the Psalms and other poetic sections of the Old Testament is that parallelism "translates" better than other poetic effects. Meter, rhyme, alliteration, etc., are almost impossible to translate from the original, but parallelism isn't. The Psalms retain their poetry and power in whatever language they are translated into. Jesus himself used parallelism:

> For in the same way you judge others, you will be judged,
> and with the measure you use, it will be measured to you (Matthew 7:2).
> Do not give dogs what is sacred;
> do not throw your pearls to pigs (Matthew 7:6).

---

all your wonders" (9:1). "The Lord lives! Praise be to my Rock! Exalted be God my Savior!" (18:46). "Sing joyfully to the Lord, you righteous; it is fitting for the upright to praise him" (33:1). "My soul will be satisfied as with the richest of foods; with singing lips my mouth will praise you" (63:5).

Praise of God is never solitary. In praising God, we want other people—and the whole universe—to join in. "Let heaven and earth praise him, the seas and all that move in them" (69:34). "Make music to the Lord with the harp, with the harp and the sound of singing.... Let the rivers clap their hands, let the mountains sing together for joy" (98:5, 8).

In many of the praise Psalms we sense a kind of *appetite for God*, an intense longing for him, the way we want to be with someone we love, feeling their absence as kind of an ache. Of course, God is never "away" from us, but our own habits and schedules (and sins) can take us away from him, so that in our quiet moments we really feel the burning desire to be *with* God. "As the deer pants for streams of water, so my soul pants for you, O God" (42:1). "I open my mouth and pant, longing for your commands" (119:131). "I have seen you in the sanctuary and beheld your power and your glory" (63:2).

You might have guessed from some of these verses that they were composed for use in the temple worship services, and the temple itself was a great inspiration for poets, since in some mysterious way it was "the house of God," even though people knew they could praise God anywhere. Later chapters will look closely at the prophets, many of whom spoke out boldly against the hypocrisy of people who lived selfish, immoral lives but who were eager participants in worship. In fact, Psalms express the pleasure of participating in the temple's worship services, but also express God's dissatisfaction with hypocritical worship. "Hear, O my people, and I will speak, O Israel, and I will testify against you: I am God, your God" (50:7). "To the wicked, God says: 'What right have you to recite my laws or take my covenant on your lips? You hate my instruction and cast my words behind you'" (50:16–17).

Several of the Psalms (120–134) are labeled as being "songs of ascents." This probably refers to their being sung by people visiting Jerusalem for the holy days of Israel, such as the Feast of Tabernacles. Israel always thought of going "up" to Jerusalem, not "up" in the north-south sense, but "up" to the place where God's house, the temple, was. The temple in Jerusalem was destroyed by the Romans in AD 70 and has never been rebuilt. Amazingly, all the Psalms that mention the temple are still being read and loved by millions of Christians and Jews around the world. One reason is that when the Psalms refer to "the house of the Lord," we don't think of the temple (even though that was the original meaning) but we think about our own house of worship—or heaven—or both.

Another reason the temple Psalms are still loved is that they rarely mention the main business of the temple, which was killing animals for sacrifices. The priests, so important in the sacrificial system, are mentioned only five times. In the Psalms, the temple is loved because it is "the house of the Lord," not because sacrifices are offered there. The people who wrote the Psalms certainly could not have imagined a temple without sacrifices—but we can, since we know faith can exist without it. The system is long gone, yet the longing to be in God's presence that we see in the temple Psalms is still very much alive. For the Psalms, what is important is the human heart focused on God: "You do not delight in sacrifice, or I would bring it; you do not take pleasure in burnt offerings. The sacrifices of God are a broken spirit; a broken and contrite heart, O God, you will not despise" (51:16–17). But the same Psalm ends with these words: "Then there will be righteous sacrifices, whole burnt offerings to delight you; then bulls will be offered on your altar" (51:19). For the writer of Psalm 51, there was no "either/or"—a person had to have the right heart *and* the right sacrifice. But once the temple was gone, the deeper truth—that the repentant heart was what mattered—still remained.

Some of the Psalms actually praise the temple itself, notably the very beautiful Psalm 84: "How lovely is your dwelling place, O Lord Almighty! My soul yearns, even faints, for the courts of the Lord; my heart and my flesh cry out for the living God.… Better is one day in your courts than a thousand elsewhere. I would rather be a doorkeeper in the house of my God than dwell in the tents of the wicked" (verses 1–2, 10). This is one of several "songs of Zion" that praise God by praising his presence in the temple on Jerusalem's Mount Zion (48, 76, 87, 122). For us, these Psalms' mentions of God's dwelling place make us think of heaven, not the temple.

DANCE AND KNOW JOY

One thing that surprises some readers is how many times the Psalms refer to dancing. We tend to associate dancing with male-female couples, but for most of human history, dancing was a group activity, often done in religious services. Remember that David "danced before the Lord with all his might" when the ark of the covenant was brought into Jerusalem (2 Samuel 6), and when the Israelites crossed the Red Sea and escaped the Egyptians, Miriam, the sister of Moses, led the women in a joyous dance. Human beings seem to have an inborn instinct to dance, especially when feeling joy. Our bodies want to move to express intense emotion, as David knew so well. "You turned my wailing into dancing; you removed my sackcloth and clothed me with joy" (Psalm 30:11). "Let them praise his name with dancing and make music to him with tambourine and harp" (149:3).

The words "joy" and "rejoice" occur more than a hundred times in Psalms. Not all the Psalms are joyful, but many are, and even the ones which start out gloomily often end with praise and rejoicing. We get the powerful impression that the life of faith is a

"Marvelous Deeds"

The Hebrew word *pala* occurs often in Psalms and, depending on the translation, is rendered "wondrous works," "marvelous deeds" and so on. One example is found in 71:17: "Since my youth, O God, you have taught me, and to this day I declare your marvelous deeds." *Pala* were things extraordinary, beyond the power of men to do, but not beyond the power, or mercy, of God. Several of the Psalms urge believers to remember God's marvelous deeds and to join in praising him for them.

joyous thing—and if troubles come (as they inevitably do), there is joy in being delivered from them, and joy in remembering how God saved us in times past. Clearly there is pleasure in knowing God, feeling so animated by him that we feel like dancing and beating on tambourines.

The Psalms seem to take as much joy in nature as we do—although to ancient Israel, *nature* wasn't what was beautiful, *God's creation* was. Think back to Genesis 1 and recall that as God created the universe, he pronounced it all "good." Even though the disobedience of Adam and Eve made the world a less pleasant place, the creation is still good, still beautiful. It is God's artwork, and it inspired some fine poetry in the Psalms. "He wraps himself in light as with a garment; he stretches out the heavens like a tent" (104:2). "The voice of the Lord is over the waters; the God of glory thunders, the Lord thunders over the mighty waters" (29:3). "He made darkness his covering, his canopy around him—the dark rain clouds of the sky" (18:11). "He provides food for the cattle and for the young ravens when they call" (147:9). This last verse is an interesting observation from an Israelite, since they regarded the raven as an "unclean" bird the people were forbidden to eat. But even the "unclean" creatures were God's creation, and he cared for them.

God isn't praised just for his beautiful creation. Most important for Israel was its awareness that God had acted on Israel's behalf in the past and would continue to do so. The most important event in the Old Testament, the Exodus from Egypt, was mentioned in many of the Psalms, notably 78: "He did miracles in the sight of their fathers in the land of Egypt, in the region of Zoan. He divided the sea and led them through; he made the water stand firm like a wall. He guided them with the cloud by day and with light from the fire all night. He split the rocks in the desert and gave them water as abundant as the seas; he brought streams out of a rocky crag and made water flow down like rivers.... He rained down manna for the people to eat, he gave them the grain of heaven. Men ate the bread of angels; he sent them all the food they could eat" (78:12–16, 24–25). This is a brief—but poetic—retelling of the crossing of the Red Sea, the pillar of cloud and pillar of fire that guided the people through the wilderness, the giving of water in the desert, the manna that kept the people fed. The same Psalm also speaks of the plagues on the Egyptians—and the ingratitude of the faithless Israelites, continually blessed and delivered by God, but always grumbling. Other notable "history Psalms" are 105, 106 and 135.

SONGS FIT FOR A KING

Some of the praise Psalms are called "songs of enthronement" because they picture God as being a king who takes his throne amid great rejoicing. One of these is Psalm 47: "Clap your hands, all you nations; shout to God with cries of joy. How awesome is the Most High, the great King over all the earth!... God reigns over the nations; God is seated on his holy throne.... the kings of the earth belong to God. He is greatly exalted" (verses 1, 8–9). Other notable enthronement Psalms are 93, 97 and 99. On the historical level, they seem to celebrate recent deliverance from a foreign enemy, such as the miraculous defeat of the Assyrians in 2 Kings 19. But Christians have read them as anticipating the future establishment of God's kingdom on earth.

The enthronement Psalms praise God as King of the earth. Some other Psalms praise an earthly king, probably one of the kings of Judah, though the king is never mentioned by name. Christians have tended to see the "royal Psalms" as "Messiah Psalms," since they seem to be prophecies of Jesus the Messiah (or Christ), and the references to the "king" or the "anointed one" seem so easy to apply to Christ.

One of the best-known royal Psalms is 2, in which God says, "You are my Son; today I have become your Father." The same Psalm also speaks of the nations that conspire "against the Lord and his Anointed One." This Psalm may have been originally written about one of Judah's kings. Kings were anointed, and when a new king was crowned, the people saw him as a kind of "son" of God. But it is impossible to read this Psalm without thinking that its deeper meaning was the "king of kings" who would be born centuries after the Psalm was written.

Psalm 72 begins, "Endow the king with your justice, O God, the royal son with your righteousness. He will judge your people with righteousness, your afflicted ones with justice." The Psalm goes on to wish for good things during his reign, bringing blessings not only on Israel, but also on all the earth. This poem might have been read aloud at the crowning of any new king—although we know from Kings and Chronicles that the real kings of Israel and Judah were a sorry lot. We reach the end of 72 and find these words: "Praise be to his glorious name forever; may the whole earth be filled with his glory. Amen and Amen." Again, the righteous king spoken of in these verses could only be the Son of God, the Christ.

It is Psalm 110 that is the most quoted Psalm in the New Testament—and 110:1 is the most quoted Old Testament verse in the New. "The LORD says to my Lord: 'Sit at my right hand until I make your enemies a footstool for your feet.' " You will understand this better if you remember that in the Old Testament, LORD is the Hebrew name Yahweh. So the verse actually says, "Yahweh [God] says to my Lord." This was probably written for the coronation of one of the kings of Judah or Israel, but after the Babylonian Captivity, when Judah no longer had a king, Jews took Psalm 110 to be a prophecy of the Messiah. The whole Psalm gives the impression that the Messiah would be a military deliverer: "The Lord will extend your mighty scepter from Zion; you will rule in the midst of your enemies. Your troops will be willing on the day of battle.... he will crush the kings on the day of his wrath." No wonder so many of the Jews were disappointed in Jesus of Nazareth, the man who said his kingdom was "not of this world." Remember that after Jesus was arrested, even his closest disciples fled. Their hopes that he would be the powerful, military Messiah of Psalm 110 were dashed.

But after Jesus' resurrection and ascension into heaven, the first Christians saw the truth: Jesus was at the right hand of God, in heaven, so 110:1 fit him perfectly: "the LORD said to my Lord, 'Sit at my right hand...'" The first Christian sermon, preached by Peter in Acts 2, quotes 110:1 and applies it to Christ. It is also quoted in Matthew, Mark, Luke and Hebrews, and Jesus at the right hand of God is also mentioned in Ephesians, Colossians and 1 Peter. Stephen, the first Christian martyr, had a vision in which he saw Christ at the right hand of God (Acts 7:56). The way the Christians understood Psalm 110:1 is one of the most radical turnarounds in the history of human thought: Instead of thinking of the Messiah as a powerful man backed by an army, driving out Israel's enemies by force, the early Christians saw that the Messiah would have a much greater power, the power of God to bring a man back from death.

A HEARTY "THANK YOU"

The line between Psalms of praise and Psalms of thanksgiving is thin, since it is hard to thank God without praising him and hard to praise him without thanking him. We see this clearly in 100:4: "Enter his gates with thanksgiving and his courts with praise; give thanks to him and praise his name." Even so, some Psalms are more gratitude-filled than others. The classic thanksgiving Psalm has to be 136:

Give thanks to the Lord, for he is good. His love endures forever.
Give thanks to the God of gods. His love endures forever.
Give thanks to the Lord of lords: His love endures forever.
to him who alone does great wonders, His love endures forever.
who by his understanding made the heavens, His love endures forever.
who spread out the earth upon the waters, His love endures forever.
who made the great lights—His love endures forever.
the sun to govern the day, His love endures forever.
the moon and stars to govern the night; His love endures forever.

This was probably intended to be recited or sung in a temple ceremony, with the temple singers singing the verse, and the people singing back the response, "His love endures forever."

Another favorite thanksgiving Psalm is 92. "It is good to praise the Lord and make music to your name, O Most High, to proclaim your love in the morning and your faithfulness at night, to the music of the ten-stringed lyre and the melody of the harp. For you make me glad by your deeds, O Lord; I sing for joy at the works of your hands. How great are your works, O Lord, how profound are your thoughts!" This and other thanksgiving Psalms (41, 66, 73, 103, 107) may have been written to be read or sung when a person made a thanksgiving offering to the Lord in the temple. We see this rather clearly in 66:13–15: "I will come to your temple with burnt offerings and fulfill my vows to you—vows my lips promised and my mouth spoke. I will sacrifice fat animals to you and an offering of rams."

Some other thanksgiving Psalms are 18, 21, 30, 32, 33, 40, 118, 124, 138, 144 and 145. Some are individual expressions of gratitude, others are collective. In most of them, the speaker invites all good men to join him in praising and thanking God. Sincere gratitude, like praise, is something people feel compelled to express—and share with others.

MANY RULES, ALL RIGHT

The feeling of "delight" in God's Law is the subject of the longest chapter in the Bible, the very long Psalm 119. It is hard for people in the modern world to grasp this attraction of the Law, but the devout people of Israel knew that God's Law wasn't given to make life a burden or to take the joy from it. God's commandments gave order to life in

---

CULTURAL INSIGHTS

Zion

In the Old Testament you'll find hundreds of references to Jerusalem—and also many references to Zion. In fact, Zion is another name for Jerusalem. The actual Zion is a hilly ridge within the city, and the name came to refer to the city as a whole. The name also became part of the political movement known as Zionism. Many Christian hymns refer to Zion—usually applying the name not to the earthly city of Jerusalem, but to the new Jerusalem, heaven. This is based on Hebrews 12:22, "Mount Zion, to the heavenly Jerusalem, the city of the living God." Zion is mentioned forty times in the Psalms, and Psalms 46, 47, 76, 84, 87 and 122 are often called the "songs of Zion" because they praise Jerusalem, and especially its temple. Zion has been a popular name for both churches and cities.

a chaotic world. They kept people out of trouble, making them aware of what a caring Father they had. Conforming to them makes life pleasant, not burdensome. "How sweet are your words to my taste, sweeter than honey to my mouth!" (119:103). Psalm 19 in its first part praises the beauty of nature, and in the second part the beauty of the Law: "The heavens declare the glory of God; the skies proclaim the work of his hands.... The law of the Lord is perfect, reviving the soul. The statutes of the Lord are trustworthy, making wise the simple. By them is your servant warned; in keeping them there is great reward. Who can discern his errors? Forgive my hidden faults." In the same hymn of praise the author could praise the beauty of the created world and the beauty of the Law that God gave mankind.

One reason Psalm 119—the "Law Psalm"—still resonates with people is that it focuses on the *moral* commandments in the Old Testament, not the *ritual* commandments. The Psalm shows little interest in the rules for sacrificing, for keeping the Sabbath, for observing the kosher rules, for observing the religious feasts. The commandments that matter to the author of 119 are the rules for the moral life. "How can a young man keep his way pure? By living according to your word" (119:9). Psalm 119 is not praising "legalism" but rather a love for the word of God as embodied in Israel's Law, since it is God's revelation of himself and his will for mankind. Psalm 15 praises the person "whose walk is blameless and who does what is righteous," but it is the keeping of the moral law that is praised, not the laws of ritual and sacrifice.

Some of the Psalms seem to be praising the author's own keeping of the commandments. "I do not sit with deceitful men, nor do I consort with hypocrites" (26:4). "Though you probe my heart and examine me at night, though you test me, you will find nothing; I have resolved that my mouth will not sin" (17:3). "Away from me, you evildoers, that I may keep the commands of my God" (119:115).

These Psalms might be a useful reminder to us that we would do well to avoid bad company. In fact, whoever compiled the Psalms into their final form saw fit to open the collection with this bit of wisdom: "Blessed is the man who does not walk in the counsel of the wicked or stand in the way of sinners or sit in the seat of mockers. But his delight is in the law of the Lord, and on his law he meditates day and night. He is like a tree planted by streams of water, which yields its fruit in season and whose leaf does not wither. Whatever he does prospers. Not so the wicked! They are like chaff that the wind blows away. Therefore the wicked will not stand in the judgment, nor sinners in the assembly of the righteous. For the Lord watches over the way of the righteous, but the way of the wicked will perish."

HOW LONG IS "FOREVER"?

The writers of the Psalms were people of their time, and they did not really believe in an afterlife. (See the sidebar on "Sheol" on page 170.) Yet if you thumb through Psalms, you will notice words like *forever, eternal, everlasting* used again and again. When Psalm 23 says "I will dwell in the house of the Lord forever," it probably means "as long as I live." Keep in mind that the ancient Israelites rarely thought of themselves as just individuals. They were part of a bigger something, a faith community, Israel, the chosen people of God. The extended family was important to these people. You identified yourself as "X, the child of Y," and you probably knew your family tree way, way back. When you thought of the future, it wasn't just your own future on earth, or in heaven, but the future of your children, their children, and so on. You wouldn't last forever, individually, but Israel would. God would keep his chosen people alive, and if they were unfaithful, at least a moral remnant would survive in Israel. And of course, God himself was eternal, and there would always be people to praise him and fellowship with him, even if the individual's own life was limited.

Christians today do not read the Psalms in that way. Forever really means *forever*, world without end. So we find a pleasure in Psalm 23 that the ancient Israelites did not: "I will dwell in the house of the Lord forever" promises eternity in heaven, one of the most comforting thoughts imaginable. "O Lord, you will keep us safe and protect us from such people forever." (12:7) "You have made known to me the path of life; you will fill me with joy in your presence, with eternal pleasures at your right hand" (16:11). "Surely you have granted him eternal blessings and made him glad with the joy of your presence" (21:6). "My flesh and my heart may fail, but God is the strength of my heart and my portion forever" (73:26). "Wealth and riches are in his house, and his righteousness endures forever" (112:3).

As comforting and inspiring as the Psalms were to their original hearers, Christians have the "enriched" version of the Psalms, for we understand *forever* and *eternal* to mean just what they say.

Old Testament Afterlife?

This Hebrew word *Sheol* occurs many times in the Old Testament, especially in Psalms, where it is found fourteen times. Sheol was the land of the dead, a gloomy place where all the dead went. It was not hell, but certainly not heaven, either. The fact is, until the very late books of the Old Testament, there is no firm belief in heaven and hell. All people ended up in Sheol, where they existed but experienced no pleasure. This explains why ancient Israel placed more emphasis on this life than on the life to come. Death was nothing to look forward to, since it ended life's pleasures, especially the pleasure of fellowship with God. Once a person went "down" to Sheol, all joys and hopes were gone. The Greeks' idea of the joyless realm called Hades was very similar.

Some Bible translations use the actual word Sheol, others translate it as "the grave" or "the pit." The King James Version translates it as "hell." For 16:10, KJV has "thou wilt not leave my soul in hell," while NIV more correctly has "you will not abandon me to the grave." For 139:8, KJV has "If I ascend up into heaven, thou art there: if I make my bed in hell, behold, thou art there," while NIV has "If I go up to the heavens, you are there; if I make my bed in the depths, you are there."

HYMNS BECOMING HYMNS

Since most of the first Christians were Jews, they continued their use of the Psalms—after all, the Psalms were addressed to the same God. For many centuries, Christians ceased to write original hymns and were content to use the Psalms—either exactly as they were in the Bible, or in *metrical* (rhymed) versions (some of which were excellent poetry, and some of which were truly laughable). Some Christian leaders were opposed to using "hymns of human composure" in church—as opposed to the Psalms, which were hymns of "divine composure." By 1562 England had a set of all 150 Psalms written in rhyming versions, sung to the tunes of popular ballads. This was *The Whole Booke of Psalmes, Collected into English Metre by T. Sternhold and I. Hopkins*. This was the only real English hymnal in the world until a new version of the Psalms was published in 1696, its chief "rhymer" being England's poet laureate, Nahum Tate. This was widely used in England and the American colonies. All these early hymnals were known as *psalters*, not *hymnbooks*, for there was still a general belief that the only words that should be sung in churches were the words of the Bible's own inspired hymnbook, Psalms.

In England, one of the first real hymnals used in churches was *The Psalms of David Imitated in the Language of the New Testament*, published in 1719 by a minister named Isaac Watts. You probably know Watts as the author of some classic hymns, such as "Joy to the World" and "When I Survey the Wondrous Cross." In his hymnal, Watts said he tried "to make David speak like a Christian." Watts paraphrased most of the Psalms and altered a lot of Old Testament words to Christian ones. For example, "Israel" often becomes "the church" in Watts's version. Psalm 72, which in the Bible begins, "His kingdom shall endure from sea to sea" comes out as "Jesus shall reign where'er the sun." It surprises some people to learn that the Christmas classic "Joy to the World" is actually Watts's version of Psalm 98, which is about praising God for his marvelous deeds, with all nature joining in with the praise.

In his youth, Watts had complained to his father that the rhymed Psalms they sang in church were dull, and his father replied, "Then write something better." Watts did, enriching the Christian world with his great hymns. He was a kind of "bridge" between rhymed Psalms of the past and distinctively Christian hymns, which were not based on the Psalms at all. In a sense he showed Christians it was permissible to sing songs other than the Psalms in church—and yet some of his greatest hymns are his Christianized version of the Psalms. Following in his footsteps, Christian writers would pen many hymns that were not based on the Psalms—and many that were.

Let's take one example of a classic hymn based on a Psalm. This is by James Montgomery (1771–1854), a Scottish journalist. You might recognize the words because they were used in the popular musical play *Godspell*:

O bless the Lord, my soul!
    His grace to thee proclaim!
And all that is within me join
    To bless his holy Name!

O bless the Lord, my soul!
    His mercies bear in mind,
Forget not all his benefits,
    The Lord to thee is kind.

> **DID YOU KNOW?**
>
> According to the inscriptions, seventy-three Psalms are "of David," twelve "of Asaph," eleven of "the sons of Korah," one each "of" Moses, Solomon, Heman and Ethan. Some are designated "for the choirmaster."

This was Montgomery's version of Psalm 103, which in the Bible reads: "Praise the Lord, O my soul; all my inmost being, praise his holy name. Praise the Lord, O my soul, and forget not all his benefits" (verses 1–2). With some fairly minor word changes, Montgomery stuck very close to the words of the Bible. Now consider a familiar hymn of Isaac Watts:

O God, our help in ages past,
    Our hope for years to come,
Our shelter from the stormy blast,
    And our eternal home.

A thousand ages in thy sight
    Are like an evening gone;

Short as the watch that ends the night
    Before the rising sun.

Watts was paraphrasing Psalm 90: "Lord, you have been our dwelling place throughout all generations…a thousand years in your sight are like a day that has just gone by, or like a watch in the night."

If you turn to the back of any hymnal, you will probably find a Scripture index, which tells you which Bible passages are the bases of the hymns in the book. Generally you will find more hymns based on Psalms than any other book of the Bible. The "Scripture songs" that have been popular in recent years continue the practice of singing the Psalms, except that instead of rhyming them, they use the words of Psalms as they were written. Whether rhymed or not, the Psalms continue to appeal to composers of music, for the words inspire people in every generation.

PUTTING THE WORD TO WORK

1. People who pay compliments easily seem to enjoy life more than people who criticize. Write down a list of things you could praise God for. Perhaps some of the Psalms we've studied today can help you get started.

2. Write down a list of things you want to thank God for. Then think: How often do you actually express to God how grateful you are? Make a resolution to set aside a "gratitude moment" at least once per day.

3. Some of the Psalms for today praise and thank God for his commandments. Is there a commandment that you especially thank God for?

4. Choose one of the Psalms from Key Passages for Today and paraphrase it—that is, restate it in your own words. See if this doesn't give you a new understanding of the Psalm.

5. Many Psalms praise the temple as being "the house of God." What locations in your own life make you feel closer to God? Why? Do you feel God's presence more when alone or with a group?

Soul Singing
THE PSALMS, PART 2

AT THE HEART OF IT ALL TODAY The Psalms express momentary frustration and doubt, but also deep faith in a God who is *Savior* and *Judge*. With this God there is forgiveness and compassion.

In the last chapter we looked at Psalms of praise and thanksgiving—Psalms in which the speaker approaches God with a smile, you might say. Today we

KEY PASSAGES TO READ TODAY

Psalms 22; 51; 73; 109; 130; 137

look at some very different Psalms, in which the speaker is frowning or in tears. About a third of the Psalms fit into the broad category of laments, in which someone asks for God's help in some crisis. In fact, there are more laments than praises and thanksgivings in the Psalms, which tells us something about human nature (we are more prone to complain than to thank). However, many of the lament Psalms begin in tears but end in triumph as the person affirms his belief that God will at last do the right thing. Some of the laments are collective—that is, it is the whole nation of Israel that is suffering. But most of the laments are individual, and among them are some of the most-loved of the Psalms.

In the Psalms we consider today, God is *Savior* and *Judge*. He comes to people's rescue in time of trouble, and he rights the wrongs that the innocent suffer. He is, as the classic hymn "Abide with Me" phrased it, "Help of the helpless."

KEY TERM FOR TODAY ## Lovingkindness

In the 1500s, translator Miles Coverdale puzzled over how to render the Hebrew word *hesedh*, which appears many times in the Old Testament, especially in Psalms. It refers to God's deep love, commitment and care for those bound to him by covenant. Coverdale chose to translate it as "lovingkindness," which was retained in the popular King James Version. Modern translations have something like "unfailing love," or even just "love," which are adequate, but "lovingkindness" does sound richer than "love," since we are talking about the deep, never-failing love of God which surpasses all human love—to quote the title of an old hymn, "O Love, That Wilt Not Let Me Go." We find this love referred to in the opening words of Psalm 51 (KJV), one of the great confessional Psalms of the Bible: "Have mercy upon me, O God, according to thy lovingkindness: according unto the multitude of thy tender mercies blot out my transgressions."

The Psalms are unique in being written over a period of six hundred years or more. Probably the earliest are from the time of David (c. 1000 BC), although one Psalm is said to be by Moses, who lived much earlier. Many of the Psalms were written for use in the first temple (Solomon's), which was completed in 960 BC and destroyed in 586 BC, and many others were written for the second temple, which was completed in 515 BC.

640–560 BC
Solon, Greek lawgiver

c. 628–c. 551 BC
Zoroaster, Persian religious founder

606 BC
Assyrian Empire is conquered by Babylonia.

Lao-tzu, Chinese philosopher, born

THE GOD-FORSAKEN MAN

No doubt the classic lament Psalm is the heart-wrenching 22: "My God, my God, why have you forsaken me? Why are you so far from saving me, so far from the words of my groaning?...I am a worm and not a man, scorned by men and despised by the people. All who see me mock me; they hurl insults, shaking their heads: 'He trusts in the Lord; let the Lord rescue him. Let him deliver him, since he delights in him.'...Dogs have surrounded me; a band of evil men has encircled me, they have pierced my hands and my feet. I can count all my bones; people stare and gloat over me. They divide my garments among them and cast lots for my clothing."

Obviously no one could read this without thinking of Jesus' crucifixion. In fact, Jesus spoke the first words of the Psalm while agonizing on the cross. The mocking, the insults, the casting lots for his clothing all came to their unpleasant fulfillment on that first Good Friday. Theologians like to argue over just why Jesus, the Son of God, could call out "My God, my God, why have you forsaken me?" How could the Son feel forsaken by the Father? The important fact is, Jesus was human, and as an innocent person suffering for a crime he did not commit, he asked one of the great questions of the Bible: *Why, God?*

The Psalm, of course, was written centuries before Jesus was born, and whoever wrote it understood the depths of degradation. He was clearly someone who held firmly to God, but whose enemies mocked his faith, skeptical that such an unfortunate person could belong to God. In this Psalm, as in many other laments, the mockers scorn both the person and God.

Bible scholars enjoy trying to figure out who the "enemies" are in particular Psalms. But part of the appeal of the Psalms is that we do *not* know who the enemies are. They could be anyone's enemies—and, more importantly, could be *our own*. This is what gives the laments such a universal appeal. People in different times and in different cultures have read Psalm 22 and it struck an immediate chord: *Yes, I have felt forsaken by God myself—I know exactly what this author was experiencing.*

We can't look at this Psalm without noting that it begins in tragedy but ends in triumph: in the closing verses, the speaker affirms that God has not hidden his face or turned a deaf ear to his cries. "The afflicted shall eat and be satisfied; those who seek him shall praise the Lord!" As it came to pass in the Gospels, Jesus the crucified became Jesus the resurrected. All the innocent who suffer will have their reward.

Another much-quoted lament is Psalm 42, with its familiar opening words: "As the deer pants for streams of water, so my soul pants for you, O God.... My tears have been my food day and night, while men say to me all day long, 'Where is your God?'... Why are you downcast, O my soul? Why so disturbed within me? Put your hope in God, for I will yet praise him." The note of hope is sounded, but then despair enters in again: "I said to God my Rock, 'Why have you forgotten me? Why must I go about mourning, oppressed by the enemy?' My bones suffer mortal agony as my foes taunt me." Then hope enters once again: "Put your hope in God, for I will yet praise him, my Savior and my God."

Psalm 69 opens with some striking visual images: "Save me, O God, for the waters have come up to my neck. I sink in the miry depths, where there is no foothold. I have come into the deep waters; the floods engulf me." Whether the author is literally in the mire is not the main point, for his real trouble is stated in verse 4: "Those who hate me without reason outnumber the hairs of my head; many are my enemies without cause." He tells God, "I endure scorn for your sake...the insults of those who insult you fall on me.... Those who sit at the gate mock me, and I am the song of the drunkards." The poor man is "scorned, disgraced and shamed" (verse 19). Even worse, in this degrading situation "I looked for sympathy, but there was none, for comforters, but I found none" (20).

One of the laments, 86, opens with "Hear, O Lord, and answer me, for I am poor and needy." But instead of continuing with the complaint, the speaker launches into a praise of the Lord, and a rather touching prayer also: "Teach me your way, O Lord, and I will walk in your truth; give me an undivided heart, that I may fear your name." Only later in the Psalm do we learn that the "arrogant" and "ruthless" are attacking the speaker.

The author of 64 is troubled by a "conspiracy of the wicked." "They plot injustice and say, 'We have devised a perfect plan!' Surely the mind and heart of man are cunning." These wicked conspirators "sharpen their tongues like swords and aim their words like deadly arrows."

It's worth pausing here to note that in most of the lament Psalms, the speaker has suffered more verbal than physical abuse. The human tongue can be used as a nasty weapon, and though it never draws blood, it does incredible harm. The Bible is fully aware of this; remember that one of the Ten Commandments forbids giving false testimony about someone, and several of the laws given to Moses forbid gossip and slander. The writers of the Psalms were well aware of the harm words could do: "Not a word from their mouth can be trusted; their heart is filled with destruction. Their throat is an open grave; with their tongue they speak deceit" (5:9). "His mouth is full of curses and lies and threats; trouble and evil are under his tongue" (10:7). "Everyone lies to his neighbor; their flattering lips speak with deception" (12:2). "Let their lying lips be silenced, for with pride and contempt they speak arrogantly against the righteous" (31:18). "Those who repay my good with evil slander me when I pursue what is good" (38:20).

"You use your mouth for evil and harness your tongue to deceit" (50:19). Murderers and thieves often get caught in their crimes, but slanderers and gossips rarely do, or rarely suffer for it. These Psalms offer us the comfort of a Judge who hears every idle word that people utter.

THE ULTIMATE JUDGE

God as judge is one of the key themes of Psalms—and the whole Bible, in fact. It is also a theme that people in our world feel uncomfortable with. But the writers of the Bible had no problem thinking of God as the Supreme Judge. "May the nations be glad and sing for joy, for you rule the peoples justly and guide the nations of the earth" (67:4). "They will sing before the Lord, for he comes, he comes to judge the earth. He will judge the world in righteousness and the peoples in his truth" (96:13).

Some of the Psalms look at judgment in global terms, nations attacking other nations without cause—something that ancient Israel, sandwiched between powerful empires, knew only too well. So naturally the Israelites who wrote the Psalms had hopes for global justice to right global injustice: "Arise, O Lord, let not man triumph; let the nations be judged in your presence" (9:19). "All the families of the nations will bow down before him" (22:27). "On no account let them escape; in your anger, O God, bring down the nations" (56:7). "Pour out your wrath on the nations that do not acknowledge you, on the kingdoms that do not call on your name" (79:6).

But more often the Psalms that speak of divine judgment—and hope for it—are focused on individuals. The key idea in hoping for judgment is that the writers feel ignored or badly treated by "the system," and for most people the system seems to work not for us but against us. The Psalms all have the hope that the divine Judge is fairer than human judges, that he won't ignore "the little people," that he won't be bribed or swayed. "He who avenges blood remembers; he does not ignore the cry of the afflicted" (9:12). "You, O God, rose up to judge, to save all the afflicted of the land" (76:9). An important—and comforting—idea in Psalms is that God alone truly knows who the real victims and oppressors are and is in a position to make right judgments.

A few of the Psalms make the point that none of us is truly innocent, truly a spotless victim in God's sight: "Do not bring your servant into judgment, for no one living is righteous before you" (143:2). More often, though, the Psalmist is someone believing in his own innocence before God: "Vindicate me in your righteousness, O Lord my God; do not let them gloat over me" (35:24). "Judge me, O Lord, according to my righteousness, according to my integrity, O Most High" (7:8).

When the Psalms speak of God as "judge," what they have in mind is not a criminal court but a civil court. The person crying out for justice in the Psalms is not saying, "Judge, please find me not guilty." By the divine standards, no person would ever be found not guilty—except Christ, of course. Rather, the person is looking for vindications after wrongful treatment. Our courts are run by human beings whose judgment can be swayed by all sorts of things. Psalm 58:1 asks the question, "Do you rulers indeed speak justly? Do you judge uprightly among men?" and, sadly, the answer is "Not much!" Sometimes human beings render right judgments, sometimes not. If they were always right, most of these Psalms pleading for God's righteous judgment would not have been written. It is the inadequacy of human justice that makes us turn to the divine appeals court: God.

IS IT "HATE SPEECH"?

Many of the lament Psalms involve praying for disaster for one's enemies. These are known as the *Imprecatory Psalms*, or *Maledictory Psalms*. (Both terms mean "calling down a curse.") They fit the "eye for an eye" sense of justice more than the love of enemies and spirit of forgiveness teachings of Jesus and the apostles. The classic Imprecatory Psalm is probably 109: "O God, whom I praise, do not remain silent, for wicked and deceitful men have opened their mouths against me; they have spoken against me with lying tongues. With words of hatred they surround me; they attack me without cause. In return for my friendship they accuse me, but I am a man of prayer. They repay me evil for good, and hatred for my friendship. Appoint an evil man to oppose him; let an accuser stand at his right hand. When he is tried, let him be found guilty, and may his prayers condemn him. May his days be few; may another take his place of leadership. May his children be fatherless and his wife a widow. May his children be wandering beggars; may they be driven from their ruined homes. May a creditor seize all he has; may strangers plunder the fruits of his labor. May no one extend kindness to him or take pity on his fatherless children. May his descendants be cut off, their names blotted out from the next generation. May the iniquity of his fathers be remembered before the Lord; may the sin of his mother never be blotted out. May their sins always remain before the Lord, that he may cut off the memory of them from the earth. For he never thought of doing a kindness, but hounded to death the poor and the needy and the brokenhearted. He loved to pronounce a curse—may it come on him; he found no pleasure in blessing —may it be far from him. He wore cursing as his garment; it entered into his body like water, into his bones like oil. May it be like a cloak wrapped about him, like a belt tied forever around him. May this be the Lord's payment to my accusers, to those who speak evil of me. But you, O Sovereign Lord, deal well with me for your name's sake; out of the goodness of your love, deliver me. For I am poor and needy, and my heart is wounded within me."

Does reading this make you uncomfortable? One reason it makes readers uneasy is not just that it is unmerciful and vindictive, but that *the Psalm expresses emotions we have all felt at one time or another.* Vindictiveness is a sin everyone battles at some point. Appealing to God to carry it out is an understandable temptation. One possible way to benefit from reading Psalm 109 is to imagine you are the person being cursed. Would you ever want to do anything to deserve such hatred?

There are many other Imprecatory Psalms. One of the best-known is 137, the beautiful lament of the exiles in Babylon—beautiful until its last verses, that is: "By the rivers of Babylon we sat and wept when we remembered Zion. There on the poplars we hung our harps, for there our captors asked us for songs, our tormentors demanded songs of joy; they said, 'Sing us one of the songs of Zion!' How can we sing the songs of the Lord while in a foreign land?…O Daughter of Babylon, doomed to destruction, happy is he who repays you for what you have done to us—he who seizes your infants and dashes them against the rocks." Killing innocent children? We could almost tolerate the words "happy is he who repays you for what you have done to us," but not throwing infants against rocks. But then, how many of us have lived through invasion, conquest and displacement by a brutal empire—and seen our own children killed by the enemy? Instead of focusing on the vengefulness of this Psalm, consider what the exiles endured that made them so distraught.

The ancient Israelites had their own manners, clearly different from ours in many ways. They made no attempt to disguise their hatred, their anger at injustice. The Imprecatory Psalms give voice to the bitter depths of human emotion that have not changed from ancient times to our own. Each of us can feel, at times, just as angry, resentful, revengeful and self-righteous as the writers of these Psalms were.

"Do I not hate those who hate you, O Lord, and abhor those who rise up against you?" (139:21). We don't like that word "hate," but consider this: the Israelites thought of God as righteous and holy. The Imprecatory Psalms never lose sight of that. God, these Psalms say, ought to avenge injustice, oppression and cruelty. And obviously the writers had a powerful sense of justice themselves. Even if they did not hate the sinners, they hated the sin and believed God hated the sin also. These Psalms had zero tolerance for sin. That is the beauty in them. Their writers were obviously not indifferent to

DID YOU KNOW?

In 1795, Samuel Seabury, the first Episcopal bishop in the United States, published *Morning and Evening Prayer with the Psalter*. He softened the Imprecatory Psalms by changing the imperative tense to the future tense. For example, Psalm 5:10 in the King James Version reads, "Destroy thou them, O God, let them fall by their own counsels, cast them out in the multitude of their transgressions." Here is Seabury's version: "Thou wilt destroy them, O God; they shall perish through their own imaginations; thou wilt cast them out in the multitude of their ungodliness." Notice the change? Instead of the Psalm asking God to harm the enemies, it is simply predicting that God will deal with them.

evil. They hated it and wanted God to punish it. In some sense their anger was a tribute to what they thought about God. "The righteous will be glad when they are avenged, when they bathe their feet in the blood of the wicked" (58:10). This is not a verse you would wish to frame and hang on your wall, and yet the desire to see wrongs righted is a good thing in itself.

Incidentally, it was not the New Testament that introduced the novel idea of forgiving one's enemies. The concept is very much alive in the Old Testament: "Do not hate your brother in your heart. Rebuke your neighbor frankly so you will not share in his guilt. Do not seek revenge or bear a grudge against one of your people, but love your neighbor as yourself" (Leviticus 19:17–18). "Do not gloat when your enemy falls; when he stumbles, do not let your heart rejoice" (Proverbs 24:17). When Jesus told his followers to love their enemies, he was not preaching something totally new. He was merely reminding the chosen people of Israel of an ethic of mercy they should have been practicing already.

For centuries, Christians allegorized the Imprecatory Psalms in this way: The enemies were not seen as human adversaries, but as the devil and his minions. The person reciting the Psalm could be seen as cursing Satan, not his fellow human beings. An interesting idea, except it twists the obvious meaning of these Psalms: The person really

---

CULTURAL INSIGHTS

Blessing and Cursing

In ancient times, people took words seriously. Blessing and cursing involved calling on one's god to do good or harm to another person, and neither was to be done flippantly—after all, one's god might really do what one asked for. So if you were briefly angry with a friend and called down a curse on him, you might regret it later (and so would he). Think back to Genesis, where old, blind Isaac mistakenly pronounced a blessing on his son Jacob, when he had meant to bless his other son Esau. Once Jacob received the blessing, it could not be taken back. You can't really understand the Old Testament unless you grasp the seriousness of blessing and cursing. The Law given to Moses made cursing of one's parents a capital crime (Exodus 21:17). Jesus told his disciples not to curse their enemies but to bless those who cursed them (Matthew 5:44).

There are plenty of both blessings and curses in the Psalms, with the Psalmists pronouncing blessings on the righteous and curses on the wicked—and they meant what they said. More often, though, the Psalms condemn people whose "mouths are full of curses."

Incidentally, the Bible never uses "cursing" to refer to profanity. In the Gospels, when Peter "curses," he is not using profanity but calling down curses on himself (Matthew 26:74).

DID YOU KNOW?

The Hebrew word *selah* occurs seventy-one times in the Psalms—and no one knows just what it means. Most Bibles have footnotes explaining that the meaning is unknown, but that it might be some kind of musical direction. The word occurs in only one other book of the Bible, Habakkuk.

was calling down God's curse on someone who had done him wrong. But, here is the most important thing to remember about these vengeance-filled Psalms: *The person does not take matters into his own hands.* He leaves retribution to God, remaining open to the possibility that God may not—at least for now—choose to punish the wicked person.

If you have time, browse through some of the other Imprecatory Psalms: 35:1–8; 58; 59; 69:22–28. Keep an open mind as you read them and ask yourself: *If I have felt such malice myself at times, what can I do to keep such feelings quiet—to love the sinner while hating the sin?*

I CONFESS

One of the beauties of the Psalms is that they do not merely lament the hurts and injustices done by others, but also lament the sins of the writers themselves. In some of the best-loved Psalms, a sinner pours out his anguish over his own sin. Christians often refer to these as the *Penitential Psalms*, and surely the best-known of these is 51: "Have mercy on me, O God, according to your unfailing love; according to your great compassion blot out my transgressions. Wash away all my iniquity and cleanse me from my sin. For I know my transgressions, and my sin is always before me. Against you, you only, have I sinned and done what is evil in your sight, so that you are proved right when you speak and justified when you judge. Surely I was sinful at birth, sinful from the time my mother conceived me. Surely you desire truth in the inner parts; you teach me wisdom in the inmost place. Cleanse me with hyssop, and I will be clean; wash me, and I will be whiter than snow.... The sacrifices of God are a broken spirit; a broken and contrite heart, O God, you will not despise."

The inscription to this Psalm reads "A Psalm of David, when Nathan the prophet went to him, after he had gone in to Bathsheba." That is, this was David pouring his heart out in guilt after Nathan confronted him with his double-edged crime: sleeping with Bathsheba and impregnating her, then arranging for her husband to be killed in battle. But as with all the other Psalms that are tied to some historical event, this confession of sin is universal—anyone under a load of guilt can pray Psalm 51.

Like most of the laments in the Psalms, this one begins in tears and ends in triumph: The sinner is certain that God will accept a broken and contrite heart—in fact, it is only the contrite heart that will make him acceptable to God, for going through the motions of a ritual sacrifice of an animal will not suffice (51:16).

People often nitpick this Psalm, especially verse 4: "Against you, you only, have I sinned." Hadn't David also sinned against Bathsheba's poor husband, Uriah? But the point of the Psalm is that, ultimately, all sin is directed against God. This doesn't mean that when we confess our sin to God, we stop there. Getting right with the person we harmed is essential also.

Consider another great Penitential Psalm, 6: "O Lord, do not rebuke me in your anger or discipline me in your wrath. Be merciful to me, Lord, for I am faint; O Lord, heal me, for my bones are in agony. My soul is in anguish. How long, O Lord, how long?" The penitential Psalm 32 begins on a more positive note: "Blessed is he whose transgressions are forgiven, whose sins are covered. Blessed is the man whose sin the Lord does not count against him." But the Psalm also states what happens when the confession is withheld: "When I kept silent, my bones wasted away through my groaning all day long. For day and night your hand was heavy upon me; my strength was sapped as in the heat of summer. Then I acknowledged my sin to you and did not cover up my iniquity."

Psalm 38 also speaks of the heavy burden of guilt: "My guilt has overwhelmed me like a burden too heavy to bear. My wounds fester and are loathsome because of my sinful folly." But he knows that God hears his confession: "All my longings lie open before you, O Lord; my sighing is not hidden from you" (verse 9). With words like "sighing" and "groaning," the Psalms do not soft-peddle the effects of sin and guilt on the individual.

Even more heart-wrenching is the Psalm known as *De Profundis*, Latin for "Out of the depths," Psalm 130: "Out of the depths I cry to you, O Lord; O Lord, hear my voice.... If

---

CULTURAL INSIGHTS

Gentiles / Nations / Peoples

You might be aware that the Hebrew word *goyim* (plural of *goy*) refers to non-Jews, also called Gentiles. The word occurs numerous times in the Psalms and the Prophets, and translators argue over whether it ought to be translated as "Gentiles" or "peoples" or "nations," and different Bible versions vary. (Israel used the Hebrew word *am*, "people," to refer to itself, so *am* was "us" and *goyim* was "everyone else.") The Israelites did not have a high opinion of the *goyim*, since they were seen as immoral idol-worshipers who were outside the covenant that Israel had with God. Also, in Israel's long history, most of the *goyim* were the Israelites' violent enemies and oppressors. This is the sentiment behind verses like these: "Why do the nations conspire and the peoples plot in vain?" (2:1). "The nations have fallen into the pit they have dug; their feet are caught in the net they have hidden" (9:15). "Pour out your wrath on the nations that do not acknowledge you" (79:6). Still, there are many indications in the Old Testament that the Gentiles/nations/peoples are not outside the orbit of God's love—the books of Ruth and Jonah, for example—something that becomes very clear in the New Testament. Later chapters will return to the word *Gentiles* and show how they were regarded by Jesus and the apostles.

Musical David

In earlier chapters we looked at the fascinating story of David, Israel's greatest king. In the Psalms, it is not David the king who is important, but David the musician and poet—and man of faith. You might recall that in 1 Samuel, gloomy king Saul needed a talented musician to help soothe his spirit: "Saul said to his attendants, 'Find someone who plays well and bring him to me.' One of the servants answered, 'I have seen a son of Jesse of Bethlehem who knows how to play the harp. He is a brave man and a warrior. He speaks well and is a fine-looking man. And the Lord is with him' " (16:17–18). Later, when David was king himself, Israel knew the joys of music: "David and the whole house of Israel were celebrating with all their might before the Lord, with songs and with harps, lyres, tambourines, sistrums and cymbals" (2 Samuel 6:5). On the brink of death, the old king was remembered for his musical and poetic talents: "These are the last words of David: 'The oracle of David son of Jesse, the oracle of the man exalted by the Most High, the man anointed by the God of Jacob, Israel's singer of songs' " (2 Samuel 23:1).

Of the 150 Psalms, seventy-three are labeled "of David," which could mean that he wrote them or inspired them. The David Psalms include some of the best-loved passages in the Bible, including 23 ("The Lord is my shepherd") and the famous confession of sin in Psalm 51. Though David did not write all the Psalms, in a sense Psalms is "David's book," since he was its chief author and the inspiration of poets and musicians who followed after him. The Psalms run deep with rich emotion, as did David himself. When Psalms was divided into five sections—known as "books"—centuries ago, those who created the divisions knew what they were doing: attributing five "books" to David just as the first five books of the Bible were attributed to the great Moses.

you, O Lord, kept a record of sins, O Lord, who could stand? But with you there is forgiveness, therefore you are feared. I wait for the Lord, my soul waits, and in his word I put my hope." The man is aware that his own failings have created a huge gulf between himself and God. If the sins were not forgiven, that gulf could not be bridged. Although this Psalm is an individual confession of sin, it is labeled a "song of ascent," so it was one of the Psalms recited by pilgrims visiting Jerusalem on the holy days. That is appropriate, since people going into the temple—to the presence of God—needed to confess their sins, so they could enter the temple with a clear conscience and a greater appreciation of the God who forgives. In the New Testament, Jesus would insist that people be on good terms with their brothers before going to worship in the temple (Matthew 5:23–24).

Let's look at one more Penitential Psalm, 143: "Do not bring your servant into judgment, for no one living is righteous before you" (verse 2). One of the beauties of this Psalm is that the poor sinner feels his own aching for God, but is aware that sin separates him from the One he loves: "I spread out my hands to you; my soul thirsts for you like a parched land.... Do not hide your face from me.... Show me the way I should go, for to you I lift up my soul.... Teach me to do your will, for you are my God." In the same Psalm the sinner asks God to rescue him from his enemies—but he is painfully aware that he cannot appeal to his own merits to ask God for favors. He has to rely on God's mercy. God will forgive, and in the future the sinner can hope to walk the right path: "Teach me to do your will, for you are my God." No wonder this is one of the best-loved passages of the Old Testament.

We'll conclude this section on confession with one of the most comforting of all the Psalms, 139, which begins, "O Lord, you have searched me and you know me. You know when I sit and when I rise; you perceive my thoughts from afar.... Before a word is on my tongue, you know it completely, O Lord." In this Psalm there is no confession of sin—on the contrary, it is a confession of openness, awareness of every word and thought being clearly known to God. "Where can I go from your Spirit? Where can I flee from your presence?"

Nowhere. Not even the darkest night is dark to God—nothing can hide us from him. But this knowledge does not have to intimidate us—rather, we can more appreciate the God who knew us from the moment of conception. "Your eyes saw my unformed body. All the days ordained for me were written in your book before one of them came to be." Oddly, the Psalm turns briefly to a prayer that God would slay the wicked. But then it ends with these words: "Search me, O God, and know my heart; test me and know my anxious thoughts. See if there is any offensive way in me, and lead me in the way everlasting." These seem to be the words of someone who was not aware of any great sin he committed, but who trusted God to keep watch over his mind and heart and lead him away from any sin. It is a lovely Psalm to read and recite in times of our own need for confession, and for expressing deep trust in God's ability to guide us.

WISDOM IN SONG

We close with a look at some passages that will guide us into the Wisdom literature of the Bible. The Wisdom books include Job, Proverbs and Ecclesiastes. Sometimes Psalms is lumped in with that group, although most of the Psalms would hardly qualify as Wisdom literature. But a few of the Psalms are referred to as "wisdom Psalms," in which the speaker reflects upon the nature of God and the nature of justice in this world, always coming back to the solid belief that God is just and his ways are always right. In most of these, the Psalm does not begin with the person speaking to God, but talking with himself, meditating, analyzing. But most of them end with an address to God—doubt and perplexity and frustration end where faith begins.

One of the best wisdom Psalms is 49: "Why should I fear when evil days come, when wicked deceivers surround me—those who trust in their wealth and boast of their great riches?…he will take nothing with him when he dies, his splendor will not descend with him. Though while he lived he counted himself blessed—and men praise you when you prosper—he will join the generation of his fathers, who will never see the light of life. A man who has riches without understanding is like the beasts that perish." The Psalm is an answer to the questions argued in the Book of Job: *Why do good men suffer and bad men prosper? Why isn't God just?* In verse 15, the Psalm hints that the justice may not occur in this life, but afterward: "God will redeem my life from the grave; he will surely take me to himself."

Psalm 37 deals with the same question about God's justice, but gives a firm answer to those who doubt: "Do not fret because of evil men or be envious of those who do wrong; for like the grass they will soon wither, like green plants they will soon die away…. For the Lord loves the just and will not forsake his faithful ones. They will be protected forever, but the offspring of the wicked will be cut off." The Psalm offers these timeless words of consolation: "Better the little that the righteous have than the wealth of many wicked" (verse 16). When our eyes see the inequities

among people, we must "refrain from anger and turn from wrath; do not fret—it only leads to evil" (verse 8). The world seems unfair, but the only right thing to do is "trust in the Lord and do good." Leave the righting of wrongs to God. Be like the author of Psalm 131: "My heart is not proud, O Lord, my eyes are not haughty; I do not concern myself with great matters, or things too wonderful for me. But I have stilled and quieted my soul."

Psalms 14 and 53 are interesting in that that they are almost word for word the same. Perhaps the compiler of the Psalms thought they contained a message worthy of repetition. Both begin with the lament "The fool says in his heart, 'There is no God.'" Here we encounter the "fool" as the Bible sees him—not a person mentally deficient, but spiritually and morally deficient, not understanding that his evil plans and deeds are being observed by God. Theologians refer to this as "practical atheism"—the person doesn't actually deny God exists (which is called "philosophical atheism"), but simply *acts* as if God is not watching and judging, and thus such a person does as he pleases. So widespread is such wickedness that the Psalm claims that "all have turned aside, they have together become corrupt; there is no one who does good, not even one" (14:3). These evildoers have their day as they "frustrate the plans of the poor," but the poor need not despair ultimately, "for the Lord is their refuge" (14:6).

"I envied the arrogant when I saw the prosperity of the wicked"—so begins Psalm 73, in which the speaker laments those from whose "callous hearts comes iniquity." "This is what the wicked are like—always carefree, they increase in wealth. Surely in vain have

---

CULTURAL INSIGHTS

Psalter

This is just another name for the Book of Psalms, but it also refers to a book that contains just the Psalms. In biblical times, there were no books, only scrolls. Sometime around AD 100, people began using what was called a *codex*, an early form of book, handwritten, with the pages bound on one side by thread. A codex could hold a lot more written matter than scrolls, so it was possible to put all the writings of the Bible together in one volume. Because the Jews—and, later, Christians—loved to read the Psalms for personal devotions, it was common for a person to own a Psalter even if they could not afford an entire Bible. (Remember that books were extremely rare and expensive before the printing press came along.) In the Middle Ages, the rich would often buy very expensive Psalters, sometimes illustrated with exquisite ink drawings, gold edges to the pages, rich leather bindings studded with jewels, etc. More often these were ways of showing off wealth than of increasing the spiritual life, but many people did treasure their Psalters and read them regularly. In fact, until the age of the printing press, a Psalter was the one book of the Bible that a Christian was likely to possess.

People often think that the first printed book was the Gutenberg Bible, printed in Germany in the 1450s, but in fact, Gutenberg's first printed book was a Psalter, followed by the whole Bible soon after. It is a testimony to people's high esteem for the Psalms that they were the first book ever printed.

I kept my heart pure…. When I tried to understand all this, it was oppressive to me." Indeed. The heart can grow bitter and hard if we dwell too long on the sufferings of the innocent and the happy lives of the wicked. But in the end, we trust: "You guide me with your counsel, and afterward you will take me into glory. Whom have I in heaven but you? And earth has nothing I desire besides you" (73:24–25).

And with that ringing affirmation, we bring to a close our study of this best and richest of the Old Testament books, one of the gems of human literature and one of the fullest revelations of God's will to humankind.

PUTTING THE WORD TO WORK

1. If you've been praying about something, try writing your own lament Psalm based on the pattern of the lament Psalms in the Bible. State your difficulty as bluntly as you can, but end the Psalm with a statement of belief in God's timing and justice.

2. Read Psalm 109 or one of the other Imprecatory Psalms. How would you change it? Which verses would you remove or alter? Read the box on Samuel Seabury for one way of changing the words.

3. What is some sin or failing—recent or in the distant past—you never confessed to God? See if you can write it down now. If it involved offending some other person, see if you can contact that person and ask forgiveness.

4. What is some injury or slight you've endured that you hoped God would set right? Be honest with yourself and ask: Do I want justice to be done, or would it be better to forgive the injury, leave it to God and move on?

5. The final section of this chapter looks at some Psalms in which people "fret" over the injustices in life. How often have you done this yourself? What recent events in your own life have caused you to fret over injustice? Do you think you'll be able to let go of the situation and trust God to make things right in his own time?

Experience as Teacher
PROVERBS

AT THE HEART OF IT ALL TODAY	Proverbs is a book of character-building, using the wisdom gained through experience to school people in leading decent, useful lives. It is a user-friendly training manual for everyday life, teaching us habits of unselfish, thoughtful living—rooted in respect for God.

Today we will look at some of the most readable, interesting, and, in parts, puzzling books of the Bible, collectively known as the Wisdom books. They are Proverbs, Job and Ecclesiastes, and some

KEY PASSAGES TO READ TODAY

Proverbs 3; 15–19; 31

people would include Psalms, since there are several "wisdom Psalms." The Wisdom books are very different from the earlier books of the Bible. In chapters 1–10 we looked at history—from the creation of the world in Genesis through God's deliverance of Israel from slavery; through the period of the judges and kings through the Babylonian exile; and finally, the return from exile and the rebuilding of the faith community in Jerusalem. We met some fascinating people and saw the working of God over a long span of time.

But in the Book of Psalms, the focus changed: Psalms is more "timeless," with not as much interest in history. Some of the Psalms do refer to God's great acts in the past—notably the deliverance from Egypt. But Psalms is mostly about *now*—God and the human soul, up close and personal. This is one reason Psalms is more often read than, say, Judges and Kings. Many people just don't like to read history. Also, you have to read

KEY TERM FOR TODAY ## The Fool

In Proverbs, a wise man and righteous man are pretty much the same thing, just as a fool and a wicked man are the same. In Proverbs, a wise man would want to be righteous, to please God and get along with his fellow man. The fool, by contrast, is probably wicked, not caring whether he pleases God or injures his fellow man, nor is he open to guidance. A "fool" in the Bible is not someone lacking education. A fool is not mentally deficient, but *morally* and *spiritually* deficient. This is what makes the Wisdom literature in the Bible distinct from the wise sayings of other cultures. In the Bible, wisdom versus folly is the same as virtue versus vice. In God's eyes, one can be well-educated and knowledgeable about many things and still be a fool.

970–931 BC
Reign of King
Solomon, main
author of Proverbs

800 BC
Invasion of
Palestine by Egypt

c. 800 BC
The Greek poet
Homer composes the
Iliad and Odyssey.

776 BC
First Olympics
held in Greece

753 BC
Founding of Rome

Traditional date for
the beginning of
Greek colonization
of southern Italy

716–687 BC
Reign of King
Hezekiah, when
the Book of Proverbs
was compiled

fairly long passages from the historical books to learn valuable lessons. Psalms is more "bite-size"—you can read one Psalm and find rich meaning in it, and you don't have to have a wide understanding of Israel's history to understand it.

The Wisdom books have that same timeless quality that the Psalms have. In fact, even though a king of Israel (Solomon) is the author of Proverbs and Ecclesiastes, there is not much in the books to connect them to any historical period—or any nation. Parts of the Book of Proverbs are attributed to two kings who were not Israelites. The Book of Job's main character is not an Israelite. The Wisdom books are timeless and practically nationless as well. The Wisdom books never once refer to Israel's history, to Moses, or the Law, or the covenant, or the dynasty of King David, or the hope of a Messiah, and only rarely mention the temple or sacrifices. (Consider Proverbs 21:3: "To do what is right and just is more acceptable to the Lord than sacrifice"—an idea that is echoed by many of Israel's prophets, as we will see later.) This lack of "Israel-ness" helps explain their wide appeal. People who could never make their way through Judges or Kings can find great pleasure and great profit in Proverbs.

Israel did not exist in a vacuum. It had its wise men and was surrounded by other nations that also honored their wise men. The Wisdom literature of the Middle East was trans-national, which is why the Bible could include in Proverbs the words of non-Israelite kings like Agur and Lemuel. Although the different countries prided themselves on their wise men, the wise sayings have little to do with divine guidance of nations, since the emphasis is clearly on the individual.

The Israelites were different from other cultures in ascribing man's wisdom to God. In both Proverbs and Job, Wisdom is something present with God through eternity. So even though Wisdom is largely "common sense," it is also divine. People have it because God gave it to us to make life better, just as he gave Israel the Law to make life better.

THE SCHOOL OF COMMON SENSE

Some people accuse Proverbs of being "secular" because the book seems to emphasize life in this world, giving little thought to God. That is not true at all. The book makes it clear that the foundation of wisdom is reverence for God. One of the most quoted verses from the book is 1:7: "The fear of the Lord is the beginning of knowledge." Here "fear" doesn't mean "trembling in terror" but "reverence and respect." We can't be truly wise unless we are rooted in God. The book also tells us to "Trust in the Lord with all your heart and lean not on your own understanding" (3:5). That is hardly a "secular" bit of advice. In fact, it seems to reinforce the message of Genesis, which showed the folly of Adam and Eve trying to be "like gods," deciding for themselves what was right and wrong—and losing paradise as a result.

It is tempting to regard the advice in Proverbs as merely practical—like believing that "honesty is the best policy" not because it is right, or because it pleases God, but because it is more effective in the long run. That attitude is totally foreign to this book, which places "the fear of the Lord" before every other consideration. The authors of Proverbs could not imagine a person being a "success" unless he or she also loved God. The unique contribution of this book is to show us that true religion can only thrive on the foundations of human decency.

The main aim of Proverbs is to form character. Day to day, character is revealed in—and formed by—ordinary small acts and habits. A good character arises from the repetition of many small acts, and it begins early in youth. Every little action of the common day makes or unmakes character. Most of the time we do not live by "rules" at all, but by habits and sensibilities. Proverbs is not about being a hero in times of crisis—like Elijah facing the prophets of Baal in 1 Kings—but about everyday life, being a good,

---

CULTURAL INSIGHTS

The Sage / Wise Man

Every head of every organization—a nation, a corporation, a church—values having wise counselors. Israel always held its wise men in high regard, with the first wise man in the Bible being Joseph, the Hebrew slave who, through his wisdom, became the right-hand man of Egypt's pharaoh, saving the land (and his own large family) from a great famine. In 2 Samuel, King David valued the wisdom of his advisor Ahitophel, who was so highly regarded that people thought that asking his advice was like asking God (2 Samuel 16:23). The other great example of a wise man in the Old Testament is Daniel, whose wisdom made him a respected counselor of the kings of Babylon and Persia. The frequent mention of kings in Proverbs gives us the hint that young men studying the Proverbs hoped they, too, might someday be another Joseph or Daniel. The wise man—the *hakham*—always hoped to be a success in the world—if not a king, the indispensable counselor of a king. "Do you see a man skilled in his work? He will serve before kings; he will not serve before obscure men" (22:29).

Wisdom has its limitations, and so do wise men. We will see this clearly when we study Job and his three extremely wise friends, who were foolish enough to think they could "explain" Job's suffering to him. The Bible has high praise for wisdom but has harsh words for those who are "wise in their own eyes." The deepest wisdom is knowing the limits of wisdom.

The Writings

Several books form the third division of the Old Testament, known as the Writings (in Hebrew, *Kethubim*). Remember from earlier chapters that the first division is the Torah, the five books of Moses—Genesis through Deuteronomy. The Prophets are the second division, divided into the Former Prophets (Joshua, Judges, 1 and 2 Samuel, 1 and 2 Kings) and Latter Prophets (Isaiah, Jeremiah, Ezekiel, the twelve Minor Prophets). The third division, the Writings, consists of all the other Old Testament books: Ruth, 1 and 2 Chronicles, Ezra, Nehemiah, Esther, Job, Psalms, Proverbs, Ecclesiastes, Song of Solomon, Lamentations, Daniel. The Writings were the last group to be accepted as divine Scripture by the Jews, with Psalms being the first book of the Writings to be regarded as inspired. As you can see, the Writings are a mixture of history (Ruth, 1 and 2 Chronicles, Ezra, Nehemiah, Esther), hymns (Psalms), wisdom (Job, Proverbs, Ecclesiastes), poetry (Lamentations, Song of Solomon), and prophecy (Daniel). Although the Jews have always valued the Torah and the Prophets more than the Writings, the books of Psalms and Proverbs are two of the most-read books of the Bible.

decent person, day to day. Part of being a decent person is coping with all the disagreeableness that life throws in our paths. Trifles make up most of our lives—little occurrences that are not particularly important in themselves, but which reveal who we are, encounters with family members, friends, neighbors and business associates, even the brief brushes with people on the street or in stores. Proverbs is about getting along with all those people, coping with them, controlling our anger and selfishness.

Bible scholars think that collections of wise sayings were originally intended for the education of kings and other government officials. That might be so, and Israel may have recorded Solomon's wise sayings in the hope that future kings of Israel would profit from them. (Based on the stories found in 1 and 2 Kings and 1 and 2 Chronicles, it appears that most of the kings did *not* follow the path of wisdom laid out in Proverbs!) Fortunately, Proverbs has been read and enjoyed by every type of person over the centuries. And although Solomon and other kings are named as the authors of the Proverbs, there is no reason to think that a lot of good plain folk wisdom didn't also make its way into the books. It is true that Solomon "spoke three thousand proverbs" (1 Kings 4:32), but God didn't reveal his wisdom—or bestow good sense—merely on kings.

REINING IN THE KNOW-IT-ALL YOUTH

Proverbs can be read profitably by people of any age—after all, it is never too late to grow wiser. But the book does give the impression that it was designed as a training manual for the young. We have all encountered the uninformed arrogance of youth, young people full of the enthusiasm of their inexperience. Proverbs seems to say to those people: *Learn that your parents, grandparents and endless line of ancestors were not all fools—in fact, over the ages they learned a lot of things that will make your life better.* The young need to hear that message—and, come to think of it, so do we all. It is difficult to see around the corner of ourselves. Wisdom helps us do that. It keeps us from being limited by our own narrow experience of life.

Wisdom literature is "history at street level." We study history because it is interesting, but, more importantly, to learn from the mistakes and successes of the human race. History teaches some obvious facts—such as, a strong nation will almost inevitably attack a weak nation nearby. The Wisdom literature is less global than that, more individual. Despite the fact that all human beings who ever lived are flawed creatures, a collective wisdom survives, floating to the surface like cream. After living on earth for many centuries, we know a lot of things, not just from our own experience, but that of our countless ancestors. Paying heed to Wisdom literature is like paying heed to some wise, experienced older person whom you respect greatly—except instead of just one wise person, there are thousands of them, all pooling their wisdom in the hope that their descendants might pay heed and make their own path through life easier.

Before we dive into Proverbs, let's consider the book's structure: It doesn't have one. The authors and editors made no attempt to organize the sayings in any way. One saying follows another; topics change. There are lots of sayings on, say, controlling one's anger, but they are not grouped together. This diversity—and lack of organization—makes the book a pleasure to browse through, since every page will have something of value.

However, the individual sayings themselves do follow certain patterns. The Hebrew word *mashal,* which we translate to "proverb," is more accurately "comparison" or "parable." Some of the couplets take the form of "the wise man does X, but the fool does Y." The familiar form is *parallelism,* which we spoke of earlier in dealing with the Psalms. In the parallels, one thing is compared—or contrasted—with another. Some examples:

Do not rebuke a mocker or he will hate you;
rebuke a wise man and he will love you (9:8).

The memory of the righteous will be a blessing,
but the name of the wicked will rot (10:7).

Hatred stirs up dissension,
but love covers over all wrongs (10:12).

Whoever loves discipline loves knowledge,
but he who hates correction is stupid (12:1).

A fool shows his annoyance at once,
but a prudent man overlooks an insult (12:16).

He who walks with the wise grows wise,
but a companion of fools suffers harm (13:20).

He who conceals his sins does not prosper,
but whoever confesses and renounces them finds mercy (28:13).

Notice that most of these are connected by the conjunction "but." We call these sayings the *antitheses*—one thing is described ("hatred stirs up dissension"), followed by its opposite ("but love covers over all wrongs"). Chapters 10–15 form almost one long block of antitheses, most of them very easily memorized.

In other cases, the sayings are *similes*—something is "like" something else. For example:

Like clouds and without rain
is a man who boasts of gifts he does not give (25:14).

As a north wind brings rain,
so a sly tongue brings angry looks (25:23).

Like a lame man's legs that hang limp
is a proverb in the mouth of a fool (26:7).

Without wood a fire goes out;
without gossip a quarrel dies down (26:20).

Obviously this parallel arrangement made the sayings fairly easy to memorize. Now lets look at some of the key themes of these wise sayings.

TONGUE TAMING

Self-control is a key theme in Proverbs, especially in regard to controlling one's tongue. You might recall that some of the Psalms in which the person laments his enemies speak more about the hurt done by words than by physical violence. Proverbs is equally realistic about the harm done by the wayward, uncontrolled tongue: "He who conceals his hatred has lying lips, and whoever spreads slander is a fool" (10:18). "When words are many, sin is not absent, but he who holds his tongue is wise" (10:19). "The tongue of the righteous is choice silver, but the heart of the wicked is of little value" (10:20). "The mouth of the righteous brings forth wisdom, but a perverse tongue will be cut out" (10:31). "A man who lacks judgment derides his neighbor, but a man of understanding holds his tongue" (11:12). "A gossip betrays a confidence, but a trustworthy man keeps a secret"

(11:13). "The words of the wicked lie in wait for blood, but the speech of the upright rescues them" (12:6). "Reckless words pierce like a sword, but the tongue of the wise brings healing" (12:18). "Truthful lips endure forever, but a lying tongue lasts only a moment" (12:19). "The tongue of the wise commends knowledge, but the mouth of the fool gushes folly" (15:2). "A wicked man listens to evil lips; a liar pays attention to a malicious tongue" (17:4). Although the Bible does not use the word "blowhard," it does speak out against such persons: "A fool finds no pleasure in understanding but delights in airing his own opinions" (18:2). The sheer delight of malicious gossip was something the wise folk of ancient times understood: "The words of a gossip are like choice morsels; they go down to a man's inmost parts" (18:8). "As a north wind brings rain, so a sly tongue brings angry looks" (25:23). "A lying tongue hates those it hurts, and a flattering mouth works ruin" (26:28). Aside from lying and gossip, boasting is also a bad thing: "Let another praise you, and not your own mouth; someone else, and not your own lips" (27:2).

It sounds like most of the emphasis is on the harm the tongue can do, but the tongue is also a force for good: "Pleasant words are a honeycomb, sweet to the soul and healing to the bones" (16:24). How much better the world would be if we spent more energy on the "honeycombs" and less on the gossip, slander and boasting! And of course, *not* saying much can often be a good thing: "A man of knowledge uses words with restraint, and a man of understanding is even-tempered" (17:27). For those who doubt their own eloquence or wisdom, the way of silence might be the wisest path: "Even a fool is thought wise if he keeps silent, and discerning if he holds his tongue" (17:28).

CURBING THE TEMPER

Just as controlling the tongue is essential, so is controlling one's temper. While the Bible doesn't say that anger is always bad (think of Jesus driving the money-changers out of the temple, or the prophet Elijah facing the prophets of Baal on Mount Carmel), most human displays of anger would be better off suppressed. "A patient man has great understanding, but a quick-tempered man displays folly" (14:29). "Better a patient man than a warrior, a man who controls his temper than one who takes a city" (16:32). "A man's wisdom gives him patience; it is to his glory to overlook an offense" (19:11). "Do not make friends with a hot-tempered man, do not associate with one easily angered" (22:24). "Like a city whose walls are broken down is a man who lacks self-control" (25:28). "Mockers stir up a city, but wise men turn away anger" (29:8). "A fool gives full vent to his anger, but a wise man keeps himself under control" (29:11).

Perhaps the most memorable saying on the subject of anger is this gem: "A gentle answer turns away wrath, but a harsh word stirs up anger" (15:1). Many people grew up with the King James Version of this verse, which speaks of the "soft answer." One of the key themes of Proverbs, and of the whole Bible, is learning to use the "soft answer" wisely.

WEALTH AND POVERTY

Critics of Proverbs claim it is very "worldly," teaching people that God wants them to be wealthy. There are indeed some verses that convey that idea, but mostly the sayings emphasize the importance of hard work and diligence—if you work, you will not go hungry, an idea few would argue with. "Lazy hands make a man poor, but diligent hands bring wealth" (10:4). "He who works his land will have abundant food, but he who chases fantasies lacks judgment" (12:11). "Do not love sleep or you will grow poor; stay awake and you will have food to spare" (20:13). "He who loves pleasure will become poor; whoever loves wine and oil will never be rich" (21:17). "One who is slack in his work is brother to one who destroys" (18:9). "Go to the ant, you sluggard; consider its ways and be wise!" (6:6). For the person who is diligent and competent, success awaits: "Do you see a man skilled in his work? He will serve before kings; he will not serve before obscure men" (22:29).

Diligence is one thing—but obsession with wealth is another: "Do not wear yourself out to get rich; have the wisdom to show restraint. Cast but a glance at riches and they are gone, for they will surely sprout wings" (23:4–5). Though Proverbs is accused of being "worldly," some of these sayings clearly point the way to the New Testament, with Jesus' teachings on the foolishness of worshipping and fretting over material things.

Proverbs is not hostile to the poor—far from it. It does take a realistic view of life: "Wealth brings many friends, but a poor man's friend deserts him" (19:4). But it also emphasizes a theme found throughout the Bible: God's people *must* help the poor. "He who despises his neighbor sins, but blessed is he who is kind to the needy" (14:21). "He who oppresses the poor shows contempt for their Maker, but whoever is kind to the needy honors God" (14:31). "He who is kind to the poor lends to the Lord, and he will reward him for what he has done" (19:17). "If a man shuts his ears to the cry of the poor, he too will cry out and not be answered" (21:13). When we study the books of the prophets later, we will hear these same messages, but uttered with more passionate intensity, as the prophets foretold disaster for a nation that had turned its back on the poor and oppressed. In fact, we will see that the great prophets often proclaimed loudly what Proverbs said calmly, in a normal tone of voice, about the need for basic human decency and compassion.

Even though Proverbs seems to tell us that there is little joy in poverty, the poor man can certainly outdo the rich man in terms of spiritual wealth. "Better to be lowly in spirit and among the oppressed than to share plunder with the proud" (16:19). "Better a dry crust with peace and quiet than a house full of feasting, with strife" (17:1). "Better a poor man whose walk is blameless than a fool whose lips are perverse" (19:1). "A rich man may be wise in his own eyes, but a poor man who has discernment sees through him" (28:11). "Wealth is worthless in the day of wrath, but righteousness delivers from death" (11:4). Wealth doesn't even guarantee pleasure in life: "He who is full loathes honey, but to the hungry even what is bitter tastes sweet" (27:7). In other words, the poor appreciate life's little comforts more than the rich do! There is balance in Proverbs, and in the Bible as a whole, which is why it is wise to become familiar with the whole book and not just read selected passages. One might read a few verses from Proverbs and conclude that it praises people who acquire wealth—overlooking the many other verses that speak of the negative aspects of prosperity.

Proverbs gives some sensible advice to people who feel like they do not have enough: Be content with what you have. "A heart at peace gives life to the body, but envy rots the bones" (14:30). Also, the people we envy may have gotten their wealth dishonestly, and their lives may be models of immorality: "Do not let your heart envy sinners, but always be zealous for the fear of the Lord" (23:17). "Do not envy wicked men, do not desire their company" (24:1). And when all is said and done, "rich and poor have this in common: The Lord is the Maker of them all" (22:2).

THE LOVE OF PLEASURE

If Proverbs has a "villain," it is the adulteress, who is spoken of at length in chapters 5–7. "These commands are a lamp, this teaching is a light, and the corrections of discipline are the way to life, keeping you from the immoral woman, from the smooth tongue of the wayward wife. Do not lust in your heart after her beauty or let her captivate you with her eyes, for the prostitute reduces you to a loaf of bread, and the adulteress preys upon your very life. Can a man scoop fire into his lap without his clothes being burned? Can a man walk on hot coals without his feet being scorched? So is he who sleeps with another man's wife; no one who touches her will go unpunished" (6:23–29).

The book's condemnation of adultery has a positive side: The writers had a very high opinion of marital fidelity. In fact, Proverbs is one of the few books in the Bible to urge husbands to stay home and enjoy the love of the women they married: "Drink water from your own cistern, running water from your own well. Should your springs overflow in the streets, your streams of water in the public squares? Let them be yours alone, never to be shared with strangers. May your fountain be blessed, and may you rejoice in the wife of your youth. A loving doe, a graceful deer—may her breasts satisfy you always, may you ever be captivated by her love. Why be captivated, my son, by an adulteress? Why embrace the bosom of another man's wife?" (5:15–20). People who claim that the Bible is "sexist" are overlooking verses like these.

We see elsewhere in Proverbs that marriage is held in high regard: "He who finds a wife finds what is good and receives favor from the Lord" (18:22). "Houses and wealth are inherited from parents, but a prudent wife is from the Lord" (19:14). (Since Solomon had hundreds of wives, these sayings may have been passed on to him by others. How would he have known the pleasure of monogamous love?)

The writers also make reference to unhappy marriages: "A wife of noble character is her husband's crown, but a disgraceful wife is like decay in his bones" (12:4). And consider this saying, which is repeated, with slight variations, several times in the book: "Better to live in a desert than with a quarrelsome and ill-tempered wife" (21:19). Perhaps had the book been compiled by women instead of men, it would have had more to say about difficult husbands! At least the book ends with lavish praise of a wife of noble character.

DID YOU KNOW?

The "loose" woman condemned in Proverbs may be a literal sexual temptress, but also there might be a second, symbolic, meaning: She represents the way of self-indulgence and wickedness, in contrast to the way of wisdom and self-control that the book promotes. Chapter 7, dealing with the wayward woman, is followed by 8, in which Wisdom is also personified as a female, inviting people to learn from her and follow in the paths God intended. The reader is invited to choose between these two "women" —the choice between temporary pleasures and wise counsel for the long run.

Contrary to what many people think, the Bible is not against pleasure, but it does condemn people who live strictly for pleasure, and this is clear enough in Proverbs. "He who loves pleasure will become poor; whoever loves wine and oil will never be rich" (21:17). "Do not join those who drink too much wine or gorge themselves on meat" (23:20). Wine and food are not wrong, but drunkenness and gluttony are. Sex itself is not wrong, but adultery and promiscuity definitely are.

LOVE REQUIRES DISCIPLINE

People who say there is no theology in Proverbs are mistaken. The book gives us a very clear picture of God as a loving Father who disciplines his children. The wise will accept and learn from the discipline instead of resisting it. "My son, do not despise the Lord's discipline and do not resent his rebuke, because the Lord disciplines those he loves, as a father the son he delights in" (3:11–12). "Whoever loves discipline loves knowledge, but he who hates correction is stupid" (12:1). "He who ignores discipline despises himself, but whoever heeds correction gains understanding" (15:32). "He who listens to a life-giving rebuke will be at home among the wise" (15:31).

Just as God the Father disciplines his children, so human parents must do the same. "He who spares the rod hates his son, but he who loves him is careful to discipline him" (13:24). "Discipline your son, for in that there is hope; do not be a willing party to his death" (19:18). "Folly is bound up in the heart of a child, but the rod of discipline will drive it far from him" (22:15). "Discipline your son, and he will give you peace; he will bring delight to your soul" (29:17).

The wise men of Israel frequently addressed their pupils as "sons," and the phrase "my son" occurs many times in Proverbs. It reminds us that throughout the ages, wisdom has primarily been passed on through the family. As great as some of the sages were—Solomon being the classic example—the passing on of many of these sayings must have been due to generations of fathers and mothers repeating the sayings to their children as they ate together, worked, traveled and worshipped God. As stated in Proverbs 22:6, "Train a child in the way that he should go, and when he is old he will not turn from it." Long before there were schools and paid teachers, there were families, and the home was the real center of learning. Solomon and the others were passing on words that had been spoken centuries earlier by Israelite parents gathered with their children sharing a meal together.

PROUD IS NOT PRUDENT

Adam and Eve are not mentioned in Proverbs, but their sin—wanting to be godlike— is condemned again and again throughout the book. While the book counsels us to be wise, it reminds us that the source of wisdom is the Lord, not ourselves. "Trust in the Lord with all your heart and lean not on your own understanding" (3:5). "Do not be

wise in your own eyes; fear the Lord and shun evil" (3:7). "All a man's ways seem innocent to him, but motives are weighed by the Lord" (16:2). "In his heart a man plans his
course, but the Lord determines his steps" (16:9). "Many are the plans in a man's heart,
but it is the Lord's purpose that prevails" (19:21). "The horse is made ready for the day
of battle, but victory rests with the Lord" (21:31). "Do not boast about tomorrow, for
you do not know what a day may bring forth" (27:1). "Do you see a man wise in his own
eyes? There is more hope for a fool than for him" (26:12).

In other words, God is in charge—not us. For this we should be thankful. "There is
no wisdom, no insight, no plan that can succeed against the Lord" (21:30). "A man's
ways are in full view of the Lord, and he examines all his paths" (5:21). "The eyes of the
Lord are everywhere, keeping watch on the wicked and the good" (15:3). Knowledge of
this should give us courage: "Fear of man will prove to be a snare, but whoever trusts in
the Lord is kept safe" (29:25).

The Book of Proverbs hates pride. This doesn't mean we ought to hate ourselves or
put ourselves down. Real humility isn't self-hatred, but realism—aware of our strengths
and weaknesses, and aware there is Someone in charge of things who is greater and wiser
than we are. We have no right to look down on others—or to think that we are gods.
"He mocks proud mockers but gives grace to the humble" (3:34). "To fear the Lord is to
hate evil; I hate pride and arrogance, evil behavior and perverse speech" (8:13). "When
pride comes, then comes disgrace, but with humility comes wisdom" (11:2). "Pride only
breeds quarrels, but wisdom is found in those who take advice" (13:10). "The Lord tears
down the proud man's house but he keeps the widow's boundaries intact" (15:25). "The
Lord detests all the proud of heart. Be sure of this: They will not go unpunished" (16:5).
"Pride goes before destruction, a haughty spirit before a fall" (16:18). "Haughty eyes and
a proud heart, the lamp of the wicked, are sin!" (21:4). "The proud and arrogant man—
'Mocker' is his name; he behaves with overweening pride" (21:24).

LOVING THY NEIGHBOR

Loving our neighbors as ourselves is not easy. People can be deceitful, disloyal, easily
offended, unforgiving. Friends easily turn into enemies. However, according to
Proverbs, "When a man's ways are pleasing to the Lord, he makes even his enemies live
at peace with him" (16:7). Difficult as it is, we are to show compassion to enemies: "Do
not gloat when your enemy falls; when he stumbles, do not let your heart rejoice"
(24:17). "If your enemy is hungry, give him food to eat; if he is thirsty, give him water
to drink. In doing this, you will heap burning coals on his head, and the Lord will
reward you" (25:21–22). Rather than prolonging quarrels, we should strive to end them:
"He who covers over an offense promotes love, but whoever repeats the matter separates close friends" (17:9).

As well as pursuing peace with our enemies, we ought to use caution in choosing our friends also. "A righteous man is cautious in friendship, but the way of the wicked leads them astray" (12:26). "Wounds from a friend can be trusted, but an enemy multiplies kisses" (27:6). "A friend loves at all times, and a brother is born for adversity" (17:17). "A man of many companions may come to ruin, but there is a friend who sticks closer than a brother" (18:24).

A wise man is generous with both his time and money. If we love our neighbor, we help them in time of need. "Do not withhold good from those who deserve it, when it is in your power to act. Do not say to your neighbor, 'Come back later; I'll give it tomorrow'—when you now have it with you" (3:27–28). "A generous man will prosper; he who refreshes others will himself be refreshed" (11:25).

A few of the sayings apply to the world of business. "The Lord abhors dishonest scales, but accurate weights are his delight" (11:1). The idea here is of a merchant weighing out his goods to a customer, making him pay for five pounds when in fact the real weight is only four. Proverbs actually repeats this saying four times—which tells us that businessmen in ancient times were no more honest than they are today!

THE ONES WITH THE POWER

Most of the sayings in Proverbs deal with everyday situations, which is one reason for the book's perennial popularity. But since the sayings were compiled by kings, some of the sayings deal with government, which in those days took only one form—monarchy. Where Proverbs has the word "king," we can mentally substitute "head of state," "president" or "government official."

The book warns against the dangers of bad government: "When the righteous thrive, the people rejoice; when the wicked rule, the people groan" (29:2). "Like a roaring lion or a charging bear is a wicked man ruling over a helpless people" (28:15). "A ruler who oppresses the poor is like a driving rain that leaves no crops" (28:3). "A tyrannical ruler lacks judgment, but he who hates ill-gotten gain will enjoy a long life" (28:16). "If a ruler listens to lies, all his officials become wicked" (29:12). "By justice a king gives a country stability, but one who is greedy for bribes tears it down" (29:4). "Arrogant lips are unsuited to a fool—how much worse lying lips to a ruler!" (17:7). Having already studied 1 and 2 Kings, we have already seen these sayings in operation!

Not all the sayings about rulers are negative in tone. "If a king judges the poor with fairness, his throne will always be secure" (29:14). "Remove the wicked from the king's presence, and his throne will be established through righteousness" (25:5). "Kings detest wrongdoing, for a throne is established through righteousness. Kings take pleasure in honest lips; they value a man who speaks the truth" (16:12–13). "When a king sits on his throne to judge, he winnows out all evil with his eyes" (20:8).

The Excellent Wife

It is true that men play a more important role in the Bible than women do, but the Book of Proverbs ends with a long hymn of praise to "the excellent wife" who is "far more precious than jewels." How fortunate her husband is, for "she brings him good, not harm, all the days of her life." Not only is she extremely industrious in the home, but she is also wise in investing money in land. Thanks to her wisdom in household management, her family never lacks for anything. But her compassion is not limited to her own family: "She opens her arms to the poor and extends her hands to the needy." She not only sets an example by her life but teaches by words as well: "She speaks with wisdom, and faithful instruction is on her tongue."

The most important verse, 30, sums up the Bible's view of what is important for every woman: "Charm is deceptive, and beauty is fleeting, but a woman who fears the Lord is to be praised." We might even go a step further and extend that truth to all people, both men and women.

This is included in the last chapter of Proverbs, 31, said to be the work of "Lemuel, king of Massa, taught him by his mother." Massa was somewhere in northern Arabia, and the inclusion of this chapter by a non-Israelite shows that Israel respected wisdom, whatever nation it came from. Lemuel certainly had a wise mother, and if she resembled the woman described in Proverbs 31, Lemuel—and everyone who knew her—was truly blessed.

"Love and faithfulness keep a king safe; through love his throne is made secure" (20:28). "It is the glory of God to conceal a matter; to search out a matter is the glory of kings" (25:2). "The lips of a king speak as an oracle, and his mouth should not betray justice" (16:10).

But, as we noted earlier, it is God who is in charge of the universe, not heads of state—for which we can all be thankful. "The king's heart is in the hand of the Lord; he directs it like a watercourse wherever he pleases" (21:1). When rulers are just and fair, we can not only thank them, but thank God, whose wisdom is present when the laws are right: "By me [wisdom] kings reign and rulers make laws that are just; by me princes govern, and all nobles who rule on earth" (8:15–16). Although Proverbs urges kings to be guided by God's wisdom, the book is reality-centered enough to know that all earthly governors have their limitations. "Many seek an audience with a ruler, but it is from the Lord that man gets justice" (29:26).

THE "FOREVER" PROBLEM

Did the writers of Proverbs believe in an afterlife? If they did, it isn't mentioned. The recurring theme is that wisdom offers people rewards on *this* side of the grave: "My son, do not forget my teaching, but keep my commands in your heart, for they will prolong your life many years and bring you prosperity" (3:1–2). "Long life is in her [wisdom's] right hand; in her left hand are riches and honor" (3:16). "Humility and the fear of the Lord bring wealth and honor and life" (22:4). "Commit to the Lord whatever you do, and your plans will succeed" (16:3).

Do we take these sayings at face value? If so, how can we reconcile them with the other Proverbs that say that a poor righteous man is better off than a rich wicked one? If wisdom (which is synonymous with righteousness in Proverbs) guarantees prosperity, how can there be *poor righteous people?*

Here is where we have to acknowledge something: Earthly wisdom has its limitations. The sayings in the Book of Proverbs are inspired by God and true. In fact, they are truer than their original writers knew. Whoever wrote that "righteousness delivers from death" (10:2) was saying more than he knew. There is, as we know (but the original writer did not), an afterlife. The promises of honor and long life for the righteous are all true—not honor and long life in this world, necessarily, but honor and eternal life afterward. Those committed to the Lord will "succeed," indeed—if not on earth, certainly afterward. As with Psalms and its visions of dwelling in the Lord's house "forever," Proverbs' promises of wealth, long life and success come to fulfillment in the Christian revelation. In the meantime, the wisdom of these wise sayings is still valid for us, teaching us to live decent, unselfish lives, honoring God in our words and deeds.

As we close this section on the Book of Proverbs, it is worth noting that some of the sayings occur more than once in the book—sometimes word for word, sometimes with a slight variation. And some of the sayings touch on the same basic ideas. If we wonder why the book repeats itself, it provides its own answer: Wisdom has to repeat itself because folly does. Consider one of the book's most unforgettable sayings: "As a dog returns to its vomit, so a fool repeats his folly" (26:11). That bit of wisdom applies not just to the individual but to the human race as a whole. The human race repeats its ancestors' mistakes; each generation does the same foolish things. But that is what the Bible's Wisdom books are designed to correct. Just because most people ignore the collective wisdom of the world is no reason we should do the same. God gave us wisdom in Proverbs. Let us absorb it and live it, driving out the old bad habits with good new ones.

PUTTING THE WORD TO WORK

1. Controlling the tongue is an important theme in Proverbs. If this is an area you'd like to improve upon, put yourself on a "word diet" for at least a day, pledging yourself to say nothing cruel or unkind, but only something kind or constructive. If the "diet" works, see how many days you can make it last.

2. Think of people you know who are prosperous and content with what they have. Think of others who are prosperous and unhappy. What makes the difference? Are the ones who are content people of faith?

3. Think of people you know who are rich in the spiritual sense. What is their attitude toward their material possessions?

4. Proverbs is blatantly anti-pride. Give yourself a "pride exam," asking yourself what you are most proud of. Looks, money, cleverness, intelligence? Are you ever aware of disliking the same kind of pride in others?

5. Think of some wise person in your life—parent, mentor, teacher, friend—whose advice made a huge difference in your life. Give that person a thank-you call, letter or e-mail.

A Deeper Wisdom

AT THE HEART OF IT ALL TODAY Why do good people suffer? What do we do when life seems meaningless? Job and Ecclesiastes probe these profound, universal questions—and give some surprising answers. The Song of Solomon is a poetic picture of intense love.

The Book of Proverbs, covered in the previous chapter, taught a message that most of the Old Testament affirms: Living wisely and morally will bring God's blessing upon you. It is a good message, but not a complete one. The fact is, we have all known very moral people who do not prosper—and

KEY PASSAGES TO READ TODAY

Job 1–3; 18–21; 38; 42

Ecclesiastes 1–2; 5:10–20; 8:14–17

Song of Solomon 2

immoral people who do. We look at the story of Moses and see a saintly and dynamic leader who endured much suffering, not only from a foreign oppressor but from his own people, the people he led out of slavery. We look at the life of Jesus and can't help but notice that he was hardly a *prosperous* or *successful* person—not by worldly standards, anyway. In a few places Proverbs even admits that it is better to be a poor person with morals than a rich person without them. But its basic message is that righteous living leads to success and prosperity.

KEY TERM FOR TODAY ## Vanity

As used in Ecclesiastes, *vanity* does not mean egotism or conceit but uselessness—doing things "in vain." It translates the Hebrew word *hebel*, which means "breath" or "vapor." It is used thirty-five times in the book, and in other places in the Old Testament, and it refers to something transient, worthless, empty. The King James Version has "vanity of vanities." (The Hebrews used this "X of X" form to indicate a superlative —"vanity of vanities" means "vanity to the utmost" or "vanity to the max"—"king of kings" means "the greatest king.") Modern translations have "utterly meaningless" or "all useless" or such—closer to the original meaning, since we no longer think of "vanity" as "something in vain." Throughout the Book of Ecclesiastes, most of the things that people pursue in life are shown to be *hebel*, worthless, useless, futile. Finding that human life is mostly "vanity" is, of course, the starting point for salvation: The vanity of the world makes us turn to God.

970–931 BC
Reign of Solomon

Ecclesiastes and
the Song of Songs
are attributed to
Solomon.

Job's author and date
are unknown, but it
probably dates from
during or before the
Babylonian exile, so
was written sometime
after 586 BC.

We find a deeper wisdom in the anonymous Book of Job, one of the gems of the Bible, and in the whole literature of the world. The story is based on the memory of a certain Job who was noted as a saintly man. The prophet Ezekiel mentions Job in the same verse as the righteous Noah, the man God chose to survive the flooding of the whole sinful world (Ezekiel 14:20). Job was not only righteous, but rich and successful, a devoted family man, respected by all who knew him. In other words, he was a living illustration of the Book of Proverbs—the virtuous man whom God blessed in every way. If you were going to raise the question of undeserved suffering, no subject could be imagined better than Job, who clearly deserved no suffering.

The story opens in "the land of Uz," which was probably somewhere in Arabia. The fact that he was not an Israelite is important. His prosperity and success prove that God blesses moral people everywhere, not just among the "chosen people," Israel. His story is universal in application, not just limited to the people of Israel.

Job is described as "blameless and upright; he feared God and shunned evil." He had seven sons and three daughters (in ancient times, no one considered himself "blessed" unless he had children, the more the better) and large flocks of livestock, plus a houseful of servants. The happy family took turns hosting dinners in the children's various homes, and Job offered sacrifices in case any of his children had sinned.

The scene shifts from Job's happy home to heaven, where the "sons of God" (probably meaning angels) assemble before the Lord. Among them is Satan, whose name means "adversary." In the Book of Job, Satan isn't the evil enemy of mankind, trying to tempt people and lead them into sin. He is a kind of heavenly prosecutor, presenting evidence against people doing wrong. He tells God he has been "roaming" the earth, and God asks him if he has seen "my servant Job," the perfectly blameless and upright man. Satan asks the question that sets the story in motion: "Does Job fear God for nothing?" (1:9). Well, of *course* Job acts like a saint—it pays off in prosperity! Take away all that he has, Satan says, and he will curse God, not praise him! God accepts the challenge: Go ahead, test Job.

One disaster follows another. Servants arrive to tell Job that raiders came and stole all the livestock, and killed the other servants to boot. Worse, all Job's children were feasting at the eldest son's house, and a storm struck the house, killing all the children. In a matter of moments the rich paterfamilias' life has completely changed. He reacted to the tragedy in the expected manner of the time, ripping his clothes and shaving his head. But then, surprisingly, he worshipped God and said, "Naked I came from my mother's womb, and naked I will depart. The Lord gave and the Lord has taken away; may the name of the Lord be praised" (1:21).

Back in heaven, Satan shows up in court again. God is pleased: Job is still his faithful servant, even though his children and his wealth have been taken away all at once. But Satan does not give up so easily. If Job is stricken physically, he will surely curse God. So Satan strikes Job with painful sores from head to toe. His wife is flabbergasted—her mind seems to work the way Satan's does. She urges Job to "curse God and die." Why would anyone serve a God who allowed such disasters? Job's reply to her: "Shall we accept good from God, and not trouble?" Poor loathsome Job goes to sit in the local dump.

ENTER THE THREE WISE MEN

Three of Job's friends hear of his troubles and come to visit. The fact that they are not local is important: They know of Job more by reputation than by actual contact. They have met him, and they have heard he is a righteous man, but they don't know him intimately, on a day-to-day basis. In what follows, their lack of intimate knowledge about him will lead them to make some rash assumptions. (It is always easier to make judgments about someone when we know little about them, isn't it?)

Their intentions are good. They go to "sympathize with him and comfort him" (2:11). They are so horrified when they actually see him, they cannot even speak for

---

CULTURAL INSIGHTS

Wisdom of the East

Job is described as a man extolled among the "people of the East." In the Old Testament, this usually referred to Edom and Arabia, nations east of Israel, and an area renowned for its wise men. In 1 Kings 5, a tribute to Solomon's wisdom is that it surpassed "all the sons of the East." The neighbor nation of Edom was frequently at war with Israel, but nonetheless there were many wise men among the Edomites, as we see in the Book of Job, whose main character lives in the "land of Uz"—Edom, or possibly Arabia, according to the scholars. The prophets Jeremiah and Obadiah condemned Edom but couldn't help mentioning its people's wisdom (Jeremiah 49:7, Obadiah 8). While most of the Book of Proverbs is attributed to "Solomon, king of Israel," chapters 30 and 31 are attributed to Agur and Lemuel "of Massa," which was an area of north Arabia. Job's three friends—Eliphaz the Temanite, Bildad the Shuhite, and Zophar the Naamathite—are all from "the East," so the original readers of the book would expect them to be full of deep wisdom. In other words, these are not three yokel blowhards spouting off their opinions in a barroom but are respected men from an area known for producing profound thinkers. They are, from a human point of view, the best minds available for "explaining" Job's sufferings—and the fact that they cannot, and only make him feel worse, sends the reader a clear message: Even at its best, human wisdom is inadequate.

seven days. They tear their own robes in agony. The fact that they say nothing—at first, anyway—is commendable. Sometimes a suffering person simply needs to know that someone is *there*, witnessing the suffering. Words are not always necessary.

Job himself breaks the silence. Instead of cursing God, he curses the day of his own birth—if only it had never happened! Or if only he had been stillborn, so he would not have had to see these days of woe! In the grave, at least there is peace, or an end of troubles! "Why is light given to those in misery, and life to the bitter of soul, to those who long for death that does not come, who search for it more than for hidden treasure?" (Job 3:20–21).

The first of the three friends to speak is Eliphaz. Since he speaks first, we might assume he is the oldest of the three, and presumably the wisest as well. He reminds Job that Job himself was a man who offered comfort to the suffering, but now he can't seem to comfort himself in his day of trouble. Then Eliphaz begins what makes up the heart of the three friends' words: He tries to *explain* the suffering. "Consider now: Who, being innocent, has ever perished? Where were the upright ever destroyed? As I have observed, those who plow evil and those who sow trouble reap it" (4:7–8). Eliphaz recalls a vision, in which a heavenly being asked him, "Can a mortal be more righteous than God? Can a man be more pure than his Maker?" God always catches evil people, even if they are skilled at hiding their sins: "He catches the wise in their craftiness, and the schemes of the wily are swept away" (5:13). Job has sinned, and God is discipling him. "Blessed is the man whom God corrects; so do not despise the discipline of the Almighty. For he wounds, but he also binds up; he injures, but his hands also heal." If Job will admit his fault, God will bless him again with prosperity. Eliphaz is sure of himself: "We have examined this, and it is true. So hear it and apply it to yourself" (5:27).

Job is not impressed with these answers. "A despairing man should have the devotion of his friends...But my brothers are as undependable as intermittent streams" (6:14–15). They are no comfort at all: "You see something dreadful and are afraid." (This is a rather human reaction to seeing something horrible: feeling fear and revulsion instead of compassion.) "Teach me, and I will be quiet; show me where I have been wrong. . . What do your arguments prove? Do you mean to correct what I say, and treat the words of a despairing man as wind?" Job is not going to submit meekly to their answers. "I will not keep silent; I will speak out in the anguish of my spirit, I will complain in the bitterness of my soul." Then he asks God the question all suffering people ask: "If I have sinned, what have I done to you, O watcher of men? Why have you made me your target?" (7:20).

The second friend, Bildad, picks up the argument: "How long will you say such things? Your words are a blustering wind. Does God pervert justice? Does the Almighty pervert what is right?" Bildad tells Job that his children died because they sinned, plain and simple. Their wise ancestors knew how these things worked. "Ask the former generations and find out what their fathers learned, for we were born only yesterday and know nothing, and our days on earth are but a shadow. Will they not instruct you and tell you? Will they not bring forth words from their understanding?" In the final analysis, "God does not reject a blameless man or strengthen the hands of evildoers" (8:20). If Job is suffering, he has sinned.

Job is not convinced. He asks an obvious question: "How can a mortal be righteous before God?" (9:2). Then he considers a painful truth: God *does* allow innocent people to suffer. "He destroys both the blameless and the wicked. When a scourge brings sudden death, he mocks the despair of the innocent. When a land falls into the hands of the wicked, he blindfolds its judges. If it is not he, then who is it?" (Note that the book does not blame Satan for mankind's woes. Even if Satan causes troubles, God *allows* him to do so.) Job again wishes he could speak to God face to face and question him: "Tell me what charges you have against me. Does it please you to oppress me, to spurn the work of your hands, while you smile on the schemes of the wicked? Do you have eyes of flesh? Do you see as a mortal sees?" (10:2–4).

Zophar, the third friend, is appalled. "Are all these words to go unanswered? Is this talker to be vindicated? Will your idle talk reduce men to silence? Will no one rebuke you when you mock? You say to God, 'My beliefs are flawless and I am pure in your sight' " (11:2–4). Job ought to realize that God can see through humans' deceit. If Job will admit his sin and turn from it, God will surely bless him again.

Poor Job becomes more sarcastic the more he hears. "Doubtless you are the people, and wisdom will die with you! But I have a mind as well as you; I am not inferior to you. Who does not know all these things?" Then he speaks one of the most painful sentences in the whole Bible: "Men at ease have contempt for misfortune" (12:5). This powerful

Redeemer

Job prays for a *goel* to come and stand up for him or relieve him from his suffering. The Hebrew word *goel* is translated "redeemer" or "avenger." The *goel* was a person's near relative who would take action on his behalf—buying him out of slavery, rescuing him from poverty, or avenging his death. In other words, this was the person whose help you relied on in dire circumstances. We can't be sure if Job was hoping for a human *goel* to aid him, or was thinking that God himself would be his *goel*—possibly he was praying for *anyone* to rescue him.

Christians often refer to Christ as *Redeemer*, the idea being that we are enslaved to sin, and Christ rescues us from it. People often read Job's words—"I know that my Redeemer lives"—as a prophecy of Christ, the divine Redeemer. In his classic choral work the *Messiah*, composer George Frederick Handel set this passage from Job to music and applied the passage to Christ. The New Testament refers many times to Jesus redeeming people from their sins.

insight may offer one "explanation" for suffering: Unless we suffer ourselves, we really can't feel deep sympathy for other people's suffering. Sympathy instructs the heart. Job is exasperated: "You are worthless physicians, all of you! If only you would be altogether silent! For you, that would be wisdom." This is a profound truth. Silence is better than giving pat answers—or trying to explain the unexplainable. Job turns their "explanation" back on them: "Would it turn out well if he examined you?" Then he gives his opinion of their deep "wisdom": "Your maxims are proverbs of ashes; your defenses are defenses of clay" (13:12). In short, words of wisdom bump up against hard reality.

Eliphaz answers again. Clearly Job is "crafty," trying to conceal his hidden sins, but he can't deceive God—or his wise friends. "Do you limit wisdom to yourself? What do you know that we do not know? What insights do you have that we do not have? The gray-haired and the aged are on our side, men even older than your father" (15:8–10). The wise know that the sinner will be caught up with, eventually. "Distress and anguish fill him with terror; they overwhelm him, like a king poised to attack, because he shakes his fist at God and vaunts himself against the Almighty" (15:24–25).

Job becomes more disgusted with his so-called friends. "I have heard many things like these; miserable comforters are you all!...But come on, all of you, try again! I will not find a wise man among you" (16:2, 17:10).

Bildad is insulted: "Why are we regarded as cattle and considered stupid in your sight?" (18:3). Doesn't Job know what "everyone" knows? "The lamp of the wicked is snuffed out; the flame of his fire stops burning."

COMFORTLESS CONSOLERS

Their "wisdom" only makes Job's plight worse: "How long will you torment me and crush me with words?" (19:2). Must they add to his pain? "I am nothing but skin and bones; I have escaped with only the skin of my teeth. Have pity on me, my friends, have pity, for the hand of God has struck me. Why do you pursue me as God does? Will you never get enough of my flesh?" (19:20–22). Job prays that some avenger will show that he is in the right—if not in this world, then afterward: "I know that my Redeemer lives, and that in the end he will stand upon the earth. And after my skin has been destroyed, yet in my flesh I will see God" (19:25–26).

Zophar counters with the familiar wisdom: Sinners get away with their sins, but are caught up with in time. Job thinks otherwise: "Why do the wicked live on, growing old and increasing in power? They see their children established around them, their off-spring before their eyes. Their homes are safe and free from fear; the rod of God is not upon them. They spend their years in prosperity and go down to the grave in peace. Yet they say to God, 'Leave us alone! We have no desire to know your ways. Who is the Almighty, that we should serve him? What would we gain by praying to him?' " The "wise" say the evil man's children will be punished for their father's sins, but that makes no sense. A man should be punished for his own sins! (21:19–21).

Eliphaz comes to the point: Job hasn't been the saint he is reputed to be: "Is not your wickedness great? Are not your sins endless?…You gave no water to the weary and you withheld food from the hungry, though you were a powerful man, owning land—an honored man, living on it. And you sent widows away empty-handed and broke the strength of the fatherless" (22:5–9).

Job will not accept these accusations: "Whoever heard me spoke well of me, and those who saw me commended me, because I rescued the poor who cried for help, and the fatherless who had none to assist him. The man who was dying blessed me; I made the widow's heart sing.… I was eyes to the blind and feet to the lame" (29:11–15). Now, the righteous man who showed compassion to all is mocked by everyone, an object of scorn. "I have become a brother of jackals, a companion of owls" (30:29). He throws out a challenge to God: "Let God weigh me in honest scales and he will know that I am blameless—the traveler—I sign now my defense—let the Almighty answer me; let my accuser put his indictment in writing.… I would give him an account of my every step."

Note that Eliphaz, Bildad and Zophar are not being mocked. They are stating what most people at the time believed. Their problem is that everything is black and white for them, no gray areas. They fell prey to the theologians' occupational hazard: not allowing for mystery. They did not conceive of the idea of serving God strictly for love. They could not conceive of the relationship to God as something more than an exchange of man's virtue for God's earthly rewards.

A fourth friend, a younger man named Elihu, arrives and scolds the "three wise men." They have defended God eloquently but not quite correctly, he says. Suffering isn't always punished, Elihu says, but can be preemptive, a warning from God "to turn man from wrongdoing and keep him from pride, to preserve his soul from the pit, his life from perishing by the sword.... a man may be chastened on a bed of pain" (33:17–19). God "makes them listen to correction and commands them to repent of their evil" (36:10). Elihu's ideas are interesting but they do not apply to Job's situation.

Another voice enters the conversation: God, speaking out of a storm. He tells Job, "Brace yourself like a man; I will question you, and you shall answer me. Where were you when I laid the earth's foundation? Tell me, if you understand" (38:3–4). In chapters 38–41, God describes the beauty and complexity of the creation. The language here is striking and poetic—doing justice to its subject. Does Job understand the weather, the ways of the birds and beasts? Does he keep the vast world in motion and care for its creatures giving birth? "Will the one who contends with the Almighty correct him? Let him who accuses God answer him!...Who has a claim against me that I must pay? Everything under heaven belongs to me" (40:2, 41:11).

After hearing all this from the mouth of God himself, Job is in awe: "I know that you can do all things; no plan of yours can be thwarted.... My ears had heard of you but now my eyes have seen you. Therefore I despise myself and repent in dust and ashes" (42:2–6). Job isn't repenting of the sins that his friends were sure he committed —he is repenting of questioning God. Clearly the ways of God are beyond human comprehension. God is great. He runs an entire universe, sustaining every atom of it. Surely he can be trusted to do what is right, even though he does not "owe" anyone anything. God says not a word about guilt or innocence, suffering or its "meaning." He doesn't need to, for a more important message got through to Job and the friends: *I am God. I rule. Trust me.*

But God is not angry with Job for his questioning. Rather, he is angry with Job's three friends. They tried to explain God—which cannot be done. This is a key theme in the book: *Suffering cannot always be explained. We have to accept that God's ways are sometimes beyond our understanding.*

But all ends happily. God restores Job's fortunes, and he fathers more children, including three beautiful daughters. Job lives to be 120, seeing his great-great-grandchildren brought into the world. "And so he died, old and full of years" (42:17).

People often say that the book answers the question of innocent people suffering. It does not. Its answer to that question is: There is no answer. God does things in his own way—always right, but not always understandable.

This is the true message of the book: Faithful people stay faithful even when life seems unbearable. Job passed Satan's test. He did not turn against God when his prosperity vanished. God hadn't purchased Job's virtue. Job was virtuous even when he lost everything God had given him.

Some readers are bothered by the end of the book. Job becomes rich and satisfied again—doesn't that negate the whole book? Wouldn't it be better if Job stayed poor and still continued to love God? Perhaps. But remember, there is no clear belief in an afterlife in the book, and Israel at this time did not believe in one. We see things differently, believing in eternal life, and we would accept it if Job stayed poor and died poor—entering heaven, which would make his earthly riches seem small by comparison. But to the original audience, the poor man had suffered much—and passed the test of faith. Someone that steadfast deserved restoration. On that point we could not disagree. And in fact, he was a greater man for having endured. The heart is stretched through suffering and enlarged.

The theme of Job: Faith must remain even when understanding fails. The fullest answer to Job's problem was written centuries later by a Christian: "I consider that our present sufferings are not worth comparing with the glory that will be revealed in us" (Romans 8:18).

In closing this section, we can ask a valid question: Does the Bible contradict itself? Doesn't Proverbs, with its basic "virtue is rewarded" morality contradict Job? Not at all. The Bible gives us two sides of the same moral coin. One side is Proverbs, with its sensible, easy-to-remember maxims about living virtuously. The other side is Job, which reminds us that living virtuously does not always and inevitably bring an earthly reward. Proverbs is full of sound advice: Control your temper, give to the poor, watch your tongue, be honest in your business dealings, work hard, discipline your children, etc. The Book of Job is not opposed to such advice, but it reminds us that righteous living does not inevitably lead to prosperity. The Old Testament's constant emphasis on

---

CULTURAL INSIGHTS ## Theodicy

This comes from two Greek words, *theos,* "God," and *dike,* "justice." Theodicy means the study of God's justice—or, put another way, trying to explain to man why God sometimes appears unfair. For the ancient Egyptians, with their strong belief in an afterlife, theodicy was never an issue. If a person behaved badly and lived painlessly on earth, they were punished afterward. If a person was saintly but suffered while on earth, things were corrected afterward. When Job was written the Israelites were still not certain about an afterlife, which is why the book has to end with Job becoming even richer than he had been before.

behaving well and expecting to be rewarded probably helped people choose the right path. But any fool could see that sometimes good people suffered while wicked people succeeded. The book raises the possibility that calamities may have some other purpose than punishment. According to Proverbs 12:21, "No harm befalls the righteous, but the wicked have their fill of trouble." To that verse, the author of Job would have tacked on "usually" or "if God wills," for there are righteous people who suffer greatly, as Job proved.

Job reminds us that morality is not a "transaction," where God "owes" us a happy life because we behave well. Life isn't that neat, and neither is morality. Most of Proverbs would lead us to believe that God owes the righteous a good life. Job provides an additional insight: The moral life ought to be pursued for its own sake, not just for the benefits it can bring us. We are supposed to be good because it's the right thing to do, not because it pays. Put another way, righteous living is "volunteer work," not "work for hire." You offer your services to the nursing home or museum or church or charity because it's a good thing to do, not because you're *paid* to do it.

ECCLESIASTES: SO WHAT'S THE POINT?

The Book of Job was written as a kind of antidote to people's reliance on wisdom. Not that wisdom is wrong—far from it! The Book of Proverbs is one of the great books of the Bible and should be studied closely. But wisdom, though it is a good *guide* in life, is not a good *explanation* for everything. That is an important theme in Job. Wisdom is a useful tool—but, like any tool, it doesn't serve every purpose.

Let's turn to another book that tries to do what Job did—question whether wisdom is all it's made out to be. It happens that the author of this book, Ecclesiastes, is supposed to be Solomon, Israel's wisest king, one whose wisdom was so renowned that people traveled from distant lands to meet the king and hear him drop pearls of wisdom from his mouth. Solomon is credited with writing Proverbs, or most of the book, anyway. So who better than Solomon to take a close look at wisdom and point out its inadequacies?

The Hebrew title for this book is *Qoheleth*, which means something like "speaker in the assembly" or "speaker on behalf of the assembly." Its Greek name, Ecclesiastes, has pretty much the same meaning. (Greek *ekklesia* is "assembly.") In the text of the book itself, the King James Version used the term "Preacher": "The words of the Preacher, son of David, king in Jerusalem." Modern translations have "Speaker" or "Teacher," since we now think of a preacher as a minister in a church, and that is not what Qoheleth was. The writer may have chosen the name Qoheleth to mean something like "speaker on behalf of the public"—a public that, like him, had grown weary of the Wisdom literature and wished to write in response to it.

Before we launch into the book, a word of warning: Its organization is frustrating. The Book of Job follows a sequence, a story, a plan, and there is a "payoff" at the end. Ecclesiastes has no clear organization. It deals with topics, drops them, picks them up again in a later chapter. It is a difficult book to summarize or outline, but, thankfully, it does have a "payoff" at its end. In fact, the book reads as if it were written by a man who couldn't sleep, whose mind was bouncing from one topic to another late at night, with him writing down his thoughts as they occurred, with no attempt to edit them or organize them later on. Read it that way and you'll find it does have an odd logic of its own.

The book opens on a sour note: "Meaningless! Meaningless!" says the Teacher. "Utterly meaningless! Everything is meaningless." Everything, he observes, goes on in a never-ending cycle of sunrise, sunset, day after day, "nothing new under the sun." Here is a slap at humans' obsession with novelty. Nothing is really new, is there? (Note that the phrase "under the sun" occurs twenty-eight times in the book. It is the author's way of saying "here on earth.")

The Teacher says he was king in Jerusalem, that he devoted himself to study, to become wise—and he succeeded admirably, as 1 Kings tells us. He understood the human mind, but all his wisdom was a "chasing after the wind"—a phrase that occurs several times in the book. "The more knowledge, the more grief" (Ecclesiastes 1:18). Wisdom, alas, does not give all the satisfaction he hoped for. (Conclusion: The intellectual life does not satisfy.)

So he turned to pleasure—the reverse of most people's method, since most human beings would seek out pleasure long before they turned to wisdom. As king of Israel, Solomon had any pleasure he liked—including his enormous harem, literally hundreds of women at his beck and call. But "laughter is foolish. And what does pleasure accomplish?" Still guided by his wisdom, he pursued the decadent life, wondering if it brought man real meaning. It did not. (Conclusion: Life in pursuit of fun does not satisfy.)

So he turned to more creative pursuits. He built houses, planted vineyards and orchards, bought slaves and flocks of livestock, became fabulously wealthy. He denied himself no pleasure, and for a while enjoyed it all immensely. In other words, he achieved all that Job had, and more—but unlike Job, he was not satisfied. "Everything was meaningless, a chasing after the wind" (2:11). He still believed that wisdom was better than folly—and who would disagree?—but then realized that the wise man and the fool both end up in the grave. He had worked more and achieved more than anyone, only to have to face death and leave his legacy to a son—and who knew if he would be wise or foolish? (The reader is expected to remember that Solomon's son, Rehoboam, was a tactless fool and a failure as king.) A man strives to achieve something yet he cannot lie down at night and sleep in peace (2:23). (Conclusion: Becoming a "success" does not satisfy.)

The wise man, the pleasure seeker, the respected successful man—all fail to find complete fulfillment "under the sun." The author's experience has turned him into a "futilitarian," finding no real meaning in life.

CONTENTMENT AND OBEDIENCE

And yet, all man's pursuits are not utterly wasted: "A man can do nothing better than to eat and drink and find satisfaction in his work. This too, I see, is from the hand of God, for without him, who can eat or find enjoyment?" (2:24–25). The Speaker repeats the same thought in 3:12–13—but also complains that God has "set eternity in the hearts of men" yet not given them the satisfaction of seeing the purpose in all things (3:11). Perhaps he had noticed that contentment is as rare among humans as it is natural among animals. Also, men die just as the animals die, and that is the end. He wonders if perhaps men's spirits go to a different place than the animals', but is not certain. (In a sense, humans are worse off than animals, since they foresee death and fear it.) In fact, the Speaker was obsessed with death, unhappy that no matter how pleasant life might seem, death awaits everyone. A person who succeeded at all he tried ends up in the grave just as an utter failure does. He envies those who have already died, for they at least no longer have the threat of death hanging over them (4:2).

He looks at human achievement again and becomes cynical: "I saw that all labor and all achievement spring from man's envy of his neighbor. This too is meaningless, a chasing after the wind" (4:4). A painful thought—but a true one. Isn't much of human effort spent on trying to impress other people, to keep up with them, surpass them? "Better one handful with tranquility than two handfuls with toil and chasing after the wind" (4:6)—indeed! In fact, the rather simple notion of being content with what you have crops up again and again in the book. After all, "whoever loves money never has money enough" and "the abundance of the rich man permits him no sleep" (5:10–12). Man comes into the world naked and penniless and leaves the same way. Some fortunate men of wealth do have the knack for enjoying their wealth, but most do not.

"Better what the eye sees than the roving of the appetite" (6:9). Again, the theme of contentment with what you have. "Go, eat your food with gladness, and drink your wine with a joyful heart, for it is now that God favors what you do. Always be clothed in white, and always anoint your head with oil. Enjoy life with your wife, whom you love, all the days of this meaningless life that God has given you under the sun—all your meaningless days. For this is your lot in life and in your toilsome labor under the sun. Whatever your hand finds to do, do it with all your might, for in the grave, where you are going, there is neither working nor planning nor knowledge nor wisdom" (9:7–10). Put another way, each day itself is blessing enough. Grand plans and high aspirations are fine, in their way, but sometimes they distract us from the small and pleasant things of life—and when our plans fail, they can indeed seem like a "chasing after the wind."

One of the curiosities of the book is that, in spite of its claim that wisdom is a "chasing after the wind," it keeps stating wise sayings—as if Solomon, the author of Proverbs, was destined to be a moral teacher no matter what his doubts about wisdom were. Some of them could easily fit into Proverbs: "As fish are caught in a cruel net, or birds are taken in a snare, so men are trapped by evil times that fall unexpectedly upon them" (9:12). "The quiet words of the wise are more to be heeded than the shouts of a ruler of fools" (9:17). "As dead flies give perfume a bad smell, so a little folly outweighs wisdom and honor" (10:1). "Whoever digs a pit may fall into it; whoever breaks through a wall may be bitten by a snake" (10:8). "If a man is lazy, the rafters sag; if his hands are idle, the house leaks" (10:18). "It is better to heed a wise man's rebuke than to listen to the song of fools" (7:5). "Do not be quickly provoked in your spirit, for anger resides in the lap of fools" (7:9). "When the sentence for a crime is not quickly carried out, the hearts of the people are filled with schemes to do wrong" (8:11). All are worthy sayings, yet they seem to fit oddly in a book where the author laments that wisdom is "meaningless."

In fact, one reason he described wisdom as "meaningless" was that he was confronted with the same problem that the Book of Job confronts: "There is something else meaningless that occurs on earth: righteous men who get what the wicked deserve, and wicked men who get what the righteous deserve. This too, I say, is meaningless" (8:14). Likewise, "The race is not to the swift or the battle to the strong, nor does food come to the wise or wealth to the brilliant or favor to the learned; but time and chance happen to them all" (9:11). As Job and his friends discovered, we cannot fully understand the ways of God. "When I applied my mind to know wisdom and to observe man's labor on earth—his eyes not seeing sleep day or night—then I saw all that God has done. No one can comprehend what goes on under the sun. Despite all his efforts to search it out, man cannot discover its meaning. Even if a wise man claims he knows, he cannot really comprehend it" (8:16–17). "As you do not know the path of the wind, or how the body is formed in a mother's womb, so you cannot understand the work of God, the Maker of all things" (11:5). Of course we can't. The same message of Job applies here: Faith has to take over where understanding fails. God gives us wisdom and expects us to use it, but wisdom can only take us so far.

As you might expect, this book—so full of doubts and puzzling—does not end with some earthshaking revelation, no "I found the Ultimate Answer!" The finish is restrained, but still worth heeding: "Now all has been heard; here is the conclusion of the matter: Fear God and keep his commandments, for this is the whole duty of man. For God will bring every deed into judgment, including every hidden thing, whether it is good or evil" (12:13–14). After all his hand-wringing and doubting and cries of "Meaningless!" the Speaker comes back to the same base as Moses and all the prophets: *Honor and obey God.*

Even if Ecclesiastes was the only part of the Bible a person ever read, it would be a great advance toward the truth, since it shows clearly that there is no ultimate satisfaction in anything on this earth.

"Of making many books there is no end, and much study wearies the body" (12:12). So said the author of Ecclesiastes, adding yet another book to the load. But it is a worthwhile, fascinating book, a reminder that a man who "had it all" did not find full satisfaction in life, that life on earth—even life lived to the fullest—seemed "meaningless, a chasing after the wind." For him, the inevitability of death—with no afterlife—took much of the joy out of life. If wise, rich Solomon could not find total fulfillment on earth, how can we? The answer of the New Testament is: *You can't, but there is something more, something better, ahead...*

THE BOOK OF LOVE

The Song of Songs, or Song of Solomon, or Canticles—it has no shortage of names—is so utterly different from the other Old Testament books that it does not fit well into any category. We include it in this chapter because it had the same author as Ecclesiastes, and because people mistakenly include it among the Wisdom books. It is one of two books in the Bible that do not mention God (Esther is the other), and there is nothing even remotely religious about it. It is a set of love poems, spoken by a man and woman who are head over heels in love and eager to express it.

How did it end up in the Bible? The honest answer is that people read meanings into it that the writer probably did not intend. From an early time the Jews treated it as an allegory: The man in the poem represented God, and the woman represented Israel. The love poems were about God and Israel expressing their devotion to each other, and everything in the poem had a meaning. Christians also interpreted the book allegorically, except that the woman represented the church—or the individual Christian soul. During the Middle Ages, scholars wrote long commentaries on the book, going into painstaking detail about what things in the poems represented: Hair represented this, apples represented that, etc. Writers outdid themselves seeing who could find the most "spiritual" interpretation of the book. Had it not been for the belief that the book was really an allegory, neither Christians nor Jews would have included it in the Bible.

Now let's ask the obvious question: Were they right? Today, most Christians and Jews would say, no. The book is what it is—a very intense expression of human love. But, unlike our ancestors, we can accept it that way. Physical attraction to another human being is not sinful in itself. And the two speakers in the Song are not just seething with lust—they appear to be in deep, true, long-lasting love, something Christians fully support. However, it is worth remembering that Israel did think of God as its "husband," and that the prophet Hosea was told that his own marriage to an unfaithful woman was a symbol of God's abiding love for faithless Israel. The apostle Paul told Christians that love between husband and wife was a picture of Christ's love for his "bride," the church (Ephesians 5:32). The many generations of Christians and Jews who read a spiritual meaning into the book were not completely wrong. Human love is a kind of echo of divine love.

Did Solomon actually write it? It is pleasant to think so—but since he had hundreds of wives and concubines, we wonder how he could single out one of the women for the intense emotion that we see in the poem. Some commentators have suggested that Solomon, who never experienced monogamous love, did not write the Song about himself and a real woman, but about the true love he never had, the one who could have made him want to forget the well-populated harem in his palace. This is all speculation, because we don't really know. However, the author and his original purpose are not as important as the book's actual content.

The book is fairly brief and, though it is not one of the spiritual high points of the Bible, it is worth reading through, if only to remind us that this kind of intense love is something God approves of—after all, he did create the human body and the sexual instinct. One thing that surprises readers is that even though the book is full of details about the two lovers' physical appearance, the feeling is romantic, not pornographic.

Reading the book is like taking a walk in the country, when spring is in the air and everything is in bloom, including love. "Awake, north wind, and come, south wind! Blow on my garden, that its fragrance may spread abroad. Let my lover come into his garden and taste its choice fruits" (Song of Solomon 4:16). "Let us go early to the vineyards to see if the vines have budded, if their blossoms have opened, and if the pomegranates are in bloom" (7:12). "Like an apple tree among the trees of the forest is my lover among the young men. I delight to sit in his shade, and his fruit is sweet to my taste" (2:3).

> **DID YOU KNOW?**
>
> The Jews read the full Song of Solomon every year at the celebration of Passover, taking the book to be a song about God's love for Israel.

One of the pleasures in reading the book is just the awareness of two people taking such delight in each other's company. "My lover spoke and said to me, 'Arise, my darling, my beautiful one, and come with me'" (2:10). "My lover is mine and I am his; he browses among the lilies" (2:16). "How delightful is your love, my sister, my bride! How much more pleasing is your love than wine, and the fragrance of your perfume than any spice!" (4:10). "How beautiful you are and how pleasing, O love, with your delights!" (7:6).

The intensity of love is expressed in the Song's most-quoted verses: "Place me like a seal over your heart, like a seal on your arm; for love is as strong as death, its jealousy unyielding as the grave. It burns like blazing fire, like a mighty flame. Many waters cannot quench love; rivers cannot wash it away. If one were to give all the wealth of his house for love, it would be utterly scorned" (8:6–7). Reading these verses, we can see why Jews and Christians could read spiritual meaning into the book. Love—the deep, eternal kind—really is the powerful force the Song says it is. When physical attraction has run its course, real love endures. When people find human love inadequate, their love hunger can lead them to God.

PUTTING THE WORD TO WORK

1. Think of an occasion when you were going through a rough time and a friend played the "blame game" with you instead of offering sympathy. How did you feel? Were you ever on the other side of this, trying to "explain" someone's misfortune instead of giving sympathy?

2. One of Job's sorrows is that people who respected him when he was wealthy mock him now that he has lost everything. Do you think it's true that people rally to winners and scorn losers? Have you known of exceptions?

3. What do you think of Elihu's notion that suffering can be a kind of warning from God, intended to humble us and keep us from sinning? Think of times in your own life when this might have occurred.

4. The author of Ecclesiastes saw most human pursuits as a "chasing after the wind." Have you known people who had the same experience? What did they turn to in order to find purpose and fulfillment?

5. The Song of Solomon has been read allegorically and realistically. Which do you think is the most profitable way to read it? What would you say to a friend who might find it amusing that a book about physical love is in the Bible?

God's Spokesmen

AT THE HEART OF IT ALL TODAY The Old Testament prophets were called by God to preach repentance, warn of disasters, and console the brokenhearted. The great prophet Isaiah emphasized the Lord's holiness and the coming of a "suffering servant" of God who would bring spiritual healing.

The final section of the Old Testament consists of the Prophets, and their writings are some of the most sublime—and disturbing—parts of the whole Bible. Traditionally they are divided into the Major Prophets (Isaiah, Jeremiah, Ezekiel) and Minor Prophets (Hosea, Joel, Amos, Obadiah,

> **KEY PASSAGES TO READ TODAY**
>
> Isaiah 6; 11:1–9; 40; 42:1–9; 49:1–6; 50:4–11; 52:13—53:12

Jonah, Micah, Nahum, Habakkuk, Zephaniah, Haggai, Zechariah, Malachi). The last twelve are called "Minor" not because they are unimportant but because their writings are so much shorter than those of the Major Prophets. In fact, the Minor Prophets together made up one scroll, and their writings were often called "the Twelve."

The prophets cover a wide span of time. The earliest, Amos, prophesied around 760 BC, while the later ones—Haggai, Zechariah and Malachi—prophesied after the Jews returned from their Babylonian exile in 538 BC. The last may have been Joel, who prophesied around 400 BC. Despite the wide time span, they all had much in common. They spoke out against sin—mostly those of their own people, but also the sins of other

KEY TERM FOR TODAY ## Sin

The Old Testament uses several words that we translate as "sin." The Hebrew word *hattat* means missing the mark, failing to do what is expected in relation to another person. The word *awon* means a twisted or distorted condition, meaning the person has deviated from the standard. The word *pesa* means rebellion, meaning one has violated the rights of another. In the case of Israel, it means being unfaithful to the covenant with God. The word *maal* also means infidelity, failing to live up to one's obligations. They had forgotten that their covenant with God, made at Sinai, mandated that they were to be a *holy people*, as God himself was holy. God spoke through the prophets to remind people that they were called to be holy.

nations—and offered consolation and hope. *Threat* and *consolation* were the two basic forms in the writings, and often the two were mingled together. The prophets spoke of God's *punishment* and *pardon*.

We think of a prophet as someone who foretells the future. Most of the prophets in the Bible did make predictions—but that was not their main purpose. The main purpose of the prophet was to be God's spokesman, his mouthpiece—which is what the Hebrew word *nabi* means. This wasn't a matter of the prophet merely "taking dictation" from God. The prophet's own personality and vocabulary did not disappear. But in some way that is impossible to explain, the prophet *heard the word of the Lord* and felt compelled to speak it to others. Jeremiah recalled God telling him, "I have put my words in your mouth" (1:9). The phrase "the word of the Lord came to So-and-So" occurs many times in these writings. Ezekiel used the phrase "the hand of the Lord was upon me." The prophet was never just his own man. He was someone who had an immediate experience of God, who saw both the present and the future through the eyes of God, and who was sent to remind people of their duty to God, bringing them back to obedience and love. As a New Testament author put it, "prophecy never had its origin in the will of man, but men spoke from God as they were carried along by the Holy Spirit" (2 Peter 1:21).

Israel's first great prophet was, of course, Moses, who conversed with God, received the divine Law, and led the Israelites out of Egypt. Following the death of Moses, there were few prophets in Israel until the reign of Ahab, when the fiery prophet Elijah spoke out against the king's many crimes. Elijah is considered the great prophet of Israel, but he and his successor, Elisha, did not write any of their prophecies down. We know these two amazing men from their stories in 1 and 2 Kings. From their time until the time of Joel, around 400 BC, there were always some prophets in Israel, trying to turn the people back to the right.

There were also plenty of *false* prophets. Most of these were the "yes men" of kings' courts, paid to put a god's stamp of approval on whatever the king proposed doing. We might think of these as "royal chaplains," hired to make the king feel good about what he was doing because God (so these prophets said) approved. But some of the court prophets, such as Nathan, said just what God wanted them to. It is a distinction of Israel that a court prophet could be so bold toward his king. Prophets in other nations did not behave this way—not if they wanted to survive.

How could people distinguish a false prophet from a true one? Often they could not. The false ones were generally the ones that told people what they wanted to hear, while the message of the true ones was often rejected. Many of the true prophets spoke out against the false prophets who promised peace and security when in fact disaster was about to strike. True prophets had no hesitation denouncing sin—individual, royal or national. The true prophets were often persecuted and unpopular, while the false ones were generally left alone. People do not like to be told they are immoral. The false prophets listened not to the word of God but to public opinion, and to the policies of the kings—which were usually at odds with the will of God.

There were "fraternities" of prophets, some of which gathered around some notable prophet, such as Elisha, whose disciples were called the "sons of the prophets." But most of the prophets of the Lord were individuals, and it is striking that the false prophets often operated in herds, such as the four hundred Baal prophets who faced Elijah, or the court prophets who wrongly counseled Ahab. The Bible gives the distinct impression that the true prophets were lone—and often lonely—individuals through whom God spoke. There is not much evidence that God ever spoke through or to the fraternities. This is something we notice throughout history: *God mostly reveals himself to individuals, not groups.* An individual is more likely to hear God's voice than a mob is.

The prophets were from very different backgrounds. Isaiah seems to have been from the upper class, while Amos and Micah were farmers, and Jeremiah and Ezekiel were from priestly families. Some ministered a long time, some only a few months. Some were called by God in their youth, others much later. All had in common the fact that God compelled them to speak out. All had a vision of God as a holy, righteous Being who loved mankind but was offended at people's immorality. God would punish people for their sins—but he preferred that they return to him in love and obedience. God is both stern and tender, demanding and forgiving, severe and kind.

GOD'S BOLD MESSENGERS

The books of the prophets contain:

a. the words of God—that is, the words of the prophet speaking on behalf of God
b. first-person narratives of the prophet's experience
c. third-person narratives of the prophet's experience

We don't know who wrote down the third-person narratives, except in the case of Jeremiah, where it was definitely his disciple Baruch. The words of God might have been written down by the prophets themselves, but could have been written down by their followers. It is clear that some of the later prophets knew and valued the older prophets, as seen in Jeremiah's quoting of Micah (Jeremiah 26:17–18).

The books of the prophets in our Bibles were probably all spoken before they were written down. In their writings we often encounter the word "oracle," which is the English translation of the Hebrew word *massa*, meaning "lifting up" the voice. It was assumed that the writings of the prophets were originally delivered orally. In ancient times, writing was considered a poor substitute for live, direct communication. However, we can be thankful that these great prophets, or their disciples, wrote down their words, since those words are able to reach out to millions of people over the centuries.

The prophets usually addressed their message to their whole nation, not to individuals, except in the case of kings, where the prophet might speak to the king and tell him of God's will for the whole nation—or demand that a wicked king change his ways, as in the case of Elijah confronting Ahab or Nathan confronting David. Since they were true prophets—not the "yes men" court prophets who were the hirelings of the kings—the men of God often got into trouble with kings, more often persecuted than listened to. Scolding kings was a privilege that nations beside Israel did not extend to prophets. We see this in the case of Ahab and his foreign-born wife Jezebel. Ahab despised the prophet Elijah but did nothing to harm him, fearing that Elijah really was God's spokesman, but Jezebel, raised in a culture where kings did whatever they pleased, made an effort to have Elijah killed. The freedom of the prophets in Israel was an indication that Israel's kings were not above God's law, that God could send prophets to chastise kings.

The prophets' primary aim was *repentance*. The people of Israel and Judah were sinning, disobeying God's law, and God intended to bring disaster on them if they did not reform. Chief among the sins was idolatry, worshipping other gods. The prophets knew that worship of false gods was more than just a matter of praying to someone other than God. *Idolatry always led to immorality.* The worship of fertility gods such as Baal and Asherah was more like a sexual orgy than a solemn worship service. There were "shrine prostitutes," both male and female, and some of the pagan worship sites were more like brothels than temples. But aside from the sexual promiscuity, there were disgusting practices such as sacrificing children to the false gods.

The false gods were not moral beings. They were forces of nature, violent, cruel, promiscuous. And the prophets understood something very profound: *People become like the things they worship.* They also worship the things they would *like* to become. The Old Testament several times mentions that people are "corrupted" by their worship of idols. The prophets saw that if the people worshipped immoral gods, they would become immoral themselves: "They followed worthless idols and became worthless themselves" (Jeremiah 2:5). If they worship a holy and moral God, they will tend to be like him. If they worship the lecherous, bloodstained gods of the pagans, they become like those gods. For the worshippers of idols there is no real connection between divinity and morality, so morality becomes purely a matter of what the majority agrees upon. There is no divine or cosmic basis for human behavior; rather, people do whatever they can get away with. (In a sense our current obsession with celebrities is the same thing. They fascinate us because they do the things we dream of doing, and usually get away with them.)

The prophets sometimes speak of the people "whoring after other gods" (Ezekiel 6:9 KJV, Hosea 4:12 KJV). The phrase had a double meaning. Literally, the people were engaging in the sexualized worship of the false gods. Figuratively, they were deserting their true "husband," God, who was thought of as a "jealous" God. You have to understand this basic concept to grasp why most of the prophets seem obsessed with Israel's "prostitution" and "adultery."

The "adultery" also took the form of *hypocrisy*—paying lip service to God. The prophets condemned idolatry, but they also condemned hypocritical worship of God. Israel's "adultery" was something like a spouse who showed up every year with expensive anniversary presents—then cheated the rest of the time. The rituals might be right, but the behavior did not match, meaning the rituals were mere mockery.

In the writings of the prophets, the all-knowing God sees through hypocrisy and detests it. The pagans feared their gods but did not have a high opinion of those gods' intelligence. The Babylonians could take a condemned criminal, dress him up in royal robes, scourge and kill him—all so that their gods would think they were in fact sacrificing the son of their king. In other words, the pagans' gods were easily fooled, so long as the religious rites *appeared* to be done correctly. But Israel's God—the Holy One of Israel, as Isaiah called him—sees into men's hearts. He even sees that the religious officials, the priests, are often corrupt and immoral. In most nations, prophets were also priests, but this was rare in Israel. The priesthood in Israel was hereditary—in other words, priests were born, not made. But prophets were those called by God, which is why they were much more important than priests. The prophets often locked horns with the priests and denounced them as unworthy of being God's servants. Two of the prophets, Jeremiah and Ezekiel, were from families of priests, but that did not stop them from rebuking priests for their immorality and corruption.

TURNAROUNDS AND BRIGHTER FUTURES

Since the prophets saw the world through God's eyes, they could see that God's chosen people, the Israelites, were a sorry lot. They had the divine Law but did not obey it. The prophets were painfully aware that Israel was a very *religious* nation—they seemed willing to worship practically anything—but not a *moral* one. People were so greedy for money that they disobeyed the commandment against working on the Sabbath. But even the people who obeyed the commandments were greedy and materialistic, ignoring the poor and oppressing them, the strong taking advantage of the weak. The prophets could see that a booming economy led to material prosperity but spiritual decay. The social injustice offended God as much as the worship of idols did.

What God desired was that people—individually and collectively—change their ways, repent, convert. The prophets often use the Hebrew word *shub*, meaning "to turn." The idea is that the person who seeks the Lord, humbles before him, directs his heart to him, learns to obey and do good, acquires a new heart. This turning, this *conversion*, is a change on the inside but it inevitably results in a change in behavior. When this occurs, the Lord is always willing, even eager, to forgive. We see this in God's word to Ezekiel: "Do I take any pleasure in the death of the wicked? declares the Sovereign Lord. Rather, am I not pleased when they turn from their ways and live?" (Ezekiel 18:23).

Although the main aim of the prophets was the repentance of God's people, most of the prophets also directed their words against enemy nations. Why so, since those enemies probably never heard or read the prophets' words? Perhaps the real audience for these was God's people, taking a word of warning from hearing their prophets denounce the evils of others. In our own time, centuries after these prophets lived, their preaching against oppressive nations like Babylon still has some value, for human pride and arrogance and oppression are still with us, even if the nation of Babylon ceased to exist long ago.

In the time of the prophets, politics was not something people could ignore. Israel existed in a dangerous location, wedged in between oppressive, expansive empires— Egypt on the southwest, Assyria and Babylon and Persia to the northeast. In the best of times, none of these was breathing down Israel's neck. But those times of peace were rare. More often one or more of the empires was menacing Israel, and Israel's kings often cozied up to one empire to protect it against the others—and the results were usually disastrous. The prophets generally opposed any kind of foreign alliance. They believed the nation would be better off relying on God as its true Protector. Inevitably the kings pursued foreign alliances, and the country suffered for it. These disasters provoked the prophets to denounce people's reliance on any kind of human institution, especially governments. The prophets' emphasis on relying on God instead of human beings is one reason their words are still stirring to read. The political situations have changed, but the choice for people to put their hopes either in politics or in faith is still with us.

The prophets were men of their own time, speaking God's word in the hope that things would change. They probably did not imagine that people living more than two thousand years later would be studying their words. But we are, and we can learn much from them about God and ethical living. We can also appreciate their words in a way their original hearers did not—mainly because so many of the sayings of the prophets were fulfilled in the life of Jesus. As we work through these books we will give attention to those prophecies.

As already noted, the prophets threatened but also consoled. After the people were taken into exile in Babylon in 586 BC, there was more consoling than threatening, for God was speaking through the prophets to tell the people that he had not abandoned them, that he would bring them back to their homeland in time and bless them. In speaking about a glorious future, the prophets were telling more than they realized. They may have envisioned a peaceful, prosperous Israel, but most of their prophecies of a blessed future have been interpreted to mean the world to come. Some of the prophets had ceased to believe that Israel as a nation would ever be holy. There would be a *remnant*, a minority of the people who were committed to God, who would endure. We see this idea in the Book of Amos: "Hate evil, love good; maintain justice in the courts. Perhaps the Lord God Almighty will have mercy on the remnant of Joseph" (5:15).

One consolation the prophets held out was the hope for a *messiah*, an "anointed one." He would be a descendant of King David who would rule as king over Israel—and even over the whole world. Other prophets foretold this anointed one as being a "suffering servant" of God, meek and humble, not a mighty king on a war horse but a gentle preacher, rejected by people, persecuted, sacrificing his own life for the salvation of others. The prophet Daniel predicted a "son of man" coming on the clouds of heaven to establish rule over the earth. The prophets did not, of course, hold a meeting and try to coordinate their prophecies of the messiah. Their words were written over several centuries, and the different prophecies aroused different expectations in people—some expecting a king who would drive away Israel's enemies, others expecting a meek man of peace, others a divine man coming on the clouds. The hope that the prophecies would be fulfilled was so strong that both before and after the time of Jesus there were false messiahs, claiming to be the anointed one the prophets had foretold, and some of these messiahs gathered large bands of followers—and many of them were killed as rebels and traitors. Jesus himself was killed, disappointing many of his followers. Not

---

CULTURAL INSIGHTS

Man of God

The Old Testament often uses the expression "man of God" to mean the same as prophet. Moses, Elijah, Elisha and several unnamed prophets are addressed as "man of God." Chronicles and Nehemiah refer to "David the man of God." Paul refers to Timothy as "man of God," and 2 Timothy 3:17 refers to every believer as "man of God."

Prophets were called by other names: *seer* (meaning one who could see what ordinary people could not), *watchman* (one who watched for the hand of God at work in events), *messenger*, *servant* (of God), *man of the Spirit*.

until after his resurrection did people understand that he was the anointed one, the messiah, the Christ, that the prophets had promised.

THE ULTIMATE VISIONARY

The longest book of prophecy, and the one most quoted in the New Testament, is Isaiah, one of the greatest prophets who ever lived. He had a long and active life and was a powerful influence of his nation's affairs during his lifetime. But his real importance is what his book has revealed to millions of readers about the will of God, and about the Messiah who was to come.

Isaiah's call is described in vivid detail in chapter 6 of his book, one of the most dramatic chapters in the Bible. In the year that Judah's King Uzziah died (740 BC), Isaiah had a vision. The Lord was in the temple of Jerusalem, and the train of his royal robe filled the temple. Six-winged seraphs (a type of angel) were flying about, calling out "Holy, holy, holy is the LORD almighty; the whole earth is full of his glory." Their voices shook the temple, which was filled with smoke. Poor Isaiah was terrified—and ashamed: " 'Woe to me!' I cried. 'I am ruined! For I am a man of unclean lips, and I live among a people of unclean lips, and my eyes have seen the King, the LORD Almighty' " (Isaiah 6:5). One of the seraphs took a live coal from the altar and touched Isaiah's lips with it. This was a sign that his sins were taken away—meaning, he was now clean enough to speak the words of God. "Then I heard the voice of the LORD saying, 'Whom shall I send? And who will go for us?' And I said, 'Here am I. Send me!' " Isaiah's eagerness is commendable, since some of the prophets were more reluctant when they were called. We can assume that before Isaiah had his life-changing vision, he was already being spiritually prepared by God for his task.

The song of the seraphs—"Holy, holy, holy"—is critical to understanding Isaiah. For him, God was *holy* above all else. Isaiah refers to God twenty-six times as the "Holy One of Israel"—a phrase used by no other prophet except Jeremiah, who used it twice. Of course, *all* the prophets thought of God as holy. But Isaiah referred to God as "Holy One" because he wanted to remind the people of their own sad spiritual state. God has spoken through Moses and told Israel they were to be a holy people, for their God was holy. But Isaiah was painfully aware that his nation was *not* holy. He was a "man of unclean lips" living among other unclean people. Like all the other prophets, he wanted them to be "clean," to be the people God intended for them to be.

In the very first chapter of his book, Isaiah denounces the people for their disobedience—and their hypocrisy as well. True, the people are going through the religious rituals, offering sacrifices, observing the religious holidays. But God sees through it all—their rituals have wearied him. How can they have the nerve to go to worship when their deeds are evil? In terms of their religious practices, they were getting everything right—except their hearts. "When you spread out your hands in prayer, I will hide my eyes from you; even if you offer many prayers, I will not listen. Your hands are full of blood; wash and make yourselves clean. Take your evil deeds out of my sight! Stop doing wrong, learn to do right. Seek justice, encourage the oppressed. Defend the cause of the fatherless, plead the case of the widow" (1:15–17).

But this scolding is followed by words of kindness: "Though your sins are like scarlet, they shall be as white as snow.... If you are willing and obedient, you will eat the best of the land; but if you resist and rebel, you will be devoured by the sword" (1:18–20).

On several other occasions Isaiah denounced people's religious hypocrisy: "The Lord says: 'These people come near to me with their mouth and honor me with their lips, but their hearts are far from me. Their worship of me is made up only of rules taught by men' " (29:13). Fasting, done as a religious duty, does not impress God if the heart is not right: "Is not this the kind of fasting I have chosen: to loose the chains of injustice and untie the cords of the yoke, to set the oppressed free and break every yoke?" (58:6).

CHARACTER CLOSE-UP ## Son Signs

Like many prophets of God, Isaiah sometimes took dramatic steps to get the attention of the faithless people. He named his first son *Shear-Jashub*, Hebrew for "a remnant will return," so the child was a living prophecy of the time in the distant future when Jewish exiles in Babylon would return to their homeland. Isaiah was told by God to name his next son *Maher-Shalal-Hash-Baz*, which was Hebrew for "quick to plunder, swift to spoil." Before the child was old enough to say "mother" and "father," the enemy nations that were threatening Judah would cease to be a threat, for they would be plundered by Assyria. Maher-Shalal-Hash-Baz has the distinction of being the longest name in the Bible.

The phrase "holier than thou" is taken from Isaiah 65:2–5 (KJV): "I have spread out my hands all the day unto a rebellious people, which walketh in a way that was not good, after their own thoughts; a people that provoketh me to anger continually to my face… which say, 'Stand by thyself, come not near to me; for I am holier than thou.'" The verse is ironic, for God is condemning idol worshippers, people who had the least right to be self-righteous.

BRIDGING THE HOLINESS GAP

After his vision of God in the temple, Isaiah could never forget that God was holy, morally and spiritually higher than man. God says to the people, "My thoughts are not your thoughts, neither are your ways my ways… As the heavens are higher than the earth, so are my ways higher than your ways and my thoughts than your thoughts" (55:8–9). "I am God, and there is no other; I am God, and there is none like me. I make known the end from the beginning, from ancient times, what is still to come. I say: My purpose will stand, and I will do all that I please…. What I have said, that will I bring about; what I have planned, that will I do" (46:9–11).

How can such a mighty Being have fellowship with human beings? He cannot—not with the proud and arrogant, anyway. But he can fellowship with the humble. "This is what the high and lofty One says—he who lives forever, whose name is holy: 'I live in a high and holy place, but also with him who is contrite and lowly in spirit, to revive the spirit of the lowly and to revive the heart of the contrite'" (57:15). "This is the one I esteem: He who is humble and contrite in spirit, and trembles at my word" (66:2).

The Holy One has no use for the arrogant. "Woe to him who quarrels with his Maker, to him who is but a potsherd among the potsherds on the ground. Does the clay say to the potter, 'What are you making?' Does your work say, 'He has no hands'?" (45:9). "You have trusted in your wickedness and have said, 'No one sees me.' Your wisdom and knowledge mislead you when you say to yourself, 'I am, and there is none besides me'" (47:10). Isaiah was aware, as all the prophets were, that people fall into the same temptation as Adam and Eve. They want to be like God, deciding for themselves what is right and what is wrong. "Woe to those who call evil good and good evil, who put darkness for light and light for darkness, who put bitter for sweet and sweet for bitter. Woe to those who are wise in their own eyes and clever in their own sight." (5:20–21) It was inevitable that people in rebellion against God would despise his prophets: "These are rebellious people, deceitful children, children unwilling to listen to the Lord's instruction. They say to the seers, 'See no more visions!' and to the prophets, 'Give us no more visions of what is right! Tell us pleasant things, prophesy illusions. Leave this way, get off this path, and stop confronting us with the Holy One of Israel!'" (30:9–11).

Like other prophets, Isaiah detested social injustice. He spoke out against the women of Jerusalem, arrogantly walking around covered in jewelry and reeking with perfume. He predicted a time when such people, indifferent to the poor, would be led away captive to a foreign land (3:13–26). While the humble would find rest for their souls, the prophet said (in more than one passage), " 'There is no peace,' says my God, 'for the wicked' " (48:22; 57:21).

A BOOK OF CONSOLATION

For all of his warnings against sin, Isaiah has many words of comfort. Part of his effort to console worried people was to remind them that despite what happened, God was still in charge. Foreign nations might threaten them on every side, but they did not have to live in fear, for they could rely on Someone more powerful than any nation: "Surely the nations are like a drop in a bucket; they are regarded as dust on the scales; he weighs the islands as though they were fine dust.… Before him all the nations are as nothing; they are regarded by him as worthless and less than nothing" (40:15–17). God, the Holy One

CHARACTER CLOSE-UP # Lucifer

Did you ever wonder why Satan is sometimes called "Lucifer"? The name is found just once in the Bible, in Isaiah 14:12 in the King James Version: "How thou art fallen from heaven, O Lucifer, son of the morning." The Hebrew word that was translated as "Lucifer" is *helal*, meaning "morning star," which is how most modern translations word it. When the Old Testament was translated into Greek centuries ago, the Greek word used here was *Luciferos*, from two Greek words meaning "light bearer." But it is clear in Isaiah 14 that the prophet is speaking not about a literal star but about the arrogant king of Babylon. Here is how the whole passage reads in a modern version: "How you have fallen from heaven, O morning star, son of the dawn! You have been cast down to the earth, you who once laid low the nations! You said in your heart, 'I will ascend to heaven; I will raise my throne above the stars of God; I will sit enthroned on the mount of assembly, on the utmost heights of the sacred mountain. I will ascend above the tops of the clouds; I will make myself like the Most High.' But you are brought down to the grave, to the depths of the pit" (14:12–15).

Although Isaiah was not writing about Satan, generations of Bible readers thought the passage perfectly described Satan, an arrogant angel who rebelled against God and was cast out of heaven and into hell. In other words, the old tradition of using Lucifer as an alternate name for Satan is based on the King James translation of the Greek texts, which interpreted Isaiah's words as a proper name and a description.

Naked

In chapter 20, Isaiah is ordered by God to go "naked and barefoot" for three years, as a sign of humiliation and degradation. This passage surprises people. A prophet from God—walking around *nude*? Probably not. In the Bible, *naked* can mean completely nude (as was the case of Adam and Eve) but more often means inadequately dressed. Probably Isaiah had on his loincloth—the equivalent of going out in his underwear. In the ancient world, to be dressed inadequately was a sign of humiliation and poverty. A man walking in public nearly naked was a sign something was seriously wrong, since only the very poor or captives would be seen this way. It was "indecent" not in a sexual sense but in the sense that it signified a state of disaster—such as being conquered, with one's possessions taken, including one's clothing. Even so, we can assume that the prophet—and also the prophet Micah, who did the same thing (Micah 1:8)—found the experience humiliating, but they did so because God wanted them to be "visual aids," warning people of coming disasters.

of Israel, "sits enthroned above the circle of the earth, and its people are like grasshoppers. He stretches out the heavens like a canopy, and spreads them out like a tent to live in. He brings princes to naught and reduces the rulers of this world to nothing" (40:22–23).

Isaiah is touching on a theme found throughout the Bible: The political powers of the world do not have the last word. "I, even I, am he who comforts you. Who are you that you fear mortal men, the sons of men, who are but grass" (51:12). More than once, the prophet spoke of human endeavors as "grass," something transient and insignificant. "All men are like grass, and all their glory is like the flowers of the field.... The grass withers and the flowers fall, but the word of our God stands forever" (40:6–8).

Fear of conspiracy was as common in ancient times as today, as we see in Isaiah: "Do not call conspiracy everything that these people call conspiracy; do not fear what they fear, and do not dread it" (8:12). Why should we fear, when God is in charge? "You will keep in perfect peace him whose mind is steadfast, because he trusts in you" (26:3). "Those who hope in the Lord will renew their strength. They will soar on wings like eagles; they will run and not grow weary, they will walk and not be faint" (40:31). "Do not fear, for I am with you; do not be dismayed, for I am your God. I will strengthen you and help you; I will uphold you with my righteous right hand" (41:10).

Living in turbulent times, Isaiah prophesied a more peaceful time. "They will beat their swords into plowshares and their spears into pruning hooks. Nation will not take up sword against nation, nor will they train for war anymore" (2:4). Perhaps, in that future state, death itself would no longer be feared: "He will swallow up death forever. The Sovereign Lord will wipe away the tears from all faces; he will remove the disgrace of his people from all the earth" (25:8).

THE MESSIAH PROPHET

One reason Isaiah has been so often read is that many of his prophecies were fulfilled in the life of Jesus. One of the best-known of these is found in 9:6: "For to us a child is born, to us a son is given, and the government will be on his shoulders. And he will be called Wonderful Counselor, Mighty God, Everlasting Father, Prince of Peace." If the words sound familiar, it may be because they have appeared on countless Christmas cards, and were beautifully set to music in George Frideric Handel's oratorio *Messiah*.

In another prophecy, Isaiah connects the Messiah with the dynasty of David: "A shoot will come up from the stump of Jesse; from his roots a Branch will bear fruit. The Spirit of the Lord will rest on him—the Spirit of wisdom and of understanding, the Spirit of counsel and of power, the Spirit of knowledge and of the fear of the Lord" (11:1–2). You might recall that Jesse was the father of King David. Like most of the prophets, Isaiah expected that the Messiah would be a descendant of David—which Jesus was, since his legal father, Joseph, traced his ancestry back to David. Isaiah predicts that under the rule of this descendant of David, peace will reign: "The wolf will live with the lamb, the leopard will lie down with the goat, the calf and the lion and the yearling together; and a little child will lead them" (11:6).

Isaiah spoke of the coming Messiah as a righteous king—an obvious contrast to the mostly unrighteous kings that have ever ruled. "See, a king will reign in righteousness and rulers will rule with justice. Each man will be like a shelter from the wind and a refuge from the storm, like streams of water in the desert and the shadow of a great rock in a thirsty land. Then the eyes of those who see will no longer be closed, and the ears of those who hear will listen. The mind of the rash will know and understand, and the stammering tongue will be fluent and clear. No longer will the fool be called noble nor the scoundrel be highly respected" (32:1–5).

Consider 60:6: "And all from Sheba will come, bearing gold and incense and proclaiming the praise of the Lord." It is impossible to read this without thinking of the wise men—magi—who came to visit the newborn Jesus, bringing their gifts of gold, frankincense and myrrh, isn't it?

Isaiah 7:14 contains the famous prophecy of the virgin birth, which in the King James Version reads, "Behold, a virgin shall conceive and bear a son, and shall call his name Immanuel: "God with us." The New Testament makes it clear that Jesus was, indeed, "God with us."

One prophecy is connected with Jesus because Jesus himself made the connection: "The Spirit of the Sovereign Lord is on me, because the Lord has anointed me to preach good news to the poor. He has sent me to bind up the brokenhearted, to proclaim freedom for the captives and release from darkness for the prisoners, to proclaim the year of the Lord's favor" (61:1–2). Jesus read this passage aloud in the synagogue of his hometown, Nazareth, and when he finished reading, said, "Today this scripture is fulfilled in your hearing" (Luke 4:21).

SONGS OF GOD'S SERVANT

Isaiah's best-known prophecies of the Messiah are found in the four Servant Songs. The first of these is found in 42:1–9. "Here is my servant, whom I uphold, my chosen one in whom I delight; I will put my Spirit on him and he will bring justice to the nations. He will not shout or cry out, or raise his voice in the streets. A bruised reed he will not break, and a smoldering wick he will not snuff out. In faithfulness he will bring forth justice; he will not falter or be discouraged till he establishes justice on earth. In his law the islands will put their hope" (42:1–4). The prophecy is interesting because it is not describing a mighty conqueror, but a gentle soul, a "servant" who "will not shout or cry out," drawing attention to himself. But in quietness and gentleness there is strength, because he will establish justice on the earth—something that was expected of kings, and the fact that Isaiah tells us the servant will establish justice means that he did think of him as a king—but one quite different from the usual type of earthly king. This servant is sent not just to save Israel, but everyone in the world, for he will be a "light to the Gentiles" (or "light to the nations" in some versions).

The second Servant Song is 49:1–6. Again, the servant is referred to as a "light for the Gentiles." In fact, Israel in this passage is identified with the divine servant, but probably Isaiah's meaning is that the servant—an individual—will be an "Israel" to the world, just as God had promised that the nation of Israel would be a blessing to the whole world. The servant had been chosen from birth to be God's messenger.

In the third Servant Song, 50:4–11, we encounter something new: The servant sent by God will endure persecution. "I offered my back to those who beat me, my cheeks to those who pulled out my beard; I did not hide my face from mocking and spitting." No one could read this without thinking of the horrible flogging Jesus received before his crucifixion, and also the mocking and spitting of the brutal Roman soldiers. Despite the suffering, the servant is confident that God is with him: "He who vindicates me is near…. It is the Sovereign Lord who helps me. Who is he that will condemn me?"

The theme of innocent suffering is even more vivid in the fourth Servant Song, 52:13—53:12. God's servant is physically abused—"disfigured" and "marred"—but afterward he is "raised and lifted up and highly exalted," which we take to be a prophecy of Jesus' flogging and crucifixion, followed by his resurrection and ascension into heaven. Before exaltation there is rejection and pain: "He was despised and rejected by men, a man of sorrows, and familiar with suffering. Like one from whom men hide their faces he was despised, and we esteemed him not. Surely he took up our infirmities and carried our sorrows, yet we considered him stricken by God, smitten by him, and afflicted. But he was pierced for our transgressions, he was crushed for our iniquities; the punishment that brought us peace was upon him, and by his wounds we are healed." When Isaiah first spoke, or wrote, these words, the world had no idea that a divine being could be abused and killed—or that his sufferings could in some way be done on other people's behalf. Yet the meaning is clear: An innocent man, with no sins of his own, willingly bears the punishment for the sins of others.

The servant was killed—"cut off from the land of the living," as 53:8 has it. He left no descendants—in ancient times, a horrible curse upon anyone. "It was the Lord's will to crush him and cause him to suffer, and though the Lord makes his life a guilt offering, he will see his offspring and prolong his days, and the will of the Lord will prosper in his hand." The phrase "guilt offering" connects the servant's death with the idea of sacrifice. Instead of an animal being slain, it is an innocent man. But after consenting to be the sacrifice, he is rewarded: "After the suffering of his soul, he will see the light of life and be satisfied; by his knowledge my righteous servant will justify many, and he will bear their iniquities. Therefore I will give him a portion among the great, and he will divide the spoils with the strong, because he poured out his life unto death, and was numbered with the transgressors. For he bore the sin of many, and made intercession for the transgressors." It was the will of God that the servant should suffer horribly—but that he would be glorified when all was done. The fourth Servant Song has been called a "dirge in reverse"—instead of speaking of past glory and present and future sorrows, it speaks of past sorrow and present and future glory.

What did Isaiah's original audience think of the Servant Songs? In fact, they did not connect them at all with their idea of a Messiah, the promised Deliverer they expected from God. Only after the death and resurrection of Jesus did anyone fully understand that their Messiah had to make the ultimate sacrifice on their behalf. Jesus himself, after his resurrection, had to explain to his disciples "what was said in all the Scriptures concerning himself" (Luke 24:27). In Acts we find the story of Philip, an evangelist, who finds an Ethiopian man reading a passage from the fourth Servant Song. He asks Philip to explain just who the "sheep to the slaughter" is in the passage. For Philip this is his opportunity to tell him the story of Jesus (Acts 8:26–40).

We close this chapter on one of the great books—and great prophets—of the Bible with this hope-filled verse: "Behold, I will create new heavens and a new earth" (65:17).

PUTTING THE WORD TO WORK

1. The prophets constantly urged the people to do a moral turnaround, a *shub*, a conversion. Many people recall one particular shub in their own lives, some can recall more than one. Have you in your own life experienced a dramatic—or maybe subtle—shub?

2. Isaiah's vision in the temple was a life-changing moment for him. What were some moments in your own life in which you were deeply aware of the majesty of God? What effect did these have on you afterward?

3. Isaiah, like other prophets, taught people to put faith in God and not fear political upheavals. What are some of your own fears about the present world situation? Commit that list to God, letting go of your fears.

4. Isaiah spoke out against people who wanted false prophets to "tell us pleasant things, prophesy illusions." What do you think a true prophet of God would warn us against today?

5. The prophecies of the "suffering servant" remind us that God moves in mysterious ways, working through a man who was a failure by worldly standards. What people have you known who were servants of God, doing their work quietly and faithfully, not trying to draw attention to themselves?

Two Men of Vision

AT THE HEART OF IT ALL TODAY	The prophets Jeremiah and Ezekiel lived through political upheavals and prophesied a time when a new covenant would exist between God and man, with God giving people new hearts to serve him.

O f all the books of the prophets, Jeremiah's contains the most personal information about the prophet himself, so in some ways we know him better than any other. In fact, his book uses "I" more than any other prophets. This is fortunate, because he is

> **KEY PASSAGES TO READ TODAY**
>
> **Jeremiah 1; 7; 9; 17; 31:27–34**
> **Ezekiel 1–2; 18; 34; 37**

an attractive personality, a sensitive soul who lived through some of the worst times in his nation's history and endured persecution and scorn. Like most great men of the Bible, he was frequently misunderstood and slandered. The theme of Jeremiah's life seems to be "God and me against the world."

Jeremiah received the call of God in the thirteenth year of the reign of King Josiah—626 BC. His call is best related in his own words: "The word of the Lord came to me, saying, 'Before I formed you in the womb I knew you, before you were born I set you apart; I appointed you as a prophet to the nations.' 'Ah, Sovereign Lord,' I said, 'I do not know how to speak; I am only a child.' But the Lord said to me, 'Do not say, "I am only a child." You must go to everyone I send you to and say whatever I command you. Do not be afraid of them, for I am with you and will rescue you,' declares the Lord. Then the Lord reached out his hand and touched my mouth and said to me, 'Now, I

KEY TERM FOR TODAY ## Circumcised Hearts

Among the Jews, circumcision was the visible sign of God's covenant with Abraham's descendants. But of course, circumcision did not make a person moral. As far back as the time of Moses, God told his people, "Circumcise your hearts" (Deuteronomy 10:16) —meaning *Don't just rely on an outward sign, but behave like God's people.* Centuries later, the New Testament would declare that physical circumcision was not necessary—but the spiritual circumcision still was: "A man is a Jew if he is one inwardly; and circumcision is circumcision of the heart, by the Spirit, not by the written code" (Romans 9:29).

have put my words in your mouth. See, today I appoint you over nations and kingdoms to uproot and tear down, to destroy and over-throw, to build and to plant.… They will fight against you but will not overcome you, for I am with you and will rescue you' " (1:4–10, 19). Like all the prophets, Jeremiah was not promised an easy time—quite the opposite! But the divine words "I am with you" gave him strength for the task he had to face.

Like all the prophets, Jeremiah was scandalized by the people's worship of false gods. In a memorable phrase, he told what bowing down to idols resulted in: "They followed worthless idols and became worthless themselves" (2:5). Judah had "changed its gods," which were not really gods at all. But when they needed help, they cried out to God (2:27). The nation had lived "like a prostitute with many lovers" (3:1), the false gods. Then the people had the gall to deny their sins: "You say, 'I am innocent; he is not angry with me.' But I will pass judgment on you because you say, 'I have not sinned' " (2:35). Yet still God, ever patient and merciful, beckons them: "Return, faithless people… for I am your husband" (3:14).

The people who worshipped worthless idols had indeed become worthless. God told Jeremiah, "Go up and down the streets of Jerusalem, look around and consider, search through her squares. If you can find but one person who deals honestly and seeks the truth, I will forgive this city" (5:1). Even the country's religious leaders were corrupt: "From the least to the greatest, all are greedy for gain; prophets and priests alike, all practice deceit. They dress the wound of my people as though it were not serious. 'Peace, peace,' they say, when there is no peace. Are they ashamed of their loathsome con-duct? No, they have no shame at all; they do not even know how to blush. So they will fall among the fallen; they will be brought down when I punish them" (6:13–15). In another memorable phrase, the prophet lamented that "They are skilled in doing evil; they know not how to do good" (4:22). The punishment for their idolatry would be perfectly fitting: "As you have forsaken me and served foreign gods in your own land, so now you will serve foreigners in a land not your own" (5:19).

Jeremiah received his divine call in the thirteenth year of Josiah's reign. In Josiah's eighteenth year, the king instituted a sweeping reli-gious reform, demolishing the idols and pagan worship sites and

605 BC
Nebuchadnezzar
becomes king of
Babylon.

c. 600 BC
Lao-tzu, Chinese
philosopher, born

commanding the people to abide by the Book of the Law (probably Deuteronomy) that had been found in the temple. Josiah was a saintly king, and 2 Kings 22–23 praises him highly. Jeremiah was pleased at the king's success in reinvigorating the country's faith. When Jeremiah reflected on the reforms of Josiah, what impressed him was not the ritual revival, but the righteousness: Josiah "'did what was right and just, so all went well with him. He defended the cause of the poor and needy, and so all went well. Is that not what it means to know me?' declares the Lord" (22:15–16). Josiah's descendants, however, were all pitiful excuses for kings, and though Josiah might have delayed the country's spiritual and moral decline, he did not halt it.

Rather foolishly, the people had come to believe that God would protect them no matter how they behaved. They saw the temple in Jerusalem as a kind of good luck charm that would save them from disaster. Jeremiah assured them this was not so. "Do not trust in deceptive words and say, 'This is the temple of the Lord, the temple of the Lord, the temple of the Lord!'" (7:4). The people themselves didn't respect the temple—they had made it into a "den of thieves" (7:11). They continued to go through their religious rituals, offering sacrifices, paying lip service to God. "When I brought your forefathers out of Egypt and spoke to them, I did not just give them commands about burnt offerings and sacrifices, but I gave them this command: Obey me, and I will be your God and you will be my people. Walk in all the ways I command you, that it may go well with you" (7:22–23). But morally the people had gone backward, not forward. Jeremiah said to the Lord, "You are always on their lips but far from their hearts" (12:2).

All the prophets understood something essential about rituals: People's "scripted" words and actions can be hypocritical. What we are when we are "off the script" shows our true selves. This is one of the great revolutions in human thought: God can see beyond our religious acts into our hearts. Pagans might doubt their gods and yet go through the motions of making sacrifices to them anyway, and all that mattered to those gods was that the rituals were performed. Israel's God was not easily fooled. As he had told Samuel centuries earlier, man looks at the outward appearance, but God looks at the heart.

Like all prophets, Jeremiah condemned sin because he wanted people to change, to do the right thing. He was a deeply spiritual and moral man who saw the world through God's eyes and was horrified that people could be so unethical. He is called the "weeping prophet" because he would literally shed tears over the moral decay he saw all around him: "Oh, that my head were a spring of water and my eyes a fountain of tears!... Beware of your friends; do not trust your brothers. For every brother is a deceiver, and every friend a slanderer. Friend deceives friend, and no one speaks the truth. They have taught their tongues to lie; they weary themselves with sinning" (9:1, 4–5). The people could hide their sins from each other, but not from the Lord: "The heart is deceitful above all things and beyond cure. Who can understand it? I the Lord search the heart and examine the mind, to reward a man according to his conduct, according to what his deeds deserve" (17:9–10).

THE PERSECUTED ONE

A sensitive soul like Jeremiah could have used the love of a faithful wife. But God told him not to marry—ever. This command must have rocked the prophet to his foundations, for in ancient times, every man wished to marry and have as many children as possible. But God sometimes used his prophets' personal lives as "living parables." The prophet Hosea was told to marry a faithless woman, their marriage becoming a parable of faithless Israel's lack of devotion to its "husband," God. Jeremiah was told to be celibate—as a sign of the disaster to come, when thousands in Jeremiah's country would be killed by war and disease. Not only could he not marry, but Jeremiah could not enter a house where someone was being mourned—or married. He was to cut himself off from the normal social rituals, living without a family of his own and not attending the family gatherings of others (chapter 16). As in the case of Ezekiel, who was forbidden to mourn when his wife died (more about that later), Jeremiah was commanded by God not to do what was expected, a fate that befalls many of God's servants.

Like most of the prophets, Jeremiah found himself discouraged many times. At times he thought God was unfair, asking him, "Why does the way of the wicked prosper? Why do all the faithless live at ease?" (12:1). He was so exasperated with his immoral people that he asked God to destroy them all. God assured him that he should prepare himself for even more exasperation: "If you have raced with men on foot and they have worn you out, how can you compete with horses?" (12:5). No prophet was ever persecuted more. For speaking the truth, Jeremiah was harassed by kings and priests—the very people who should have embraced him as one who spoke the Lord's words. Pashhur, the priest in charge of the temple, had the prophet beaten and placed in the stocks for public humiliation (chapter 20). This would not be the first or last time in Scripture that a priest—a minister of God, supposedly—persecuted a prophet of God. Jeremiah asked the Lord, "Why did I ever come out of the womb to see trouble and sorrow and to end my days in shame?" (20:18).

One of the strangest incidents in Jeremiah's career was the fate of a scroll he sent to the wicked king Jehoiakim, a scroll containing his prophecies. Jehudi, the king's secretary, read aloud from the scroll, and when he finished reading a portion of the scroll, Jehoiakim cut off that portion and threw it into the fire. Such was the contempt that the kings had for prophets (chapter 36). Yet the king and people gladly listened to the glib words of the false prophets, those that "speak visions from their own minds, not from the mouth of the Lord" (23:16). The sinful people were pleased to hear them lie and say "The Lord says: 'You will have peace' and 'No harm will come to you' (23:17). They knew Jeremiah as a prophet of doom—but sometimes prophets of doom are right. In the time of Zedekiah, Judah's last king, Jeremiah was accused of deserting to the Babylonians, so he was beaten and imprisoned. Later he was given more freedom, but for prophesying that the city would fall to Babylon (which it did), many said he should be put to death for discouraging the soldiers. They threw him into a muddy cistern and left him to die, but one of the palace officials—a foreigner, as it happened—protested and Jeremiah was taken out. However, Zedekiah threatened Jeremiah with death if he repeated his prophecy that the city would be captured (chapters 37–38).

Despite all the threats and warnings, the Lord also spoke consolation through Jeremiah. In fact, some of the tenderest words in the Bible are found here, as God assures his wayward people of his compassion: "I have loved you with an everlasting love; I have drawn you with loving-kindness" (31:3). "You will seek me and find me when you seek me with all your heart" (29:13). The holy, righteous God hated sin, but never failed to love the sinners.

The people did not repent, and what Jeremiah had long prophesied came to pass: The Babylonians conquered Judah, burned the Lord's temple and carried many of the people off into exile. Jeremiah was not among the exiles, but he did send a letter to them, with words given to him by God: "Build houses and settle down; plant gardens and eat what they produce. Marry and have sons and daughters; find wives for your sons and give your daughters in marriage, so that they too may have sons and daughters. Increase in number there; do not decrease. Also, seek the peace and prosperity of the city to which I have carried you into exile. Pray to the Lord for it, because if it prospers, you too will prosper" (29:5–7). In time, God would bring the exiles home—but not soon. The exiles did as Jeremiah said and settled—not happily, at first—into their new situation in faraway Babylon. In time they would learn the lesson that God could be worshipped anywhere, that faith could survive disasters and that the temple was not necessary.

In ancient times, people thought of their gods as having a certain "turf"—that is, they seldom thought of any god as being everywhere at once. When Solomon dedicated the Jerusalem temple to the Lord, he raised the question: Could the God of the universe be contained within a building? The obvious answer is no, and yet the Jews did think that in some way God "dwelled" in their temple. They would learn differently in their years of exile in Babylon. God was everywhere. Even after they returned to Jerusalem and built a new temple, the lesson would not be completely forgotten.

The Babylonians had served as God's instrument in punishing Judah, and in fact the Lord himself referred to the Babylonian king Nebuchadnezzar as "my servant" (an

Babylonians / Chaldeans

Depending on the Bible translation you use, you might find *Chaldeans* or *Babylonians*, or both, mentioned often in Jeremiah and Ezekiel. Both refer to the same people, the people of the empire with its capital at Babylon. In this period, when the mighty king Nebuchadnezzar ruled, the people called themselves Chaldeans. Later on (as in the Book of Daniel), the name *Chaldeans* often referred specifically to the Babylonian priests, magicians and astrologers. With good reason the Jews always associated the Babylonians/Chaldeans with sorcery and the occult. You might recall from Genesis 12 that the great patriarch Abraham was living in the Chaldean city of Ur when God called him and had him settle in Canaan.

unwitting servant, of course). Even so, Jeremiah prophesied a day of doom for the brutal empire. Chapters 50 and 51 predict that the mighty city "will be a heap of ruins, a haunt of jackals, an object of horror and scorn, a place where no one lives.... Babylon sinks to rise no more" (51:37, 64). That prophecy did in time come to pass, and even before the city became a ruin, it would be conquered by a more humane empire, the Persians, and the Persians would allow the exiles to return home.

Jeremiah was still a prisoner, bound in shackles, when the Babylonians conquered Jerusalem. He was released not by one of his own people, but by the commander of the Babylonian army, who suggested Jeremiah go to live with Gedaliah, a Jew whom the Babylonians had appointed to govern the Jews who remained in the land—mostly the poor. Gedaliah was assassinated by some of his own people, and the assassins and many other Jews fled to Egypt, even though God, speaking through Jeremiah, told them not to. The fugitives took Jeremiah with them, against his will. Tradition says that Jeremiah died in Egypt, stoned to death by his own people for speaking the truth. The tradition is probably true, because, as Jesus observed, his own people had a habit of killing God's messengers.

Jeremiah was a failure by worldly standards. He left behind no wife and children—God had told him not to marry—and he was at best ignored and at worst persecuted by his people. He was "despised and rejected by men," as the prophet Isaiah described the Suffering Servant of God. But God does not see things as man sees, and in his eyes, Jeremiah was anything but a failure.

WRITING ON THE HEART

Jeremiah's most important spiritual contribution was his prophecy of a new covenant. It would not replace the old covenants with Abraham (circumcision) and Moses (the Law given at Sinai). Rather, it would add something new: an inward motivation to please God.

" 'The time is coming,' declares the Lord, 'when I will make a new covenant with the house of Israel and with the house of Judah. It will not be like the covenant I made with their forefathers when I took them by the hand to lead them out of Egypt, because they broke my covenant, though I was a husband to them.... This is the covenant I will make with the house of Israel after that time.... I will put my law in their minds and write it on their hearts. I will be their God, and they will be my people. No longer will a man teach his neighbor, or a man his brother, saying, "Know the Lord," because they will all know me, from the least of them to the greatest.... For I will forgive their wickedness and will remember their sins no more' "(31:31–34).

The old covenant with Moses had been written on stone tablets. The new covenant would be written on people's hearts. God's commandments would be "internalized." Most of the time we do not live by rules at all, but by habits and sensibilities—habits rooted in the fact that we love and respect someone else and try to please them, even if that means not pleasing ourselves at times. When we know God—intimately and personally—we form those habits, so the covenant with him is written on the heart, not set down in a long list of rules.

In the New Testament, the Letter to the Hebrews quotes from Jeremiah 31 and says that the new covenant Jeremiah predicted was achieved through Jesus Christ, and that the old covenant—the laws of sacrifices and other rituals—is done away with. Under

---

CULTURAL INSIGHTS

The Recabites

In Genesis, most people were nomads, living in tents instead of houses. When the Israelites settled in Canaan, they built houses and put the nomadic life behind them— or at least, most did. A group known as the Recabites (descended from a man named Recab, naturally) made up a kind of "simple life" movement, taking a vow to live in tents and never drink wine or cultivate crops. Their lifestyle was intended to remind people of the years when the Israelites lived in the wilderness, before they settled in Canaan and became materialistic and corrupt. The Recabites must have been valiant for God, because in 2 Kings 10 they joined in with Jehu's revolt against the wicked dynasty of Israel's king Ahab.

They appear in Jeremiah 35. The prophet was told by God to invite the Recabites to the temple and offer them some wine. The Recabites came but refused the wine, saying they had never been unfaithful to their ancestors' vows. God approved their fidelity to their vows, which contrasted with the other Israelites who so flagrantly disobeyed God's laws. The Recabites were steadfast and honest in a country where promises and vows had ceased to matter.

The prophet Jeremiah had a knack for memorable phrases. In speaking of his people's habit of sinning, he asked, "Can the Ethiopian change his skin or the leopard its spots? Neither can you do good who are accustomed to doing evil" (13:23). Wondering what could heal the moral wound of the people, he asked, "Is there no balm in Gilead? Is there no physician there? Why then is there no healing for the wound of my people?" (8:22). Despairing of his people's ever repenting of their sins, he said, "The harvest is past, the summer has ended, and we are not saved" (8:20).

the new covenant, Jesus himself is both sacrifice and priest. This allows us to "draw near to God with a sincere heart in full assurance of faith" (Hebrews 10:22).

Something else was different about the new covenant: The covenants with Abraham and Moses were *collective*—made between God and Israel. The new covenant would be *individual*. Each person was responsible for his own sins. "In those days people will no longer say, 'The fathers have eaten sour grapes, and the children's teeth are set on edge.' Instead, everyone will die for his own sin; whoever eats sour grapes—his own teeth will be set on edge" (Jeremiah 31:29–30). It's still true we can suffer the consequences of our parents' sins—if our parents don't work, we grow up in poverty—but we are not *judged* for their sins. We are judged by what we make of our own lives—no shifting of the blame to parents or anyone else.

Under the new covenant, each individual, no matter what his condition, would have access to God. Everyone could know God—which, in the Bible, is the greatest good that mankind can hope for. "Let not the wise man boast of his wisdom or the strong man boast of his strength or the rich man boast of his riches, but let him who boasts boast about this: that he understands and knows me, that I am the Lord, who exercises kindness, justice and righteousness on earth, for in these I delight" (9:23–24).

We close this section on Jeremiah with a look at his prophecies of a Messiah. Matthew's Gospel repeats the words of Jeremiah 31:15: "A voice is heard in Ramah, mourning and great weeping, Rachel weeping for her children and refusing to be comforted, because her children are no more." Rachel, you might recall, was the beloved wife of the patriarch Jacob. Jeremiah is using her name figuratively: As the mother of some of the tribes of Israel, she was lamenting the loss of her descendants. Matthew quoted the verse in his description of one of the most brutal incidents in the Bible, the slaughter of the infants of Bethlehem by order of King Herod, who was trying to kill the newborn Messiah (Matthew 2:18).

But Jeremiah spoke a happier prophecy. In two different passages he predicted the coming of a wise and righteous king, a descendant of David: " 'The days are coming,' declares the Lord, 'when I will raise up to David a righteous Branch, a King who will reign wisely and do what is just and right in the land. In his days Judah will be saved and Israel will live in safety. This is the name by which he will be called: The Lord Our Righteousness'" (23:5–6, repeated almost word for word in 33:15–16). In the New Testament, Jesus was taken to be this righteous king, though he ruled a spiritual kingdom, not an earthly one.

Jeremiah advanced spirituality by emphasizing that true religion could go on without the temple and without Israel as a nation. For him, religion consisted primarily in an individual's personal relationship to God.

THE MAN OF DIZZYING VISIONS

Ezekiel and Jeremiah were contemporaries, although we don't know if they ever met. Their fates were very different, for Ezekiel's mission was mostly carried out in faraway Babylon, where he was taken in 597 BC in the "first wave" of exiles, ten years before the "second wave" that followed the destruction of the temple in Jerusalem. (The prophet Daniel was also in this first wave of exiles.)

CHARACTER CLOSE-UP ## Jeremiah the Lamenter

Tradition says that Jeremiah wrote the brief Book of Lamentations, found between Jeremiah and Ezekiel. Jews refer to it by its Hebrew name Qinoth, "Elegies." True to its name, the book is a sad dirge over the conquered city of Jerusalem, the city that ignored Jeremiah's call to repent before disaster struck. Jeremiah took no pleasure in seeing his prophecy come to pass—he would have preferred that a moral turnaround would have averted the catastrophe. Sad as the event was, it was evidence of God's justice, and no one had the right to ask *Why did this happen*? Jeremiah asked, "Why should any living man complain when punished for his sins?" (3:39).

But all was not lost. There were survivors, including the prophet himself, and the faith would go on even without the temple and its priests. Hope could live on because God lived on. "Because of the Lord's great love we are not consumed, for his compassions never fail. They are new every morning; great is your faithfulness.... The Lord is good to those whose hope is in him, to the one who seeks him; it is good to wait quietly for the salvation of the Lord" (3:22–26).

The Jews read Lamentations aloud every year on the holy day commemorating the destruction of the temple. Some Christian churches read it during Good Friday services, since it is full of sadness.

Because of the sadness of Lamentations, and also many passages in the Book of Jeremiah, and because 2 Chronicles 35:25 says that Jeremiah lamented over the death of King Josiah, the word *jeremiad* is used to refer to any lament or sad complaint.

The prophet's call by God occurred in Babylon—which was surely a sign that he was God everywhere, not just in Judah. "While I was among the exiles by the Kebar River, the heavens were opened and I saw visions of God." The Kebar was actually a canal off the Euphrates River in Babylon, and many of the Jewish exiles lived nearby. The year was 592, since the prophet tells us it was the fifth year of King Jehoiachin's exile. Ezekiel begins his story with a familiar phrase of the prophets: "the word of the Lord came" to him. In a windstorm—not an ordinary storm, but a cloud with brilliant light—he saw four "living creatures." They were manlike, but with four wings and four faces each, the faces being those of a man, an ox, a lion and an eagle. They glowed like fire as they moved. Strange wheels "full of eyes all around" moved the creatures about. Above them was a vast expanse sparkling like ice, and above it a throne of sapphire, on which was seated a manlike figure surrounded by light. "This was the appearance of the likeness of the glory of the Lord. When I saw it, I fell facedown" (1:28).

Apart from this vision, Ezekiel's call was amazingly similar to Jeremiah's: "He said to me, 'Son of man, stand up on your feet and I will speak to you....' He said: 'Son of man, I am sending you to the Israelites, to a rebellious nation that has rebelled against me; they and their fathers have been in revolt against me to this very day.... And whether they listen or fail to listen—for they are a rebellious house—they will know that a prophet has been among them. And you, son of man, do not be afraid of them or their words. Do not be afraid, though briers and thorns are all around you and you live among scorpions. Do not be afraid of what they say or terrified by them, though they are a rebellious house' " (2:1–6). You might notice that this passage is repetitious—something that is true throughout the book. The prophets did not consider this a failing—they repeated for emphasis, as all good teachers do.

God calls the prophet "son of man." In fact, he calls him this ninety-three times in the book. The Hebrew words were *ben adam*—which can mean both "son of man" and "son of Adam." It is simply the Hebrew way of saying "human being," and some modern translations of the Bible use "mortal man." Like the prophet Isaiah, Ezekiel had a lofty view of God, so great, so holy, so powerful that his presence was overwhelming. The prophet could only think of himself as a "mere mortal" when God was speaking to him. When we study the Gospels in a later chapter, we will look at Jesus' use of the name "son of man" for himself.

Two phrases are unique to Ezekiel. Six times he says "the hand of the Lord was upon me," and six times he says "the Spirit lifted me up." When he speaks of "the hand of the Lord," he means that the power of God came upon him—bringing to mind the earlier prophets Elijah and Elisha, who were at times empowered by the "hand of the Lord." When the Spirit "lifted up" Ezekiel, he was probably in a trance or visionary state: physically not moving, but spiritually discerning things that other mortal eyes could not see. Most of the other prophets saw visions at times, but Ezekiel is the visionary par excellence, and this visionary quality makes his book fascinating—but also puzzling—to read.

But back to Ezekiel's vision: Commentators love to speculate about just what this odd vision meant. What were the "living creatures"? Angels? That seems the logical conclusion, and in chapter 10 they are called *cherubim*, recalling the cherubim figures on the ark of the covenant, which were figures of winged angels—probably like winged lions but with human faces. Possibly the meaning of these bizarre creatures Ezekiel saw was that they represented the forces of nature, since they had *four* faces and *four* wings each, and in symbolism this usually meant the four winds. Some commentators say the four faces represented the four "excellencies" of creation: the lion, greatest of the wild beasts; the ox, greatest of domestic beasts; the eagle, greatest of the birds; and man, greatest of all created things.

The Jews believed that God's "throne" was in the temple in Jerusalem, but these exiles in Babylon were far from the temple. In his vision, Ezekiel saw that God's throne was everywhere—even in pagan Babylon. It is tempting to pick the passage apart and analyze each detail, asking, *What does the eagle's head mean?* and so on. Focusing on the trees can make us miss the forest, however. The main point of this vision is that Ezekiel had an encounter with Almighty God, even more dramatic and awe-inspiring than Moses' encounter with God in the burning bush. The "living creatures" are best understood as "attendants" in God's "court." Like the Lord himself in the vision, they are somewhat human in appearance, but also quite different—something quite removed from Ezekiel himself, who was merely a "son of man."

WORDS THAT STICK IN THE HEART

"You adulterous wife! You prefer strangers to your own husband!" (16:32). So the prophet addressed his people, the faithless "wife" of God, never faithful to her "husband." In chapter 23 of his book he spoke of two "sisters," Oholah and Oholibah, representing the two nations of Israel and Judah. Both were notoriously promiscuous—meaning they went after other gods, dating back to their days as slaves in Egypt. The two sisters were chronically unfaithful to the one God who was actually real. Chapter 23 is difficult to read. In fact, if translated literally it is almost obscene, as the prophet seems to rub our noses in the two sisters' sexual escapades. But he is not trying to titillate, nor is he speaking of literal adultery. He is speaking of spiritual and moral corruption, which inevitably happened among the people who worshipped idols.

What had caused the people to stray so far from the right path? Certainly the herds of false prophets had not helped the situation. "This is what the Sovereign Lord says:

Bone Valley

One of Ezekiel's most famous visions is found in chapter 37. "The hand of the Lord was upon me, and he brought me out by the Spirit of the Lord and set me in the middle of valley; it was full of bones.... He asked me, 'Son of man, can these bones live?' I said, 'O Sovereign Lord, you alone know' " (37:1–3). The prophet was ordered to "prophesy" to the bones, "Dry bones, hear the word of the Lord." "And as I was prophesying, there was a noise, a rattling sound, and the bones came together, bone to bone. I looked, and tendons and flesh appeared on them and skin covered them, but there was no breath in them" (37:7–8). The bodies had re-formed, but were not alive quite yet. "Then he said to me, 'Prophesy to the breath; prophesy, son of man, and say to it, 'This is what the Sovereign Lord says: Come from the four winds, O breath, and breathe into these slain, that they may live.'" So I prophesied as he commanded me, and breath entered them; they came to life and stood up on their feet—a vast army" (37:9–10).

The prophet in this passage uses a Hebrew word that can mean *breath* or *wind* or *spirit*—or all three at once. This was probably his intention. A *wind* was blowing upon the bones, and it became *breath* and brought them to life, but the true source of the new life was God's *Spirit*. The bones represented God's people, Israel—spiritually dead, but never hopeless as long as God's Spirit could breathe new life into the people.

Woe to the foolish prophets who follow their own spirit and have seen nothing! Their visions are false and their divinations a lie. They say, 'The Lord declares,' when the Lord has not sent them; yet they expect their words to be fulfilled....they lead my people astray, saying, 'Peace,' when there is no peace" (13:3–6, 10).

The false prophets had led the people astray, but so had the leaders such as the priests and nobles. Like all prophets, Ezekiel's harshest criticisms were for the leaders, who set a bad example when they should have been role models of decency. The prophet called them "shepherds" who had failed miserably at their task of guarding their sheep. "Son of man, prophesy against the shepherds of Israel; prophesy and say to them: 'This is what the Sovereign Lord says: Woe to the shepherds of Israel who only take care of themselves! Should not shepherds take care of the flock? You eat the curds, clothe yourselves with the wool and slaughter the choice animals, but you do not take care of the flock. You have not strengthened the weak or healed the sick or bound up the injured. You have not brought back the strays or searched for the lost. You have ruled them harshly and brutally' " (34:2–4).

God had compassion on these sheep with their scapegrace shepherds. Something better was in store for the flock. "I will save my flock, and they will no longer be plundered. I will judge between one sheep and another. I will place over them one shepherd, my servant David, and he will tend them; he will tend them and be their shepherd. I the Lord will be their God, and my servant David will be prince among them. I the Lord have spoken" (34:22–24). Perhaps, centuries later, Jesus had this passage in mind when he told his followers, "I am the good shepherd. The good shepherd lays down his life for his sheep" (John 10:11).

When the flock finally had a righteous shepherd, it would no longer be divided. God said to Ezekiel, "I will make them one nation in the land, on the mountains of Israel. There will be one king over all of them and they will never again be two nations or be divided into two kingdoms" (37:22). The old division into two kingdoms—Israel and Judah—would be healed. The people would be morally pure, and finally they would have a righteous leader: "My servant David will be king over them, and they will all have one shepherd. They will follow my laws and be careful to keep my decrees" (37:24).

Although Ezekiel spoke of restoring Israel, he shared with Jeremiah an emphasis on the individual. The old idea that salvation was collective was gone. "What do you people mean by quoting this proverb about the land of Israel: 'The fathers eat sour grapes, and the children's teeth are set on edge'? As surely as I live, declares the Sovereign Lord,

---

CULTURAL INSIGHTS

Merkabah Mysticism

Merkabah is the Hebrew word for "chariot." Centuries ago, some Jewish readers of Ezekiel were impressed by the prophet's vision of God and the "living creatures," which were thought of as God's "chariots." Ezekiel's visions were the basis of what is called *merkabah mysticism*, in which a person tries to have a vision of God, aided by reciting hymns praising God's power and majesty. The person hopes to pass through seven heavens, seeing angels and celestial palaces along the way. Since he would meet hostile spirits along the way, he had to know spells (or "passwords") that would keep them away. The goal was to see what Ezekiel saw, the throne of God.

While the goal of seeing God is commendable, merkabah mysticism had no moral content, and the mystics showed little interest in studying the Bible as a whole. This form of spirituality—more like magic and occultism than faith—is a good example of what happens when people focus on an isolated part of the Bible and forget the importance of its overall teachings. In later chapters we will look at Gnosticism, which borrowed some of its ideas from merkabah mysticism.

you will no longer quote this proverb in Israel. For every living soul belongs to me, the father as well as the son—both alike belong to me. The soul who sins is the one who will die" (18:2–4). At this point we need to be reminded: God does not wish *any* soul to die. "Do I take any pleasure in the death of the wicked? declares the Sovereign Lord. Rather, am I not pleased when they turn from their ways and live?… Rid yourselves of all the offenses you have committed, and get a new heart and a new spirit. Why will you die, O house of Israel? For I take no pleasure in the death of anyone, declares the Sovereign Lord. Repent and live!" (18:23, 31–32). Anyone who believes that God in the Old Testament is cruel and unkind ought to read this passage—often.

And now we get to the deepest, richest part of the book: the new covenant. Here God speaks: "I will give them an undivided heart and put a new spirit in them; I will remove from them their heart of stone and give them a heart of flesh" (11:19). Does this sound like the New Testament phrase "born again"? It should, for both are speaking of a spiritual rebirth. "I will give you a new heart and put a new spirit in you; I will remove from you your heart of stone and give you a heart of flesh. And I will put my Spirit in you and move you to follow my decrees and be careful to keep my laws" (36:26–27).

The phrase "they will know that I am the Lord" occurs more than fifty times in Ezekiel. The only other book where the phrase occurs often is Exodus, where it is referring to the many miracles God performed in liberating the Israelite slaves from Egypt. Ezekiel probably knew this and chose the phrase deliberately to remind people that the age of miracles was not in the distant past. Miracles still occurred, God's people could still be delivered out of foreign lands. Ezekiel 40–48 is a long description of a restored Jerusalem, which the prophet saw in a vision. He was correct in predicting that the exiles would return there and rebuild the temple, and no doubt his vision gave them hope. But the more important prophecy was the promise of a "heart of flesh" to replace the "heart of stone." A "new heart and new spirit" seem more miraculous than the rebuilding of a temple.

The book ends with these words: "The name of the city from that time on will be: THE LORD IS THERE." He wasn't really thinking of an earthly Jerusalem anymore. He and Jeremiah had both lived through events that let them see a profound truth: All political structures are sand castles standing too close to the tides of time. Israel would some day be restored—but its ultimate restoration would not be on this earth, but beyond it, in a kingdom that would endure. In chapter 47 he described a river flowing out of the temple, big enough for fishermen to ply their trade in, and on its banks grew trees that bore fruit in all seasons. The river flowed into the salty Dead Sea and made it fresh, full of living things. As much as Ezekiel, who was from a family of priests, may have longed for the rebuilding of the temple in Jerusalem, his vision is clearly of something else, something beyond this life, a place where the people with the "new hearts" may live in peace and know no fear.

CHARACTER CLOSE-UP ## Ezekiel's Unmourned Wife

When people try to read Ezekiel, they seldom get beyond the first chapter with its description of the bizarre "living creatures." Ezekiel is often dismissed as the strange prophet who saw weird visions no one fully understands. This is unfortunate, because there is moral and spiritual depth in the book, and Ezekiel was as sensitive a soul as Jeremiah was. He received a bitter word from God: his wife, the "delight of his eyes," would die. Even worse, he was told not to mourn her. The usual signs of grief—going bareheaded and barefoot—were not to be observed. God told him to "groan quietly," but otherwise hold in his unrelievable grief. He was not even to eat the food that sympathetic mourners brought to him. The people were told that the prophet was a "living parable": just as he was not mourning his beloved wife, so they were not to grieve when they received horrible news from Jerusalem, news that the Lord's temple was destroyed by the Babylonians.

This is a hard command for anyone to obey, but surely harder for Ezekiel than for us. Our culture encourages us to hold in our grief, even at funerals, but in ancient times, people let their tears and wails flow with no feeling of shame. We can have no doubt that "groaning quietly" was not easy for this man raised to believe that the death of a loved one was a reason for demonstrative emotion. He held it in, and for the same reason the Jews were told to hold in their grief over the destruction of the temple: It was a grief too deep to mourn.

PUTTING THE WORD TO WORK

1. Jeremiah endured rejection and persecution for speaking the truth. Who are some people you have known who were persecuted for the same reason? How did they cope with it?

2. Jeremiah watched in horror as his prophecy was fulfilled: The people continued in their immoral ways, and as punishment they saw the temple destroyed, and people taken into exile. How do we respond in faith and sympathy when we see people suffering the consequences of their own actions?

3. Both Jeremiah and Ezekiel condemned the false prophets for telling people what they wished to hear, giving them false security. Who are some "false prophets" of today who peddle glib, easy answers to people's problems? How do we respond to friends and acquaintances who are taken in by such messages?

4. Ezekiel is considered one of the most difficult Old Testament books to understand. What did you gain most from our brief study of the book?

5. Ezekiel spoke of a time when God would give his people an "undivided" heart. What do you think this means? What are some things that "divide our hearts," keeping us from being fully devoted to God?

Five Voices Worth Hearing

**AT THE
HEART
OF IT ALL
TODAY**

In the books of five of the Minor Prophets we see the theme of divine mercy: Man repents, God relents. The prophets' messages mingle God's justice with his patience and everlasting love.

I n Hebrew Bibles there is a long book known as "the Twelve," meaning twelve prophets. We call these the Minor Prophets, not because they were unimportant (far from it!) but because their writings are much briefer than the Major Prophets (Isaiah, Jeremiah and Ezekiel). When the Bible was translated into Greek centuries ago, the twelve men's writings were known as the *Dodekapropheton*—twelve prophets. The Book of Daniel is a special case, which we'll talk more about in the next chapter.

KEY PASSAGES TO READ TODAY
Hosea 1; 3; 6
Amos 2:6–8; 5:7–24
Jonah
Micah 4:1–5; 6:1–8; 7:1–7
Zephaniah 1:14–18; 3:9–17

The books of the Major Prophets appear in the Bible in chronological order. The Minor Prophets do not. In fact, Amos was the earliest of the twelve, even though his book is third in the Bible, and Joel, probably the latest of the twelve, is second in the Bible, and frankly, scholars aren't quite sure why (or when) the sequence was established. In today's chapter we'll look at them in chronological order, throwing in a disclaimer that some of them—Joel, Obadiah and Jonah—aren't easy to date. However, their spiritual content is much more important than the precise dates of when these prophets lived.

They were a mixed and interesting group—men of different occupations and living in different times. Only two—Amos and Hosea—prophesied in the northern kingdom,

KEY TERM FOR TODAY ## Slow to Anger

Three of the minor prophets—Joel, Jonah, and Nahum—refer to God as "slow to anger," meaning he is patient, forbearing, not eager to punish quickly. The actual meaning of the Hebrew wording is "long of nose." To the Hebrew mind the "hot nose" was the sign of anger—the person breathed heavily, noisily. To be "long of nose" meant the nose didn't overheat easily—in other words, a patient person. Although almost all the prophets speak of God's righteous anger, they all emphasize how ready God is to forgive—and how long he delays punishing offenders.

Israel. The others prophesied in Judah, which doesn't mean God sent more prophets to Judah, only that more of their writings were preserved. Some of their writings, especially Hosea, had a profound effect on Jews and Christians, while others (the one-chapter Book of Obadiah) are almost unread today, which is unfortunate, for there are good things in all twelve of these books. They are not studied as often as the Major Prophets, but there are spiritual gems in them, and we will look at these in detail.

MR. JUSTICE

Amos is often called the "prophet of justice," and the name fits perfectly, although it is a little unfair, since most of the prophets spoke out in favor of social justice, love for the poor and honesty in business dealings.

Amos was a shepherd—or to be more precise, a sheep farmer, meaning he owned flocks of sheep and was not merely a hired hand. He also was a "tender of sycamores," which refers to the tedious task of piercing holes in the figs produced on sycamore-fig trees, so the fruit will ripen. The jobs could be done at the same time, since sheepherders often grazed their flocks among the fig orchards, watching the sheep while at the same time tending the figs. In other words, Amos was a manual laborer, not afraid of hard work or soiling his hands.

His hometown was Tekoa, a village in Judah not far from Bethlehem—the home of a more famous shepherd, David. For several years of Amos' lifetime, Judah and Israel were on friendly terms, their kings—Uzziah of Judah and Jeroboam II of Israel—forming an alliance. Both kings had long reigns beginning and ending almost at the same time, so this was a rare lull in the usual hostilities between the two nations. Travel between the two countries was easy during this period. Amos is the only case in the Bible of a prophet going from one country to the other to prophesy. The fact that he was still a foreigner as far as Israel was concerned did not make his task any easier.

As might be expected of a man from Judah, he saw the worship of God as being centered in Jerusalem, so his prophecy opens with "The Lord roars from Zion," Zion being an alternate name for Jerusalem. When the Lord roars, "the pastures of the shepherds dry up." Amos, the sheepherder, is opening his book with a touch of drama: God Almighty is about to speak. In chapter 1, the Lord condemns the brutal nations nearby—Aram, the Philistines, Tyre, Edom, Ammon and Moab. The nations raid their neighbors, sell the captives as slaves, and cut open the bellies of pregnant women. For their brutalities, these nations would eventually all be punished.

But Amos' main concern is for his own people, the two nations that are supposed to be devoted to God. They too will be punished. Judah has not kept God's laws, but has worshipped idols and loved false gods.

Then he launches into his sermon against the northern kingdom, Israel. At this period, Israel was materially prosperous. Peace had made it easy to make—and spend—money. We would say that the country had a booming economy. But Amos could see the downside of prosperity. "This is what the Lord says: 'For three sins of Israel, even for four, I will not turn back [my wrath]. They sell the righteous for silver, and the needy for a pair of sandals. They trample on the heads of the poor as upon the dust of the ground and deny justice to the oppressed. Father and son use the same girl and so profane my holy name' " (2:6–7). God reminds faithless Israel that he had destroyed the pagan Canaanites, and he could destroy Israel as well. Why had the people been such ingrates after God had delivered them out of Egypt and sent them prophets for spiritual guidance? They had stifled the prophets, and for that, there would be retribution.

Israel had grown complacent. They were God's chosen people, so that gave them special status. Indeed it did, as Amos puts it so forcefully: "You only have I chosen of all the families of the earth; therefore I will punish you for all your sins" (3:2). The chosen people would not be given a "pass"—quite the opposite. They had been especially blessed by God, so their ingratitude was even worse than the behavior of the pagans. There was no privilege without responsibility.

The prophet gets specific about the people's sins. He scolds the women of Samaria, Israel's capital, calling them "cows" who oppress the poor and needy and order their husbands to bring them drinks. "You lie on beds inlaid with ivory and lounge on your couches. You dine on choice lambs and fattened calves" (6:4). They guzzled wine and idled away their time listening to music. Their wealth was all ill-gotten: "You hate the one who reproves in court and despise him who tells the truth. You trample on the poor and force him to give you grain. Therefore, though you have built stone mansions, you will not live in them; though you have planted lush vineyards, you will

525–465 BC
Aeschylus, Greek dramatist

520 BC
Foundations of new Jerusalem temple laid
(Ezra 3–6)

515 BC
Completion of the temple
(Ezra 6:13–18)

499–479 BC
Persian wars against Greek states

c. 473 BC
Esther made queen of Persian king Xerxes
(Esther)

450–400 BC
Flowering of Greek culture under Pericles

c. 450–c. 377 BC
Hippocrates, "father of medicine"

445–443 BC
Restoration of Jerusalem's walls
(Nehemiah 2–6)

431–404 BC
Peloponnesian War

c. 427–348 BC
Plato, Greek philosopher

399 BC
Death of Greek philosopher Socrates

396 BC
Plato writes the *Apology* in defense of Socrates.

not drink their wine. For I know how many are your offenses and how great your sins. You oppress the righteous and take bribes and you deprive the poor of justice in the courts" (5:10–12). For their lack of compassion, God will "tear down the winter house along with the summer house; the house adorned with ivory will be destroyed and the mansions will be demolished" (3:15). The "cows" would eventually be led away into captivity with hooks.

Like all the prophets, Amos condemned hypocrisy. True, the people were going to the shrines and making sacrifices to God. They were generous with sacrifices—but it was all for show. Their minds were on material things, not on God. "Hear this, you who trample the needy and do away with the poor of the land, saying, 'When will the New Moon be over that we may sell grain, and the Sabbath be ended that we may market wheat?'—skimping the measure, boosting the price and cheating with dishonest scales, buying the poor with silver and the needy for a pair of sandals, selling even the sweepings with the wheat" (8:4–6). Did they think God didn't see through them? "I will turn your religious feasts into mourning and all your singing into weeping. I will make all of

KINGS OF JUDAH	PROPHETS	KINGS OF ISRAEL
Amaziah 796-781 BC (2 Kings 14:1-22)		
	Amos [reign of Jeroboam II]	Jeroboam II 783-743 BC (2 Kings 14:23-29)
	Hosea [reign of Jeroboam II]	
	Jonah [reign of Jeroboam II]	
Uzziah 781-740 BC (2 Kings 15:1-7)		Zechariah, for 6 months in 743 BC (2 Kings 15:8-13)
		Shallum, for 1 month in 743 BC (2 Kings 15:13-16)
Jotham 740-736 BC (2 Kings 15:32-38)	Micah [reign of Jotham]	Menahem 743-738 BC (2 Kings 15:17-22)
		Pekahiah 738-737 BC (2 Kings 15:23-26)
Ahaz 736-716 BC (2 Kings 16)		Pekah 737-732 BC (2 Kings 15:27-31)
		Hoshea 732-723 BC (2 Kings 17:1-4)
Hezekiah 716-687 BC (2 Kings 18-20)		
Josiah 640-609 BC (2 Kings 22; 23:1-30)	Zephaniah [reign of Josiah]	

you wear sackcloth and shave your heads. I will make that time like mourning for an only son and the end of it like a bitter day" (8:10).

In what is probably his most quoted passage, Amos spoke of the Lord's distaste for hypocritical religion: "I hate, I despise your religious feasts; I cannot stand your assemblies. Even though you bring me burnt offerings and grain offerings, I will not accept them. Though you bring choice fellowship offerings, I will have no regard for them. Away with the noise of your songs! I will not listen to the music of your harps. But let justice roll on like a river, righteousness like a never-failing stream!" (5:21-24).

The people were such fools that they claimed they hoped for the "Day of the Lord," the time when God would come and judge the nations. It would not be a good day for them! "Woe to you who long for the day of the Lord! Why do you long for the day of the Lord? That day will be darkness, not light. It will be as though a man fled from a lion only to meet a bear, as though he entered his house and rested his hand on the wall only to have a snake bite him. Will not the day of the Lord be darkness, not light—pitch-dark, without a ray of brightness?" (5:18-20).

And yet, as with all the prophets, Amos spoke with a loving purpose: God wanted the people to change, not be destroyed. "Seek good, not evil, that you may live. Then the Lord God Almighty will be with you, just as you say he is. Hate evil, love good; maintain justice in the courts. Perhaps the Lord God Almighty will have mercy on the remnant of Joseph" (5:14-15). Here "Joseph" refers to the two large tribes of Ephraim and Manasseh, the sons of Joseph in Genesis. These were the largest tribes in Israel. Amos was telling Israel that some of them—a righteous remnant—might survive the day of judgment. In another passage, Amos speaks of a shepherd saving a sheep from a lion—not saving the entire sheep, but perhaps only a leg or an ear (3:12). As with all the prophets, the idea of Israel being saved *collectively* was passing away. They were God's chosen people but had not followed God. So salvation was not to be for an entire nation, but for righteous individuals—a remnant of the people.

As often happened with prophets, the religious leaders of their people opposed them. Amos locked horns with Amaziah, the priest at Bethel. Amaziah told Amos to go home to Judah and do his prophesying there. He had no business at Bethel, since it was the *king's* worship center. Amos would have been aware that the king's name was Jeroboam—the same as the *first* king Jeroboam, who had built the shrine at Bethel centuries earlier. The prophets never ceased to condemn Jeroboam I for this sin, setting up a rival sanctuary to the one temple of God in Jerusalem.

Amos informed the priest he was not a prophet nor did he belong to one of the fraternities of the prophets. He was a simple farmer, but God had called him to prophesy, and prophesy he would (7:14-16). The priest was a fool to harass a prophet of God, for even worse than hearing the condemnation of a prophet was to have no prophets at all.

" 'The days are coming, declares the Sovereign Lord, 'when I will send a famine through the land—not a famine of food or a thirst for water, but a famine of hearing the words of the Lord. Men will stagger from sea to sea and wander from north to east, searching for the word of the Lord, but they will not find it' " (8:11–12).

But the Lord's compassion is irrepressible. The Book of Amos ends on a hopeful note: A time of healing will come. " 'New wine will drip from the mountains and flow from all the hills' " (9:13). God would not *utterly* destroy Israel—not the righteous anyway.

Amos gives a sign that God is not just Israel's God—he loves all people. He has extended his blessing even to the Philistines (9:7). We will meet again with this theme in the other prophets. Calling them "prophets of Israel" isn't fully accurate, for they were speaking on behalf of the God of the whole world.

MAN WITH A DIFFICULT MARRIAGE

The longest book in the twelve Minor Prophets is Hosea's, and in some ways he is the most interesting, since he had a "colorful" life—to put it mildly. God sometimes made great demands on his prophets. He ordered Jeremiah not to marry, Ezekiel not to mourn when his wife died—and Hosea to marry a prostitute.

Or so people believe. God told Hosea, "Go, take yourself a wife of harlotry"—or "adulterous wife" in some translations. We don't know for sure if this woman—who had the catchy name Gomer—was a prostitute by trade, a temple prostitute for one of the pagan gods, or simply a "loose woman" who would prove to be an unfaithful wife. Any is possible. Whichever she was, her marriage to poor Hosea was intended by God to be a "living parable," her infidelity a painful sign of how Israel was unfaithful to God, chasing after other gods.

The badly matched couple had three children, all with highly symbolic names. The first was a son named Jezreel, in memory of the bloody massacre of wicked king Ahab's family at Jezreel by the rebel Jehu. In fact, God himself had ordered Jehu to exterminate Ahab's vile dynasty, but Hosea's disapproval suggests that Jehu had gone overboard with his bloodbath. Hosea's next child was a daughter named Lo-Ruhamah—Hebrew for "not loved," for God intended to withdraw his love from faithless Israel. The third child was a son, Lo-Ammi—"not my people." The people had not kept their covenant with the Lord, and he intended to cast them off.

Israel, the "wife" of God, had aroused the anger and jealousy of her "husband," God. He was furious and would punish her—but only with a view to bringing her back and restoring to her the joys of their first love. Faithless Gomer became the slave or concubine of another man, but Hosea brought her back because he loved her in spite of her sins.

You might recall from earlier chapters that the great prophet Elijah had confronted the prophets of Baal in the famous contest on Mount Carmel. Elijah's God proved real, hundreds of the Baal prophets were killed, and it seemed Baal worship was vanquished. It was not. It continued —sin is very hard to eradicate—and so another prophet anointed Jehu to exterminate the Baal-worshipping dynasty of Ahab. Jehu went further and staged a massacre of Baal devotees inside their temple. But only a few years later, Baal worship was back with a vengeance, as Hosea's book makes clear. How could it be otherwise?

The religion of God called people to a high morality. Baalism did not—getting Baal's attention did not require moral living but quite the opposite: having sex with a temple prostitute—of either gender! Baalism was bound to appeal to the worst side of human nature. And Israel had a long, sad history of serving the god of fertility. Speaking through Hosea, God says, "When I found Israel, it was like finding grapes in the desert; when I saw your fathers, it was like seeing the early fruit on the fig tree. But when they came to Baal Peor, they consecrated themselves to that shameful idol and became as vile as the thing they loved" (9:10). Baal Peor was the site on the border of Canaan where the Israelites first fell into Baal worship. Note the last sentence here, a familiar idea in the Bible: People who worship vile, immoral gods become like them. Man's ingratitude to God is as old as the human race itself: "Like Adam, they have broken the covenant" (6:7).

Not only did many of the people worship false gods, but their worship of God was tainted with hypocrisy. They paid lip service to him, but their deeds showed how rotten they were at the core. "They make many promises, take false oaths and make agreements; therefore lawsuits spring up like poisonous weeds in a plowed field....you have planted wickedness, you have reaped evil, you have eaten the fruit of deception" (10:4, 13). Yet they continued to go through the motions of their religious rituals. In probably the most-quoted phrase of the book, God tells them "I desire mercy, not sacrifice, and acknowledgment of God rather than burnt offerings" (6:6). With such immorality and hypocrisy, judgment was inevitable. "They sow the wind and reap the whirlwind" (8:7). They had sowed immorality and would reap destruction.

"When Israel was a child, I loved him, and out of Egypt I called my son" (11:1). What ingrates the Israelites could be—victims of their own spiritual amnesia. If God were nothing more than cosmic justice, he would cast away the people and say "Good riddance!" But Hosea is the book of divine love and mercy. "I will not carry out my fierce anger, nor will I turn and devastate Ephraim. For I am God, and not man—the Holy One among you. I will not come in wrath" (11:9).

Aware of this mercy, Hosea summons the people: "Come, let us return to the Lord. He has torn us to pieces but he will heal us; he has injured us but he will bind up our wounds. After two days he will revive us; on the third day he will restore us, that we may live in

Prostitution

This may not be the "world's oldest profession," but it certainly is old, as the Bible proves. Some prostitutes were simply women making their living that way, but many more were "temple whores" in the service of some of the pagan gods and goddesses. Many of the so-called temples were basically brothels, dedicated to a god or goddess of fertility. Even the Greeks, thought of as being so refined, had temples to their goddess Aphrodite, which were nothing more than whorehouses staffed by "priestesses," overseen by "priests" who were nothing more than pimps. When you understand how widespread—and accepted—such practices were, you see how very different the worship of God was—no idols, no fertility rituals, no promiscuous sex.

Whenever the people of Israel were tempted to abandon worshipping God and to worship false gods, the Bible authors refer to it as "prostitution." Sometimes it literally was, with a man of Israel having intercourse with one of the temple whores (some of whom were *male*, by the way). But worshipping a false god was also a kind of spiritual infidelity. The Israelites' true master and "husband" was God himself. To worship another god was like being unfaithful to one's spouse—only much more serious.

When you read the Old Testament, particularly the books of the Prophets, you'll find frequent references to prostitution and adultery, most often in reference to this spiritual infidelity. The classic example is the Book of Hosea, where poor Hosea endures his unfaithful wife. Gomer symbolizes Israel, the "unfaithful wife" who forsakes her true husband (God) and takes other lovers (the false gods of the surrounding nations).

his presence" (6:12). Sincere repentance could avert disaster. The names Hosea gave to his children could change, as God made abundantly clear: "I will plant her for myself in the land; I will show my love to the one I called 'Not my loved one.' I will say to those called 'Not my people, ' 'You are my people'; and they will say, 'You are my God' " (2:23).

The book ends on a hopeful note—hopeful, but realistic in observing that not all people will accept God's love and mercy. There will always be rebels—remember Adam and Eve?—who choose their own way instead of God's. "Who is wise? He will realize these things. Who is discerning? He will understand them. The ways of the Lord are right; the righteous walk in them, but the rebellious stumble in them" (14:9).

Hosea was a contemporary of Amos, but Hosea's ministry lasted much longer, and he may have lived to witness the Assyrian conquest of Israel in 721 BC. If so, it could not have pleased him that his threats of coming disaster had come to pass. A prophet can only preach repentance; he cannot enforce it. Hosea's image of God as a righteous holy being who is also brimming over with mercy and love is appealing, but people then and now reject it, following their own inclinations.

In closing this section, it is worth remembering this: Most of the prophets spoke of Israel's "adultery" and "whoring" and how deeply these offended God. Hosea knew about it "up close and personal"—he was the good and faithful husband married to the wayward wife. His marital pain helped him see the world through God's eyes—an unpleasant but life-changing, soul-enriching experience. His heart was enlarged through his suffering.

A SAVIOR FROM BETHLEHEM

Isaiah was not the only prophet active in the reigns of Ahaz and Hezekiah, for Micah of the village of Moresheth was also prophesying about and addressing many of the same issues. His book is small compared to Isaiah's, but it is full of good things.

Though he lived in Judah, Micah prophesied to both Judah and Israel, as did most of the other prophets. Although Israel had broken away and set up its rival worship centers, the prophets of Judah never wrote off Israel as a total loss. God still cared for both kingdoms.

In Micah's day, both kingdoms were being menaced by the Assyrians. The threat of disaster hangs over the book. Samaria, the capital of Israel, would become a heap of ruins. Jerusalem was threatened also. Why? Because of the people's greed and immorality. "Woe to those who plan iniquity, to those who plot evil on their beds! At morning's light they carry it out because it is in their power to do it. They covet fields and seize them, and houses, and take them. They defraud a man of his home, a fellow-man of his inheritance. Therefore, the Lord says: 'I am planning disaster against this people, from which you cannot save yourselves. You will no longer walk proudly, for it will be a time of calamity'" (2:1–3). As usual, the false prophets could not tolerate warnings of disaster. Why not, Micah asks—God's words are not a threat to the righteous but to the wicked. "Do not my words do good to him whose ways are upright?" (2:7). Yet the foolish people prefer a prophet who is a liar. The false ones say anything that will get them a free meal. But Micah himself is filled with the Spirit and must speak the truth.

The people's leaders are given a thrashing. Instead of doing their people good, they devour them. They take bribes, the priests and prophets lie for money. Then they foolishly believe the Lord is on their side, so they have nothing to fear. Because of their sins and hypocrisy, "Jerusalem will become a heap of rubble" (3:12).

It is not just the leaders who are corrupt. No one can be trusted. "Do not trust a neighbor; put no confidence in a friend. Even with her who lies in your embrace be careful of your words. For a son dishonors his father, a daughter rises up against her mother, a daughter-in-law against her mother-in-law—a man's enemies are the members of his own household" (7:5–6). Who can we turn to that can be relied on? "As for me, I watch in hope for the Lord, I wait for God my Savior; my God will hear me" (7:7). We see this theme often in the prophets: only God can be relied on totally.

God wants a change of the heart more than sacrifices and other meaningless rituals. "He has showed you, O man, what is good. And what does the Lord require of you? To act justly and to love mercy and to walk humbly with your God" (6:8). This is Micah's high point. He has summed up morality in only a few words. Pleasing God is a simple matter, and people know the right thing to do. They simply have to *do* it—and few do.

Some will. They are the "remnant" the prophets speak of. "Who is a God like you, who pardons sin and forgives the transgression of the remnant of his inheritance? You do not stay angry forever, but delight to show mercy. You will again have compassion on us; you will tread our sins underfoot and hurl all our iniquities to the depths of the sea" (7:18–19). No wonder Micah is often called the "prophet of mercy."

Where there is true devotion—where people do justly and love mercy and walk humbly with God—there is blessing. "He will judge between many peoples and will settle disputes for strong nations far and wide. They will beat their swords into plowshares and their spears into pruning hooks. Nation will not take up sword against nation, nor will they train for war anymore. Every man will sit under his own vine and under his own fig tree, and no one will make them afraid, for the Lord Almighty has spoken. All the nations may walk in the name of their gods; we will walk in the name of the Lord our God for ever and ever" (4:3–5).

A delightful vision. But probably the most famous verse in Micah is, without a doubt, 5:2: "But you, Bethlehem Ephrathah, though you are small among the clans of Judah, out of you will come for me one who will be ruler over Israel, whose origins are from of old, from ancient times." The verse is quoted in the New Testament as a prophecy of the birth of Jesus, born in Bethlehem. Micah no doubt had in mind the birth of the great king David there centuries earlier. It was in the divine plan that someone much greater than David would be born there, one who would be a spiritual ruler, not a man of war and conquest as David was. When the magi—wise men—came seeking the newborn Jesus and called on King Herod, Herod's advisors searched the Scriptures and determined that the new "king of the Jews" would be born in Bethlehem—and so the wise men traveled there and, sadly, so did Herod's soldiers, ordered by that vile leader to kill the infant boys in the town. Herod failed to exterminate the child: The family had departed, thanks to a dream sent to Joseph by God.

TALE OF THE WHALE

For such a short book, Jonah has generated a tidal wave of controversy. Can a man really be swallowed by a whale—and live to tell about it? Actually, yes. But concentrating on the whale is to miss the main points of the book.

However, we can't discuss the book without dealing with the whale issue. First of all, the book itself says Jonah was swallowed by a "great fish." The Hebrew word *dag*, "fish," is used here. The people of ancient times did not know, as we do, that whales are mammals, not fish. They used the word that seemed to fit, *dag*, and added the modifier for "large." A sperm whale *can* swallow a man, and has done so. In all likelihood, this is the creature the book of Jonah refers to.

With the whale issue aside, consider the book itself. It is the story of Jonah, the son of Amittai—a prophet mentioned in 2 Kings 14:25. Based on that passage, Jonah would have lived in Israel, the northern kingdom, during the reign of Jeroboam II, making him a contemporary of Amos and Hosea. The mention of Jonah in 2 Kings would have been long ago forgotten if the Book of Jonah had not provided us with a touching—and amusing—story about a reluctant prophet.

The book begins in the usual fashion of a prophet: "The word of the Lord came to Jonah." But instead of being sent to Judah or Israel, Jonah was sent to, of all places, Nineveh, capital of the Assyrian Empire. Jonah was to go there and warn of the wicked city's imminent destruction. Without any analysis of his motives or moods, the book simply says that he went to the port of Joppa and paid fare on a ship bound for Tarshish—the place we now call Spain. This was about as far as one could get from Israel in those days. Jonah hoped to go "from the presence of the Lord." If there was a place on earth where God was not present, Tarshish would be the place. (Worth noting: The Israelites were not a seafaring people, and the fact that Jonah boarded a ship bound for *anywhere*, let alone faraway Tarshish, proves he was desperate to get away from God.)

But of course, you can't flee God's presence. Out on the sea, God sent a mighty windstorm, which threatened to break up the ship. The crew jettisoned some cargo, and each sailor cried out to his own god. Amazingly, down in the ship Jonah was fast asleep. He was awakened by the desperate captain telling him to call on his god. How did he know Jonah's god might be effective in this situation? The crew cast lots to determine just who might be the cause of this tempest. The lot fell on Jonah. Who are you, they asked him, and who are your people? Jonah identified himself as a Hebrew, "and I worship the Lord, the God of heaven, who made the sea and the dry land" (1:9). The men already knew that Jonah was fleeing from the Lord's presence because he had told them so. What do we do now, they asked. Jonah, apparently aware that no one could flee from God, told them: Throw me overboard and the storm will cease. The reluctant prophet was not lacking in compassion. Why should the whole ship perish when it was him God wanted? When the storm grew worse, they threw him overboard—all the while praying to God not to blame them for what they were doing. The men offered sacrifices to Jonah's God when, as he'd predicted, the storm ceased when he was thrown overboard. Consider the irony: Jonah had tried to flee God, and instead his flight became a means of evangelizing some pagans!

God was ready: He had "prepared" the great fish to swallow the prophet. This, of course, is the key point in the whale/fish part of the story: *The beast was there to keep Jonah from drowning*. Whatever the creature was, it was Jonah's life preserver.

Jonah prayed—and who wouldn't? His prayer reads like a psalm of lament, but also of thanksgiving. Some readers wonder why his prayer condemns "worthless idols." It is obvious: The gods the sailors prayed to were worthless. They had no power to save a man—or pursue him across the ocean! After three days, the whale vomited Jonah onto dry land.

God spoke again to Jonah, telling him to go preach to Nineveh. This time, not surprisingly, he obeyed. No doubt he was a changed man. Reaching the metropolis, he preached the message of doom: In forty days Nineveh would be overthrown. The Ninevites were more responsive than Jonah had been: They did repent. Everyone put on sackcloth—that is, burlap, the usual sign of mourning or repentance. The king issued a decree, ordering everyone to cry out for mercy to God. Man repented, and God relented.

"But Jonah was greatly displeased and became angry" (4:1). *Angry?* Yes. God had compassion on Nineveh, but Jonah did not. Jonah was overlooking something rather obvious: *He himself had been spared God's judgment*. Now Jonah admits the truth to God: He had fled from God for the very reason that he did *not* want the Ninevites to repent. Once it has happened, though, he prays to God to take his life. After preaching repentance to the Ninevites, he is sorry they listened. He'd had more compassion for the pagan sailors on his ship than he had for the thousands of people in Nineveh.

DID YOU KNOW?

Jonah's name means "dove." While the Bible often associates doves with purity and innocence—and their habit of mating for life—they could also symbolize silliness (Hosea 7:11). The prophet in the book does indeed have his silly side. Perhaps there is a symbolic aspect to the dove image. At the time God called him, Jonah may have wished he was a literal dove, with wings to fly away from the mission he detested.

The pouting prophet went out of the city, made himself a shelter from the sun, and sat down to see what would happen. Perhaps God would change his mind and destroy those blasted Ninevites! He did not—but God did make a plant grow up over Jonah's shelter, providing more shade. But the next day a worm made the plant wither, taking away some of the shade, then the sun beat down on Jonah's head—and he wished again he would die.

Jonah was angry—about Nineveh and about the plant withering away. He was angry because God was "slow to anger." God pointed out the irony: "You have been concerned

Jonah II

It is definitely true that a man who was swallowed by a sperm whale survived. An Englishman named James Bartley had signed on as a crew member of the whaling ship *Star of the East* in 1891. Near the Falkland Islands, in the Atlantic Ocean off the coast of South America, the crew sighted a sperm whale. The harpooners in the ship's long-boats pursued the whale, which submerged, then suddenly surfaced, sending the boats into the air. But the harpooned whale soon died, and the crew hoisted it alongside the ship and carved it up.

A shock awaited the crew when the whale's stomach was pulled onto the deck: It moved! The ship's doctor cut it open and found James Bartley, who was unconscious—and worse for wear, as the whale's digestive acids had burned all the hair off his body and bleached his skin ghostly white. Thanks to the acid he was nearly blind also. He had been inside the whale about fifteen hours.

Weeks later, he recalled being jettisoned into the air when the whale surfaced, then falling into its toothy mouth. He went down its esophagus and into its belly, where he blacked out because of lack of oxygen. This was his first voyage on a whaling ship—and *last* as well. He went back to England and settled far from the sea and took up the very un-nautical trade of shoemaking. His tombstone had an appropriate inscription: "A Modern Jonah."

Bartley was in the whale fifteen hours—could he have survived longer? Three days, as Jonah did? We don't know. Bartley blacked out, while the Bible says Jonah was conscious, and that he prayed inside the whale. Bartley was cut out of the whale's belly by his shipmates, but the Bible says Jonah was vomited out onto the land by the whale. If Jonah's hair was all gone, and his skin bleached, as Bartley's was, we could see why the people of Nineveh paid attention to him—he would have seemed like a visitor from another world!

about this vine, though you did not tend it or make it grow. It sprang up overnight and died overnight. But Nineveh has more than a hundred and twenty thousand people who cannot tell their right hand from their left, and many cattle as well. Should I not be concerned about that great city?" (4:10–11). On that note, this odd, touching, funny, irony-saturated story ends.

The Jews read the Book of Jonah every year on their Day of Atonement, a reminder that the Gentiles too can be reconciled to God if they repent. That is, after all, the theme of the book: Even the most wicked can be accepted by God if they repent. It is a testament to the Bible's broadmindedness that this story is included, for the prophet himself is an unappealing character, while the heathens of Nineveh, the heathens on the ship—and God, of course—come across very well. God moves in mysterious ways, reaching far beyond Israel with his tender mercies, calling on a selfish, foreigner-hating prophet to do his will—and going to great lengths to make that prophet perform his assigned task.

Before we close this section, we ought to turn the Jonah story back on ourselves. True, Jonah seems selfish and remarkably intolerant of the Ninevites. But then, Israel had a long and unpleasant history of dealing with Assyria. It was a notoriously brutal empire, one of the worst in ancient times. When God told Jonah to go to Nineveh, the prophet might have thought: *Nineveh, Lord? If you're going to send me to some foreign country, fine—but those vile, gore-loving, corpse-mutilating Assyrians, of all people? Them?* Imagine your own worst enemies, and ask: Would I really want them to repent or be saved? That was the situation Jonah faced. Perhaps we are more like him than we would care to admit. But the point of the story is to be more like God—slow to anger, eager to accept the repentant sinners.

ROYAL DOOMSTER

The prophet Zephaniah opens his book with his ancestry—not unusual, except that he does not stop with "Zephaniah son of Cushi," but goes back three more generations, all the way to Hezekiah, one of the few saintly kings of Judah. It may seem as if the prophet is boasting of his royal blood, but since prophets of the Lord were routinely ignored or even persecuted, we cannot fault him for wanting to boost his credibility in any way possible.

Zephaniah prophesied during the reign of Josiah, another saintly king. But apparently he was active *before* Josiah instituted the sweeping reform of the nation's religion, for as Zephaniah describes Judah, it was one step away from being utterly destroyed by the Lord. In fact, it would be valuable to read Zephaniah, then turn to 2 Kings 22–23 to see how startling the change was under Josiah. Zephaniah's words did not take, however, since there was almost immediate backsliding after Josiah's death. In a sense, moral warnings like Zephaniah's never go out of date.

The prophet opens with a loud, jarring trumpet call from God: "I will sweep away everything from the face of the earth…both men and animals." The Lord is tired of the people's bowing down to Baal idols and worshipping the stars and planets, even worshipping the horrible god Molech, to whom children were sacrificed. The people had gotten away with their wickedness for so long, they were sure no one was watching them. "I will search Jerusalem with lamps and punish those who are complacent, who are like wine left on its dregs, who think, 'The Lord will do nothing, either good or bad' " (1:12).

The day of the Lord is coming, a "day of wrath, a day of distress and anguish." No one will escape, not even the smug rich: "Neither their silver nor their gold will be able to save them on the day of the Lord's wrath. In the fire of his jealousy the whole world will be consumed, for he will make a sudden end of all who live in the earth" (1:18). Jerusalem "obeys no one, she accepts no correction" (3:2). Her leaders are more like predators than shepherds, her prophets are false and arrogant, her priests corrupt. "The unrighteous know no shame" (3:5).

The neighbor nations will not escape punishment either. Moab and Ammon will be destroyed as surely as Sodom and Gomorrah were in Genesis. The Lord will destroy their false gods. Mighty Nineveh, capital of Assyria, will be "utterly desolate." That "carefree city" will be a haunt for owls and wild beasts (a prophecy that did come true, by the way, when Nineveh was destroyed in 612 BC).

And yet…God is *slow to anger*. Perhaps he will relent. "Seek the Lord, all you humble of the land, you who do what he commands. Seek righteousness, seek humility; perhaps you will be sheltered on the day of the Lord's anger" (2:3). God wishes to "purify the lips of the peoples, that all of them may call on the name of the Lord and serve him shoulder to shoulder" (3:9). The day of the Lord is doom—but not for all: "On that day you will not be put to shame for all the wrongs you have done to me, because I will remove from this city those who rejoice in their pride. Never again will you be haughty on my holy hill. But I will leave within you the meek and humble, who trust in the name of the Lord" (3:11–12). Here again we meet with that familiar theme of the prophets: the remnant. "The remnant of Israel will do no wrong; they will speak no lies, nor will deceit be found in their mouths. They will eat and lie down and no one will make them afraid" (3:13).

For all the threats in the book, love and mercy shine through: "The Lord your God is with you, he is mighty to save. He will take great delight in you, he will quiet you with his love" (3:17). We can envision a frightened child curling up in his father's lap, with the father saying, *Have no fear, my child. I love you.*

PUTTING THE WORD TO WORK

1. Amos, the "prophet of justice," told people to let "justice roll on like a river." What are some ways you can be more fair and just with the people you come in contact with?

2. The Lord is "slow to anger" and quick to forgive those who repent. In what ways is this a model for us to follow? Think of people you know who are slow to anger, and talk to one of them about what helps them control their emotions.

3. The prophets speak often of God preserving a faithful "remnant" of his people. What do you think are some signs that a person is part of the "remnant"?

4. The story of Jonah shows a man who was peeved at God's forgiveness of the repentant people of Nineveh. Have there been times in your own life when you've actually been sad or jealous to see that someone has undergone a change for the better? If so, why did you feel that way?

5. Zephaniah stated that "neither silver nor gold" could save people on the day of the Lord. In what ways does money distort our perspective, giving us a false sense of security and power?

Visionaries and Dreamers

AT THE HEART OF IT ALL TODAY	The Minor Prophets challenge and comfort us with their prophecies of the "day of the Lord" and the coming of the Messiah and the outpouring of the Holy Spirit. Daniel's dream-visions affirm the afterlife and the triumph of persecuted people of faith.

We continue today with the Minor Prophets, moving forward in time so that with the last of them, Joel, we are within four centuries of the time of Jesus. We probe into the deep doubts of the prophet Habakkuk, the Messiah prophecies in Zechariah, the notion of God as "refiner" in Malachi, and the foretelling of the outpouring of the Spirit in Joel. We'll also look at the visions in

> **KEY PASSAGES TO READ TODAY**
>
> Joel 2:10–14; 28–32
>
> Habakkuk 2
>
> Zechariah 7:8–13
>
> Malachi 4
>
> Daniel 7:13–14; 12:1–4

the Book of Daniel, with their puzzling images and their affirmation of an afterlife and ultimate triumph of God's persecuted saints.

GOOD-BYE, CRUEL EMPIRE

If you want to know how cruel and brutal the ancient Assyrians were, read the brief Book of Nahum. It is one long rant—and prediction of doom—for that evil empire. In chapter 1, the prophet describes God as "slow to anger," yet he will not leave the guilty unpunished. The capital of Assyria, mighty Nineveh, is doomed. It is a "city of blood, full of lies, full of plunder, never without victims!" (3:1). Bodies pile up, corpse on corpse, victims of an idolatrous, violent nation. Yet the city will fall, as other mighty

KEY TERM FOR TODAY ## The Day of the Lord

This term is used by the prophets to refer to a future time when God will punish sin and reward his righteous ones—in other words, Judgment Day. The first prophet to speak of it was Amos, who warned people that if they were sinners, they were fools to hope for the day to come: "Woe to you who long for the day of the Lord! Why do you long for the day of the Lord? That day will be darkness, not light" (Amos 5:18). Frightening as the day would be, it would finally bring justice on the earth.

753 BC
Founding of Rome

640–560 BC
Solon, Greek lawgiver

c. 628–c. 551 BC
Zoroaster, Persian
religious founder

606 BC
Assyrian empire
conquered by
Babylonia

c. 600 BC
Lao-tzu, Chinese
philosopher, born

586 BC
Jews taken into exile
in Babylon after the
fall of Jerusalem
(2 Kings 25:18–21).

c. 582–c. 507 BC
Pythagoras, Greek
philosopher and
mathematician

c. 563–c. 483 BC
Buddha, Indian
religious founder

551–479 BC
Confucius, Chinese
philosopher

539 BC
Persians conquer
Babylon
(Daniel 5:24–31).

cities have fallen over the centuries. Across the nations people will clap their hands when they hear of Nineveh's fall, "for who has not felt your endless cruelty?" (3:19). When Nineveh lies in ruins, the people of Judah can breathe a sigh of relief and celebrate their holy days with no more fear.

The book mentions the fall of the Egyptian city of Thebes, which occurred in 663 BC, and the fall of Nineveh which the prophet foretold was in 612 BC, so Nahum wrote his book sometime between those years. Here we have a very clear case of a prophecy coming true. However, Judah didn't have long to enjoy the demise of Nineveh, for another empire, Babylonia, would prove to be an even greater menace.

Nahum is the "flip side" of Jonah, which relates that the Ninevites repented when Jonah preached to them. Obviously their moral turnaround was not permanent, for they reverted to their cruelty and barbarity.

Although the book makes people uncomfortable—it takes obvious delight in disaster falling on Nineveh—we have to look at the situation through God's eyes. Nineveh and the Assyrians had caused widespread harm, including the conquest of Israel in 722 BC. Evil empires wreak havoc, but eventually they too are destroyed. This is the way things are—but how much better it would be if nations never practiced such cruelty!

"I HAVE A FEW QUESTIONS, LORD…"

The Book of Job asked a question all human beings have asked: Is God fair? The prophet Habakkuk asked that question, but it was not his own sufferings that prompted him. He questioned God's dealings with nations, not individuals, but in a way the question remains the same: Why do evil men prosper while good men suffer?

Habakkuk's book is in the form of a dialogue. He asks, God responds. "Destruction and violence are before me; there is strife, and conflict abounds. Therefore the law is paralyzed, and justice never prevails" (1:3–4). Habakkuk had his own nation, Judah, in mind here. God's answer surprised him. "Look at the nations and watch… I am raising up the Babylonians, that ruthless and impetuous people…. They are a feared and dreaded people, they are a law to themselves" (1:5–7). They are "guilty men, whose own strength is their god" (1:11).

Habakkuk questions God again: God's eyes are "too pure to look on evil"—so how can he use the loathsome Babylonians as his instrument? The people of Judah have sinned, true—but they are better morally than the Babylonians are. He asks God, "Why are you silent while the wicked swallow up those more righteous than themselves?" (1:13). God answers: there is an "appointed time" for his revelation. "Though it linger, wait for it. It will certainly come and not delay" (2:3). The Babylonians are proud—"puffed up"— greedy for loot. "Woe to him who builds his realm by unjust gain to set his nest on high, to escape the clutches of ruin!" (2:9). The Babylonians have "plotted the ruin of many peoples"—but a day of reckoning is coming. The evil ones will "be filled with shame instead of glory" (2:16).

What does the good person do while he awaits the punishment of the wicked? "The righteous will live by his faith" (2:4). At some time in the future, God's purposes will be plain. "The earth will be filled with the knowledge of the glory of the Lord, as the waters cover the sea" (2:14).

Chapter 3 of the book is a kind of praise Psalm, in which God is depicted as a warrior, riding in a chariot, brandishing his bow and arrows. God defeated the Egyptians when they pursued the Israelites into the Red Sea. He will defeat Israel's enemies in the future. The prophet "will wait patiently for the day of calamity to come on the nation invading us" (3:16). Though things seem to be in a sorry state—"the fig tree does not bud and there are no grapes on the vines"—people of faith will be sure that God is in charge. They will rejoice in God, their Savior. The mighty God is their strength.

One of the beauties of this brief book is that it has served a purpose far beyond what the prophet intended. He was thinking of a specific situation: the wicked Babylonians as a threat to his homeland. Remove the word "Babylonians" from the book and suddenly the book's questions apply to everyone: Why do the wicked prosper? Why are they allowed to oppress the good? Will justice never be done to them?

The answer comes back to something simple: "the righteous will live by his faith." In the New Testament, the apostle Paul quoted this verse—in fact, he made it a key point of his theology (Romans 1:17, Galatians 3:11). This is crucial to the spiritual life: *Trust God to do*

538 BC
Decree of Persian king Cyrus allows Jews to return home (Ezra 1).

525–465 BC
Aeschylus, Greek dramatist

520 BC
Foundations of new Jerusalem temple laid (Ezra 3–6).

515 BC
Completion of the temple (Ezra 6:13–18)

499–479 BC
Persian wars against Greek states

496–454 BC
Alexander I ruled Macedonia.

c. 473 BC
Esther made queen of Persian king Xerxes (Esther).

450–400 BC
Flowering of Greek culture under Pericles

c. 450–c. 377 BC
Hippocrates, "father of medicine"

445–443 BC
Restoration of Jerusalem's walls (Nehemiah 2–6)

c. 427–348 BC
Plato, Greek philosopher

399 BC
Death of Greek philosopher Socrates

right. The Hebrew word Habakkuk uses is *emunah*—translated "faith," and referring to loyalty and steadfastness, the trait of a person who holds on to God confidently even when things go wrong.

"The Lord is in his holy temple; let all the earth be silent before him" (2:20). God judges the world. The wicked seem to prosper for a time, but justice will be done. Those who oppress and abuse their neighbors, who live for money and possessions, who think they are gods—they are being watched by the Judge of all the world.

In closing this section, it is worth noting that the book seems to have been written to be sung or chanted. It ends with these words: "For the director of music. On my stringed instruments." Chapter 3 opens with "A prayer of Habakkuk the prophet. On *shigionoth*." After verse 3:3 occurs the word *Selah*—found in many of the Psalms. No one knows what these Hebrew terms meant, except they were probably some kind of musical direction. Habakkuk's book, with its questioning of God and God's responses, may have been set to music and sung in the temple services, a way of teaching a solid bit of theology in song.

ONE-CHAPTER WONDER

Obadiah, whose name means "servant of the Lord," is the shortest book in the Old Testament, one brief chapter with one clear purpose: to condemn the nation of Edom for its crimes. After the Babylonians conquered Judah in 586 BC, the nearby nations enjoyed their share of looting the defeated people—in other words, they poured salt into the wounds the Babylonians made. Edom had been at war with Judah and Israel for centuries, and the Edomites saw a chance for vengeance and took it. (They had certainly not forgotten being conquered by Israel's king David centuries earlier.) They must have been in their glory, thinking their old rival was vanquished forever.

Obadiah's book is a long passionate rant against Edom. It is understandable he would react so, but a question arises: Did he think anyone in Edom would ever hear or read his words? Probably not. It was intended for his fellow Jews, and was a release of his, and their, own righteous anger against the opportunistic Edomites and their crimes. Edom would become "small among the nations...utterly despised" (verse 2). The Edomites were famous for their numerous wise men, but the wise men would be slaughtered along with the rest of the people. They would be sorry they gloated over Judah's defeat.

"The day of the Lord is near for all nations. As you have done, it will be done to you; your deeds will return upon your own head" (verse 15). What goes around, comes around. They might think Judah is utterly ruined, but God would in time deliver his people. Judah would some day be a fire—and Edom would be stubble. Their land will be taken over by others, just as Judah had suffered occupation. "And the kingdom will be the Lord's" (verse 21).

Obadiah's prophecy came true in an unexpected way. In the period between the Old and New Testaments, Judah did achieve self-rule once again—and conquered Edom. This was more than a political conquest: The Edomites were forced to accept the Jews' religion. The region came to be called Idumea—and, in one of history's great ironies, an Idumean, Herod, became king of the Jews.

Obadiah's prophecy that Edom would eventually be destroyed came true. After the Romans destroyed Jerusalem in AD 70, the Edomites vanished from history.

DANIEL REVISITED

On Day 10 we looked at the first six chapters of the Book of Daniel, since our focus then was on the history of the Babylonian exile. Today we revisit Daniel for the prophecy the book contains. It is worth noting that in the Hebrew Bible, Daniel was not among the Prophets but among the mixed collection known as the Writings. This puzzles some people since Daniel definitely was a prophet, and in most Bibles his book follows the Major Prophets—Isaiah, Jeremiah and Ezekiel. Perhaps the Jews lumped in Daniel with the Writings because of the unique nature of his book—part history, part prophecy.

To refresh your memory, Daniel was among a group of Jewish youths carried off to Babylon when the Babylonian king Nebuchadnezzar besieged Jerusalem in 605 BC. Daniel was probably in his early or midteens at that time, and he and three friends were put into a kind of internship program, training them to serve in the Babylonian court. Daniel rose to high office because he could interpret the puzzling dreams of Nebuchadnezzar. When the Persians conquered Babylon in 539 BC, Daniel was made a court official to the king of Persia.

CULTURAL INSIGHTS

Burden

Nahum, Habakkuk and Malachi title their prophecies "burdens." In the King James Version, Nahum opens his book with the words "The burden of Nineveh," Habakkuk with "The burden which Habakkuk the prophet did see," Malachi with "The burden of the word of the Lord to Israel by Malachi." The Hebrew word used here, *massa*, refers to something heavy—that is, God has given the prophet a message of great weight and importance. Modern translations usually have "oracle" instead of "burden." Isaiah and Jeremiah also use "burden," and on one occasion Jeremiah's enemies punned on the word, claiming that Jeremiah's prophecies were indeed a "burden" to them (Jeremiah 23:33–40).

The book changes dramatically at chapter 7. Chapter 1–6 had been told in the third person. From chapter 7, the prophet Daniel speaks in the first person, "I, Daniel." He is not telling his own story now but revealing what God showed him.

Chapter 7 relates a vision he saw in a dream when the Babylonians were still in power. Four beasts come up from a turbulent sea—a winged lion, a bear, a four-headed winged leopard, and a ferocious ten-horned beast with iron teeth. Then the prophet saw a throne with the "Ancient of Days" seated on it, dressed in white and with white hair, attended by thousands of angels. "The court was seated and the books were opened" (7:10). "There before me was one like a son of man, coming with the clouds of heaven. He approached the Ancient of Days and was led into his presence. He was given authority, glory and sovereign power, all peoples, nations and men of every language worshipped him. His dominion is an everlasting dominion that will not pass away, and his kingdom is one that will never be destroyed" (7:13–14). Daniel, who had so skillfully interpreted Nebuchadnezzar's dreams, could not interpret his own. So a heavenly interpreter intervened: The four beasts were four kingdoms. "But the saints of the Most High will receive the kingdom and possess it forever" (7:18). But not before the horrible fourth beast trampled everyone on earth, with one particularly evil king who persecutes the saints. But in the end he too will be defeated.

As you might imagine, this passage has been pored over, commented on, and preached on for centuries. No one agrees on just what the "four kingdoms" were, or will be. In times past, it was assumed that the fourth beast with his iron teeth and his persecution of the saints, was the Roman empire, which so brutally persecuted Christians. But a useful guideline for the Bible is to study the parts that are clear and put aside those that are in doubt. In this passage, there is no doubt that the Ancient of Days is God, since Ancient of Days is another way of saying the Eternal One. What about the "one like a son of man"? You might recall that "son of man" was the Hebrew way of saying "human being." But this figure is "like" a son of man—meaning "not quite the same." From the New Testament period on, people have interpreted this figure as Christ, since Jesus used the term "son of man" for himself many times. In Daniel's vision, God is handing over the dominion of the world to Christ. The saints are persecuted, but in the end good triumphs. This is what we know for certain about chapter 7, while the rest—the beasts, the kings, the ten horns—remains in doubt. (In dreams and prophecies, a horn is always a symbol of power, while white, the color of the Ancient of Days, is always a symbol of holiness, also of eternity.)

Daniel's second dream, two years later, is found in chapter 8. He dreams of a ram and a goat—but in this case the heavenly interpreter explains that the ram represents the Medo-Persian empire and the goat the Greek empire. The interpreter says this is a vision of the "time of the end" (8:17). Daniel is told to "seal up the vision."

Seven

Since "sevens" play such an important part in the prophecies in Daniel, let's look at the significance of the number in the Bible. God created the world in six days, then rested on the seventh, so seven symbolizes *completion*. The Israelites used the number seven in many ways. Mourning periods were seven days. Priests sprinkled sacrificial blood seven times. The unclean were isolated from the community for seven days. Seven Israelite priests marched around the city of Jericho seven times, then the city walls fell. Among the Israelites, every seventh year was a "sabbatical" year, and after seven times seven years (forty-nine, that is) came the "jubilee" year. Samson's wedding feast lasted seven days. Jesus told his followers to forgive people "seventy times seven" times. The symbol of the nation of Israel today is the menorah, the seven-branched candlestick.

The number seven is mentioned eleven times in Daniel, such as in 3:19, where king Nebuchadnezzar orders a hot furnace heated "seven times hotter than usual" before Daniel's three friends are thrown into it. As poetic justice, the great king loses his sanity for seven years (4:16). The other "sevens" in the book are a puzzle to Bible readers, such as the "seventy sevens" mentioned in 9:24. A "seven" could mean "week," so in some passages "seventy sevens" could mean "seventy weeks"—but then, interpreters think the "weeks" might be referring to years—or periods. Daniel is a fascinating but sometimes frustrating book to read.

In chapter 9 we learn who Daniel's interpreter is: the angel Gabriel, mentioned here for the first time in the Bible. Centuries later, it would be Gabriel who would visit the virgin Mary and announce to her she was to give birth to the son of God. Later in the book we meet another angel, Michael, known as the "great prince," head of the heavenly armies.

In the final chapter, 12, we encounter something entirely new in the Bible: belief in an afterlife. Remember from earlier chapters that for centuries Israel had no clear belief in either heaven or hell. They believed in *Sheol*, the dark and gloomy land of the dead, where all people went, good or bad. But in God's own good time, and according to his plan, Israel would see that Sheol was not the end. "Multitudes who sleep in the dust of the earth will awake: some to everlasting life, others to shame and everlasting contempt. Those who are wise will shine like the brightness of the heavens, and those who lead many to righteousness, like the stars for ever and ever" (12:2–3). By the time of Jesus, most Jews believed in reward and punishment after death. Some, known as the Sadducees, did not, nor did they accept Daniel as inspired Scripture, for they only accepted the Torah, the first five books of the Bible, which do not mention an afterlife.

Daniel's visions were to have a powerful connection to Jesus and his apostles. Jesus, who called himself "son of man," more than once spoke of coming to earth on the clouds of heaven, as Daniel had prophesied in 7:13–14. Jesus told his followers, "At that time the sign of the Son of Man will appear in the sky, and all the nations of the earth will mourn. They will see the Son of Man coming on the clouds of the sky, with power and great glory" (Matthew 24:30). In another setting, he would seal his own fate by identifying himself with Daniel's "son of man": "Jesus remained silent. The high priest said to him, 'I charge you under oath by the living God: Tell us if you are the Christ, the Son of God.' 'Yes, it is as you say,' Jesus replied. 'But I say to all of you: In the future you will see the Son of Man sitting at the right hand of the Mighty One and coming on the clouds of heaven' " (26:63–64). At this point the high priest tears his robe in anguish. To him, Jesus is a blasphemer, deserving death.

CULTURAL INSIGHTS

Abomination of Desolation

Among the many puzzling things in the Book of Daniel is the "abomination that causes desolation" mentioned three times. "On a wing of the temple he will set up an abomination that causes desolation, until the end that is decreed is poured out on him" (9:27). The "he" here is the "ruler who will come," an evil figure who will do horrible things. "His armed forces will rise up to desecrate the temple fortress and will abolish the daily sacrifice. Then they will set up the abomination that causes desolation" (11:31).

In the period between the Old Testament and the New, the crazed Syrian ruler Antiochus Epiphanes horrified the Jews by setting up an altar to the god Zeus in the temple and sacrificing a pig. Remember that in the kosher laws, the pig was an "unclean" animal. Antiochus was "dirtying" the temple of God in the worst way.

Was this what Daniel foretold? Not according to the New Testament. Jesus indicated the "abomination of desolation" was still in the future. "When you see 'the abomination that causes desolation' standing where it does not belong—let the reader understand —then let those who are in Judea flee to the mountains" (Mark 13:14). This occurs in a passage where Jesus is telling his followers of the signs that the world is coming to an end. He predicted great persecution—as Daniel had. Note the phrase "let the reader understand": these are not Jesus' words but the words of the Gospel writer. He is providing a kind of "footnote," saying to the reader, "Remember, this is the abomination spoken of by the prophet Daniel."

The Bible's last book, Revelation, also borrows some images from Daniel. "Among the lampstands was someone 'like a son of man,' dressed in a robe reaching down to his feet and with a golden sash around his chest" (1:13). "I looked, and there before me was a white cloud, and seated on the cloud was one 'like a son of man' with a crown of gold on his head and a sharp sickle in his hand" (14:14). Revelation is here speaking of the resurrected Christ.

THE TEMPLE'S CHEERING SECTION

Scholars spent countless hours debating when the books of the Bible were written. One that is refreshingly easy to date is Haggai. We are almost certain he spoke his brief prophecy in 520 BC, when he directed the Lord's word to Zerubbabel, the governor of Judah, and the priest Joshua. The exiles had returned from Babylon in 538 BC. Why wasn't the temple rebuilt? The people had built nice homes for themselves—didn't they care for the temple, God's house? The Lord reminded the people: "I am with you." The work on the temple began.

A few weeks later, Haggai spoke again. Were the older people disappointed? Were they fearing that the new temple would be inferior to the old? Not to worry! "The glory of this present house will be greater than the glory of the former house" (2:9).

Haggai is not one of the high points of the Bible, to be sure, but it is a reminder that God was still sending his prophets to the people in this period.

PROPHESYING CHRIST

Zechariah is the second-longest book among the Minor Prophets, but his real importance is that he is quoted several times in the New Testament because of the uncanny way his prophecies were fulfilled in the life of Jesus.

Zechariah was a contemporary of Haggai, and both were given the task of encouraging the completion of the temple in Jerusalem. Zechariah's first prophecies were spoken in the year 520 BC. The first chapters of the book are symbolic visions in which God assured the people of Jerusalem that he was with them as they rebuilt the community of faith. Zerubbabel, the governor, and Joshua, the priest, appear in the visions. These chapters are puzzling to read, but they contain some gems: " 'Not by might, nor by power, but by my Spirit,' says the Lord Almighty" (4:6). "Who despises the day of small things?" (4:10).

The prophet was obsessed with the temple, yet he was also obsessed with justice and fairness. A faith community had to have more than a temple and rituals, it had to have ethical behavior: "Administer true justice, show mercy and compassion to one another. Do not oppress the widow or the fatherless, the alien or the poor. In your hearts do not think evil of each other" (7:9–10). Note carefully that last sentence: We are already on the verge of the New Testament, learning that not only our outward behavior is important

but our inner attitude as well. It is wrong for people to make their hearts "as hard as flint" and to ignore God's words. God hates deceit and injustice in the courts, people who plot against their neighbors (8:17).

Now, on to the prophecies of Christ. Zechariah 9 foretells the coming of a "king" to Jerusalem: "Rejoice greatly, O Daughter of Zion! Shout, Daughter of Jerusalem! See, your king comes to you, righteous and having salvation, gentle and riding on a donkey, on a colt, the foal of a donkey" (9:9). In the next verse, Zechariah draws a contrast: the day of the war horse and chariot is done, the battle bow will be broken. The king on the donkey will proclaim "peace to the nations," and his "rule will extend from sea to sea…to the ends of the earth" (9:10–11). Prisoners and captives will be set free.

The prophecy of the king coming on a donkey was fulfilled in the Gospels when Jesus rode into Jerusalem on the very week he would die—and live again. We celebrate this event on Palm Sunday, remembering that the people of Jerusalem greeted him by waving palm branches and shouting "Hosanna!" (Matthew 21:6–9). While we find the image appealing, it is even more impressive when you realize that in ancient time, no king would ride a lowly donkey. A king would ride a large horse, or be driven in a chariot. The Jesus who said "my kingdom is not of this world" was the kind of king Zechariah had in mind: not a mighty conqueror but a meek gentle soul, a man of the people.

In chapter 12, God says, "I will pour out on the house of David and the inhabitants of Jerusalem a spirit of grace and supplication. They will look on me, the one they have pierced, and they will mourn for him as one mourns for an only child, and grieve bitterly for him as one grieves for a firstborn son." In John's Gospel, this is quoted at the time of Jesus' crucifixion, when one of the soldiers pierces his side with a spear: "Another scripture says, 'They will look on the one they have pierced' " (John 19:37).

Zechariah 13:7 reads "Strike the shepherd, and the sheep will be scattered." Jesus quoted the words at the Last Supper: "Jesus told them, 'This very night you will all fall away on account of me, for it is written: "I will strike the shepherd, and the sheep of the flock will be scattered." The actual "scattering" occurred at the time of Jesus' arrest in Gethsemane, when the disciples fled and Jesus was left to face his torments alone.

The book ends with a prophecy of the "day of the Lord." The prophecy begins darkly: All nations will join together to fight against Jerusalem. "The city will be captured, the

Satan, Again

Zechariah is the only one of the prophets who mentions Satan. You might recall in the Book of Job that Satan is not an evil tempter opposed to God but a kind of heavenly prosecutor, telling God that Job is a saint only because God blesses him. With God's permission, Satan sends calamities on Job to find out whether his accusation is true. (It isn't.) In Zechariah, the prophet has a vision of a heavenly courtroom, where the high priest Joshua is being accused by Satan. The angel of the Lord says, "The Lord rebuke you, Satan" (3:2). Apparently Satan had made some accusation against the high priest, one that has no substance to it, judging from the angel's reply. Although Satan still seems to be playing the prosecutor role here, the story gives a hint that Satan is the enemy of mankind, something that will be very clear when we get to the New Testament.

houses ransacked, and the women raped" (14:2). But the Lord will come and stand on the Mount of Olives east of Jerusalem. The day will be like no other—night will never come. "Living water will flow out from Jerusalem.... the Lord will be king over the whole earth. On that day there will be one Lord, and his name the only name." Jerusalem will be secure and safe from then on. Plagues will strike Israel's enemies, and their wealth will be given to Jerusalem. The survivors will go up to Jerusalem to celebrate the feast.

The last verse is curious: In the New International Version, it reads, "There will no longer be a Canaanite in the house of the Lord Almighty." But a footnote states that "Canaanite" could also be translated "merchant." You might recall that Jesus drove the moneychangers out of the temple. "Get these out of here! How dare you turn my father's house into a market!" (John 2:16). If Jesus had in mind the last verse of Zechariah, then his act of driving out the moneychangers was a sign that the "day of the Lord" the prophet foretold had arrived.

WRAPPING UP A TESTAMENT

Our Old Testament ends with the Book of Malachi. Although this was probably not the last of the prophets (Joel was slightly later), the book does in a way prepare the reader for the New Testament.

Malachi lived around 460 BC, in the period after the temple had been rebuilt. Although the land was technically part of the Persian empire then, Malachi shows no interest in foreign affairs. The country was fortunate at that time—no worries about invaders or conquerors, something that all the other prophets were concerned

Angels or Human Messengers?

Our English word *angel* translates the Hebrew word *malakh*, which simply meant "messenger," and could refer to either a human or divine being. The same is true for the Greek word *angelos* in the New Testament. We have to determine from the context whether the messenger is a human or angel, and sometimes we aren't quite sure, especially since many of the angels in the Bible could appear deceptively human.

about. The nation was at peace, the temple had been rebuilt—but things were not well spiritually.

The book, like Habakkuk, is a kind of dialogue between prophet and Lord—except that in Malachi, it is God who initiates the conversation. "I have loved you," God says. Israel wonders: How so? Long ago, God had chosen Jacob to be the father of his people —and rejected Jacob's twin brother Esau. Why? Because Jacob was a better man? Definitely not! Malachi makes it clear that God's choosing of Jacob over Esau was his own choice. Genesis does not make Jacob a particularly lovable character—he is a sneaking deceiver, in fact. Yet God had blessed Jacob's descendants, Israel, more than Esau's descendants, Edom. For that divine choice, Israel should have been grateful—but seldom was.

They were ingrates, people with spiritual amnesia, forgetting the good things God had done for them. Even the priests were not what they should be. They were disobeying the laws of Moses and offering up blemished animals as sacrifices—when the law said that the sacrifice was to be the best of the flock, not the worst. Instead of offering God their best, they were just going through the motions of the sacrifices. They were not paying their required tithes, and God was not blessing them as a result.

But rituals were not Malachi's only concern. In fact, none of the prophets neglected the *social* aspects of God's laws. On the contrary, Malachi spoke out boldly against "adulterers and perjurers, against those who defraud laborers of their wages, who oppress the widows and the fatherless, and deprive aliens of justice" (3:5). The people were wondering, "Where is the God of justice?" He was watching—and in his own time would bring justice to the land.

An important idea in Malachi is that God's judgment is a "refining." "But who can endure the day of his coming? Who can stand when he appears? For he will be like a refiner's fire or a launderer's soap. He will sit as a refiner and purifier of silver; he will purify the Levites and refine them like gold and silver. Then the Lord will have men who will bring offerings in righteousness" (3:2–3). We see this refining theme in other books: "For you, O God, tested us; you refined us like silver" (Psalm 66:10). "See, I have refined you…I have tested you in the furnace of affliction" (Isaiah 48:10).

The "day of the Lord" will be a refining, a fire that burns up the "stubble," the evil and the arrogant. But for the good, "the sun of righteousness will rise with healing its wings" (4:2). Those who serve God faithfully will be his "treasured possession" (3:17). Finally, "you will again see the distinction between the righteous and the wicked, between those who serve God and those who do not" (3:18).

Then the great prediction: "See, I will send you the prophet Elijah before that great and dreadful day of the Lord comes. He will turn the hearts of the fathers to their children, and the hearts of the children to their fathers; or else I will come and strike the land with a curse" (4:5–6). Although Malachi is one of the least-read books of the Old Testament, this prophecy at the end of his book was one that the people never forgot. The great prophet Elijah, you might recall from an earlier chapter, was always associated with *fire*: calling down God's fire from heaven to light a sacrifice and to destroy enemy soldiers, being taken into heaven by a chariot and horses of fire. The Elijah prophecy fits in perfectly with Malachi's emphasis on refinement, being "tested in the fire."

At the time Jesus lived, faithful Jews all awaited the second coming of the prophet Elijah, who would usher in the "great and dreadful day of the Lord." Many had no doubts about who that was: the wilderness prophet John the Baptist. Many people thought Jesus himself was Elijah come back to earth. We will speak more about the "second Elijah" in later chapters.

Malachi's name means "my messenger." No name could have been more appropriate for one of God's prophets.

> **DID YOU KNOW?**
>
> Malachi prophesies a "sun of righteousness" rising with "healing in its wings." The early Christians in the Roman empire celebrated the birth of Jesus on December 25 because it was an old Roman holiday in honor of *Sol Invictus*, the Unconquered Sun. While the Romans had literally worshipped the sun, the Christians paid their homage to Jesus, the "sun of righteousness."

THE PLAGUE AND THE SPIRIT

Most of the prophets open their books by giving their name and then the names of the kings of Judah and Israel in their time, making it fairly easy for us to know when they lived. Joel, however, is more of a mystery: "The word of the Lord that came to Joel, the son of Pethuel." We don't have a clue when he lived, and scholars have made guesses as early as 830 BC and as late as 400 BC. The fact that he does not mention any king makes the late date (400 BC) the strongest possibility, since Judah had no king at that time. Much as we would like to know when the prophet lived, we cannot, so it is best—as with several other books of the Bible—to concentrate on the book's spiritual and moral value, which is considerable.

Whoever Joel was and whenever he lived, he had a way with words—or, more accurately, a way with *God's* words. He opens his book with images of one of the greatest disasters humans can face, a plague of locusts, devouring every green in sight. Commentators have suggested Joel was speaking figuratively, that the "locusts" in chapter 1 are really foreign invaders, wreaking destruction. This is possible, but the detail given here suggests Joel was speaking of real insects, and his eye for detail gives the impression he was someone close to the soil himself. Whether the locusts were six-legged insects or two-legged humans, the devastation they caused led the people to call on God—something typical of us when hard times come.

For Joel, the disaster is important as a kind of "preview" of something else: the day of the Lord, the day of judgment. This is true of any natural disaster: earthquakes, hurricanes, tornadoes, floods, fires—they remind us of how little control we have over such things, how close we are—despite our financial security, our insurance policies—to utter ruin. "Blow the trumpet in Zion; sound the alarm on my holy hill. Let all who live in the land tremble, for the day of the Lord is coming. It is close at hand—a day of darkness and gloom, a day of clouds and blackness. Like dawn spreading across the mountains a large and mighty army comes, such as never was of old nor ever will be in ages to come" (2:1–2). Here the trumpet is an alarm signal. Something terrifying is on its way. "The day of the Lord is great; it is dreadful. Who can endure it?" (2:11).

Here they are, on the brink of divine judgment. Yet God the Judge does not wish to punish. He is overflowing with love. " 'Even now,' declares the Lord, 'return to me with all your heart, with fasting and weeping and mourning.' Rend your heart and not your garments. Return to the Lord your God, for he is gracious and compassionate, slow to anger and abounding in love, and he relents from sending calamity" (2:12–13). People repent—and God relents. Note that phrase "rend your heart and not your garments." Tearing one's clothing was a sign of anguish, mourning—and repentance. Joel is telling people that the literal rending of clothing is not the important thing, but "rending the heart" is. When the heart is torn apart, God can enter into it.

Where there is true repentance, God will pour out his blessings. The people will be paid back in full for what the locusts destroyed. But here the prophet goes beyond what his hearers expected: something much greater is in store than merely their material well-being. "I will pour out my Spirit on all people. Your sons and daughters will prophesy, your old men will dream dreams, your young men will see visions. Even on my servants, both men and women, I will pour out my Spirit in those days. I will show wonders in the heavens and on the earth, blood and fire and billows of smoke. The sun will be turned to darkness and the moon to blood before the coming of the great and dreadful day of the Lord. And everyone who calls on the name of the Lord will be saved" (2:28–32).

If this passage sounds familiar, it might be because it is quoted in Acts 2, where the apostle Peter is preaching the first Christian sermon. Peter chose the quote because he and the other apostles, filled with the Spirit, were accused of being drunk early in the day. We are drunk, Peter said—we are inspired by God! And his quoting of the passage from Joel introduced a new theme into religious belief: *Everyone* could have God's Spirit. In the Old Testament, God endowed selected individuals with his Spirit. But a new age began with Peter's sermon: *All people could have God's Spirit*, for all who called upon God could be saved. Peter's famous sermon occurred on the day of Pentecost, and Joel is often referred to as the "prophet of Pentecost."

The final chapter of Joel is a prophecy of war. The nations will war with Israel in a site called the Valley of Decision and also the Valley of Jehosphahat (which is Hebrew for "God judges"). Joel speaks in martial terms: "Proclaim this among the nations: Prepare for war! Rouse the warriors! Let all the fighting men draw near and attack. Beat your plowshares into swords and your pruning hooks into spears. Let the weakling say, 'I am strong!' " (3:9–10). Was the prophet speaking of a literal battle—or a spiritual one? Perhaps Joel's original hearers thought of literal war, but generations of readers have preferred a spiritual interpretation. The enemies of Israel—meaning all God's people—will face great enemies in the Valley of Decision, but they will triumph, for God is on their side. Even the weakling can say "I am strong!" when God is at his side. "The Lord will be a refuge for his people" (3:16).

For such a brief book, Joel is an inspirational delight. People who have suffered the devastation of a natural disaster like a tornado or flood take great comfort from it. Those more fortunate may read the book as a reminder that the "day of the Lord" could be any day, that life and property are precarious, that we ought to always be spiritually ready for whatever life sends us. In any situation a person can say "I am strong!" if he makes the Lord his refuge.

Here we end our study of the prophets, and of the Old Testament—but not really, because the Old is constantly quoted and referred to in the New, and much of what happened in the life of Jesus and the apostles was considered a "fulfillment" of things prophesied in the Old. Our "bridge" into the New Testament from the Old is that important concept "the word of the Lord," the word that God spoke to, and through, his prophets. In the New Testament, the Word—with a capital W—was going to be spoken again after a long dry spell when no prophets spoke.

PUTTING THE WORD TO WORK

1. The coming "day of the Lord" was a reality to the prophets, something they knew would occur, in God's own good time. Think of ways you can be prepared, spiritually, for that day.

2. Have you ever had doubts about God's fairness, as Habakkuk did? Try writing a brief "Habakkuk dialogue," where you ask God about things in your own life that seem unjust. Then try writing the responses God might give—that is, try to see the situation from the divine point of view.

3. The Book of Nahum seems "mean-spirited," since it looks forward to the destruction of Nineveh, but it also celebrates the coming release of the people whom Nineveh oppressed. Are these two points of view compatible with each other? Is the destruction of an oppressor or an abuser justified by the liberation of the people who suffered?

4. In the Book of Malachi, God is spoken of as "refining" his people. Think of ways in your own life that God has tested and refined you.

5. Natural disasters such as the prophet Joel described remind us how uncertain and fragile life is. Think of times in your own life or the lives of friends when some disaster helped you turn to the Lord.

Immanuel, God with Us

AT THE HEART OF IT ALL TODAY At the time of Jesus' birth, the Jewish people prayed for the coming of God's "anointed one," the Christ, the king who would lead them to victory over their oppressors. The Christ that God sent was born in a stable, into a working-class family, and was destined never to wield military or political power. Most people were disappointed, yet others would perceive that the Christ had a spiritual power that made earthly power seem petty. God's view of power is very different from ours. And God's answer to our prayers is not always what we pray for, but what we truly need.

Some good news: For the next few days you'll be getting very familiar with the four books of the Bible called "good news"—better known as the four Gospels. Our English word "gospel" comes from the Old English *godspell*, which meant "good news." It's a translation of the Greek word *euangelion* used in the New Testament. One of the four Gospels,

KEY PASSAGES TO READ TODAY

Matthew 1:18—2:23
Luke 1:26–38; 2:1–20; 41–51
John 1:1–5; 10–14
Hebrews 1:1–2

Mark's, opens by referring to itself as "the good news [*euangelion*] about Jesus Christ, the Son of God." Mark and the other Gospel authors weren't just reporting events, but presenting *good* news, something that people could respond to with joy and gladness.

Today we will begin at the beginning of the good news, looking at Jesus' birth and the troubled, violent, expectant world he was born into. Be warned: You will learn some things about the familiar "Christmas story" that will surprise and even shock you. First, though, we need to take a look at the time that elapsed between the Old and New Testaments.

KEY TERM FOR TODAY ## Incarnation

You won't actually find the word in the Bible, but the idea is certainly there. The word is from Latin, meaning "in the flesh," and it refers to God becoming a human being, the man Jesus of Nazareth, known as the Son of God and the Word of God—truly human, but also truly divine. John's Gospel states that God's Word "became flesh and made his dwelling among us" (1:14). The entire New Testament affirms that Jesus was *fully human* and yet also the Son of God, the Word-made-flesh.

CHANGING OF THE POWERS

Recall that in 538 BC the Persian emperor Cyrus allowed the Jewish exiles in Babylon to return to their homeland. Many did return, and by 515 BC they had built a new temple, and by 445 BC they had rebuilt the city walls of Jerusalem. Their religion was re-established on its former site, and the Jews had a fair amount of political freedom living as a province of the Persian empire, where the common language was Aramaic.

Now, in between the two Testaments, a new power conquered the Persians: the Greeks, under the leadership of Alexander of Macedon, better known as Alexander the Great. Alexander had been tutored under the Greek philosopher Aristotle, and like all Greeks, he thought of his own culture as far superior to the "barbarians" who lived outside Greece. He spread his empire to the edge of India, and Judea was conquered in 333 BC, with Alexander showing a fair amount of respect to the Jews and their temple.

He created new cities (several of them egotistically named "Alexandria"), with the usual Greek facilities of gymnasiums, open-air theaters, and libraries. He encouraged the conquered people to settle in these model cities, where their ethnic quarters would have a certain amount of independence but also could be part of the city's life and governing. He assumed that in time the minorities would see the superiority of Greek culture and would adopt Greek dress, speak Greek, give their children Greek names, and discuss the great philosophical and literary works of Greece. One of the many cities named Alexandria was in Egypt, and it had an enormous Jewish population. It was in this city that Jewish scholars completed the famous translation of the Old Testament into Greek, known as the Septuagint. It is this Old Testament, not the Hebrew or Aramaic, that the writers of the New Testament quoted. In fact, the Septuagint had the distinction of being one of the few "barbarian" writings ever translated into Greek. Rendering the Old Testament into Greek made it available to a much wider readership than the Hebrew originals ever had. Countless pagans, unhappy with their crude religious myths and dry philosophies, were drawn to the high morality and spirituality of the Greek Old Testament. When Alexander conquered the Jews, he would never have imagined that in time the religion of a Jewish carpenter would have a far greater impact on the world than Alexander himself ever had.

Alexander died, still a young man, in 323 BC—in, of all places, the palace that Nebuchadnezzar built in Babylon centuries earlier. Alexander left no successor, and by 301 BC his empire had been divided up into two Greek-speaking empires, the Ptolemies ruling from Egypt, the Seleucids ruling from Syria. It was inevitable that poor Judea was going to be dominated by one or the other of these two powerful neighbors—first the Ptolemies (323–200 BC) and then the Seleucids (200–166 BC). Under these two powers, the Jews accepted their conquered status pretty well, since their rulers were fairly tolerant of different religions—for a while, anyway. Had things continued on the same path, there was a danger of Judaism becoming so thoroughly Hellenized as to become unrecognizable. (Alexander's policy of "show toleration and in time the people will go Greek" had worked very well.) But then the Seleucid king Antiochus IV decided Judea wasn't sufficiently "civilized" (meaning, totally Greek in its culture), so he issued decrees against Jews keeping the Sabbath, owning any copies of the sacred Scriptures, or performing circumcisions. Even worse, he offered a sacrifice—of *pigs*—to the god Zeus in the Jews' temple. The maniacal Antiochus, who apparently thought he in fact *was* Zeus in the flesh, ordered that every Jewish village offer similar sacrifices. This sparked a revolt, led by a priest named Mattathias and his five sons, the whole family being known as the Maccabees. (Antiochus didn't know the history of the Jews. If he had, he would have known that they could tolerate foreign domination just fine—*until their religion was interfered with*.) The Maccabees' long war with the Seleucids is detailed in 1 and 2 Maccabees, two books of the Apocrypha. By 142 BC the Maccabees had won full independence for the Jews, and the Maccabee descendants, known as the Hasmoneans, ruled Judea as priests and kings until 63 BC. Their nation had roughly the same boundaries as Israel had had under King David. For a brief moment in time, the Jews thought the golden age had come, that they could settle down and be the holy nation God wanted them to be.

THE UNEASY MIXTURE OF JEW AND GREEK

However, in spite of gaining their political independence and ending religious persecution, the Jews weren't free of Greek culture. Many Greek-speaking peoples had settled in the towns of Judea and Galilee, so the pure Jewish population that Ezra and Nehemiah had hoped for was not even remotely possible. Aside from that, the Jewish upper classes felt the draw of Greek culture with its poetry, drama, philosophy, art and architecture. Young upper-class Jewish men, exercising nude in the Greek gymnasiums,

c. 6 BC
Birth of Jesus in Bethlehem

4 BC
Death of Herod the Great

c. 3 BC
Beginnings of the Zealot sect of anti-Roman Jews

AD 2
Japanese farmers at Kyoto cultivate rice for the first time, using seed imported from China.

AD 6
Judea placed under direct Roman rule

AD 18
Caiaphas becomes high priest of the Jews.

AD 26
Pontius Pilate becomes Roman governor of Judea.

Hellenism

The name for Greece is the same today as it was in New Testament times: *Hellas*. Its people were (and still are) known as Hellenes, and people who promoted Greek culture were Hellenists, or Hellenizers.

In the New Testament period, "Greek" (the actual word was *Hellenos)* had ceased to mean just "person of Greek blood." It was also a cultural term, not just an ethnic or national one. There were some Jews who thought of themselves culturally as more Greek than Jewish. Many gave their children two names—one Greek, the other Jewish, as in the case of Saul, who went by his Greek name Paul when spreading the faith to non-Jews. However, not all Hellenized Jews gave up their faith. Some—such as Paul, Stephen and Apollos in the Book of Acts—applied the Greek mental habits (reason, logic, debate) to their faith, making them the perfect men to spread Christianity to both Jews and non-Jews.

The Septuagint, the Greek translation of the Old Testament, not only served the Greek-speaking Jews, but also made Judaism more easy to transport, and laid the groundwork for the Septuagint-quoting Christians. Christians could also be grateful to the Jews for having already formed monotheistic religious communities everywhere, having written apologetics for monotheism, for practicing a high morality and family life that pagans both admired and mocked, and having emphasized a God who revealed himself through Scriptures.

wanted to fit in so badly with non-Jews that some of them had surgery to try to conceal their circumcision. The Jews became a divided culture, the lower and middle classes sticking close to their religious roots and speaking Aramaic, the upper classes more or less abandoning their faith and "going Greek." The priests were mostly of the upper class, so for the most part they went through the motions of the rituals, such as sacrifices in the temple, but culturally they thought their own people backward and primitive. There were cases of Jewish priests leaving their sacrifices half-burned on the Jerusalem altar, as the priests scurried off to watch athletic contests—a rather early example of men preferring sports to worship. While Herod the Great reigned as king in Judea, he appointed only Hellenized, unreligious men as high priests. During this period, the more pro-Greek Jews became known as the Sadducees, while the more faith-centered, Law-centered Jews became known as Pharisees. We will have more to say about those two important factions in later chapters. For now, it is worth noting that *both* parties had a certain contempt for the common people of the land, and that contempt would have a powerful effect on the life of Jesus.

The Maccabees had made a political alliance that would come back to haunt the Jews: They allied themselves with a rising power called Rome. In fact, 1 Maccabees gives a glowing description of what decent, faithful allies the Romans were! But alliances always come with a price, and in 63 BC a bloody civil war among the Jewish rulers gave Rome an excuse to move in, kill thousands of Jews, and make the region part of their empire. The Jews would have no political independence from 63 BC to AD 1948. (Obviously the author of 1 Maccabees, with his lavish praise of Rome, was *not* a prophet!)

Culturally, there was no major change. The Romans had immense respect for anything Greek, and in the eastern part of the empire, Greek, not the Romans' language (Latin), was the common language of trade and commerce. The Greek language united a huge area, an area the Romans had united politically. Jews who engaged in any business relations with Greeks and Romans knew some Greek, so Jesus, a carpenter living in a region with many non-Jews, probably knew enough Greek to engage in conversation. (Two of Jesus' disciples, Andrew and Philip, had Greek names, and at one point

---

CULTURAL INSIGHTS

BC and AD

BC means "before Christ," and AD means *Anno Domini*, Latin for "year of our Lord." The practice of dating years from the time of Jesus' birth has been around for centuries. But, strangely enough, it is slightly wrong. In the year 525, Pope John I asked a scholar named Dionysius Exiguus to calculate the year of Jesus' birth. It was a good choice, because Dionysius was not only a theologian and Bible scholar, but also a competent mathematician. However, his calculation was off by a few years. We now know that Herod the Great died in 4 BC, and that Jesus' birth occurred before that (see Matthew 2). So Jesus was not born in AD 1 (as Dionysius believed) but in 6 or 5 BC. Strange as it sounds, Christ was born "before Christ."

Dionysius' purpose, incidentally, was to provide the world with a *Christian* chronology to replace the old Roman one, which numbered years from the time of the founding of Rome. So the Roman year 753 became the Christian AD 1. It might please Dionysius to know that his dating—even though slightly wrong—is now used globally.

Using the phrase "the year of our Lord" in legal documents and historical records was common for centuries and is still sometimes used.

By the way, there is no year 0. The year 1 BC was followed by AD 1. The Jews have had their own calendar for many centuries, with their year 1, the year of the creation of the world, corresponding to the year 3761 BC. Modern Jews often use the abbreviations CE ("common era") and BCE ("before common era") instead of AD and BC.

they brought to Jesus some Greeks who wished to see him (John 12:20–23). Some of the apostles, especially Paul, were perfectly at home writing and speaking Greek, which was to prove a tremendous advantage as they began to spread their faith.

Although most Jews detested their Roman conquerors (they regarded them as even more immoral than Greeks), and there were frequent rebellions, the Romans' empire maintained public order and was relatively peaceful and safe to travel in. The combination of a common language (Greek) and secure roads and seaways meant that ideas—good and bad—could move quickly from one end of the empire to the other. Jesus' apostles would find this to be a great advantage in spreading their message.

To summarize: When Jesus was born, his part of the world was mostly Jewish in religion, Roman in politics, and mostly Greek in culture. These three elements sometimes existed peacefully together, sometimes not. But in the providence of God, Jewish men would spread a vital new faith over the vast Roman world, using the Greek language that Alexander the Great had spread by conquest. God moves in mysterious ways: empires conquered and oppressed, but they made it possible to spread a religion that had its roots in a small region of the world called Canaan.

FOUR PORTRAITS, ONE CHRIST

Let's look at the four sources for our knowledge of Jesus, the Gospels that go by the names of their authors: Matthew, Mark, Luke and John. Why four, when one would have sufficed? We should be glad there are four, just as a court of law is glad when there is more than one witness to an event. The more witnesses, the clearer idea we have of what took place. Each of the four Gospels in our Bible included material that the others chose to leave out. Altogether, they give us a vivid picture of the amazing man that people of his time and afterward called the "Son of God."

Probably the oldest, and definitely the briefest, is Mark's Gospel. Mark was a close friend of Peter, one of Jesus' twelve disciples, so Mark's Gospel is based on Peter's eyewitness testimony. Matthew's Gospel, written by another one of Jesus' disciples, uses most of Mark's material but also adds a lot of important teachings of Jesus. Matthew quotes the Old Testament frequently, showing how Jesus' life and deeds fulfilled prophecies. Luke's Gospel also uses Mark's material, and some of the teachings used in Matthew's, but Luke's is tilted more toward readers who weren't familiar with the Old Testament. John's Gospel is very different from the first three. He begins Jesus' story not with Jesus' birth or with his family tree, but at the beginning of time itself: Jesus was "the Word" of God, present with God even before the world existed. Jesus was God's ultimate revelation of himself to human beings: As John's Gospel puts it, "the Word was made flesh, and dwelled among us." Matthew's Gospel has the same idea, referring to

Jesus as "Immanuel," meaning "God with us." As we work through the next few chapters, you'll learn more about the four different Gospel authors.

Matthew, Mark, Luke and John are sometimes known as the "Evangelists." The Greek word *euangelion*, meaning "good news," in time morphed into the word "evangel," so the ones who presented the evangel (good news) to the world were known as Evangelists. Obviously "evangelism" means "spreading the good news."

In spite of their differences, the Gospels have much in common because they center around the same amazing man. And all four were written for the same purpose, which we find stated near the end of John's Gospel: "These [things] are written that you may believe that Jesus is the Christ, the Son of God, and that by believing you may have life in his name" (John 20:31). This is the good news: Jesus, the Son of God, gives people life—deeper and more meaningful life in this world and beyond.

CULTURAL INSIGHTS

Evil Empires: Rome

In our day, "imperialism" has become a dirty word. We think it's terrible that a nation would try to impose its values and beliefs and political system on another nation. After all, shouldn't each country manage its own affairs?

At the time of Jesus, most Jews agreed with this sentiment. Most Jews lived within the enormous Roman Empire, and it galled them that the Romans controlled the land of Israel, the Jews' homeland—a Jewish country ruled by unbelievers! The Romans wouldn't even use the name Israel, but carved up the area into three districts they called Judea, Samaria and Galilee.

The Romans' heavy taxation of the people they conquered was deeply resented, as was their air of superiority, their lax morals and their worship of numerous gods. Paying taxes so that upper-class Romans could idle away time drinking and feasting with their concubines did not seem right to people of deep faith. No wonder so many Jews prayed for the coming of God's "anointed one," the Messiah.

The Romans themselves thought they were bringing peace and culture to the people they ruled. While they taxed heavily, they also built roads and maintained order. In fact, the Romans pretty much left their subject peoples alone, unless public order was threatened. Their civic religion, offering sacrifices to the old Roman gods, was more a matter of form than faith, and generally the Romans had a hands-off attitude toward religions. The good communications and relative peace of the Roman Empire would allow Christianity to spread thousands of miles from the land of its birth.

Although we talk about the "four Gospels," this isn't quite accurate. There is really only one *euangelion*, one story of good news, that being the story of Jesus. In the original Greek, the Gospels are titled "According to Matthew," "According to Mark," and so on. One Son of God, one story, but four witnesses, so four accounts "according to" those four writers. Four portraits, one Savior.

All four Gospels—and the other books of the New Testament—were written in Greek, a perfect choice, because the language was spoken throughout the wide Roman empire. But Greek wasn't the native tongue of Jesus and his first followers. They spoke Aramaic, a language similar to the Hebrew of the Old Testament. In a few places in the Gospels, the writers actually give us the Aramaic words that Jesus used (John 1:42 and Mark 5:41, for example). Jesus and other Jews probably knew enough Greek to communicate with the Romans and other foreigners who lived among them.

THE MESSIAH'S FAMILY TREE

Matthew's Gospel begins with something that some readers find long and dry: a family tree. But this genealogy is there for a purpose. It traces Jesus' ancestry all the way back to Abraham, the man of faith who was ancestor of all the Jews. In between Abraham and Jesus was Israel's great king David, a man with many glaring faults (think back to Day 8) but a true man of faith, someone later generations remembered as the best type of king, one who loved and followed God and fought off Israel's oppressors.

David was remembered as God's "anointed one." Anointing was the ritual involving daubing the person's head with a small amount of fragrant oil, indicating the person was marked for a special purpose for God. Kings and priests were anointed. But over the centuries most of the Jewish kings were so corrupt and immoral that people began to hope for a good king like David, another "anointed one." The Jewish prophets predicted the coming of such a person, and it was assumed he would be a descendant of David. Many people believed—or hoped—that the "anointed one" would not only be loyal to God but would also use military power to boot out the foreign powers that controlled the Jewish homeland. In the time of Jesus, that power was the Roman Empire. When Jesus was born, most of Israel was ruled by a Roman puppet, the immoral and murderous King Herod. With such earthly powers governing them, no wonder the Jews longed for an anointed, heaven-sent king. The prophets had promised a time of peace and security when every man could dwell securely "under his own vine and fig tree." But that time never seemed to come: Foreign conquerors kept coming, and the people pined for God's anointed one to bring in a new age.

In the Old Testament, the Hebrew word for "anointed one" was *messiah*, and in the New Testament, the Greek word was *christos*. So "Jesus Christ" meant "Jesus the Anointed

One." Jesus' followers then and now believe Jesus was the anointed one the prophets had predicted. But the people who expected this anointed one to be a king and military leader would be very disappointed. He was sent by God not to save the Jews from the Romans but to save all people from their sins (Matthew 1).

THOSE PEOPLE FROM NAZARETH

Jesus' family tree in Matthew 1:1–17 may seem tedious, but the story picks up steam at 1:18, where we are introduced to Mary, a young woman in the village of Nazareth. Her amazing story is told there and in Luke 1, where we learn that an angel, Gabriel, tells Mary she will bear "the Son of the Most High," God's son. The child is to be named "Jesus"—an important part of the story, since the Jews had a tradition that the Messiah would be named by God before his birth.

Mary is engaged to a man named Joseph and is still a virgin, but Gabriel tells her that the child will have no human father ("for nothing shall be impossible with God"). Gabriel also tells Mary that her elderly cousin, Elizabeth, has conceived. Miraculous conceptions are taking place, signs that God is about to do something wonderful on earth. In the meantime, Joseph is also visited by an angel, who tells him to go ahead and marry Mary, who will bear a son conceived by the Holy Spirit.

But as we all know, Jesus wasn't born in Nazareth, but in Bethlehem. Why? Luke's Gospel tells us that Caesar Augustus, the Roman emperor, ordered a census, which required people to return to their ancestral homes. Joseph's was Bethlehem, which also was the home of David centuries earlier. So he and the pregnant Mary journey south from Nazareth to Bethlehem, and finding no inn in which to lodge, Mary gives birth to Jesus in a stable—a curious beginning for God's "anointed one," descended from the kings of Israel! But the birth doesn't go completely unnoticed: angels announce the birth to some shepherds in the fields near Bethlehem. It must have jarred the ears of the shepherds to learn that this "Savior, who is Christ the Lord" would be found not in a palace but in a manger, a food trough for livestock! The Savior was meeting working-class people on their own turf.

But Matthew's Gospel (chapter 2) tells us that the humble birth was known to people besides the poor shepherds. From "the east"—probably Persia or Arabia—there came "wise men" (or "magi") who were astrologers. By watching the stars they knew that a "king of the Jews" had been born. What was the "star of Bethlehem" anyway? Comet, nova, meteor? Some experts believe it was a rare conjunction of the planets Saturn and Jupiter, aligned closely, that occurred in 7 BC. The magi would have been watching this unusual occurrence closely. They would have known that the planetary conjunction took place in the constellation Pisces—known as the "House of the Hebrews" by ancient stargazers. Since Pisces was associated with Israel, this may explain the wise men's journey to that land. They may even have known of the mysterious prophecy in Numbers 24:17: "A star will come out of Jacob; a scepter will rise out of Israel."

The magi showed up in Jerusalem, the Jews' capital, and the reigning king of the Jews, wicked Herod, was not pleased to learn about the birth of a rival king. Herod's advisors, familiar with the writings of the prophets, tell the wise men that this "anointed one" would be born in Bethlehem. The magi make their way there, led by the star they followed from their homeland. Finding Joseph, Mary and the baby Jesus in a house, they fall down and worship the infant and present him the famous gifts: gold, frankincense and myrrh, gifts fit for a king. Clearly these wise travelers who journey so far have high expectations for this newborn. While "wise men" may not be a totally accurate translation of the Greek word *magi* that Matthew uses, the visitors really *were* wise men, for of all the people on earth, they alone realized that this baby born into a working-class family deserved to be worshipped and honored.

Time for a historical correction: Much as we love our familiar Nativity scenes showing the wise men and shepherds together in the stable, no such scene took place. The shepherds (Luke 2) visited the newborn Jesus while he was still in the stable, but the

CHARACTER CLOSE-UP ## How Many Wise Men?

Were there *three*? The Bible doesn't say so. The tradition of three developed because Matthew's Gospel mentions three *gifts* (gold, frankincense and myrrh). We have no idea how many wise men there were. In fact, some very early Christian artworks show as many as twelve of them. There is no basis for the tradition that the wise men were kings. Matthew refers to them as *magi*, which means they practiced astrology and other magic arts, and magi were never kings. Mostly likely they were from Persia (Iran) and were priests of the religion called Zoroastrianism, which worshipped one god. Some early Christians read Isaiah 60:3 (KJV)—"the Gentiles shall come to thy light, and kings to the brightness of thy rising"—and applied it to the magi. Since there were Jews living in Persia (as we know from Esther, Nehemiah and Daniel), the magi probably knew Jews and took some interest in their prophecies of a Messiah, especially since Jews and magi both worshipped one God.

The story that the three men were named Gaspar, Melchior and Balthasar is very old, but not based on the Bible. Many towns in Iran and Iraq claim to possess the tombs—or homes—of the magi. The cathedral of Cologne, Germany, claims to possess their remains, and the spire of the cathedral is topped with a star, in remembrance of the men following the star to Bethlehem. The word "magi," in case you hadn't guessed already, is the root of the word "magic."

King Herod "the Great"?

One of the Bible's nastiest characters is known to history as "the Great," which proves that "great" people aren't necessarily good. He was "king of the Jews," although he had no Jewish blood at all. He was an Idumean, the same as the Edomites, the descendants of Esau in the Book of Genesis. In the period between the Old and New Testaments, the Jews had conquered the Idumeans and forced them to convert to the Jewish faith. Though religiously the Idumeans were "brothers" to the Jews, the Jews were horrified to have an Idumean ruling over them.

In his younger days, Herod had impressed the Roman ruler Augustus, and the Roman Senate made Herod king over the Jews (though he was still under the Roman thumb) for thirty-two years. Herod knew the Jews despised him for being a Roman puppet, so he tried to impress them with lavish building projects, notably rebuilding the temple in Jerusalem. He made it much more impressive than the original built by Solomon, but though the Jews loved the temple, they still detested Herod. Not only his secular building projects offended the Jews; Herod also replaced the high priests at his pleasure, always choosing thoroughly Hellenized, unreligious men.

He may have been a "great" builder, but his morals were rock-bottom. Herod was pathologically suspicious and paranoid, growing worse as he aged. He murdered two of his wives (he had eight) along with one wife's sons and brother, and killed his own firstborn son. His massacre of the infants of Bethlehem (Matthew 2) was in keeping with his cruel nature. In later chapters we will meet some of Herod's vile descendants.

wise men came later (Matthew 2), when the family has moved into a "house." Even so, it must have deeply impressed Mary and Joseph to be visited first by shepherds and then by the richly dressed magi from a foreign land.

King Herod, notoriously paranoid, had asked the wise men to report back to him when they found the child, but his intentions were despicable: He wanted to find this rival king and kill him. To a man of Herod's mentality, there was some political logic here: He ruled by the grace of Rome, and the magi probably came from Persia, part of the Parthian empire that opposed Rome. So the pro-Roman Herod had reason to be worried about Parthian visitors paying their respects to a newborn "king of the Jews." At any rate, the Bible tells us that the wise men learned in a dream that they should not report back to Herod, and this must have fed his suspicions of their motives. Joseph also had a dream, telling him to leave Bethlehem and live for a while in Egypt, for Herod was about to do a horrible thing. So the beautiful story of Christmas is marred by a cruel king doing one of the most gruesome things reported in the Bible: He orders the slaughter of all the male infants in the region of Bethlehem. Many years later, Jesus' followers were aware that Herod's slaughter of the infants of Bethlehem was shockingly similar to the Pharaoh's slaughter of the Hebrew children in the Book of Exodus. In Exodus, God had guarded the life of the infant Moses, the future deliverer of Israel, and in Matthew he guarded the life of the infant Jesus, the future deliverer of the world.

We hear the Christmas story so often that we miss some of its deeper meaning. Note what happened: The Jews had been praying for the messiah, Christ, the "anointed one," to be born. When he actually was born (in a stable!), it brought joy to the common Jewish people (the shepherds) and even to non-Jews (the wise men), but caused terror to the Jews' king (Herod). Rather than honoring the child, Herod tried to destroy him.

Have you ever wondered what Joseph and Mary did with the expensive gifts of the magi? One possibility: They sold them so they would have enough to live on while staying as refugees in Egypt.

While living in Egypt, Joseph learned from an angel that the loathsome Herod had died. Joseph, Mary and the child left Egypt and went to live in the small town of Nazareth, hence the familiar name "Jesus of Nazareth." Unlike Bethlehem, which was connected with David and with the Book of Ruth, Nazareth had no connections with great events in the history of Israel. It was such an unimportant place that when Jesus became an adult, some people would sneer that nothing significant could come from a bump-on-the-highway like

---

CULTURAL INSIGHTS

Christmas and Epiphany

The word Christmas does not occur in the Bible. Matthew and Luke give us a lot of information about Jesus' birth—but no hint of what time of year it was. Frankly, we have no idea. The Romans celebrated December 25 as the festival called *Natalis Solis Invicti*, "birthday of the unconquered sun." This was a winter holiday celebrating the lengthening of days. As Christianity spread, the church adopted the old holiday, so as early as AD 336 Christians were celebrating it as the birthday of Christ, the "Sun of Righteousness," based on the prophecy in Malachi 3:2. In time it was called the Feast of the Nativity, "nativity" coming from a Latin word meaning "birth."

The holy day called Epiphany, celebrated on January 6, commemorates the visit of the wise men, or magi, to the baby Jesus. The Greek word *Epiphaneia* means "appearance" or "manifestation." The wise men's visit means Christ has appeared to the Gentiles (non-Jews). The "twelve days of Christmas" refer to the span from Christmas to Epiphany. (Thus the twelfth day of Christmas would be January 5.) In some countries, people exchange gifts on Epiphany instead of Christmas, in memory of the gifts the wise men brought.

Joseph

The advantage of having four Gospels is that they offer different perspectives on the life of Jesus. Luke's Gospel tells the story of Jesus' birth with a focus on Mary, while Matthew's Gospel gives more attention to Joseph, each account complementing the other.

Joseph found himself in a difficult situation: The woman he was engaged to was pregnant—an awkward dilemma if he had been the father, but even more awkward since he was not. The natural assumption would be that she had been with another man. We don't know what thoughts ran through Joseph's mind, but Matthew tells us Joseph was "a righteous man and did not want to expose her to public disgrace"—a more compassionate reaction than most men were capable of. "He had in mind to divorce her quietly"—in those days an engagement was binding and had to be legally dissolved. This was the loving option—as opposed to allowing her to be stoned as an adulteress. But there was a third option: Go ahead and marry her.

An angel appeared to Joseph in a dream and told him the amazing news: Mary was pregnant by the Holy Spirit, not by any man. Joseph should take her as his wife, and the son she would bear would save people from their sins (Matthew 1:18–21). He was a righteous man—and he obeyed the message God sent him.

Joseph was descended from King David. This was important, for though Joseph was not Jesus' biological father, he was his legal father, and thus Jesus was, through Joseph, a descendant of David, as the Messiah was expected to be. In a few places in the Gospels, Jesus is referred to as the "son of Joseph," so people knew him as the child of Joseph and Mary.

Joseph is mentioned in Luke's story of the twelve-year-old Jesus in the temple. After that, he is not mentioned again, which suggests he died sometime between then and when Jesus began his ministry around age thirty. Joseph would have taught Jesus his own trade, carpentry, and, more importantly, taught him to be a good man, a man guided by God's commandments. He probably taught Jesus to speak some Greek, since Nazareth was surrounded by Greek-speaking villages, so their trade would have given Jesus a view of a wider world than just the Jews in their own village.

We can well imagine being Jesus' father was not always easy. Joseph may have at times been in awe of the boy he raised. But God had his own good reasons for choosing the working-class couple from Nazareth. Jesus was blessed in having a righteous Father and a righteous father.

Nazareth. God has his own way of doing things, and that "insignificant" village in Galilee is known all over the world because of the carpenter who grew up there.

Regarding the name Jesus: In Jesus' native language, Aramaic, it was *Yeshua*, and it was a common one in those days. It was the Aramaic form of the Old Testament Hebrew name Joshua, which meant "Yahweh [the LORD] saves." Both Mary and Joseph were told by an angel to give this very meaningful name to the child. People in those days took naming very seriously, and there could not have been a more appropriate name for the Son of God than "the LORD saves."

THE MESSENGER IS THE MESSAGE

You might remember from previous chapters that God's prophets were his spokesmen, which is why their writings often contain the formula "The word of the Lord came to X…" The prophets believed the Lord was speaking to, and through, them. But after the latest Old Testament prophets—Haggai, Zechariah, Malachi and Joel—there was no prophecy at all, none. In the Maccabean period, when the courageous Jewish fighters managed to re-establish worship in the temple and cast off their oppressors, no prophet spoke a word from the Lord. The more devout Jews turned to the obvious source of God's revelation, the Scriptures, what we know as the Old Testament. In this long period the Jews became the "People of the Book."

> **DID YOU KNOW?**
>
> John's Gospel (1:41) is the only book of the New Testament to use the word *Messiah*. John immediately explains to his Greek-speaking readers that the Hebrew word *Messiah* means "the Christ," the Anointed One.

John's Gospel does not open with a genealogy of Jesus, as Matthew's Gospel does. It goes back much further in time—in fact, back before time even existed. "In the beginning was the Word, and the Word was with God, and the Word was God. He was with God in the beginning. Through him all things were made; without him nothing was made that has been made. In him was life, and that life was the light of men" (1:1–4). John was choosing his words carefully here. He knew he was beginning his book exactly the way the Book of Genesis began: "In the beginning…" He also knew that the Greek word *Logos* was the same as the Hebrew word *dabhar*, "word"—not the "word" on a page, but the spoken, active, living communication, the self-revelation from God that the prophets of old times received. That revelation to mankind had a purpose: salvation.

That vital Word was with God from the beginning. So far every Jewish reader of John's words would have been nodding in agreement. God brought the universe into being by his Word, as they all knew from Genesis.

But in the next phrase, John made a decisive break with the Jewish religion: "The Word was God." A few verses later, he says that "the Word became flesh and made his dwelling among us" (1:14). Here the word of God does not "come to" a prophet, but *is* that prophet. We will see that in the Gospels, Jesus was regarded as a prophet—but he does not use the familiar phrase of the prophets, "Thus says the Lord…" Instead, he says, "I say to you…" The spokesman, the "middleman," the prophet, has been eliminated. The Word of God is speaking directly to human beings, and the Word *is* a human being. The Messenger is the Message.

Although the other New Testament writings do not use *Logos* as a title for Christ, they share with John the concept of "the Word" as God's revelation to man, the proclamation of salvation. Whereas the Old Testament speaks often of "the word of the Lord" being revealed to the prophets, the New Testament states that the word of the Lord is finally revealed in its ultimate form, the Word incarnate, Jesus Christ.

In Matthew's account of Jesus' birth, he quotes a centuries-old prophecy of Isaiah: "The virgin will be with child and will give birth to a son, and they will call him Immanuel—which means, 'God with us' " (Matthew 1:23, quoting Isaiah 7:14). Since the first century AD, theologians have been explaining—or *trying* to explain—just how it was that God was "with us," how the Word of God "became flesh," how God appointed his Son "heir of all things." How could a person be both fully human and fully divine? How do the divine and human natures exist together? When all the explanations have been written, debated and debated again, the wisest of the writers end up where they started, saying that God becoming a human being is a great *mystery*, something we should be eternally grateful for even if we cannot grasp it.

When he made the first translation of the New Testament into English in 1536, William Tyndale had this footnote for Matthew 1:23, explaining "Immanuel" in this way: "Where Christ is, God is." In five words he had rather neatly summarized what the first Christians believed about Jesus Christ. John, Matthew and the other New Testament writers all agree on the key idea: The child born to the virgin Mary in a stable in Bethlehem during the reign of King Herod was "God with us." He was the Messiah, the Christ, the Anointed One the Jews had expected and prayed for—although he was so different from what they expected that most of them would reject him. His birth in a stable to a working-class family—visited by shepherds and a band of astrologers from Persia—was proof that God is full of surprises.

SILENT BUT NOT EMPTY

Jesus' childhood is often called the "silent years" because we know so little about it. In fact, although we don't know the details, we have a general idea of what Jesus would have lived through, thanks to a few details in Luke's Gospel. Mary and Joseph were devout Jews, as shown by the fact that they took the newborn to Jerusalem to the temple to dedicate him to the Lord—which was required of every family's firstborn son. In the temple they encountered an old man named Simeon, who had been promised by God that before he died he would see the Christ. Perhaps Simeon had been expecting to see an *adult* Christ, but in the temple he was somehow informed by the Holy Spirit that the child brought to the temple by Mary and Joseph was the Christ. Simeon blessed the family and thanked God for letting him see God's salvation (Luke 2:21–35). An elderly and devout woman, Anna, also praised God for letting her see the Christ child.

"The child grew and became strong, he was filled with wisdom, and the grace of God was upon him" (2:40). This sentence sums up the "silent years," although we can guess that Jesus would have been taught in the synagogue school in Nazareth, that his own parents and the local rabbi would have made him familiar with the Jewish Scriptures, that he would have been taught a high moral code. For the most part he absorbed his teaching in the home, which was typical of all Jewish children. Based on the deep familiarity with Scripture that he showed as an adult, he must have lived among people who cherished the sacred writings.

At age twelve, Jesus was taken to Jerusalem to celebrate the Jewish Passover—something that was the family's custom, and a sign they took their faith seriously. Amazingly to us, they left Jerusalem without him. This doesn't mean they were neglectful parents, but that they probably traveled with a large family group and that, somehow, Jesus was not with the group when it departed. Three days later they found him—not only safe, but also discussing things with the Jewish teachers, who marveled at his wisdom. Mary and Joseph had been frantic, of course. "Why were you searching for me?" he asked. "Didn't you know I had to be in my Father's house?" (Luke 2:49). The family departed, and Jesus "was obedient to them.... And Jesus grew in wisdom and stature and in favor with God and men" (2:51–52). The Gospels say nothing else about Jesus until he reached adulthood. All we know for certain is that God spent all the "silent years" preparing his Son thoroughly for his task.

One incident that occurred in Jesus' childhood merits a mention: the Zealots, Jews who were hostile to Roman rule, staged a major rebellion, led by a man named Judas (not the Judas who would be Jesus' disciple). The Zealots captured the city of Sepphoris, not far from Nazareth. The Romans stepped in to put down the revolt and crucified thousands of Zealots. Jesus would have known of this and most likely saw men hanging on crosses. He would have learned at an early age what rebelling against Rome could lead to, but in the future would learn that even nonviolent men could be crucified.

The next time we encounter Jesus in the Gospels, he is about thirty years of age. Somehow, amazingly, thirty years in a working-class home in an unimportant village in Galilee had prepared the Son of God for his mission to the world. For thirty years, only a handful of people knew that the Christ existed. A wider audience was about to learn what Immanuel, "God with us," was like.

PUTTING THE WORD TO WORK

1. The Jews' faith was in serious danger of being diluted by Hellenism. What are some ideologies and beliefs today that seem in danger of watering down our faith? How can we resist these?

2. How do you, in your heart more than your head, perhaps, understand Jesus as "the Word made flesh"?

3. The first people to learn of Jesus' birth were humble shepherds. What do you think was God's purpose in giving them the news first?

4. The magi brought rich gifts they thought were fitting for an earthly king. Since we know Jesus was not that kind of king at all, what gifts can we give him that are fitting?

5. Compare and contrast the story of Herod "the Great" with some of the other kings we have studied in this book—say, David or Solomon or Josiah.

Heeding the Call of God

AT THE HEART OF IT ALL TODAY John the Baptist, the great wilderness prophet of repentance, paved the way for the ministry of Jesus, who was baptized, then resisted the temptations of the devil. Jesus chose twelve disciples, learners, from among the common people of the land.

Six months before the birth of Jesus, an amazing child was born, one whose life would intertwine with Jesus' in a dramatic way. This was John, known as the Baptist. His parents were a saintly aged couple named Zechariah and Elizabeth, childless and beyond childbearing age. Zechariah was a priest, and

> **KEY PASSAGES TO READ TODAY**
>
> **Matthew 3:1—4:22**
> **Luke 1: 5–25; 39–45; 57–66**
> **John 1:6–51**

Luke 1 records that the old man was given his once-in-a-lifetime duty of entering the temple and burning incense for the Lord—a great honor and, at his age, one he would not repeat.

Zechariah got a surprise he had not expected: Standing by the incense altar was the angel Gabriel. Zechariah reacted in the way people in the Bible always reacted to angels: He was terrified. The angel calmed him and told him he and Elizabeth would have a son, who was to be named John. "Many of the people of Israel will he bring back to the Lord their God. And he will go on before the Lord, in the spirit and power of Elijah, to turn the hearts of the fathers to their children and the disobedient to the wisdom of the righteous—to make ready a people prepared for the Lord" (Luke 1:16–17). Zechariah would have known immediately that the angel was referring to the prophecy

KEY TERM FOR TODAY ## Devil

The actual Greek word in the New Testament is *diabolos*, meaning "slanderer." This harks back to the Book of Job, where Satan scoffs at Job's righteous behavior and tells God that Job is a saint only because good behavior brings him prosperity. In the story of Jesus' temptation, the slanderer casts doubts on Jesus being the real Son of God.

In the Greek New Testament there is only one *diabolos*, Satan himself. Some Bible translations refer to "devils," plural, but this is never correct, because the Greek word *daimonia* should always be "demons"—one *diabolos*, but numerous *daimonia*.

of Malachi, that Elijah would return to earth before the great "day of the Lord." He would also have shared the common Jewish belief of his time: The Messiah would not come until Israel fully repented, and Israel would not repent until Elijah came.

The old man was devout—but doubtful. Father a child at his age? Gabriel, the angel who stands "in the presence of God," told Zechariah that because he doubted, he would be struck with muteness till the day of the child's birth. When poor Zechariah emerged from the temple, he could not share his good news with the people—who had no clue what had occurred. But Elizabeth did indeed conceive, and for this she praised God. She was the latest in a long line of long-barren women who finally conceived, and who dedicated their children to the Lord even before their birth. In fact, Gabriel had instructed Zechariah that his son John would be a Nazirite, the same as Samson and Samuel (who had also been born to long-barren mothers). As a Nazirite, John would never touch wine and never cut his hair. He would be a remarkable character in many other ways as well.

Elizabeth received a visit from a relative—a young woman named Mary, who had herself received some amazing news from the angel Gabriel. Both women were overjoyed at their miraculous conceptions. Elizabeth, six months further along in pregnancy, felt her son move in her womb when Mary arrived—almost as if the unborn John was saluting the unborn Jesus. We can well imagine that the two women, so different in age, did some emotional bonding during this period, both of them unexpectedly pregnant with children who would change the course of history.

The aged Elizabeth gave birth to John, and on the eighth day he was circumcised, the usual Jewish custom, and on that day he was to be named. When the subject of the name came up, the mute Zechariah wrote down "His name is John," and at that time his voice returned. The old man's choice of words was interesting: "His name is John," not "We will call him John." As far as Zechariah was concerned, the angel had already named the child, and that was that. He was not going to question God again—not after being mute for all those months! Not surprisingly, he began praising God, and everyone who knew the family was filled with awe, wondering, "What then is this child going to be?" Zechariah knew that the son would be "a prophet of the Most High" (Luke 1:76). "And the child grew

43 BC–AD 18
Ovid, Roman poet

27 BC–AD 180
The Pax Romana, years of relative peace in the Roman empire

c. 6 BC
Birth of Jesus in Bethlehem

4 BC
Death of Herod the Great

c. 3 BC
Beginnings of the Zealot sect of anti-Roman Jews

AD 5
The Roman legions defeat Lombard tribes that have established themselves on the lower Elbe River.

AD 6
Judea placed under direct Roman rule.

AD 14–37
Reign of Roman Emperor Tiberius

AD 18
Caiaphas becomes high priest of the Jews.

AD 26–36
Pontius Pilate is Roman governor of Judea.

c. AD 27–28
Ministry of John the Baptist; baptism of Jesus and beginning of his ministry
(Matthew 3, Mark 1, Luke 3, John 1:6–35)

AD 29
Execution of
John the Baptist
(Matthew 14:3)

AD 30
Death and
resurrection
of Jesus
*(Matthew 27–28,
Mark 15–16,
Luke 23–24,
John 18–21)*

and became strong in spirit; and he lived in the desert until he appeared publicly to Israel" (1:80).

John's mother and father were both from priestly families, and John's father learned of John's conception while on-duty as a priest in the temple. As the son of a priest, John could have been a priest himself, but if he ever served as one, he clearly abandoned that life and sought out his own spiritual path. John may have had some contact with the Jewish community called the Essenes, who were responsible for the Bible manuscripts we call the Dead Sea Scrolls. The Essenes withdrew into the wilderness and thought of themselves as the spiritual community that would "prepare the way of the Lord," far removed from the corrupt and unspiritual priesthood in Jerusalem. John's father, Zechariah, is one of the few priests mentioned approvingly in the New Testament. Jesus would have a fateful—and unpleasant—encounter with priests later in his life.

PROPHECY FINDS ITS VOICE AGAIN

We noted in the last chapter that after the close of the Old Testament, there were no more prophets in Israel. People tried to live by the Laws that God gave to Moses, and in that sense they listened to the "word of the Lord." But the priests and the scribes were merely passing on what God had already communicated through the prophets. There were no new prophets, no men claiming that God was speaking to, and through, them. That was about to change, for the prophet Elijah that Malachi had spoken of was about to return—"in spirit"—to the people.

You might recall from an earlier chapter that Elijah was a bold but also mysterious character, the man who confronted a horde of Baal prophets on Mount Carmel and made them look like fools, also the man who called down fire from heaven on his enemies, and who was taken to heaven in a chariot of fire. No mention was ever made of his home or family, and apparently he lived alone in the wilderness most of the time. In other words, he was a kind of "holy hermit," living mostly apart from the corrupt, materialistic cities. Zechariah's son John was to be just that type of man. Luke 3:2 records that "the word of God came to John"—he had received the word. Israel had a true prophet once again.

John's message was simple: "Repent, for the kingdom of heaven is near" (Matthew 3:2). Matthew often quotes the Old Testament prophets, and he observed that John was "a voice of one calling in the desert, 'Prepare the way for the Lord, make straight paths for him,' " a quotation

> **DID YOU KNOW?**
>
> Some churches observe May 31 as the Feast of the Visitation, in remembrance of Mary's visit to Elizabeth in Luke 1.

from Isaiah 40. John had a distinctive look: a rough coat of camel's hair, a wide leather belt around his waist. (This was not the suedelike camel-hair coat we wear today, but a hide with the unfinished camel hair still attached. It was no coincidence that the prophet Elijah dressed this way.) No doubt the long hair of the Nazirite added to John's distinctiveness. Even his food was unusual: "locusts and wild honey." (Locusts could mean actual grasshoppers—which are edible—or could mean pods from the locust tree, what we today call carob.) Simple clothing, simple food, living in the wilderness—an unusual man, to say the least.

Yet he drew people like a magnet. In response to his call to repent, they were baptized by him in the Jordan River, the immersion in water being a symbol of washing away their sins. Some who came were Pharisees and Sadducees, people of the two major religious factions among the Jews. John did not give them a warm welcome: He called them a "brood of vipers." He knew they were spiritually proud, and pride and repentance do not fit together at all. Too many Jews thought their descent from the patriarch Abraham would be their salvation. (It was popularly believed that Abraham sat at the

CHARACTER CLOSE-UP ## Gabriel

Many people think of Gabriel as the angel whose trumpet blast will announce the end of time. An interesting idea, but not based on the Bible. Gabriel appears in only two books of the Bible: Daniel and Luke. In Daniel he is the heavenly interpreter of the puzzling dreams of the prophet (8:16, 9:21) and is the one who granted Daniel wisdom and understanding. In Luke, he announces the conception of John the Baptist to Zechariah and the conception of Jesus to the virgin Mary. Since he makes these two important announcements, it is natural to think of him as the "announcing angel," but where did the idea of the trumpet come from? Jesus said that at his Second Coming, angels would sound the trumpet and gather God's people together (Matthew 24:31). Paul spoke of the Rapture of the saints with these words: "The Lord himself will come down from heaven with a loud command, with the voice of an archangel, and with the trumpet call of God" (1 Thessalonians 4:16). Also, the Book of Revelation depicts seven angels with trumpets, announcing the horrible plagues on mankind. None of these mentions Gabriel by name. Also, the Bible never refers to Gabriel as an *archangel* (meaning "ruling angel"), a title that is only used for Michael.

Thanks to his being the announcer of Jesus' conception to Mary, he is a major figure in artworks, with countless paintings titled *The Annunciation*. Some churches celebrate the Feast of the Annunciation every year on March 25, nine months before Christmas.

The Jordan River

Compared to major rivers such as the Nile or Amazon or Mississippi, the Jordan River is insignificant, but though it is small by world standards, it is important in the Bible, being the only river of any real size in Israel. Also, key events are connected with the river. When the Israelites entered into Canaan, they crossed the Jordan—on dry land—when it was at flood stage. This was a sign to the Israelites that God was still with them, that the age of miracles (such as God parting the Red Sea for them) was not over (Joshua 3). On another occasion the great prophet Elijah struck the waters of the Jordan with his mantle, and the river parted, a miracle that his disciple Elisha repeated (2 Kings 2:8, 14). Elisha healed the Syrian commander Naaman of leprosy by having him bathe in the Jordan (2 Kings 5).

In the New Testament, the river is remembered as the site of John's ministry of baptism. Jesus himself was baptized in the Jordan, of course, which is why many churches with baptisteries—pools used for immersion baptisms—have a scene of the Jordan River painted on the wall behind the pool.

The phrase "crossing over Jordan" occurs in many Christian hymns. It harks back to the Israelites crossing the Jordan into Canaan under Joshua. Christians often interpret Canaan, the "Promised Land," in a spiritual way, meaning heaven, so "crossing the Jordan" means leaving this world and passing into heaven.

gate of Gehenna—hell—to make sure none of his descendants entered there. Abraham's righteousness was so great, so they thought, that all Jews benefited from it.) But John said descent from Abraham was not enough: People had to repent, and had to "produce fruit in keeping with repentance"—in other words, repent, and show by their actions that their repentance was sincere. Otherwise they would be cut down like fruitless trees and thrown into the fire. Already the divine "ax" was aimed at the roots of the unfruitful trees.

Do phrases like these sound familiar? They should. John spoke exactly like one of the prophets of the Old Testament, warning people to change their evil ways before the wrath of God came upon them. No wonder people so readily accepted John as a prophet. We wonder why it was that centuries had passed when no man had spoken this way. Four hundred years, and not one person spiritually on fire, calling for repentance? Puzzling, and yet God had his own reasons, no doubt. Perhaps it made the people all that more eager to pay heed to John, this unusual, fiery voice in the wilderness.

Some people who came to John for baptism were unexpected. Tax collectors—among the most despised people alive—showed up, asking John what was expected of them morally. John told them to collect no more than was legal—no more lining their own pockets with ill-gotten gains. Soldiers came also, and John told them to be content with their pay and not use their position to extort money from people. (Americans have such a good impression of our own soldiers—with good reason—that we forget the bigger historical picture is very different. Through the ages, soldiers have been notorious for looting and raping, especially when among foreigners.) It is certainly worth noting that John did not tell the soldiers or tax collectors to leave their jobs—only to deal honestly and fairly, and to be content with their pay.

But John had a more important task than baptizing: He was paving the way for someone greater than himself. People wondered if he was the Christ, the Messiah. He was not, but by heightening their expectations, he was readying them for the Messiah's arrival. "I baptize you with water for repentance. But after me will come one who is more powerful than I, whose sandals I am not fit to carry. He will baptize you with the Holy Spirit and with fire"—fire that burns up the useless hulls left over from wheat threshing. John was using the familiar image of fire burning up what was useless, leaving behind what was worth saving. His words here are one of the reasons that fire is so often used as a symbol of the Holy Spirit. His hearers would probably recall fire as a sign of God's presence—as in the encounter of Moses and the burning bush, or the fire that Elijah called down from heaven on Mount Carmel, or the fire on the altar in the temple, always burning, never allowed to die out. It is interesting that the Gospel refers to John preaching the "good news"—and that the "good news" includes his teaching about the "unquenchable fire." While to us the fire sounds threatening, to John's receptive hearers it really was "good news": Until what is evil and useless are overthrown and destroyed, there is no "good news."

Of course, we all know who it was that John was speaking of—his distant kinsman, Jesus, who had made the trip from his home province, Galilee, south to the Jordan. Clearly he did not just "happen" to be there—he made the trip specifically to meet John and be baptized. John at first resisted: "I need to be baptized by you, and do you come to me?" He did not think it fit for the lesser man to baptize the greater. But Jesus replied, "Let it be so now; it is proper for us to do this to fulfill all righteousness" (Matthew 3:15). Theologians love to argue over this passage. If Jesus was sinless, as most people believed, why did he need to be baptized at all? He had nothing to repent of, as John was aware. What did Jesus mean by "fulfill all righteousness"? Frankly, we aren't sure. The usual interpretation is that Jesus was being a model of what others should do: Be baptized and begin a new moral and spiritual life. He was not a sinner himself, but he identified himself with them—that is, with all mankind. To save sinners, he was willing to be among them. He did not go into the Jordan to cleanse himself but to show that his second life was beginning. In a sense, his baptism is a prelude to his crucifixion

—he was willing on both occasions to be the innocent man standing in place of sinful mankind. It is no coincidence that he would speak of his death as a "baptism" (Mark 10:38, Luke 12:50).

THE SIGN OF THE DOVE

Jesus' baptism was a dramatic turning point in his own life: "At that moment heaven was opened, and he saw the Spirit of God descending like a dove and lighting on him. And a voice from heaven said, 'This is my Son, whom I love; with him I am well pleased'" (Matthew 3:16–17). People puzzle over what "like a dove" meant. Was an actual dove present? Or something *like* a dove? We don't know. The passage is, of course, the reason that the dove is a symbol of the Holy Spirit. The descent of the Spirit upon Jesus is his "anointing." Jesus was technically never anointed with oil as kings and priests were, yet he was the *Christos*, the Anointed One, in a more important way: He had been anointed with the Holy Spirit by God himself.

The Father's words of approval spoken at the moment are strikingly similar to a verse in Isaiah 42: "Here is my servant, whom I uphold, my chosen one in whom I delight; I will put my Spirit on him and he will bring justice to the nations." This is one of the Servant Songs from Isaiah. It is clear that the Gospel writers saw Jesus the Son as the divine servant prophesied by Isaiah.

Jesus' baptism is recorded with almost the same words in Matthew, Mark and Luke. John's Gospel gives a slightly different version. The Baptist recalls that it was at the moment of Jesus' baptism, when he saw the Spirit come down from heaven like a dove, that he was aware that Jesus was the Son of God (John 1:32–34). John's Gospel takes pains to show that the Baptist was not "the light" that God sent into the world, but was a "witness to the light." The Baptist had made such an impression upon people that some Jews asked him if he was the Christ. He specifically said no. He was merely the one that Isaiah had prophesied, preparing the way of the Lord.

The Baptist bestowed a title on Jesus that no one would ever forget: "Look, the Lamb of God, who takes away the sins of the world!" (John 1:29, 35). For the first time in the Gospels we are introduced to the idea of Jesus being a sacrifice for people's sins. Jesus was the spotless "sacrificial lamb" offering himself up voluntarily.

The Jewish historian Josephus refers to John the Baptist as "a good man, who urged the Jews to practice virtue, uprightness toward one another and reverence toward God, and so to come to baptism." Josephus was not a Christian nor was he a disciple of John. Like most people, he accepted that John had been sent by God for a special purpose. Jesus himself went further and told his followers that John was indeed the "Elijah who was to come" (Matthew 11:14). In fact, Jesus said, "Among those born of women there has not risen anyone greater than John the Baptist.... For all the Prophets and the Law prophesied until John" (Matthew 11:11, 13). In other words, the Prophets and Law were a kind of prelude to John, and John himself was a prelude to Christ.

FROM MULTITUDE TO SOLITUDE

At Jesus' baptism he was given the wholehearted approval of his Father. God was "well pleased" with his Son. But this "spiritual embrace" was followed immediately by spiritual warfare. The Son was going to be put to the test by an old enemy of mankind. As all human beings endure temptation, so must the One who comes to save us.

Jesus went alone into the wilderness and fasted for forty days—led there by the Spirit. This is an important detail: God himself had planned this confrontation. It was not just a matter of Jesus and the devil bumping into each other in the wilds. It was meant to

---

CULTURAL INSIGHTS

Baptism, Pre-Christian

Most religions feature some kind of ritual washing that symbolizes that a person is made clean and pure. The Laws given to Moses had intricate rules for washing after contact with anything "unclean." Baptism, though, is different, because it involved full immersion of the body in water. When a non-Jew (Gentile) converted to the Jewish faith, a baptism was required (and, for men, circumcision as well). These converts were called proselytes, and it was assumed that every proselyte had undergone baptism as a way of "cleaning off" the old Gentile habits. The baptisms done by John were radically different because he was inviting *Jews* to be baptized. Their baptism was a reminder that they could not rely on their descent from Abraham to save them. Everyone needed to repent of their sins and be baptized, and afterward begin a new moral and spiritual life. God does not show favoritism—a radical idea we will explore further when we study Acts and the Epistles. The water itself was just a symbol, however. The real baptism, the cleansing, was the repentance itself. In later chapters we will look closely at some deeper meanings that Christians found in the ritual of baptism. It is worth remembering that in Acts 19, the apostle Paul encountered disciples of John the Baptist in Ephesus—thirty years after the Baptist had died. Although John saw himself as only the herald of the Messiah, it is clear that his preaching and baptism had a powerful hold on his admirers.

Luke the Obsessive Historian

Luke, the author of the third Gospel and also of the Book of Acts, states that he "carefully investigated" the story of Jesus in order to write his "orderly account" of his life and work, and in this way readers could "know the certainty" of the story (1:1–3). He was indeed fussy over details, and he includes more historical references than the other Gospels. We see this first in Luke 2:1–2: "In those days Caesar Augustus issued a decree that a census should be taken of the entire Roman world. (This was the first census that took place while Quirinius was governor of Syria.)"

Luke 3 makes another attempt at dating: John the Baptist began his public ministry "in the fifteenth year of the reign of Tiberius Caesar—when Pontius Pilate was governor of Judea, Herod tetrarch of Galilee, his brother Philip tetrarch of Iturea," etc., and "during the high priesthood of Annas and Caiaphas." We know that Pilate became governor in AD 26. Caiaphas was high priest from AD 18 to 36. However, Luke was honest in admitting he did not know Jesus' *precise* age: "Jesus himself was about thirty years old when he began his ministry" (3:23).

It is natural that with such an important figure as Jesus we would like to know precisely when he lived. After all the dust has settled, however, the important thing is that he *did* live, and that we know for certain that his life overlapped with those of historical persons such as Augustus, Pilate, Tiberius and others.

occur. The devil, also called the "tempter" here, began his assault with an appropriate temptation: "If you are the Son of God, tell these stones to become bread." Jesus did not. Instead, he quoted the Law of Moses: "It is written, 'Man does not live on bread alone, but on every word that comes from the mouth of God' " (Deuteronomy 8:3).

Jesus clearly had the power to turn stones into bread—but chose not to. His power from God wasn't for his own use, even for the legitimate use of taking necessary nourishment. We know that later on Jesus would use his power to multiply loaves and fishes to feed a hungry crowd—but would not use it here to end his own hunger.

So, the Son of God had countered temptation with Scripture. Well, the devil himself could quote Scripture too. Somehow, perhaps in a vision, he "transported" Jesus to the highest point of the temple in Jerusalem: "If you are the Son of God, throw yourself down. For it is written: 'He will command his angels concerning you, and they will lift you up in their hands, so that you shall not strike your foot against a stone' " (Psalm 91:11–12). Jesus countered Scripture with Scripture: "It is also written, 'Do not put the Lord your God to the test' " (Deuteronomy 6:16).

Satan is quoting the Bible—but *twisting* it, which is a temptation we all face. The comforting words of Psalm 91 were obviously *not* intended to make people think they could throw themselves from a cliff or in front of a rampaging bull. God does expect us to use our common sense. Psalm 91 had been around for centuries, but there was no pattern of devout Jews putting themselves in mortal danger as a sign they trusted God. Jesus proved he had a better command of Scripture than Satan did. Jesus had no intention of performing a wonder just to please a mob and gain a following. Jesus could heal leprosy and turn water into wine—but he always rejected people's pleas to do a miracle "just for show." Jesus wasn't sent to entertain or dazzle people who were bored with life. He was sent to reach out to the spiritually hungry.

A popular belief of the time was that the Messiah would stand on the temple and announce to Israel that the time of deliverance had come. Clearly, Jesus was *not* to be that type of Messiah—it was Satan that had brought him there! God had promised his people a Messiah and, through the prophets, given hints of what he would be like, but the people's own wild imaginations led them in their own direction, expecting a very *worldly* king and deliverer.

In another vision, the devil transported them to a high mountain, showing Jesus all the kingdoms of the world and their splendor. "All this I will give you if you will bow down and worship me." Jesus would have none of it: "Away from me, Satan! For it is written, 'Worship the Lord your God, and serve him only' " (Deuteronomy 6:13).

This must have been the greatest of the three temptations, and which of us could have resisted it? Dominion over the whole world—including those detested, high-taxing, immoral Romans! Surely this was what most of Jesus' own people thought of as the ultimate destiny of their Messiah: to rule righteously over an immoral world. But Satan was honest enough to admit there was a catch: Jesus could not have the world without serving Satan himself. Jesus could be the "king of the Jews" the magi had come to see— king of the whole world, in fact! He could have a crown instead of a cross—but such a price tag! Worshipping Satan—the very being whose work he came to destroy!

Was Satan bluffing? Was dominion over the world something he really had the power to bestow? Absolutely! In several places the New Testament refers to Satan as the "prince of this world" (John 12:31, 14:30, 16:11, 2 Corinthians 4:4, Revelation 13:2 are just a few). God, of course, was in ultimate control—but he gave Satan leeway, and, after all, the people's own selfishness and their own contempt for divine authority made it easy for him.

Note that the temptation story speaks of the "splendor" of the world's kingdoms. The Gospel writers didn't take that splendor too seriously. They knew the splendor was a veneer over immorality and corruption. Goodness and decency have never flourished amid wealth and power. Jesus knew that. His hometown of Nazareth was near Sepphoris, the largest city in Galilee, a mostly Gentile city that the corrupt Herod Antipas had made into a showplace of stunning Greco-Roman buildings. As a carpenter, Jesus may have supplied furniture to the people of Sepphoris. Their fine homes and urban splendor were a cover for decadence and a poverty of spirit. If Sepphoris was corrupt, how much more so mighty Rome, a grand marble metropolis built over a moral cesspool! Even the people who loved Rome admitted its corruption. If Jesus even for a second considered the option of ruling over such "splendor," we would be surprised. Splendid, yes—but spiritually disgusting. No wonder Jesus could cry, "Get away from me, Satan!" Who would want to bow down and worship the evil ruler of such hollow-hearted splendor? At a later point in his life, Jesus would say, "My kingdom is not of this world."

The devil departed, and angels came and attended Jesus. Luke's story of the temptation adds an important detail: "When the devil had finished all this tempting, he left him until an opportune time" (Luke 4:13). The temptation was not a once-and-for-all event, clearly. Jesus had passed the initial test, but there would be more testing ahead. Since temptation faces us all, every day, it must have been the same with Jesus as well, since he was fully human. The temptation story tells of something Jesus experienced soon after his baptism, but perhaps the larger truth is that these three key temptations were things he faced throughout his time on earth. Satan never sleeps or rests, and neither can we. Later on in the story, Jesus' own followers will tempt him again to be the Messiah king with worldly dominion.

Entire books have been written on the temptation of Jesus. In fact, one of the masterpieces of poetry tells an extended version of the story. The great English poet John Milton wrote the epic *Paradise Lost*, telling of Adam and Eve's being tempted and disobeying God. Milton's sequel was *Paradise Regained*, telling of Jesus' temptation and how he resisted—in a sense, "undoing" what Adam and Eve had done. Satan tempted both Adam and Jesus—both of them sinless at the time they were tempted. Adam failed the test, Jesus did not. Jesus had proven that falling into sin and disobedience was not inevitable. Adam could have resisted, but chose not to. Jesus resisted. God was making a new beginning with mankind.

Note that Satan begins his three temptations with a kind of tease: "If you are the Son of God, then…" He is suggesting doubt: "I don't think you really are God's Son, Jesus, because if you were, you could…" Remember that Satan had tempted Adam and Eve by dangling the prospect of being "like gods" in front of them. Jesus really was "like God," so Satan approached from the other direction, implying that the Son of God would behave in a certain way.

The Roman empire at this period of history had plenty of charlatans and lunatics referring to themselves as "sons of God," often performing fake miracles to prove it. For Jesus, being the one Son of God meant obeying God, not performing showy miracles. In other words, Satan was offering him the choice: Be the "son of God" that many people expect, or be true to who you really are, the Son of God, obedient to God in all things.

The story of Jesus' temptation was meant to remind all Christians, individually and collectively, of the temptation to abuse their powers. Obviously Christians throughout history have fallen into all three temptations, and failed the test. The fact that Jesus fasted for forty days in the wilderness reminds readers of Israel's forty years of testing after the exodus from Egypt.

We might well wonder: How did the writers of the Gospels know about the temptation? The obvious answer: Jesus told his disciples. He would have done so not only to relate some crucial information about himself, but to warn his followers that they would face the same temptations as he did.

One element of the temptation story is often overlooked: Jesus responded to Satan with three quotations from the Law, all three beginning "It is written…" He would use this phrase many times in his career. For him the sacred writings—the Law, the Prophets, the Psalms—were the foundations of truth and could answer the taunts of Satan—or human opponents. In time he would use "it is written" against the scribes and the Pharisees, who valued their own traditions about the Scriptures more than the Scriptures themselves.

Closing this section, we might well ask: Why did both John and Jesus retreat into the wilderness? In the case of Jesus, his fasting and solitude were a preparation for the mission that lay ahead. In the wilderness there were no distractions from spiritual realities—no work, no social activities, nothing but a barren landscape and God—and the devil. John's ministry in the wilderness is harder to explain. Shouldn't he have taken his powerful message of repentance into the heart of Jerusalem where it would reach the most people? Surely he had his reasons for being in the wilderness—other than the proximity to the river, that is. The people had to come to him to hear his message, so they were drawn out of their towns and villages where life seemed predictable and secure. It is a basic rule of any kind of mental or spiritual change: Get the person away from familiar surroundings and they are more receptive to a life-changing message.

> **DID YOU KNOW?**
>
> The forty-day season of Lent, observed in some churches, is based on Jesus' forty days of fasting in the wilderness.

TWELVE NEW TRIBES

Israel had long regarded itself as twelve tribes, the descendants of the patriarch Jacob's twelve sons. The old tribal borders had disappeared long ago, thanks to the invasions and conquests of various empires. Technically, Israel did not exist on a map any more—but it did exist in people's minds, Israel as God's special "chosen people." People were still aware of their tribal connection, Paul, for example, tracing his ancestry to the tribe of Benjamin. But Paul himself was aware that Jesus had created a new *spiritual* Israel, open even to people who had not a drop of Jewish blood in their veins.

Twelve

Twelve, like seven, was a significant number for the Israelites. The significance of twelve lies in the stars—literally. The Israelites and other people of the Middle East divided the calendar into twelve months, based on the changes of the moon. The nations of the Middle East also were aware of the twelve signs of the zodiac. Israel did not dabble in astrology as its neighbor nations did, but people were aware of the zodiac.

Because of its significance in the calendar, twelve became a key number. Jacob, also named Israel, had twelve sons, each one the founder of one of the "tribes" of Israel. There were twelve Minor Prophets—their writings collected in one book that Jews still refer to simply as "the Twelve." Jesus chose twelve men to be disciples, and when one (the traitor, Judas) killed himself, the remaining eleven felt obligated to replace him. The disciples are sometimes referred to as "the Twelve." The Letter of James, addressed to Christians throughout the world, goes out to "the twelve tribes scattered among the nations."

The Book of Revelation, with its visions and symbols, paints a picture of heaven that is filled with twelves—twelve pearl gates, twelve angels, twelve gems, twelve foundations, twelve kinds of fruit on the tree of life, the names of the twelve apostles and the twelve tribes of Israel.

Jesus' life definitely changed after his baptism. If he ever went back to the trade of carpentry, we are not told of it. Nor did he ever reside permanently in Nazareth again. He went "on the road"—an unusual practice for a teacher or rabbi. To accompany him, and learn from him, he chose twelve men to be *disciples*, learners, pupils. They were the beginning of a new Israel, and being a part of that new Israel was not based on descent from one of the twelve sons of Jacob, but on following the Son of God.

At least two of the disciples had been followers of John the Baptist, and these two followed Jesus when John told them Jesus was "the Lamb of God." One of the two was the fisherman Andrew, who was so enthusiastic he told his brother Simon, "We have found the Messiah." Simon, later to be called Peter, became a disciple also. Jesus told Andrew and Simon that from then on they would be "fishers of men" (Mark 1:17). Another who joined up early was Philip, who was from the same town as Andrew and Simon. Philip told his friend Nathanael that he and his friends had found "the one Moses wrote about in the Law, and about whom the prophets also wrote—Jesus of Nazareth." Nathanael scoffed. Nazareth? Obscure little Nazareth? Philip invited him to meet the man from Nazareth. Jesus impressed Nathanael—he had seen him sitting under his fig tree. Perhaps this man from Nazareth did have some great power!

Nathanael called him "the Son of God" and "the king of Israel." Jesus responded by referring to himself as "the Son of Man." Clearly, Jesus understood that there was no glory without humility. This was the first occasion in the Bible where he calls himself "Son of Man," and it was his usual way of referring to himself.

Nathanael himself did not become one of the twelve disciples of Jesus. Two who did were the brothers James and John, fishermen on the Sea of Galilee. While they were mending their fishing nets one day, Jesus called to them to follow him, and they did, leaving behind their livelihood as had the others.

Another man going about his work was called. This was Matthew, a tax collector. They were as despised then as they are today—more so, in fact, because they lined their own pockets by charging more tax than the law required. Any Jew who collected tax for the hated Romans was utterly detested. It must have jarred many people when Jesus said the words "Follow me" to Matthew. Sometime soon after, Matthew held a feast in his house, at which other tax collectors were present. Jesus was criticized for hobnobbing with such "sinners," but he claimed it was not his mission to save the righteous, but to save sinners (Matthew 9:9–13).

Other than Andrew, Simon (Peter), James, John, Philip and Matthew, we know nothing about how the other disciples came to be called. The other six in the lists were Bartholomew, Thomas, James son of Alphaeus, Thaddeus, Simon the Zealot, and Judas Iscariot (Matthew 10:1–4). We know four of them were fishermen, one a tax collector (probably the wealthiest of the twelve). Since Simon is called "the Zealot," he would have been zealous for Israel and strongly opposed to the Romans and anyone who collaborated with them—in other words, he would have had reason to detest Matthew the tax collector (unless Matthew totally abandoned his former occupation, which is possible). All the twelve probably came from Galilee, Jesus' home province, although scholars think Judas Iscariot came from the southern province, Judea.

In any group this size, there was bound to be an "inner circle," and it consisted of Simon (Peter), James and John, who would be present with Jesus at some occasions when the larger group was not. Frankly, the Gospels do not give many details about the others, and some of them are not recorded as speaking in the Gospels. Jesus must have had his reasons for choosing them, must have known their purpose in his ministry, must have believed that fishermen and tax collectors had some great spiritual aptitude.

In the period after the New Testament, many legends sprang up about the twelve disciples—perhaps based on truth, perhaps based on vivid imaginations. In the legends, each disciple traveled to some foreign land, spread the gospel and was eventually martyred. That last element is probably true, given Jesus' prophecy that they would be persecuted as he had been—and as most of the great prophets had been (think back to Moses and Jeremiah). Whatever became of them all after the New Testament closes, we don't know, but we do know that while they were with Jesus they were incredibly slow to learn and seemed to constantly misunderstand and misconstrue his words. When Jesus was finally arrested, they all fled and abandoned him. And yet, amazingly, in the Book of Acts they were changed men, dynamic in spreading their faith in the risen Jesus. In other words, the Bible gives us the disciples as they really were, in no way sugarcoating their fickleness and failings. There is an obvious lesson here: Jesus chose his disciples from among ordinary folk. He didn't entrust his teaching to the scholars or to generals or princes, but to some John Does from small towns in an unimportant corner of the Roman empire. We see in Luke's Gospel that Joseph and Mary were devout working-class folks who went regularly from Nazareth to Jerusalem to celebrate the great holy festivals of the faith. That was Jesus' own background, and probably the background of the disciples also—ordinary people, but with a deep faith, not the well-thought-out faith of the rabbis and wise men, but a simpler, more direct faith. Jesus would always bypass the religious "professionals" and aim at the *am haaretz*, the Aramaic term meaning "people of the land." It was among them that Jesus would show himself to be *Immanuel*, "God with us."

PUTTING THE WORD TO WORK

1. John told the people he baptized to be honest in their business dealings. Look at your own employment situation and ask yourself if you are being thoroughly honest in every way. If not, correct that situation.

2. John and Jesus both withdrew into the wilderness at certain times, probably to think clearly and draw nearer to God. Give some thought to planning a spiritual retreat—perhaps for just a day or two—to some place where you can be free from distractions and free to think deeply about your spiritual state.

3. Review Jesus' three temptations and ask yourself: Which have you come closest to giving in to? Why?

4. Jesus answered Satan's three temptations by quoting Scripture. What were some times in your own life when remembering a verse of Scripture kept you on the right moral path?

5. Jesus chose to reveal himself and his message to a group of ordinary people of faith. Take a few moments to reflect on that choice, knowing Jesus is "God with us" and that you are included in "us."

Signs and Wonders

AT THE HEART OF IT ALL TODAY Jesus announces that the kingdom of God is at hand, and the signs of the kingdom are his compassionate miracles. His power over demons, disease and the forces of nature reveal that a new age has arrived.

People often think of Jesus as a great teacher, which he was. The people of his own time recognized this, but what impressed them was the divine power he manifested, the power to do wonders of healing and other miracles. In using this power, he was announcing to the world that the kingdom of God was at hand. Miracles were Jesus' way of reminding people: *God rules.*

> **KEY PASSAGES TO READ TODAY**
>
> Matthew 8:1–17
> Mark 6:30–56
> Luke 8:26–39; 9:37–50; 10:1–21
> John 2:1–11; 11

The Bible sees God as the Creator of all that is. He makes the universe and also the natural laws that apply. In Bible times, when most people believed in God or gods, the unexplainable was usually attributed to the supernatural. Interestingly, in the Bible these unusual occurrences are always for a *purpose.* Jesus never did miracles at random. He healed people and worked other miracles for them because he loved them. God is not a cosmic entertainer who likes to show off. He is a loving Father who does amazing things for a purpose. Like human beings, he is free. Being free, he can sometimes act in a way different from the natural processes in the world. A miracle is a reminder that God is free to do this.

KEY TERM FOR TODAY ## Demon Possession

In the ancient world, people believed that demon possession was possible. Even the great Greek philosopher Aristotle, known in his day as a "scientific" thinker, stated that demons were a reality. In the New Testament period, demons (Greek *daimonia*), also called "unclean spirits" (*pneumaton akarthon*), were very real and widespread. There is only one devil (*diabolos*), Satan, but numerous *daimonia*. As the Gospels make clear, a demon-possessed person was sometimes a danger—to himself and to others. Jesus drove out demons by the power of God; this was a sign that the kingdom of God— God's rule over the earth—was near.

RAISING A TOAST TO THE KINGDOM OF GOD

After Jesus' baptism and temptation, the great prophet John the Baptist was put in prison by the wicked Herod Antipas. Jesus returned to his home province, Galilee, and began to preach: "Repent, for the kingdom of heaven is at hand."

The Gospel of John records that Jesus attended a wedding in the Galilean village of Cana. His disciples were there, and so was his mother—one of the few occasions in the Gospels where Mary is mentioned after Jesus' birth. The wedding party ran out of wine. Mary told Jesus, who replied with the puzzling words, "Dear woman, why do you involve me? My time has not yet come." Mary obviously expected Jesus to do something about the lack of wine. Did she know already that he had miraculous powers? We aren't sure, but she did say to the servants in the house, "Do whatever he tells you to do." Jesus told the servants to fill up the stone water jars—holding more than twenty gallons each—with water. They did so, and Jesus told them to draw some liquid out and take it to the head of the wedding party. The man was deeply impressed—this was fine wine, more surprising since the custom was to drink the best wine at the beginning of the party and save the cheaper wine for later. The head of the wedding party told the groom, "You have saved the best till now."

Jesus "thus revealed his glory, and his disciples put their faith in him" (John 2:11). John here uses a word that is special for him: "sign." Jesus' miracles are "signs" that he is the Son of God, that the kingdom of God has begun on earth. It is, in a way, an undramatic beginning—a quiet sort of "household miracle" that most of the people at the banquet were hardly aware of. But it was done for a good purpose: A wedding party had run out of wine and was in an embarrassing and awkward situation. Jesus helped them. And keep in mind here that shortly before, while he was fasting in the wilderness, Satan had tempted him to turn stones into bread. Obviously Jesus did have the power to transform material objects into other material objects. He did not do so for himself—but did it at the wedding in order to help others. This was the pattern for his miracles—they were acts of compassion, sometimes small, sometimes grand. His disciples were now aware that the man they were following was no ordinary teacher.

Jesus' first miracle of healing occurred in the town of Capernaum on the large lake called the Sea of Galilee. Jesus was teaching in the synagogue on the Sabbath when a demon-possessed man cried out, "What do you want with us, Jesus of Nazareth? Have you come to destroy us? I know who you are—the Holy One of God!" (Mark 1:24). Here is a curious occurrence: following Jesus' baptism, the first being to acknowledge Jesus' divine origin is not a human being but a demon— or perhaps several demons, since the demon referred to himself as "us."

Jesus handled the situation quickly and firmly. In a stern voice he said, "Be quiet! Come out of him!" The man shook violently—the demon (or demons) came out of him "with a shriek."

The people in the synagogue were in awe. Jesus not only taught as "one with authority," but also spoke with authority to the demon—who obeyed him! To fully appreciate this miracle, you have to realize that in ancient times, various "exorcists" claimed to have the power to cast out demons. They often went into long incantations and "spells," calling on the power of some god, making quite a spectacle. Jesus did not do this: He gave the demon a short, sharp command—making it clear he expected to be obeyed. The Son of God did not have to plead or negotiate with demons—he simply

AD 29
Execution of John the Baptist
(Matthew 14:3)

AD 30
Death and resurrection of Jesus
(Matthew 27–28, Mark 15–16, Luke 23–24, John 18–21)

CULTURAL INSIGHTS

Galilee

In Jesus' time, the old land of Israel did not exist on a map. The territory comprised three districts of the Roman Empire: Judea in the south, Samaria in the center, Galilee in the north. Though he was born in Bethlehem in Judea, most of his life was spent in Galilee, in his hometown of Nazareth and, once his ministry began, all around the province. Roughly fifty miles from north to south and thirty miles from east to west, Galilee was tiny by our standards, but it would have seemed larger to Jesus and his disciples, since they traveled on foot.

Judeans looked down on Galileans, something we will see clearly when Jesus goes to Jerusalem. The Judeans saw themselves as more faithful to God than Galileans. Many Gentiles (non-Jews) had settled in Galilee, and Judeans often spoke of "Galilee of the Gentiles," and they did not mean it as a compliment. Centuries earlier, Galilee had been conquered by the Assyrians, who settled various foreigners in the region. Racially and religiously, Galilee had a more "mixed" population than Judea.

God clearly had his reasons for having his Son grow up in Galilee. The area was mostly immune to the influence of the Jewish scribes and Pharisees. The people of Galilee took their religious beliefs from the Scriptures, not from the "traditions of the elders," the "oral law" that many Judeans obsessed over. When Jesus said that he was sent to the "lost sheep of Israel" (Matthew 15:24), he probably had in mind the common folk of Galilee, who were more receptive to God's word than the "establishment" Jews of Judea.

told them to go away. Jesus, Immanuel, "God with us," was sending them back to the abyss from which they came. Jesus came to drive Satan from the earth just as his Father had driven Satan (then known as Lucifer) out of heaven. In the words of one of his own apostles, "The reason the Son of God appeared was to destroy the devil's work" (1 John 3:8).

Jesus' next miracle also happened in Capernaum. The disciple Simon Peter, a fisherman, lived there, and his mother-in-law lived in his house. She was sick in bed with a fever. Jesus took her hand and helped her out of bed. The fever had left her—"and she began to wait on them" (Mark 1:29–31). The next miracle involved a leper, a man afflicted with the horrible disease called leprosy, which caused deformity and, worse, forced the afflicted one to live apart from other people. The leper who approached him did so in faith—or, at least, in optimism. "If you are willing, you can make me clean." Jesus was "filled with compassion" for the man. "I am willing. Be clean!" Jesus actually *touched* the leper—something no one ever did, since it rendered one "unclean." But the man's leprosy was gone as quickly as the spirit had left the demon-possessed man. Although Jesus told the man specifically *not* to tell how he was cured, the leper did—who could have kept such news to himself? Word of Jesus spread even more (Luke 5:12–16).

Back in Capernaum, Jesus was mobbed by people wanting to be cured. He was preaching inside a house and the crowd was so thick no one could get through the door. A paralyzed man had been brought on a pallet by four men. They were so desperate to reach Jesus that they were not going to let the press of the crowd stop them. They literally cut through the roof—not all that difficult, since the roofs of many houses were just a layer of clay over strips of cane. They lowered the paralyzed man down into the house, impressing Jesus with their faith. Jesus said to the man, "Son, your sins are forgiven." This did not sit well with some of the scribes, who thought of Jesus as a blasphemer—after all, no one but God could forgive sins. Jesus knew their thoughts. What was easier, he asked them—to forgive someone's sins, or to tell them to get up and walk? He said to the paralytic, "Get up, take your mat, and go home." The man did, to everyone's amazement (Mark 2:1–12).

Jesus' words to the scribes here are important: They thought he considered himself divine—and he did. His miracle proved that he had the power to heal disease—and that power came from God, who also gave him the power to forgive sins. He could heal the body as well as the soul. Jesus' words to the scribes apply to us all: Like the man on the mat, we all need spiritual healing, whatever our physical condition might be.

The man with the mat was not the only paralytic in Capernaum. A centurion, a Roman soldier, came to Jesus and told him he had a paralyzed servant in his home. Jesus said some words that must have shocked his followers: "I will go and heal him." Faithful Jews did *not* set foot in the homes of Gentiles. Living among Jews, the centurion knew this, of course. He told Jesus he did not even deserve to have Jesus come under his roof. But he understood Jesus had divine power—and authority. The centurion—typical of the Romans' mentality

—understood authority. The centurion had soldiers who would do as he told them. Jesus had power over demons and diseases—if he told them to be gone, they would be.

Note the contrast between this story and the previous one: The scribes, the Jews who studied the Law so closely and were regarded as highly religious, thought Jesus was a blasphemer. The centurion did not; he saw Jesus as a man with divine power who could work miracles. Jesus said to him, "I have not found anyone in Israel with such great faith" (Matthew 8:10). Then Jesus spoke of the great banquet in heaven where faithful Jews expected to sit down with the patriarchs Abraham, Isaac and Jacob. But, Jesus said, there will be surprises there! He explained that people of faith—even this Gentile centurion—would be there, and many people who thought they would be there would not!

Jesus did not go to the centurion's home. He did not need to. He told the centurion to go home, the healing had taken place "just as you believed it would." Jesus had the power, but the recipient's faith was necessary too.

In the eyes of Jesus' critics, he had come very close to doing the unthinkable: setting foot inside a Gentile's home. On another occasion the critics found him doing something else improper. He was in a synagogue on the Sabbath, and a man with a shriveled hand had come to him for healing. No faithful Jew was supposed to do any work on the Sabbath—and the critics thought of healing as work. Jesus could have said to the man, "I will heal you after the Sabbath ends." He did not. He had the man stand up and stretch out his hand. The hand was completely restored.

Hard as it is for us to believe, the Pharisees were so provoked by this healing that they began to plot how they might destroy Jesus. Why? The Sabbath was an obsession for them. They had developed a whole body of regulations about what could—but mostly could not—be done on the Sabbath. The Ten Commandments simply said that man should not work on the Sabbath. The scribes and Pharisees became very specific about what constituted "work." They were so nitpicky they would not even eat an egg that a hen laid on the Sabbath! When Jesus asked the Pharisees whether it was lawful to do good and heal on the Sabbath, they said nothing. They were more concerned about their rigid Sabbath rules than about compassion. They might have been pleased if Jesus had told the man, "Wait until after the Sabbath, and then I will heal you." But had Jesus done that, it would have showed that he submitted to the Pharisees' rule-centered religion, and he had no intention of doing that.

Jesus' home province, Galilee, was fortunate in not having many scribes or Pharisees living there. But the Gospels note that as Jesus' fame spread, scribes and Pharisees came all the way from Jerusalem to monitor his "questionable" activity. On one occasion they accused him of having power to drive out demons because he was in league with Beelzebub, the prince of demons. Jesus asked them, "How can Satan drive out Satan? If a house is divided against itself, that house cannot stand." Jesus assured them: Satan was not driving out the demons (Mark 3:23–30).

Here Jesus spoke of what many people call "the unpardonable sin": All sins and blasphemies could be forgiven, he said, except one: blasphemy against the Holy Spirit, which is an "eternal sin." People often quote his words about the sin and forget the context: He had just been accused of doing miracles of compassion through the power of Satan. A person who "blasphemes against the Holy Spirit" is accusing God of doing evil, mistaking Satan for God. A blasphemer against the Spirit is doing what the prophet Isaiah condemned: one who calls good evil, and evil good (Isaiah 5:20).

Jesus did not allow his critics to deter him from his mission. In the region of the Gerasenes, he encountered a thoroughly agitated man who lived among tombs and was possessed of such strength, no one could bind him, "not even with a chain" (Mark 5:3). He was, as the King James Version puts it, "exceeding fierce," a danger to anyone passing nearby. The demons gave him strength but also agony, for he would cry out and cut himself with stones. When he—or, rather, the demons—saw Jesus, he threw himself at Jesus' feet. "What do you want with me, Jesus, Son of the Most High God? Swear to God that you won't torture me!" Jesus asked him his name. "My name is Legion, for we are many." The demons begged a favor: Let them go into a nearby herd of pigs instead of sending them to the abyss from which they came. Jesus gave them permission, and the demons went into the herd of two thousand pigs, which rushed into the lake. The keepers of the pigs spread the news—and, not surprisingly, they asked Jesus to leave their region. The pigs were apparently worth more to them than the fact that Jesus had healed a pitiful man possessed by a herd of demons (Mark 5:1–20).

In another town, Jesus was followed by a woman who had spent practically everything she had on doctors. She had endured uterine bleeding for twelve years, but nothing seemed to help her. Apparently she was so shy she feared to speak to Jesus—how could she speak of her affliction with a crowd of people around?—but though lacking in boldness, she did not lack faith. She touched Jesus' robe, believing that simple gesture alone would cure her. Somehow Jesus sensed what had happened. He asked his disciples who had touched his robe. The disciples were aghast: In this crowd, how could he ask "Who touched me?" Jesus looked around him, and the poor woman came and fell at his feet, trembling, and told him what she did. "Daughter, your faith has healed you. Go in peace and be freed from your suffering" (Mark 5:34).

In the same town, a man named Jairus had sent word to Jesus that his daughter was dying, and he wished Jesus to come and heal her. But before Jesus went to the house, some messengers arrived: The daughter was already dead. But Jesus told Jairus, "Don't be afraid;

just believe." He took three of the disciples—the "inner circle," Peter, James and John—to the house, where people were already in loud mourning. Jesus asked why they were wailing: "The child is not dead but asleep." The people were astonished—was the famous healer being cruel, or was he crazy? Jesus entered the girl's room with her parents and the three disciples. He took her by the hand and said, "Little girl, I say to you, get up." The girl, who was twelve, stood up immediately and walked (Mark 5:42). This is the first sign in the Gospels that Jesus could not only heal diseases but perhaps even bring back a person from the dead.

In the town of Nain, Jesus and his disciples encountered a funeral procession at the town gate. A widow was burying her only son. Jesus' heart went out to her and he told her, "Don't cry." He went to the bier and said, "Young man, I say to you, get up!" He sat up and began to speak. The people were jubilant: "God has come to help his people!" (Luke 7:11–17). Indeed, that was the purpose of all the miracles of Jesus.

PROPHET WITHOUT HONOR

It should be obvious now that faith plays a role in miracles: God gave Jesus the power, but the faith of the recipient of the miracle mattered. In one story, Jesus encountered a definite *lack* of faith. Jesus had returned to his hometown, Nazareth, and taught in the synagogue on the Sabbath. The people were amazed at his teachings, and at the rumors of his miracles. But they were more offended than amazed. "Isn't this the carpenter?" (Mark 6:3). Jesus told his disciples that a prophet was not without honor—except among his own people. "He could not do any miracles there, except lay his hands on a few sick people and heal them. And he was amazed at their lack of faith" (Mark 6:5–6). We can assume that the few people he healed did have faith, but apparently the town as a whole was against him. To the people of Nazareth he was not the great healer, teacher or prophet. He was just "the carpenter."

There was more faith to be found elsewhere. On one memorable occasion, Jesus taught a crowd of five thousand people. Jesus "had compassion on them, because they were like sheep without a shepherd." Indeed they were! Generation after generation of bad kings and false teachers, and now they were, understandably, spiritually hungry. Late in the day they were physically hungry as well. As Jesus continued teaching the crowd, his disciples reminded him that they were in a remote place, and it was late in the day. Perhaps he should dismiss the people so they could travel to some village and find food. Jesus told the disciples to feed them. Impossible, they said—who had enough money to feed such a crowd? Jesus sent them out among the crowd—perhaps there was some food the people could share. The disciples did not find much—five loaves of bread and two fish—hardly enough for one family, much less a crowd of five thousand.

Jesus told the people to sit down on the grass. Jesus took the bread and fish and gave thanks to God for the food. He broke the loaves of bread and divided up the fish.

"They all ate and were satisfied;" in fact, there were even twelve baskets full of leftovers (Mark 6:30–44).

Think back to Jesus' first miracle—turning water into wine—and also think back to his first temptation, to turn stones into bread to feed himself. He did not use his great power for his own selfish reasons, but chose to use it on this occasion to feed others. In the Old Testament, the prophets Elijah and Elisha both performed miracles of food, extending a small amount of food to make it last. But their miracles only involved a few people. Jesus had fed five thousand with five loaves of bread and two fish. Remember that at his temptation to turn stones into bread, Jesus said to Satan that man does not live on food alone, but on the words of God. The crowd of five thousand had followed him to hear his teaching. They had hungered for the word of God, and Jesus gave them that, then saw to their physical need as well.

Bread—figuratively—played a role in another miracle. Jesus was in the region of Phoenicia, the land of the Mediterranean coast. A Phoenician woman came to him, fell at his feet, and begged him to heal her demon-possessed daughter. Jesus' words to her seem almost cruel: "First let the children eat all they want, for it is not right to take away the children's bread and toss it to their dogs." The woman understood: He was a Jew, and his mission was to his fellow Jews. But she would not be put off so easily. "Even the dogs under the table eat the children's crumbs," she said. Jesus was touched—she was not a Jew, but she had faith, and that was what mattered. He told her to go home. Her daughter was healed (Mark 7:24–30).

Jesus went from there to the region called the *Decapolis*—Greek for "ten cities." This was a mostly Gentile region near Galilee. There some people brought him a man who was deaf and almost mute. On this occasion Jesus took the man away from the crowd. He touched the man's ears and his tongue and said, "Be opened!" The people were in awe. They had never known a deaf man to be healed (Mark 7:31–37).

A greater miracle occurred in the town of Bethsaida. A blind man was brought to Jesus, and Jesus led him outside the town. He touched the man's eyes and his sight was restored—partially. The man said, "I see people; they look like trees walking around." Then Jesus touched his eyes again. His sight was fully restored (Mark 8:22–26).

Note what happened in these last two miracles: Jesus took the person away from the crowd before he performed the healing. He knew word of his healings was spreading, so he began doing miracles out of the crowd's sight.

Let's pause here and observe that Jesus' miracles were always done out of compassion — never to impress a crowd. Jesus never performed a miracle "on demand." When some of the Pharisees and scribes asked him to perform a miraculous sign, Jesus answered, "A wicked and adulterous generation asks for a miraculous sign!" (Matthew 12:38–39). Their request was insincere. They already knew about Jesus' miracles, and he knew that performing another one for them would not make them change their minds. The people who came to him to heal their own diseases could count on his compassion, but he had no intention of showing off just to impress the hypocritical Pharisees. God's power did not work that way.

So far we have looked at Jesus' power to heal diseases, cast out demons, and multiply food. On certain occasions he also had power over the weather. In a boat with his disciples, Jesus fell asleep. A furious storm came up and threatened to swamp the boat. Amazingly, Jesus still slept. His disciples awakened him: "Teacher, don't you care if we drown?" Jesus "rebuked" the wind and waves: "Quiet! Be still!" Suddenly all was calm. He scolded the disciples: Why were they afraid? After knowing him so long, did they not have faith? The Bible says the disciples were "terrified." Who was this, they wondered, that even the wind and waves obeyed him? (Mark 4:35–41). Wasn't the answer obvious? It was the person they had spoken of in the Psalms they had sung from childhood. This was the God who calmed the storm and ruled over the sea.

At another time, Jesus' disciples were in a boat on the Sea of Galilee, straining at the oars because the wind was against them. Jesus came to them, walking on the waves. They were terrified, thinking he was a phantom. He quieted their fears. "Take courage! It is I." He got into the boat and the wind died down (Mark 6:45–52).

CHARACTER CLOSE-UP Luke the Doctor

In his Letter to the Colossians, the apostle Paul refers to Luke as "the beloved physician" (4:14 KJV). Since Paul remarks that Luke was not among those "of the circumcision," it is assumed that Luke was a Gentile, not a Jew, which would make him the only non-Jew to write part of the Bible. Luke was clearly familiar with the Old Testament, and his Gospels show he had a great reverence for the Jewish temple, so it's likely he was either a God-fearer or proselyte (a Gentile who practiced the Jews' religion). The fact that his is the only Gospel to mention the large group of disciples known as "the Seventy" has led people to think he might have been one of the Seventy himself. If this were so, he would have actually seen Jesus face-to-face.

Since Luke was a physician, he had great interest in Jesus' miracles of healing. In fact, he adds some interesting details in the miracle stories. When Matthew and Mark report the healing of Peter's mother-in-law, they speak of a fever, but Luke adds it was a "high" fever (Luke 4:38). In the story of healing a leper, Luke adds the detail that the man was "full of leprosy," meaning it was an advanced case (5:12 KJV). However, in the story of the woman healed when she touched Jesus' robe, Luke *omits* a detail: Matthew and Mark report that she had spent all her money on doctors, but Luke leaves this out! Luke's is the only Gospel to record the parable of the beggar named Lazarus, who was covered with sores and licked by dogs.

The Possessed Magdalene

So much of what people know—or *think* they know—about Mary Magdalene is quite wrong. The New Testament, which mentions her only a few times, does *not* say she was a prostitute, nor that there was even a hint of any romantic attraction between her and Jesus. The Bible does say, however, that Jesus had driven "seven demons" out of her (Luke 8:2). We aren't told if these had caused her some kind of physical distress or perhaps mental anguish, or both. Whatever they were, Jesus' rescue of her caused her to feel eternally grateful, which is why she became one of his devoted followers, one among a group of several women who had been cured of their ailments and who gave financial support to Jesus and the disciples. The Bible makes no mention of the men Jesus healed ever giving him any sort of aid; Mary Magdalene was one of the women who were more generous in spirit than the men were.

It is easy to overlook the fact that in these miracles, Jesus "rebukes" the elements. They are threatening people he loves, and he authoritatively commands them to let up. The message here is clear: In this world human beings are surrounded by seemingly hostile forces—demons, diseases, a natural world that seems indifferent to man's security and safety. It is easy for us, when things are peaceful and calm, to admire the "beauties of nature." The disciples in the boat did not find nature beautiful at that moment! Nature could be lethal! But all the natural world was under God's control. Jesus could feed the hungry, heal the sick and blind and deaf, cure the horrible condition of leprosy, even quiet the winds.

Jesus expected those closest to him to follow in his footsteps. "He called his twelve disciples to him and gave them authority to drive out evil spirits and to heal every disease and sickness" (Matthew 10:1). Clearly, the twelve were not just with him to learn his words of wisdom, but to be agents of God's power. They were to go out and preach that the kingdom of God was near, and they were to show that God's power was already at work in the world: "Heal the sick, raise the dead, cleanse those who have leprosy, drive out demons. Freely you have received, freely give" (10:8).

Did the disciples do miracles themselves? On at least one occasion their lack of faith failed them. A man came to Jesus and lamented that his son was possessed by a demon, which not only made him deaf and mute, but also gripped him with seizures and caused the child to foam at the mouth and throw himself into fire or water. In other words, the demon wanted its host's body dead. The man had brought the boy to the disciples, but they could not heal him. Jesus lamented their lack of faith. The father said to Jesus, "If you can do anything, take pity on us and help us." Jesus told him, "Everything is possible for him who believes." The father tearfully exclaimed, "I do believe; help me overcome my unbelief!" This is one of the great moments in the Gospels: The man has faith but realizes he needs more. God gives more faith to the person who realizes his own need. But there must already be *some* faith present. The father's emotional honesty is touching.

Jesus had the boy brought to him. He rebuked the demon, and it left the boy immediately. It caused such a violent convulsion that the boy appeared dead, but Jesus took him by the hand and raised him to his feet.

The disciples wondered: Why couldn't *we* do this? Jesus knew their minds, and said to them, "Because you have so little faith." If they had only a little faith—something as tiny as a mustard seed—they would have the power to move mountains (Mark 8:14–29; Matthew 17:14–21).

Jesus' disciples may have failed in their efforts to heal and drive out demons, but others were more successful. Oddly, this bothered the disciples. They reported to Jesus that they saw a man driving out demons in Jesus' name, and they told him to stop because he was not one of their band. Jesus told them, "Do not stop him, for whoever is not against you is for you" (Luke 9:49–50). We sense some obvious envy in the disciples. They were Jesus' chosen ones, yet their own lack of faith caused them to fail at driving out demons, so they resented someone else having that power. But, Jesus said, the unnamed man who was successful at driving out demons was to be praised, not censured.

Luke's Gospel records that there was a larger group of Jesus' followers than the main twelve. Jesus sends out "the Seventy" to preach the kingdom of God. Jesus warns them they are going out as lambs among wolves. But after some time "on the road," they return with good news: "Lord, even the demons submit to us in your name." Jesus said, "I saw Satan fall like lightning from heaven" (Luke 10:17–18). These words puzzle people. Was he referring to the distant past, when Satan rebelled against God and was cast out of heaven? Or was he referring to what his followers just told him, that the demons were being cast out, and thus Satan's grip on the world was being challenged? He tells the jubilant followers not to rejoice because they have power over demons but because their names are written in the Book of Life. In other words, don't enjoy power for its own sake—it can go to a person's head, just as the proud angel Satan fell and was expelled from heaven.

The double meaning here was probably deliberate. Jesus himself is ecstatic over the news the Seventy has brought him. He thanks God for hiding spiritual things from the wise and revealing them to "the little children"—the trusting, faith-filled Seventy, whose faith at this point seems more solid than the faith of the twelve disciples. Interestingly, when he sent out the Seventy, he did *not* tell them to drive out demons. Thanks to their own faith, they discovered they had the power to do so. Contrast them with the twelve disciples, who were told to drive out demons, but could not. God is full of surprises!

Jesus in the Eyes of His Critics

Even Jesus' critics did not try to deny that he possessed some sort of power. The Jewish historian Josephus admitted that Jesus performed miracles—although Josephus, no friend of Christianity, called the miracles "paradoxical deeds." In the Talmud, the large body of Jewish legal traditions, Jesus is referred to as a miracle-worker—but, the Talmud says, his power came not from being the Son of God, but from having gone into Egypt as a child. According to the Talmud, Egypt, always considered the home of sorcery and the occult, had taught Jesus the magic that he used to work miracles.

MIRACLES THAT ASTOUND—AND OFFEND

In Jerusalem, Jesus and his disciples came upon a beggar who had been blind from birth. The disciples' question to Jesus is peculiar: "Rabbi, who sinned, this man or his parents, that he was born blind?" By asking if the man was being punished for his parents' sin tells us the disciples didn't know their Bible very well, for God most emphatically did not punish people for their parents' failings. The disciples may have been parroting what was popularly believed. But why did they ask if the man was being punished for his own sins? Could a person be "pre-punished" for sins he was going to commit in his life?

Whatever the disciples may have thought about punishment, Jesus brushed it all aside. "Neither this man nor his parents sinned, but this happened so that the work of God might be displayed in his life." Jesus spit on the ground, made a small daub of mud, and put it on the man's eyes. He told him to go wash in a nearby public pool. The man did, and he was able to see. People were so shocked to see this lifelong beggar suddenly walking about that they couldn't believe their own eyes.

Jesus' healing displeased his enemies, the Pharisees, because Jesus had healed on the Sabbath again! The man was brought to them, and they assured him his healer was not from God, for no man of God would heal on the Sabbath. But some weren't so sure. How could a sinner do such miracles? The formerly blind man had his own opinion: Jesus was a prophet, not a sinner. The Pharisees were still skeptical. They had the man's parents brought in, who identified the man as their son. They also feared the Pharisees because they had heard that people on Jesus' side could be expelled from their synagogues. The blind man himself claimed he could not say for certain whether or not Jesus was a sinner—but he did say, "One thing I know, I was blind but now I see!" The Pharisees were furious. Obviously this man was "steeped in sin at birth" (John 9:34). How dare he side with Jesus!

So many of the people Jesus healed are nameless. One who stands out and whose name is remembered was Lazarus, who, with his sisters Mary and Martha, were close friends with Jesus. When Lazarus fell sick, the sisters sent word to Jesus: "Lord, the one you love is sick." Jesus told his disciples that "this sickness will not end in death." Yet he did not go to their house immediately.

There were reasons to avoid going to the family. The three lived in Bethany in Judea, and there were plots there against Jesus. When Jesus told his disciples they were returning to Judea, they reminded him of the risk (John 11:8). He insisted on going. Lazarus was "asleep," and Jesus intended to "wake him up." The disciples, as usual, misunderstood. They took his words literally and assumed he meant Lazarus was in a healing sleep. Jesus made it plain: Lazarus was dead.

When Jesus and the disciples reached Bethany, Lazarus was not only dead but buried—in the tomb for four days, in fact. The house was full of mourners. Martha came out and told Jesus that if he had been there, Lazarus would not have died. Jesus assured her that her brother would rise again. Martha thought he was speaking of the resurrection at the end of time. Did she believe, he asked her, that Jesus had the power over life and death now? Yes, she believed—she knew he was the Son of God.

The other sister, Mary, came out to meet him, full of tears. Jesus was touched by her weeping. He asked to be taken to Lazarus' tomb. Then occurs one of the great moments of the Bible: "Jesus wept." While this is not the only occasion when Jesus shed tears, it is special, for Jesus was weeping over the loss of a dear friend—not only that loss, but the grief it caused the sisters and their friends. Death was a terrible thing, and Jesus understood. Knowing death was inevitable did not take away people's pain, even if they believed in a

---

CULTURAL INSIGHTS

Leprosy

Technically, true leprosy is *Hansen's disease*, a disfiguring skin condition that affects the sense of touch and also the voice. Victims—lepers—lose sensation in some parts of the body and suffer agonizing pain in others, while lumps growing on the skin, especially the face, give them a grotesque appearance. It can be treated today, but for most of history there was no treatment, and people knew that it was contagious. Lepers—with their frightening appearance and strange voices—had to live apart from other human beings, wear torn clothing and, if they approached people, call out "Unclean, unclean!" so people could steer clear of them. Leprosy was a kind of "living death," making a person an outcast from society, with no hope of recovery. People afflicted with leprosy had to endure watching themselves literally rot away.

Jesus' healing of lepers was more than a matter of curing illness. He was rescuing the poor creatures—shunned by their fellow man—from a living death. In a way his healing of lepers was as dramatic as raising his friend Lazarus from the dead.

One Grateful Leper

Near the border of the provinces of Galilee and Samaria, Jesus encountered ten lepers. From a distance they called out to him, "Jesus, Master, have pity on us!" He called out to them, "Go, show yourselves to the priests"—a regulation from the Law of Moses requiring those healed of any impurity to be examined by a priest before being pronounced well. The ten were cured as they went on their way. One of them, seeing that he was healed, ran back to Jesus, praising God loudly. He threw himself at Jesus' feet and thanked him. Jesus asked, "Were not all ten cleansed? Where are the other nine?" (Luke 17:11–18). The one grateful leper was a Samaritan—the people so despised by the Jews. If the other nine lepers were Jews—which the story implies—how ironic that the only one to thank this Jewish healer was a Samaritan! In one of his parables, Jesus had spoken of a fictional Samaritan who took pity on a Jewish traveler on the road, showing kindness to him when no one else did. In the story of the lepers, here was a real Samaritan who showed a faith that Jesus commended.

greater reward after death. Jesus was not some Stoic philosopher, keeping his face stony and sighing, "What must be, must be." He ran rich with emotion, even the emotion of grief.

Jesus asked the people to move away the stone from Lazarus' rock-cut tomb. Martha protested: He had been in the tomb four days, so there would be the foul smell of decay. Jesus brushed aside the protest. Had he not told her she was going to see the glory of God? Jesus prayed to his Father. Then he called out, "Lazarus, come out!" Wrapped in the strips of linen used for the bodies of the dead, Lazarus came out from his tomb. This time there was no doubt about the miracle. In the cases of the daughter of Jairus and the son of the widow of Nain, critics might say that the "dead" person had merely been in a deep coma. But Lazarus had been in the tomb four days. He was most assuredly dead—but Jesus was stronger than death.

Bethany was a mere two miles from Jerusalem. Word of the great miracle reached Jerusalem quickly. The Sanhedrin, the great ruling council of the Jews, was called into session. The priests were worried. They feared this healer from Nazareth would stir things up. Perhaps the Romans would use this as an excuse to shut down the temple and end the priesthood forever! The high priest, Caiaphas, put the matter simply: This Jesus had to die. It was better "that one man die for the people than that the whole nation perish" (John 11:50). Jesus was not going to die for being a teacher. The priests knew their own religion's history well enough to know that a great moral and spiritual teacher was no real threat to the powers that be—there had been plenty of teachers like that! But a man manifesting divine power—now, *that* was a threat! They were obviously envious of Jesus, who was popular with the people, while they held their office through heredity alone and were not particularly well-liked.

In a way this is one of the saddest episodes in the Bible—following upon the heels of one of the gladdest. Jesus had raised a man from the tomb. Lazarus' friends and family rejoiced. Instead of sharing in the jubilation, the priests and other rulers saw it as a threat to their own position. They wanted Jesus dead. John's Gospel tells us they even plotted to kill Lazarus. Perhaps it never crossed their minds that Jesus could raise Lazarus again—or, more importantly, that Jesus himself might not stay in his own tomb.

We end this chapter by going back to the basic message that Jesus preached: "Repent, for the kingdom of God is at hand." *The point of the miracles was to let people see the power of God so that they would repent of their sins.* And, thanks to human blindness to spiritual realities, most people who witnessed the miracles—or benefited from them—did *not* repent. Jesus lamented this, comparing some of the cities—including Capernaum, where he lived for part of the time—to wicked Sodom. The cities that had witnessed the power of miracles were as spiritually wretched as Sodom—or worse, for Sodom never had a mighty prophet preaching repentance to its people and working miracles of compassion in its streets.

PUTTING THE WORD TO WORK

1. Some of Jesus' miracles show his willingness to reach out to the "unclean," such as lepers and Gentiles. Make an effort today to reach out to someone you would normally avoid.

2. Jesus' enemies, the Pharisees, seemed more concerned about rule-keeping than loving people. Try to think of areas of your own life where you might be too legalistic or unforgiving.

3. Can you recall an incident in your own life, or the life of someone close to you, when you felt a miracle had taken place? How did you respond? In what way did you thank God?

4. The seventy disciples Jesus sent out were amazed at their power over demons. Try to think of times in your own life when God pleasantly surprised you, giving you more courage and ability than you thought you had.

5. The father who told Jesus, "I do believe—help me overcome my unbelief!" recognized the imperfect state of his faith. Make it a point today to pray that your own faith will increase so that you will remain more open to miracles in your life.

Teacher and Storyteller

AT THE HEART OF IT ALL TODAY	Directly in sermons and indirectly in parables, Jesus teaches what the kingdom of God is like, turning the world's values upside down and showing that our thoughts and motivations are as important as our outward behavior.

In the previous chapter we looked at Jesus the miracle worker. His miracles of healing, casting out demons, controlling nature, and even raising the dead were signs that what he called "the kingdom of God" was at hand. Today we look at Jesus' profound teaching about the kingdom and the sort of people who would be part of it.

KEY PASSAGES TO READ TODAY

Matthew 5–7; 25:31–46

Luke 10:25–37; 15:1–31

When Jesus said "kingdom of God," he did not mean "kingdom" in the sense of a nation or any place that could be found on a map. As he would tell Pontius Pilate, "my kingdom is not of this world." When Jesus spoke of the "kingdom of God," he meant "sovereignty of God" or "rule of God." In other words, not a location, but a spiritual reality.

Didn't Jesus believe that his Father was already Ruler of everything? Of course! But think back to the garden of Eden, where Adam and Eve chose to disobey and rebel against God. God gives us freedom. We don't *have to* obey him or accept him as King. You might say that the first sin was man thumbing his nose at God and saying, "I'm in charge, God, not you." God rules the universe, yes—but does not force us to accept him as Ruler. He is not a puppet master but a Father. Part of Jesus' mission was to help people realize what Adam and Eve had forgotten: to put oneself under the protective authority of God is to be free.

Also, think back to the chapter where we looked at Jesus' temptation by Satan. The devil offered him the splendor of the world's kingdoms—*if* Jesus would worship him,

KEY TERM FOR TODAY ## The Kingdom of God

The kingdom of God—in Greek, *basileia tou theou*—means the rule or reign of God, not a location or an institution. Jesus announced that it was "near." Did he mean it was sometime in the future—or already present—or both? The answer is both. Jesus' casting out of demons was a sign that the kingdom had already arrived on earth (Matthew 12:28). Whenever people submit to the rule of God in their lives, the kingdom already exists. For each of us the kingdom is present when we allow God to rule.

that is. Jesus resisted that temptation. Were the kingdoms really the devil's to give? In a sense, yes. The New Testament makes it clear that Satan and his legions of demons exercise great—and always harmful—power in this world. You might say that they have established a rival government to God's rule. But Jesus' power to drive out demons was a sign that God's rule was reasserting itself. Jesus' miracles were a witness to this, and so were his teachings.

Jesus also speaks of a more glorious time in the future when the kingdom will be "fulfilled." In the parable of the sheep and the goats, for example, the saints who showed compassion while they lived on earth are told at the Last Judgment that they may now enter "the kingdom prepared for you since the creation of the world" (Matthew 25:34). In other words, in time to come, heaven and the kingdom of God will be the same thing. At the end of time, as we see in Revelation, "The kingdom of the world has become the kingdom of our Lord and of his Christ" (11:15).

THE PROPHET LIKE MOSES

Toward the end of Moses' life, God made him a promise: "I will raise up for them a prophet like you from among their brothers; I will put my words in his mouth, and he will tell them everything I command him" (Deuteronomy 18:18). "Them" here refers to Israel. Moses had been the great (and also persecuted and underappreciated) leader of Israel, leading the slaves out of Egypt and delivering God's laws to them, as well as performing many miracles. As centuries passed, God did raise up many other prophets for Israel, including the miracle-working Elijah and Elisha. But Israel always hoped for a special prophet, *the* prophet that God would send them, one as great as Moses, or greater. In time they came to speak of their hope for "the Prophet," and many expected he would be the same as the Messiah, the Christ. But for several centuries, Israel had no prophets at all. Then along came John the Baptist, Jesus' kinsman and forerunner. John was a great prophet—in fact, Jesus said that no prophet was greater than John. But the Gospels make it clear that Jesus himself was "the prophet like Moses" foretold in Deuteronomy.

The early Christians saw Jesus as a "second Moses," even greater than the first one. This is especially clear in Matthew's Gospel, which was primarily written for Jewish readers to show that Jesus was not

43 BC–AD 18
Ovid, Roman poet

27 BC–AD 180
The Pax Romana, years of relative peace in the Roman empire

c. 6 BC
Birth of Jesus in Bethlehem

4 BC
Death of Herod the Great

c. 3 BC
Beginnings of the Zealot sect of anti-Roman Jews

AD 5
The Roman legions defeat Lombard tribes that have established themselves on the lower Elbe River.

AD 6
Judea placed under direct Roman rule

AD 14–37
Reign of Roman Emperor Tiberius

AD 18
Caiaphas becomes high priest of the Jews.

AD 26–36
Pontius Pilate is Roman governor of Judea.

c. AD 27–28
Ministry of John the Baptist; baptism of Jesus and beginning of his ministry *(Matthew 3, Mark 1, Luke 3, John 1:6–35)*

AD 29
Execution of
John the Baptist
(Matthew 14:3)

AD 30
Death and
resurrection of Jesus
(Matthew 27–28,
Mark 15–16, Luke
23–24, John 18–21)

only the Messiah but also the great prophet Moses himself had foretold. And he was very much like Moses—speaking the words of God to man, performing miracles—and enduring scorn and persecution.

Chapters 5 through 7 of Matthew's Gospel are some of the most quoted passages of the Bible. They are the essence of Jesus' teaching, and are often called the Sermon on the Mount, based on the opening words: "Now when he saw the crowds, he went up on a mountainside and sat down. His disciples came to him, and he began to teach them." Note that the sermon was delivered on a mountain, just as Moses was on Mount Sinai when he received the Law of God.

The Sermon on the Mount opens with the passage called the Beatitudes, meaning "blessings": Jesus pronounces God's blessing on the poor in spirit, mourners, those who hunger for righteousness, the meek, the pure in heart, the merciful, the peacemakers, and those who are persecuted for righteousness. Such people are "sons of God" and part of his kingdom. The Beatitudes turn the world's values upside down. In this world, people are not esteemed for being meek, merciful peacemakers—quite the opposite! But the kingdom of God is not like this world. In God's kingdom, many people who are losers by the world's standards are winners in the eyes of God. The hearts of the poor in spirit are stretched through suffering and enlarged, so their hearts have more room for God.

Luke's version of the famous Sermon balances the famous blessings with a set of "woes": Jesus pronounces "woe" upon those who are rich and well-fed now, for they have received their comforts on earth, but not in the world to come. (On another occasion, Jesus said that "it is easier for a camel to go through the eye of a needle than for a rich man to enter the kingdom of God" [Matthew 19:24].) Jesus also pronounces woe upon those who are praised by men, "for that is how their fathers treated the false prophets" (Luke 6:2–26).

Jesus tells his listeners that they are to be the "salt of the earth" and "light of the world"—"seasoning" an evil world and "lighting" it with their acts of compassion. In Jesus' day, salt was a valuable commodity, not as cheap as it is today. In fact, some soldiers were paid in salt instead of coin, and our word *salary* comes from the Latin *salarium*, meaning "salt money." Human beings cannot live without salt, and the world cannot exist without good and decent people in it.

The Sermon shows how differently Jesus viewed human behavior from the religious teachers of his time. To begin, Jesus said, "Do not think that I have come to abolish the Law or the Prophets; I have not come to abolish them but to fulfill them" (Matthew 5:17). He was making it clear that the moral teachings in the Old Testament were still binding. But Jesus went beyond those teachings, emphasizing that our feelings and motivations are as important as our actual deeds. "You have heard that it was said, 'Do not commit adultery.' But I tell you that anyone who looks at a woman lustfully has already committed adultery with her in his heart" (Matthew 5:27–28). This was a new teaching: God not only prohibits adultery, but also prohibits fantasizing about it. Jesus also tells his listeners that not only is murder forbidden, but so is hating someone—or even calling him a fool! Why did he teach this? Because murder is only the final carrying out of a *feeling*. From anger follow evil words, from evil words evil deeds. It is not enough to forbid the final act, which is only the result of an interior process that has made it inevitable. The right thing to do is to cut at the root of the evil, to destroy the evil plant of hate, which bears the poisonous fruit. Put another way, if we could all stop hating, there would be no murder, and if we could all stop lusting, there would be no adultery. It is easier—and more effective—to nip evil in the bud than to deal with it full-grown and dangerous. But people nurse their hate and lust and greed on the inside, thinking no one knows their hearts—but God does.

"If your right hand causes you to sin, cut it off and throw it away. It is better for you to lose one part of your body than for your whole body to go into hell." Did Jesus mean this literally? No, but he did mean it *seriously*. We ought to be conscious of anything in our lives that leads us astray and be willing to "amputate" rather than keep on sinning. "You have heard that it was said, 'Eye for eye, and tooth for tooth.' But I tell you, Do not resist an evil person. If someone strikes you on the right cheek, turn to him the other also." The "eye for eye" rule came from the Law of Moses, and as we saw in an earlier chapter, this was a good law, for it *limited* vengeance—eye for an eye, instead of *two* eyes for an eye. "Eye for an eye" was just and fair—but how much better not to seek vengeance at all! Instead of striking back, turn the other cheek. Hard to do, indeed, but Jesus himself would demonstrate that it was possible.

CULTURAL INSIGHTS

Rabbi

The Hebrew word *rab* meant "great," and *rabbi* meant "my great one" and was used as a title of respect for teachers. Although Jesus' disciples and others sometimes called him rabbi, he warned against the vanity of the scribes and Pharisees who loved to be called rabbi and other honorifics (Matthew 23:7–8), and he made it clear that the kingdom of God was made up of people who humbled themselves, not delighting in pompous titles (23:11–12). Luke's Gospel, written by a Gentile for Gentiles, never calls Jesus *rabbi* but always uses the Greek word *didaskolos*, "teacher."

"You have heard that it was said, 'Love your neighbor and hate your enemy.' But I tell you: Love your enemies and pray for those who persecute you, that you may be sons of your Father in heaven. . . If you love those who love you, what reward will you get?" This is one of the most radical statements in whole Bible: *love your enemies*. He does not say it is easy—but it is possible. Loving those who love us back is a good thing, of course—certainly better than returning love with ingratitude, which happens far too often! But Jesus tells us to stretch ourselves morally and spiritually, praying for those who do us harm. We aren't told to *like* or *admire* them, but *love* them, just as God loves people who do not love him in return. If our love does not change our enemies—and on occasion it does—it changes *us* on the inside.

ALL FOR SHOW

Jesus was the great enemy of religious hypocrisy, and nowhere is this clearer than in the Sermon on the Mount. "Be careful not to do your 'acts of righteousness' before men, to be seen by them. If you do, you will have no reward from your Father in heaven" (Matthew 6:1). Jesus notes that the hypocrites "announce it with trumpets" when they give to the needy, but the people in God's kingdom should do it quietly. We should do good deeds "by stealth": "Do not let your left hand know what your right hand is doing, so that your giving may be in secret. Then your Father, who sees what is done in secret, will reward you." Likewise, our prayers and religious devotions ought to be done out of love for God, not to impress others. In fact, our prayers ought to be direct and simple— eloquence may impress our fellow man, but not God.

Matthew 6:9–13 is the most-quoted prayer of all time, and since it is brief, let's quote the entire text: "This, then, is how you should pray: 'Our Father in heaven, hallowed be your name, your kingdom come, your will be done on earth as it is in heaven. Give us today our daily bread. Forgive us our debts, as we also have forgiven our debtors. And lead us not into temptation, but deliver us from the evil one.' " Note that Jesus does not tell people to specifically pray this prayer: We are to pray *like this*—that is, the Lord's Prayer is a *model* prayer. It begins with reverence and praise for God, then asks for what the person needs (*needs*, not *wants*), asks for God's forgiveness (which is conditional—we have to forgive other people also), and ends with a request for deliverance from the power of the evil one. Entire books have been written on the Lord's Prayer, and we can hardly do it justice in a few sentences. However, it is worth remembering that there is no "magic" prayer in the Bible, and we aren't saved by repeating the same prayer day after day. The Lord's Prayer is a model or outline for our own personal prayers to follow.

After quoting the prayer, Jesus emphasizes one aspect of it: forgiveness of sins. His words are blunt: "If you do not forgive men their sins, your Father will not forgive your sins" (Matthew 6:15). We can't expect God to forgive if we cannot do it ourselves. We should not even try to approach God in worship if we harbor hate and grudges in our hearts: "If you are offering your gift at the altar and there remember that your brother has something against you, leave your gift there in front of the altar. First go and be reconciled to your brother; then come and offer your gift" (5:23–24). God's kingdom will be a kingdom of people of forgiveness and mercy.

It definitely will *not* be a kingdom of material splendor. Jesus tells people not to lay up treasure on earth, but "treasures in heaven, where moth and rust do not destroy, and where thieves do not break in and steal. For where your treasure is, there your heart will be also" (6:20–21).

We cannot, Jesus said, serve two masters—God and money. The actual word he used was *mammon*, which is better translated "material goods." Nothing is wrong with money and possessions—except that too often we worship them instead of accepting them as good gifts from God. We simply cannot worship our possessions and worship God too, so we have to choose. To truly enjoy life we ought to rejoice in what we *do* have and not obsess over what we *don't* have.

Jesus understood that even when we do not worship money and possessions, we still fret over material things: "Do not worry about your life, what you will eat or drink; or about your body, what you will wear. Is not life more important than food, and the body more important than clothes?" After all, God feeds the birds and animals—and aren't we more valuable to him than they are? The pagans spend their lives fretting over what they will eat and what they will wear, and such anxiety saps the joy from life—and also expresses our lack of confidence in God. "Seek first his kingdom and his righteousness, and all these things will be given to you as well" (6:33). In other words, get your priorities straight. Our first concern ought to be our moral and spiritual health. When that is our first priority, God will take care of our other needs. We ought to *become* something valuable, not *acquire* something valuable. Imagine how radically different the world would be if people took these anxiety-killing words to heart!

After all, God gives us what we really need. Human fathers have their failings, and yet no father would give his son a stone if he asked for bread. If human fathers can show love and generosity when their children ask, how much more generous the heavenly Father is! (7:7–11).

"Do not judge, or you too will be judged" (7:1). Did Jesus mean we should have no opinions—or that we could never serve on a jury or act as judge in court? Of course not. He was telling people not to see themselves as the Supreme Judge, the one who is above criticism himself. Only God is that Judge, and he alone can judge every person and situation rightly. When we judge people harshly, we are playing God. "How can you say to your brother, 'Let me take the speck out of your eye,' when all the time there is a plank in your own eye?' " (7:4). Our first priority ought to be judging *ourselves*, not others. "So in everything, do to others what you would have them do to you, for this sums up the Law and the Prophets" (7:12). Sums up, yes, but how difficult to follow! Jesus did not promise it was easy: "Enter through the narrow gate. For wide is the gate and broad is the road that leads to destruction, and many enter through it. But small is the gate and narrow the road that leads to life, and only a few find it." Jesus had in mind something that we have seen throughout the pages of the Bible: the *righteous remnant* of mankind, the few faithful ones willing to obey God. "Not everyone who says to me, 'Lord, Lord,' will enter the kingdom of heaven, but only he who does the will of my Father who is in heaven" (7:21).

ALAS, THE LAWYERS!

Matthew's Gospel concludes Jesus' Sermon on the Mount with these words: "When Jesus had finished saying these things, the crowds were amazed at his teaching, because he taught as one who had authority, and not as their teachers of the law" (7:28–29). Greek scholars tell us that the word translated "amazed" or "astonished" here actually means "alarmed" also. There was something so radical in his teachings that they were rattled, not just amazed. This is not surprising—his words are still alarming, since they go against our human inclinations to be selfish and judgmental. He also was harsh on "religious" folk, making it clear that much of their "deep faith" was just for show. He understood that people who are hollow at the core tend to focus on external things.

The King James Version speaks of "lawyers," while other versions have "teachers of the law" or "scribes." These weren't courtroom lawyers but were experts in interpreting the Laws of Moses—or so they believed. Remember that in earlier chapters we studied the Jews returning from Babylonian exile and rebuilding their temple and religious life in Judea. Knowing that the exile had been punishment for disobeying God's laws, their leaders were determined that they would not let that happen again. From then on they would observe the Law of Moses strictly. One problem, though, was that the Law did not cover every situation in life. So the scribes, the "experts," studied the Law closely and determined how to apply the Law to every detail of life, no matter how trivial.

The scribes believed in the *oral law*. Supposedly God had not only given Moses the laws written in the Torah, but also laws that were passed on by word of mouth to later generations. In time, these orals laws were regarded as "traditions of the elders" and were seen as binding as the written laws were. But in practice, the scribes were *more* obsessed with the tradition of the oral law than with the Torah itself. Jesus did not share their reverence for the oral law, the "traditions." He honored only the Law and the Prophets, the words that God gave to man. This is why he could so often say "it is written" and "have you not read"—always referring to the Bible, not to the traditions.

This is why his teachings were amazing *and* alarming to his listeners. He didn't cite the oral law that the scribes cited, but quoted only the Law and Prophets. But, even more alarming, he spoke *with his own authority*. Throughout the Sermon on the Mount we see a pattern: "You have heard it said…but I say to you…" The scribes had a flair for quoting from the oral law—you might say they "footnoted" themselves when they taught. Jesus did not. He would quote from the Law and Prophets, yes, but when he gave his own interpretation of the verses he quoted, he did it on his own authority, not the "traditions of the elders." Jesus scolded the scribes and Pharisees by saying, "You have let go of the commands of God and are holding on to the traditions of men" (Mark 7:8). The Pharisees had spoken of the "traditions of the elders," but Jesus turned it into "traditions of men," contrasted with the "commands of God." Clearly, the commands of God took precedence.

The scribes often claimed they were bringing out the deeper meanings of the Law, so that even in the most minute details of life people could know they were obeying God. Jesus himself sought the Law's deeper meaning—but for him the deeper meaning was mostly an inward thing, not outward. For him, "You shall not murder" also meant "You shall not hate," and "You shall not commit adultery" meant "You shall not lust in your heart." The scribes were not concerned about such matters. Here is one example of the pickiness of their oral law: The Law told the people not to work on the Sabbath. According to the scribes, one could look into a wall mirror on the Sabbath—that was not considered work—but not into a hand mirror, since hand mirrors often contained tweezers, so looking into a hand mirror on the Sabbath might lead to tweezing a gray hair. Also, cutting one's hair or nails on the Sabbath was a mortal sin, and an egg laid by a hen on the Sabbath could not be eaten. Jesus called the scribes "hypocrites" because they went to the bother of tithing their herbs—mint, dill and cumin—"but you have neglected the more important matters of the law—justice, mercy and faithfulness." In other words, they were getting everything right—except the things that really mattered!

To the scribes, this web of regulations was a good thing, the application of God's holy laws to the minute details of life. To Jesus, it was burdening down people with bothersome details, leading them to think that the heart of faith was in the details of the law, not in loving God and neighbor. Jesus saw that the scribes had laid a "heavy yoke" of regulations upon the people. His own yoke was easy and his burden was light

(Matthew 11:28–30). He didn't mean that the life of faith was a breeze, but that obeying God was easier than constant fussing over the scribes' endless regulations. He told his followers that their righteousness had to *exceed* the righteousness of the scribes—not by being more fussy about the rules than they were, but by being better people on the inside (Matthew 5:20).

Think back to earlier chapters when we studied the prophets of Israel. They often introduced their words with the phrase, "Thus says the Lord…" Jesus did *not* speak that way, ever. People saw him as a prophet, in fact, as *the* prophet, the one like Moses that they had hoped for. But Jesus did not do what the earlier prophets did, speaking as the "middleman," the "mouthpiece" for the words of God. He spoke on his own authority—which was entirely appropriate, since he was God's Son. But, needless to say, the people accustomed to bowing to the "experts," the scribes, were irked at his teaching. To them, it was arrogance to say "I say to you…" But if such bold teaching offended the scribes and their admirers, it impressed others deeply. For many of them, it was as if God himself was speaking directly to them—and what a joy for those who recognized it!

THE "LIKE" STORIES

Jesus concluded his Sermon on the Mount with these words: "Everyone who hears these words of mine and puts them into practice is like a wise man who built his house on the rock.…" The storms and floods came, but the house stood firm, being built on a rock, whereas the foolish man builds on a foundation of sand. This is an example of a teaching technique that Jesus was famous for, the *parable*. Parables were in long use, and many are found in the Book of Proverbs, for example: "Like clouds and without rain is a man who boasts of gifts he does not give" (25:14). "As a north wind brings rain, so a sly tongue brings angry looks" (25:23). A parable is simply a simile, comparing one thing to another, always using situations and objects from everyday life. Jesus was not an abstract philosopher tossing out technical words for people. He communicated at the layman's level, and when he wanted to speak of spiritual realities, he spoke in concrete images people could easily understand—farmers sowing seed, housewives baking bread, fishermen letting down nets into the water.

Some of the parables are extremely short: "The kingdom of heaven is like treasure hidden in a field. When a man found it, he hid it again, and then in his joy went and sold all he had and bought that field" (Matthew 13:44). "The kingdom of heaven is like a merchant looking for fine pearls. When he found one of great value, he went away and sold everything he had and bought it" (13:45–46). The meaning here is obvious enough: The kingdom of God is something of great value—but the concrete images of the parable help the idea stick in the mind. In another parable, Jesus spoke of the kingdom as arriving by "stealth": It is like yeast mixed in flour, in time leavening the whole loaf of bread (13:33). We can imagine Jesus' original listeners nodding and thinking, "Yes, I know exactly what he means."

Some of the parables were longer, more storylike: "The kingdom of heaven is like a net that was let down into the lake and caught all kinds of fish…" (Matthew 13:47). When the fishermen lifted the net out of the water, they collected up the edible fish and threw the others away. This, Jesus said, would be like what happens at the end of time, when the angels will come and separate the righteous—the "keepers"—from the wicked (Matthew 13:47–50). In a similar parable, a man sows a field with wheat, but at night his enemy comes and scatters weed seeds in the field. The farmer allows the wheat and weeds to grow up together, but at the time of harvest, the wheat will be harvested while the weeds will be pulled up and burned (Matthew 13:24–30).

Jesus' most famous "farm parable" is the story of the sower. A farmer sows seed, with some falling among the path, where birds eat it. Some falls on rocky soil, where it sprouts but does not take root, and the plants wither in the sun. Some falls among thorns, which

---

CULTURAL INSIGHTS

Scribes / Teachers of the Law

The Hebrew word was *sofer*, the Greek word *grammateus*. The scribe was the expert in applying the Laws of Moses—and the "traditions of the elders"—to all of life. Among the Jews of Jesus' time, a scribe had clout—he was to be believed, no matter what he said, and it was believed he would have a great reward in heaven. Although there were legends of scribal academies dating back as far as the time of Shem (Noah's son), the scribes had their origin in the time of Ezra and Nehemiah, after the return from Babylon. In that period, the Persians allowed the Jews self-rule under the Torah, but since the laws in the Torah did not cover everything, the scribes were the interpreters, applying it to all situations. They were both legal scholars and teachers. In their eyes, the laws of God were so detailed and complex that the average person could not possibly understand or interpret them. Their motto could be summed up as "Trust us, we're experts!" Jesus most definitely did not *trust* them, and he believed their focus on the details made them miss the larger goals of loving God and neighbor.

Sinners

Several times in the Gospels, Jesus' enemies rebuked him for fraternizing with "sinners." While this may have included people who really were notorious sinners, the scribes and Pharisees actually used "sinners" to refer to Jews who were not as obsessive about the laws as they themselves were. By the standard of the scribes and Pharisees, Jesus himself was a "sinner." They could not imagine that salvation was available for people who did not observe the thousands of tedious regulations found in the "traditions of the elders."

choke the new plants out before they can mature. The rest of the seed fell on good soil, where it produced a crop of a hundred times what was sown. This parable was complicated enough that Jesus had to explain it to his disciples: The seed was the word of God, the message of the kingdom. Some fell along the path, but was eaten by the birds—that is, the devil. The seed on the rocky soil represents the message received by the shallow person, who does not allow it to take root in him and who will not endure in times of trouble. The seed among the thorns stands for the person who receives the word but who allows the worries of life to kill the word. The good soil, of course, stands for the person who receives the word gladly and lets it grow within him (Matthew 13:1–9, 18–23).

LOVE STORIES

Some of Jesus' best-known parables were stories driving home the point that God loves all people and wishes to save them, if they are willing. The scribes and Pharisees, who had a high opinion of their own virtue, groused about Jesus hobnobbing with "sinners," and Jesus responded with parables. God, he said, is like the farmer who has a hundred sheep in his flock. One goes astray, and the farmer leaves the ninety-nine and goes after the lost one, rejoicing at finding it and inviting his neighbors to share his joy. "There will be more rejoicing in heaven over one sinner who repents than over ninety-nine righteous persons who do not need to repent" (Luke 15:1–7). God is also like the housewife who loses one of her ten silver coins, and she searches every cranny of the house until she finds it (15:8–10).

No doubt the most famous parable of divine love and forgiveness is found in Luke 15:11–32, known as the parable of the prodigal son, although parable of the forgiving father would be more appropriate. In the familiar story, a man has two sons, and the younger asks for his share of the inheritance. The young fool proceeds to go abroad and squander it all—on what the King James Version calls "riotous living."

Finding himself in dire straits, he takes a job tending pigs—we can imagine how Jesus' Jewish listeners reacted to this part of the story!—and considers that the pigs are better fed than he is. The young man, chastened by his experience, resolves to go home and beg his father's forgiveness. He is even willing to serve his father as a hired hand. His father sees him at a distance and runs to meet him. He hugs and kisses his boy, who confesses his wrong. The father calls for suitable clothing and orders up a feast to celebrate the return. "This son of mine was dead and is alive again; he was lost and is found."

The story would be wonderful enough if it ended there, but more follows: The elder son, who had stayed home and been dutiful and obedient, hears the sound of a feast. The fatted calf has been killed to celebrate the brother's return—and the older son is angry. Why hasn't his father ever rewarded him for his good behavior? But the father won't have any jealousy. We must celebrate, he says, for the scapegrace son has learned a hard lesson and changed his ways. Like several other parables, this one has a twist ending: Instead of the prodigal son dying in poverty far from home, he turns shamefully

STORIES WORTH REMEMBERING: Beggar in Paradise

In the parable found in Luke 16:19–31, the poor beggar Lazarus lies outside the gate of a rich man who lives in luxury. Both men die, and Lazarus is carried to heaven, where he fellowships with the patriarch Abraham. The rich man has another destination: He is tormented in fire, and he looks to heaven and begs Abraham to allow Lazarus to dip his finger in water and cool his tongue. Abraham reminds the dead rich man that things are reversed: He had comforts while on earth, and now he is in torment, while for Lazarus the reverse is true. The rich man realizes there is no hope for himself now, but he begs for someone to go warn his family so that they will not meet the same fate. Abraham reminds him that they have already received ample warning—through Moses and the Prophets. The rich man pleads: if someone comes back from the dead, then they will repent. Abraham says, no, not even that would convince them.

When Jesus' disciples told the parable later, they were aware that Jesus himself had returned from the dead. In other words, he was exactly the person that the rich man had said would bring his family to repentance. But Abraham knows this would not happen. The problem was hardness of heart: The rich man had not the slightest concern for the beggar at his gates—even though Moses and the Prophets taught the necessity of caring for the poor. Someone coming back from the dead would change nothing—a man lacking in basic compassion won't be changed just because someone rose from the dead.

homeward—and becomes a more sympathetic character than the well-behaved older brother. The message to Jesus' critics was clear: Instead of criticizing me for drawing "sinners" to me, you ought to rejoice that they are turning back to God.

A twist ending wasn't the only way Jesus could make a story memorable: In one of his most loved parables, the hero is the person his listeners least expected. One of the self-righteous scribes decided to test Jesus with the question: "What must I do to inherit eternal life?" Jesus asks him what the Law says. The scribe replies that we are to love God with all our hearts and love our neighbor as ourselves. This is the perfect answer—in fact, on another occasion, Jesus told his listeners that these two commands sum up the whole Law perfectly. Jesus commends the scribe's answer, but the scribe wants some clarification: Since the Law tells us to love our neighbor, just who is my neighbor?

Jesus replied with the story of a man journeying from Jerusalem to Jericho. He fell among robbers, who beat him and left him half dead. A priest came along, saw the poor

---

CULTURAL INSIGHTS

Samaritans

If it weren't for Jesus' famous parable of the good Samaritan found in Luke 10, most people probably would never have heard of the Samaritans. In the Old Testament, the city of Samaria was the capital of the kingdom of Israel, the northern kingdom that fell to the Assyrians in 722 BC. The Assyrians settled foreigners in the land, and over time the population was notoriously "mixed," with descendants of the Israelites inter-marrying with Assyrians and other foreigners. Most were idol worshippers, although some continued to worship God. Collectively, the motley group was called Samaritans. When the Jews returned from the Babylonian exile in 539 BC and started to rebuild the temple in Jerusalem, some Samaritans offered to help—and were heartily snubbed. From this period grew the hostility between Jew and Samaritan. The Samaritans built their own temple to God on Mount Gerizim, but the Jews destroyed it, adding fuel to the hostilities. Around the year AD 7, some Samaritans desecrated the temple in Jerusalem by scattering human bones in the courts. From that time on they were banned from the temple. In the time of Jesus, hatred of Samaritans was so intense that Jews in Galilee, Jesus' home province, would take a long roundabout route to get to Judea, avoiding the shortest route, passing through Samaria. Jesus himself, as we see in his parable, was more open-minded about the Samaritans, and in the Book of Acts, many of them received the gospel.

The Samaritan religion still exists. They still worship on Mount Gerizim, the site of their former temple, and they still treasure their own version of the Torah, the Law of Moses.

The Rich Fool

Some things never change: Rich people are admired and respected. Jesus taught quite the opposite, for "a man's life does not consist in the abundance of his possessions." In one parable he spoke of a rich man who had a bumper crop—in fact, his barns weren't big enough to contain the harvest that year. So he resolved to tear down his barns and build bigger ones. Then life would be grand: He told himself the words that are part of our language—"eat, drink and be merry." But as in many parables, surprises were in store. The man got a message from God: "You fool! This very night your life will be demanded of you. Then who will get what you have prepared for yourself?" Anyone who thinks he controls the future is a fool. The man is a fool for another reason: His prosperity could have led him to share with the less fortunate, but he could only think of himself. He had told himself, "You have plenty of good things laid up for many years." We can imagine a smug smile on his face. Everything seemed perfect—but even the rich can die unexpectedly (Luke 12:13–21).

One thing that is easy to overlook is that the parable isn't just directed against the wealthy. Jesus told his listeners to "guard against all kinds of greed." Even the poor can be fixated on material things. The parable is a warning to *all* of us.

man—and passed by on the other side of the road. A Levite—one of the servants in the temple—came by and did the same thing. The third man to come by was—of all things—a Samaritan, one of the mongrel people north of Judea that the Jews despised. While the priest and Levite—ministers of God's temple—showed no compassion at all, the Samaritan went to the man and bandaged up his wounds, then took him to an inn on his donkey, where he not only paid the innkeeper to lodge the man but promised to reimburse him for any other expenses on his return trip. Given the amazing compassion of the Samaritan, we can assume the innkeeper believed he would keep his word.

Jesus posed the obvious question to the scribe: Which of the three men acted as a neighbor to the beaten man? The scribe apparently could not bring himself to say "the Samaritan," so he said, "The one who had mercy on him." Jesus replied, "Go and do likewise." Obviously the kingdom of God was open to all types of people—even a Samaritan—as long as they loved God and loved their neighbor. It is no wonder the parable of the good Samaritan is one of the best-known and best-loved stories of all time.

It is worth noting here that "love of neighbor" was not something that the ancient world—except for the Jews—understood. It understood passion for a woman, friendship for a friend, affection for family members, justice for the citizen—but not love of neighbor. The Old Testament gave the command: "Love your neighbor as yourself." It was left to Jesus and the apostles to clarify just what neighbor love was all about. The ancient world also had no concept of humility—not outside the Bible, that is.

One parable that clarifies neighbor love is found in Matthew 25. Jesus speaks of himself as the great Judge and King at the end of time, when he will separate all people as a herdsman separates his flock into sheep and goats. The "sheep," the righteous, are those who gave the king food when he was hungry, water when he was thirsty, comfort when he was sick and in prison. The sheep are puzzled: When did we do that for *you*, Lord? The King replies, "Whatever you did for one of the least of these brothers of mine, you did for me." The "goats," the unrighteous, are in the opposite situation: They neglected to aid the hungry, the thirsty, the sick—and by neglecting them, they neglected the King himself. The goats "go away to eternal punishment, but the righteous to eternal life" (25:31–46). In this beautiful—and disturbing—parable, we see the merging of love for God and love for neighbor. As the King sees it, we show our love for him by loving our neighbor—even "the least" among them. If we ignore and neglect our neighbor, we show we have no love for God.

In closing this section about the parables, we must deal with something that puzzles many readers: The Gospels make it sound like Jesus deliberately intended his parables to be incomprehensible, that only his disciples were told the true meaning of them: "He told them, 'The secret of the kingdom of God has been given to you. But to those on the outside everything is said in parables so that, "they may be ever seeing but never perceiving, and ever hearing but never understanding; otherwise they might turn and be forgiven!' " (Mark 4:11–12, quoting Isaiah 6:9–10). Surely this can't mean that Jesus did not want all people to understand and be saved. People on the outside perceived the spiritual truth in the parables, but refused to *act* upon it. They "understood" mentally, but not morally or spiritually, which meant the parables were wasted on them. "With many similar parables Jesus spoke the word to them, as much as they could understand" (Mark 4:33). It might be more accurate to say "as much as they were willing to *accept*." In God's view of things, you don't fully *understand* a truth unless you put it into practice. Remember what we said in this book's introduction: The Bible is never about someone else. It's about God speaking to you personally. Jesus did not teach about the kingdom of God to entertain people, but to save them.

Before ending this chapter, think back to Day 1, where we looked at Adam and Eve and their yielding to the temptation to be "like gods." Jesus proposed something similar: *Be like God.* Be merciful, forgiving, compassionate, loving people that do not, by our usual standards, "deserve" love. When we follow Adam and Eve and strive to be like gods, disaster happens, and we make a wreck of our lives. When we try to be like God—not as King, but as the fount of love and kindness—we enrich our own lives and the lives of everyone around us.

PUTTING THE WORD TO WORK

1. Jesus' Beatitudes speak of what brings blessedness, "success" in spiritual terms. Reread the Beatitudes—Matthew 5:3–12—and pick one to meditate on today.

2. Jesus warned that people on the side of the right would be persecuted, but that in this they would be "blessed." One meaning of this is that persecution has a way of separating true believers from the lukewarm. Think of a time in your own life when you felt you were harassed or persecuted because of your moral stand. What resulted from the harassment?

3. It is clear from the Sermon on the Mount that if we want God's forgiveness, we must forgive others. Today, think of someone you know that you have not forgiven. Make a real effort—personal contact, phone, e-mail—to let that person know you genuinely forgive them.

4. In Jesus' view of the Ten Commandments, "Do not murder" extended to "Do not hate" and "Do not call people names." If you harbor any ill feeling toward anyone, resolve to nip that hate in the bud. Stop all outward shows of hostility toward that person and (this is the hard part!) try to let go of the hostility you feel on the inside.

5. Today's lesson takes a hard look at how our religious actions are too often done for show. We can all too easily become "scribes," fussing over outward details and neglecting the larger aims of loving God and loving neighbor. Do a "true religion inventory" on yourself at the end of the day, asking yourself what you did—or didn't do—out of love for God and neighbor.

Encounters with the Master

AT THE HEART OF IT ALL TODAY

Some of the most powerful passages in the Bible show Jesus' compassionate, insightful encounters with some of the "lost" people he was sent to save. Equally powerful are his encounters with those who misunderstood or opposed him, including his own family.

You don't have to read far in the Gospels without being struck by this fact: *For Jesus, the individual soul mattered.* He taught—and modeled—not a generalized love for "mankind" or "the world," but for individual human beings. He taught his twelve disciples and crowds numbering in the thousands, yet

> **KEY PASSAGES TO READ TODAY**
>
> Mark 8:27—9:9; 10:17–31
>
> Luke 7:36–50
>
> John 4:1–42

many of his teachings focus on individuals. In the previous chapter we looked at Jesus' parables, including one in which a shepherd with a large flock of sheep went looking for the one who was lost (Luke 15:1–7). God rejoices over the return of one lost soul just as the shepherd rejoiced over finding the lost sheep. Likewise the famous parable of the prodigal son shows the father (God) tearfully rejoicing over the son's return. Today we will focus not on the parables but on Jesus' actual encounters with individuals, most of them resulting in an entirely new life for the people he encountered. We will also look at his encounters with people who misunderstood him—including his closest disciples, his own family and the spiritual leaders of his own religion.

THE WOMAN WITH A PAST

We have already looked at Jesus' famous parable of the good Samaritan, a story known around the world for its depiction of compassion that breaks down barriers of ethnicity

---

KEY TERM FOR TODAY ## Salvation

The Greek word *sozo*, "to save," is used often in the New Testament to refer to deliverance from illness, demon possession and other trials. But the word *soteria*, "salvation," never refers to physical healing, political liberation or release from demonic powers. Salvation means being brought into a right relationship with God—spiritual healing, being released from sin and selfishness and inner brokenness. Jesus is the *soter*, the Savior of all who accept the offer of salvation.

and race. Being the best type of teacher, Jesus proved by his own actions that God loved the Samaritans and desired their salvation as much as he loved the Jews, in spite of the age-old hostility between Samaritan and Jew.

Jesus and his disciples had been ministering in Judea for a time but decided to return to Galilee, their home territory. Samaria lay in between the two regions, and devout Jews often took a long round-about route to avoid passing through the region. Recall from earlier chapters that the hostility went back centuries, to the time after the Babylonian exile, when the Jewish exiles returned to rebuild the temple in Jerusalem. They were offered aid by the Samaritans, the Israelites who had remained in the land north of Judea and in many cases intermarried with the Assyrians who conquered them. The Jews snubbed the Samaritans and their offer—and, much later, destroyed a rival temple that the Samaritans had built. The grudge ran deep, and neither group considered the other to be true children of God.

But on this occasion—no doubt at Jesus' insistence—the disciples did pass through Samaria, through a town called Sychar, "near the plot of ground Jacob had given to his son Joseph" (John 4:5)—an interesting detail that reminds the reader that the region had historic associations with Jacob, the ancestor of the Israelites. In fact, Jesus went for a drink of water at "Jacob's well," where he saw a Samaritan woman who had come to draw water. Jesus asked her for a drink, and the woman responded, "You are a Jew and I am a Samaritan woman. How can you ask me for a drink?" We aren't told how she recognized that he was a Jew—his accent, perhaps? However it was that she knew he was a Jew, she was certainly surprised he would ask her for water—or would even speak to her at all. If she had some sort of dipper with her for drinking, she would have known that no Jew would have drunk from it.

Jesus' next words must have surprised her even more: "If you knew the gift of God and who it is that asks you for a drink, you would have asked him and he would have given you living water" (John 4:10). There was a double meaning in Jesus' words: "living" meant fresh, flowing water—as opposed to stagnant. But clearly Jesus intended a spiritual meaning as well. The woman was, it seems, somewhat literal-minded, for she wondered how he could draw this

43 BC–AD 18
Ovid, Roman poet

27 BC–AD 180
The Pax Romana, years of relative peace in the Roman empire

c. 6 BC
Birth of Jesus in Bethlehem

4 BC
Death of Herod the Great

c. 3 BC
Beginnings of the Zealot sect of anti-Roman Jews

AD 5
The Roman legions defeat Lombard tribes that have established themselves on the lower Elbe River.

AD 6
Judea placed under direct Roman rule.

AD 14–37
Reign of Roman Emperor Tiberius

AD 18
Caiaphas becomes high priest of the Jews.

AD 26–36
Pontius Pilate is Roman governor of Judea.

c. AD 27–28
Ministry of John the Baptist; baptism of Jesus and beginning of his ministry
(Matthew 3, Mark 1, Luke 3, John 1:6–35)

AD 29
Execution of
John the Baptist
(Matthew 14:3)

AD 30
Death and
resurrection of Jesus
(Matthew 27–28,
Mark 15–16, Luke
23–24, John 18–21)

living water, since he had nothing to draw with and the well was deep. She also mentioned "our father Jacob, who gave us the well and drank from it himself." In saying "our father Jacob," she was reminding Jesus that the Samaritans as well as the Jews traced their ancestry to the patriarch Jacob.

Jesus told her that whoever drank the well's water would be thirsty again—but that Jesus knew of "a spring of water welling up to eternal life." Being a practical woman, she asked him for this eternal water—which would save her the trouble of walking to the well every day! Jesus' next words must have caught her off guard: "Go, call your husband and come back." She replied, "I have no husband." Jesus saw that she was telling the truth—but not quite the whole truth: "You are right when you say you have no husband. The fact is, you have had five husbands, and the man you now have is not your husband" (John 4:16–18).

This woman with a rather sordid domestic history did what many of us would do in such a situation: She tried to change the subject. "Sir, I can see you are a prophet. Our fathers worshipped on this mountain, but you Jews claim that the place where we must worship is in Jerusalem." She was speaking of Mount Gerizim, where the Samaritans had their own temple to God—a temple that the Jews did not believe was legitimate, since the only true temple of God was in Jerusalem. Jesus told her that a time was coming when all the true worshippers of God would worship on neither mountain, but would worship "in spirit and in truth." Location would not matter, and neither would one's ethnic identity.

The woman replied that she believed that when the Messiah, the Christ, came, he would explain all these things. We can imagine her astonishment when Jesus said, "I who speak to you am he" (John 4:26).

At this point the disciples, who had gone to buy food, "returned and were surprised to find him talking with a woman." By the standards of the time, a man alone did not engage in conversation with an unescorted woman. But the Son of God was walking the earth, and barriers were being broken down. Jesus was talking not only with a woman, but also a woman with a past.

Forgetting her errand of fetching water, the woman left her jar at the well and went into the town, where she told the people, "Come, see a man who told me everything I ever did. Could this be the Christ?" In her excitement, she was exaggerating—he did not tell her "everything she ever did." But he saw through her, saw the kind of life she had led, yet he did not snub her for being an immoral woman—or for simply being a woman. She had three strikes against her—a Samaritan, a woman and several times married. Yet Jesus revealed himself to her as the Messiah and promised that a time was coming when the hostility between Samaritans and Jews would no longer matter. The woman became a convert—and so did others in the town, because of what she told them.

"When the Samaritans came to him, they urged him to stay with them, and he stayed two days." It is unfortunate that John's Gospel does not record what else happened during Jesus' sojourn in Samaria. Whatever he taught them, it led to many more Samaritans becoming believers (John 4:39–42). He had proven that he was not just the Messiah for the Jews, but even for the Samaritans.

We should be thankful for this beautiful story of what transpired between the righteous Son of God and the woman at the well, the woman with a past. Meeting the Master changed her life forever.

PERFECTLY LOST

We turn now from the story of a woman of a despised ethnic group, a woman with an irregular marital history, to someone quite the opposite: a "golden boy," a young, wealthy Jewish man with no stains on his record at all. The Samaritan woman might have seemed like the classic "lost" person that needed salvation. But this young man seemed in need of nothing at all. He was a man with a bright future. But Jesus had a way of seeing beyond the obvious.

"As Jesus started on his way, a man ran up to him and fell on his knees before him. 'Good teacher,' he asked, 'what must I do to inherit eternal life?'" Jesus' answer somewhat surprises us: "Why do you call me good?... No one is good—except God alone." This was a point of etiquette. The Jews referred to a respected teacher as "rabbi" or "master," but without adding "good" to the name, since all the rabbis taught that God alone was good. The man may have been intending to flatter Jesus. At any rate, Jesus did answer his question: "You know the commandments: 'Do not murder, do not commit adultery, do not steal, do not give false testimony, do not defraud, honor your father and mother.'" The man replied, "All these I have kept since I was a boy."

Matthew's version of the story adds the detail that the man was young. Luke's version describes him as a "ruler"—probably not meaning that he held any kind of political office, but that he was of the local elite, the ruling class. Mark's version adds this interesting detail: "Jesus looked at him and loved him." Apparently there was something appealing about the earnest fellow, perhaps the mere fact that a young man of the ruling class was the last person we would expect to be interested in eternal life.

Though he loved the man, Jesus' words hit him like a sledgehammer: "One thing you lack…Go, sell everything you have and give to the poor, and you will have treasure in heaven. Then come, follow me." The young man's face fell. "He went away sad, because he had great wealth" (Mark 10:17–22).

This brief interchange had not occurred in private but in full view of Jesus' disciples. Jesus took it as an opportunity to teach: "How hard it is for the rich to enter the kingdom of God!… It is easier for a camel to go through the eye of a needle than for a rich man to enter the kingdom of God." The disciples were amazed. Weren't the rich people the ones who were especially blessed by God? The disciples asked him, "Who then can be saved?" Note that they did not ask, "How can the rich be saved?" Their question "Who then can be saved?" suggested exasperation. If the rich, with all their advantages in life, can't be saved, who can? Jesus looked at them and said, "With man this is impossible, but not with God; all things are possible with God" (Mark 10:23–27).

Jesus' demand to the rich young man has puzzled readers for centuries. He asked the man to sell *everything he had* and give it to the poor—then follow Jesus. Did Jesus intend that every follower had to give away all he had in order to have eternal life? Over the centuries, some have interpreted the passage that way—and done what Jesus asked. These are rare individuals. Most of us can't, or won't, do something so drastic. The main point of the encounter seems to be this: the young man seemed to think of salvation as something that could be *earned*. One of the clear messages of the New Testament is that it cannot be. It is impossible on our own—but God makes it possible.

However faithful the young man had been in keeping the Jewish commandments —something that Jesus found lovable—his wealth was an obstacle between him and salvation.

The young man was not willing to follow Jesus. But others had made that radical choice: "Peter said to him, 'We have left everything to follow you!' " Jesus assured the disciples that those who had given up the comforts of home and family for the sake of the gospel—and endured persecutions—would surely inherit eternal life. "But many who are first will be last, and the last first" (Mark 10:31). The world's values are radically different from God's.

It is worth pausing here to note that in ancient times the Jews were almost alone in showing concern for the poor. Among the Gentiles, old or sick slaves were thrown out to die in the street, and many people thought that feeding them or giving them money only prolonged their wretched existence. Poverty and riches were both decreed by the gods, or fate, and there was no point in the "haves" feeling any obligation to the "have-nots." Many people agreed with the Roman historian Tacitus that human life was only one great farce—or, more accurately, tragedy. The people with money and possessions had their comforts (in this life, anyway), but the poor were worthy only of contempt. Yet the Jewish Scriptures made it clear that God had a special concern for the poor and that faithful Jews were commanded to respect the poor and aid them whenever possible. However, Jesus' disciples' reaction to his words about the difficulty of a rich man finding eternal life shows us that even among the Jews, the belief that the rich were especially favored by God was strong.

We end this section with a brief story found in three of the Gospels: While in the temple, Jesus saw the rich putting their large gifts of money into the offering box—while a poor widow put in two small copper coins. "This poor widow has put in more than all the others. All these people gave their gifts out of their wealth; but she out of her poverty put in all she had to live on" (Luke 21:1–4). The rich gave much more—but also had much more left for themselves. The widow gave a little—but had almost nothing left for herself. What counts with God is not the size of the gift but the size of the heart that gives it.

THE JOHN 3:16 ENCOUNTER

The rich young man who would not follow Jesus was a case of a person who encountered Jesus but did not profit from the meeting. A more life-changing encounter is found in John 3, one of the great chapters of the Bible, which contains some of its most-quoted verses. It involved another "golden boy," a Pharisee named Nicodemus, who was also a member of the Sanhedrin, the Jews' ruling council. He came to see Jesus at night—a sign that he did not wish to be seen one-on-one with the teacher from Nazareth, which is not surprising, given the contempt that so many of the Pharisees showed to Jesus. But Nicodemus was an admirer, as we see in his first words to Jesus: "Rabbi, we know you are a teacher who has come from God. For no one could perform the miraculous signs you are doing if God were not with him."

In reply Jesus declared, "I tell you the truth, no one can see the kingdom of God unless he is born again." Jesus' words here can mean both "born again" and "born from above." But either way, Nicodemus did not understand: "How can a man be born when he is old?... Surely he cannot enter a second time into his mother's womb to be born!" Jesus had to explain himself: Being part of God's kingdom required a spiritual rebirth. We were born once in the flesh. What saves us is the second birth, the spiritual one. "How can this be?" Nicodemus asked. "You are Israel's teacher," said Jesus, "and do you not understand these things?" Nicodemus was both a Pharisee and a member of the Sanhedrin —he was "Israel's teacher," yet so slow to grasp spiritual realities.

Nicodemus had begun the conversation by stating that he believed that Jesus' miracles proved that he had been sent by God. When he sought Jesus out by night, he had no clue

Only Begotten Son

One of the most difficult Greek words to translate is found in the often-quoted John 3:16, in which Jesus refers to himself as God's "only begotten Son," as the King James Version has it. The Greek word here is *monogenes*, which meant both "only" and "beloved" when referring to a child. In normal conversation, it was used to refer to what we would call an "only child." In terms of Christian theology, the word is appropriate, because Jesus was God's "only child" in a unique sense. The New Testament teaches that all believers are God's sons and daughters, but Jesus is clearly different, the unique and divine Son of God in a way that we are not. So how do we translate *monogenes* the right way? The King James Version uses "only begotten"—the idea being that God the Father "begat" Jesus as Son, but most modern readers don't grasp the meaning of "begotten," so contemporary translations have "one and only" Son or "only" Son or even "unique" Son. None of these quite catch the nuance of *monogenes*, a term that John uses not only in 3:16, but also in 1:14—"We have seen his glory, the glory of the One and Only, who came from the Father"—and 1:18—"No one has ever seen God, but God the One and Only, who is at the Father's side, has made him known." It is also found in 1 John 4:9: "This is how God showed his love among us: He sent his one and only Son into the world that we might live through him."

he was seeking an audience with the Son of God himself. We have to wonder how he reacted to these words of Jesus: "God so loved the world that he gave his one and only Son, that whoever believes in him shall not perish but have eternal life. For God did not send his Son into the world to condemn the world, but to save the world through him."

The Gospel does not tell us Nicodemus' response at that encounter. We learn later that when some of the other Pharisees were discussing Jesus and how they might trap him, Nicodemus protested and noted that the Jews' law did not allow for condemning a man without a hearing. Apparently he was not ready at that point to identify himself as a follower of Jesus—only to remind his fellow Pharisees that it was wrong to condemn without investigating the matter (John 7:45–52).

The last mention of Nicodemus is in connection with the burial of Jesus. He went with Joseph of Arimathea—"a disciple of Jesus, but secretly because he feared the Jews"—to give Jesus a proper burial with several pounds of spices (John 19:38–40). Clearly the night-time encounter with Jesus had produced some sort of spiritual fruit in Nicodemus. Could he have been the first person to experience that second birth that Jesus told him was necessary?

A PUZZLED FAMILY

In an earlier chapter we saw that when Jesus returned to his hometown of Nazareth, most of the people rejected him as a prophet, and he did few miracles there because of lack of faith in him (Mark 6:1–6). To the locals of Nazareth he was merely "the carpenter." Sadly, Jesus was misunderstood not only by the people of his hometown but also by his own family. "Only in his hometown, among his relatives and in his own house is a prophet without honor."

In the Gospels, there is an episode involving the adult Jesus and his family. After Jesus had begun his public ministry and chosen his twelve disciples, he began to draw crowds. On one occasion he and his disciples were invited to a meal at a house but were not able to eat, so thick was the crowd that followed them. "When his family heard about this, they went to take charge of him, for they said, 'He is out of his mind' " (Mark 3:21). Later, family members including his mother arrived at the house and sent someone inside to tell him, "Your mother and brothers are outside looking for you." Jesus posed a rhetorical question: "Who are my mother and my brothers?" Looking at those seated around him, he said, "Here are my mother and my brothers! Whoever does God's will is my brother and sister and mother" (Mark 3:31–35).

Was Jesus rejecting his own family? Of course not. But it is clear from the first reaction cited in Mark that some members of his family neither understood nor approved what Jesus was doing. This could be one of the reasons that Jesus' "base" during his itinerant ministry was not Nazareth but Capernaum. Jesus was a man with a divine mission, doing the will of his Father, and he could not be restrained by the tug of family members trying to make him lead a normal, settled life. As Jesus made clear, the spiritual family—people united in the common purpose of doing God's will—is more important than the biological family. These words must have been remembered often by the first Christians, who found themselves misunderstood or even ostracized by their blood families.

While it is somewhat unsettling to read of this episode, we learn later, in the Book of Acts, that Jesus' mother and brothers were named among the believers (1:14), and his brother James became one of the key leaders among the Christians in Jerusalem (15:13). Clearly at some point they had discovered that far from being "out of his mind," he was the Messiah and Son of God.

We need to pause here to mention the different interpretations of the word "brothers" in referring to Jesus' relatives. While some Bible scholars believe these "brothers" were sons of Mary and Joseph, other scholars note that "brothers" (the Greek word *adelphoi*) could also refer to Jesus' cousins or to other male relatives that are not siblings.

SINNERS AND PHARISEES

Throughout the Gospels, Jesus and the disciples had numerous encounters with the Pharisees—most of them hostile. Usually the Gospels simply refer to "the Pharisees" collectively, but on a few occasions, such as with Nicodemus, Jesus engaged in dialogue with an individual Pharisee. Another such occasion was at the home of a Pharisee named Simon, who had invited Jesus and the disciples to dine at his home—surely a sign that he was more receptive to Jesus' message than many of his fellow Pharisees were. But at the dinner, an unexpected event occurred.

"When a woman who had lived a sinful life in that town learned that Jesus was eating at the Pharisee's house, she brought an alabaster jar of perfume, and as she stood behind him at his feet weeping, she began to wet his feet with her tears. Then she wiped them with her hair, kissed them and poured perfume on them" (Luke 7:37–38). We aren't told what constituted her "sinful life," although the usual assumption is that she had been a prostitute or an adulteress. Whatever she was, her presence and her action did not please Simon the Pharisee, who thought to himself that if Jesus had been a true prophet of God, he would not have wanted this sinful woman making such a display of emotion. Jesus understood Simon's thoughts, and he responded to them with a parable.

"Two men owed money to a certain moneylender. One owed him five hundred denarii, and the other fifty. Neither of them had the money to pay him back, so he canceled the debts of both. Now which of them will love him more?" Simon replied, "I suppose the one who had the bigger debt canceled." "You have judged correctly," Jesus said (Luke 7:43). Since Simon did not seem to see how the parable applied to what the sinful woman had done, Jesus had to explain: a person who has been forgiven much will love much, while the person who has been forgiven little will love little. The people known to be sinners were more grateful to God for his mercy than were people like the Pharisees, who thought of themselves as almost sinless. The woman knew her own heart, and approached Jesus with humility, sorrow and an emotionally overwhelming respect. Jesus pointed out to Simon that when he entered Simon's home, he did not greet him with a kiss—the usual greeting for a respected guest. The sinful woman seemed richer in genuine human feeling than the socially respectable Pharisee.

Jesus told the woman her sins were forgiven. "Your faith has saved you. Go in peace" (Luke 7:50). Luke does not tell us her name or the name of the town where this took place. Her spontaneous act of love and devotion, and Jesus' response to her, are the important elements in the story. The unnamed woman is the prototype for all of us, showing our love for God when we are most conscious of our own sins and his willingness to forgive.

On another occasion, Jesus told the self-righteous religious people that "the tax collectors and the prostitutes are entering the kingdom of God ahead of you" (Matthew 21:31). Indeed, he had a tax collector (Matthew) among his own disciples, and another tax collector named Zacchaeus had a life-changing encounter with Jesus. But perhaps the most famous tax collector in the Gospels is found in the parable Jesus directed at "some who were confident of their own righteousness and looked down on everybody else." Two men, a Pharisee and a tax collector, went to the temple to pray. The Pharisee expressed gratitude for God—because "I am not like other men," robbers, adulterers, "even like this tax collector." The Pharisee reminded God of his good behavior: He tithed and fasted twice a week. The tax collector's prayer was quite different: He beat his breast and said, "God, have mercy on me, a sinner." It was the tax collector, not the Pharisee, who "went home justified before God." The interesting thing about the Pharisee's prayer is that God is not important at all: The Pharisee's attention is focused on himself, a fine

Zacchaeus the Tax Collector

Tax collectors have never been popular people, and the New Testament makes it clear that Jews who collected taxes for the Romans were intensely despised by their fellow Jews. Jesus had a tax collector (Matthew) among his twelve disciples, which was surely a sign that even these hated people were not beyond the reach of God's love. Luke 19 contains the touching story of a man named Zacchaeus—not merely a tax collector, but a chief tax collector, which probably meant he was head over the local collectors, and no doubt wealthier and even more despised.

Jesus was passing through the ancient town of Jericho, and Zacchaeus wanted to see him. Perhaps he had heard that the great teacher from Nazareth had a tax collector among his own disciples. Zacchaeus was short—"a wee little man," as the familiar Sunday school song has it—and could not see Jesus for the crowd, so he climbed a sycamore tree to get a look. The sight of this wealthy, and hated, man clambering up a tree must have amused the townspeople. Jesus, spotting him, said, "Zacchaeus, come down immediately, I must stay at your house today." Zacchaeus "welcomed him gladly."

The locals were not so pleased, and began muttering about Jesus being the guest of a sinner. But Zacchaeus was so overjoyed at Jesus being his guest that he promised to give half his possessions to the poor—and to pay back anyone he had cheated.

Jesus announced that salvation had come to Zacchaeus' house. "The Son of Man came to seek and to save what was lost."

specimen of mankind, especially when he contrasts himself with others. The Pharisee does not really need God at all—he has saved himself (so he thinks) by his own good behavior. But the tax collector is aware of his own sins—and God's holiness, because when he prayed, "he would not even look up to heaven." He knows he needs God. Jesus concluded the parable with words echoed many other times in his teachings: "Everyone who exalts himself will be humbled, and he who humbles himself will be exalted" (Luke 14:11).

Jesus' dinner at the home of Simon was not the only time he was invited to a Pharisee's home. In fact, despite Jesus' harsh words about the Pharisees, the Gospels never show him declining an invitation to be their guest. He knew part of his mission was to reach out to these people who had a high opinion of their own righteousness. Luke 14 tells of an invitation from an unnamed Pharisee, but this time an ulterior motive is mentioned: "He was being carefully watched." A man suffering from dropsy (accumulation of fluid in the body) was present. It was the Sabbath, and by Jewish law—as the Pharisees interpreted it—no healing could be done on the Sabbath, for healing constituted work. As on other Sabbath occasions, Jesus healed the man anyway. Sensing the Pharisees' disapproval of what he had done, he asked them if they would not rescue their own donkey or ox that had fallen into a well on the Sabbath. And weren't human beings of far more value than livestock? (Luke 14:1–6).

Luke records another occasion of Jesus dining with a Pharisee. To the Pharisee's surprise, Jesus did not wash his hands before eating. All the Pharisees took cleanliness with the utmost seriousness, washing their hands many times each day. Jesus did not take issue with cleanliness itself but with the Pharisees' priorities. Outward cleanliness counted for something, but inner cleanliness was the important thing. Jesus must have jarred his host when he said, "You Pharisees clean the outside of the cup and dish, but inside you are full of greed and wickedness" (Luke 11:39). Jesus made it clear that "nothing outside a man can make him 'unclean' by going into him. Rather, it is what comes out of a man that makes him 'unclean.'… For from within, out of men's hearts, come evil

STORIES WORTH REMEMBERING

Martha and Mary

John's Gospel records the awesome miracle of Jesus raising his friend Lazarus, brother of Martha and Mary, from the tomb. Luke's Gospel records an earlier story of that friendship, where in a certain village "a woman named Martha opened her home to Jesus." Martha was what we would call a gracious hostess, but "she had a sister called Mary, who sat at the Lord's feet listening to what he said." Martha was "distracted by all the preparations that had to be made," which is not surprising, given that food preparation in ancient times was much more time-consuming than now (grinding out flour and making one's own bread, just to name one example). Martha was exasperated enough that she went to Jesus and said, "Lord, don't you care that my sister has left me to do the work by myself? Tell her to help me!" Jesus was not lacking in sympathy, but in his eyes, Martha's priorities were not right. She was, he told her, "worried and upset about many things, but only one thing is needed. Mary has chosen what is better, and it will not be taken away from her" (Luke 10:38–42). Mary was not being lazy or negligent of her duties. She was focusing her mind on an amazing man, whose presence was gracing their home. Martha must have been working to spread an elaborate table for Jesus—which is what is suggested by "distracted by all the preparations." She wanted everything to be "just right" for the guests, especially the guest of honor. Mary had chosen "what is better"—giving her divine guest her undivided attention and devotion.

thoughts, sexual immorality, theft, murder, adultery, greed, malice, deceit, lewdness, envy, slander, arrogance and folly. All these evils come from inside and make a man 'unclean' " (Mark 7:14–23).

Jesus, who had no fear of "soiling" himself by associating with sinful people, was well aware of the Pharisees' obsession with washing their hands and dishes. They were especially concerned to wash their hands after leaving the marketplace (Mark 7:3–4). Their concern with outward purity made them avoid the common people—whom they considered "cursed"—as much as possible and to do business only with their own kind, people fussy about cleanliness. But Jesus made it clear he had come to save these "unclean" people that the Pharisees held in contempt.

O FOOLISH DISCIPLES!

One reason we can trust the Gospels' historical reliability is that they do not sugarcoat Jesus' disciples. These twelve men, with him constantly, were also constantly misunderstanding his purpose and his teachings. This was even true of the three disciples closest to Jesus, the "inner circle" of Peter, James and John.

On one occasion, John told his Master, "we saw a man driving out demons in your name and we tried to stop him, because he is not one of us." "Do not stop him," Jesus said, "for whoever is not against you is for you." Later, a Samaritan village did not welcome Jesus, so the brothers James and John asked Jesus, "Lord, do you want us to call fire down from heaven to destroy them?" Jesus rebuked them (Luke 9:49–56). The two brothers apparently deserved the nickname "sons of thunder" that Jesus bestowed on them (Mark 3:17), but at times their zeal was misguided.

At other times they could show they understood the true nature of the Master they followed. In the region of Caesarea Philippi, Jesus asked the disciples, "Who do people say I am?" They replied, "Some say John the Baptist; others say Elijah; and still others, one of the prophets." Jesus' public had, it seems, recognized him as a prophet. "But what about you?" Jesus asked. "Who do you say I am?"

Peter's answer is one of the great moments in the Bible: "You are the Christ" (Mark 8:29). After so many days with the man from Nazareth, Peter had discerned the deep truth: His master was a prophet, a teacher, a healer—but more than that, he was the Christ, the Messiah the Jews had long expected. This much Peter grasped—but he would learn that Jesus was not the kind of Messiah they had all expected. Jesus began to teach them that he "must suffer many things and be rejected by the elders, chief priests and teachers of the law, and that he must be killed and after three days rise again." *A suffering and dying Messiah?* Surely not! Peter took Jesus aside to rebuke him, but was rebuked himself, for Jesus told him, "You do not have in mind the things of God, but the things of men." Yes, Jesus was the Christ, but not the kind the people had long expected—not a king or military leader who would drive out the Romans, but a man who would give up his life. Here was the deep truth that the disciples would be slow to accept: "If anyone would come after me, he must deny himself and take up his cross and follow me. For whoever wants to save his life will lose it, but whoever loses his life for me and for the gospel will save it" (Mark 8:27–35).

This episode—known as "Peter's confession" because he was the first of Jesus' followers to identify him as the Christ—is followed by the curious, mysterious incident called the Transfiguration. Jesus took Peter, James and John with him to a high mountain. There he was transfigured before them. His face shone like the sun, and his clothes became as white as the light. Just then there appeared before him Moses and Elijah, talking with him. For the Jews, Moses represented the divine Law, and Elijah repre-

STORIES WORTH REMEMBERING
The Adulterous Woman

Jesus' enemies decided to test whether he was the righteous man that people said he was. While he was teaching in the temple courts in Jerusalem, some of the scribes and Pharisees brought in a woman they had caught in adultery. The meaning here is clear: she was not just rumored to be an adulteress, but *caught in the act*, so there was no question of her guilt. The scribes and Pharisees reminded Jesus that the Jewish law mandated stoning for this offense. "Now what do you say?"

Jesus stooped down and wrote on the ground—we aren't told why, or what he wrote. But finally he stood up and said, "If any one of you is without sin, let him be the first to throw a stone at her."

The accusers went away, one by one. We can well imagine the emotional state of the woman at this moment. Jesus asked her, "Has no one condemned you?" She replied, "No one, sir."

Jesus' reply was beautiful and for every generation: "Then neither do I condemn you. Go now and leave your life of sin" (John 8:1–11).

The story is often quoted today as an illustration of Jesus' compassion and forgiveness. It is that, definitely, but the real point of the story is "leave your life of sin." The woman was a sinner, deserving punishment—but she was released. The compassionate judge had given her a second chance. That possibility is offered to us all.

sented the prophets. Both these departed saints had been persecuted in their lifetimes, and, given Jesus' earlier words prophesying his own death, the three men were discussing the suffering that Jesus was soon to endure. The voice of God spoke and said, "This is my Son, whom I love; with him I am well pleased. Listen to him!" The three disciples were so terrified they fell facedown on the ground. When they looked again, they were alone with Jesus (Matthew 17:1–8).

What was the meaning of it all? Jesus had prophesied his coming death—something the disciples had trouble accepting. But then the voice of God himself approved of his Son, and the presence of Moses and Elijah was a reminder to the disciples that God's holy men are persecuted. The Transfiguration was a brief glimpse of divine glory for Jesus and his three closest followers before Jesus met his destiny in Jerusalem.

Later, on the way to Jerusalem, James and John showed they still did not grasp what was about to happen to their Master. The two brothers asked him a favor: "Let one of us sit at your right and the other at your left in your glory." Jesus asked them if they were able to drink the cup of suffering that he was about to drink. "We can," they answered. Jesus prophesied that someday they would. But the other disciples became indignant with James and John—understandably so! Jesus scolded them all. It was normal human practice to jockey for position in any group—but his followers had to be different: "Whoever wants to become great among you must be your servant, and whoever wants to be first must be slave of all." He would show them how by his own example. "For even the Son of Man did not come to be served, but to serve, and to give his life as a ransom for many" (Mark 10:35–45).

WHAT WAS THE "SON OF MAN"?

We conclude this chapter with a closer look at a phrase that has been used several times already, "Son of Man." This was the name Jesus used for himself—in fact, it almost never occurs in the New Testament except on Jesus' own lips. Preachers and writers often explain it by saying that it emphasized Jesus' human nature, while "Son of God" (a phrase he himself never used) emphasized his divine nature. This explanation is reasonable enough, but it does not go to the heart of Jesus' real meaning.

In Hebrew and Aramaic speech, "son of man" was simply another way of saying "human being." This is the way it was used often in the Book of Ezekiel, where God often referred to the prophet as "son of man," meaning "mortal" or "human being." Every person on earth is a *ben-adam*, a "son of man." But why did Jesus use the name for himself? For one thing, he was identifying with all human beings. He understood himself to be God's unique Son, the Messiah, the Savior—yet chose to call himself by a phrase that meant only "human being." He was willing to identify himself as one of us rather than demand—or even encourage—people to call him by some lofty title.

Daniel's "Son of Man"

The Jews of Jesus' time were familiar with the Book of Daniel and its vision of "one like a son of man, coming with the clouds of heaven," who was given authority by God to rule over an everlasting kingdom (Daniel 7:13–14). People have long accepted this as a prophecy of Christ, which it certainly was. Daniel was reporting a vision of four evil worldly kingdoms, symbolized by four beasts. The everlasting kingdom of the saints is symbolized by "one like a son of man"—in other words, a human being, in contrast to the beasts that symbolized the kingdoms of this world. What Daniel foresaw was an eternal kingdom, a kingdom of people as God intended them to be, not the tyrannical, oppressive kingdoms of history, rightly symbolized by beasts.

Throughout the Gospels we see him constantly urging people to keep his divine nature a secret. He is the Son of God who came to us as the Son of Man.

One person who understood what Jesus meant by "Son of Man" was the apostle Paul, whom we will study later. Paul saw Christ as the second Adam. The first Adam, the "prototype" for the human race, disobeyed God and lost paradise. The second Adam, Christ, obeyed God and regained paradise (Romans 5:12–19). The second Adam was what God intended human beings to be. In a sense, "son of man" is what all religions are about. Every religion is based on the assumption that people are not all that they should be. Jesus is the model of "the man" as God intended. In Genesis, God created man "in the image of God," but this image was marred through Adam's disobedience. Looking at Jesus, we see what the image of God in man was intended to be. Adam and Eve had given in to the serpent's temptation to "be like gods," while Jesus told his disciples that if they wished to be great, they would need to be *servants*. True greatness is in giving, not taking.

In this chapter, and in the previous chapters dealing with Jesus as teacher and healer, we have seen him exemplifying the role of servant, not standing aloof from humankind but entering into it fully, not afraid to rub shoulders with lepers and prostitutes and tax collectors. All his actions supported his compassionate words: "Are not two sparrows sold for a penny? Yet not one of them will fall to the ground apart from the will of your Father. And even the very hairs of your head are all numbered. So don't be afraid; you are worth more than many sparrows" (Matthew 10:29–31). The Son of Man made an awesome offer to his followers: "Come to me, all you who are weary and burdened, and I will give you rest. Take my yoke upon you and learn from me, for I am gentle and humble in heart, and you will find rest for your souls. For my yoke is easy and my burden is light" (Matthew 11:28–30).

PUTTING THE WORD TO WORK

1. In the story of Jesus meeting the Samaritan woman at the well, a racial and ethnic gap was bridged. What are some occasions in your own life when a chance meeting gave you an opportunity to reach out to a fellow human being outside your own group?

2. Jesus' encounter with the rich young man who would not follow him is a sad example of someone's material possessions keeping him apart from God. Think of people you have known who followed that pattern—but also think of others who were able to lead a life of faith even while living a life of affluence.

3. The Pharisees represent the human desire to equate cleanliness with moral purity. Stop and consider whether you have been tempted to make this equation, and give some thought to Jesus' strong words about inner cleanliness.

4. Reflect on the story of Jesus being misunderstood by his own earthly family. Have you known people of deep faith who were misunderstood or ostracized by family members? Were they successful in finding a place within a "spiritual family"?

5. Reflect on Jesus' use of the title "Son of Man" for himself. How do you think his disciples reacted to his constantly referring to himself by this name?

Passion, Despair, Triumph

AT THE HEART OF IT ALL TODAY The events of Holy Week—Jesus' triumphal entry into Jerusalem, his confrontations with the religious authorities, his betrayal and abandonment by his followers, his arrest and trial, his mocking and crucifixion, and his resurrection—are the very core of the New Testament, demonstrating God's power to bring triumph out of suffering.

In the previous chapter, we saw Jesus' disciples declaring that he was the Christ, the Messiah that the Jews had long expected and prayed for. But we also saw Jesus taking pains to explain to the disciples that in the days ahead he would suffer greatly, falling into the hands of the leaders of his own religion, and would be executed. It would soon become clear that the twelve disciples—and the many other people who admired Jesus—could not accept a suffering Christ.

> **KEY PASSAGES TO READ TODAY**
>
> Mark 11:1–19; 12:13–17;
> 14:32–42; 15:1–47
> John 20

THE LORD IN HIS TEMPLE

Jesus and the twelve headed for Jerusalem to celebrate Passover. We see in the Gospels that the band had made previous visits to the city, going there as faithful Jews to observe the Jewish holy days. Passover was unique among the Jewish feasts, since it commemorated the key event of the Old Testament, the liberation of the Israelite slaves from Egypt. It was not only a religious festival, but also a festival of freedom, and the many Jews who hated being dominated by the Roman Empire could not help but hope for a second Passover, freeing them from their political bondage. The Romans were aware of this, and the Roman governor, who normally resided in the port city of Caesarea, stayed

KEY TERM FOR TODAY ## Glory

Jesus endured opposition, abandonment, condemnation, unspeakable physical suffering and death—all as a prelude to a glorified life following his resurrection. "Did not the Christ have to suffer these things and then enter his glory?" (Luke 24:26). This is a key theme of the New Testament: God is greater than whatever tribulations people endure, and the way of suffering leads to glory.

in Jerusalem at the time of Passover, his soldiers keeping a watchful eye on the thousands of Jewish pilgrims who thronged the city. Any Passover would have been a likely time for the Jewish freedom fighters, the Zealots, to attempt some violence against the Romans.

One event that may have escaped the Romans' notice completely was the entry of a humble teacher from Nazareth, who was in the company of twelve followers. A few miles outside Jerusalem, Jesus sent two of his disciples into a village to fetch a young donkey. The disciples took their cloaks and made a sort of saddle for their master, and Jesus rode the donkey into Jerusalem. The teacher from Nazareth had quite a following among the common people, and the ride into Jerusalem turned into a sort of triumphal parade, with people laying their cloaks and palm branches along the path, calling out "Hosanna to the Son of David!" and "Blessed is the king who comes in the name of the Lord!" (Luke 19:38). The "king" was, of course, seated on a little donkey—hardly the picture of a mighty king! But the crowds probably shared the hope of Jesus' own disciples—that he would at some point drop his guise as a peaceful, gentle carpenter and reveal himself to be the political liberator they had hoped for. When their hopes were dashed, they would prove to be fickle in their loyalties, as crowds often are.

What followed the entry into Jerusalem may have intensified their hopes for this kind of Messiah. As expected, Jesus made his way to the temple. What was not expected was the one violent act he ever committed. "Jesus entered the temple area and drove out all who were buying and selling there. He overturned the tables of the money-changers and the benches of those selling doves. 'It is written,' he said to them, 'My house will be called a house of prayer, but you are making it a den of robbers' " (Matthew 21:12–13).

Some words of explanation are in order. Every Jew had to pay an annual temple tax, one half-shekel, and it had to be paid in Jewish coinage, not the "heathen" coins in use everywhere in the land—Greek, Roman, Persian, Egyptian, Syrian. The money-changers would normally ply their trade in the towns prior to Passover, then, closer to the feast itself, move to the temple courts in Jerusalem. (Interestingly, many of the priests considered themselves exempt from the temple tax.)

In earlier times, people of Israel brought their own sacrificial animals to the feast, but with so many Jews living far away, provision was made to sell sacrificial animals, and obviously some profit was involved in the transaction. Also, people bringing their own animals had to have the beasts inspected and approved by the priests, and if the priests found any defect, the animal could not be used in sacrifice, so the person would have to buy their animals from the temple merchants. Clearly, some of the priests could be overly finicky in finding "defects" in animals, forcing many people to buy from the merchants. The whole system was hardest on the poor, the ones who could only afford to offer doves as sacrifices. The mark-up on doves was a mere pittance to the wealthy, but to the poor it could seem exorbitant. In the cleansing of the temple, Matthew and Mark specifically mention that Jesus overturned "the benches of those selling doves" (Matthew 21:12, Mark 11:15). In John's version, Jesus says to the sellers of doves, "Get these out of here! How dare you turn my Father's house into a market!" (2:16). The doves were sold to the poorest people. In specifically mentioning the doves, Jesus and the Gospel writers were showing their sympathy for the poorest.

AD 29
Execution of John the Baptist
(Matthew 14:3)

AD 30
Death and resurrection of Jesus
(Matthew 27–28, Mark 15–16, Luke 23–24, John 18–21)

Jewish pilgrims who had traveled long distances to Jerusalem found their worship space was in fact a farmer's market. In cleansing the temple of its "marketers," Jesus was showing far greater reverence for it than the priests themselves did.

Jesus' act is referred to as the "cleansing of the temple." The act apparently pleased the crowd, but certainly not the priests, who saw such an act as a threat to their own livelihood. Also, such an action might attract the attention of the Romans. The priests themselves could have used their own temple guards to arrest Jesus, but they sensed his popularity with the crowd and did not want to provoke a riot. Nonetheless, at this point they "began looking for a way to kill him" (Mark 11:18).

All this took place on the first day of the week, a day that in the years ahead people of faith would refer to as Palm Sunday.

QUESTIONS AND CONFRONTATIONS

The following day, the priests and the scribes (teachers of the law) found Jesus teaching in the temple courts. The events of the previous day were no doubt fresh in their minds, as well as in the minds of Jesus' followers. The priests asked him, "By what authority are you doing these things?" Their question was not surprising: A ruling elite is never pleased to see a grassroots hero whose words are more highly regarded than their own.

We have seen before that Jesus showed amazing shrewdness in dealing with confrontations and questions. He posed a question to his questioners: "John's baptism—

was it from heaven, or from men?" Jesus was speaking of his kinsman, the great prophet John the Baptist, who had been beheaded by order of the wicked Herod. John was highly regarded as a great man, a prophet and martyr. The priests knew this, and they knew there was no right answer to Jesus' question. If they said John's ministry was merely human in origin, the people would be enraged. If they said John was sent by God, Jesus would ask why they did not believe and follow John. So the priests answered, "We don't know." Jesus replied, "Neither will I tell you by what authority I am doing these things" (Mark 11:27–33).

Jesus' quiet but firm air of authority in his teaching was, of course, the main reason the Jewish religious elite hated him. Although he showed himself a faithful Jew, coming to Jerusalem for the holy days, he made no pretense of submitting to the authority of the Pharisees or Sadducees or priests. In fact, he spoke out openly against the hypocrisy of many of them, and this fearless preaching earned him their hatred—and the admiration of the mass of people. The Gospels mention several times that the Pharisees and Sadducees were "envious" or "jealous" of Jesus, and this was at the root of their contempt. Rather than admit to jealousy of a mere carpenter from Galilee, they preferred to label him a "dangerous" character whose actions might upset the status quo in the land. So eliminating him was—so they reasoned—the best and safest course for the people and their religion.

Another confrontation involved the Pharisees and the Herodians, the cronies of the corrupt Herod dynasty. Hoping to trap Jesus with his own words, they went to him and posed a question, which they sugarcoated with great flattery: "Teacher, we know you are a man of integrity. You aren't swayed by men, because you pay no attention to who they are; but you teach the way of God in accordance with the truth. Is it right to pay taxes to Caesar or not?"

Jesus saw through their hypocrisy—although, ironically, their words of praise were actually quite true! "Why are you trying to trap me?" he asked them. He asked that someone bring him a Roman coin, a denarius. To his deceitful questioners, he asked, "Whose portrait is this? And whose inscription?" They replied, "Caesar's." Jesus' reply was perfect, and it completely silenced them: "Give to Caesar what is Caesar's, and to God what is God's" (Mark 12:13–17). With that answer, he showed that he was no threat to the Roman government—if taxes were due to the Romans, then pay them. But the duty to give God his due satisfied every religious Jew.

The next question—a truly ridiculous one—was posed by the Sadducees, who did not believe in an afterlife. Yet their question concerned a woman whose husband died, leaving her childless. By the law of Moses, the widow would marry her husband's brother and have children by him, and these would be considered the children of her first husband. But the second husband died, leaving her childless again. She married another brother—and the pattern continued until the poor woman had married seven brothers, but had children by none of them. The Sadducees asked Jesus, "At the resurrection, whose wife will she be, since the seven were married to her?" Jesus knew that his questioners did not even believe in a resurrection—but he did, and he used their mocking question as an opportunity to teach: In the afterlife, people would not be married, but would be "like the angels in heaven." As for the Sadducees' disbelief in the afterlife, he reminded them of Moses' encounter with God in the burning bush, when God identified himself with the words, "I am the God of Abraham, the God of Isaac, and the God of Jacob"—not, "I *was* the God of Abraham," but "I *am*." The patriarchs Abraham, Isaac and Jacob had died—but were alive with God. Jesus told the Sadducees, "He is not the God of the dead, but of the living. You are badly mistaken!" (Mark 12:18–27).

CULTURAL INSIGHTS

The Sadducees

The Pharisees and Sadducees were the two most important factions among the Jews of Jesus' day. Although not mentioned in the Gospels nearly as often as the Pharisees, the Sadducees actually played a much larger role in the arrest and condemnation of Jesus. The Sadducee party consisted of the priests and their cronies, and for the most part they were worldly and materialistic, gladly collaborating with the Romans, since the Romans helped maintain the status quo, allowing the Sadducees to live off the earnings of the temple. The Sadducees hated Jewish rebels as much as the Romans did, for any uprising might give the Romans an excuse to curtail the priests' privileges or even destroy the temple—which, indeed, would occur in AD 70.

The Sadducees were an unspiritual bunch, not even believing in an afterlife. For them, religion consisted of the temple rituals. The Pharisees took faith more seriously, and for that reason the two groups disliked each other intensely, with the Sadducees seeing the Pharisees as meddling laymen. Both groups had reason to hate Jesus, but the Sadducees had more political power than the Pharisees, so they were much more responsible for what befell Jesus. Jesus' cleansing of the temple made it clear to them that Jesus was a dangerous rebel who had to be disposed of.

One of the scribes (who, unlike the Sadducees, would have believed in the afterlife) was pleased with Jesus' answer, and he came forward and asked, "Of all the commandments, which is the most important?" Jesus replied that the first in importance was "Love the Lord your God with all your soul and with all your mind and with all your strength." The second greatest was "Love your neighbor as yourself." "And from then on no on dared ask him any more questions" (Mark 12:28–34).

PROPHESYING TROUBLES

Jesus warned the crowds in the temple precincts about the hypocrisy of the Pharisees and the scribes. Jesus noted that these "religious" people built monuments to the prophets and martyrs, yet throughout Israel's history the saintly men were persecuted and even killed by religious hypocrites. Jerusalem was the center of the Jews' religious life, and yet it was the city where the prophets were stoned to death (Matthew 23:1–39).

Destruction was coming, and Jesus knew it. As he and his disciples left the temple, the disciples marveled at the size and craftsmanship of the temple. Indeed, the temple that the wicked Herod the Great had lavished such attention on was one of the noted sights in the Roman Empire, impressing all who saw it. But Jesus told his followers that in the time to come, not one stone of the temple would be left upon another. His prophecy would come to pass in the year 70, when a Jewish revolt led to the Romans' destruction of the temple—and the end of the corrupt priesthood.

Jesus took his closest disciples to the Mount of Olives, where they questioned him about the end times. Jesus warned of the coming of false Christs. There would be "wars and rumors of wars," and one nation against another. For the faithful there would be persecution. Believers would be dragged before kings and councils—but this would be an opportunity to witness to the faith. "All men will hate you because of me, but he who stands firm to the end will be saved" (Mark 13:13).

False prophets will appear, deceiving many people. After great worldwide distress, Jesus would return to earth, "coming in clouds with great power and glory." When would this all occur? No one knew except the Father in heaven. Therefore, "Be on guard! Be alert!" Be spiritually ready at all times, and do not be weighed down by the cares of this earthly life (Mark 13:21–37, Luke 21:34–36). Judgment is coming upon the earth, just as it came in the time of Noah, when only Noah and his family were prepared for the flood that destroyed everyone else (Matthew 24:37–41).

CONSPIRACY AND BETRAYAL

For Jesus himself, destruction would come much sooner. The chief priests and scribes were plotting to arrest him and kill him, but they would not do it openly in the daylight, for the crowds of Passover pilgrims might riot over the arrest of a popular teacher.

"Then Judas Iscariot, one of the Twelve, went to the chief priests to betray Jesus to them. They were delighted to hear this and promised to give him money. So he watched for an opportunity to hand him over" (Mark 14:10–11). In these few words the Gospel records one of the most horrible agreements ever made. What on earth made Judas do this? Luke's Gospel states that Satan entered into Judas (22:3–6), but we have to wonder: How did Satan goad the man to betray his master? And why did Jesus choose this man to be one of his closest disciples? Surely there must have been some good, or some potential for good, in Judas. Other than mentioning Satan, the Gospels do not try to "explain" Judas. People like to speculate that Judas, like many admirers of Jesus, hoped that at some point Jesus would reveal himself as the Christ and become the political liberator, driving out the Romans. Betraying Jesus to the priests would force Jesus' hand—he would show himself to be the liberator Messiah, and all Jews would follow him. We can't know this for sure. However, remember that at the beginning of Jesus' ministry, Satan tempted Jesus with worldly power. Satan entered into Judas, so it is conceivable that Judas's act was a final temptation of Satan: Jesus, the Son of God, would be tempted to reveal his divine power in a dramatic way.

While Judas plotted, the other disciples prepared to celebrate the Passover supper with their Master. On the second floor of a house in Jerusalem, the group gathered for the solemn meal. It became even more solemn when Jesus told them that one of them would betray him. The disciples, greatly distressed, each began to ask, "Is it I?" But the meal continued, with Jesus breaking the unleavened Passover bread and giving it to the disciples, saying, "This is my body, given for you; do this in remembrance of me." Afterward he took a cup of wine and said, "This cup is the new covenant in my blood, which is poured out for you" (Luke 22:14–23).

The event we call the Last Supper has great meaning for us. We have to wonder what it meant to the disciples at the time. Their Passover meal—a solemn but joyous occasion, when devout Jews thanked God for the exodus from Egypt—had ended with Jesus speaking of his body being broken and his blood poured out.

Leaving the house, Jesus and the disciples went to the Mount of Olives. Jesus told them, "You will all fall away." Peter, always the most blunt and outspoken of the group, protested: "Even if all fall away, I will not." Jesus corrected him: Before the rooster crowed the next morning, Peter would deny him three times. Peter declared he would never deny him, and the other disciples said the same (Mark 14:27–31).

On the Mount of Olives was a kind of park or garden, called Gethsemane, which had been an olive orchard.

> **DID YOU KNOW?**
>
> The night of the Last Supper is often called Maundy Thursday. The name comes from *mandatum novum,* Latin for "new command," based on John 13:34: "A new command I give you: Love one another."

Farewell and Footwashing

In John's Gospel, the account of the Last Supper omits any mention of the bread and wine, but includes a long speech in which Jesus encourages the disciples and prays for them. Before the speech, Jesus "got up from the meal, took off his outer clothing, and wrapped a towel around his waist. After that, he poured water into a basin and began to wash the disciples' feet" (John 13:4–5).

Peter protested—understandably, for in his eyes, this was all wrong. Jesus was the master, they were his disciples. Washing the feet was the duty of a servant, not the master. But Jesus told him, "Unless I wash you, you have no part in me." Peter relented. When all the disciples' feet were washed, Jesus explained his actions. He was their master—but had acted as a servant. They were to do the same—not lording it over each other, but acting as servants. Love and service were to be the signs of faith. "By this all men will know that you are my disciples, if you love one another" (13:35). Many churches continue the practice of footwashing during Holy Thursday services, as a sign of mutual servitude to each other.

Looking at what lay ahead in a short time, Jesus told the disciples, "Greater love has no one than this, that he lay down his life for his friends." As his friends, they would be persecuted, as he was. In fact, "a time is coming when anyone who kills you will think he is offering a service to God" (16:2). "In this world you will have trouble. But take heart! I have overcome the world" (16:33).

Jesus took Peter, James and John with him as he went away to pray. He told these three, his closest companions, "My soul is overwhelmed with sorrow to the point of death" (14:34). He told them to keep watch while he walked a little farther away and began to pray.

Let's pause here to remind ourselves of a key belief of the New Testament: Jesus was fully human—divine, yes, but truly human. No human being wants to die at the age of thirty, especially by an unjust stoning or crucifixion, in unfathomable agony while his enemies mocked. Jesus knew it was part of God's plan that he die, but he prayed that this "cup" of suffering would be taken away—if it was God's will. Jesus was not some Stoic philosopher, accepting death as a natural part of life. If he approached this death without fear, he would not have been a human being—not a sane one, at any rate. "Being in anguish, he prayed more earnestly, and his sweat was like drops of blood falling to the ground" (Luke 22:44).

He asked to be spared—and God said no.

He returned to his closest friends—they were asleep, unable to keep watch for him in his hour of distress. "The spirit is willing, but the flesh is weak" (Mark 14:38 KJV). The traitor had come with "a crowd armed with swords and clubs, sent from the chief priests." Judas had arranged a signal: In the dark garden he would kiss his Master to identify him. At the signal, the men seized Jesus. Peter drew a sword, cutting off the ear of a servant of the high priest. Jesus told him to sheath his sword—the way of violence was not his way. He touched the ear of the servant and healed him—an act of compassion bestowed on an enemy.

"Then everyone deserted him and fled" (Mark 14:50). Jesus had prophesied rightly. They had all fallen away. Why did they flee? They were willing to use force to defend Jesus, but when he told them not to, they did not know what to do. They were not only afraid for themselves, but also perhaps deeply disappointed in the submissiveness of the man they hoped would be their king. Certainly Simon the Zealot had hopes for a political Messiah, probably Judas also, and, based on their actions, Peter, James and John as well, since these were the most outspoken of the group. The others probably felt the same. In spite of the fact that Jesus had told them over and over what was going to happen to him in Jerusalem, they were not prepared for it. They had not listened to their master's words and had not taken them to heart.

CHARACTER CLOSE-UP # Peter

The Galilean fisherman named Simon was given a new name by Jesus: *Cephas* in Aramaic, *Petros* in Greek, both words meaning "rock." The new name was bestowed when Simon was the first to state the belief that Jesus was "the Christ, the Son of the living God" (Matthew 16:16). Although the most outspoken and openhearted of the twelve disciples, *Petros*, or Peter, proved to be an unsteady "rock," exemplified in his denying three times that he knew Jesus. Yet, in spite of this and other failings, Peter is a lovable man, deeply devoted to Jesus, as evidenced by his wielding a sword in the garden of Gethsemane, and by his entering the priest's courtyard to learn what was happening to the master he had abandoned. Peter's bitter weeping after his third denial of Jesus is one of the most emotional episodes in the Gospels. Later, Peter would run to the tomb of Jesus, eager to learn if the women's story of the empty tomb was true. When we study the Book of Acts, we will see Peter's boldness put to good use among the first Christians, as he preaches the first sermon and is first to carry the gospel message to the Gentiles.

JUDGING THE SON OF GOD

Peter had fled like the others—yet he had not totally abandoned his master, for he followed the armed mob at a distance as Jesus was taken to the house of Caiaphas, the high priest, the man who had told his cohorts that Jesus must die (John 11:50). A fire was kindled in the house's courtyard, and Peter sat by the fire among the servants. A man looked at him and pointed him out as a follower of the man who was arrested. Peter denied it. Another servant identified him as a follower of Jesus. Again, he denied it. Yet another, hearing Peter's Galilean accent, identified him. Peter denied a third time—and then the rooster crowed. Peter "went outside and wept bitterly" (Matthew 26:75). Another of Jesus' prophecies had proved true—to the great shame of Peter, the blunt, impulsive, deeply emotional Galilean fisherman.

The Sanhedrin, the Jews' ruling council, had gathered at Caiaphas' house. Jesus, to the council's amazement, remained silent as false accusers came forward. Caiaphas bluntly asked Jesus, "Are you the Christ, the Son of God?" At long last Jesus spoke: "Yes, it is as you say." Caiaphas tore his robe—the Jewish sign of intense anguish—and denounced Jesus as a blasphemer, condemned by his own words. The council pronounced Jesus worthy of death. The guards began abusing Jesus, mocking him, spitting in his face and slapping him.

As Peter was painfully aware, morning had come. The Sanhedrin sent Jesus off to Pontius Pilate. John's Gospel adds the interesting detail that the Jews would not enter Pilate's home, since entering a Gentile's quarters would render Jews ritually unclean before Passover. The men had no qualms about condemning the Messiah, the Son of God, to death, but were concerned about small matters of ritual! (John 18:28). So Pilate had to come out to them. They told Pilate that Jesus was "subverting" the nation—and lied when they said that he opposed paying taxes to Caesar (Luke 23:2). Pilate, who could not have been pleased at having to try a case so early in the day, told the Jews to judge Jesus by their own law. The Jews reminded him that they did not have the right of capital punishment, only the Romans did. By the Jewish law, Jesus should have been stoned, since that was the mode of execution for blasphemers. They could have gone to Pilate and asked his permission to stone the blasphemer. But, knowing Jesus' popularity as a religious teacher, that might have incited a riot. Better to maneuver Pilate into condemning Jesus as a political criminal.

Summoning Jesus inside, Pilate asked him, "Are you the king of the Jews?" Jesus responded with his own question: "Is that your own idea, or did others talk to you about me?" Pilate asked Jesus what he had done to be handed over by his own people. Jesus replied, "My kingdom is not of this world." Pilate, a practical-minded Roman, probably could not grasp what a "kingdom not of this world" was. When Jesus told him he had been sent to the world to testify to the truth, Pilate replied, "What is truth?" (John 18:33–39). The Roman governor had no interest in discussing abstractions like truth with a Jew. But it was clear Jesus was no political threat to Rome, and for Pilate, that was all that mattered. He told the priests that he found no crime in Jesus. According to Roman practice, that settled things—Pilate had rendered his official judgment—the case was closed for lack of evidence. But the priests and their cronies—who apparently were moving among the crowd—told Pilate that Jesus was stirring up people all over the land.

CULTURAL INSIGHTS

Anti-Semitic Gospels?

Matthew's Gospel states that Pilate washed his hands in front of the crowd, saying, "I am innocent of this man's blood. It is your responsibility." Then, "all the people answered, 'Let his blood be on us and on our children!'" (Matthew 27:24–25). What did Matthew mean by "all the people"? Didn't Jesus have admirers among the Jews? He did, but 27:20 states that the chief priests had persuaded the fickle crowd to ask for Jesus' death.

"Let his blood be on us and on our children"—these words, according to some Jewish spokesmen, have led to persecution of Jews. Supposedly, some Christians have thought of Jews as "Christ-killers," who are accursed because of what their ancestors said. Whether this verse ever actually led to persecution is difficult to prove. Certainly the Old Testament shows that anti-Semitism existed centuries before the time of Jesus.

The accusation that the Gospels are anti-Semitic does not hold water. Jesus was a Jew, as were his twelve disciples, and the Gospels (with the exception of Luke) were written by Jews. Non-Christian writings from this period of history give an unflattering picture of the Jewish priests, and Jewish writers of the period sternly denounced the corruption of the priestly families. The large collection of Jewish writings known as the Talmud is harsh in condemning Caiaphas, Annas, and every other priest of that period. Annas was particularly noted for the corruption of the judges who served under him. It was not the Jews as a whole that the Gospels condemned, but the narrow-minded priests and officials who saw Jesus as a trouble-maker whose followers might stir up strife and bring down the wrath of Rome on the temple bureaucracy.

The Sanhedrin

The supreme ruling council of the Jews was known as the Sanhedrin (some translations have "Council") and was composed of 71 men, presided over by the high priest. The members were from three groups: the chief priests, the elders (prominent laymen) and the scribes (also called teachers of the law). Prior to the Roman conquest, the Sanhedrin ruled in all matters, political and religious, but the Romans restricted the Sanhedrin to religious matters. As we see in the Gospels, it could condemn an offender to the death penalty but had to hand him over to the Romans for the actual execution.

The Sanhedrin presented in the Gospels is a decidedly unspiritual group, particularly the high priest Caiaphas and his father-in-law, the former high priest Annas. While some members—Nicodemus and Joseph of Arimathea—were inclined to show fairness to Jesus, the council as a whole saw Jesus not as the Messiah all Jews had longed for but as a blasphemous troublemaker who needed to be disposed of. Knowing Jesus had support among the people, the council was eager to have Pilate condemn Jesus as a political criminal instead of a blasphemer. After some hesitation, Pilate caved in, but the writers of the Gospels were certain that though the Romans carried out the crucifixion, the Sanhedrin—the highest representatives of Jesus' own religion—was really responsible.

Luke's Gospel adds an interesting episode that the other Gospels omit: Pilate, learning that Jesus was from Galilee, decided to rid himself of this troublesome legal case by sending Jesus to be judged by Herod, the ruler of Galilee, who was in Jerusalem for Passover. Herod, son of Herod the Great, was as corrupt as his famous father, and had beheaded the great prophet, and Jesus' kinsman, John the Baptist. Pilate had given Herod the opportunity to condemn Jesus as well, but Herod did not. In fact, the cynical Herod tried to get Jesus to perform a miracle. Not only did Jesus not do so, but he said nothing at all to Herod—the one single case of Jesus refusing to speak to a person. Despite his cynicism, Herod found no grounds to condemn Jesus. Herod's men mocked Jesus and sent him back to Pilate (Luke 23:6–12).

The Romans had a custom of releasing one Jewish prisoner at the time of Passover. One prisoner was a notorious murderer and revolutionary named Barabbas—exactly the kind of trouble-maker Pilate would have gladly executed, for Barabbas was a real threat to Roman power. But to his great surprise and vexation, the crowd—which probably included many of the same people who had cheered Jesus a few days earlier—yelled for the release of Barabbas, not Jesus. Pilate asked what should be done with Jesus. "Crucify him!" the mob shouted (Mark 15:13).

What made the crowd want Jesus' blood? The Gospels tell us that the priests' men were among the crowd, leading the shouting. But the people may have turned against Jesus because he had disappointed them. The Palm Sunday procession had them hoping for something dramatic from the prophet from Nazareth. They were perhaps expecting a quick and violent revolution, and he had not given them that. The priests, of course, despised the crowds, yet they were willing to use them to get what they wanted. How ironic, since only hours earlier the priests had arrested Jesus by night, fearing how the crowd might react if Jesus was arrested in broad daylight!

Pilate caved in to the crowd. He feared a riot was in the making, and, even worse, the priests had told him that if he released Jesus, he was no friend of Caesar. Pilate took water and washed his hands before the crowd, saying he was innocent of Jesus' blood—not quite true, for he had allowed an unruly mob, and the fear of being called disloyal to Caesar, make him condemn a man he knew was innocent. The shouting of evil men had won the day.

Reading the story of Jesus' arrest and trial, we often overlook something important: The religion that condemned Jesus was the highest that had ever existed. The government that condemned him was, at the time, probably the best on earth. Jesus hadn't fallen into mankind's worst, but its best, people. And yet a horrendous injustice had been done—had to be done, for the sake of the world.

Jesus had been betrayed by one disciple, deserted by the others, condemned by the leader of his own religion, condemned by the secular government, and condemned by the public. He had no one on his side—except God. Being fully human, Jesus experienced what we all experience at one time or another—abandonment by our friends, our institutions, by the world at large.

ONE HORROR AFTER ANOTHER

Pilate ordered Jesus scourged or flogged. This involved stripping a man to the waist, tying him to a post, and beating him with a whip, its thongs studded with pieces of bone and metal. It was a brutal punishment, one that proved fatal for some men. Jesus would have

Pontius Pilate

At the time of Jesus' arrest, the governor (*prefect*) of the Roman province of Judea was Pontius Pilate, who was a protégé of the unscrupulous, ambitious Sejanus, advisor to the emperor Tiberius. Sejanus was notoriously anti-Jewish, and so was Pilate. When Pilate took office in Judea in the year 26, he horrified the Jews by having Roman military flags, bearing the emperor's image, brought into Jerusalem. To the Jews, these were idols, and Pilate finally removed them, though he continued to have a contentious relationship with the people he ruled. On one occasion he had his soldiers club to death a crowd of Jewish protesters, an incident alluded to in Luke 13:1. His mentor Sejanus fell from the emperor's favor in the year 31, and as a Sejanus protégé, Pilate's own loyalty to the empire was under suspicion. This situation helps explain why he caved in to the Jews' taunts of being "no friend of Caesar" if he released Jesus.

Pilate's rule in Judea ended in 36, and he went to Rome, with the Jews pleased to see him go. Some old legends say that both he and his wife became Christians, while another tradition says he committed suicide.

As a minor Roman official, Pilate would have been long ago forgotten had he not crossed paths—briefly but fatefully—with Jesus of Nazareth. Thanks to the phrase "suffered under Pontius Pilate" that is part of most Christian creeds, Pilate's name has been recited countless times over the centuries. Thanks to the spread of Christianity, he might be the most famous Roman in history.

been extremely weak and covered in blood when, after the scourging, Pilate's soldiers made sport of him, putting a scarlet robe on his beaten back, plaiting a crown of thorns for his head and putting a reed in his hand—a parody of a king's royal robe, crown and scepter. They spit on him and struck him, saying, "Hail, king of the Jews!" (Mark 15:16–20). Pilate's men, none of whom were Jews themselves, found delight in tormenting one of these people they so detested.

The convicted criminal always carried on his own shoulders the horizontal beam of his cross. Jesus was so weak from the scourging that a bystander named Simon of Cyrene was forced to carry the beam to Golgotha, the execution site. Jesus was offered the usual anesthetic, wine mingled with myrrh, but he refused it.

"They crucified him." The Gospels provide that bare statement of the crucifixion, giving no details. They did not need to, for the original readers would have been very familiar with crucifixions, since they were always done along highways and hillsides, as public as possible. The man would have nails through his wrists and feet, and over a period of hours, sometimes even days, would slowly die from exhaustion and heart failure. It was an unimaginably horrible form of death, one the Romans reserved for slaves, pirates and revolutionaries. The Roman writer Cicero spoke of crucifixion as "the most cruel and repulsive of punishments." The Romans crucified men nude—but made an exception for Jews, allowing them to wear their loincloth. Normally a plaque called the *titulum* was placed over the head of the criminal, stating the charge he was convicted of. Jesus' read "King of the Jews"—wording that Pilate chose deliberately to irk the priests (John 19:19–22).

The physical agony was not all that Jesus endured. He had to watch as the callous soldiers took his clothing and cast lots to determine who would get them. Speaking about them or perhaps about everyone involved in the cruel process, Jesus said, "Father, forgive them, for they know not what they do" (Luke 23:34). Like any crucified criminal, he had to endure the taunts of the public, mockers calling out, "If you are the Son of God, come down!" The priests and the scribes taunted him with "He saved others but cannot save himself." He was even taunted by one of the two men crucified with him, two called "thieves," although the Greek word *lestai* was also used for Zealot revolutionaries, which is probably what they were. One of them mocked Jesus, but the other, more reflective, said they were receiving their just punishment, while Jesus was innocent. He said, "Jesus, remember me when you come into your kingdom." Jesus answered, "Today you will be with me in paradise" (Luke 23:39–43).

The Gospels say that around "the sixth hour"—noon—there was darkness over the land, lasting three hours. Around the ninth hour, Jesus called out in Aramaic, "Eloi,

STORIES WORTH REMEMBERING

The Traitor's Death

Judas Iscariot is one of the great villains of history—and yet he was not totally without a conscience, for Matthew's Gospel says that when Judas saw that Jesus had been condemned to death by the Sanhedrin, "he was seized with remorse." He took the thirty pieces of silver the priests had paid him back to them and told them, "I have sinned, for I have betrayed innocent blood." The worldly priests had no interest in him—he had served the purpose of leading them to Jesus at night and was no longer needed. Judas threw the money into the temple—then went and hanged himself.

The priests had their money back—but it was "blood money," tainted by its use, so they could not put it back into the temple treasury. They used the money to buy a field to be used as a cemetery for foreigners—a plot of ground known as the Field of Blood (Matthew 27:1–10).

Thirty pieces of silver was, incidentally, the price of a slave, as stipulated in the Law of Moses (Exodus 21:32).

Eloi, lama sabachthani?"—the first words of Psalm 22, which in English are "My God, my God, why have you forsaken me?" The words have aroused much speculation. Did Jesus really feel abandoned by his Father? Perhaps—and understandably so. But Psalm 22 begins in despair and ends in trust, as the oppressed man affirms, at the end, that he knows God will rescue him. Jesus could not have spoken the beginning of the Psalm without recalling the ending.

Where were Jesus' disciples? Probably in hiding. But John's Gospel states that while on the cross, Jesus saw "his mother there, and the disciple whom he loved standing nearby." It is usually assumed this was the disciple John, though we aren't certain. From the cross, Jesus commended his mother to the keeping of this disciple (John 19:25–27).

With a loud voice, Jesus called out, "Father, into your hands I commit my spirit!" (Luke 23:46). Then he died. Watching from a distance were some of the faithful women who had been among his followers. Closer at hand was one Roman centurion, who said, "Surely this man was the Son of God!" (Mark 15:39).

MOURNING AND VINDICATION

It was Friday afternoon, and the Jews' Sabbath began at sunset. A wealthy member of the Sanhedrin, Joseph of Arimathea, had secretly been an admirer of Jesus. He went to Pilate and asked for Jesus' body. Aided by Nicodemus, the Pharisee who had visited Jesus by night, he had Jesus' body wrapped in linen cloth and placed in a tomb cut out of rock. A huge stone was rolled over the entrance of the tomb. Mary Magdalene and another woman follower of Jesus saw where Jesus was laid to rest (Mark 15:42–47).

The priests and their cronies had seemingly triumphed. But they were not satisfied. Someone recalled that Jesus prophesied that he would be crucified, but then raised to life again on the third day. The priests secured from Pilate some guards, who would watch the tomb to ensure that Jesus' disciples did not steal the body and start the rumor that Jesus rose from the dead (Matthew 27:62–66).

The Jews would normally bury a body with spices and perfumes. This had not been possible on Friday because the Sabbath was approaching, nor was it possible on Saturday, the Sabbath itself. On Sunday morning at sunrise, Mary Magdalene and two other women brought spices to the tomb, then realized they had no way to roll away the stone from the tomb.

They did not need anyone. The stone had been rolled away—not by men, but by an angel, who told the women, "He is not here, he has risen, as he said." The angel told the women to tell the disciples. The women hurried from the tomb—"afraid yet filled with joy" (Matthew 28:8). They gladly told the disciples—who, not surprisingly, did not believe them, "because their words seemed to them like nonsense." Peter, however, went to the tomb and indeed it was empty, the linen gravecloths lying there (Luke 24:9–12).

The Gospels differ in their accounts of what followed. In John's Gospel, the first person to actually see the risen Jesus was Mary Magdalene, who at first did not recognize him. Apparently his risen body was different from his earthly body, yet recognizable. In fact, we see in the Gospels' accounts of the risen Jesus that his own resurrection was different from the cases of three people he had restored to life: his friend Lazarus, the daughter of Jairus, and the son of the window of Nain. All three of these were brought back to the same kind of life they had before, but Jesus, as the Gospels make clear, was in a new condition, a "glorified" life similar to yet very different from his previous existence. Jesus hadn't just been brought back to life but in some mysterious way had conquered death, something that would be made known to all believers in the course of time. Instead of resuscitation, there is transformation. A new sort of life has begun. Later in the New Testament, the apostle Paul would describe it in this way: "It is sown a natural body, it is raised a spiritual body" (1 Corinthians 15:44).

Toward evening on the day of resurrection, when his disciples were gathered together, Jesus appeared among them, showing them the crucifixion wounds in his hands and side. Absent from the group was the disciple Thomas, who heard what happened later and could not accept it. "Doubting Thomas" would not believe until he saw and touched Jesus himself. A week later, Jesus appeared again, and Thomas believed. To him, Jesus said, "Because you have seen me, you have believed. Blessed are those who have not seen and yet have believed" (John 20:29).

In a sense, Jesus was pronouncing a blessing on every future Christian who would take it on faith, not sight, that the crucified Jesus had indeed risen from the dead. The "criminal" that the Romans and the Jewish priests condemned to public humiliation and agonizing death had been declared "not guilty" by God himself. This is the key miracle—and the key belief—of the New Testament. It has never been easy to believe—and yet is the only explanation for the transformation of

> **DID YOU KNOW?**
>
> Some people puzzle about the chronology in the Gospels. If Jesus was crucified on a Friday and rose on the third day, didn't that mean he was resurrected on a *Monday*? Not by the Jewish way of dating. For the Jews, Jesus was in the tomb three days—Friday, Saturday and Sunday, even though he was not in the tomb a full day on either Friday or Sunday. By that reckoning, Sunday was indeed "the third day."

the frightened, disillusioned band of disciples into the bold apostles who would preach the faith to the world, an amazing story that unfolds in the rest of the New Testament.

Recall that our first chapter about Jesus was titled, "Immanuel, God with Us." That is what Jesus was. God came to us as a man, suffered as a man and died as a man—but was victorious over death, giving humankind an imperishable sign of hope. This is the message of the Gospels.

PUTTING THE WORD TO WORK

1. Jesus told his listeners in Jerusalem that the greatest commandments were to love God with all our souls and love our neighbors as ourselves. As you go through the day, keep these two commandments in mind, particularly at moments when you may feel tempted to say or think something harsh about someone you encounter.

2. How do you react to the story of Peter's denial? As you respond to the question, remember that Peter was the only one of the disciples who made an effort to follow Jesus and see what happened after his arrest.

3. Jesus' words from the cross—"Father, forgive them, they know not what they do"—is the classic statement of compassionate forgiveness. Have there been times in your life when you were genuinely able to forgive people who had wronged you? Is there someone in your life now that you need to forgive? If you feel someone has wronged you deeply, compare what they did to what Jesus endured and forgave.

4. In light of the brutality that the soldiers heaped upon Jesus, what do you think prompted the centurion at the cross to say, "Surely this was the Son of God"?

5. The disciples expressed disbelief when Mary Magdalene told them she had seen the risen Lord. How do you think you would have responded to the news? How would you have reacted upon seeing the risen Jesus yourself?

Twelve Simple Men Take on the World

**AT THE
HEART
OF IT ALL
TODAY** Empowered by the Holy Spirit, Jesus' apostles boldly spread the gospel, enduring persecution and coping with controversies within the new community of faith. Two men give up their lives for the faith, yet the message of salvation attracts more and more converts, even among the Gentiles.

The Book of Acts, also called the Acts of the Apostles, is one of the great books of the Bible, the story of Jesus' closest followers obeying his command to "go and make disciples of all nations" (Matthew 28:19). The apostles not only preach

KEY PASSAGES TO READ TODAY

**Acts 2; 4:1–21; 32–35;
5:17–42; 7:51–60; 10**

dynamically but also perform great miracles. And—as Jesus foretold—they suffered persecution, some of them even giving up their lives for their faith.

The book was written by Luke, author of the third Gospel. As in his Gospel, Luke addresses the work to someone named Theophilus—a Greek name meaning "one who loves God." Theophilus was a common enough name in those days, and this Theophilus may have been an actual individual—perhaps an official of high rank, since he is referred to as "most excellent Theophilus" (Luke 1:3). But even if this were the case, Luke did not address his Gospel and Acts to only one individual. Both writings are directed to every Theophilus—every person who loves God.

In the opening of Acts, Luke mentions his "former book," meaning the Gospel he wrote. Acts is the sequel to the Gospel of Luke, a sequel we should all be eternally grateful for, since without it our knowledge of the early Christians would be greatly diminished.

KEY TERM FOR TODAY ## The Holy Spirit

The prophet Joel predicted a time when the Spirit would empower not just a select few, but *all* of God's people: "your sons and daughters will prophesy, your old men will dream dreams and your young men will see visions" (Joel 2:28). Joel's prophecy came to pass at Pentecost, and Peter quoted the prophecy in his fiery sermon. Peter and all the apostles were "filled with the Spirit," and when Peter invited his listeners to repent and be baptized, he promised that "you will receive the gift of the Holy Spirit" (Acts 2:38). The early Christians thought of the Spirit as "God within," guiding and empowering them.

Luke was a gifted storyteller with an eye for details that bring the characters and events to life. Some of the later passages of Acts are narrated in the first person—the so-called "we" passages. Thus Luke was an eyewitness to some of the events he narrates, and since he was a companion of the apostle Paul, he would have heard from Paul's own lips the story of the stoning of Stephen, which Paul himself witnessed.

In Acts, Luke made no attempt to tell *all* the facts about the spread of Christianity. Regarding some events, Acts tells us little; for example, it records that the apostle James was put to death with a sword by order of Herod, but provides no other details (12:1–2). It says nothing about how Christianity was first taken to the great cities of Rome and Alexandria, something that would have greatly interested Luke's readers (and us as well). This reticence tells us that Luke was a reliable historian—giving us details when he knew them, but not filling in details where he did not know them. It is clear in Acts that Luke had close connections with the city of Antioch, so he has much to tell us about the Christians' activity in that city. It would have been tempting to make up colorful, highly detailed stories about other locales and about all twelve apostles, and indeed, in later times such fiction came to be written. But Luke confined himself to the facts he knew could be verified, believing that the power of God was decisively at work among the first Christians. The more historians and archaeologists study ancient times, the more they are impressed by the reliability of Luke's written record in his Gospel and in Acts.

Acts opens with the event that closes Luke's Gospel, Jesus' ascent into heaven. After his resurrection, Jesus was on earth another forty days. At the end of that time, his disciples asked him, "Lord, are you at this time going to restore the kingdom of Israel?" (Acts 1:6). That question indicates they were still clinging to the old expectation the Jews had, that their Messiah would be a political liberator. Instead of answering the question, Jesus promised them they would be endowed with the power of the Holy Spirit and would carry their faith "to the ends of the earth" (1:8). Then he was taken up into heaven, hidden from their sight by a cloud. Two "men dressed in white"—understood to be angels—told the disciples that someday Jesus will return to earth in the same way he departed.

The disciples returned to Jerusalem, where they formed part of a faith community that included Jesus' mother Mary and his brothers (1:14). (A reminder: When the Gospels and Acts refer to Jesus' "brothers," they may be referring to sons of Mary and Joseph, but might also be referring to cousins or other male relatives of Jesus. Whoever they were, they did not come to faith in him until after his resurrection.) Judas Iscariot, the traitor among the original twelve disciples, had committed suicide after his betrayal of Jesus, and the disciples chose a better man, named Matthias, to take his place among the twelve. Clearly the disciples saw the importance of having twelve men, no doubt aware that Jesus deliberately chose twelve disciples to symbolize the beginning of a new Israel—not twelve tribes based on physical descent, but twelve men of deep faith. Presumably Matthias was someone who had already shown a devotion to Christ, and perhaps was one of the wider band of disciples known as "the Seventy" (Luke 10:1–20).

PENTECOSTAL POWER

The disciples were gathered for the Jewish feast called Pentecost, which fell on the fiftieth day after the Passover holy day. In the house where they were staying, "suddenly a sound like the blowing of a violent wind came from heaven and filled the whole house where they were sitting. They saw what seemed to be tongues of fire that separated and came to rest on each of them. All of them were filled with the Holy Spirit and began to speak in other tongues as the Spirit enabled them" (Acts 2:2–4).

CULTURAL INSIGHTS

Clouds

In describing Jesus' ascension into heaven, Acts says that "he was taken up before their very eyes, and a cloud hid him from their sight" (1:9). This is one of many passages in the Bible in which clouds symbolize the divine presence. When Moses ascended Mount Sinai to meet with God, a cloud covered the mountain (Exodus 24:15), and many other times in the Moses saga a pillar of cloud indicates God's presence. At Solomon's dedication of the Lord's temple in Jerusalem, a cloud filled the temple (1 Kings 8:10). At Jesus' transfiguration, when he was speaking with the long-dead Moses and Elijah, a "bright cloud" enveloped the three men (Matthew 17:5). Jesus prophesied that when he again returned to earth on the Day of Judgment he would appear "on the clouds of the sky" (Matthew 24:30). The Letter to the Hebrews uses the interesting phrase "a cloud of witnesses," referring to the departed saints who are now in the presence of God (12:1).

A key prophecy had been fulfilled: Jesus' disciples had been baptized with the Holy Spirit and with fire (Matthew 3:11; Luke 3:16; Acts 1:6). Fire was often an indication of God's presence, as in the encounter of Moses with God in the burning bush (Exodus 3) and in the prophet Elijah's amazing departure into heaven (2 Kings 2). Wind, also, could indicate his presence, as in the encounter of Elijah with God at Mount Horeb (1 Kings 19:12), and in Ezekiel's famous vision of the valley full of dry bones, where a wind from God brought the bones to life (Ezekiel 37). Jesus told Nicodemus that the Spirit of God was like a wind that "blows where it pleases. You hear its sound, but you cannot know where it comes from or where it goes. So it is with everyone born of the Spirit" (John 3:8).

CULTURAL INSIGHTS

Pentecost

The Old Testament Law prescribes the celebration of a holy festival; sometimes it is called the Feast of Weeks, at other times the Feast of Harvest (Exodus 23:16; 32:22; Deuteronomy 16:9–11). It fell on the fiftieth day after the more important Feast of the Passover, so at times it was called Pentecost, from the Greek word for "fiftieth." It was one of three special pilgrim feasts of the Jews, meaning that on these days every adult Jewish male was expected to visit Jerusalem and worship in the temple. Although it was originally a harvest festival, by the time of the apostles, the Jews celebrated the day as a commemoration of God giving the Law to Moses.

Because of the events recorded in Acts 2, this Jewish holiday took on a distinctively Christian meaning. The Holy Spirit came upon the apostles at Pentecost, giving them the power to speak the languages of the ethnically diverse Jewish pilgrims who had come to Jerusalem for the feast. The early Christians remembered the day as "the birthday of the church," when the Spirit endowed the apostles with the power to preach eloquently and perform miracles. Just as the Jews had celebrated the holiday fifty days after Passover, so the Christians began the custom of celebrating it fifty days after Easter. (Jews today almost never refer to their own festival as Pentecost, preferring to use the Hebrew name *Shavuot*.)

Many Christians refer to themselves as Pentecostals. These are believers who emphasize the power of the Holy Spirit. Because the apostles were given the ability to speak in unknown tongues, Pentecostal Christians pray for the gift of speaking in tongues, as well as for other gifts of the Spirit described in Paul's letters (Romans 12:3–8; 1 Corinthians 12–14). Pentecostal churches often use a flame as the symbol of the Spirit, based on Acts 2, where the Spirit descended upon the apostles as "tongues of fire."

Jewish pilgrims from many lands had come to Jerusalem for the Pentecost celebration, and they were amazed that the twelve disciples—all men from Galilee—were suddenly able to communicate in other languages. Devout Jews would have remembered the story of the tower of Babel in Genesis 11, in which humans went from speaking a common language to speaking many, resulting in failure to communicate and in the scattering of people over the earth. The apostles' gift of being able to speak in other languages was a reversal of what happened at Babel. Some saw it as a miracle—the more skeptical said, "They have had too much wine" (Acts 2:13).

A crowd had gathered, and Peter, who had always been the most outspoken of Jesus' disciples, saw an opportunity to preach to the people—the first Christian sermon. Peter responded to the skeptics: No, the disciples were not drunk—it was too early in the day for drinking! Rather, something wondrous had come to pass. The centuries-old prophecy of Joel—that God's Spirit would be poured out on many people who would prophesy in God's name—was being fulfilled.

Joel's prophecy said that "everyone who calls on the name of the Lord will be saved" (Acts 2:21). Now Peter explained how that salvation could be obtained. Jesus, "a man accredited by God," had worked many miracles, but he had been handed over treacherously to the authorities and crucified—but God had raised him from the dead. The disciples themselves had seen Jesus after his resurrection. The Jesus so wrongly crucified was now "both Lord and Christ" (2:36).

"When the people heard this, they were cut to the heart and said to Peter and the other apostles, 'Brothers, what shall we do?' Peter replied, 'Repent and be baptized, every one of you, in the name of Jesus Christ for the forgiveness of your sins. And you will receive the gift of the Holy Spirit'" (2:37–38). That very day, three thousand people accepted Peter's message and were baptized. Afterward, the converts formed a community of faith, meeting together to learn from the apostles and to pray and share meals.

Chapter 2 of Acts concludes with this reminder of the appeal of the faith that was spread: "The Lord added to their number daily those who were being saved." Earlier in the chapter it is noted that the Jews present on the day of Pentecost were from many distant lands—including Rome. Before his ascension, Jesus had told the disciples they would carry the message of faith to "the ends of the earth." Devout Jews thought of Jerusalem as the "center" of the earth and the pagan capital of Rome as "the end of the earth," both geographically and morally. It is possible that among the many converts on the day of Pentecost were some of the Jews from Rome. If that was the case, then within

Apostles

In the Gospels, Jesus' twelve closest followers were almost always called "disciples," those who followed a master and learned from him. In Acts, these twelve are almost always referred to as "apostles," meaning "those sent out." The Greek word *apostolos* could refer to a messenger, ambassador or envoy. The twelve are no longer "learners" but "doers," sent out by the risen Christ to be his representatives on earth, preaching, baptizing and even performing miracles. As Christ himself was persecuted, so were his apostles.

Acts also applies the title "apostle" to others who were not members of the original band of twelve. These include James (not the disciple, but another James, the brother or relative of Jesus), Barnabas, and Paul. We know that Paul had a vision of the risen Christ (Acts 9), and that before his ascension into heaven Christ appeared to James (1 Corinthians 15:7). So it seems one important qualification for being an apostle was an encounter with the risen Lord. This is understandable, since the original disciples (now apostles) had witnessed the reality of the greatest miracle of all time, the resurrection of Jesus.

Although the Book of Acts is often called "Acts of the Apostles," its actual title in Greek is simply *Praxeis*—"acts" or "deeds" or "achievements." And although its most prominent characters are the apostles, the ministry of several other key people—such as Stephen and the evangelist Philip—form part of the story.

a few months of Jesus' crucifixion, resurrection and ascension, the salvation message proclaimed by Peter would already have reached Rome, the capital of the mighty empire.

THE PERSECUTION BEGINS

In the early chapters of Acts, the apostles are all in Jerusalem, engaging in frequent worship at the temple. This was a logical place for their mission to be based, since at all times Jews from all over the world were coming, forming an audience ripe to hear the message of Jesus the Messiah. In Acts 3, Peter and John are on their way to pray in the temple when they encounter a beggar, a man who had been crippled from birth. The detail that he had been lame for many years is important. There were fake cripples in those days and afterward, and if the apostles had been charlatans, they might have "planted" such a man and then pretended to heal him in order to gain fame. But Acts makes it clear that this poor man was a familiar sight at the temple gate, lame from the day he was born, a hopeless case—but perhaps not too hopeless in the divine view of things.

The crippled beggar asked the two apostles for money. He received something more than expected. Peter said to him, "Silver or gold I do not have, but what I have I give to you. In the name of Jesus Christ of Nazareth, walk." The man not only was able to walk, but, Acts says, was "jumping and praising God" (3:8). People who had seen him frequently begging were in awe of his radical transformation.

A crowd gathered, and Peter asked the people why they were so amazed. The power that healed the lame beggar did an even more amazing thing, bringing Jesus back to life. He told the crowd, "Repent, then, and turn to God, so that your sins may be wiped out, that times of refreshing may come from the Lord" (3:19). A miracle had given Peter a grand opportunity to witness to the crowd about his faith.

However, it also became the occasion of persecution. The soldiers employed by the temple's priests seized Peter and John and threw them in jail. While five thousand people had responded to Peter's call for repentance, the priests were alarmed. The following day the two apostles were brought before the priests for questioning. The group included Caiaphas and his father-in-law Annas, and the two apostles must have recalled that these were the same corrupt, unspiritual men who had condemned their Master to death. Yet Peter boldly said that the miracle had been done through the power of

STORIES WORTH REMEMBERING Ananias and Sapphira

Acts 4 tells of the generosity of the first Christians, with people selling property and using the money to aid the less fortunate among them. Acts 5 tells of a married couple that was generous—but only to a point. The couple owned a plot of land, which they sold, bringing the money to the disciples. But Ananias, with his wife's knowledge, kept part of the money for himself.

Peter confronted him. Ananias was perfectly free to keep part of the profits for himself—but not to lie to the apostles and claim that *all* the money had been given. Peter told him, "You have not lied to men but to God" (5:4). Ananias was so mortified at being caught in his lie that he fell down and died. Men took him out and buried him, and all who heard of what happened were in awe.

Sapphira had not been present when all this occurred. She came in later, and Peter tested her honesty. Was the amount she gave to the apostles the amount they received for the land? She said yes. Peter replied that she was foolishly trying to test God by her deceit. Like her husband, she fell down dead. "Great fear seized the whole church and all who heard about these events" (5:11).

Many readers are disturbed by this story, since it raises the question: Would God kill someone for just one lie? In fact, Acts does not say that God caused the two to die. The main point of the story is that a compassionate faith fellowship had been formed, and there was no place for deceit or hypocrisy in it.

Christ, and that the healed man was witness to that power. The council ordered the apostles to cease preaching their message about the Christ. "But Peter and John replied, 'Judge for yourselves whether it is right in God's sight to obey you rather than God. For we cannot help speaking about what we have seen and heard'" (4:19–20). This is one of the key verses of the New Testament: Those who had witnessed the risen Christ could not be muzzled. The priests threatened the apostles but then released them, sensing that punishing men for a miracle of healing would horrify the people.

It is worth noting in Acts that the Sanhedrin makes no accusation that Jesus was *not* truly raised from the dead. Obviously they did not believe he was, yet they had no evidence to prove it false. For all the authority they wielded, they could find no way to refute the apostles' teaching that the crucified Jesus was no longer in the tomb.

While the priests worried over the apostles and their message, the apostles themselves continued preaching, witnessing the growth of a faith community in which "all the believers were one in heart and mind" (4:32). Believers who were rich in material goods shared with those who had little, with some of them selling property and giving the money to the disciples to aid the needy.

THE ROAD TO MARTYRDOM

As Jesus prophesied, the apostles performed many miracles, so many that people from the towns near Jerusalem brought in the sick and demon-possessed so the apostles could heal them. The priests and other leaders among the Jews were "filled with jealousy" at seeing these working-class men from Galilee exercising such power—and finding favor with the public (5:17). (Remember that the Jewish leaders were also jealous of Jesus' popularity with the people.) Once again they threw them in jail—not just Peter and John this time, but apparently the whole band of twelve men. The priests did not foresee a miracle: An angel released the apostles from prison that night, and the next morning they were preaching again in the temple courts. The priests sent the temple soldiers out and had the apostles brought in for questioning.

The chief priest asked them why they had disobeyed the order to cease preaching in Jesus' name. Peter replied with one of the great ethical declarations of the Bible: "We must obey God rather than men!" (5:29). Having the priests' attention, he reminded them that they had arranged to have Jesus killed—but God had brought him back to life, and the apostles had seen him alive. The priests were furious and wanted to kill the apostles, but one member of the ruling council, a teacher named Gamaliel, counseled leniency. The council released the apostles after having them flogged—a cruel punishment in itself, one their own Master had suffered. But instead of complaining, the apostles rejoiced that they were suffering on behalf of Christ. None of them had been called upon to give up their lives for their faith—not yet.

Acts 6 tells of a dispute among the early Christians. The Greek-speaking Christians complained to the apostles that their widows were being slighted by the Aramaic-speaking Christians in the distribution of charity. This sounds like a minor matter, and it probably was, but what was likely at issue here was an age-old antagonism between Greek-speaking and Aramaic-speaking Jews. Put another way, the two groups had a history of being slightly suspicious of each other, and the Greek-speaking people felt they were not receiving their fair share. Whatever the problem was, the apostles had greater tasks that needed their attention, so they told the believers to choose seven good, respectable men who would take responsibility for the distribution of food among them. Two of these seven would become known for much more than distributing charity. In fact, since all seven of the men had Greek names, and since two of the men proved to be great preachers, the seven appear to be the spiritual standouts in the large group of Greek-speaking Christians, just as the twelve apostles were most prominent among the Aramaic-speaking group.

One of the seven was a man named Stephen—"full of grace and power," able to perform miracles among the people. Stephen was apparently an eloquent speaker on behalf of Christianity, and some of his opponents, unable to outdo him in open debate, claimed they heard Stephen blaspheme both Moses and God—charges that had also been made against Jesus while he was on earth. The Jewish leaders were so stirred up that they had Stephen brought in before the Sanhedrin, the Jews' ruling council. False witnesses lied and said Stephen was preaching against the temple—an accusation that would certainly get the attention of the priests and other leaders, since their livelihood depended on the temple. The Sanhedrin asked Stephen if the charges against him were true.

CULTURAL INSIGHTS

The Seven Deacons

Acts 6 tells of the dispute that resulted in the apostles appointing seven men "full of the Spirit and wisdom" to aid in their ministry. Two of these men—Stephen and Philip—play important roles in Acts. Tradition refers to the group as "the seven deacons," although Acts never actually calls them "deacons," merely referring to them as "the Seven" (21:8). Our word "deacon" comes from the Greek *diakonos*, usually translated "helper" or "servant." In some of Paul's letters, he speaks of the qualifications needed in a *diakonos* in the church (1 Timothy 3:8–13). In another letter he greets the "overseers and deacons" in the church (Philippians 1:1). Based on Acts 6, and Paul's mention of deacons, some churches give the title "deacon" to laymen who have special responsibilities.

Jewish Executions

Alert readers sometimes wonder about the execution of Stephen. Don't the Gospels say that the Sanhedrin, the Jews' ruling council, had no authority to execute men (John 18:31)? They do indeed, but that doesn't rule out the possibility of an occasional mob execution, particularly in a situation like Stephen's, where his words sent his enemies into such a rage that they weren't going to be bothered by the finer points of the law. Remember that at the time of Jesus' crucifixion, the Roman governor Pilate was in Jerusalem, keeping things orderly during the Passover festival. But most of the time the Roman governor would have resided in the city of Caesarea, far enough away that the Jews would have felt safe in executing a blasphemer without getting the Romans' approval.

Pilate was removed from office in the winter of AD 36–37. A few months elapsed before a new Roman governor took his place, and it is possible Stephen's execution took place in the interim, in the period when the Sanhedrin would not have feared Roman interference.

Later in Acts, the Jewish king Herod Agrippa I had the apostle James put to death. During Herod's reign (AD 41–44) there was no Roman governor, so Herod could execute whomever he pleased (Acts 12).

Stephen, whose "face was like the face of an angel," defended himself. Acts 7 contains his eloquent and heartfelt defense, in which he gives a capsule history of the Jews, starting with the call of the patriarch Abraham in Genesis. Continuing through the story of Moses, he reminds his listeners that Moses had prophesied the coming of a great prophet (whom the first Christians knew was Christ). He also reminds them of how rebellious the Israelites were under Moses, making the infamous golden calf idol while Moses was on Mount Sinai receiving the commandments from the hand of God.

If Stephen had confined himself to his recitation of Israel's history, he would have offended no one. After all, his listeners were quite familiar with the stories from Genesis and Exodus. However, he reminded his listeners that "the Most High does not live in houses made by men" (7:48)—a belief he confirmed by quotations from the Bible, but which riled the Sanhedrin, who saw his words as an insult to the temple. (Perhaps Stephen had heard from the apostles themselves the prophecy of Jesus that the temple would some day be destroyed [Mark 13:2], a prophecy which would come to pass in AD 70, when the Romans destroyed the temple.) Throughout his speech in Acts 7, he made it clear that God was not restricted to one city or one building—after all, the Israelites in the wilderness had no temple but were very much aware of God's presence. Stephen was presenting an idea that we will encounter in later books of the New Testament: God's saving message is not tied to any locale or tribe, and the true "temple of God" is not made of stones but of people. This profound message would survive the coming destruction of the temple in Jerusalem.

Stephen pushed his listeners over the brink when he told them, "You are just like your fathers: You always resist the Holy Spirit! Was there ever a prophet your fathers did not persecute?" And the last prophet, Christ, the greatest of all, they had killed.

The Sanhedrin was furious, its members grinding their teeth in their fury. Like many people of deep faith, Stephen was calm in a crisis because his mind was fixed on God, not on the eruption going on around him. He looked up to heaven and said that he saw Christ standing at the right hand of God. For his listeners, this was blasphemy—claiming that the "heretic" Jesus was now in heaven with God! His opponents dragged him out of the city and gave him the punishment given to blasphemers: stoning. His last words were "Lord, do not hold this sin against them" (7:60). The Christians who heard these words would have remembered Jesus' words on the cross: "Father, forgive them, they know not what they do" (Luke 23:34).

CHARACTER CLOSE-UP ## Gamaliel

In Acts, Jews seem to react to the gospel in one of two ways—total acceptance or total rejection. But a third option was exemplified by the respected rabbi Gamaliel, a Pharisee and member of the Sanhedrin. When the apostles were brought in for questioning, Gamaliel reminded the Sanhedrin that in the recent past, several would-be messiahs had arisen—but the movements they headed proved short-lived. He advised a "wait and see" policy toward the followers of Jesus: "If their purpose or activity is of human origin, it will fail. But if it is from God, you will not be able to stop these men; you will only find yourselves fighting against God." As a result of his sensible counsel, the Sanhedrin released the apostles—after flogging them (Acts 5:33–40). Given Gamaliel's words, we might well wonder if at some point he himself became a Christian.

Years before this incident, the revered rabbi had been the teacher of a devout young Jewish man named Saul—later to be known as the great Christian apostle Paul (Acts 22:3). Fortunately for the history of Christianity, Saul/Paul would not take the cautious "wait and see" approach to Christianity, but would be a devoted persecutor—and, later, one of its greatest preachers.

Christendom had its first martyr. As Christ had foretold, he himself would be condemned to death—and so would some of his followers. However, Acts records Stephen's death with these words: "He fell asleep" (7:60). The early Christians saw death as only a temporary victory of evil. Christ had been raised from the dead. So, in time, would all of his followers.

One man who witnessed the stoning of the saintly Stephen was "a young man named Saul" (7:58), who thoroughly approved of what happened. We will take a much closer look later at this man Saul, better known by the name Paul.

BREAKING DOWN BARRIERS

Thus far in Acts all the converts to the faith were Jews. Jesus had prophesied that the faith would spread to all the world, beginning in Judea but moving far beyond, and in Acts 8 we witness the prophecy coming true. After the martyrdom of Stephen, a great persecution broke out in Jerusalem against the Christians. One result of this was that the scattered believers would witness to the faith wherever they went. In Acts, and in fact throughout the history of Christianity, persecution does not destroy faith, but rather it seems to increase the number of converts.

One of the first locales outside of Judea to hear the gospel was Samaria, the region so despised by devout Jews. The faith was carried there by Philip, one of the seven men who had been chosen to aid in distributing charity to the Greek-speaking Christians. (One of the twelve apostles was also named Philip, but none of his activities are reported in Acts. The Philip we are speaking of here is sometimes known as Philip the evangelist to distinguish him from Philip the apostle.) Like Stephen, Philip worked miracles and preached boldly. The apostles who remained in Jerusalem heard of Philip's ministry to the Samaritans, and they sent Peter and John to aid in the mission (8:4–25).

Guided by an angel, Philip witnessed to the faith in a surprising way. The angel took him to a desert road, where he encountered a eunuch, who was an official of the queen of the faraway land of Ethiopia. The eunuch was apparently a God-fearer—a Gentile drawn to the Jewish religion—because he had been worshipping at the temple in Jerusalem. When Philip found him, he was in his chariot, reading the words of the prophet Isaiah. Philip asked him if he understood what he was reading in the scroll. The eunuch replied no—how could he, without an interpreter? He was reading from Isaiah 53—one of the "Servant Songs" that prophesied

DID YOU KNOW?

In ancient times people always read aloud, never silently. In the story of Philip and the Ethiopian eunuch in Acts 8, we are told that Philip "heard the man reading Isaiah the prophet" (8:30). In the ancient world, people believed that the written words themselves were lifeless, that they were not truly effective unless spoken aloud.

a divine Servant of God who was "led like a sheep to the slaughter." Philip explained that the words of Isaiah were a prophecy that had been fulfilled in the life of Jesus Christ. Philip "told him the good news about Jesus," and the eunuch responded in faith. Seeing a body of water nearby, Philip baptized the new convert. Philip was the first, but definitely not the last, evangelist to apply Isaiah's Servant Songs to the life of Jesus.

In our time of instant communications and jet travel, we miss the importance of the story. Philip had spread the faith not only to Samaria—not that many miles away from Jerusalem—but to a man from faraway Ethiopia. Presumably the eunuch would carry his newfound faith back to his homeland and make new converts there. To the original readers of Acts, this was awesome: The gospel was being taken to a land that seemed like the far reaches of the earth.

The fact that the man was a eunuch was important also. The Old Testament law prohibited eunuchs from being full converts to the Jewish faith (Deuteronomy 23:1). So the story shows that the faith was being spread to people who had been excluded from the old religion. This fulfilled a prophecy of Isaiah, who spoke of a future time when even the eunuchs would be included among the people of God (Isaiah 56:3–5). The eunuchs could not produce physical descendants to carry on their name, but according to Isaiah they could have something even better, an "everlasting name" in God's kingdom.

CHARACTER CLOSE-UP ## Simon Magus

Matthew's Gospel records that *magi* (generally translated "wise men") came to honor the infant Jesus. These *magi* were probably astrologers from Persia, but the other *magi* of the New Testament were charlatan magicians, plying the trade of working fake miracles. According to Acts 8, a *magus* named Simon dazzled the Samaritans so much that they referred to him as "the Great Power" (8:10). Simon lost some of his following as many Samaritans converted to Christianity, and in fact "Simon himself believed and was baptized" (8:13). He was intrigued by the evangelist Philip's ability to work *true* miracles (done for compassion, not for show).

Simon was even more impressed by the apostles Peter and John, who laid their hands on people who then received the Holy Spirit. Simon did an audacious thing: He offered them money for the secret of their power. Peter rebuked him harshly, telling him he had no part in the ministry because his heart was not right with God. Peter told him to repent of his wickedness. Simon responded, "Pray to the Lord for me." Did Simon in fact repent? Acts does not say. A very old tradition credits Simon as one of the early Gnostics, who mingled elements of Christianity with pagan beliefs.

Simon's attempt to buy spiritual power is the root of the word *simony*, referring to the corrupt practice of paying money to obtain a high office in the church bureaucracy.

Philip disappears from Acts for a while, but chapter 21 mentions that the apostle Paul stayed with him awhile, and that Philip "had four unmarried daughters who prophesied" (21:8–9).

THE WONDERS CONTINUE

Following the great persecution that came after the death of Stephen, there was an interlude of peace for the Christians. Traveling about the country, the apostle Peter went to the town of Lydda, where he encountered a man named Aeneas, a paralytic who had been bedridden for eight years. Peter worked a miracle with the words "Jesus Christ heals you," and the man got up from his mat and walked.

In the town of Joppa, a devout woman named Tabitha, well known for her generosity to the poor, had died. Before she was buried, some of the believers sent word to Peter, who came to Joppa. Here was a true test of the apostles. They had healed the sick, but could they, like their Master, raise the dead? Indeed, they could. Peter brought her to life with the words, "Tabitha, get up" (9:32–42).

Soon after this, a death occurred among the twelve apostles. James, the brother of John, was put to death by beheading. With Peter and John, James had formed a kind of "inner circle" among Jesus' twelve disciples, the three men being present at such important events as the Transfiguration and Jesus' agony in the Garden of Gethsemane. In the Gospels, James and John were ambitious enough that they asked Jesus for the privilege of sitting at his right and left hand when he received his kingdom. Jesus asked them, "Are you able to drink the cup that I drink?" They replied that they were, not knowing then that the "cup" might mean martyrdom (Mark 10:35–40), as proved to be the case for James.

> **DID YOU KNOW?**
>
> In Christian art, the apostle James is often depicted with a sword, since Herod had him beheaded with a sword (Acts 12:1–2).

Acts 12 says the execution of James was done by order of "King Herod." There are several men named Herod in the New Testament, and sometimes this can be confusing. The Herod mentioned here was Herod Agrippa I, the grandson of Herod the Great, the brutal king who ordered the massacre of the infants of Bethlehem (Matthew 2:16). He was also the nephew of Herod Antipas, who had beheaded John the Baptist (Mark 6:17–29) and mocked Jesus (Luke 23:6–12). Like the other men in his family, Herod Agrippa I was a Hellenized sophisticate, utterly lacking in spirituality. Through the will of the Romans he ruled over a territory as large as his grandfather's, but unlike him, Herod Agrippa was popular with his Jewish subjects. He liked to impress them as being faithful to their religion. He executed James to please the Jews—to them, the execution would have seemed like getting rid of a bothersome heretic—and finding that this increased his standing, he had Peter arrested, presumably for the purpose of executing him also. The fact that Peter had begun fraternizing with Gentiles (Acts 10–11) must have been widely known, and the Jews who were not Christians would have taken this as further proof that these followers of Jesus could not be tolerated. (Note the irony here: In his private life, Herod Agrippa hobnobbed with immoral Gentiles, but to curry favor with the Jews, he pretended to be a devout Jew, not tolerating "heretic" Jews like Peter who mingled with Gentiles.)

Herod held Peter in prison, planning to put him on trial at the time of the Passover—something the apostles would have found ironic, since Jesus had been executed at the Passover season. Peter must have wondered if he was about to suffer the same fate as James—or as Christ himself.

Cornelius and Peter

One of the most touching stories in the Bible concerns a Roman centurion named Cornelius, stationed in the city of Caesarea. He and his household were "devout and God-fearing"—meaning they followed the Jewish teachings even though they were Gentiles. One afternoon when Cornelius was praying, an angel appeared and commended his faith and generosity. The angel told him to send for a man named Peter, who was staying not far away (Acts 10:1–6).

The following day, Peter, on the rooftop of the house where he was staying, had a curious vision: He was hungry, and in the vision he saw a great sheet, or tarp, filled with all sorts of "unclean" animals—animals prohibited as food by the Jews' kosher laws. A voice told the apostle, "Get up, Peter. Kill and eat." Peter protested—he would never eat anything unclean. The heavenly voice responded, "Do not call anything impure that God has made clean." While Peter puzzled over the vision, the men sent by Cornelius found Peter and invited him to Cornelius' house. Peter was doing the unthinkable—a devout Jew entering the home of a Gentile.

Peter addressed a gathering of Cornelius' relatives and friends. He told them, "God has shown me that I should not call any man impure or unclean.... God does not show favoritism, but accepts men from every nation who fear him and do what is right" (10:28; 34–35). Peter then presented the gospel message: Jesus, God's anointed one, went about doing good, was crucified but then raised to life again. Much to the amazement of Peter's companions, the Gentiles accepted the message and were baptized. Later, some Jewish Christians scolded Peter for hobnobbing with Gentiles. But after Peter explained all that happened, they understood: "God has granted even the Gentiles repentance unto life" (11:18).

God had other plans for Peter, however. In prison, Peter was bound with chains, with a soldier on either side of him. An angel appeared to the sleeping Peter, roused him, and the chains fell off him. Peter followed the angel out of the prison, so perplexed at what was happening that he thought he was dreaming. They walked past the guards and found the iron gate open for them. The angel disappeared suddenly, and Peter was in awe at the power of the Lord.

He went to the home of a fellow believer, the mother of a man named Mark. (He was presumably the author of the Gospel that bears his name, and this is the first mention of him in Acts. Later on in the book we will meet him again as a missionary.) Peter knocked at the outer entrance, and a servant girl named Rhoda answered. Recognizing Peter's voice, she was overjoyed—so caught up in the emotion that she neglected to let Peter in! She ran to tell the news to the others, who thought she was out of her mind. But to the joy of everyone, it was indeed Peter, miraculously delivered by the Lord.

Not everyone was joyful at the deliverance. The soldiers who had guarded Peter were understandably aghast at what had happened. Herod ordered a search for Peter, and when he was not found, Herod had the poor guards executed. (Herod was of a paranoid, suspicious nature like his infamous grandfather, and he may have suspected some kind of plot at work.)

The story ends with a demonstration of divine justice. Herod, it seems, had been having a quarrel with some of the residents of the territory he ruled. To make an impression for public relations purposes, he put on his royal robes and delivered a public address to the people. The Jewish historian Josephus tells of the same incident, adding the detail that Herod wore a robe made of silver, and that his speech was made when the morning sun's rays struck the robe, creating a dazzling sight. According to both Josephus and Acts, some of the people present were so in awe of him that they shouted, "This is the voice of a god, not of a man." The words must have pleased the vain, pompous, wicked man, but he had little time to savor the words, because immediately he fell down dead (12:23).

"But the word of God continued to increase and spread." Time and again, some member of the infamous Herod family had killed good, innocent people in an effort to destroy the new faith. But nothing, not even a wicked, persecuting ruler, could put a stop to the power of the Lord.

In closing this chapter on the first part of Acts, it is worth rereading 4:13, which tells us that when the priests "saw the courage of Peter and John and realized that they were unschooled, ordinary men, they were astonished and they took note that these men had been with Jesus." Only a few weeks earlier, these men who "had been with Jesus" ran away in fear when their Master was taken prisoner. But much had happened since then.

They had seen their Master alive again after his death, and they had been given new power through the Holy Spirit, as Jesus had promised. The fact that they were "unschooled, ordinary men" was of no importance. Peter and John were working-class men from Galilee, as was the Teacher they had followed—laymen, not rabbis or scholars. But such men were being used by God in a dramatic way.

PUTTING THE WORD TO WORK

1. Acts praises the generosity of the first Christians, who made an effort to share with their poorer brothers and sisters. Think of ways that you can share—either materially or spiritually, or both—with fellow believers who are less fortunate than you.

2. The story of Ananias and Sapphira is a painful reminder of the pervasiveness of hypocrisy, with the couple wanting to be considered more religious than they actually were. Make a resolution to be honest always—with others and with yourself—about your spiritual condition.

3. In Acts, the apostles use their arrests by the authorities as opportunities to witness to others about their faith. Have there been occasions in your own life when having your faith questioned gave you an opportunity to be a witness?

4. Acts notes that Stephen's face was "like the face of an angel"—probably not referring to physical attractiveness, but to some deep spiritual quality that people perceived in him. Have you known anyone who radiated their spirituality this powerfully?

5. The story of Peter and Cornelius is a reminder that even good people can regard certain other people as "unclean." Who are some people—groups or individuals—that you have sometimes tried to avoid? Are there ways you can try to reach out to those people?

From Persecutor to Apostle

**AT THE
HEART
OF IT ALL
TODAY**
Paul, the persecutor of Christians, becomes an apostle and missionary, enduring confrontations, conspiracies and many trials as he carries the gospel far and wide, ending in the capital of the Roman empire.

Shipwreck, earthquake, prison, floggings, stonings, riots, murder plots, hair's-breadth escapes, trial before kings...the story of Paul the apostle told in Acts contains all these and much more, a saga so vivid no fiction writer could have invented it. From being

> **KEY PASSAGES TO READ TODAY**
>
> **Acts 9:1–30; 14:8–20; 15:1–21;
> 22:30—23:11; 26:1–32**

the most devoted persecutor of Christians, Paul became the devoted apostle, evangelist, missionary, pastor, and (through his many letters that Christians kept and treasured) the greatest theologian of all time. Thanks to Acts and his letters, we know Paul more intimately than almost any other figure of ancient times. Next to Jesus himself, he is the most important player in the drama of the early church, a man worth knowing in detail.

As we take a close look at Paul's story in Acts, here is something to keep in mind: Acts presents Paul for the most part addressing people *outside* the church, while Paul's letters deal with concerns *inside* the church. Put another way, Acts shows us Paul the missionary and evangelist, while his letters show us Paul the pastor and theologian.

IN HIS OWN WORDS

We are fortunate that Luke, the author of Acts, knew Paul personally and was present at many of the events he records. He was familiar with Paul's life both before and after he

KEY TERM FOR TODAY ## Brothers

The New Testament uses the word Christian only three times. The common term used by the first Christians themselves was the Greek word *adelphoi*—"brothers." The term (including the singular form, *adelphos*) is used 235 times in the New Testament—fifty times in Acts and 130 times in Paul's letters. Those first believers understood that by putting their faith in Christ, *the* Son of God, they had been adopted as the sons and daughters of God, so fellow believers were spiritually brothers and sisters. Some churches still hold to the old custom of members referring to each other as "brother" and "sister."

became a Christian, and so Acts gives us a lot of information about Paul's youth, usually in Paul's own words. Paul describes himself as "a Jew, born in Tarsus of Cilicia," but reared in Jerusalem. Under the revered Rabbi Gamaliel, "I was thoroughly trained in the law of our fathers" (Acts 22:3). Paul was what we might call "bicultural." Reared in Tarsus, a fairly cosmopolitan city, he was Hellenized, that is, familiar with Greek culture and with the way the Greek mind worked. Greek was probably his first language. But having studied in Jerusalem, he also spoke Aramaic (and probably Hebrew as well, since it was the language of the Scriptures). Like many Hellenized Jews, he had two names— Saul being his Jewish name, Paul his Greek one. Though he wasn't aware of it in his youth, everything in his background prepared him to be the apostle to the Greek-speaking Gentiles in the Roman empire.

"The Jews all know the way I have lived ever since I was a child… They have known me for a long time and can testify, if they are willing, that according to the strictest sect of our religion, I lived as a Pharisee" (26:4–5). We encountered the Pharisees in chapters dealing with the life of Jesus and know that they were the Jews most zealous for keeping the Law in all its details. Most of the Pharisees were hostile to Jesus, and most were equally hostile to his followers.

The first mention of Paul is in Acts 7:58, where he witnesses the stoning of the saintly Christian martyr, Stephen—and he approves it. Soon after, Paul "began to destroy the church. Going from house to house, he dragged off men and women and put them in prison" (8:3). Acts gives the impression that there was not a more dedicated persecutor of the first Christians. But God had his own plans for harnessing the zeal and energy and intellect of this man.

Acts 9 shows that Paul did not confine his persecution to Jerusalem but received a commission from the Jewish high priest to go to the Jews in Damascus, the chief city of Syria, to arrest "those who belonged to the Way," the Christians. But "as he neared Damascus on his journey, suddenly a light from heaven flashed around him. He fell to the ground and heard a voice say to him, 'Saul, Saul, why do you persecute me?' 'Who are you, Lord?' Saul asked. 'I am Jesus, whom you are persecuting,' he replied. 'Now get up and go into the city, and you will be told what you must do'" (9:3–6). The men traveling with Saul heard the voice but saw nothing. The divine light had blinded Saul, and he had to be led by the hand to the city.

AD 14–37
Reign of Roman
Emperor Tiberius

AD 35
Stoning of Stephen
(Acts 6–7)

Conversion of Saul,
later called Paul
(Acts 9:1–31)

AD 37–41
Reign of Roman
Emperor Caligula

AD 41–54
Reign of Roman
Emperor Claudius

AD 46–47
Paul's first
missionary journey
(Acts 13–14)

AD 48–49
Apostles' council
in Jerusalem
(Acts 15, Galatians 2)

AD 49
Smallpox appears for
the first time in China.

AD 49–51
Paul's second
missionary journey
(Acts 16:1—18:22)

AD 52–57
Paul's third
missionary journey
(Acts 18:24–20:38)

AD 54–68
Reign of Roman
Emperor Nero

AD 58
Paul's arrest
in Jerusalem
(Acts 21–23)

AD 58–60
Paul in prison
in Caesarea
(Acts 24)

AD 60
Paul's trial before
Festus and Agrippa
(Acts 25–26)

AD 60–61
Paul's journey to
Rome and shipwreck
(Acts 27:1–28:15)

AD 61–63
Paul under house
arrest in Rome
(Acts 28:16–31)

AD 62
Alexandrians witness
a lunar eclipse on the
evening of March 13
at eleven o'clock.

AD 63
Pompeii, the city
at the foot of Mount
Vesuvius, is heavily
damaged by a strong
earthquake.

We should pause here to consider the words of Jesus. He asks Saul, "Why do you persecute me?" Saul wasn't literally persecuting Jesus, of course—he was persecuting his followers. But already among the Christians was a consciousness that they were Christ's representatives on earth, so in a spiritual way they *were* him. In a very real sense, persecuting Christians was persecuting Christ himself. Saul would never forget the words, "I am Jesus, whom you are persecuting," for in later years, as a Christian apostle writing letters to guide Christian fellowships, he spoke of Christians as being the "body" of Christ (1 Corinthians 12:12–26).

In Damascus, a Christian named Ananias had his own troubling vision: God told him to go to a certain house and lay his hands on a man named Saul and restore his sight. Ananias was horrified, knowing this Saul was the great persecutor of Christians. But God assured Ananias that "this man is my chosen instrument to carry my name before the Gentiles and their kings" (Acts 9:10–16). Ananias—no doubt with fear and trembling—did as he was instructed, finding Saul, who had been blind for three days. Addressing him as "Brother Saul," he restored his sight. The persecutor was baptized—a sign that he was part of the faith community.

In one of the great spiritual turnarounds in history, Saul joined with the Christians and began preaching in the synagogues that Jesus was the Son of God. He had set out from Jerusalem with a commission from the high priest to arrest Christians, but that was overruled by a higher authority, a commission from Christ himself. The Christians of Damascus, who had been dreading his coming, now were calling him "Brother."

Thoroughly trained in the Scriptures, Paul devoted his eloquence and energy to the movement he had intended to stamp out. The fact that he was able so quickly to begin preaching the Christian message tells us he was already quite familiar with it. Perhaps in his zeal to stamp it out he had learned its teachings—and now was passing them on to others. This pleased the Christians but made the Jews furious—they saw him as a dangerous turncoat and renegade—and they plotted to kill him. He escaped by night, lowered in a basket over the city walls—the first but not the last hair's-breadth escape in his story (9:20–25). From this point on in Acts, Paul's life is almost always in danger.

DID YOU KNOW?

In William Tyndale's 1526 New Testament—the first English translation from the Greek—he gave this title to Acts: "The Acts of the Apostles, written by St. Luke Evangelist which was present at the doings of them." The long title recognizes that Luke was an eyewitness of many of the events in the book.

He returned to Jerusalem, and the Christians there were at first—and with good reason—highly suspicious of him. How did they know he wasn't a "mole" trying to gain their trust before betraying them? But Saul found a sponsor in Barnabas, a Jew from the island of Cyprus who had generously sold some land and donated the money to the needy Christians. Barnabas accepted the reality of Saul's amazing conversion and took him to meet the apostles. As in Damascus, a murder plot developed among the Jews, and the Christians—"the brothers"—sent him off to his hometown, Tarsus, for his safety's sake.

MAN WITH A MISSION

In the previous chapter we saw that the apostle Peter preached the faith to the Roman centurion Cornelius, who became a convert. The faith was being spread to the Gentiles, and the center of the Gentile mission was the great city of Antioch in Syria. The Christians in Jerusalem sent Barnabas, "a good man, full of the Holy Spirit and faith," to Antioch to investigate the growth of the church there. He approved of what he saw

CULTURAL INSIGHTS

Antioch

Apart from Jerusalem, no city is more important in the Book of Acts than Antioch, capital of the Roman province of Syria. It was the third-largest city in the empire (after Rome and Alexandria) and renowned for its culture (and also the immorality of its pagan residents). Christianity reached there following the persecution and scattering of Jerusalem Christians after the martyrdom of Stephen (Acts 11:19), and the road between Jerusalem and Antioch was well-traveled by the early Christians, with the Jerusalem believers sending Barnabas to Antioch to minister to the growing faith community (11:22). It was the first primarily Gentile church and also the place where believers were first called Christians (11:26). Antioch became the starting place of Paul's three missionary journeys (13:1–3) and was also the locale where Jewish Christians tried (but eventually failed) to convince Gentile believers that they had to be circumcised (15:1–2). The city could rightly be called the Cradle of Gentile Christianity.

Because of its importance in Acts, Antioch has been a popular name for churches. The city still exists today, known as Antakya in the nation of Turkey, although few of the buildings of the New Testament period still exist. Those buildings would have included the enormous amphitheater known as the Circus, remembered as the site of the famous chariot race in the film *Ben-Hur*.

Church

The New Testament used the secular Greek word *ekklesia* to refer to the Christian fellowships. We usually translate it as "church," but the word literally means "assembly" or "congregation." The idea behind the word was that a king or some official summoned his people to meet together. For the Christians, they had been summoned by their King, Christ. They followed the Old Testament habit of speaking of Israel, the Lord's people, as the *qahal,* the Hebrew word that also means "assembly."

When William Tyndale made the first English translation of the Bible in the 1520s, he translated *ekklesia* as "congregation." He chose not to use "church" because in his own time (and in ours) "church" referred to a building. In the New Testament, the word *ekklesia* never refers to a building but always to the assembled believers. While local fellowships existed, there was also a consciousness that the Lord's *ekklesia* encompassed all Christians everywhere.

Related to the word *ekklesia* is another important word *klesis,* meaning "call" or "summons." The Christian understood that he had been summoned by God. He was a *kletos*, a called person. While all Christians were called by God, some were called for a special purpose, as in Acts 13:2: "While they were worshipping the Lord and fasting, the Holy Spirit said, 'Set apart for me Barnabas and Saul for the work to which I have called them.' " Paul never forgot he was God's *kletos* man, as we see in the opening of his Letter to the Romans: "Paul, a servant of Christ Jesus, called to be an apostle and set apart for the gospel of God."

and sent word to Saul in Tarsus that he was needed. For a full year Barnabas and Saul ministered to the believers in Antioch and made new converts. Acts 13:1 names the two men as being part of a group of five "prophets and teachers" in the city.

Somehow the Holy Spirit communicated to the group at Antioch that Barnabas and Saul were to be "set apart" for the work of carrying the faith far and wide. Here began what is called Paul's first missionary journey. With Barnabas's young cousin John Mark accompanying them, they set sail for Barnabas's homeland, the island of Cyprus, where they first preached the faith to the Jews in their synagogue. The local ruler, named Sergius Paulus, expressed interest in the new faith, but the missionaries were opposed by a sorcerer named Elymas. No doubt the sorcerer saw the new religion as a threat to his own livelihood as a charlatan magician. (This is not the first nor last time in Acts that someone making a profit from false religion felt threatened by the bringers of the true religion.) For hindering the progress of the faith, the sorcerer was temporarily struck with blindness, so impressing Sergius Paulus that he became a believer. At this point in the narrative, Acts begins referring to Saul as Paul (13:4–12).

For some unstated reason, John Mark returned to Jerusalem, a departure from the mission that would shortly cause conflict. Barnabas and Paul went to the city of Antioch of Pisidia. (There were several cities named Antioch in ancient times.) Paul's first sermon recorded in Acts was preached in this city's synagogue. Paul addressed his words to "men of Israel and you Gentiles who worship God." Paul's message that Jesus was the Messiah that the Jews and God-fearing Gentiles had hoped for won many converts—but also stirred up the wrath of many of the Jews. This would become a familiar pattern for the missionaries. It was at this point that Paul understood that his mission was chiefly to the Gentiles (13:46–48)—to be specific, to the God-fearers, Gentiles who had already been drawn to the Jewish religion and were spiritually ready to hear the proclamation of the Messiah. The Jews themselves for the most part rejected the gospel message and, more importantly, did what they could to oppose it.

The two men traveled to the town of Lystra, where they encountered a man who had been lame from birth. With the words "Stand up on your feet!" Paul healed him—not the last time the apostle would perform a miracle. The healing so impressed the local pagans that they shouted, "The gods have come down to us in human form!" They believed Barnabas was the Greek god Zeus, while Paul was the god Hermes. The local priest of Zeus intended to sacrifice bulls to the two "gods," but the two men assured the crowd that they were merely human. Some Jewish opponents arrived and stirred up the people against Paul. They dragged him outside the city, stoned him, and left him for dead. But, through the power of God, Paul proved to be a survivor. In fact, despite all the opposition they encountered, the first mission was a great success. Paul and Barnabas returned to Antioch and reported joyfully how God had "opened the door of faith to the Gentiles" (14:27).

THE CRISIS AND THE COUNCIL

Some Jewish Christians came to Antioch and announced that true Christians had to be circumcised according to the Laws of Moses. Paul and Barnabas sharply disagreed, seeing that such a requirement would do immeasurable harm to their mission. Why should a person's salvation depend on circumcision? The two traveled to Jerusalem to meet with the apostles and other Christian leaders and settle this troubling issue.

The meeting is generally called the "council of Jerusalem," and it was one of the decisive moments in the history of the faith. The basic question was: Is Christianity a unique and universal faith, or is it merely a Jewish sect? To require circumcision of converts would be to remain under the Jewish Law. The Jewish religion attracted many Gentiles, but many more of them found it distasteful, seeing no spiritual purpose in circumcision or the kosher food laws. The many God-fearers who were converting to Christianity had long been attracted to the Jewish morality, but not to the requirements

Synagogues

Synagogues, Jewish houses of worship, developed due to the Babylonian conquest and exile of the Jews. The Babylonians destroyed the Jerusalem temple in 586 BC, and after that, Jewish religious life centered around synagogues, where Jews gathered on the Sabbath to worship and read from the Law and the Prophets.

Even after a new temple was built, serving as the center of sacrifices and the Jewish holy days, the Jewish faith remained centered in the synagogues, which were found throughout the Roman empire and elsewhere. Synagogue services were open to everyone, and Gentiles interested in the Jewish faith—the God-fearers and proselytes—were sometimes faithful attenders.

We see in Acts that the apostle Paul always started his missionary activity in a city by going to the synagogue and trying to convince the Jews and God-fearers that Jesus was the Messiah the Scriptures had prophesied. Although he was the "apostle to the Gentiles," he felt it his duty to preach first to his own people, the Jews. In each locale he made converts but also made enemies, since most Jews would not accept his message. As Jesus predicted, his followers would be persecuted in the synagogues because of their faith (Matthew 10:17).

Depending on the locale, the language of the synagogue service might be in Aramaic or Greek. In most of the synagogues mentioned in Acts, the language was Greek, so Paul would have preached his faith by quoting from the Septuagint, the Greek translation of the Old Testament.

for circumcision and food taboos. The time seemed right to release the faith from these arguably useless regulations.

It is worth noting here that in a couple of passages (13:45, 17:5), the Jews were said to be "jealous" of the Gentiles who accepted the Christian message. Why? The Jews had always welcomed God-fearing Gentiles to their synagogue services. Yet many Jews still felt themselves to be God's "chosen people," and Acts makes it clear that many of them were not happy to see the God-fearers respond so positively to the apostles' preaching. In fact, Acts gives us the impression that some Jews rejected the gospel because they saw the Gentiles responding to it. They wanted to retain their position as God's chosen people, while Paul and the other apostles wanted *all* people to be saved.

At the Jerusalem council, the apostle Peter reminded the people that he himself had carried the faith to Gentiles. God made no distinction between Gentile and Jew, for all could be saved through faith in Christ. Paul and Barnabas vouched for this with their stories of making many converts among the Gentiles. Clearly, many people had already been saved without being circumcised.

Presiding over the council was James, a brother of Jesus, who had not been a follower during Jesus' lifetime but came to faith later. (Just a reminder: Some Bible scholars believe James and the other "brothers" of Jesus mentioned in the Gospels were the children of Mary and Joseph, while other scholars note that "brothers" in these contexts could also refer to cousins, or to other male relatives.) A prominent figure in the Jerusalem church, James announced that "we should not make it difficult for the Gentiles who are turning to God" (15:19). The council agreed with James, however, on other points, asking Gentile converts to refrain from sexual immorality and from eating food offered to idols.

Paul and Barnabas returned to Antioch and ministered to the Christians there. Paul proposed a second mission, revisiting the converts they had made on their first trip. Barnabas agreed, but wanted to take along John Mark, who had gone on the first journey but for some unstated reason left them along the way. They disagreed so sharply that they went their separate ways, Barnabas setting out on a mission with John Mark, Paul taking a new missionary partner named Silas. We can feel a little sadness at this dispute between Paul and Barnabas—even saints are human—but also observe that it resulted in the sending out of two missionary pairs instead of just one. God moves in mysterious ways. The account of the dispute also reminds us that sincere people of faith can disagree without hating each other. It also reminds us how truthful Luke was being when he wrote Acts. In writing about the early Christians, it might have been tempting to smooth over such disagreements, but Luke reported the incident, without passing judgment on either Paul or Barnabas. The two partners parted, but the faith continued to

CHARACTER CLOSE-UP ## Silas

After his disagreement with Barnabas, Paul took on Silas as his missionary partner. Silas was a prominent member of the faith community in Jerusalem (Acts 15:22), and, like Paul, he was a Roman citizen. Silas was with Paul at Philippi, where both were beaten and imprisoned—and then (following the dramatic earthquake that knocked the prison down) released by the embarrassed locals, who were horrified to learn they had punished two Roman citizens without due process (Acts 16:35–39).

The name Silas is probably a variant of the Greek name Silvanus, and Silas may be the Silvanus named in Paul's salutations of the two letters to the Thessalonians. A Silvanus is praised as a "faithful brother" as well as the scribe of 1 Peter (5:12), and it is likely that the well-written Greek of the letter is a case of Silvanus/Silas polishing the thoughts of the Aramaic-speaking fisherman, Peter. If this is the same person, Silas was indeed a privileged man to have been a companion of both Paul and Peter. Unlike Paul and Barnabas, Silas is never referred to as an "apostle," but he was clearly a dedicated worker in carrying the faith to the Gentiles in the eastern Roman Empire.

spread, and that was what mattered. When we study Paul's letters later on, we will see that, happily, Paul and John Mark worked together once again (Colossians 4:10) and the dispute with Barnabas had ended.

EVEN TO EUROPE

On Paul's second missionary journey, he had other companions besides Silas. One of these was a young man named Timothy, whom the childless Paul would come to regard as his spiritual son. Another companion was the author of Acts himself, Luke, and in Acts 16:10 begins one of the book's "we passages," in which Luke narrates in the first-person plural. The "we passages" are very special, for we know Luke is an eyewitness to what he describes.

The missionary group had decided to take the gospel to Europe, for Paul had had a vision of a man of Macedonia, begging him, "Come over... and help us" (16:9). The men sailed for Macedonia (part of Greece) and stopped in the city of Philippi. Apparently there was no synagogue in the city, for the Jews and God-fearers met for prayer by a river. One of the God-fearers was Lydia, a dealer in cloth. She became a convert and opened her home to the missionaries (16:15).

One of their encounters in Philippi was much less pleasant. A slave girl who supposedly could foretell the future followed the missionaries around, shouting: "These men are servants of the Most High God, who are telling you the way to be saved." Her words were true, but apparently she was so disruptive that Paul ordered the demonic spirit inside her to depart. Her owners were not pleased, since her prophetic powers made them money. Paul and Silas were dragged to the marketplace and accused of disturbing the peace. The two men were stripped and beaten, then thrown in jail, with their feet put in stocks. To the amazement of the other prisoners, Paul and Silas sang hymns to God in the night. A violent earthquake shook the prison so that the prisoners' chains fell off. The jailer, seeing that the prisoners were loose, was about to kill himself, but Paul stopped him. No doubt in a highly emotional state, the jailer asked them, "Sirs, what must I do to be saved?" The two presented the gospel to him and he was baptized —and washed the wounds from their beating. Under the most unlikely circumstances a new convert was made. In fact, his whole family was baptized with him.

Paul and Silas took the gospel to the Greek city of Thessalonica, where they made some converts but, as usual, found opponents. They had more success in Berea, where the people were of "noble character" and more receptive to the message (17:11).

Paul then went on alone to the great city of Athens, renowned for its beauty and culture. However, Paul was "greatly distressed to see that the city was full of idols." He was equally distressed that the shallow, pretentious Athenians "spent their time doing nothing but talking about and listening to the latest ideas" (17:21). Athens was full of temples to various gods, but the Athenians had heard too many ideas to have much enthusiasm for any. It seemed an unlikely place to make converts, yet Paul never passed up an opportunity to preach. Some of the locals referred to him as a "babbler," but he was given the chance to present his message, since the people were intellectually curious (and spiritually skeptical). Paul's address was delivered at the site called the Areopagus—"hill of the war god Ares." Paul told the crowd that he had seen an altar inscribed with the words *Agnosto theo*—"To the Unknown God." It was this unknown God that he wished to proclaim to them. Since he was speaking to a pagan audience, he did not follow his usual pattern of preaching about Jesus as the fulfillment of Old Testament prophecies. Rather, he spoke in more general terms about the Creator God who made all men and would someday judge them for their deeds. And he spoke of the resurrection of Jesus, at which some of them sneered. Not surprisingly, he made only a few converts in Athens.

NEW FRIENDS, NEW ENEMIES

Paul left Athens for the large (and notoriously immoral) port city of Corinth, where he made friends with a Christian couple, Priscilla and Aquila, who would prove to be a great

---

CHARACTER CLOSE-UP # Priscilla and Aquila

Two of Paul's dearest friends were husband and wife, Aquila and Priscilla, both Christians. They were living in Rome when the emperor Claudius expelled all Jews from the city, a fact recorded in Acts 18:2. The Roman historian Suetonius states that the expulsion occurred because the Jews had been quarreling about "Chrestos," and most likely he was referring to a dispute between Jews who had become Christians and those who had not. Since the expulsion was in the year 49 or 50, we know that Aquila and Priscilla had become Christians at an early date. For a time they lived in the city of Ephesus, where a Christian fellowship met in their home, and where they taught the eloquent speaker Apollos the deeper meanings of the faith (Acts 18:18–28). We gather from Paul's Letter to the Romans that at some point the couple returned to Rome, and the same letter states that they risked their own lives for Paul's sake (Romans 16:3). Paul commends them as "my fellow workers in Christ Jesus." Although Paul chose the single, celibate life and commended it because it freed the Christian to devote himself wholeheartedly to the Lord's work (1 Corinthians 7), the courage and dedication of Priscilla and Aquila show the value of a married couple operating as a spiritual team.

Tent-Making

Paul is referred to as a *skenopoios*, a Greek word usually translated "tent-maker" but more generally meaning "leatherworker." The leather tents on which Paul's livelihood was based were not camping equipment but the large tents used by the Roman legions for their winter quarters. The typical tent would have housed eight men. Paul's dear friends Aquila and Priscilla were also tent-makers (Acts 18:3). Because tents and other leather goods were needed in every locale, Paul, Aquila and Priscilla could make a living anywhere, an obvious advantage as they spread the faith.

In 2 Corinthians, Paul drew an image from his vocation, referring to the Christian's earthly body as a "tent," a temporary dwelling that will, in time, no longer be needed (5:1–4).

Paul's occupation as tent-maker has added a term to the religious vocabulary: a "tent-making ministry" refers to a minister earning his livelihood not by his church work but through a secular job. (In fact, there were *no paid ministers* in the New Testament.) Paul no doubt learned what all tent-making ministers have learned: It is easier to speak the truth to people—including speaking out against immorality—when one isn't relying on those people as a source of income.

help to him. He made many converts in Corinth, but, as usual, made enemies among the Jews, who accused him in front of the local ruler as being a troublemaker. The ruler, Gallio, brushed the matter aside as a Jewish issue that was no concern of his (Acts 18:12–17).

Paul stayed a long time in Corinth—and no doubt his pastoral care was needed in this den of vice (something we will learn more of later when we study his two letters to the Corinthians). He then took the gospel to Ephesus, where he met a Christian Jew named Apollos from the great metropolis of Alexandria, Egypt. Apollos was an eloquent speaker and well-versed in the Scriptures, but before being sent out as a missionary himself, he received further instruction in the faith from Priscilla and Aquila (18:24–28).

Ephesus, where Paul spent two years, was in a region known for its peculiar religious sects and occult practices. Some of the Christian converts in Ephesus showed they had forsaken their former ways by bringing out all their writings on sorcery and burning them publicly (19:17–20). Historians tells us that in ancient time, the term "Ephesian writings" often referred to these scrolls.

However, the many conversions to Christianity riled up a silversmith named Demetrius. Ephesus was the site of the Artemision, the famous temple to the goddess Artemis, regarded as one of the Seven Wonders of the World. Curiously, the Artemis of Ephesus was not the slim, tomboyish, virginal woodland goddess depicted in many Greek myths, but a matronly fertility goddess, shown with her body covered over with breasts—a rather bizarre contrast to the graceful refinement of the temple itself. The many pilgrims to the temple would purchase silver Artemis shrines (probably small replicas of the temple or of the goddess) that Demetrius and his cohorts made. For the silversmiths, Christianity seemed both a religious and economic threat. Demetrius whipped up the local people into a frenzy. Gathering in the local amphitheater, they shouted out "Great is Artemis of the Ephesians!" for two hours. Paul's friends wisely prevented him from addressing the angry mob (19:23–41). Luke's account of this bizarre riot contains the interesting detail that "Most of the people did not even know why they were there"—which shows that Luke understood how utterly irrational a mob could be.

Despite the riot, Paul's ministry in Ephesus was mostly a success. Acts 20 contains Paul's very emotional farewell to the leaders of the Ephesian church. At the end of his speech, "they all wept as they embraced him and kissed him. What grieved them most was his statement that they would never see his face again" (20:37–38). Paul had a premonition that great trouble awaited him in Jerusalem.

PAUL THE PRISONER

On the trip back to Jerusalem, Paul met a Christian prophet named Agabus, who foretold that the Jews of Jerusalem would arrest Paul and hand him over to the Gentiles. Paul's friends begged him not to go on, but Paul insisted on going, sensing some divine purpose in what would happen.

James and the other Christian leaders in Jerusalem received Paul warmly, of course. However, the Jews accused Paul of doing the unthinkable, taking a Gentile into the

---

CULTURAL INSIGHTS

"Civilized" Greeks?

We see pictures of exquisite Greek sculpture and architecture and think of the Greeks as a civilized, rational people. They were—at times. But as in all cultures throughout history, there was a wild and irrational side to them, especially in the area of religion. We see this clearly in the story of the long, impromptu "pep rally" for the goddess Artemis in Ephesus, when the local mob saw Paul and his faith as a threat to the local religion. Paul and his companions were active in Phrygia, a region notorious for its frenzied religious practices. One of the most popular cults in the Roman empire originated in Phrygia, the cult of Cybele, the Great Mother of the Gods, or Mountain Mother. Her priests, the Galli, were self-emasculated, and in the orgiastic worship rites the Galli, dressed in women's garb and their long hair anointed with fragrant oil, would dance wildly and often slash themselves with knives. In the early days of Christianity, the Great Mother cult was a major rival of the new faith.

Sleeping Eutychus

People in ancient times could listen to a speaker for hours, particularly if he was a charismatic one. We can assume that Paul was surely worth listening to. However, even the most dynamic speaker might witness a listener falling asleep. Acts 20 tells of Paul addressing a house fellowship in the city of Troas. He talked on past midnight in a third-story room, and a young man named Eutychus, seated on a window sill, dozed off and fell to the ground. He appeared dead, but Paul went down, threw his arms around the young man, and revived him. Despite this dramatic interruption, Paul continued to talk on until daybreak. "The people took the young man home alive and were greatly comforted" (20:12).

temple area, which was strictly off-limits to non-Jews. The charge was false, but many people believed it, and the whole city was in an uproar. The mob dragged Paul out of the temple area and would have beaten him to death if the commander of the Roman troops had not intervened. The commander gave Paul permission to address the crowd. Speaking in Aramaic, Paul told of how he had persecuted the Christians until his experience on the road to Damascus. The people listened quietly until Paul stated that he had been sent as an apostle to the Gentiles, then they began shouting again, demanding that Paul die.

The commander saw that they were getting nowhere with the mob, so he had Paul taken to the soldiers' barracks. He was about to have Paul flogged, but Paul informed him that he was a Roman citizen and thus could not be punished or put in chains without standing trial first (Acts 22:25).

The following day, Paul—no longer in chains—was allowed to speak to the Sanhedrin, the Jews' ruling council. The Sanhedrin was quieter than the lynch mob, but no less hostile to him. Paul knew that there were both Pharisees and Sadducees on the council, and that the Sadducees did not believe in the resurrection of the dead. Willing to use the division to his advantage, Paul told the council, "I am a Pharisee... I stand on trial because of my hope in the resurrection of the dead." An uproar resulted, with the Pharisees rallying around Paul as one of their own. Sensing violence in the air again, the Roman commander had Paul taken back to the barracks (23:1–10).

In the midst of all these troubles, Paul received a word of comfort from the Lord: "Take courage! As you have testified about me in Jerusalem, so you must also testify about me in Rome" (23:11).

The predators were still after the apostle. More than forty Jewish men took a vow not to eat food again until Paul was dead. Paul's nephew learned of the plot and reported it to the Roman soldiers. By night, Paul was taken from Jerusalem to Caesarea, where he was kept under guard.

The plotters learned their intended victim had escaped. The high priest and some of his cronies went to Caesarea and informed the Roman governor, named Felix, that Paul was a troublemaker, "a ringleader of the Nazarene sect" who had defiled the Jews' holy temple. Felix gave Paul a chance to defend himself, and Paul denied that he had defiled the temple. Felix had a Jewish wife named Drusilla and was "well acquainted with the Way," meaning that he was somewhat familiar with Christianity, though definitely not a Christian himself. The Roman historian Tacitus wrote that Felix carried out his duties "with all sorts of cruelty and lust." He tried to rid the region of Jewish zealots by crucifying hundreds of them. In fact, he kept Paul prisoner because it pleased the Jews he ruled over—and also because he hoped that Paul or his friends might offer him a bribe. For two years Paul was kept under guard, until the greedy Felix was succeeded by a better man, Festus.

TRIALS AND VOYAGES

Festus had only been three days at his post when the Jewish leaders, still eager to take Paul's life, requested that he allow Paul to be tried in Jerusalem. Instead, Festus summoned the leaders to Caesarea and called upon Paul to defend himself. "I have done nothing wrong against the law of the Jews or against the temple or against Caesar," Paul said, in all truth. Festus asked him if he was willing to be tried in Jerusalem. Having no

---

CULTURAL INSIGHTS

Roman Citizenship

Being a *resident* of the Roman empire was not the same as being a *citizen*. Essentially, a Roman citizen was anyone who had the same civil rights as the natives of the city of Rome. An emperor could reward service to the empire (or himself) by granting citizenship to an individual, a family, a city or an entire province. Once citizenship was granted to a family, the children automatically became citizens. Acts 22:28 states that Paul was "born a citizen," and his citizenship was based on his being born in the cosmopolitan city of Tarsus, whose residents had been granted citizenship by the emperor Augustus.

Citizenship carried certain civic responsibilities, but also privileges, such as immunity from flogging and crucifixion, and the right of appeal to the emperor—always referred to as *Caesar*—himself. Two Latin phrases carried great legal weight: *Ciuis Romanus sum*—"I am a Roman citizen." *Ad Caesarem prouoco*—"I appeal to Caesar." The apostle Paul was not lacking in courage, but more than once in Acts he is willing to take advantage of his rights as a Roman citizen. In one of his letters, he told his fellow Christians that "our citizenship is in heaven," which tells us he prized his faith infinitely more than his Roman citizenship (Philippians 3:20).

In the New Testament, the actual Greek word we translate as "citizen" is *polites*, rooted in the word *polis*, "city."

---

desire to be handed over to the hostile Jews, Paul availed himself of his right as a Roman citizen: He appealed to Caesar. Festus replied, "To Caesar you will go!" (Acts 25:12). Paul, raised as a devout Jew, expected more fairness from the Roman emperor than from the leaders of the faith he was raised in.

Before sending Paul to Rome, however, Festus received two guests: Agrippa, one of the infamous Herod family, and his sister Bernice. This Agrippa is known to historians as Herod Agrippa II, son of Herod Agrippa I, who had ordered the execution of the apostle James. Agrippa II had an incestuous relationship with his sister Bernice, and even the jaded Romans with their lax morality were scandalized at his behavior. Hearing of Paul's curious case, Agrippa expressed an interest in hearing the prisoner speak. The next day Agrippa and Bernice "came with great pomp," and Paul was brought before them. (Luke could not resist pointing out the contrast of Paul, the prisoner in chains, with the "great pomp" of Agrippa and Bernice. In the divine view of things, the insignificant prisoner in his chains was a far greater man than these two bejeweled, immoral sophisticates.)

Paul spoke of his past life as a persecutor and of his life-changing conversion experience, and stated that the Jews hated him because of his mission to the Gentiles. Festus, a practical-minded Roman, found all this religious talk bizarre, and he interrupted Paul, saying, "You are out of your mind, Paul!... Your great learning is driving you insane" (26:24). Agrippa was equally skeptical, saying to Paul, "Do you think that in such a short time you can persuade me to be a Christian?" (The answer was yes, for Paul never passed up an opportunity to witness to his faith.) While these two very worldly officials may have scoffed at Paul's faith, from a legal standpoint they saw he was perfectly innocent. They would have released him—except that he had appealed to Caesar, and so had to be sent to Rome.

Acts 27 is the account of the trouble-filled voyage to Rome. This is one of the "we passages," so we know Luke himself was also on the ill-fated trip, and it is obvious that the unpleasant details of the voyage were still very clear to him. At first, unfavorable winds made the ship's going slow, but then, worse, a hurricane-force "northeaster" struck the ship. Luke admits that they "gave up all hope of being saved" as the storm persisted for several days. But in the midst of the trouble, Paul assured them though the ship would be destroyed, not one life would be lost, an assurance he had received from God (27:22).

The crew and passengers (276 people in all) went several days without eating—though we can well imagine that the tossing of the ship ruined their appetites! Finally, daylight broke through and the ship ran aground on a sandbar. The soldiers intended to follow the usual Roman practice and kill all the prisoners to prevent them from running away, but a centurion who had taken a liking to Paul prevented this. As Paul had prophesied, not one life was lost in the ordeal.

They had run aground on the Mediterranean island of Malta, where the locals received them hospitably. Paul made a deep impression on the people when he survived the bite of a poisonous viper, and even more so when he healed the sick father of the local governor (28:1–10).

Eventually the group took another ship and finally arrived in Italy. In Rome, Christian brothers eagerly awaited the arrival of the renowned apostle Paul. In light of the trouble Paul had had with the Jews in his travels, he spoke to the leaders of the Jews in Rome and assured them that he was no troublemaker. The Jews agreed to give him a fair hearing, and of course, his meetings with them were an opportunity to witness to his faith in Christ.

At the end of Acts, Paul has lived for two years in Rome, under house arrest, but with freedom to receive visitors. "Boldly and without hindrance he preached the kingdom of God and taught about the Lord Jesus Christ" (28:31). In light of all that Paul had endured, this is certainly a happy ending. But many readers wonder: Why does Acts end here? Why doesn't Luke tell of Paul's trial before Caesar? The simple truth is, we don't know why the book ends where it does. It is possible Luke died before he continued the story—or, more likely, he thought that Paul preaching the gospel in Rome was a perfectly good way to end the book. It is conceivable Luke had planned to write a sequel, telling more about Paul and the other Christian leaders. Acts was probably written before AD 64, since that was the year that Nero began persecuting Christians in Rome.

Some old, and possibly reliable, traditions say that Paul was tried before Caesar, released, whereupon he did further missions, but was executed by beheading in the persecution of Christians under emperor Nero. We can't know for certain, although, given what we know of Paul from Acts, his martyrdom does seem highly probable. The zealous Pharisee-turned-Christian was bound to make friends—and bitter enemies—wherever he went. Most of the Jews of his time saw him as a traitor to his religion. Paul and other Jewish converts

DID YOU KNOW?

New Testament scholars agree that the most difficult part of the New Testament to translate is Acts 27, the story of Paul's sea voyage and shipwreck. Luke uses many nautical terms for the weather and parts of the ship that had translators puzzling for centuries. One example: 27:17 refers to *boetheiai*, the Greek word meaning, "helps," which is how the King James Version renders it. James Smith, both a scholar and an experienced seaman, aided modern translators immeasurably with his 1848 book *The Voyage and Shipwreck of St. Paul*. We now know that the word in this context refers to large ropes or cables used to hold a ship's hull together in a storm.

to Christianity did not see it that way at all. They saw themselves as faithful Jews, who joyfully accepted Jesus of Nazareth as the Messiah that the Jews had long prayed for.

At the opening of Acts, the risen Jesus told the apostles, "You will be my witnesses in Jerusalem, and in all Judea and Samaria, and to the ends of the earth" (1:8). When the book ends, Paul—though a prisoner—is preaching the gospel in faraway Rome. Jesus' words had come to pass. And despite more opposition and persecution, the faith would continue to spread.

PUTTING THE WORD TO WORK

1. Paul's dramatic conversion experience is one of the classic turnarounds in world history, with the persecutor becoming an apostle. Can you think of people you have known who have had spiritual and moral turnarounds? Was it always a dramatic event that caused it?

2. The dispute between Paul and his missionary partner Barnabas shows that people of faith can disagree without hating each other. Have you ever "agreed to disagree" with a fellow believer, allowing the relationship to continue? What were some other times when you wish this had happened?

3. Several times in Paul's story he receives a comforting word from the Lord in the midst of trouble. Can you look back to some occasions in your own life when you sensed God consoling and encouraging you in a time of crisis?

4. Paul's experience in Athens was a classic case of intellectuals and sophisticates failing to respond to deep religious faith. Do you know anyone who considers himself "too sophisticated" to believe? How could your own faith appeal to them?

5. Paul's dear friends Priscilla and Aquila are the New Testament's classic example of a Christian couple devoted to spreading the faith, even having their own home serve as a center of fellowship. Have you known married couples who also seemed to work together as a spiritual team, whose home gave a warm welcome to fellow believers?

Ageless Letters

AT THE HEART OF IT ALL TODAY	Paul's three greatest letters—Romans and 1 and 2 Corinthians—probe some of the deepest truths of the faith, including the nature of true love and the difficulty of living morally in a fallen world. In the same letters we also see the power of God at work in sustaining the apostle through his trials.

In this chapter and the next we will dive into the deep waters of the mind of the apostle Paul. Thanks to his many letters and the Book of Acts, we know more about Paul than any other person of the New Testament, including Jesus himself. As we saw in the previous chapter, Paul was a dynamic mission-ary and concerned pastor, the former persecutor of Christians who became the most widely traveled of the apostles. Paul established many churches in his travels, and in his letters he continued to be the faithful, caring pastor *in absentia*. Reading the letters is poignant, since we feel Paul's regret at not being able to deliver his messages in person. But in the providence of God, Paul's extreme busyness spreading the gospel was a good thing, for the letters he sent to counsel the churches have been read and taken to heart for almost two thousand years.

Before we proceed, let's answer a question: What is the difference between a *letter* and an *epistle*? As far as your New Testament is concerned, none. Some Bibles have "Epistle to the Romans," others have "Letter to the Romans," both referring to the same thing. Strictly speaking, though, the writings we are studying in this chapter were letters, not

> **KEY PASSAGES TO READ TODAY**
>
> **Romans 1; 8; 12**
> **1 Corinthians 7; 13; 15**
> **2 Corinthians 5; 6:14–18; 12:1–10**

KEY TERM FOR TODAY ## Adoption

The Bible does not actually teach that all people are God's children. Rather, as is clear in Romans and other New Testament writings, we *become* sons and daughters of God, being *adopted* by him when we put our faith in Christ. We see the idea at the beginning of John's Gospel: "To those who believed in his [Christ's] name, he gave the right to become children of God" (1:12). The word we translate as "adoption" is *huiothesia*, literally, "son-making." Adoption is both present and future. We are already sons and daughters of God, but we "come into our inheritance" only after death.

epistles. In the New Testament period, an epistle (from the Latin *epistola*) was a literary work, words carefully chosen, directed to a wide audience or to the public at large—not so different from today's "open letter" in a major newspaper, published by a political action group to make a public statement of its opinions on some contemporary issue. The New Testament epistles don't fit that formula, since they are often full of personal greetings and other items that would normally be part of a personal letter. Obviously Paul's brief Letter to Philemon is a letter, not an epistle, but even in his more "formal" writings, there is a warm, personal tone in Paul, with his various "shout-outs" to people he knows. In other words, a letter was private, while an epistle was public. However, Paul (except in the case of Philemon) always wrote as a "public Christian," never as just Paul the individual. He was well aware of the sharing of his letters and encouraged it, as we see in Colossians 4:16: "After this letter has been read to you, see that it is also read in the church of the Laodiceans and that you in turn read the letter from Laodicea." Perhaps it would have surprised him that millions of Christians around the globe read the letter over a period of two millennia too.

In Paul's time, letter writing took three forms:
1. writing it oneself, word for word
2. dictating it word for word
3. dictating the sense, but leaving the choice of words to the scribe

Philemon verse 19 states that Paul wrote this brief letter with his own hand, but we are pretty certain that he dictated the others, and that sometimes he signed his own name to validate them, as in Galatians 6:11: "See what large letters I use as I write to you with my own hand!" Paul was putting his "John Hancock" on the letter. It is possible that the variations of style and vocabulary in Paul's letters may indicate method 3, particularly if the scribe was someone he trusted.

Paul's letters follow a familiar formula:
1. his own name, and his co-senders' names, if any
2. the name of the recipients, a church or group of churches
3. a greeting, usually some variation of "Grace and peace be yours from God our Father and the Lord Jesus Christ"
4. thanking the person or group for favors done
5. the main message, doctrine followed by moral instruction

6. personal news and specific advice for individuals

7. closing, some variation of "The grace of our Lord Jesus Christ be with you"

Paul's longest, most studied and most influential letter was to the Christian community in Rome. It is also the least typical of his letters, because, unlike his other letters, he was writing to a church he had not founded himself. In his other letters he wrote as the "founding father" of the fellowship, but in Rome the foundation had been laid by others. In other words, he was writing not to converts he had made but to Christians who knew him by reputation. For that reason his tone in the letter is somewhat formal, less conversational than the others. He is also much more organized, not jumping from topic to topic as he does in his other letters. He wasn't responding, as in his other letters, to some theological or ethical crisis. Romans is the closest he came to writing a systematic, well-thought-out, reflective summary of Christian belief and practice, which is why the letter has always been considered one of the greatest Christian writings ever.

Christianity reached Rome at an early date—partly because in those days, all roads literally did lead to Rome, so any teaching that sprang up in the empire would soon reach the capital city. Rome had a very large Jewish community, and as far as we know the Christian community there was a mix of both Jews and pagans. Paul wrote the letter around AD 57, as he was wrapping up his third missionary journey.

Paul opens the letter with "Paul, a servant of Christ Jesus, called to be an apostle and set apart for the gospel of God." Most translations have "servant," but a more literal translation is "slave," for that is the meaning of the Greek word *doulos*. A servant worked for wages, while a slave was *owned* by his master—and Paul and the other apostles had no qualms about gladly doing whatever their Master, God, asked them to do. Paul addresses his readers, "To all in Rome who are loved by God and called to be saints." He tells the readers that he has longed to meet them face to face (a wish that would be granted years later, when he was taken to Rome as a prisoner, as we saw in the last chapter).

Then he launches out into deep waters: All people, everywhere, have a sense that God exists. "Since the creation of the world God's invisible qualities—his eternal power and divine nature—have been clearly seen, being understood from what has been made, so that men are without excuse" (Romans 1:20). In other words, no human being can claim to be completely ignorant of the existence of God. But instead of glorifying God, men have worshipped worthless idols, and their corrupt religion has led to corrupt morals (a key teaching of the prophets centuries earlier). They have committed all sorts of vile sins, something the residents of Rome would have known all too well. They have become "filled with every kind of wickedness, evil, greed and depravity" (1:29). Rejecting God, "they are senseless, faithless, heartless, ruthless" (1:31). Worst of all, "they not only continue to do these very things but also approve of those who practice them" (1:32).

Slaves of Christ

In several of the New Testament epistles, the author introduces himself as the *doulos Christou*, "slave of Christ." Many Bible translations have "servant," but this is not as accurate, since a servant could work for pay, but a slave was the property of its owner and had to do whatever the owner asked. In our own age, where we value independence and freedom, we may wonder why a person would choose to call himself a slave of anyone. Paul, the "slave of Christ," believed that all people were slaves to sin before they came to Christ. By becoming slaves of Christ, they exchanged the worst master (sin) for the best (Christ). Unlike human masters, Christ would only require his slaves to do what was best for them. Being "owned" by Christ is not a burden. Instead, it brings the only true freedom possible, freedom from our own selfish impulses, freedom to do what is right. Also, remember that Christians thought of themselves not just as slaves, but also as the adopted children of God. And also note that the New Testament writers —Paul, Peter, James and Jude—who called themselves "slaves of Christ" used the name as a sort of title for themselves, just as they used "apostle." For them it was a badge of honor to be able to spread the faith in their Master, Christ. Perhaps they remembered that Christ had told his disciples that "whoever wants to be first must be your slave" (Matthew 20:27). In other passages, Christians are referred to as *diakonoi*, "servants." Whether servants or slaves, they were in the service of Christ.

The word "approve" here is crucial: For Paul, this is the sign that people have morally and spiritually hit rock-bottom—not just sinning or tolerating sin in others, but *saying that sinning is a good thing*. Here Paul was echoing the words of the prophet Isaiah from centuries earlier: "Woe to those who call evil good and good evil" (Isaiah 5:20).

This delight in wickedness isn't just limited to the Gentiles. The Jews were God's chosen people, entrusted with the Law of Moses, but the Jews have not kept the Law. Both Jews and non-Jews have sinned: "All have sinned and fall short of the glory of God" (3:23)—one of the most profound statements about the human condition.

But there is hope for everyone, for all people can do as the patriarch Abraham did: Be saved by faith. Putting our faith in Christ is what saves us. "Since we have been justified through faith, we have peace with God through our Lord Jesus Christ" (5:1). We are justified—made right, declared not guilty—by God, thanks to the sinless Christ offering himself as a sacrifice on our behalf. "God demonstrates his own love for us in this: While we were still sinners, Christ died for us" (5:8). Just as Adam's disobedience of God resulted in all men being condemned as sinners, so Christ's self-sacrifice makes it possible for all to be saved (5:18). In a sense our old selves and our sins "die" with Christ on the cross. "Count yourselves dead to sin but alive to God in Christ Jesus" (6:11). Out of gratitude to God we cannot let ourselves be slaves to sin any longer. "For the wages of sin is death, but the gift of God is eternal life in Christ Jesus our Lord" (6:23).

In chapter 7, Paul touches on a sore point: We may want to do good but our sinful nature still leads us to do wrong. Here Paul is not pointing the finger just at others, but at himself as well. All Christians, even the apostle himself, feel the pull of sin. "What a wretched man I am! Who will rescue me from this body of death? Thanks be to God— through Jesus Christ our Lord!" (7:24–25). In this famous passage, Paul was pointing out a deep truth: Men can know what is right, even *want* to do it, but still fall short. So often our powers don't seem equal to our intentions. This was a distinction from the idea of the Greek philosophers, like Plato, who believed that if people know what is right and good, they will do it. Paul was more of a realist than Plato.

But, thankfully, Christians, the saved people, are no longer under the complete control of their sinful nature but under the power of the Spirit. Thanks to the Spirit, we are "adopted" as sons of God. As sons, we can speak to God with the Aramaic expression *Abba*—"dear Father." Here and elsewhere in the New Testament we see the key theme of being adopted as God's children. We are "co-heirs" with Jesus, the Son of God—but as co-heirs, we will inevitably suffer as he did. But "our present sufferings are not worth comparing with the glory that will be revealed in us" (8:18). Following this line of thought, Paul utters one of the greatest spiritual messages of all time: "We know that in all things God works for the good of those who love him, who have been called according to his purpose" (8:28). In a sense he has answered the question of the Book of Job: Why do good people suffer? They will suffer, but ultimately will prevail. After all, "if God is for us, who can be against us?" (8:31). "Nothing can separate us from Christ"— in fact, we are "more than conquerors through him who loved us" (8:37). Paul had traveled wide, seen much, and suffered much, and after all his experience, he could say with confidence, "I am convinced that neither death nor life, neither angels nor demons, neither the present nor the future, nor any powers, neither height nor depth, nor anything else in all creation, will be able to separate us from the love of God that is in Christ Jesus our Lord" (8:38–39). Romans 8 is one of the great chapters of the Bible.

In chapter 9, Paul returns to the subject of Jews and Gentiles in God's plan. In the church in Rome, Jews and Gentiles probably did not entirely like or trust each other, even if they were all now part of the Christian family. Here, as in other letters, he emphasizes that what they now have in common is far more important than whether they were born Jew or Gentile. As he states elsewhere in his letters, the true descendants of the faithful patriarch Abraham are not his physical descendants, the Jews, but all people who believe in Christ, the *spiritual* descendants. Faith, which Abraham had, is the key thing: "If you confess with your mouth, 'Jesus is Lord,' and believe in your heart that God raised him from the dead, you will be saved" (10:9). Paul echoes a theme of the prophets: a righteous "remnant" of the human race will be saved by faith (9:27, 11:5). Paul, reared as a devout Jew, laments that most Jews have not accepted the Messiah they had so long awaited. God has not rejected his people—rather, they have rejected him.

In Paul, the line between theologian and poet is thin. He often stated that he was not eloquent, but he underestimated himself, for on occasion his delight in God unloosed a flow of words: "Oh, the depth of the riches of the wisdom and knowledge of God! How unsearchable his judgments, and his paths beyond tracing out!" (11:33). For Paul, salvation—something that was a gift from God, not something we earned or deserved—was the most beautiful thing ever.

As in all his letters, Paul follows his theological teaching with moral teaching. Those who have accepted Christ should show their gratitude to God: "I urge you, brothers, in view of God's mercy, to offer your bodies as living sacrifices, holy and pleasing to God— this is your spiritual act of worship" (12:1). The phrase "living sacrifice" is interesting: we need no longer offer animal sacrifices, as done under the Old Testament Law. Rather, we ourselves are the sacrifice, living our lives to please God.

"Do not conform any longer to the pattern of this world, but be transformed by the renewing of your mind. Then you will be able to test and approve what God's will is— his good, pleasing and perfect will" (12:2). This commandment wasn't easy for the people in first-century Rome to follow, nor is it easy for us today. But it is one of the great ethical commands of the Bible. In fact, all of chapter 12 is rich ethical instruction, much of it echoing Jesus' own teaching, beautifully summed up in the final verse: "Do not be overcome by evil, but overcome evil with good" (12:21).

In chapter 13, Paul tells Christians, "Everyone must submit himself to the governing authorities, for there is no authority except that which God has established. The authorities that exist have been established by God" (13:1). The King James Version has the more familiar wording "the powers that be are ordained of God." One reason Paul and others told Christians to behave and obey the government was that the Jews had a long history of getting treated better by the government than by the population at large. This was true of the Christians as well, since they too were persecuted unofficially by their unbelieving neighbors long before the government itself persecuted them. Paul's words about obeying the government have always affected Christians' attitude toward the government, along with Jesus' words about rendering to Caesar what is Caesar's. His words also bring to mind the Book of Acts, where we saw Paul being treated decently by most of the Roman officials he dealt with. Paul, of course, had no illusions about the Roman emperor's depraved court, and the Christians in Rome probably knew only too well how immoral "the powers that be" really were. Still, in the great scheme of things, even a government run by flawed men played a role in maintaining order on earth. Christians were told to *submit* to the government, not *admire* it.

Later in chapter 13, Paul repeats Jesus' teaching that all the Old Testament commandments can be summed up in "Love your neighbor as yourself." Paul adds: "Love does no harm to its neighbor. Therefore love is the fulfillment of the law" (13:10). We ought to work at pleasing our neighbors, not ourselves (15:1–2).

In the closing chapter, Paul greets people he knows in Rome, including his dear friends Priscilla and Aquila, who "risked their lives for me." Always thinking as a fatherly pastor, Paul interrupts his greetings to tell the readers, "I want you to be wise about what is good, and innocent about what is evil" (16:19). We see that Paul employed a scribe, or secretary in the letter: "I, Tertius, who wrote down this letter, greet you in the Lord" (16:22). We may well wonder if Tertius was aware that the words he was writing down would influence generations to come throughout the world.

CULTURAL INSIGHTS

Roman Morality

Paul's depiction of the decadence of pagan life in Romans 1 is no exaggeration. Even some of the Romans themselves bewailed the immorality, including the historian Suetonius, whose *Lives of the Caesars* still shocks us with its depictions of the emperors' depravities. Women were "liberated," which meant they tended to imitate the vices of men, particularly in regard to sexual morals. Unwanted babies were aborted or abandoned soon after birth, to die of neglect or be eaten by dogs, or raised to be prostitutes. (Sadly, an abandoned infant was more likely to be adopted to be raised as a prostitute than as a beloved son or daughter.) Women, especially in the upper class, divorced at will and joked about their number of husbands. While Paul's condemnation of homosexuality provokes controversy today, he was correct in stating that some men and women, bored with their promiscuity with the opposite sex, tried homosexuality as one option among others. Even aside from sex, the Roman Empire was still a den of iniquity, with people taking it for granted that businessmen would cheat and that politicians were all bribed. People looked upon each other as things to be used, not beings made in the image of God. No wonder many people gladly turned to a moral religion like Christianity—and no wonder they were mocked by their immoral neighbors.

THE CHURCH IN THE DEN OF INIQUITY

Rome had a well-deserved reputation as a wicked city, but if there was one city in the Roman empire with an even worse reputation, it was the Greek port city of Corinth. The phrase "to live like a Corinthian" meant to live a life of depravity, and "Corinthian girl" was a slang term for prostitute. Being a Christian in such a place was not easy, which is why several letters were exchanged between Paul and the Christians in Corinth. We possess only two of them, two of the greatest writings in the Bible, amazingly contemporary in their depiction of the difficulty of living morally in an immoral society.

Acts 18 tells of Paul founding the church in Corinth on his second missionary journey, making more converts among the Gentiles than among the Jews. Sometime around AD 55, while on his third missionary journey, Paul learned about the immorality and squabbles among the Christians in Corinth. He was compelled to write to the flock and remind them they were God's people and should act accordingly.

CULTURAL INSIGHTS

The Goddess of Love

Aphrodite was the Greek goddess of love—although goddess of *lust* is more accurate, since faithful and enduring love was not her sphere, nor was marriage, as proven by her own frequent cheating on her unattractive husband, the god Hephaestus. Erotic love, with all its passion and selfishness and destructive power (and tendency not to last) was what Aphrodite was all about. "Golden Aphrodite," as the Greeks often called her, represented all that was bad about the pagan view of love. Not surprisingly, Aphrodite was the patron deity of the loose-living city of Corinth, and her temple dominated the city. It had a thousand "priestesses," who were nothing but prostitutes. Essentially the temple was a religious brothel, with the priests as pimps, living off the funds paid to the "priestesses." Corinth was a port town, and the randy sailors kept the temple in business. Perhaps when Paul was writing his famous "love chapter," 1 Corinthians 13, he had in mind the awesome contrast between *agape*, the unselfish love Christians should practice, and *eros*, the selfish, fickle and often destructive love represented by the goddess Aphrodite.

The more sensitive pagans lamented that their gods and goddesses were, morally speaking, hardly deserving of worship. Some of the pagans tried to allegorize the old myths about the promiscuous and violent gods, finding spiritual meaning in crude stories that, frankly, had no spiritual content. Other pagans moved in the direction of believing in one God, a moral being, and these people were open to Christianity, finding in it a satisfaction that the old polytheistic religion did not provide.

CHARACTER CLOSE-UP   Apollos

According to Acts 18, Apollos was a Jew from the city of Alexandria in Egypt. We can gather from his name (think of the Greek god Apollo) that his Jewish family was Hellenized, steeped in Greek culture. (Apollos is actually the short form of the longer name Apollonius.) Acts describes Apollos as a man well-versed in the Scripture, eloquent, fervent in the Spirit. In Ephesus he met Paul's friends Priscilla and Aquila, who led him into a deeper understanding of Christian truth. He went to Corinth as a missionary and was an eloquent debater with the Jews there, arguing from the Scriptures and convincing many that Jesus was the Messiah the Jews had hoped for.

Paul apparently had a high opinion of Apollos (Titus 3:13), but we see in 1 Corinthians that in the factious church in Corinth there was an "Apollos party" opposed to the "Paul party," with people claiming to follow one or the other. This divisiveness was wrong, Paul said, for he and Apollos and all other preachers of the gospel were mere servants of God. In Corinth, "I planted the seed, Apollos watered it, but God made it grow" (1 Corinthians 3:6). Doubtless Apollos himself would have agreed. The divisiveness among the Corinthians shows that "stardom" among ministers can result not just from a minister's own ego, but from the human tendency to form a "fan club" around a notable person, even if that person doesn't want one.

There is some speculation that the eloquent Apollos might have written the Letter to the Hebrews, which is in the most elegant Greek in the New Testament.

As always, the letter opens on a positive note, with Paul expressing gratitude and affection for the people. Then he launches into the issues. There were divisions in the church, some of the people claiming to follow him, others Peter, others Apollos. These divisions, Paul says, are wrong. Christ is not "divided." Christians should be united in their minds (1 Corinthians 1:10). If there is any kind of "personality cult" among believers, it should be centered on Christ, not any "star" among the teachers and preachers.

Then Paul digresses, as he often did, speaking of the gospel as being "foolishness" by the world's standards, often mocked by both Jews and Gentiles. But "the foolishness of God is wiser than man's wisdom, and the weakness of God is stronger than man's strength" (1:25). As always in the Bible, God's standards are different from the world's standards: "We have not received the spirit of the world but the Spirit who is from God, that we may understand what God has freely given us" (2:12). Thanks to the Spirit, "we have the mind of Christ" (2:16). Since that is so, we ought to recall that it is God who judges us, not any human judge (4:3–5). Ignoring what the world thinks, Paul and the apostles are mocked and persecuted, "the scum of the earth, the refuse of the world." But, "When we are cursed, we bless; when we are persecuted, we endure it; when we are slandered, we answer kindly" (4:12–13). It is impossible to read these words without recalling Jesus' teaching about "turning the other cheek."

Inevitably, since the people live in Corinth, Paul has to address the issue of sexual morality. In chapter 5, Paul speaks out boldly against immorality, his first example being one of the members who is having relations with his own stepmother—and the other members tolerate it! This, Paul insists, is wrong: "Don't you know that a little yeast works through the whole batch of dough?" (5:6). A little immorality can infect the entire congregation. Paul reminds them it is their duty to chastise and correct believers who are doing wrong, while judging people outside the church is left to God (5:12–13). This is an important point, for Paul makes it clear that a fellowship of faith ought to "clean up its own backyard" instead of denouncing the sins of the outside world.

Paul also scolds the people for suing each other in court. How does this look to unbelievers, Paul asks? As brothers, part of the family of God, shouldn't they try to settle matters among themselves?

Paul returns to the issue of sexual immorality. Our bodies, Paul says, belong to God, so how can we abuse them through visiting prostitutes or other sexual sins? Our bodies are the "temple of the Holy Spirit, therefore honor God with your body" (6:20). Later in the letter, Paul reminds the readers that sexual temptation, or any kind of temptation, can be resisted: "No temptation has seized you except what is common to man. And God is faithful; he will not let you be tempted beyond what you can bear. But when you are tempted, he will also provide a way out so that you can stand up under it" (1 Corinthians 10:13). Paul also reminds the Corinthians that in the past many of them were notoriously immoral, "but you were washed, you were sanctified, you were justified in the name of the Lord Jesus Christ and by the Spirit of our God" (6:11). *Justified*, by the way, is an important word in Paul's letters, expressing the key belief that, thanks to the sacrificial death of Christ, we have been put in a right relationship with God.

Chapter 7 is Paul's famous, and infamous, chapter on marriage. Paul himself was single—which doesn't rule out the possibility he had been married and widowed, and following standard Jewish practice, it is highly probable he was married earlier in life. However, when he wrote to Corinth, he was single, and glad that his single state allowed him to be completely devoted to the work of God. Paul recommends the single state—for those who can accept it without falling into sexual immorality. Most people can't, and for them it is better to marry than to sin (7:9). For people like Paul, who can remain chaste, singleness frees them from the worries of marriage and allows them to serve God with fewer distractions.

What about a believer married to an unbeliever? If the unbelieving spouse leaves, so be it—after all, "God has called us to live in peace" (7:15). But the believing spouse should not desert the unbelieving one. There were, and are, cases of unbelieving spouses who in time come to accept the faith of the believing spouse, but Paul is enough of a realist to observe that there is no certainty this will happen.

Then Paul touches on slavery. Some of the early Christians were slaves. Should they flee their masters? No, Paul says—but if they can earn their freedom legally, fine (7:21). Slaves should remember that as sons of God, they are already free in the deepest sense. As Paul would observe in other letters, the distinction between "slave" and "freeman" doesn't exist in Christ. Whether slave or free, they all serve one Master, Christ.

In chapter 8, Paul deals with an issue also covered in Romans: eating food sacrificed to the pagan gods. Some Christians had scruples about eating food that had been dedicated to these false gods, while other Christians mocked this fussiness since, after, the idols were not real gods anyway. This is, for us, "ancient history," but the core issue is still with us. How do we react to believers who seem fussier about these little details than we are? Paul commands us to take our fellow believers' feelings into account (8:9). We can't let the fussier brothers dictate to our own consciences, but we also can't let our own sense of freedom cause others to stumble.

As an apostle, Paul is free, the slave of God but not the slave of any man—and yet, "I have become all things to all men so that by all possible means I might save some" (9:22). All believers are free, and yet "nobody should seek his own good, but the good of others" (10:24). Whatever we do, we should "do it all for the glory of God" (10:31). Imagine what lives we might lead if we asked ourselves, often, *Is what I'm doing now something that glorifies God?*

Chapter 12 is one of the key chapters of the letter, dealing with the issue of spiritual gifts. Believers make up a body, and the head of that body is Christ. No part of a body can say it doesn't need the other parts. The body needs all its parts to function. There should be no division in the body, but, rather, "its parts should have equal concern for each other" (12:25). There are many parts, but one body, one Spirit. Within the body there are apostles, prophets, teachers, miracle-workers, healers, administrators, people who can speak in other tongues. All are needed in the church.

This leads to one of the most quoted passages of the entire Bible, chapter 13, Paul's famous *love chapter*. After talking about the various spiritual gifts, Paul says "now I will show you the most excellent way," the way of *agape*, the Greek word for unselfish, compassionate love. "If I speak in the tongues of men and of angels, but have not love, I am only a resounding gong or a clanging cymbal" (13:1). Speaking in tongues, or exercising any other spiritual gift, does not matter if the

Speaking in Tongues

"Speaking in tongues" literally translates the Greek word *glossolalia*. In the letters of Paul it refers to the early Christian practice of what we might call "prayer language," the believer speaking syllables and sounds that resemble no known language. In a state of ecstasy or closeness to God, the believer expresses what words cannot express. Paul saw it as one of the many gifts the Spirit bestowed on believers. In 1 Corinthians 14, Paul states that he himself spoke in tongues often—but he was aware that in the worship services in Corinth, Christians speaking in tongues were causing a commotion. Apparently some believers had the gift of interpreting the messages of tongues, and Paul stated that tongues-speaking in worship services was fine if an interpreter were present. In worship, "I would rather speak five intelligible words...than ten thousand words in a tongue" (14:19). Speaking in tongues privately was fine, but in worship it needed interpretation.

As is clear in 1 Corinthians, speaking in tongues was a divisive issue among the first Christians and has continued to be so. Some churches encourage it, some tolerate it, others condemn it, even attributing it to the power of Satan. Based on the Bible, the practice should not be condemned, though we should follow Paul's advice about not allowing the practice to disrupt worship.

person does not love. "Love is patient, love is kind. It does not envy, it does not boast, it is not proud. It is not rude, it is not self-seeking, it is not easily angered, it keeps no record of wrongs." In other words, *agape* is far from being the passionate, selfish feeling most of the world calls "love." "It always protects, always trusts, always hopes, always perseveres. Love never fails" (13:7–8). Gifts like prophesying and speaking in tongues will some day pass away, but love never will. "These three remain: faith, hope and love. But the greatest of these is love" (13:13).

No wonder this beloved passage is so often read at weddings. But in fact, Paul's poetic description of *agape* ought to apply not only to spouses, but also to all our relations—parents and children, siblings, friends, neighbors, co-workers. Paul, the single man who commended the single state to all who could accept it, might be pleased to know that his description of love—*real* love—is often read when two people enter into the married state.

THE HEAVENLY HOPE

In chapter 15, Paul speaks of one of the key beliefs of Christians: Jesus Christ was raised from the dead, and his resurrection is a preview of what will in due course happen to all believers. Apparently some people were teaching that there would be no resurrection.

For Paul, belief in Jesus' resurrection is not "optional": "If Christ has not been raised, our preaching is useless and so is your faith" (15:14). If there is no future resurrection of the dead, "we are to be pitied more than all men" (15:19). But there will be this glorious event. Adam's disobedience brought death into the world, but Christ's saving work undoes the work of Adam (15:22). We all "died" in Adam, but are made alive in Christ, who is the "firstfruits," his resurrection being a sign of what will eventually happen to us all. Finally, death itself will be destroyed.

At the resurrection, we will possess, as the risen Christ did, a "spiritual body"—a definite oxymoron. Paul was stretching language to its limits, since he was trying to express something the mind cannot grasp. "The body that is sown is perishable, it is raised imperishable; it is sown a natural body, it is raised a spiritual body. If there is a natural body, there is also a spiritual body.... And just as we have borne the likeness of the earthly man, so shall we bear the likeness of the man from heaven" (15:42–44, 49). We are reminded here of the Gospels' accounts of Jesus after the resurrection, when his body was like, but different from, his earthly body.

How will the resurrection take place? Here Paul waxes poetic: "Listen, I tell you a mystery: We will not all sleep, but we will all be changed—in a flash, in the twinkling of an eye, at the last trumpet. For the trumpet will sound, the dead will be raised imperishable, and we will be changed" (15:51–52). The words are familiar not only from our reading, but also from George Frideric Handel's *Messiah*, where a trumpet solo adds to the effect of the words when sung.

It is worth noting here that neither the Greeks nor Romans had a firm belief in an afterlife. There was a vague notion that some notable people—emperors and military heroes, for example—might dwell forever in a lovely place called the Elysian Fields. But Greco-Roman religion as a whole saw death as the end of existence—or as entry into Hades, a gloomy place deep in the earth. One of the most appealing aspects of Christianity was its unwavering belief in heaven. Paul wasn't about to let this critical belief be denied or neglected.

Paul ends his letter with greetings to friends in Corinth, commending those who "refreshed my spirit" (16:18), a beautiful phrase that sticks in the mind. He reminds them all: "Be on your guard; stand firm in the faith; be men of courage; be strong. Do everything in love" (16:13–14). He tells them to "greet one another with a holy kiss," and then adds a closing in his own handwriting. Thus ends one of the most profound and moving letters ever written.

THE PAINFUL FOLLOW-UP

Paul's first letter to Corinth did not settle all the issues there, as is obvious from his writing of 2 Corinthians. However, he opens the letter not with scolding, but with hearty thanks to God, who gave him comfort in some recent hardships. God "comforts us in all our troubles, so that we can comfort those in any trouble with the comfort we ourselves have received from God" (2 Corinthians 1:4). This verse reminds us of a painful truth: People who don't suffer generally lack compassion for those who do, while those who do suffer can sympathize with others who suffer. And, Paul says, suffering also teaches us to rely on God instead of ourselves (1:9).

In fact, suffering is a key theme of this letter: "We are hard pressed on every side, but not crushed; perplexed, but not in despair; persecuted, but not abandoned; struck down, but not destroyed. We always carry around in our body the death of Jesus, so that the life of Jesus may also be revealed in our body" (4:8–10). Paul looks at life's adversities from the heavenly point of view: "we fix our eyes not on what is seen, but on what is unseen. For what is seen is temporary, but what is unseen is eternal" (4:18). Paul, who plied the trade of tentmaker, refers to the earthly body as a "tent," a temporary dwelling, not ultimately important in itself, because "we have a building from God, an eternal house in heaven, not built by human hands" (5:1). We can remember truths such as this because "we live by faith, not by sight" (5:7). Because we see our neighbors through the eyes of faith, "we regard no one from a worldly point of view" (5:16).

At this point, Paul writes one of his deepest truths: "If anyone is in Christ, he is a new creation; the old has gone, the new has come!" (5:17). A key word in this passage is *reconciliation*, bridging the gap between righteous God and unrighteous man. "God was reconciling the world to himself in Christ, not counting men's sins against them" (5:19). God's ministers, such as Paul, have a ministry of reconciliation. In fact they are "Christ's ambassadors, as though God were making his appeal through us" (5:20). This ministry doesn't lead to success in the worldly view—on the contrary, as Paul well knew, it led to persecution and great suffering. He was often "sorrowful, yet always rejoicing; poor, yet making many rich; having nothing, and yet possessing everything" (6:10).

Since he was writing to Christians living among immoral pagans, Paul had to take a stand on Christians hobnobbing with unbelievers. Christians cannot totally separate themselves from others, of course, and even if they could, they could not win people to the faith if they had no contact with them. Even so, believers ought not to be "yoked," closely joined with unbelievers. "What fellowship can light have with darkness?" (6:15). Christians have argued a great deal over this "yoke" passage and the extent to which people of faith ought to separate themselves from people of no faith. But the basic message is plain enough: We can't allow unbelievers' proximity to us compromise our own walk of faith. Put another way, if our behavior isn't distinct from that of people with no faith, we must be doing something wrong.

Chapters 8 and 9 deal with the collection of an offering for the poorer believers in Jerusalem. These chapters remind us that, although many of the first Christians were poor themselves, they were often generous in helping the poorest among them. (In fact, surveys show that even today, the poor often give proportionally more of their income to charities than middle- or upper-income people.) Paul praises generosity: "Remember this: Whoever sows sparingly will also reap sparingly, and whoever sows generously will also reap generously. Each man should give what he has decided in his heart to give, not reluctantly or under compulsion, for God loves a cheerful giver" (9:6–7). As an example of generosity, Paul points to Christ, the son of God, who gave himself.

In chapters 10 and 11, we see that Paul, who had founded the church in Corinth, was not always highly regarded. The poor man was put in the position of having to defend his own ministry as an apostle. The Corinthian church should have regarded him as its spiritual father, but some of them were rejecting him—something as painful as a biological father rejected by his own children. Some of the Corinthians had said that Paul was "weighty" in his letters but unimpressive in person (10:10). On top of that, there were some "super-apostles" (Paul's word) who seemed to be regarded as superior to Paul himself. In fact, some of these super-apostles were really false teachers: "false apostles, deceitful workmen, masquerading as apostles of Christ" (11:13). This was not unexpected, "for Satan himself masquerades as an angel of light" (11:14). Some of these false apostles and their admirers claimed to be wise but were in fact fools. Paul becomes a bit sarcastic here: "You gladly put up with fools since you are so wise!" (11:19). (The King James Version of this verse is the source of our phrase "suffer fools gladly.") As always, the Bible warns against conceited people who have a high opinion of their own wisdom. As in Proverbs, those who are wise in their own eyes are often the biggest fools of all.

For those who might doubt Paul's qualifications as an apostle, he makes one thing clear: he has certainly suffered in order to spread the faith. His "persecution resume" is indeed impressive: "Five times I received from the Jews the forty lashes minus one. Three times I was beaten with rods, once I was stoned, three times I was shipwrecked, I spent a night and a day in the open sea" (11:24–25). With no settled home, he had often gone without food or adequate clothing, in danger from both Jews and Gentiles. We can assume Paul's body bore scars on it—from God's point of view, these

DID YOU KNOW?

In 2 Corinthians 11:24, Paul states that five times he had endured "forty lashes minus one." This does not refer to the Roman punishment of scourging, which Jesus endured and which Paul was exempt from due to his Roman citizenship. Rather, he is referring to the Jewish punishment of flogging, beating the offender with rods or four-thonged whips across the bare back and chest, stipulated in the Mosaic law (Deuteronomy 25:2–3). Although the maximum punishment was forty lashes, it was Jewish practice to administer only thirty-nine—on the possibility that the person doing the flogging might not count accurately and administer more than forty!

Perfection

At the end of 2 Corinthians, Paul tells his readers to "aim for perfection" (13:11). The word translated "perfection" here is the Greek *teleios*. It definitely does not refer to a state of being absolutely without fault. Rather, it could be translated "whole," "complete," "undivided," "full" and especially "mature." Put another way, "aim for perfection" could be rendered as "strive to be all that God intended you to be." The idea was found in Jesus' Sermon on the Mount: "Be perfect, therefore, as your heavenly Father is perfect" (Matthew 5:48). In another of Paul's letters, he spoke of the goal of presenting "everyone perfect in Christ" (Colossians 1:28).

were signs of a saintly man's dedication to the good. Aside from his physical adversities, Paul was constantly concerned about the spiritual welfare of his many converts—evident enough in this very letter. Also, he was at times betrayed by "false brothers"—fellow believers who let him down or neglected him (11:26). The poor man faced enemies outside the fellowship and unstable brothers inside it.

Despite all the sufferings, there were "mystic moments" now and then. In chapter 12, Paul speaks of "a man" he knew of, years earlier, who was "caught up to the third heaven…caught up to paradise," where he "heard inexpressible things." Bible commentators suspect the unidentified "man" is Paul himself, and that he felt greatly privileged to experience whatever these heavenly visions were. But to keep him from becoming conceited about these revelations, an unnamed "thorn in the flesh" tormented him. He prayed to God to relieve him, but God answered, "My grace is sufficient for you, for my power is made perfect in weakness" (12:9). There has been endless speculation about what Paul's "thorn" was—some recurring physical ailment, some mental anguish he did not wish to reveal, who knows? Perhaps we should be glad the problem was unidentified, since each of us can take comfort from Paul's endurance of his "thorn." The consolation for any of us is that, like Paul, our own sense of powerlessness can make us more reliant on God.

In chapters 10 through 13, we sense that Paul deeply regrets having to defend his own apostleship. The Corinthians certainly should have remembered the labors of the great man. But there was rivalry among some of the Christian ministers in those days, and some had apparently been trying to turn Paul's own flock against him—turning the children against their father, spiritually speaking. In a way we should be glad, for otherwise we might not possess this letter and its painful details about the sorrows Paul experienced. The letter reminds us that Paul was no "stained-glass saint," but very much a flesh-and-blood person who endured hardships that might have led lesser men to abandon their faith. We see Paul at his most emotional, most *vulnerable* in 2 Corinthians, and the revelations deepen our admiration for him. Perhaps it would benefit us, when we are enduring our own sorrows, to read 2 Corinthians 12 again, reminding us of the amazing power of God to sustain his people through great trials.

We close this chapter by recalling that Romans and 1 and 2 Corinthians are often called Paul's Great Letters, the three longest and most important of his writings. When he wrote them all those centuries ago, he wrote as a missionary and pastor concerned about the spiritual and moral health of fellow Christians, a spiritual father wanting his children to walk the right path and grow in the faith. Thanks to the veneration the first Christians had for these writings, and for the amazing man who wrote them, generation after generation of readers have benefited from the apostle's heartfelt concern for people of faith.

PUTTING THE WORD TO WORK

1. Paul told Christians to do everything "for the glory of God." As you go through the day, ask yourself, when deciding what to do, if your acts glorify God.

2. In Romans, Paul told Christians to "overcome evil with good." Think of times in the past week when you, or someone you know, confronted evil with good.

3. Think of some "thorn in the flesh," some recurring physical or mental pain that bothered you for a long time, but which did not go away, even after you prayed about it. Did this affliction, like Paul's, lead you to rely more on God?

4. Read Paul's love chapter, 1 Corinthians 13, closely. Can you think of anyone you've known who consistently demonstrated this kind of unselfish love, this *agape*, in their lives?

5. In 2 Corinthians, Paul spoke of being "ambassadors for Christ," acting as full representatives for Christ on earth. What are some ways you can be an "ambassador" in your daily life?

A Universal Mind

AT THE HEART OF IT ALL TODAY In ten classic letters, the apostle Paul defines spiritual freedom and gives timeless advice on marriage and child-rearing, enduring hardships, finding joy and contentment in all circumstances, and looking forward to eternity with God.

In this chapter we continue with the letters of the apostle Paul, including the letters that may well be the oldest writings in the New Testament. The letters today also include Paul's last writings, when he sensed his martyrdom was not far off, and he was passing on his hard-earned wisdom to his protégés, the pastors Timothy and Titus. As with the letters of the previous chapter, these writings are amazingly contemporary in regard to the theological and moral issues that Paul and his followers dealt with.

KEY PASSAGES TO READ TODAY

Galatians 3:26—4:20; 5:16–26

Ephesians 2:1–13; 6:10–18

Philippians 2:1–11; 4:1–19

Colossians 3

1 Thessalonians 4:13–18

2 Thessalonians 2:1–12

1 Timothy 4

2 Timothy 2:8–13; 3:10–17

THE FREEDOM LETTER

The Greek words *eleutheros* and *eleutheria*—"free" and "freedom"—show up again and again in the New Testament. Jesus told his followers that the truth would set them free, and "if the Son sets you free, you will be free indeed" (John 8:36). Paul told the Christians in Rome that they were free from sin and death (Romans 8:2) and the Christians in Corinth that "where the Spirit of the Lord is, there is freedom" (2 Corinthians 3:17). Christians were free from the ritual requirements of the Laws of Moses, from sin, from

KEY TERM FOR TODAY Redemption

In an age when slavery was common, redemption (the Greek word was *apolutrosis*) meant buying a person out of slavery. Paul and other apostles used the word in a figurative sense: Christians were redeemed from their slavery to sin and the fear of death. Redemption is both present and future: If we put our faith in Christ, we are already redeemed. But our "full" redemption lies in the future, in heaven (Romans 8:23). It is worth noting that among the early Christians, redemption was not always figurative; Christians often collected money to redeem fellow believers who had been made slaves.

death—and yet, strangely enough, we see in the New Testament that the first Christians were constantly tempted to make themselves slaves again to man-made rules. This is one of the key themes of Paul's amazing Letter to the Galatians, sometimes called the Magna Carta of Christian Freedom.

Galatia was a province of the Roman Empire, roughly in the center of what is today Turkey. Paul was an active missionary in this region, as we saw in the Book of Acts, where he established Christian communities in the cities of Iconium, Lystra and Derbe on his first missionary journey, revisiting them on his two later journeys. The Letter to the Galatians has the distinction of being addressed not to one particular city but to a group of cities, although we know that all of Paul's letters were circulated beyond their original destinations. Some scholars think Galatians might be the earliest of Paul's letters, possibly written around AD 49, but most think it was written between AD 54 and AD 57, when Paul was busy with his third missionary journey. But he was never too busy to lend his wisdom to a distant fellowship that needed his advice.

The religious atmosphere of Galatia and the surrounding regions was, to put it mildly, diverse. Greece lay to the west, Syria, Judea and Egypt to the south, the Parthian empire to the east, so there was a mingling of religious and philosophical beliefs. Phrygia, nearby, was notorious for its wild and often violent religious cults. People of the region were open to Christianity when it was preached to them, but, as Paul found, they did not readily grasp that Christianity was a distinctive faith that could not be merged with ideas and beliefs from other faiths. We call this mixing of beliefs *syncretism* (think of it as a kind of buffet approach to religion, with a person heaping his religious plate with various items that he likes). In several of the letters of today's chapter we see Paul speaking out boldly against syncretism. For him, faith in Christ was sufficient for salvation and it was wrong to try to add to it.

Paul opens the letter by identifying himself as "an apostle—sent not from men nor by man, but by Jesus Christ and God the Father, who raised him from the dead." This is an important point for his readers, as he is making it clear to them that the faith he preached to them is not just another religion for them to dabble in: It is *the* faith that God wants all men to adhere to. "I want you to know,

AD 60–61
Paul's journey to
Rome and shipwreck
(*Acts 27:1–28:15*)

AD 61–63
Paul under house
arrest in Rome
(*Acts 28:16–31*)

AD 64
Persecution of
Christians in Rome
under Nero

**PROBABLE DATES
OF PAUL'S LETTERS**

AD 51
1 Thessalonians
AD 51–52
2 Thessalonians
AD 54–57
Galatians
AD 55–56
1 Corinthians
AD 56–57
2 Corinthians
AD 56–57
Philippians
AD 57–58
Romans
AD 61–63
Ephesians
AD 61–63
Colossians
AD 61–63
Philemon
AD 64–65
1 Timothy
AD 64–65
Titus
AD 66–67
2 Timothy

brothers, that the gospel I preached is not something that man made up. I did not receive it from any man, nor was I taught it; rather, I received it by revelation from Jesus Christ" (Galatians 1:11–12). He preaches not to please men or win their approval, but to please God.

He reminds the Galatians of his personal history: He was an avid persecutor of Christians until his conversion. Afterward he was accepted by Jesus' own apostles, and he teaches the same true faith of those apostles, who extended to him the "right hand of fellowship," and approved his going as a missionary to the Gentiles. He speaks of the famous Council of Jerusalem, at which the apostles determined that Gentiles could become Christians without being bound by the Jewish laws—one of the pivotal moments in the history of the faith (2:9). He recalls that some of the Jewish Christians —even the apostle Peter—were for a time backsliding into their old habits, behaving as if there was some distinction between a Jewish Christian and a Gentile Christian. Paul called this "hypocrisy," and would not stand for it. Gentile Christians were freed from the Jewish law, not needing to be circumcised or to observe any of the old requirements.

And yet...the old obsession with rules was sneaking back in. "You foolish Galatians! Who has bewitched you?" Paul was furious— were they going to give up their freedom? He reminds them of a truth we saw earlier in the Letter to the Romans: The true "children of Abraham" are not the Jews, but all people who have faith in Christ. Faith, not descent from Abraham, is what counts. The old distinction between Jew and non-Jew is meaningless: "There is neither Jew nor Greek, slave nor free, male nor female, for you are all one in Christ Jesus" (3:28). Through faith, we are all children of God, and because we are his children, God sent the Spirit of his Son into our hearts, the Spirit who calls out, " 'Abba, Father' " (4:6).

Paul reminds the Galatians that in their pagan days, "you were slaves to those who by nature are not gods"—that is, idols, false gods. The Galatians had abandoned those old habits, but now "you are observing special days and months and seasons and years" (4:10). Meaning what, exactly? We aren't certain, but clearly some people were teaching that it was necessary to observe certain holy days—perhaps Jewish ones, or, given the diverse religious mix of the region, possibly some festivals of the pagans. They were in danger of abiding by "weak and miserable principles" of man-made religions (4:9). Perhaps we can be thankful that we don't know for certain what beliefs and practices the Galatians were engaging in, for Paul is just vague enough about the false teachings that his words can apply not only to his own age, but to any, because there have always been (and no doubt always will be) people trying to complicate the life of faith by mandating "rules" that have no basis in the Bible, and no real value in increasing our love for God or our neighbor.

"It is for freedom that Christ has set us free. Stand firm, then, and do not let yourselves be burdened again by a yoke of slavery" (5:1). This is one of the great declarations of the Bible. Man-made religions and rules count for nothing. "The only thing that counts is faith expressing itself through love" (5:6). He repeats some familiar words of Jesus himself: "The entire law is summed up in a single command: 'Love your neighbor as yourself' " (5:14). A religion of rules versus a religion of love—for Paul the choice was abundantly clear.

Preaching freedom to people has its hazards, as Paul was aware. People tend to think that being free means they can live as they like, throwing off all moral restraint. Paul warns against this: "You, my brothers, were called to be free. But do not use your freedom to indulge the sinful nature; rather, serve one another in love" (5:13). In case the readers were unclear about what constituted an immoral life, Paul made it clear: "The acts of the sinful nature are obvious: sexual immorality, impurity and debauchery; idol-

---

CULTURAL INSIGHTS

Asceticism

The New Testament refers often to self-control and self-denial, rooted in love for God and love for our neighbor. We are told not to worship money or material goods, and to emphasize the spiritual over the physical. However, at its root Christianity is not an *ascetic* faith—that is, it doesn't see any value in self-denial *for its own sak*e. In the New Testament period, various religious cults taught the merit of doing without wine or meat, or regarding certain foods as "unclean," or men emasculating themselves, or forgoing marriage, or fasting for long periods, or wearing rough clothing, or sleeping on the bare ground or out in the cold. In the view of the Bible, such strict behavior does not "score points" with God. Most of the letters in this chapter deal with false teachers who pressured Christians to be ascetics, to pursue a "higher" sort of Christianity by various forms of self-denial. Paul and the other apostles could see that such behaviors never seemed to result in a deeper spirituality, or in loving God and neighbor more dearly. Usually the ascetic person is trying to draw attention to himself, to gain a reputation as a "spiritual" person through outward appearances. God, as the Bible often reminds us, sees the heart and does not judge by what is on the outside.

atry and witchcraft; hatred, discord, jealousy, fits of rage, selfish ambition, dissensions, factions and envy; drunkenness, orgies and the like. I warn you, as I did before, that those who live like this will not inherit the kingdom of God" (5:19–21).

If Paul is sounding like he's scolding in this passage, he shows his readers the more positive side of living as free people: "The fruit of the Spirit is love, joy, peace, patience, kindness, goodness, faithfulness, gentleness and self-control" (5:22–23).

We see in Galatians, as well as in other New Testament writings, that freedom involves a delicate "balancing act." On the one hand, people of faith are freed from legalism. On the other hand, they aren't free to please themselves in an immoral fashion. Loving God and loving our neighbors as ourselves are what help us "maintain the balance," keeping us from behavior that shows lack of love for others or lack of respect for the Lord.

In the final chapter, Paul urges the believers to deal gently with a brother who is caught in sin. They should "carry each other's burdens, and in this way you will fulfill the law of Christ" (6:2). Also, "as we have opportunity, let us do good to all people, especially to those who belong to the family of believers" (6:10). In other words, remember that the *adelphoi*, the "brothers," are due special consideration. Paul's words here call to mind a later critic of Christianity, a certain pagan named Celsus, who had little good to say about the Christians but had to grudgingly admit, "How these Christians love one another!" The love of believers for each other was a powerful influence on many converts, who saw that the "every man for himself" attitude of the pagan world was not appealing. In the 300s, the Roman emperor Julian tried to reinvigorate paganism and undercut Christianity by trying to mimic the Christians' charitable societies, but his efforts failed, for the pagans inclined to brotherly love had all joined with the Christians.

In closing this section on Galatians, let's look at 2:20, in which Paul summarizes his life's purpose after his conversion: "I have been crucified with Christ and I no longer live, but Christ lives in me. The life I live in the body, I live by faith in the Son of God, who loved me and gave himself for me."

YOU WERE ONCE DARKNESS...

When we studied Acts, we looked at Paul's ministry in the busy, cosmopolitan city of Ephesus, where he established a faith community on his second missionary journey, and where the famous riot on behalf of the goddess Artemis took place. The Letter to the Ephesians dates from years after that, probably between AD 61 and AD 63, when Paul was living in Rome under house arrest. It is one of his later writings and also one of the richest in its theology.

A word about the name of the letter: Paul spent a lot of time in Ephesus and had many contacts there, so it strikes some readers as very odd that the conclusion of the letter does not have Paul's usual greetings and advice to people he knows. The best explanation for this is that Paul intended it as a "circular letter" like Galatians, passed around to the Christians in more than one city. (Galatians also lacks the greetings and personal advice found in the other letters.) Probably the letter was sent first to Ephesus, then circulated or copied for Christians in nearby cities.

In the first chapter, Paul speaks of Christians being chosen by God "before the creation of the world" (Ephesians 1:4). In the eternal plan, God will eventually put all things under the authority of Christ, and believers will be seated with Christ "in the heavenly realms" (2:6). Paul reminds these former pagans that they were dead in their sins in the days when they followed "the ways of this world," which for now is under the dominion of Satan (2:2). But thanks to God, "by grace you have been saved, through faith—and this not from yourselves, it is the gift of God—not by works, so that no one can boast" (2:8–9). But, lest they think that now that they are saved, their behavior does not matter. Paul adds, "we are God's workmanship, created in Christ Jesus to do good works" (2:10). In other words, saved people are not saved *by* their works, but they inevitably do good works out of gratitude to God.

Paul, a "prisoner for the Lord," urges his readers to "live a life worthy of the calling you have received. Be completely humble and gentle; be patient, bearing with one another in love. Make every effort to keep the unity of the Spirit through the bond of peace. There is one body and one Spirit—just as you were called to one hope when you were called—one Lord, one faith, one baptism" (4:1–5). In fact, *unity* is the great theme of this letter. As in Galatians, the old distinctions between Jew and Gentile, slave and free, no longer matter. Christ has brought us all together.

As in all his letters, Paul urges these people who are surrounded by pagans to live moral lives. People not familiar with the Bible often assume that "immorality" always refers to sexual behavior, but that is not the case, for here and in other letters Paul warns, "get rid of all bitterness, rage and anger, brawling and slander, along with every form of malice" (4:31). Also, "do not let the sun go down while you are still angry, and do not give the devil a foothold" (4:26–27). Rather, forgive others, as Christ forgave you.

In chapter 5, Paul reminds the people "you were once darkness, but now you are light in the Lord. Live as children of light" (5:8). They should live as wise men, not fools, and should not be intoxicated with wine but with the Spirit. They should "submit to one another out of reverence for Christ" (5:21). Wives are told to submit to their husbands—a teaching that many readers today find unpalatable, but Paul is also careful to command husbands to love their wives as they love themselves. Paul had a high view of marriage and saw that it had to be based on mutual respect, especially in the case of two Christians married to each other. For him, the unselfish love of Christ for his saints was the model for how a husband and wife should love each other.

He tells children to obey their parents, but also reminds fathers "do not exasperate your children; instead, bring them up in the training and instruction of the Lord" (6:4). Christian slaves should obey their masters, while Christian masters should treat their slaves with decency and respect.

The Letter to the Ephesians concludes with one of the great chapters of the Bible, in which Paul urges Christians to fend off the devil and his "spiritual forces of evil" by putting on "the full armor of God," with its belt of truth, breastplate of righteousness, shield of faith, helmet of salvation, and the "sword of the Spirit, which is the word of God" (6:13–17). Perhaps Paul, "an ambassador in chains" in Rome, saw the armor of the Roman soldiers on a regular basis and thought of a more spiritual and more effective armor.

> **DID YOU KNOW?**
>
> In Christian artwork, Paul was often depicted holding a sword. This was based on his description of the "full armor of God" in Ephesians 6. In many pictures, the sword he holds is inscribed with the Latin words *Spiritus Gladius*, "the sword of the Spirit" (6:17). The other reason Paul is shown with a sword is that, according to tradition, he was executed by being beheaded by a sword—the privilege of a Roman citizen.

THE JOY LETTER

Adversity brings out the best in some people. It certainly did in the case of Paul, whose faith seemed to grow stronger the more he suffered. The heart is stretched through suffering, and enlarged. This is very clear in the brief Letter to the Philippians, written while he was in prison, but, amazingly, overflowing with joy.

Recall from our study of Acts that Philippi was in the Greek region of Macedonia. Paul and Silas took the gospel there on Paul's second missionary journey, but the two were flogged and thrown into prison, where an earthquake resulted in their release and the conversion of their jailer. Paul retained great affection for the generous Christians in Philippi, and the warmth comes through in the letter. Paul was in prison when he wrote the letter—possibly his Roman captivity (AD 61–63), but more likely an earlier imprisonment in Ephesus (AD 56 or 57).

Paul thanks the people for their past kindnesses and observes that his imprisonment has had the good effect of leading other Christians to speak out boldly for the faith. (Persecution has always had this effect on faith. It causes the lukewarm believers to fall away, but brings the more dedicated ones out of the shadows.) Paul knows that some men preach more for their own ego than for love of God, but their motive does not matter, because "whether from false motives or true, Christ is preached" (Philippians 1:18). (These words are worth remembering at moments when we are prone to criticize ministers for their failings. Even less-than-admirable ministers can further the gospel through their work.) For Paul himself, martyrdom may be inevitable, but he does not fear it: "For to me, to live is Christ and to die is gain" (1:21). In fact, he longs to go on to his heavenly home, but also longs to remain on earth and continue to serve God. He leaves the decision in the hands of the Lord. Suffering for the sake of Christ is not a burden but a privilege (1:29).

As always, he tells his readers to be humble and unselfish—the supreme model of this being Christ himself, who "being in very nature God, did not consider equality with God something to be grasped, but made himself nothing, taking the very nature of a servant, being made in human likeness" (2:6–7). That is, if Christ humbled himself, so can we. If we live as Christ lived, we will be "children of God without fault in a crooked and depraved generation," in which we "shine like stars in the universe" (2:15–16). No matter what happens to us in this world, we can take comfort in knowing that "our citizenship is in heaven" (3:20), where our earthly bodies will be transformed like the glorified body of Christ.

"Rejoice in the Lord always. I will say it again: Rejoice!" (4:4). The words "joy" and "rejoice" occur several times in the letter, which is remarkable, considering that Paul's situation was one that would hardly make most people joyful. Paul's hardships had taught him this profound truth: "Do not be anxious about anything, but in everything, by prayer and petition, with thanksgiving, present your requests to God. And the peace of God, which transcends all understanding, will guard your hearts and your minds in Christ Jesus" (4:6–7). Having faced more difficulties than most of us ever deal with, the apostle could state "I have learned to be content whatever the circumstances" (4:11). He could do "all things" through the strength of Christ (4:13). For himself, and for every believer, there was this assurance: "My God will meet all your needs according to his glorious riches in Christ Jesus" (4:19).

SYNCRETISM, ONCE MORE

The brief Letter to the Colossians is the only one of Paul's letters sent to a church and city that are not mentioned in the Book of Acts. It was written while Paul was in prison in Rome (AD 61–63), dealing with a problem (syncretism) dealt with in the earlier Letter to the Galatians. A Christian named Epaphras, who was probably the founder of the church in the city of Colosse, had come to Rome and informed Paul that some false teachers in Colosse were teaching that Christianity was incomplete. As in Galatians, Paul had to assure them that Christ was all that was needed for salvation. For this reason, he speaks of just what an exalted Person the risen Christ is: "He is the image of the invisible God, the firstborn over all creation. For by him all things were created: Things in heaven and on earth, visible and invisible, whether thrones or powers or rulers or authorities; all things were created by him and for him. He is before all things, and in him all things hold together" (Colossians 1:15–17).

Because Christ is all they need, Paul commands them to "see to it that no one takes you captive through hollow and deceptive philosophy, which depends on human tradition and the basic principles of this world rather than on Christ" (2:8). Apparently some of the false teachers were claiming that Christians had to avoid certain foods and drinks and had to observe certain holy days. Such rules, Paul said, were useless and foolish. They "have an appearance of wisdom, with their self-imposed worship, their false humility and their harsh treatment of the body, but they lack any value in restraining sensual indulgence" (2:23). Here, Paul identified one of the key problems of the false teachers: They imposed new rules on people, but none of the rules were directed at anything that mattered morally. In other words, they were rules for the rules' sake, not rules for the sake of being better people. The great appeal of legalism is that there will always be people who enjoy making rules and boasting of how they kept them. This love of rules by no means ended with the New Testament period.

The Letter to the Colossians intrigues historians of religions because the false teachings Paul opposes seem to be an early form of what is called Gnosticism, a sort of amalgam of elements from various religions. Generally, Gnostics saw matter as evil, which seems to be the case of the false teachers and their food laws. This particular group of Gnostics (or "pre-Gnostics") seem to have borrowed the practice of circumcision from the Jews, and borrowed Christ from Christianity, while viewing Christ as only one among a whole hierarchy of angelic powers. Colosse was in the province of Asia Minor, which, like nearby Galatia, was a breeding ground for syncretistic cults and their mishmash of beliefs.

While such cults, cocktails of myths and foggy thinking, never resulted in genuine moral transformation, Paul says, true Christianity always does. Believers are to be kind and compassionate and forgiving, and "over all these virtues put on love, which binds them all together in perfect unity" (3:14). In regard to unbelievers, people of faith should "be wise in the way you act toward outsiders; make the most of every opportunity. Let your conversation be always full of grace, seasoned with salt, so that you may know how to answer everyone" (4:5–6).

Near the end of the letter, Paul says, "After this letter has been read to you, see that it is also read in the church of the Laodiceans and that you in turn read the letter from Laodicea" (4:16). Laodicea was a city twelve miles away, and this verse reminds us that Paul's letters were circulated among several churches.

The letter ends with these sobering words: "Remember my chains." But despite his own situation, Paul's chief concern in the letter was not his plight as a prisoner, but the spiritual welfare of a flock of Christians far away. Spiritually, the apostle had his priorities straight.

WHEN WILL CHRIST RETURN?

If Paul's letters were in chronological order, 1 and 2 Thessalonians would come first, since they were written, a few months apart, around AD 51. Although some scholars think the Letter of James might be older, the two letters are probably the oldest writings of the New Testament. In both letters, Paul, along with his fellow missionaries Silas and Timothy, was writing to the church at Thessalonica in Greece, which Paul had founded on his second missionary journey.

STORIES WORTH REMEMBERING

Paul and Onesimus

The one letter Paul wrote entirely with his own hand is the brief Letter to Philemon, one of the little gems of the Bible. Philemon was a friend of Paul and a leader in the Christian fellowship at Colosse. Philemon had a slave named Onesimus, who stole some money or property from his master and ran away to Rome where he encountered the imprisoned Paul and, under his guidance, became a Christian. In the letter, Paul greets "Philemon, our dear friend and fellow worker" who had at times "refreshed the hearts of the saints."

Paul announces he has a new son—not a physical son, but a spiritual one, the slave Onesimus. The name is Greek for "useful." In the past he was useless, but now he really is useful, both to Paul and to Philemon. Paul would like to keep Onesimus with him for companionship in his time of imprisonment, but he sends him back to Philemon, "no longer as a slave, but better than a slave, as a dear brother." In sending him back, Paul tells Philemon, "welcome him as you would welcome me." Ever mindful of honesty and fair dealing, Paul promises that he himself will pay Philemon back whatever Onesimus took from him.

Many readers of the Bible are puzzled that the New Testament never actually condemns slavery. In fact, on more than one occasion Paul urges slaves to serve their masters faithfully. But we see in the Letter to Philemon that, among the Christians themselves, slavery was doomed, for it was clear that no true Christian could "own" another human being, especially one who was a fellow believer.

Paul praises the faith of his readers, who apparently have endured some persecution from their unbelieving neighbors. Living among mockers and skeptics, Christians should "lead a quiet life" so that in time their daily life will win the respect of outsiders (1 Thessalonians 4:11–12). They should live moral lives, "for God did not call us to be impure, but to live a holy life" (4:7).

Then he proceeds to the main issue: The believers are worried about their brothers who have died ("fallen asleep"). Since the Lord has not yet returned to earth, will those who have died already be raised or are they lost forever? Paul tells them not to worry: when Christ returns, "with a loud command, with the voice of the archangel, and with the trumpet call of God, the dead in Christ will rise first" (4:16). Those still living "will be caught up together in the clouds to meet the Lord in the air" (4:17)—an event often referred to as the Rapture, although Paul does not use this word himself.

But when will the great event occur? Jesus himself had said that no one could know for certain the time of his return. Paul warns that "the day of the Lord will come like a thief in the night. While people are saying, 'Peace and safety,' destruction will come on them suddenly, as labor pains on a pregnant woman, and they will not escape" (5:2–3). The image of the "thief in the night" is used more than once in the New Testament to emphasize how unexpected the return will be. In the meantime, Paul says, live good and decent lives, spiritually prepared at every moment to meet the Lord.

This letter did not settle the Thessalonians' minds. Some of them believed Jesus was returning to earth very soon, so they had ceased working. So, a few months after the first letter, Paul wrote again. He assured them that before the Lord's return, certain events had to take place first. An evil "man of lawlessness" would appear. "He will oppose and will exalt himself over everything that is called God or is worshipped, so that he sets himself up in God's temple, proclaiming himself to be God" (2 Thessalonians 2:4). He will work all sorts of counterfeit miracles to deceive the people, and many will be led astray, but this evil one will be destroyed when Christ returns. Paul does not actually use the word Anti-Christ here, but clearly this is who he has described, building on Jesus' own prophecies of false Christs appearing near the end of time. Later we will see in the Book of Revelation the sinister "Beast" who is probably identical with the "man of lawlessness" Paul described in 2 Thessalonians.

In the meantime, Paul lays down this rule: "If a man will not work, he shall not eat" (3:10). Waiting for the Lord's return is no excuse for idleness, and people who are not busy tend to become busybodies (3:11).

The two Letters to the Thessalonians are the most "brotherly" of Paul's writings, for he uses the word "brothers" twenty-one times, twice even calling them "brothers loved by the Lord." (By comparison, he uses "brothers" eighteen times in Romans, ten in Galatians.)

PAUL THE MENTOR

We move now from Paul's earliest letters to his latest ones, the three known as the Pastoral Letters, written to his two protégés, Timothy and Titus. The letters are known as the Pastorals because Paul was giving the men advice on how to be a proper minister of Christ. (*Pastor*, incidentally, was the Latin word meaning "shepherd," and you might recall that Jesus called himself the "Good Shepherd.") They were all probably written after Paul's release from his Roman imprisonment, 1 Timothy and Titus written AD 64–65, 2 Timothy AD 66–67.

So far as we know, the apostle Paul had no biological children. But thanks to his preaching of the gospel far and wide, he had numerous "spiritual children," and he was especially close to some who were his fellow missionaries, including both Timothy and Titus. Timothy, at the time Paul wrote his two letters, was head of the Christian fellowship in Ephesus, Titus head of the fellowship on the island of Crete.

In the opening of 1 Timothy, we see that old problems haven't gone away. False teachers were still urging people to believe in "myths and endless genealogies," leading to pointless controversies (1 Timothy 1:4). Believers are engaging in "meaningless talk," when in fact the goal of the Christian life is "love, which comes from a pure heart and a good conscience and a sincere faith" (1:5–6).

Paul urges Timothy to pray for everyone—including kings and all government authorities, "that we may live peaceful and quiet lives in all godliness and holiness" (2:2). Paul no doubt heard of the brutal persecution of Christians in Rome under the vile emperor Nero, which took place after Nero blamed the great fire of Rome (in the year 64) on the Christians. The fact that Paul urged prayer for rulers tells us he held out hope for mercy from the emperor. (Nero's persecution was extremely harsh but, fortunately, short-lived.)

In chapter 3, Paul refers to the qualifications for being an *episkopos* and *diakonos*—two Greek words that have been translated in various ways. *Episkopos* literally is "overseer," while *diakonos* is literally "helper" or "servant." When William Tyndale made the first English translation of the Bible in the 1530s, he rendered *episkopos* as "overseer," which riled the church authorities, who believed the word should be rendered "bishop." Tyndale was correct in seeing that the *episkopos* of Paul's day was nothing like the worldly, wealthy church bishops of his own day. However, most English translations do have "bishop." At any rate, the *episkopos* Paul was describing was a leader (one among several) in a local Christian fellowship, and Paul stated that he had to be a decent and moral man, and one who wielded authority within his own family (3:5).

Diakonos is the source of the word "deacon." We gather from these letters that the *diakonoi* (plural) played some important role in the churches, apparently ranking below the "overseers." Paul not only talks about the moral qualifications for the deacons, but their wives as well. Perhaps he was aware that in any fellowship, a minister's wife has to be mindful of how she presents herself. Later in the letter, Paul speaks of leaders called *presbuteroi*, literally "elders," whose work involved preaching and teaching (5:17–19). Paul's use of the terms *episkopoi*, *diakonoi* and *presbuteroi* in the letter obviously had a powerful effect on Christian denominations, as is clear in the names Episcopalian and Presbyterian, and in the presence of deacons in many Christian churches.

Paul returns to the subject of false teachers. Some of them "forbid people to marry and order them to abstain from certain foods, which God created to be received with thanksgiving by those who believe and who know the truth. For everything God created is good, and nothing is to be rejected if it is received with thanksgiving" (4:3). Avoid, Paul tells Timothy, "myths and old wives' tales" (4:7). False teachers have "an unhealthy interest in controversies and quarrels about words," resulting in strife and suspicion (6:3–5).

From 1 Timothy we get a fairly clear idea of what Christian worship was like in those early years: "Devote yourself to the public reading of Scripture, to preaching and to teaching" (4:13). Paul tells Timothy that as a leader in the church, he should treat the people as family members (5:1–3).

> **DID YOU KNOW?**
>
> "Money is the root of all evil" is an often-quoted proverb, but what the Bible actually says is, "the love of money is the root of all kinds of evil" (1 Timothy 6:10). Money itself is morally neutral and can do a great deal of good, but *love* of it, as Jesus himself pointed out, is spiritually destructive. Paul's words about money echo the New Testament's essential teaching about it: We ought to work to *become*, not to *acquire*.

Near the close of the letter, Paul urges, "Fight the good fight of the faith. Take hold of the eternal life to which you were called when you made your good confession in the presence of many witnesses" (6:12).

Paul's Letter to Titus, dating from the same time as 1 Timothy, was sent to the Greek island of Crete, where his protégé Titus headed the fellowship. To him, Paul offered some sage advice on dealing with Christians of different ages: "Teach the older men to be temperate, worthy of respect, self-controlled, and sound in faith, in love and in endurance. Likewise, teach the older women to be reverent in the way they live, not to be slanderers or addicted to much wine, but to teach what is good. Then they can train the younger women to love their husbands and children, to be self-controlled and pure, to be busy at home, to be kind, and to be subject to their husbands, so that no one will malign the word of God. Similarly, encourage the young men to be self-controlled" (Titus 2:2–6). Besides teaching, set a good moral example. A worthy minister who lives an honorable life can "encourage and rebuke with all authority" (2:15).

The Letter to Titus often goes unread, but its first chapter contains a rather profound insight of Paul's. Speaking of the ever-present false teachers and their pointless regulations about food and what-not, Paul observes that "to the pure, all things are pure, but to those who are corrupted and do not believe, nothing is pure" (1:15). Paul was echoing a key teaching of Jesus, who stated that it was not what went into a man that defiled him, but what came out of him—that is, his words and actions (Matthew 15:11). Paul's point was that external things like food don't determine our inner, spiritual state. If we are pure on the inside, external things cannot contaminate us. There was in Paul's day, and probably always will be, the sort of person who sees religion as a matter of surfaces, exteriors, in contrast to the New Testament faith, which emphasizes the interior transformation of the person.

A few years later, Paul penned his last letter, 2 Timothy, probably written from his second (and last) imprisonment in Rome. The apostle is literally in chains—"I am suffering even to the point of being chained like a criminal. But God's word is not chained" (2 Timothy 2:9). Pondering his plight, Paul quotes what might have been an early Christian hymn: "If we died with him, we will also live with him; if we endure,

---

CULTURAL INSIGHTS

Timothy

Judging from his many mentions in Paul's letters, Timothy was the apostle's closest companion over a long period of time. Paul thought of him as his "true son in the faith" (1 Timothy 1:2) and "dear son" (2 Timothy 1:2). He is first mentioned in Acts 16, where we gather that he lived in the town of Lystra, in which Paul preached the gospel. He had a Greek pagan father and a devout Jewish mother, named Eunice, whose own devout mother was named Lois, and the two women had apparently nurtured young Timothy in their Jewish faith, so that he had deep knowledge of the Scriptures. The two women converted to Christianity, then so did Timothy. This occurred on Paul's first missionary journey. When Paul and Silas came to Lystra on Paul's second journey, Timothy joined in the missionary enterprise. Timothy went with the two into Greece and was also active in the Christian communities in Asia Minor, especially Ephesus.

In 1 Corinthians, Paul speaks highly of his aide: "I am sending to you Timothy, my son whom I love, who is faithful in the Lord. He will remind you of my way of life in Christ Jesus, which agrees with what I teach everywhere in every church" (4:17). He reminded the Philippians that "Timothy has proved himself, because as a son with his father he has served with me in the work of the gospel" (2:22). He must have been an active worker for the Lord, in spite of his having frequent illnesses (1 Timothy 5:23) and being somewhat timid by nature (2 Timothy 1:7).

we will also reign with him. If we disown him, he will also disown us" (2:11–12). As Paul is painfully aware, "everyone who wants to live a godly life in Christ Jesus will be persecuted" (3:12).

Paul turns his attention from his own imprisonment to the end of time, when "people will be lovers of themselves, lovers of money, boastful, proud, abusive, disobedient to their parents, ungrateful, unholy, without love, unforgiving, slanderous, without self-control, brutal, not lovers of the good, treacherous, rash, conceited, lovers of pleasure rather than lovers of God—having a form of godliness but denying its power" (3:1–4). In the meantime, false teachers were everywhere, but God has given us something to keep us wise: "All Scripture is God-breathed and is useful for teaching, rebuking, correcting and training in righteousness, so that the man of God may be thoroughly equipped for every good work" (3:16–17). When Paul uses "Scripture" here, he is in fact referring to the Old Testament, the only "Bible" that Christians of this period had. Within a fairly short time, Paul's own letters would come to be accepted as part of the sacred collection of "God-breathed" writings that believers would take as their guide for life. (We see this as early as 2 Peter 3:16, where Paul's writings are already being called "Scriptures.") Earlier versions of the English Bible used the word "inspired" in the verse, but the New International Version and several others literally translate the Greek word *theopneustos*, "God-breathed," which has an advantage over "inspired" in that it is clear that the writings have their origin in God himself.

Toward the close of 2 Timothy, Paul mentions a desire to see Mark, who is "helpful to me in my ministry" (4:11). Remember that in Acts, Paul and Barnabas had quarreled about Mark, Paul not regarding Mark as being a reliable aide. We get the impression from 2 Timothy that any hostility between Mark and Paul has long since been forgotten.

Looking back on his life, Paul can feel some satisfaction: "I have fought the good fight, I have finished the race, I have kept the faith" (4:7). He concludes the letter with a remembrance that at some point "I was delivered from the lion's mouth." Recalling this, he is confident that "the Lord will rescue me from every evil attack and will bring me safely to his heavenly kingdom" (4:18). Based on what we know of this amazing, dynamic, warmhearted, deepminded, intense, fearless, God-intoxicated man, we can feel confident that he did indeed arrive safely in the heavenly kingdom. He is a true champion and shaper of the faith.

PUTTING THE WORD TO WORK

1. In Galatians, Paul said the old divisions between slave and free, Gentile and Jew, no longer existed among people of faith. Think of situations in your own life where sharing a common faith has broken down social barriers between people. Can you think of people now who might share your faith, but whom you avoid for social reasons? Give some thought to reaching out to those people.

2. Reread Paul's list of the "fruit of the Spirit" in Galatians 5:22–23. Which of these "fruits" are evident in your own life now? Which would you like to see more of in yourself?

3. One of the great quotes of today is Philippians 4:11, in which Paul says, "I have learned to be content whatever the circumstances." Try to think of people you know, or knew in the past, who had this ability. What kept them content in any circumstances?

4. Paul told the Colossian Christians, "Let your conversation be always full of grace, seasoned with salt." How do you interpret this? Keep in mind that here Paul was talking about how to interact with "outsiders," unbelievers. As a believer, how can you make your conversations "full of grace"?

5. Paul's letters to Timothy and Titus talk of how disruptive people can be by introducing quarrels and controversies into a religious fellowship. Make a pledge to be a "peacemaker" in your own group, avoiding quarrels and working to build bridges between people, seeking for common ground instead of trying to divide and disrupt.

Letters to the World

AT THE HEART OF IT ALL TODAY The anonymous Letter to the Hebrews shows us Christ as the heavenly priest sympathizing and interceding for mankind. The Letters of James, 1 and 2 Peter, and Jude tell of persevering in the faith when facing persecution and false teaching.

Today we look at letters *not* written by the apostle Paul. These include two attributed to the best-known of Jesus' disciples, Peter, one attributed to Jesus' brother, James, and another to Jesus' brother, Jude. (A reminder: When the New Testament refers to Jesus' "brothers," it may be referring to cousins or other male relatives.) There are three short letters attributed to the apostle John, but we will look at them in the book's final chapter, since they have some connection with the Bible's last book, Revelation. Today's chapter also looks at one of the most intriguing anonymous books in the world, the so-called Letter to the Hebrews.

> **KEY PASSAGES TO READ TODAY**
>
> Hebrews 1:1–4; 2:14–18; 9:1–28; 11–12
> James 1:19–27; 2:5–11; 14–17; 3:3–6; 5:7–11
> 1 Peter 2:9–12; 3:1–6; 4:12–16
> 2 Peter 1:16–21; 3:8–13

WHO WERE THE "HEBREWS"?

One of the greatest—and, in parts, most difficult—writings in the New Testament is the Letter to the Hebrews. It puzzles many readers, and often people will give up after the first few chapters. It puzzles scholars also, since they don't know who wrote it, or when,

KEY TERM FOR TODAY ## Perseverance

"We consider blessed those who have persevered" (James 5:11). Hebrews, James, and both 1 and 2 Peter emphasize *hypomone*, the Greek word we translate as "perseverance." People of faith have to keep their eyes fixed on Christ, who himself suffered persecution, and on heaven, which is the reward for the faithful. The testing of our faith through suffering develops perseverance even more—in other words, the more we endure, the more we realize we *can* endure. When we grow in perseverance, we can become "mature and complete, not lacking anything" (James 1:4).

or even who its intended readers were. We will try to solve some of those puzzles and put aside the ones that don't matter.

First of all, its author is not named. This sets it apart from all the letters of Paul, James, Peter and Jude. Some older versions of the Bible title the letter "The Epistle of St. Paul to the Hebrews," but it is definitely *not* by Paul, which is obvious in translation and even more so in the Greek original. (The letter does mention Timothy at the end, and Timothy was a close friend of Paul, which is what has led some readers to assume Paul wrote it.) Its style is like no other New Testament writing—in fact, it is the most elegant Greek in the Bible. It may be the only New Testament letter directed toward a "sophisticated" audience. Because it is so well written, one possible author is Apollos, mentioned in Acts 18 as "eloquent." Hailing from the cultured Greek-speaking city of Alexandria, Apollos is indeed a likely candidate, but this is only a guess. We find ourselves in the position of the early Christian scholar Origen, who said, "God only knows who wrote Hebrews." Whoever it was, he was one of the deepest thinkers among the first Christians. God saw fit to pass on his message, not his name.

The second puzzle is the title. In the period when it was written, there were no "Hebrews," an Old Testament term that no longer had any meaning. Jews thought of themselves as, collectively, Israel. The Hebrew language was still studied by the rabbis and scribes, but there were no people who actually thought of themselves as Hebrews. The usual explanation of the title is that it was addressed to Christians who had been Jews, which makes sense, because the letter takes pains to show that the Jewish system of priests and sacrifices is no longer necessary. We saw in the Book of Acts that there was some division between Greek-speaking Jews (the Hellenists) and the Aramaic-speaking Jews of Judea and Galilee. In fact, the Gospels and Acts sometimes use "Hebrew" to refer to the Aramaic language, so the epistle might have been addressed to Aramaic-speaking Jews—except that it is written in elegant Greek! A more plausible suggestion is that its intended readers were Jewish priests, or former priests, which makes sense, given the concern about sacrifices. If priests were its original readers, the letter has, thankfully, found a much wider audience over the centuries.

But the original readers weren't necessarily Jews. If you think back to earlier chapters, you might recall that the translation of the

AD 69–79
Reign of Roman
Emperor Vespasian

**PROBABLE DATES
OF LETTERS**

AD 49
James
(possibly AD 58)
AD 64
1 Peter
AD 65–69
Hebrews
AD 67
2 Peter
AD 70–80
Jude

Old Testament into Greek—the Septuagint—meant that the Old Testament had a wide readership. By the New Testament period, the Old Testament was no longer just "the Jews' book." In a sense it belonged to the world. There were numerous Gentiles interested in the Jews' religion, many of them attending synagogue services and even becoming full-fledged converts. Known as "God-fearers," some of these converts knew the Old Testament as well as, or even better than, many people who were born Jews. We've seen that Paul often quoted the Old Testament when writing to Gentiles. Luke, the author of the third Gospel, was a Gentile, yet his Gospel shows he was very much attracted to the Jewish temple and its rituals. The Gentiles who were drawn to the Jews' religion thought of themselves as included in God's "chosen people," his Israelites, his "Hebrews." So the title could be referring to Jews or Gentiles who had followed the Jewish faith, or both. Consider this possibility: The author thought of the "Hebrews" as all of God's people on earth, passing through this world temporarily as the Hebrew slaves passed through the wilderness on their way to their final home in Canaan. The fact that people of faith are referred to as "aliens and strangers on earth" (Hebrews 11:13) makes this view plausible. The "old" Hebrews were passing through the wilderness on the way to Canaan. The "new" Hebrews are passing through this world on their way to heaven.

When was the letter written? We don't know, but we do know that the Romans destroyed the Jewish temple in AD 70, bringing the system of priests and sacrifices to an end. Since the Letter to the Hebrews speaks as if the sacrifices were still being done, we can assume the letter was written before AD 70. It's true that the letter never once mentions the temple as the place of sacrifice. Instead, it refers to the Tabernacle, the large tent that was the Israelites' worship center during their long journey from Egypt to Canaan. Why does it refer to the Tabernacle, which had not been used in centuries? Probably because the Tabernacle symbolized the time of passing through the wilderness on their way to Canaan. Unlike the temple, the Tabernacle was known to be temporary, just as the time in the wilderness was. Christians were in the same position: passing through on their way to a better world.

But after all the debates over authorship and readership and date are done, we are left with only one solution: Read the letter for its *content* and be glad it is part of our Bible.

THE ULTIMATE REVELATION

The letter opens with words remarkably like the opening of John's Gospel: "In the past God spoke to our forefathers through the prophets at many times and in various ways, but in these last days he has spoken to us by his Son, whom he appointed heir of all things, and through whom he made the universe. The Son is the radiance of God's glory and the exact representation of his being, sustaining all things by his powerful word. After he had provided purification for sins, he sat down at the right hand of the Majesty in heaven" (Hebrews 1:1–3). There is a lot of theology packed into these verses. The Son of God was the agent through whom God made the universe. The Son is the final revelation of God to mankind, superseding the former revelations through the prophets of Israel. He has purified believers from their sins and is now in heaven, glorified. This much seems clear enough. But when readers progress further into chapter 1, they become puzzled; as the letter speaks of Jesus as being superior to the angels, something most readers today have no doubts about. The original readers had possibly been exposed to an early form of Gnosticism, in which various angelic beings were important. (As in the Letter to the Colossians, the simple gospel—Jesus, God's Son, as Savior of mankind—was in danger of being complicated and corrupted.)

Chapter 2 is in some ways the flip side of chapter 1. Jesus, the Son of God who is now glorified in heaven, was fully human. "Both the one who makes men holy and those who are made holy are of the same family. So Jesus is not ashamed to call them brothers.... Since the children have flesh and blood, he too shared in their humanity" (2:11, 14). Then the letter introduces one of its key themes: Jesus as the only priest that mankind needs. "He had to be made like his brothers in every way, in order that he might become a merciful and faithful high priest in service to God, and that he might make atonement for the sins of the people. Because he himself suffered when he was tempted, he is able to help those who are being tempted" (2:17–18). This is one of the few passages in the New Testament that refers to Jesus being tempted by the devil. It is a comforting reminder that Jesus, though he is now exalted in heaven, had to endure what all humans endure. The Letter to the Hebrews is like the Gospel of John in emphasizing that Jesus was both fully human (and thus able to sympathize with us) and fully divine (able to rescue us from our sins). Both John and Hebrews mention Jesus weeping.

According to chapter 3, Jesus is greater than Moses—meaning that the new faith based on Christ is superior to the old faith based on the laws God gave to Moses. The old faith was a "house," but Christ himself is the "builder," and the builder is always greater than the house itself. This chapter reminds readers that the constantly grumbling Israelites whom Moses led through the wilderness were always in danger of turning away from God, and that temptation is one that believers still face. The letter's original readers apparently were at some risk of falling away from the faith, and the letter encourages them to persevere, looking for the "Sabbath-rest for the people of God" (4:9). God is watching us at all times: "Nothing in all creation is hidden from God's sight. Everything is uncovered and laid bare before the eyes of him to whom we must give account" (4:13). But this stern warning is followed by a reminder that Jesus, our high priest, is able to "sympathize with our weakness," for he was tempted just as we are—but did not yield to the temptation. With this sympathetic mediator on our side, we can "approach the throne of grace with confidence, so that we may receive mercy and find grace to help us in our time of need" (4:16).

Chapter 5 is interesting because it is one of the few places outside the Gospels that refers to Jesus' agony in Gethsemane before his arrest and trial. Jesus "offered up prayers and loud cries and tears to the one who could save him from death" (5:7). Like any human, Jesus had no desire to die a violent death, yet he obeyed God and accepted the cross. By obeying, even though it involved great suffering, he was able to bring salvation to mankind (5:8).

In chapter 7 the letter returns to the idea of Jesus as priest. The Jewish priests traced their descent to Aaron, the brother of Moses and the first high priest. In Hebrews, Jesus is spoken of as being superior to Aaron. He is a priest like Melchizedek, the priest-king in Genesis to whom the patriarch Abraham paid tithes. Here the letter introduces a way of thinking that modern readers find difficult: The letter sees Melchizedek as a *type*, a pattern, a foreshadowing of an even greater priest, Jesus. Melchizedek is a unique character in the Bible, for there is no mention of his father (remember that in the Old Testament, a person was identified as "X, son of Y"). For the writer of Hebrews, this makes Melchizedek a sort of "timeless" character, just as Jesus is the eternal priest. Since Abraham paid tithes to Melchizedek, and since the Jewish priests were all descendants of Abraham, the Abraham-Melchizedek incident shows that Melchizedek's priesthood is superior to the priesthood of Aaron. (Melchizedek had "seniority," so to speak.) The eternal priesthood is superior to the temporary priesthood exercised by Aaron's descendants. Jesus is a priest like Melchizedek—without beginning or end. And not only is Jesus eternal and sinless—the perfect priest—but he is also the perfect sacrifice as well. (The Hebrew name Melchizedek means "king of righteousness"—an appropriate name for Jesus.) The sacrifice of Jesus is done not in the Jewish Tabernacle, but in heaven (8:2). In fact, the sacrifices offered on earth were a kind of "copy" of the real sacrifice taking place in heaven.

At this point the letter quotes a long passage from Jeremiah, the prophecy of a new covenant: "This is the covenant I will make with the house of Israel after that time, declares the Lord. I will put my laws in their minds and write them on their hearts. I will be their God, and they will be my people. No longer will a man teach his neighbor, or a man his brother, saying, 'Know the Lord,' because they will all know me, from the least of them to the greatest" (Hebrews 8:10–11, quoting Jeremiah 31:31–32). You might recall that at the Last Supper, Jesus spoke of his "blood" of the new covenant (Luke 22:20). The offerings and sacrifices done under the old covenant (the laws of Moses) "were not able to clear the conscience of the worshipper. They are only a matter of food and drink and various ceremonial washings—external regulations" (Hebrews 9:9–10). Here we are reminded of Jesus' criticism of the scribes and the Pharisees, with their fussy attention to handwashing and other rituals. These no longer have any meaning under the new covenant.

Jesus' great sacrifice—himself—cleanses us from our sins in a way the old sacrifices and rituals could not. "The law is only a shadow of the good things that are coming—not the realities themselves. For this reason it can never, by the same sacrifices repeated endlessly year after year, make perfect those who draw near to worship" (10:1). Since Jesus has made the perfect sacrifice on our behalf, "let us draw near to God with a sincere heart in full assurance of faith, having our hearts sprinkled to cleanse us from a guilty conscience" (10:22).

CULTURAL INSIGHTS

Mediator

In the New Testament the Greek word *mesites* means, literally, "middleman." It was used to refer to what we would call an umpire, arbitrator, negotiator, intermediary. The key idea was that a third party helped bring two parties together, settling disputes and establishing harmony. In terms of the life of faith, the mediator is the one who reconciles holy God and sinful man. Several Old Testament saints were mediators. Abraham tried to mediate for Sodom, although the city was so wicked that God decided to destroy it anyway. Moses was the mediator many times for the rebellious Israelites, whom God was on the verge of destroying. Israel's high priest was, in theory, the nation's chief mediator, but as was clear in the case of the wicked high priest (Caiaphas) of Jesus' time, priests were often corrupt and immoral men. Israel longed for a godly mediator. Moses himself had prophesied the coming of a great prophet like himself, and many believed this prophet—who might also be the Messiah—would be a mediator just as Moses was.

According to the New Testament, and particularly the Letter to the Hebrews, the ultimate Mediator between God and man was Jesus Christ—the perfect Mediator because he is both God *and* man. In Hebrews, Jesus' role as the great high priest in heaven is emphasized. No longer must people look to worldly, corrupt human priests to mediate between them and God. Jesus is not only the sinless priest but also the perfect sacrifice. In three passages, Hebrews refers to Christ as the "mediator of a new covenant," doing away with the old Sinai covenant and its system of sacrifices.

Being freed from sin is a great thing—but it is not an excuse for us to become complacent. God still judges his people, and "it is a dreadful thing to fall into the hands of the living God" (10:31). The letter reminds the readers of their earlier zeal in the faith, when they had suffered insults and persecution and showed sympathy to fellow believers who were sent to prison. We don't know when exactly this persecution took place, but for some of them it resulted in confiscation of their property. The letter reminds them that their "better and lasting possessions" are in heaven (10:34).

There follows one of the great chapters of the Bible, the "Faith Hall of Fame," chapter 11. "Now faith is being sure of what we hope for and certain of what we do not see. This is what the ancients were commended for" (11:1–2). The first to be commended is Abel, who offered a righteous sacrifice to God, unlike his brother Cain. Then there is Enoch, the man who "walked with God" and never died. Then Noah, who built the ark to save his family. Then Abraham, who left his native country at God's command, and who offered up his only son Isaac. Then Moses, who gave up his position in Pharaoh's court, willing to share the slavery of his own people, then lead them out of Egypt. The chapter commends many others: Isaac, Jacob, Joseph, Gideon, Barak, Samson, Jephthah, David, all the prophets. "Through faith (they) conquered kingdoms, administered justice, and gained what was promised; who shut the mouths of lions, quenched the fury of the flames, and escaped the edge of the sword; whose weakness was turned to strength; and who became powerful in battle and routed foreign armies" (11:33–34). Yet there was persecution, inevitably: "Some faced jeers and flogging, while still others were chained and put in prison. They were stoned; they were sawed in two; they were put to death by the sword.... destitute, persecuted and mistreated—the world was not worthy of them" (11:36–38). Indeed not!

At this point is one of the great revelations in the New Testament: The saints of the Old Testament, which expresses no clear faith in an afterlife, are nonetheless rewarded with heaven: "These were all commended for their faith, yet none of them received what had been promised. God had planned something better for us so that only together with us would they be made perfect" (11:39–40).

Chapter 12 speaks of these people of faith as a "cloud of witnesses." The Greek word here, *martyr*, literally means "witness," but was coming to mean "one who dies for his faith," as many of these witnesses had done. The use of "cloud" is a reminder that many times in the Bible a cloud is the sign of God's presence. The witnesses, the great people of faith, are now with God—"surrounding" those of us still on earth, reminding us that we too can persevere under trials.

Hardships are a reminder that God is our Father, since there is no father who does not discipline his children. "God disciplines us for our good, that we may share in his holiness. No discipline seems pleasant at the time, but painful. Later on, however, it produces a harvest of righteousness and peace for those who have been trained by it. Therefore, strengthen your feeble arms and weak knees" (12:10–12).

The reward for perseverance is heaven, which is compared to a mountain—not Mount Sinai, the symbol of the old covenant with Moses, but Mount Zion, Jerusalem, "with thousands upon thousands of angels in joyful assembly" (12:22). Clearly, this is not the earthly Jerusalem but the "new Jerusalem," also described in Revelation. This is our "kingdom that cannot be shaken" (12:28), a reminder that Jesus' kingdom, the kingdom of God, is "not of this world."

Like Paul's letters, the Letter to the Hebrews ends with moral instructions. Christians are reminded to give sympathy aid to those in prison, to keep away from sexual sin and the love of money. They are to honor and imitate godly leaders, and to share with those in need. Although ritual sacrifices are no longer needed, God is pleased with the "sacrifice" of good deeds and generosity —the "living sacrifices" that Paul spoke of in Romans.

One closing thought: Many Bible scholars think that Hebrews was not originally an epistle at all, but a sermon that (thankfully) was written down, then later circulated widely. If so, it is the longest sermon in the Bible, and probably one of the deepest and most beautiful ones ever preached.

> **DID YOU KNOW?**
>
> The phrase "angels unaware" is from the King James Version for Hebrews 13:2: "Be not forgetful to entertain strangers: for thereby some have entertained angels unawares." The verse is referring to Genesis 18, where three angels, appearing human, visit the patriarch Abraham.

THE "AMOS" OF THE NEW TESTAMENT

Some passages of Hebrews are difficult to fathom, so it is a relief to turn to the highly readable, easily understood Letter of James, with its clear message of "walking the walk, not just talking the talk" of faith. There are several men in the New Testament named James, including two among Jesus' twelve disciples. But it is generally agreed that the author of the Letter of James was "James, the Lord's brother," mentioned by Paul in Galatians 1:19. This was the same James who held a key leadership position among the Jerusalem Christians, as we saw in the Book of Acts. (A reminder: When the New Testament refers to Jesus' "brothers," it may be referring to cousins or other male relatives.) The letter may well be the oldest part of the New Testament, possibly written as early as AD 48.

James introduces himself as "a servant of God and of the Lord Jesus Christ." His letter is to "the twelve tribes of the dispersion"—not the twelve tribes of Israel, but God's "new Israel," the Christians. Along with 1 and 2 Peter, 1–3 John, and Jude, James is classed among the "Catholic Epistles"—"Catholic" in its original sense of "universal." These letters weren't addressed to a particular locale, as Paul's were, but to Christians in general. (Happily, *all* the epistles in the New Testaments became "universal" very quickly, with Paul's recipients sharing his writings with others.)

The Diaspora

Jews who lived away from the homeland (Judea) were known as the Diaspora, a Greek word meaning "dispersion" or "scattering." They were scattered mainly because of the Babylonian conquest of Judea in 586 BC, in which huge numbers of people were exiled to Babylon. At the same time, many Jews in Judea fled into Egypt, starting a very large Jewish colony there. In the New Testament period, there were far more Jews living away from Judea than in it. Jews were scattered across the Roman Empire, mainly in large cities like Rome, Antioch and Alexandria. The Christian faith spread widely because of the Diaspora, since (as we saw in Acts), missionaries like Paul generally began their preaching in the synagogues wherever they traveled.

We see in the Letters of James and 1 Peter that "Diaspora" was taking on a new meaning. Christians, whether they were former Jews or not, thought of themselves as God's people scattered far and wide. James addressed his letter to "the twelve tribes scattered among the nations," and Peter to "God's elect, strangers in the world, scattered throughout" various provinces. James clearly did not have in mind the twelve tribes of Israel, but the "new Israel," based not on nationality or descent but on faith.

James jumps immediately into one of his main themes: persecution. He is not talking here about official government persecution but about the petty harassment by unbelievers, a theme we will also find in 1 Peter. As in Hebrews, James reminds us that testing develops perseverance, making us mature and complete. The great example of persevering in the midst of suffering is Job (James 5:11). A person who endures his trials will receive the "crown of life" from God (1:12). God himself does not tempt us—on the contrary, our own evil desires are the cause (1:14).

Another key theme of the book is the sin of showing favoritism toward the rich and snubbing the poor. James is sometimes called the "Amos" of the New Testament because of his concern for the poor, a concern voiced eloquently by the prophet Amos. Like Jesus, James sees rich and poor from God's viewpoint: the rich are really "low," the poor are really "high." The rich man's goods will someday wither away like the grass (1:11). Christians are "brothers," fellow believers in Christ, and there is no place for favoritism. James provides concrete details: A well-dressed man with a gold ring comes to a meeting, then a shabbily dressed man comes in. The rich man is given a nice seat, while the shabby man is told to sit on the floor. In God's eyes this is wrong. Those who are poor by worldly standards can be "rich in faith." Why do people favor the rich when it is the rich who exploit them? Favoritism is a violation of what James calls the "royal law of Scripture": "Love your neighbor as yourself" (2:8).

James has some harsh warnings for the wealthy: "Now listen, you rich people, weep and wail because of the misery that is coming upon you.... Look! The wages you failed to pay the workmen who mowed your fields are crying out against you" (5:1, 4). Those who live in luxury and self-indulgence have fattened themselves for the day of slaughter.

Then James speaks of his main theme, an issue that, like concern for the poor, is an echo of the Old Testament prophets: Our deeds must match our words. "What good is it, my brothers, if a man claims to have faith but has no deeds? Can such faith save him?...faith by itself, if it is not accompanied by action, is dead" (2:14, 17). Again, James gives a concrete example: seeing a brother who lacks food and clothing and saying to him, "Go, I wish you well." If faith is only words, it is no faith at all. He brings up the example of Abraham, who proved his faith when he was willing to sacrifice his son Isaac: "His faith and actions were working together" (2:22). There is no salvation or justification without good works. Saying "I believe in God" is not enough—as James points out, "even the demons believe that—and shudder" (2:19). We're reminded here that when Jesus encountered demons, they recognized him as the Son of God—but their *belief* did not save them!

We have to pause here and admit that James has been criticized for teaching "salvation by works," whereas Paul taught that faith, not works, is what saves us. But there is no real contradiction. Both men agreed on the basic point: If a person really does have faith, his deeds will show it.

James then addresses an area where we all fall short: taming our tongues. Just as a bit steers a horse and a rudder steers a ship, the tongue, though small, steers a human being— usually in the wrong direction! The tongue "corrupts the whole person, sets the whole course of his life on fire, and is itself set on fire by hell. All kinds of animals, birds, reptiles and creatures of the sea are being tamed and have been tamed by man, but no man can tame the tongue. It is a restless evil, full of deadly poison. With the tongue we praise our Lord and Father, and with it we curse men, who have been made in God's likeness. Out of the same mouth come praise and cursing. My brothers, this should not be" (3:6–10). James also echoes the words of Jesus: "Who are you to judge your neighbor? (4:12). We should not grumble against each other, since "the Judge is standing at the door" (5:9). We need to control not only our tongues, but our tempers as well: "Everyone should be quick to listen, slow to speak, and slow to become angry" (1:19). People who consider themselves religious and can't control their tongues are only fooling themselves (1:26).

The letter turns to the topic of wisdom. Apparently James knew of Christians who thought themselves smarter than others. Fine, James says: "Let him show it by his good life, by deeds done in the humility that comes from wisdom" (3:13). The real wisdom from God is "peace-loving, considerate, submissive, full of mercy and good fruit, impartial and sincere" (3:17). Worldly wisdom only leads to boasting, envy and other evils.

James

Acts 15 shows James succeeding the apostle Peter as leader of the Christians in Jerusalem, with James presiding over the council, which debated allowing Gentiles into the church. Although James was not one of the original twelve disciples, Paul refers to him as "apostle" (Galatians 1:19), probably because, like Paul himself, James had seen the risen Jesus (1 Corinthians 15:7). The Letter of James shows James as a moral teacher, echoing many of the teachings of Jesus himself, such as the importance of not judging others and of loving our neighbor as ourselves.

A fairly reliable tradition says that James was stoned to death in AD 62 at the instigation of the Sadducees. He was often known as "James the Just" for the uprightness of his life.

James's actual name, by the way, was Jacob, which is also true of the other Jameses of the New Testament. Centuries ago his name—in Greek, *Iakobos*—evolved into Jacobus, then (oddly) into Jacomus, and finally James.

Worldly greed is wrong too. It leads to coveting and quarreling. "Don't you know that friendship with the world is hatred toward God? Anyone who chooses to be a friend of the world becomes an enemy of God" (4:4). But God can help us keep our worldly urges in check: "Submit yourselves, then, to God. Resist the devil, and he will flee from you. Come near to God and he will come near to you" (4:7–8).

At this time in history, Christians were expecting the speedy return of Christ to earth—a theme we already saw in Paul's two letters to the Thessalonians. Like Paul, James reminds people to be patient—like the farmer patiently waiting for his crops to bear fruit (5:7).

The letter ends with a reminder for believers to confess their sins to each other and pray for each other, for "the prayer of a righteous man is powerful and effective" (5:16). If we find a brother wandering from the faith, we should bring him back and "save him from death" (5:20).

You can see why James is a well-loved letter. There is no hard-to-fathom theology here, no poetry—just very blunt, no-holds-barred ethical teaching, telling believers to show their faith by how they act—enduring trials patiently, showing no favoritism to the rich, aiding the poor, controlling our tongues. Many readers have pointed out that its words would fit perfectly into Jesus' Sermon on the Mount.

THE FISHERMAN AS TEACHER

We have already met Peter the devoted but sometimes unstable disciple, then Peter the fiery Christian leader in the Book of Acts. Now we meet Peter the wise counselor of the early Christians, Peter the letter writer. He apparently wrote the letter while in Rome, which he refers to as "Babylon" in 5:13. He states that the letter was written "with the help of Silas," presumably the same Silas who was a missionary partner of Paul. This use of an aide, or "secretary," may explain why the letter is in such excellent Greek—probably too eloquent for a Galilean fisherman—but then again, perhaps not. After all, Peter's brother Andrew bore a Greek name, which tells us the family had some familiarity with Greek culture. While it is tempting to think of Peter as some bluff, dimwitted, working-class man, incapable of writing the letter known as 1 Peter, he may have been more at home in Greek than we might imagine. Since we know Silas was a Roman citizen, he might have helped "polish" Peter's words.

Peter's first letter, written around AD 64, is addressed to "God's elect, strangers in the world, scattered throughout" five Roman provinces in the area we today call Turkey. Like Paul, Peter opens his letter with "grace and peace." Like Hebrews and James, he addresses the issue of persecution. Again, this is not the official Roman persecution of a later time, but the mocking and hostility of unbelieving neighbors, who scorned the Christians for their high moral standards, for being "unworldly." As in the other epistles, Peter reminds his readers that their sufferings are painful, but that they are God's way of testing and refining their faith. They should rejoice, for there is "an inheritance that can never perish, spoil, or fade" awaiting them (1 Peter 1:4). He reminds them that Christ himself suffered, but was later glorified (1:11).

They should live lives of hope and holiness, remembering they are "strangers" here on earth—an idea echoed in Hebrews. They were purchased for salvation not by gold and silver but by the blood of the sinless Christ, chosen for his task before the world began. "You have been born again, not of perishable seed, but of imperishable, through the living and enduring word of God" (1:23). (The phrase "born again" is not only found in John's Gospel.) Christ is the "living Stone"—rejected by men but precious to God, and Christians themselves are living stones, built into a spiritual house. Then follows the most-quoted passage of the letter: "You are a chosen people, a royal priesthood, a holy nation, a people belonging to God, that you may declare the praises of him who called you out of darkness into his wonderful light" (2:9). These people of God are "aliens and strangers in the world," and these aliens live such good lives that some of the pagans will in time turn to the faith (2:12).

Peter then echoes a teaching of Paul, as stated in an earlier chapter: Submit to earthly authorities, for they are given by God to maintain order and restrain evil. One reason Paul, Peter and others told Christians to behave and obey the government was that the Jews had a long history of getting treated better by the government than by the population at large. They saw—with good reason—the government as their protection against mob violence. Peter's admonition to "honor the king" is interesting in light of the fact that his letter is said to come from "Babylon," that is, Rome. He had no illusions about Rome—it was as immoral as ancient Babylon was—yet even a bad government played a role in maintaining the peace.

Like Paul, Peter tells slaves to obey their earthly masters—not only the good masters, but the harsh ones as well. Suffering for doing good is commended by God, but suffering for doing wrong is not. (In other words, if your master beats you because he is a cruel man, shame on him. If he beats you because you stole from him, shame on you.) Christ himself set the example of meekly enduring persecution. Christ put his case in the hands of the one righteous Judge (2:23). Again, like Paul, Peter urges wives to submit to their husbands, partly in the hope that unbelieving husbands will be won over to the faith by their wives' actions. Women ought not to fuss over their hair, jewelry and clothing, but cultivate "the unfading beauty of a gentle and quiet spirit, which is of great worth in God's sight" (3:4). Husbands are told to treat their wives with respect—a bit of advice we take for granted today, but it was not taken for granted in those days, when men could easily get away with abusing their wives and children.

Again, Peter turns to the subject of persecution. Believers should always be ready to speak out on behalf of their faith—but gently and respectfully. Peter reminds them of how in times past they wasted themselves in the same sensuous pleasures the pagans enjoyed, which is why the pagans now cannot understand the remarkable change in the Christians' behavior. Inevitably they will heap abuse on their former partners in sin—but God will judge them for it (4:3–5). "Dear friends, do not be surprised at the painful trial you are suffering, as though something strange were happening to you. But rejoice that you participate in the sufferings of Christ, so that you may be overjoyed when his glory is revealed" (4:12–13). They can take heart that their brothers throughout the world are undergoing the same trials (5:9).

Like James, Peter counsels believers to resist the devil, who "prowls around like a roaring lion" (5:8). He also counsels them to humble themselves, that God may lift them up (5:6). In perhaps the most comforting verse of the letter, he tells them to "Cast all your anxiety on him, because he cares for you" (5:7).

At the end of the letter, Peter sends a greeting from "my son Mark," probably not his biological son, but his "son in the faith," the same Mark who accompanied Paul on a missionary journey. This mention of Mark supports the old tradition that Mark based his Gospel on the eyewitness accounts of Peter.

This is one of the great letters of the Bible, albeit sadly neglected, since people tend to give more attention to the letters of Paul. It is rich in theology and moral teaching, and in words of comfort for those who were persecuted. Interestingly enough, shortly after writing the letter in Rome, Peter would witness the first *official* persecution of Christians, for after the great fire of Rome in AD 64, the depraved emperor Nero blamed the fire on Christians, touching off a wave of crucifixions and other tortures and executions, which delighted the Romans. The populace's contempt for the Christians—the unofficial persecution spoken of in 1 Peter—preceded and laid the foundation for the official persecution, a pattern that would become familiar in the years ahead.

FOR THOSE LED ASTRAY

Two brief letters, 2 Peter and Jude, are very similar, both dealing with the issue of false teachers—a problem among the early Christians that remains even today.

An old tradition says that Peter was martyred during the persecution in Rome following the great fire in AD 64. Supposedly he was about to be crucified and told his executioners that he did not deserve to die in the same way his Master did. The cruel executioners obliged him by crucifying him upside down. If he was martyred at this time, then 2 Peter must have been written earlier, or possibly Peter survived and was martyred at a later time.

In chapter 1, Peter reminds his readers that, in contrast with false teachers, he himself was an eyewitness of Jesus' glory. Aside from that, the false teachers were apparently contradicting the Scriptures (the Old Testament) in some way, and Peter reminded his readers that "no prophecy of Scripture came about by the prophet's own interpretation. For prophecy never had its origin in the will of man, but men spoke from God as they were carried along by the Holy Spirit" (2 Peter 1:20–21). This is one of the key passages in the Bible regarding what is meant by the "inspiration" of Scripture. Peter recalls that in the days of the Old Testament prophets, there were false prophets as well. He warns that judgment is coming upon these greedy exploiters, just as God cast the rebel angels out of heaven, sent the great flood in the time of Noah, and destroyed wicked Sodom and Gomorrah. Remembering how God rescued Lot and his family from Sodom, Peter writes that "the Lord knows how to rescue godly men from trials and to hold the unrighteous for the day of judgment, while continuing their punishment" (2:9).

Apparently the false teachers condemned in the letter were not just going astray over words and beliefs, but morals as well. They "carouse in broad daylight" and "never stop sinning" (2:13–14). "They promise freedom, while they themselves are slaves of depravity —for a man is a slave to whatever has mastered him" (2:19). Like the prophets in the Old Testament, the apostles in the New were aware that false religions were more than

> **DID YOU KNOW?**
>
> Outside the Gospels, 2 Peter is the only book to refer to the voice of God heard at Jesus' baptism and Transfiguration, with God on both occasions referring to Jesus as his "beloved Son." You might recall that Peter, James and John were the only three disciples present at the Transfiguration. According to 2 Peter 1:18, "We ourselves heard this voice when we were with him on the sacred mountain."

just a matter of words and doctrines: where beliefs were wrong, morals would be wrong also. The worst cases are believers who fall back into sin—worse off than if they had never known Christ (2:21).

Peter also criticizes those who scoff because Christ has not yet returned to earth—a problem also mentioned by James and Paul in their letters. The letter offers a profound insight into God's view of time: "Do not forget this one thing, dear friends: With the Lord a day is like a thousand years, and a thousand years are like a day" (3:8). Aside from this, the Lord is delaying the day of judgment to give sinners more time to repent. The day will come unexpectedly, "like a thief" (3:10), an image also found in 1 Thessalonians and Revelation. Peter prophesies what we see at the end of Revelation, "a new heaven and a new earth" (3:13). Knowing this, people should live blameless lives, always ready for the Lord's return.

Curiously, almost at the end of the letter Peter refers to the writings of his fellow apostle, Paul: "His letters contain some things that are hard to understand, which ignorant and unstable people distort, as they do the other Scriptures, to their own destruction" (3:16). These words have proven to be true over two thousand years, with people eagerly distorting the Bible for their own purposes. The verse also makes us realize that at this point in time Christians were already beginning to think of Paul's writings as inspired Scripture.

One thing in 2 Peter that should not be overlooked: Peter speaks of the "tent" of his body—a common image among the early Christians, since a tent is only a temporary dwelling place. He claims his "tent" will soon be put aside, "as our Lord Jesus Christ has made clear to me." Apparently the apostle received a revelation that he was to die soon, probably as a martyr to the faith. The letter was his last opportunity to speak to the faithful about true and false teachings, and the importance of being ready for the Lord's return.

The very brief Letter of Jude covers much of the same ground as 2 Peter, warning of false teachers. In the opening, Jude refers to himself as "a servant of Jesus Christ and a brother of James," which almost certainly refers to the same James who wrote the Letter of James. Thus Jude was, like James, a "brother" of Jesus who came to faith only after the resurrection. Jude's actual name was Judas, a common name in the New Testament period, but thanks to the bad reputation of the notorious traitor Judas Iscariot, tradition prefers to call this *good* Judas by the name Jude.

Unlike James, we know nothing about Jude and his role in the early church, other than writing this letter. We don't know when or to whom the letter was written, only that Jude was disturbed by the "godless men who change the grace of our God into a license for immorality and deny Jesus Christ as our only Sovereign and Lord" (Jude verse 4). Like 2 Peter, the letter refers to the rebel angels and the cities of Sodom and

Gomorrah as examples of wickedness that God punished. Instead of following the Spirit, they follow their own natural instincts (verse 19). Believers should show mercy to those who doubt and snatch them from the fire.

In our final chapter we will continue with some of the same themes as today—persecution and false teachings. Both will reach a fever pitch in the closing book of the Bible, Revelation.

PUTTING THE WORD TO WORK

1. Hebrews makes the point that Jesus is able to sympathize with our human weaknesses. In the course of the day, when you experience a moment of weakness, picture Jesus standing by your side, giving you sympathy and strength.

2. Following Hebrews 11, write down your own "Faith Hall of Fame," naming great role models of faith—either people you have known personally or through history.

3. Hebrews speaks of the "cloud of witnesses" that surround us. As you go through the day, try to imagine the great heroes of the Bible watching you.

4. In light of James's words, make today your day to be "quick to listen, slow to speak, slow to be angry."

5. Think about Peter's words on "the unfading beauty of a gentle and quiet spirit, which is of great worth in God's sight." Consider how much time you devote to your own physical appearance, and ask yourself what you can do to cultivate unfading inner beauty.

Love, Judgment and Amen

AT THE HEART OF IT ALL TODAY Love and perseverance are the two key themes in this study of the three letters of John and the mystifying but inspiring Book of Revelation, with its images of persecution and the final triumph of good over evil.

We conclude our walk through the Bible with four books, all written by a man named John. We aren't certain if they are by the same John, since John (in the Greek, *Ioannan*) was a common name then as now. But all four are associated with John

KEY PASSAGES TO READ TODAY

1 John 1:5–10; 2:15–17; 4:7–11
Revelation 1–3; 19:11—22:21

the apostle who, tradition says, was the last of the twelve apostles to die. Since he was the last of Jesus' original band of followers, it is appropriate that his writings wrap up the New Testament, and the entire Bible. All four writings have a great deal to say about divine love—and divine judgment as well.

WALKING THE WALK

John the apostle wrote not only the Gospel that bears his name but also three brief epistles found near the end of the Bible. The three form a kind of appendix to the Gospel, addressing some of the same themes and warning believers against some new challenges to the faith.

At the beginning, John tells us that his purpose in writing is to "make your joy complete" (1 John 1:4). God, he reminds us, is light, and if we have true fellowship with him, we can't "walk in the darkness." Being "in the light" doesn't mean we are perfect, of course. In fact, "if we claim to be without sin, we deceive ourselves and the truth is not in us. If we confess our sins, he is faithful and just and will forgive us our sins and purify us from all

KEY TERM FOR TODAY Victory

You might already know that the Greek word *nike* means "victory." That word, or some form of it, occurs numerous times in Revelation and the letters of John, where believers are assured that ultimately they will *nikao* (overcome, conquer, be victorious). "Everyone born of God overcomes [*nika*] the world" (1 John 5:4). Every faithful believer is a *nikon*, a victor, conqueror, overcomer (21:7).

unrighteousness" (1:8–9). Notice the balance here: we are called to "walk in the light," but not to become so proud that we fool ourselves into thinking we are sin-free. When we do sin, there *is* a remedy.

You might recall that in John's Gospel, Jesus tells his disciples, "If you love me, keep my commandments." The same idea is found in the epistle. "The man who says, 'I know him [Christ],' but does not do what he commands is a liar, and the truth is not in him. But if anyone obeys his word, God's love is truly made complete in him" (2:4–5). And if we follow Christ's commands, hate is out of the question: "Anyone who claims to be in the light but hates his brother is still in the darkness" (2:9).

Another sign we are in the darkness is that we become too attached to material things. "Do not love the world or anything in the world. If anyone loves the world, the love of the Father is not in him" (2:15). Of course, God made the world and everything in it for us to enjoy. But John understands how easily we can worship the gifts instead of the Giver. Besides, we are called to set our minds on the things that endure: "Everything in the world—the cravings of sinful man, the lust of his eyes and the boasting of what he has and does—comes not from the Father but from the world. The world and its desires pass away, but the man who does the will of God lives forever" (2:16–17). In other words, we can be "successful" in worldly things, but our success is transitory, while fellowship with God is eternal. John even reminds us that the world is under the sway of the evil one, Satan (5:19), but "everyone born of God overcomes the world. This is the victory that has overcome the world, even our faith" (5:4).

John uses a word that no other book of the Bible (except his own second letter) uses: *antichrist*. "Dear children, this is the last hour; and as you have heard that the antichrist is coming, even now many antichrists have come" (2:18). This verse catches people off-guard. Isn't there supposed to be one *antichrist*? Not according to 1 John. There are *many* antichrists. Who are they: "Who is the liar? It is the man who denies that Jesus is the Christ. Such a man is the antichrist—he denies the Father and the Son" (2:22). For John, antichrist is not the Beast of Revelation, the one figure who will do horrible things at the end of time. John is here referring to false teachers who teach something other than Christ as the Son of God. Here "anti" does not mean "opposed to" but "instead of"—that is, a false

AD 35
Stoning of Stephen
(*Acts 6–7*)

Conversion of Saul,
later called Paul
(*Acts 9:1–31*)

AD 43–44
Execution of the
apostle James
(*Acts 12*)

AD 60–61
Paul's journey to
Rome and shipwreck
(*Acts 27:1–28:15*)

AD 61–63
Paul under house
arrest in Rome
(*Acts 28:16–31*)

AD 64
Persecution of
Christians under
Roman Emperor Nero

AD 70
Jewish revolt
provokes the Romans
to destroy the temple,
bringing the Jewish
priesthood to an end.

AD 87–96
Persecution of
Christians under
Roman Emperor
Domitian

c. AD 90
Writing of 1, 2, 3 John

AD 95
Writing of Revelation

AD 96–180
Starting with Emperor
Marcus Nerva,
Rome is ruled by five
individuals who
became known as the
"Good Emperors."

AD 100
Traditional date for
the death of John

Eschatology

The Greek word *eschaton* means "end," and eschatology is the study of the end times, based on the Bible. Various parts of the Bible make predictions about the end of the world—Daniel, Revelation, and even some parts of the Gospels, where Jesus warned his disciples about some of the signs of the end. Many Bible readers make an effort to "coordinate" the various passages concerned with the end times, but there is no general agreement about how they all fit together, so eschatology is one area of belief where there is no final, definitive, authoritative statement of "This is what will happen in the future." Throughout the centuries, speculations about the end of time have led people into some wild (and occasionally dangerous) beliefs and practices. Various people claiming to know the "true" interpretation of Revelation have occasionally banded together some followers and gone somewhere to await the end times—only to be disappointed. In fact, eschatology ought to be a comfort, not a puzzle to be solved. The best use of the Bible's prophecies of the end time is to find hope and consolation in them and be aware that no matter what happens, the world will have a happy ending, thanks to God.

Christ, not the one the believers have been taught. Later in the epistle, John urges believers to be wise: "Dear friends, do not believe every spirit, but test the spirits to see whether they are from God, because many false prophets have gone out into the world" (4:1). In his brief second letter, John speaks of the "many deceivers, who do not acknowledge Jesus Christ as coming in the flesh" (2 John verse 7). John was battling a false teaching that was around for centuries, the belief that Christ was not fully a human being.

A key theme of the whole Bible is that our deeds must harmonize with our words. Like James, John assures us that good words without good deeds do not fool God: "If anyone has material possessions and sees his brother in need but has no pity on him, how can the love of God be in him? Dear children, let us not love with words or tongue but with actions and in truth." (1 John 3:17–18). "If anyone says, 'I love God,' yet hates his brother, he is a liar. For anyone who does not love his brother, whom he has seen, cannot love God, whom he has not seen" (4:20). This might be the most profound statement in the book, and one of the most profound in the entire Bible. *There is no true love for God unless we love other people.* John is actually using "brother" in the epistle to refer to a fellow believer, but it could easily apply to any human being.

We can thank 1 John for raising a crucial question: How is true Christianity to be identified—and verified? The answer is to be found in the moral life and love of the brethren.

John's other two letters are brief, only one chapter each. The second is addressed to the "chosen lady and her children," which might mean a Christian woman but probably refers to a church and its members. In the brief letter John reiterates the importance of brotherly love. The third letter, written to a friend named Gaius, commends the friend's hospitality in receiving visiting believers. In both of these letters, John refers to himself as "the elder," a title of respect. It does not mean John was old at the time (though he may have been), but that he was a revered leader among the Christians. There is a long old tradition that John the apostle had a devoted follower known as John "the elder," and this John wrote down the apostle's recollections in the Gospel and also wrote the epistles we know as 1, 2 and 3 John.

CHRIST VERSUS CAESAR

The Book of Revelation has been called the "victory song of the persecuted church." By the time it was written, persecution was no longer the petty harassment and mocking spoken of in the earlier New Testament writings. Rather, there was some serious, horrible, government-sponsored persecution of believers. Blood was being shed, which is why Revelation is one of the "bloodiest" books in the Bible. It all ends happily, but not before people of faith have endured unthinkable horrors.

The book identifies its author as "John," who was exiled on the bleak, rocky island of Patmos in the Mediterranean Sea. Tradition says this was John the apostle, who also wrote the Gospel of John and the epistles 1, 2 and 3 John. It is possible the author was "John the elder," who was a disciple of John the apostle. Whichever John it was, he was exiled for preaching the faith, and some of his fellow believers were suffering worse things than exile. Probably the persecution took place under the Roman emperor Domitian, who reigned from AD 81 to AD 96. The Roman emperors were, in theory, divine, and there were old myths claiming they were descended from some of the Roman gods. No one took the emperor's divinity very seriously, since it was more a matter of "public relations" than religious belief. (The Romans themselves had borrowed the idea of a "divine king" from Egypt and Babylon.) But Domitian actually took his divinity seriously and insisted that all inhabitants of the far-flung empire pay homage to him as a god. This the Christians would *not* do.

If you think back to the Book of Acts, you might recall that there was no Roman persecution of Christians in the earliest days. In fact, the apostles were persecuted by their fellow Jews, and the Roman officials at times intervened to save the apostles' lives. But in between then and the time of Revelation, things had changed. Public opinion had changed. As Christianity spread, pagans became more and more aware of the Christians, feeling more and more threatened by their growing numbers. The Christians were countercultural—they didn't participate in pagan festivals or attend the gory games in the arena or the immoral, sex-saturated plays in the theatres. The Christians seemed decent and harmless, but unbelievers were not so sure. Perhaps these people with their peculiar new religion were dangerous. The empire was waiting for some catastrophe to occur so the Christians could be blamed and punished.

A turning point was in the reign of the vile emperor Nero. A great fire had burned much of the city of Rome, and there were rumors (possibly true) that Nero had the fire started so he could rebuild Rome to his liking. Nero blamed the fire on Christians, and soon there was fierce persecution in Rome, with Christians crucified, coated with pitch and burned alive, devoured in the arena by wild beasts, or killed by gladiators—all in full view of the Roman crowds, who enjoyed the spectacle. Tradition says that both Paul and Peter were martyred under Nero. After his death, Nero (who committed suicide before the mob could kill him) was remembered as a great persecutor of Christians, but in fact more widespread persecutions took place under later emperors, notably Domitian.

He ordered everyone to address him as *Dominus et Deus*—"Lord and God." His imperial dispatches began "Your Lord and God instructs you to…" When he ordered all citizens to swear oaths to his "Genius" and to offer sacrifices to his image, faithful Christians and Jews refused, and for this "treason" they were executed or sent into exile. Domitian's persecution was particularly fierce in the province of Asia—the very region to which John addressed the Book of Revelation.

Years earlier, the apostles Paul and Peter had both counseled Christians to respect the government (Romans 13:1, 1 Peter 2:17). Respect was one thing—calling the emperor "God" was quite another. Jesus told people to render to Caesar what was Caesar's—but divinity was *not* Caesar's. Most pagans went through the motions of acknowledging Domitian as a god—which proves not that they had a high opinion of their emperors, but a low opinion of their gods. But the Christians and many Jews would not call a cruel, lustful tyrant "God," and for this they were punished.

LETTERS FROM HEAVEN

"The revelation of Jesus Christ, which God gave him to show his servants what must soon take place." Thus opens the final book of the Bible, which was revealed by Christ to "his servant John." "Blessed is the one who reads the words of this prophecy, and blessed are those who hear it and take to heart what is written in it, because the time is near" (Revelation 1:3). Exiled on the island of Patmos, John saw a vision on a Sunday—"the Lord's Day." John was "in the Spirit"—meaning, probably, he was in a God-inspired vision. He heard a loud voice like a trumpet and saw Christ—"one like the Son of Man," recalling that Jesus always referred to himself as "Son of Man." He is no longer the simply clad carpenter of Nazareth, but the heavenly Christ, with a gold band around his chest, his face shining like the sun. John "fell at his feet as though dead." But this awesome figure is still the loving, compassionate Christ: "He placed his right hand on me and said: 'Do not be afraid. I am the First and the Last. I am the Living One; I was dead, and behold I am alive forever and ever! And I hold the keys of death and Hades.'" Here "keys" symbolize power. He has power over death and Hades—Hades being not hell, but the realm of death. As God raised Christ from the dead, so Christ can raise his followers from the dead also.

Christ gives John messages to be delivered to seven Christian communities in Asia. At this time, the name Asia didn't refer to the entire continent but to the region that is today the western part of Turkey. The area had been evangelized at an early date, and the apostle Paul was active there. In fact, one of the cities in which Paul was most active was Ephesus, the first of the churches mentioned in Revelation.

Christ begins by commending the Christians at Ephesus, which was the capital of the province of Asia: "You have persevered and have endured hardships for my name, and have not grown weary. Yet I hold this against you: You have forsaken your first love. Remember the height from which you have fallen! Repent and do the things you did at first. If you do not repent, I will come to you and remove your lampstand from its place" (Revelation 2:3–6). The church at Ephesus was obviously a vibrant faith community— as evidenced by Paul's own letter to the Ephesians, and to the warmth that the Ephesian Christians showed to Paul in the Book of Acts. But something was lacking. The brotherly love the fellowship had known in the past was fading. Christ was asking the people to rekindle the love they had known in the past. "To him who overcomes, I will give the right to eat from the tree of life, which is in the paradise of God" (2:7).

CULTURAL INSIGHTS

Apocalyptic Writing

The Greek word *apokalypsis* means "revelation," and in some Bibles the Book of Revelation is called the Apocalypse. Over the centuries, Jews and Christians wrote books claiming to reveal things about the future, supposedly revealed to the writer by God himself. The apocalyptic writings are usually highly symbolic instead of straightforward. While the prophets sometimes foretold the future in their writings, they were usually clear about who or what they were addressing—Assyria, Babylon, Judah, etc. In apocalyptic writing, things are rarely called by their true names. In the Book of Revelation, for example, "Babylon" does not refer to the Babylonian empire (which had ceased to exist by the time Revelation was written) but to some other wealthy and tyrannical government. One reason that apocalyptic writings hid their meanings under symbols is that they were often written under persecution. One key purpose of these writings was to give encouragement to people who were persecuted, reminding them that God was in control and that evil would in time be vanquished. The last chapters of the Old Testament's Book of Daniel are apocalyptic, but the best-known example of the writing is the Book of Revelation.

The fellowship at Smyrna received high commendation: "I know your afflictions and your poverty—yet you are rich!...Do not be afraid of what you are about to suffer. I tell you, the devil will put some of you in prison to test you, and you will suffer persecution for ten days. Be faithful, even to the point of death, and I will give you the crown of life.... He who overcomes will not be hurt at all by the second death" (2:9–11). More persecution lay ahead, but those who endured would have nothing to fear, for though they might experience physical death, they would never experience the "second death," the death of the soul.

The third message was to the Christians at Pergamum, "where Satan has his throne" (2:13). What was the "throne"? From the time of the emperor Augustus, the city had been a center of emperor worship. Augustus may have been only halfhearted about emperor worship, using it only as propaganda, but Domitian had recently set up a statue of himself in Pergamum, and this image of the "god" Domitian would qualify as "Satan's throne." It is likely that Domitian had decided to show the city just how serious he was about his own divinity, for Christ says to the church in Pergamum, "you remain true to my name. You did not renounce your faith in me, even in the days of Antipas, my faithful witness, who was put to death in your city—where Satan lives."

The fourth message was to Thyatira, remembered as the home of Lydia, the merchant woman who was a convert of Paul. The faith community at Thyatira was alive and well: "I know your deeds, your love and faith, your service and perseverance, and that you are now doing more than you did at first" (2:19). But all was not quite right: "Nevertheless, I have this against you: You tolerate that woman Jezebel, who calls herself a prophetess. By her teaching she misleads my servants into sexual immorality and the eating of food sacrificed to idols." We don't know exactly who this "Jezebel" was. Obviously she had tried to lead the people into false religion, as wicked queen Jezebel had done in the Old Testament. Christ counsels the church to put aside all false teaching and immorality.

The fifth message was to Sardis, which apparently had a fellowship that had fallen upon bad times: "I know your deeds; you have a reputation of being alive, but you are dead. Wake up! Strengthen what remains and is about to die, for I have not found your deeds complete in the sight of my God" (3:1–2). We don't know the precise nature of the church at Sardis. Perhaps there was too much compromise with the pagan environment in which it existed. Christ issues it a stern warning: "Remember, therefore, what you have received and heard; obey it, and repent. But if you do not wake up, I will come like a thief, and you will not know at what time I will come to you." This, of course, is a message for everyone to bear in mind: Be spiritually prepared at *all* times, ready to give account to Christ if he appears.

The sixth message was to the fellowship at Philadelphia, whose name is Greek for "brotherly love." The church there receives no scolding, only praise: "I know your deeds. See, I have placed before you an open door that no one can shut. I know that you have little strength, yet you have kept my word and have not denied my name" (3:8). The believers there have been mocked by the "synagogue of Satan," but their faith has remained strong. "Since you have kept my command to endure patiently, I will also keep you from the hour of trial that is going to come upon the whole world to test those who live on the earth." This sounds ominous: A time of testing is coming to the world, but for those who remain faithful, good things await: "Him who overcomes I will make a pillar in the temple of my God. Never again will he leave it. I will write on him the name of my God and the name of the city of my God, the new Jerusalem, which is coming down out of heaven from my God." Later in Revelation we will learn much more about the "new Jerusalem."

> **DID YOU KNOW?**
>
> England's King James I, for whom the King James Version of the Bible is named, wrote *A Fruitful Meditation,* a commentary on Revelation. The mysterious book has attracted numerous "amateur theologians" over the years, including English novelist D. H. Lawrence, whose last work was *Apocalypse*, his commentary on Revelation.

The seventh message was to the spiritually lazy fellowship at Laodicea. Christ has nothing good to say to them: "I know your deeds, that you are neither cold nor hot. I wish you were either one or the other! So, because you are lukewarm—neither hot nor cold—I am about to spit you out of my mouth" (3:15–16). Cold water was for drinking, hot water for bathing or cooking, but lukewarm water was useless. Laodicea was the classic "lukewarm" church, not quite dead but certainly not "on fire" with its faith. Christ did not criticize any particular faults as he found in the other churches, just an overall spiritual tepidity, brought on by self-satisfaction. The city was wealthy, and apparently the local Christians were also, and they were overly complacent in their material wealth.

After this scolding, Christ reminds them of why he speaks so harshly: "Those whom I love I rebuke and discipline. So be earnest, and repent." This is "tough love," the only kind the Bible ever attributes to God or Christ. Love for believers does not mean letting them do whatever they like, but disciplining them, urging them on to be the tough, patient, persevering spiritual warriors they were intended to be.

The message to Laodicea ends with these familiar, and beautiful words: "Here I am! I stand at the door and knock. If anyone hears my voice and opens the door, I will come in and eat with him, and he with me" (3:20). Christ does not force his way in. He knocks, and leaves it to the believer to open the door. Then true spiritual fellowship can begin. The message was intended for the believers in Laodicea, but this much-quoted verse has been applied to everyone.

A MAP THROUGH THE MAZE

Before proceeding further, though, we have to ask the difficult question: Was John speaking of events that have already taken place, or will take place in the future—or is there some other interpretation?

There are four views of how to interpret the prophecies:

1. The *preterist*, or *contemporary-historical* interpretation understands the book from the standpoint of its first-century historical setting. In this view, the major prophecies of the book were fulfilled within a hundred years of John's writing. In this view, John was writing strictly to his own contemporaries. If this view is correct, we can read the book today for its historical interest, to remind ourselves that God triumphed over evil in ancient times and will do so in the future.

2. The *historicist* interpretation sees Revelation as a kind of survey of history leading up to John's own time. In other words, John is writing to people who are "in the middle of the story," looking forward to the end (the new Jerusalem). Chapters 13 and 17, which may be referring to previous persecutions of Christians, give some credence to this interpretation.

3. The *futurist*, or *eschatological*, interpretation is the most common, but also the most difficult. Ever since it was written, people have read Revelation and believed that it was describing events taking place in their own times. Countless people through history have been identified as the Beast, countless governments as Babylon, countless events as the millennium. One reason this interpretation is so common is that Christians have been persecuted throughout history, so there are plenty of "Beasts" and "Babylons" we can point to and wonder, *Was this the one John was referring to?* For most readers today, the futurist interpretation involves viewing the book as revealing things yet to come.

4. The *idealist* or *timeless* interpretation removes the book from history—or, more accurately, it sees the book as describing a pattern that repeats itself, the ongoing struggle between good and evil, between God's kingdom and Satan's kingdom. Viewing the book this way does not rule out the possibility that at some time in the future the events would have their final unfolding, that evil would be conquered once and for all.

What did John think was the purpose of his book? Probably he intended it for fellow Christians of his own time, threatened with persecution by the Roman empire ruled by its megalomaniac emperor. But as we know from studying the Old Testament prophets, sometimes prophecies mean more than the original author intended. John may have advanced the preterist interpretation, but that doesn't mean that the futurist and idealist interpretations are wrong. No interpretation necessarily excludes the others. In a sense, John's theme has not changed: *Christ versus Caesar* still applies, as long as we take "Caesar" to mean any persecuting power that demands Christians renounce their religion.

John wrote down a prophecy he received from Christ, a prophecy intended to warn and encourage people of faith. Throughout history it has served that function very well. It has given hope to millions of believers over the centuries. In fact, we might say that only a persecuted believer can fully appreciate the book. Only for people who have *not* experienced persecution does the book become a kind of puzzle to be solved, trying to "decode" the events and connect them with events in the news. The whole Bible is a book of faith and a book of salvation. The key message of Revelation is: *Be ready for the Lord's coming.* Each generation may well be the last on earth, so in that sense the time of judgment is always "near."

Now, let's plunge into the deep waters of Revelation.

THRONES IN HEAVEN, WOES ON EARTH

Chapters 1 through 3 are relatively easy to interpret. Christ is in heaven, offering warnings and encouragement to Christians on earth. But from chapter 4 on to the end, we are in the realm of a vision full of symbols, and our puzzlement begins. However, we can make some general observations about what the symbols in the book mean:

woman = a nation or people	purple = luxury, royalty
horn = power	black = death
eyes = knowledge	dragon, sea monster = evil
trumpet = a divine voice	lamb = sacrifice
wings = mobility	lion = royalty
sword = the word of God	six = incompleteness, imperfection
palms = signs of triumph	seven = fullness, perfection
white = joy, victory, glory	twelve = the people of God

In chapter 4, John has a vision of the throne of God. The throne is surrounded by twenty-four other thrones, on which are seated "elders" dressed in white and wearing gold crowns. The throne gives off lightning and thunder, and four "living creatures" covered with eyes are also around the throne. The living creatures, each with six wings, "never stop saying: 'Holy, holy, holy is the Lord God Almighty, who was, and is, and is to come' " (Revelation 4:8). Remember that eyes represent the divine ability to see all things. The "living creatures" might be familiar, since they are like the ones Ezekiel saw in his own vision. Chapter 4 is showing us Almighty God, enthroned in heaven, surrounded by his court—a scene of awe-inspiring beauty.

In chapter 5, God holds a scroll, sealed with seven seals in his hand. No one is worthy to unseal the scroll, until the Lamb appears. The Lamb is Christ, who with his blood "purchased men for God." In chapter 6 the Lamb breaks open the first seal on the scroll. "I looked, and there before me was a white horse! Its rider held a bow, and he was given a crown, and he rode out as a conqueror bent on conquest." Much fuss has been made over who, or what, the rider on the white horse is, but John's meaning is clear: This is conquest, which always bring devastation on the earth. "Then another horse came out, a fiery red one. Its rider was given power to take peace from the earth and to make men slay each other. To him was given a large sword." Clearly this represents warfare. "I looked, and there before me was a black horse! Its rider was holding a pair of scales in his hand. Then I heard what sounded like a voice among the four living creatures, saying, 'A quart of wheat for a day's wages, and three quarts of barley for a day's wages, and do not damage the oil and the wine!' " This horseman represents famine. "I looked, and there before me was a pale horse! Its rider was named Death, and Hades was following close behind him. They were given power over a fourth of the earth to kill by sword, famine and plague, and by the wild beasts of the earth." The Greek word describing this fourth horse is *chloros*, which means not "pale" but "sickly green"—the color of a rotting corpse. Obviously death follows in the wake of conquest, war and famine.

These "four horsemen of the Apocalypse" have called forth a million interpretations, but the basic meaning seems clear: Horrible things have occurred on earth. More horror follows as the Lamb opens the fifth seal and John beholds "under the altar the souls of those who had been slain because of the word of God and the testimony they had maintained. They called out in a loud voice, 'How long, Sovereign Lord, holy and true, until you judge the inhabitants of the earth and avenge our blood?' " When the sixth seal is broken, an earthquake occurs, and the people on earth see that the day of God's wrath has come.

Chapter 7 is one of several "interludes" in Revelation. They interrupt the flow of the horrifying events to give believers on earth a kind of "preview" of heaven. John sees a great multitude of people in white robes, holding palm branches and praising God. (The color white is mentioned fourteen times in Revelation, usually symbolizing heavenly glory, joy and victory.) These are those who have come out of the "great tribulation," and now they are in the presence of God, and "God will wipe every tear from their eyes" (7:17). This and the other interludes in the book are a kind of pause, a spiritual "breather" in which the prophet says, "Hold steady, my brothers, and consider your fellow sufferers who have already crossed over into eternity." The interludes also contrast the joys of the saints in heaven and the troubles befalling the people still on earth.

In chapter 8 the seventh seal is broken, meaning that the scroll in God's hand can finally be opened and read. In succession, seven angels blow trumpets, and various horrors are unleashed on earth, including a star that falls from the sky and poisons the earth's waters. Another horror is a plague of locusts and scorpions, although these are not meant literally, for the "king" over them is the "angel of the Abyss," also named Abaddon, the Hebrew word for "destruction." These "locusts" and "scorpions" are probably demons, but God prevents them from harming his own people, who have his seal on their foreheads (9:4). Other horrible plagues came upon the unbelievers, killing many, but those who survived still would not repent of their immorality and idolatry.

The two witnesses described in chapter 11 are, most interpreters think, Moses and Elijah—the same two men who appeared with Jesus at his Transfiguration, symbolizing the Law (Moses) and the prophets (Elijah). The witnesses prophesy with great power, but a Beast from the Abyss kills them. The earth gloats over these saints' deaths and lets them lie in the streets unburied. Then God brought them to life again and drew them into heaven.

CULTURAL INSIGHTS

Armageddon

Thanks to Revelation 16:16, the word Armageddon has come to mean any decisive battle, but particularly the final end-time confrontation between good and evil. In Revelation, the kings of the earth gather "together in the place that in Hebrew is called Armageddon." The site was Mount Megiddo, which in the Old Testament had been the scene of many battles, including Gideon defeating the Midianites, King Saul in his last fight against the Philistines, and King Josiah's final battle against the Egyptians. We don't know if John, author of Revelation, meant that the world's last battle would literally take place at Megiddo, or whether he was speaking figuratively, using the name of the locale because of its many associations with brutality and bloodshed.

COSMIC CONFLICT, THEN THE CITY OF BLISS

In the last half of Revelation, things build toward the ultimate showdown between God and evil. In chapter 12, a woman "clothed with the sun" is pursued by a horrible red dragon. Since she has a crown of twelve stars on her head, she represents Israel—or, more precisely, the new Israel, Christians. She gives birth to a child, who represents Christ. The archangel Michael and his army of angels fight with the dragon and his evil angels. The dragon—Satan—is cast down to the earth and he pursues the woman, but the earth protects her. The dragon then makes war on the woman's children, who represent people of faith (12:17).

The well-known Beast symbolized by the number 666 is described in chapter 13. Rising up from the sea, the first bizarre Beast is given his power by the dragon. Blaspheming against God, the Beast makes war on God's people and forces all people to worship him. Another Beast rises up from the earth and causes everyone to receive a mark on their right hand or forehead so that they can buy or sell. The second Beast is in the form of a lamb—which is the reason interpreters of the book refer to this person as the Antichrist. Christ is the true Lamb of God in Revelation, and this second Beast is "like" a lamb, and because he can do amazing miracles (as Christ did), he deceives people. He looks like a lamb but speaks like a dragon (13:11). (Remember Jesus' warning about wolves in sheep's clothing.) It is this second Beast who is symbolized by 666 (3:18). Oceans of ink have been spilled trying to explain just who, or what, 666 refers to, but probably the most certain explanation is that it is intended as the number of incompleteness, falling short. Seven is a "good" number in the Bible, and 777 would be a sort of ideal number, perhaps the number of God himself. The probable meaning of 666 is that the Beast regards himself as divine, but in fact falls short of divinity. (Writing around the year 180, the theologian Irenaeus admitted that the specific individual that 666 referred to had been forgotten. If he did not know in 180, we are unlikely to figure it out in the twenty-first century!)

But not everyone has followed the Beast and received his mark on them. In chapter 14 we have another "heavenly interlude." We see the Lamb (Christ) surrounded by 144,000 faithful people who have God's name on their foreheads. In spite of all the harm the two Beasts have done, there are still blameless people who cling to God. Three angels flying in the air warn people to repent of their sins, for those who follow the Beast will be tormented forever. But God's people will endure forever, despite their persecution by the Beast: "Blessed are the dead who die in the Lord from now on.' 'Yes,' says the Spirit, 'they will rest from their labor, for their deeds will follow them' " (14:13).

Because of the persecution of the saints, angels pour out seven bowls of God's wrath on the earth. The plagues are similar to, but worse than, the plagues God sent on the

Egyptians in the Book of Exodus. The plagues cause people to curse God but not to repent of their evil ways (16:11).

An angel shows John a luxuriously dressed woman sitting on a scarlet beast. The woman is "Babylon the great, mother of prostitutes and of the abominations of the earth." Remember from the Old Testament that the prophets often used "prostitution" figuratively, meaning idolatry. Babylon here is not the literal city of Babylon, which had fallen centuries earlier, but symbolizes any tyrannical power. This woman, Babylon, is "drunk with the blood of the saints" (17:6). She has taken delight in persecuting God's people.

But wicked Babylon is doomed: " 'Fallen! Fallen is Babylon the Great! She has become a home for demons and a haunt for every evil spirit…. Come out of her, my people, so that you will not share in her sins, so that you will not receive any of her plagues; for her sins are piled up to heaven" (18:2, 4). The evil city that was the envy of all the earth is destroyed. Her days of tormenting the saints are over. For John's first readers, Babylon's doom was a promise—but for the time being, they suffered in one of the great dramas of human history, persecuted by a succession of depraved emperors.

CHARACTER CLOSE-UP ## Anti-Christ

The Bible has several prophecies of an evil figure who will appear before the end of time to persecute God's people. In Revelation 13, he is the Beast from the sea who dazzles people with miracles he performs through the power of the dragon (Satan). Revelation says that the number of the Beast is 666—which has caused endless speculation since the time it was written. Many political figures throughout history have been accused of being the Beast. In Revelation 19, Christ finally casts the Beast into the lake of fire.

In 2 Thessalonians 2, Paul spoke of the "man of lawlessness" who will exalt himself over everything that is called God and is "worshipped," and will even proclaim himself as God. He will deceive people through counterfeit miracles, but will be destroyed when Christ returns to earth. Jesus himself warned of "false Christs and false prophets" who appear near the end, performing signs and miracles to deceive people (Mark 13:22).

In all these prophecies, this evil figure is able to work miracles and deceive many people, so he is "Anti-Christ" not only because he opposes Christ and his people, but because he is a *false* Christ. As God sends Christ to earth to do good and save people, so Satan sends his Anti-Christ to do evil and lead people to destruction. While some people believe the Anti-Christ will be an individual person, others believe he symbolizes all persons or groups who persecute people of faith.

The actual word *antichrist* occurs only in 1 and 2 John, where it refers to all false teachers who deny that Christ was fully human.

The Christians were fighting the swords of the empire with the Word and making new converts out of the sensitive few who found more to admire in the decency of the martyrs than in the vileness of the Romans, who called themselves the "master race" of the world. It was right that John used the name "Babylon," for the name would remind readers that all earthly kingdoms passed away, just as mighty Babylon had done.

At 19:11 begins the final clash between God and evil: A rider named Faithful and True, also called the Word of God, rides forth on a white horse. He is Christ, the King of Kings and Lord of Lords. He rides out to battle the Beast and the kings of the earth. The Beast and his false prophet are thrown alive into the lake of burning fire, and the kings of the earth die in battle (19:21).

Chapter 20 predicts a thousand-year period (millennium) in which Satan is bound in the Abyss (the bottomless pit), and in which God's saints who had been martyred for their faith are brought to life again, reigning with God. At the end of the thousand years, Satan is released, and he gathers together an evil army to surround God's saints. But the armies are devoured by fire from heaven, and the dragon, Satan, is thrown into the fiery lake where the Beast had been thrown, to be tormented forever (20:10). Satan, who took the form of a serpent and led mankind astray in the beginning of the Bible, is at the end of the Bible finally vanquished. Mankind can have paradise again, but this time without the evil tempter present.

Around a great white throne, all people are judged. "I saw the dead, great and small, standing before the throne. . . The dead were judged according to what they had done as recorded in the books. . . If anyone's name was not found written in the book of life, he was thrown into the lake of fire" (20:21).

After all the horror and drama of persecution and spiritual warfare have ended, the book ends in a vision of blissful beauty—no longer an "interlude," but eternity itself: "Then I saw a new heaven and a new earth, for the first heaven and the first earth had passed away, and there was no longer any sea. I saw the Holy City, the new Jerusalem, coming down out of heaven from God, prepared as a bride beautifully dressed for her husband. And I heard a loud voice from the throne saying, 'Now the dwelling of God is with men, and he will live with them. They will be his people, and God himself will be with them and be their God. He will wipe every tear from their eyes' " (21:1–4). The people of faith, those who have "overcome" through their suffering, live here forever as the children of God (21:7).

Some of the images of the new Jerusalem are already familiar to us. Its streets are of gold and its twelve gates are of pearl (21:21). Unlike the earthly Jerusalem, this one has no temple, and no need for one, for the entire place is God's dwelling. It is lighted not by the sun or moon but by the glory of God himself.

Heaven has "the tree of life, bearing twelve crops of fruit, yielding its fruit every month" (2:1–2). John surely had in mind the tree of life in Eden, the paradise that our original parents lost for us. In a sense the human story has come full circle—from the first paradise (Eden) to the final one (heaven).

The book ends with a warning from Christ: "Behold, I am coming soon! My reward is with me, and I will give to everyone according to what he has done." But the warning is followed by an invitation: "Whoever is thirsty, let him come; and whoever wishes, let him take the free gift of the water of life" (22:17). As was true of the rest of the Bible, Revelation is full of threats and warnings from the Lord, who hates evil and wants us to do right. God takes evil seriously, and so should we. But in the end, it is the divine invitation of bliss that draws us to God.

PUTTING THE WORD TO WORK

1. Focus on 1 John's words about loving not in words but in deeds. Today, make it a point to show love to everyone you encounter, and notice how it makes you feel.

2. According to 1 John, we can't hate a brother and love God. Think of someone you know that you've had a quarrel with. Make some effort to heal the old wounds.

3. Think of someone you know who has been persecuted for his or her faith at some point. Call, e-mail or write that person, let them know you've recognized what they endured and that it has inspired your own faith walk.

4. Take a few minutes and pray earnestly for people around the world who are persecuted for their faith. As you pray, focus not just on their distress, but on Revelation's message of comfort and hope for such people.

5. Revelation contains the promise that "God will wipe every tear" from the eyes of his people. Make it a point to read slowly the final chapter, and let the vision of the new Jerusalem melt away any pain that you have in your life today.

WHO DECIDED WHAT WENT INTO THE BIBLE?

The traditional answer to this question is: God did. But how? That question leads us to two important—and elusive—concepts: *inspiration* and *canon*.

What does "inspired" mean? We can read a book, view a painting, hear a symphony, and say it is an "inspired" work or that the author was "inspired." We might also say that the book/painting/symphony "inspires" us. Meaning what? That it is a cut above the ordinary? That there is some hard-to-define spiritual quality about it? That it moves or touches us?

The Bible, so Christians believe, is definitely above the ordinary and definitely has a spiritual quality, and over the centuries it has moved and touched millions of lives. When we say the Bible is "divinely inspired," we mean that God—in some mysterious way—moved the authors to write what they wrote. They were not just "taking dictation," because it is obvious in different parts of the Bible that the authors' very different personalities shine through the writing. God was speaking his words through theirs. You might say he was the unseen co-author. In one of Paul's letters, he refers to the holy writings with the Greek word *theopneustos*—literally, "God-breathed." Paul stated that the "God-breathed" writings were given so that believers "may be competent, equipped for every good work" (2 Timothy 3:16). Another letter, 2 Peter, states that the holy writings were not mere human products, "but men spoke from God as they were carried along by the Holy Spirit" (1:21).

People sometimes say that the Bible is *inerrant*—no errors in it at all. This makes sense. After all, God would not make mistakes, would he? No, but human beings would. And so we encounter places in, for example, the Gospels, where Matthew, Mark and Luke tell of the same event, but the details differ slightly. Was one correct, and the other two in error? A better explanation is this: Human beings making tiny errors, or differing on details, was not a huge concern for God. He is more concerned about the Big Picture. And the Big Picture is this: The Bible is a book revealing God's will to humankind. He created human beings and wants them in a close personal relationship with him. The Bible is intended to build and nurture that relationship. It is not intended to be a textbook on science, history, etc.—even though the archaeologists continue to find that the Bible got most of its historical details correct. As noted in the previous paragraph, the Bible is given so people may be "equipped for every good work."

The sixty-six books that make up our Bible were studied over the centuries and found to have a spiritual depth that other books do not possess. Christians believe it is no accident that, over the course of time, these books came together in one volume. They were inspired, and they inspire.

No one thinks the inspiration was equally distributed. Some parts of the Bible are skippable. Most of Leviticus is dry reading, as are the endless genealogies in the Old Testament. The books of Esther and Song of Solomon do not even mention God. These parts can't compare with the teachings of Jesus, Paul's letters, some of the Psalms, the powerful preaching of Isaiah and Jeremiah, the timeless story of Moses and the Exodus. But in spite of all the variety within it, the Bible is a unity, since the same God reveals himself throughout it. We do the Bible, and ourselves, a disservice when we focus on our favorite parts and neglect the rest, for the Bible as a whole will give us the deepest knowledge of God. The whole Bible, Genesis to Revelation, is what God intended us to have—no more, no less.

This idea has been seriously questioned in recent years. There is a huge interest in the "hidden Gospels," writings that lay literally buried in the dust for centuries but are now translated and selling (sometimes very well) in bookstores. The editors and translators of these ancient writings would have us believe that the early Christians were in on a vast conspiracy. They deliberately suppressed some fine writings that contained the "real" or "deeper" truth of what Jesus taught. The fans of the "hidden Gospels" accuse the early Christians of "cultural imperialism," spreading a narrow Christianity that was far from what Jesus intended. To mention one notable example, the phenomenally popular novel *The Da Vinci Code* spread the idea (one that is centuries old) that Mary Magdalene, a minor character in the Bible, was really one of Jesus' closest followers and the recipient of his deepest teachings—which the Christians wrongly suppressed. *The Jesus Papers* and *The Gospel of Judas* offered readers "revisionist" views of Jesus, catering to a centuries-old urge to prove the Bible itself misrepresents the "real" Christ.

Any truth to this "conspiracy theory" at all?*

The fans of the non-biblical Gospels are correct about one thing: The writings in the New Testament were not the only writings of the early Christians. There were dozens of other Gospels, and epistles as well, most of them claiming to be written by some of the apostles, and many claiming to contain "secret" and "higher" teachings that were not given to most of Jesus' followers. One of the best-known of these is called the Gospel of Thomas, and it was included (along with the four New Testament Gospels)

---

*One of the best books on this subject is Philip Jenkins's *Hidden Gospels: How the Search for Jesus Lost Its Way* (New York: Oxford University Press, 2001).

in a recent book titled *The Five Gospels*. The editors of this book take the interesting position of judging the truth of the four New Testament Gospels by comparing them to the Gospel of Thomas.

What happened among the early Christians was just the opposite: They used Matthew, Mark, Luke and John to judge the numerous Gospels that did not make it into the Bible. Some of those Gospels mingled sayings from the four Gospels with teachings that sound radically different from the Jesus of Matthew, Mark, Luke and John. In a sense the non-biblical Gospels were "parasitic"—that is, they could not have existed if the four Gospels of the New Testament weren't already in circulation.

And how do we know for certain that Matthew, Mark, Luke and John were the Gospels that God intended us to have? We don't, actually—not if you demand scientific proof, anyway. There is an element of faith here—you can believe that those four Gospels give us a pretty accurate view of what Jesus said and did. Or you can take a leap of faith in the other direction: believing that the "hidden" Gospels give us the "real" Jesus. The fans of the hidden Gospels have no way of proving they were suppressed and that Christians have been duped by the wrong writings for all these centuries.

The simple fact is that most of these "suppressed" writings finding their way to bookstores today were written much later than the writings of the New Testament—more than a century later, in most cases. The Gospels and epistles of the New Testament were all written down by AD 100, perhaps even by AD 70. They were all written within the lifetimes of Jesus' first followers, meaning there were plenty of people around who could vouch for the accuracy of the writings. The Gospel of Thomas (which, by the way, is definitely *not* by the apostle Thomas) came much later. What do you think would be more accurate—a biography written within fifty years of the life of its subject, or one written two hundred years later?

The early Christians produced hundreds of writings—some based on the memories of Jesus' apostles, some not. Over time, some of the writings continued to inspire people, so they were preserved and duplicated. The false writings had their fans, of course, but mostly they ended up (literally) on the ash heap of history.

Now let's revisit a word mentioned at the beginning of this appendix: *canon*. It's a Greek word that meant "rule" or "standard." As time passed, Christians debated among themselves about which of the writings were uniquely inspired by God. They already accepted the Jews' sacred books—what they came to call the Old Testament—as inspired. What was taking shape was the New Testament, which eventually included twenty-seven writings—the four Gospels (telling the story of Jesus), Acts (telling of the activities of the earliest Christians), the epistles (early Christian leaders giving instruction about belief and morals), and Revelation (a vision of the end of time). There was no precise date when it was decided, once and for all, that these books were the Christian canon. But we have writings from the mid-300s that show that Christians spread out over a wide area had pretty much agreed about these twenty-seven books. There were a few "almosts," some popular epistles (one was called the Epistle of Barnabas) that continued to be widely read. But one thing was certain: By the mid-300s, the "hidden" Gospels had been finally rejected by the vast majority of Christians. There was no "conspiracy," no sinister group trying to suppress deep spiritual writings. There was just a powerful sense, existing over a long period of time, that certain writings were rooted in what really happened to Jesus and his apostles—and some writings that clearly were not.

In fact, the early Christians were very suspicious of writings that seemed to be mere fiction—even if those writings were produced for a good purpose. A bishop wrote the Acts of Paul, which contained some inspiring and miraculous stories. His intentions were good, but when it was revealed that the work was pure fiction, he was removed from his post as bishop around AD 190. The Christians were equally dead set against the many fictional Gospels circulating, many of which replaced the historical Jesus of Nazareth with a mythical Jesus who sounds more like a guru attached to no particular time and place.

So why are these old documents being published now? One obvious answer: They sell. And they sell because people enjoy a good conspiracy theory. Also, after two thousand years of Christianity, people can point to a lot of bad things done in the name of Christ—which might lead people to believe that maybe the "real" teachings of Jesus got lost along the way and deserve a hearing. You might say the "hidden" Gospels have the attraction of being both really old (which they are) and really new (since for centuries no one read them). Pop culture makes a big fuss over these writings, with people never bothering to ask the most obvious question: Might there be a good reason why these writings were rejected by most Christians—like, maybe, the fact that they weren't regarded as true?

Most of these Gospels that were not accepted into the Bible were produced by people loosely known as Gnostics. There isn't space enough here to fully explain Gnosticism, but in general the Gnostics (some of whom considered themselves Christians) saw themselves as spiritually "higher" people, believing in "secret" teachings that were not intended for the great mass of Christians (or for mankind in general). There were numerous Gnostic Gospels floating around, most of them mixing parts of the four biblical Gospels (a nice "hook" to get Christians' attention) with the "secret" teachings that the risen Jesus supposedly passed on to Thomas, Mary Magdalene, Judas or others. (Tacking on the name of one of Jesus' actual followers was another "hook," obviously.) In general, the Gnostic Gospels emphasize these "secret" teachings at the expense of the moral teaching that is so important in the four Gospels found in our Bibles. The Gnostics saw themselves as being saved not by faith, nor by righteous living, but by the knowledge that only they possessed. (*Gnosis* is the Greek word for "knowledge.") Gnosticism was, you may say, "spirituality from the neck up." In other words, Gnosticism spread via the age-old appeal of intellectual snobbery—the feeling of superiority that comes from knowing things that most people don't. As proof that some things never change, the same appeal can be found today among those who read the "suppressed" Gospels and find Gnosticism more to their taste than the Christianity of the New Testament. Add intellectual snobbery to the belief in a conspiracy theory, and the current vogue for these old writings is understandable.

WHAT ABOUT THE APOCRYPHA?

One key question when discussing the Bible: *Just which writings does the Bible include?* Jews, Catholics and Protestants do not agree on which books are included in the Bible. Jews, of course, don't regard the Christian writings known as the New Testament as part of their Bible. They only accept the books that Christians know as the Old Testament. But Christians themselves disagree about just which books to include in the Old Testament.

Here is the standard list of the books that Jews and Protestant Christians regard as part of the Bible:

Genesis	1 and 2 Kings	Song of Solomon	Obadiah
Exodus	1 and 2 Chronicles	Isaiah	Jonah
Leviticus	Ezra	Jeremiah	Micah
Numbers	Nehemiah	Lamentations	Nahum
Deuteronomy	Esther	Ezekiel	Habakkuk
Joshua	Job	Daniel	Zephaniah
Judges	Psalms	Hosea	Haggai
Ruth	Proverbs	Joel	Zechariah
1 and 2 Samuel	Ecclesiastes	Amos	Malachi

These books are found in *all* Bibles—Jewish, Protestant or Catholic. However, Roman Catholic Bibles include these other books in the Old Testament:

Tobit	Ecclesiasticus (*not* the same as Ecclesiastes)
Judith	Baruch
1 and 2 Maccabees	Additions to Esther
Wisdom	Additions to Daniel

Confused? This last group of books, known as the *Apocrypha*, have been the subject of controversy for many centuries. Apocrypha is a Greek word meaning "hidden things." But these books never were, strictly speaking, hidden. They were widely read, just like the other books of the Old Testament. But the Jews did not hold them in quite as high regard as the other Old Testament books, partly because they were written later (in the period between the Old and New Testaments) and hadn't been read and cherished as long as some of the other books.

Keep something in mind: For many centuries, there was no standard list of books of the Bible. The individual "books" were actually written on scrolls, meaning that people in ancient times didn't have the luxury we have of having all the writings together under one cover (or on one scroll). Over time, though, both Jews and Christians thought it was important to lay down a *canon* (meaning "rule" or "standard")—that is, to make it clear that certain books were inspired by God and were to be used as the basis for morals and belief. Books that were not included were "outside the canon." They might still be read, but were not as important as the writings "within the canon."

Sometime around AD 100, a council of rabbis met in the town of Jamnia in Palestine to debate which books the Jews included in their canon. The Jews read a popular Greek translation of the Old Testament known as the Septuagint, and it included all the writings that we now call the Apocrypha. However, the council at Jamnia chose not to include those books in the Jewish canon.

The early Christians were mostly Jews, and they knew the Old Testament through the Septuagint translation. However, the books of the Apocrypha are never quoted or even referred to in the New Testament, which gives us the impression that the early Christians did not regard them as divinely inspired. The books of the Apocrypha did continue to be read, even though many Christians followed the lead of the Jewish council of Jamnia and questioned whether the books of the Apocrypha ought to be considered sacred.

In AD 382, a Christian scholar named Jerome was commissioned by the pope to prepare a standard Latin version of the Bible. Jerome learned Hebrew so he could translate the Old Testament from the original language. In discussing the Old Testament with rabbis in Palestine, Jerome became convinced that the Apocrypha should not be included in the Old Testament. However, the pope ordered him to include them in the new Latin Bible, so for centuries they were, even though many Christian scholars had doubts about whether they truly belonged there. From the time Jerome completed his Latin Bible (about AD 404) until the early 1500s, it was the only Bible available in Europe, so for more than a millennium most Bibles contained the disputed books.

In the 1500s, when Martin Luther began the Protestant Reformation in Germany, he translated the Old Testament from Hebrew into German, and he had the same doubts about the Apocrypha that Jerome had. Luther made an important change:

While the Latin Bible had the books of the Apocrypha scattered through various places in the Old Testament, Luther put them in a separate section, bestowing the name "Apocrypha" on them. He said they deserved to be read but were not on par with the other parts of the Bible. The other Protestant leaders agreed, and the first complete English Bible, published in 1535, placed the Apocrypha after the New Testament. The Protestants agreed that quotations from the Apocrypha could not be used as the foundation for Christian beliefs—one reason being that the Catholic belief in purgatory is based solely on a single verse in 2 Maccabees. By affirming that the Apocrypha could not be used as a foundation for Christian beliefs, the Reformers demolished all the ideas and practices connected with the Catholics' belief in purgatory.

Catholics reacted to this: At the 1546 session of the Council of Trent, they made it clear that the books of the Apocrypha *were* part of the divinely inspired Bible—although they were given the name *deutero-canonical*, meaning "of the second canon." To this day, Catholics do not refer to "the Apocrypha" but to "the deutero-canonical writings." For Catholics, Judith and 1 Maccabees are as much a part of the Old Testament as Genesis and Psalms are.

Let's throw in another complication: The Eastern Orthodox churches (Russian, Greek, Romanian, etc.) have a canon that differs from both the Catholic and Protestant canons. In 1672 an Orthodox council meeting in Jerusalem chose to include Tobit, Judith, Wisdom and Ecclesiasticus in their Old Testament, but omitted Baruch and 1 and 2 Maccabees.

Since the Protestants had pushed the books of the Apocrypha into a separate section of the Bible and made it clear that they were "second-class" at best, it was only a matter of time before Protestants dropped the Apocrypha entirely. Protestant scholars weren't writing commentaries on the books, and Protestant preachers rarely quoted from the Apocrypha or preached on it, so finally, by the 1800s, most Protestant Bibles did not include the Apocrypha.

What about today? Some Protestant Bibles today do include the Apocrypha, partly for historical purposes, since 1 and 2 Maccabees contain some important history about the period between the Old and New Testaments. Also, many people find the books of Wisdom and Ecclesiasticus useful to read, containing some of the same kind of wisdom found in Proverbs. However, Protestants have serious doubts about the historical value of Tobit and Judith, even though the stories are inspiring. And the simple fact is that the Apocrypha as a whole has never inspired people in the same way that the other books of the Bible have done.

Should you read the Apocrypha? Instead of answering that with a simple Yes or No, here is our answer: First get familiar with the sixty-six books that *all* Christians agree are part of the divinely inspired Bible. That is what the book you are now holding was intended to help you do.

PUTTING YOUR HEADS TOGETHER: ORGANIZING A BIBLE STUDY GROUP

The Old and New Testaments present a community faith, not a private faith. You can, and should, study the Bible on your own. But you can gain a lot—and so can other people—by studying the Bible in a group setting. Keep a key motive in mind: There is safety in numbers. An individual can (and often has) come up with some pretty kooky interpretations of the Bible. A group could do this also, but it's more likely that someone in the group will say (tactfully, of course), "That's a kooky idea." On the positive side, in the group setting you can share insights. Someone in the group will perceive some aspect of a Bible passage that you didn't see.

1. Get in touch with people you think would be interested.

You might do this through your church, but it can be done with fellow workers, neighbors, whomever. You might even post a notice on your supermarket's bulletin board, stating your name, phone number, and what you're trying to organize. Churches should, of course, have regular Bible study groups. But there is something to be gained from groups outside the church. For one thing, such a group could be interdenominational—which makes for an interesting mix of viewpoints. It also allows members to shoot for the "meat" of the Bible, not for things that only confirm people's denominational biases. It also allows you to include seekers who are (for the present) more interested in the Bible than in attaching themselves to a church.

2. Aim for a group of between six and twelve people.

As Jesus was aware, twelve was a good number for a group. (It's a commonly used number in the Bible.) Anything more than twelve allows shyer members to fade into the wallpaper. A group smaller than six or seven has the danger of too much agreement, not enough creative discussion.

3. Set up the study as a real study time, not a social hour.

People have come to expect food and drink in any kind of human encounter, and eating does seem to mellow people out. But if you want the group to focus on the Bible, keep the munching to a minimum.

4. Set up the meetings for a definite time.

A weekly meeting usually works best. Generally, an hour is too cramping, but two hours is more than some people want to commit. So compromise with ninety minutes, and try to begin and end the meetings on time.

5. Pick a place.

Private homes are cozy and relaxing, but there may be a problem with adequate parking in some residential areas. Some other possibilities: a room in a church (not necessarily your own church), a public room available for use in a library or community center, or the club room in your apartment complex (only make sure you can shut the door and have quiet). Rooms like these can seem chilly compared to someone's den, but public rooms do seem more "serious" than private homes.

For many reasons, men's study groups often choose to meet over breakfast. If a local restaurant is open to this, why not schedule a weekly meeting over a breakfast? The only flaw with breakfast meetings: If a lively discussion gets started, it can't continue too long, since most of the people have to leave. Then again, this limitation could be a blessing.

Note: If you expect the group to include people very unfamiliar with the Bible—maybe even people who don't consider themselves believers yet—you should not hold the meetings in a church. Many people have, alas, had unpleasant experiences with churches. It's possible for people to be interested in the Bible but not (for the time being, anyway) the least bit interested in attending a church. Holding a meeting in a church suggests to many people that you intend to get them involved in church—that church and its denomination, to be specific. So if you're casting a wide net, hoping to include seekers who may not yet be pro-church, choose your place carefully.

6. Choose the book or passage or topic the group will study.

Go for the obvious: one of the four Gospels, one of Paul's great letters (Romans, Galatians, Ephesians), Acts, Psalms, Proverbs, Isaiah. In the case of a long book like Psalms or Isaiah, you might opt for only part of the book, not the whole. A warning: If this is your first venture with the group, avoid any book that is surrounded by controversy—like Revelation, Daniel or Genesis.

7. During your first meeting, decide on the format the meetings will follow.

One logical method: Assign for the week ahead a portion of the book to be read ahead of time and discussed at the meeting. For example, if you're studying John's Gospel, assign chapter 1. The group members will read that chapter before the next meeting and be prepared to discuss it then. Discussing the passage involves members telling what they've gotten from the reading, what problems they encountered, how they might apply the text to their lives.

8. Designate a leader.

This doesn't necessarily mean a lecturer or teacher. It means an organizer, a monitor, one who will arrange the meetings, keep in touch with members and guide the discussion. The leader will always come to the group prepared, having read the text (even if no one else did) and jotted down some discussion questions, suggestions on how the text applies to human life, and so on. One necessary role of the group leader is to keep very talkative members from dominating the discussion. The flip side of this: the need to draw out comments and questions from the quieter members.

The leader does not need to be a certified Bible scholar or someone with a degree in religion. The leader of a Bible study does need to come prepared. This means not just reading through the assigned passage but consulting at least one good commentary or Bible dictionary to help explain problem areas.

9. Keep the group focused on what they're studying.

First, try to stay focused on the Bible itself. Anyone who has worked with a Bible study group knows how easily the members can get derailed, off the track of actually discussing the Bible. If you sense that a particular group member wants to discuss a personal problem (which may or may not relate to the Bible passage you're studying), you might just want to call that person at home at another time. The group might not be the ideal setting.

Second, keep them from focusing too much on minute details so that they don't miss the big picture of what they're studying. In every group you'll have someone who likes to discuss little historical or theological details. This person can be helpful—or a real hindrance if he dominates the group discussions. You may also get a person who simply likes to argue. The group leader needs tact and a gentle and firm hand in steering the group back to the material.

A little historical reminder here: Until the printing press in the 1400s, mass production of Bibles wasn't possible. So before then, and for a long time afterward, Bible reading and study was usually a group thing, not a private thing. It was possible for an individual to read the book (or scrolls, in ancient times), but most people were exposed to the Bible in a group setting—in worship, in a family study, in church classes. Much of people's exposure to the Bible came from hearing it read aloud and then being discussed or preached on.

So group study of the Bible is an old and respectable custom. When your group meets together, it is carrying on a tradition as old as the Bible itself. The apostle Paul wrote to one of his assistants, "Until I come, devote yourself to the public reading of Scripture, to preaching and to teaching" (1 Timothy 4:13).

WHY YOU DON'T NEED AN EXPERT TO STUDY THE BIBLE

Throughout this book I've mentioned ways you can get help from Bible scholars, the "experts." You probably can't meet them personally, but you'll find their work available in Bible dictionaries, commentaries, and thousands of other books on the market. This is comforting—knowing you aren't getting in over your head when you start to read the Bible. The scholars have studied the Bible closely. Some of them make their living this way. They are pleased to make their knowledge available to you.

But you don't need to become expert-dependent. Millions of people over the centuries have read the Bible—and *understood* it—with little or no aid from experts. I have to believe that God is present when a commentary or Bible dictionary helps to enlighten a Bible reader. But I believe that God can work without such books.

One problem with the scholars: They swim in the world of the Bible, as easily as a fish swims in water. It is their element. But for most readers, this isn't so. The fish says to the man, "Just jump on in, use your gills, and you can breathe underwater." Easier said than done! Most of us are trying to live our lives, making a living in jobs that have little or nothing to do with the world of the Bible. At the end of a workday, we approach the Bible, not as if we belong in it, but hoping to get some good out of it. We want to "use" it. This isn't selfishness—just being practical. Unlike the Bible scholars, we can't spend an entire day speculating about Assyrian emperors and the exact date that one of them invaded Israel. "That's nice for them," we say, "but please, let's get back to reality. I have a job, a family, hobbies, a retirement plan. I also have problems. What I *don't* have is a huge amount of time to decipher the Bible."

Well, happily, we don't need huge amounts. We do need the dedication to read the Bible with some sense of purpose. It does take some commitment. And why not? Dieting does, and so does exercise—and people gladly fling themselves into weight loss and workout programs.

But again, you can do this with little help from the Bible pros. You do need some help. For many people, what they need is a study partner—a fellow seeker. Think of times in your school days when you benefited from studying with a group. Maybe your teacher was excellent, but when you asked him for help he a) explained things you understood already, b) gave you a lot of information you didn't need, or c) failed to address the thing that really puzzled you. The teacher often forgets what it was like to be a learner, a beginner. A fellow student knows less than the teacher—but maybe he understands your needs and questions better than the teacher does. He has gotten snagged at the same places you have. He may have untangled some of those—and you may have untangled some that he is still struggling with.

So don't underestimate the power of a fellow seeker. Two people beginning from the same point can aid each other. Also helpful: someone who is, say, just a few steps ahead of you in what he has learned. Think of it as the high school junior telling the sophomore, "What, you're hung up on geometry? Hey, I had that just last year. Here, let me help you out…"

Here's a simple, everyday example: A neighbor and I were discussing talk radio. I raised a question that had puzzled me, "Why are so many of the callers calling from their cars?" My neighbor replied, with no hesitation, "Because those call-in shows put them on hold for such a long time. If they're sitting in their cars, they have the cell phone at hand. If they were at home and they stay on hold for a long time, they get antsy and start wanting to move around." A simple, and no doubt correct, answer. I hadn't thought of it, but once he said it, it seemed so obvious. Sometimes two heads really are better than one.

A little historical note: Martin Luther, the great Christian leader in the 1500s, wrote and preached a great deal about the Bible. Yet he went on record as saying, "O that God would grant that my commentaries and those of all other teachers were destroyed. For every Christian should take the Bible in his own hands and read God's word for himself. He would then see that there is a vast difference between the word of God and the words of man."

WHY YOU SHOULDN'T FLY SOLO

The Bible has no conception of a solitary faith. In the Old Testament, the faith community is Israel. In the New Testament, it is the Christian community. An individual can interact with God, and an individual can read and grasp the Bible—sometimes. But not always. An individual can experience the revelation of God. But the Bible pictures people experiencing that revelation in a community.

When you read the Bible, you are reading the words of more than forty authors. In the course of time, their words have been studied and interpreted by thousands of people. Some of these interpretations have been weird, misguided, and maybe just plain wrong. But with the passage of time, some agreement develops, too. Readers, century after century, find some of the same meanings in the words of the Bible—not in every verse, but in many, especially the most important ones.

If you read the Bible on your own, never bothering to find out how other people have interpreted it, you can still gain a lot of insight. But you would be depriving yourself of a lot of other people's viewpoints. For two thousand years people have been making some intelligent observations on the Bible. Doesn't it make sense to know what their comments were?

You may find that your own insights into the Bible were the same as theirs. If so, wonderful. You can feel some satisfaction that your own mind (and heart, also) are part of the mainstream. You'll find many times that your own fresh discovery may be two thousand years old. But it's still valid. It just means your own mind works in ways similar to other readers' minds.

And occasionally you'll find that your own interpretations are radically different from what the commentators thought. Does that mean they were right and you're wrong? Not necessarily. But it doesn't mean they're wrong and you're right, either. Over the years a lot of weird religious groups have begun because someone had a new insight into the Bible. An example: the Adamites, a group that read Genesis 2:25 and had a new insight. The verse reads: "The man and his wife were both naked, and they felt no shame." The Adamites concluded that if God made Adam and Eve naked, then that was the normal human state, so let's be naked. So, a group calling itself Christian concluded from the Bible that nudity was the norm. Needless to say, most readers have *not* drawn that conclusion.

As part of the human family, we owe it to each other to share insights and ideas. (Sharing is not the same as forcing ideas down people's throats, by the way.) If you find that reading the Bible gives you insights into how to handle stress, find purpose in life, deal with problems and so on, others can benefit from your sharing those insights. Other people might not agree with all of them—just as you might not agree with their insights. But there's a lot to be gained by sharing. This is why Christians have, for two thousand years, chosen to worship and study together, not just in isolation.

WHAT'S A FAMILY TO DO?

Charity begins at home, and so does Bible literacy. Attending Sunday school and weekly worship are essential to a knowledge of the Scriptures, but can we really expect two or three hours of church activity each week to give us enough Bible? Relying on those few hours communicates a message to children: The Bible is just "a church thing," something reserved for Sunday mornings, largely separate from the rest of the week and from real life. Here are some modest proposals for families wanting to become more biblically literate.

1. Study the Bible together and use a plan.

Yes, the contemporary family is supremely busy, but every family ought to set aside a time daily for systematic study of the Bible. Many parents have found that immediately after dinner (assuming all members can be assembled together for one meal a day) is a good time.

2. Read.

The decline of Bible literacy is connected with the general decline in literacy. For many people, books—especially older books—do not seem "user-friendly." How much easier to turn on the TV or surf the Web! Yet consider how many centuries passed without video or audio, which meant that families entertained themselves by reading, playing games together, making their own music, etc. If you are out of the habit of reading, it may take some nudging to force yourself. (Consider it a worthwhile personal investment—like dieting or exercising.) Communicate this message to the children: Reading is a pleasant way to pass the time. More importantly, make it clear that private reading of the Bible is a normal part of everyday life.

3. Play with the Bible.

There is no reason parents can't combine education with play, and all Christian bookstores (and many secular stores as well) sell Bible board games and quiz books for all age levels. While we should never lose sight of the fact that the Bible's teachings are to be taken with the utmost seriousness, Bible trivia games can be a delightful way for a family to spend time together.

4. Encourage memorization.

Memorizing is a good thing. Why should Sunday school be the only place where memorization takes place? As a modest beginning, have the entire family aim to memorize one Bible verse per month—an important verse (John 3:16, for example, or any one of the Beatitudes in Matthew 5) that is fairly short. From one new verse per month you might increase it to one every two weeks, and so on. Use such a plan as a way of memorizing longer passages—for example, memorizing two of the Ten Commandments per month, so that in five months the family can recite all ten.

Do you think the human memory is limited? Listen closely to the man who can rattle off sports statistics from the last fifty years. Listen to the aging baby boomer who knows the words to a limitless number of rock-and-roll oldies. Most educational experts agree that human beings underuse their memories even more than they underuse their bodies' muscles.

See pages 497–502 for tips on memorizing the Bible.

5. Discuss the day's events in light of the Bible.

This can occur during the family's daily Bible study, or at any time parent and child are interacting. Where a healthy parent-child situation exists, the child will probably feel comfortable discussing events of the school day. On a broader level, if the family watches the evening TV news together, discuss world, national and local news in the light of the Bible's view of God's will for mankind. You can also discuss any TV show—a sitcom, talk show, drama, even a sports event—in the light of what the Bible teaches about God and human beings.

The Bible, like anything written hundreds of years ago, helps us put things in perspective by reminding us that human nature never really changes. The evening news will assure you that human beings are often greedy, immoral, militaristic, cruel, hypocritical—in short, just plain selfish. The Bible will assure you that none of this is new. There were saints and heroes in Bible times, as there are today. There were also lying politicians, unjust laws, religious persecution, oppression of the weak, wars, broken homes, alcohol dependence…does the world really change much?

THE BARE MINIMUM TO KNOW: JUST WHAT IS "BIBLE LITERACY"?

Several years ago I interviewed several Christian leaders, asking them about Bible literacy. What, I asked them, are the key things—the basics—that a person should know about the Bible?

The Ten Commandments

This is the core of the Old Testament moral law, given by God to Israel. Survey after survey shows Americans' ignorance of this crucial Old Testament passage. *Living Bible* author Kenneth Taylor, father of ten and author of several books for children, mentioned that children, properly taught at an early age, have no trouble memorizing the Ten.

Most of us don't like to memorize things—especially rules. On the other hand, we do so when we feel the need. We're glad to learn rules of the road so we can get our driver's license. Rather than viewing the Ten Commandments as an outdated series of rules irrelevant to a high-tech world, we can look at them as the basic rules God intended for us to follow—for our own best interests.

The names and sequence of books of the Bible

Bible drills in which children were taught to locate—quickly as possible—particular verses have fallen into disuse. Still, we do need to know where to find the passage referred to in the pastor's sermon or in the book we are reading.

An overview of salvation history

No one has to know the names of all the kings of Israel, but all the Christian leaders I interviewed mentioned the necessity of knowing the high points of salvation history —creation and man's fall; Noah and the flood; Abraham, Isaac and Jacob; Moses and

Israel's Exodus from Egypt; the kingdom under Samuel, Saul, David and Solomon; Israel's spiritual decline and exile; the messages of the prophets (particularly Elijah, Isaiah, Jeremiah and Ezekiel); Jesus' life, death, resurrection and teachings; the growth of the church in Acts and the Letters, especially the work of Paul; the final judgment.

The Sermon on the Mount

Matthew 5–7 contain the essence of Christian ethical teaching. Memorization of such a long passage may be too much to hope for, but every Christian should have at least a familiarity with the Beatitudes, the Lord's Prayer, and the words on salt and light.

Key ethical passages

Besides the Ten Commandments and the Sermon on the Mount, a familiarity with Proverbs is useful. Matthew 19 (on divorce) is perhaps crucial in the modern church, as are Paul's teachings on marriage and family (particularly Ephesians 5–6, Colossians 3–4).

The Apostles' Creed

A creed is a basic summary of Christian beliefs. Not all churches use a creed, but many do, and knowing (better, *understanding*) the points of this ancient formula are essential. Kenneth Taylor adds one disclaimer: "The Creed is sparse in regard to the Holy Spirit, and this needs expansion regarding the gifts and fruit of the Spirit. We need to know that help is available from the Spirit in crippling the sin nature and helping us in good works and thoughts."

Pastors have preached sermon series on the Apostles' Creed. It could be called a "Bible creed," since all parts of it are drawn from the Bible. And in case you're not familiar with the creed, here it is:

> I believe in God the Father Almighty, Maker of heaven and earth;
> And in Jesus Christ his only Son our Lord; who was conceived by the Holy Spirit, born of the virgin Mary, suffered under Pontius Pilate, was crucified, dead and buried; on the third day he rose from the dead; he ascended into heaven, and sits at the right hand of God the Father Almighty; from thence he shall come to judge the living and the dead.
> I believe in the Holy Spirit, the holy universal Church, the communion of saints, the forgiveness of sins, the resurrection of the body, and the life everlasting.

You may know this creed already, or it may surprise you to know that for many years, people recited it (by heart, not by reading) in churches all over the world. It's a good summary of the Bible's teaching about God and Christ.

Basic doctrines

The Apostles' Creed is a good summary of doctrine, but it leaves out some critical points (sin and our need of redemption, for example). A more complete summary was given by pastor Brett Griffith, whose congregation studies the Westminster Confession of Faith: "Creation, the nature of God, the Trinity, Christ as true man and true God, the nature of sin (Genesis 3 and Romans 5), the atonement, salvation through faith, sanctification ('made holy by union with Christ'), the last things (particularly the implications of Judgment for our walk with God)."

THANKS FOR THE MEMORY: WHY WE SHOULD MEMORIZE THE BIBLE AND HOW WE CAN

When I was in high school, my church's pastor introduced something new into our Sunday evening worship: memory time. Shortly before his sermon, the congregation would stand and recite (if they could) a Bible verse that he had given them the previous week. He didn't select the verse at random; he chose a verse that related to his sermon on that Sunday.

Most of us liked doing this. We had an entire week to roll the verse around in our minds, and there was a good feeling of doing something as a congregation. Sometimes peer pressure can be a good thing.

Do I now remember what all those verses were? No. I doubt if even the pastor remembers them all. Yet I don't think they've left my mind completely. I'm sure they're in my brain somewhere, probably more accessible than the hundreds of things I learned in college but have had no reason to recall since then.

Memorizing passages from the Bible is an old practice. For centuries, any educated person in Europe and America was expected to know the Bible very well. Even if you weren't a college graduate, it was assumed you would know certain verses, or at least phrases, from the Bible (which, until recently, always meant the King James Version of 1611). This was something that united people of all social classes and backgrounds. The bank president, the college professor, the housewife and the farmhand would all share a basic knowledge of the Bible. Until the last fifty years or so, we were a "people of the Book."

There was more to this than just learning the materials you were taught in church and home. Most people assumed that the Bible was a moral guide for life. You remembered it, not just to be smart, but to help yourself and others in all seasons of life.

An example: It was not unusual to call to mind, when someone close to you died, a verse like John 11:25: "I am the resurrection, and the life." These words of Jesus brought a lot of comfort to grieving people over the years, and still do. But of course, most of us don't walk around with a Bible in our hands all the time. In times of stress or anxiety we may not have a Bible nearby, and even if we do, we may not feel like reading it, searching through it for some word of comfort. This is the advantage of having a "Bible memory bank."

Take an obvious example: A married man away on a business trip strikes up a conversation with a woman he has just met. If he's had any exposure to the Bible at all, the words "You shall not commit adultery" may cross his mind. If the precise words do not, at least the basic thought will. And if he's lucky (and if his wife is lucky), his remembering those words will affect his behavior.

I'll use another example from my own life: My grandmother frequently repeats a verse that was a favorite of her own mother, Hebrews 10:25: "Not forsaking the assembling of ourselves together." In context, the verse refers to the need Christians have to meet together for worship. In fact, Hebrews presents this as a command, and so my grandmother (and her mother) interpreted it. Whenever I get the urge to skip church, I can practically hear my grandmother's voice saying those words. (Amazing what repetition can do, isn't it?) She did her work well, and apparently so did her own mother. Good. That verse from Hebrews is important. I'm happy to say it isn't the only Bible verse that has been part of my grandmother's "memory bank."

Two friends of mine, a married couple, went through some marital strife a few years ago. They're on the mend now, and the husband mentioned to me that one thing that pulled them through was the verse that says that love "beareth all things, believeth all things, hopeth all things, endureth all things." He couldn't remember exactly where that verse is (it's 1 Corinthians 13:7), but he said the "love endureth all things" part stuck in his mind through twelve years of marriage.

In case you were wondering, this practice of tucking away Bible verses in our minds is urged by the Bible itself. Consider a few of these verses:

"But in your hearts set apart Christ as Lord. Always be prepared to give an answer to everyone who asks you to give the reason for the hope that you have" (1 Peter 3:15).

"Your commands make me wiser than my enemies, for they are ever with me. I have more insight than all my teachers, for I meditate on your statutes. I have more understanding than the elders, for I obey your precepts" (Psalm 119:98-100).

"I have hidden your word in my heart that I might not sin against you" (Psalm 119:11).

"Let the word of Christ dwell in you richly as you teach and admonish one another with all wisdom, and as you sing psalms, hymns and spiritual songs with gratitude in your hearts to God" (Colossians 3:16).

These are just a few of the Bible's words concerning memorizing and meditating on God's word. Keep in mind that for hundreds of years most people did not have their own private copies of the Bible. Bibles were rare and fairly expensive, so people had to share.

A person's exposure to the Bible may have happened only in church or around the family Bible. In such a situation, if a person wanted access to the Bible (and many people did), they had to store it in their minds.

The situation has changed, obviously. Most people can afford a Bible, and if you can't, organizations like the American Bible Society and the Gideons give them away. But the human need to "hide the word in our heart" hasn't changed. Having the words in the printed book is fine, but there's nothing quite like having them engraved on the mind.

PACKAGING A MEMORY

Religious publishers work on the same principle as all publishers: Find a need and fill it. So at least one, NavPress, has found a need (a system for Bible memorization) and filled it (with their Topical Memory System). The system is wonderful. It uses cards (about the size of a business card) that you take with you in a plastic pocket pack. Carrying them wherever you go, you can look at the verses when you have spare moments, brushing up on ones you memorized previously or learning new ones. The System uses verses on key topics of the Bible (temptation, for example), so you usually memorize several verses on the same topic. The verses are usually the most important verses on a particular topic, and also the easiest to memorize. The System also comes with the memory verses printed in several different Bible versions—that is, you can buy the System with the King James Version, the New International Version or other editions.

But, of course, a homemade version of this system is easy to create. Using small file cards (which are more durable than slips of paper), you can write a favorite verse on one side and then the reference (book, chapter and verse) on the other side. You could write on one side of a card, "God was reconciling the world to himself in Christ." On the other side of the card you can write "2 Corinthians 5:19" and maybe the topic ("Salvation" or "Jesus Christ"). As you begin to memorize verses, you can test your memory by looking at the back side (with the reference) and trying to recite the verse. And, by the way, writing out a verse is a helpful part of memorizing. (And it's a lot more fun and rewarding than in your younger days when you had to write "I will not talk in class" five hundred times.)

As with the Topical Memory System, you can carry your cards with you to work, to the gym, anywhere. Modern life is full of frustrating spare moments—often waiting in line or waiting on the phone while you're on hold. Instead of doing what most people do (fuming), you can put these useless minutes to good use, rereading your memory verses. Or give your brain something to do while you're working your muscles on a StairMaster or a treadmill.

If you're new at this, try one verse, a short one. Try 1 John 4:8: "Whoever does not love does not know God, because God is love." (If you feel intimidated by this, try the short form, "God is love.") Read the verse, and then write it on a slip of paper or a card. Read it aloud. Then put the paper face down and see if you can say the verse from memory. Check the paper. If you missed a word or two, don't be frustrated.

When you've chosen a verse you want to memorize, try *paraphrasing* it—that is, restating it in your own words and then writing those down. Understand that "restating it in your own words" doesn't mean "rewording it in a way that suits you." Take one of the Ten Commandments: "You shall not commit adultery" (Exodus 20:14). Although that's a pretty straightforward verse, and easy to remember, you could write it down this way: "I must not be unfaithful to my spouse." That's a pretty accurate paraphrase. It would *not* be accurate to paraphrase it "I should not be unfaithful to my wife, except that the last few weeks she's really getting on my nerves and we don't love each other like we used to anyway, so..." Putting your own "spin" on the Bible is something all human beings do—but in doing so, we're missing out on what the Bible really says.

You'll find paraphrasing a great aid in memorizing a verse. But make up your mind to *memorize the verse as it is in the Bible* (whatever translation you're using). Your own paraphrase is just an aid, helping you connect the words on the page to your own mind.

Besides paraphrasing, you can aid your memorizing by *visualizing* whenever possible. In our video-saturated age, we are probably more visual than people ever were. We've already said that it helps your memory by writing a verse down, actually seeing it on the page. But even words in ink and paper are less stimulating to us than actual pictures. Take a favorite verse, a saying of Jesus: "Come to me, all you who are weary and burdened, and I will give you rest" (Matthew 11:28). This isn't a very "visual" verse, except notice the word *burden*. Can you visualize a person—yourself, maybe?—carrying a huge load on your back? Picture yourself with an enormous bundle strapped on you. You are bending low, maybe sweating, your face pained. Up ahead on the path is someone—Jesus, however you actually picture him—saying "I will give you rest." Perhaps he has his arms extended, indicating he is ready to take the burden you're carrying (or maybe catching you just before you fall down from fatigue). Does visualizing the verse this way help you? It seems to aid most people. Even if you are no Rembrandt, you might want to make a quick sketch of how you visualize the verse, using stick figures. (If you have a copy of the Good News Bible, also called Today's English Version, it has some excellent drawings showing how Bible verses can be illustrated very simply but dramatically.)

Another example is Jesus' words on worry: "Who of you by worrying can add a single hour to his life?" (Matthew 6:27). You could sketch a stick figure of a person, a worried expression on his face, staring at a large clock. Or try this verse: "All a man's ways seem right to him, but the Lord weighs the heart" (Proverbs 21:2). Here the most visual words are *heart* and *weigh*. Try sketching a heart (in the usual shape, that is) sitting on a scale (maybe the old-fashioned balance-type scales, not your bathroom scales).

A little mental effort is required to do this sort of thing, of course. You have to do it yourself—whereas MTV producers are happy to put the latest song in visual images, while advertisers package their newest ad slogans with dynamic images. Don't let it be said that you're completely lacking in imagination. And remember, you don't have to show your "artworks" to anybody. They're for your own use.

Incidentally, make a habit of memorizing the book, chapter and verse of what you've memorized. The actual words of the verse are more important, of course, but it helps you to memorize its location as well. You may want to turn back to the Bible to refer to it again, show it to a friend and so on. Remember how in your grade-school spelling bees you were supposed to say the word, spell it and then say it again? Do that with your chapter and verse references. Let's say you've memorized Psalm 19:1, an easy verse to remember. Repeat it to yourself in this way: "Psalm nineteen, one: 'The heavens declare the glory of God; the skies proclaim the work of his hands.' Psalm nineteen, one."

Most of us are "soft" in the memory, just as a couch potato feels during a first work-out at a gym. But a couch potato can, with determination, change as muscles gradually come into use again. So with the human memory. The capability for incredible memorization is there—if we put it to use.

FIRST STEPS: SOME SUGGESTED MEMORY VERSES FOR BEGINNERS

There is no "official list" of Bible verses worth memorizing. Still, over the centuries, certain verses have become favorites of many people. Probably one of the most loved and most quoted passages in the Bible is Matthew 5:3–12, a part of Jesus' teaching known as the Beatitudes. (The word is from the Latin *beatus*, meaning "blessed.") The Beatitudes are a list of "blessed are," with Jesus describing the sorts of people who are the people of God's kingdom. The whole passage is worth memorizing, and some of its parts are in the list of verses below. If you're feeling ambitious someday, try memorizing the whole passage of the Beatitudes. (It's shorter than the lyrics to your average pop song—but without the rhymes, unfortunately.)

This list here is arbitrary—which means, any author of a book like this is bound to pick some of his own personal favorites. However, I selected these on the basis of brevity, popularity with several generations of Bible-readers and coverage of several basic themes of the Bible.

The verses as they are quoted below are from the New International Version of the Bible, a popular contemporary translation published in 1978. Many people (including this author) grew up with the King James Version of 1611, a version that was old-fashioned in its language but also (perhaps for that reason) very "quotable." Some people still find the older version easier to memorize—maybe because its language seems dignified and different from everyday speech. Our recommendation if you're interested in memorizing some Bible verses: Memorize from the version(s) that you're most comfortable with. You might find the King James Version very memorizable, or you might prefer a newer translation like the New International Version (NIV). One advantage of the NIV is that in many cases it retains the wording of the King James, or uses very similar wording. The New King James Version does the same.

One command of memorizing verses: Don't just pick a verse (including the verses below) without reading it in context. That is, read the paragraph or chapter surrounding it so you'll understand the verse in relation to what precedes and follows it. (Consider: In Shakespeare's *Hamlet*, Prince Hamlet makes his famous "To be or not to be" speech in which he considers committing suicide. The speech is famous, and readable, all by itself. But it helps your understanding of the speech if you've read the rest of the play and understand *why* this young man is considering suicide.)

As you study the Bible and become more familiar with it, you'll probably become an underliner, marking verses that you find especially meaningful. Thanks to the human mind's underused capacities, you may find yourself memorizing these special verses without even trying (just as you probably memorize pop song lyrics without meaning to). This is fine—memorizing without trying to. But it's also kind of fun, and challenging, to push yourself a little bit to memorize verses on the Bible's key teachings. That is what the verses below are all about.

About the Bible itself:

"All Scripture is God-breathed and is useful for teaching, rebuking, correcting and training in righteousness" (2 Timothy 3:16).

"Your word is a lamp to my feet and a light for my path" (Psalm 119:105).

About nature:

"The heavens declare the glory of God; the skies proclaim the work of his hands" (Psalm 19:1).

About God's love:

"God so loved the world that he gave his one and only Son, that whoever believes in him shall not perish but have eternal life" (John 3:16).

"Whoever does not love does not know God, because God is love" (1 John 4:8).

"God does not judge by external appearance" (Galatians 2:6).

"God demonstrates his own love for us in this: While we were still sinners, Christ died for us" (Romans 5:8).

"We know that in all things God works for the good of those who love him, who have been called according to his purpose" (Romans 8:28).

About God's guidance:

"Trust in the Lord with all your heart and lean not on your own understanding" (Proverbs 3:5).

"The ways of the Lord are right; the righteous walk in them, but the rebellious stumble in them" (Hosea 14:9).

"It is better to take refuge in the Lord than to trust in man" (Psalm 118:8).

"The Lord disciplines those he loves" (Proverbs 3:12).

About our love for God:

" 'Love the Lord your God with all your heart and with all your soul and with all your strength and with all your mind'; and, 'Love your neighbor as yourself' " (Luke 10:27).

"Whom have I in heaven but you? And earth has nothing I desire besides you" (Psalm 73:24).

"The fear of the Lord is the beginning of knowledge" (Proverbs 1:7).

"This is love for God: to obey his commands" (1 John 5:3).

"May the words of my mouth and the meditation of my heart be pleasing in your sight, O Lord, my Rock and my Redeemer" (Psalm 19:14).

About love for other human beings:

"These three remain: faith, hope and love. But the greatest of these is love" (1 Corinthians 13:13).

"Do to others what you would have them do to you, for this sums up the Law and the Prophets" (Matthew 7:12).

"Love your enemies and pray for those who persecute you, that you may be sons of your Father in heaven" (Matthew 5:44-45).

"The only thing that counts is faith expressing itself through love" (Galatians 5:6).

"He has showed you, O man, what is good. And what does the Lord require of you? To act justly and to love mercy and to walk humbly with your God" (Micah 6:8).

"He who refreshes others will himself be refreshed" (Proverbs 11:25).

"Rejoice with those who rejoice; mourn with those who mourn" (Romans 12:15).

About human failings:

"He who conceals his sins does not prosper, but whoever confesses and renounces them finds mercy" (Proverbs 28:13).

"All have sinned and fall short of the glory of God" (Romans 3:23).

"All a man's ways seem right to him, but the Lord weighs the heart" (Proverbs 21:2).

"There is a way that seems right to a man, but in the end it leads to death" (Proverbs 16:25).

"The wages of sin is death, but the gift of God is eternal life in Christ Jesus our Lord" (Romans 6:23).

"Blessed is he whose transgressions are forgiven, whose sins are covered" (Psalm 32:1).

"The heart is deceitful above all things and beyond cure. Who can understand it?" (Jeremiah 17:9).

"Man looks at the outward appearance, but the Lord looks at the heart" (1 Samuel 16:7).

About weariness in living:

"Come to me, all you who are weary and burdened, and I will give you rest" (Matthew 11:28).

"In this world you will have trouble. But take heart! I have overcome the world" (John 16:33).

"I can do everything through him who gives me strength" (Philippians 4:13).

"If God is for us, who can be against us?" (Romans 8:31).

"Blessed is the man who perseveres under trial" (James 1:12).

"The eyes of the Lord are on those who fear him, on those whose hope is in his unfailing love" (Psalm 33:18).

About priorities and worldly success:

"What good will it be for a man if he gains the whole world, yet forfeits his soul?" (Matthew 16:26).

"Whoever wants to become great among you must be your servant" (Mark 10:43).

"Where your treasure is, there your heart will be also" (Luke 12:34).

"Everyone who exalts himself will be humbled, and he who humbles himself will be exalted" (Luke 14:11).

"The love of money is a root of all kinds of evil" (1 Timothy 6:10).

About salvation:

"God was reconciling the world to himself in Christ" (2 Corinthians 5:19).

"God did not send his Son into the world to condemn the world, but to save the world through him" (John 3:17).

"Jesus answered, 'I am the way and the truth and the life. No one comes to the Father except through me'" (John 14:6).

"Here is a trustworthy saying that deserves full acceptance: Christ Jesus came into the world to save sinners" (1 Timothy 1:15).

"In repentance and rest is your salvation, in quietness and trust is your strength" (Isaiah 30:15).

About eternal life:

"Surely goodness and love will follow me all the days of my life, and I will dwell in the house of the Lord forever" (Psalm 23:6).

"Jesus said to her, 'I am the resurrection and the life. He who believes in me will live, even though he dies'" (John 11:25).

"As in Adam all die, so in Christ all will be made alive" (1 Corinthians 15:22).

"Our citizenship is in heaven" (Philippians 3:20).

"The world and its desires pass away, but the man who does the will of God lives forever" (1 John 2:17).

"Blessed are the dead who die in the Lord" (Revelation 14:13).

About personal renewal:

"If anyone is in Christ, he is a new creation; the old has gone, the new has come!" (2 Corinthians 5:17).

"Do not conform any longer to the pattern of this world, but be transformed by the renewing of your mind" (Romans 12:2).

"Whatever you do, whether in word or deed, do it all in the name of the Lord Jesus" (Colossians 3:17).

"A broken and contrite heart, O God, you will not despise" (Psalm 51:17).

"Those who hope in the Lord will renew their strength. They will soar on wings like eagles" (Isaiah 40:31).

"Blessed are those who hunger and thirst for righteousness, for they will be filled" (Matthew 5:6).

About freedom:

"Where the Spirit of the Lord is, there is freedom" (2 Corinthians 3:17).

"If the Son [Jesus] sets you free, you will be free indeed" (John 8:36).

About temptation:

"Resist the devil, and he will flee from you" (James 4:7).

"God is faithful; he will not let you be tempted beyond what you can bear" (1 Corinthians 10:13).

About loving people we don't like:

"Do not be overcome by evil, but overcome evil with good" (Romans 12:21).

"Above all, love each other deeply, because love covers over a multitude of sins" (1 Peter 4:8).

"Let us not love with words or tongue but with actions and in truth" (1 John 3:18).

"Blessed are the merciful, for they will be shown mercy" (Matthew 5:7).

About forgiveness:

"Do not judge, and you will not be judged. Do not condemn, and you will not be condemned. Forgive, and you will be forgiven" (Luke 6:37).

"Be kind and compassionate to one another, forgiving each other, just as in Christ God forgave you" (Ephesians 4:32).

"Forgive as the Lord forgave you" (Colossians 3:13).

About joy in living:

"The cheerful heart has a continual feast" (Proverbs 15:15).

"[Jesus:] 'I have come that they may have life, and have it to the full'" (John 10:10).

"Light is shed upon the righteous and joy on the upright in heart" (Psalm 97:11).

"The peace of God, which transcends all understanding, will guard your hearts and your minds in Christ Jesus" (Philippians 4:7).

A NOTE FROM THE EDITORS

G uideposts, a nonprofit organization, touches millions of lives every day through prod- ucts and services that inspire, encourage and uplift. Our magazines, books, prayer network and outreach programs help people connect their faith-filled values to their daily lives. To learn more, visit www.guideposts.com or www.guidepostsfoundation.org.